3rd Edition

CONTEMPORARY BEHAVIOR THERAPY

ALSO OF INTEREST FROM BROOKS/COLE

Abnormal Psychology

Abnormal Psychology: An Integrative Approach by Barlow/Durand
Abnormal Psychology: An Introduction by Durand/Barlow
Casebook in Abnormal Psychology by Brown/Barlow
Exploring Psychological Disorders, a CD-ROM for Mac and Windows
    by Chute/Bliss
Seeing Both Sides: Classic Controversies in Abnormal Psychology
    by Lilienfeld
Looking into Abnormal Psychology: Contemporary Readings by Lilienfield

Behavior Change

Self-Directed Behavior: Self-Modification for Personal Adjustment
    by Watson/Tharp

Clinical Psychology

Clinical Psychology by Phares and Trull
Interpersonal Process in Psychology: A Guide for Clinical Training
    by Teyber

Psychopathology

Exploring Psychological Disorders, a CD-ROM for Mac and Windows
    by Chute/Bliss
Seeing Both Sides: Classic Controversies in Abnormal Psychology
    by Lilienfeld
Looking into Abnormal Psychology: Contemporary Readings by Lilienfield
Culture and Mental Illness by Castillo
Meanings of Madness: A Reader by Castillo

Forthcoming Titles

Abnormal Child Psychology by Wolfe/Mash

3rd Edition

CONTEMPORARY BEHAVIOR THERAPY

Michael D. Spiegler
Providence College

David C. Guevremont
Blackstone Valley Psychological Institute

Brooks/Cole Publishing Company
I(T)P® An International Thomson Publishing Company

Pacific Grove • Albany • Belmont • Bonn • Boston • Cincinnati • Detroit • Johannesburg • London
Madrid • Melbourne • Mexico City • New York • Paris • Singapore • Tokyo • Toronto • Washington

Sponsoring Editor: *Marianne Taflinger*
Marketing Team: *Lauren Harp, Deborah Petit, Alicia Barelli*
Editorial Assistant: *Scott Brearton*
Production Coordinator: *Karen Ralling*
Interior Design: *E. Kelly Shoemaker*
Cover Design: *Vernon T. Boes*

Editing and Production Services: *Graphic World Publishing Services*
Typesetting: *Graphic World, Inc.*
Cover Printing: *The Courier Company, Inc.*
Printing and Binding: *The Courier Company, Inc.*

COPYRIGHT © 1998 by Brooks/Cole Publishing Company
A division of International Thomson Publishing Inc.

I(T)P The ITP logo is a registered trademark under license.

For more information, contact:

BROOKS/COLE PUBLISHING COMPANY
511 Forest Lodge Road
Pacific Grove, CA 93950
USA

International Thomson Publishing Europe
Berkshire House 168-173
High Holborn
London WC1V 7AA
England

Thomas Nelson Australia
102 Dodds Street
South Melbourne, 3205
Victoria, Australia

Nelson Canada
1120 Birchmount Road
Scarborough, Ontario
Canada M1K 5G4

International Thomson Editores
Seneca 53
Col. Polanco
11560 México, D. F., México

International Thomson Publishing GmbH
Königswinterer Strasse 418
53227 Bonn
Germany

International Thomson Publishing Asia
221 Henderson Road
#05-10 Henderson Building
Singapore 0315

International Thomson Publishing Japan
Hirakawacho Kyowa Building, 3F
2-2-1 Hirakawacho
Chiyoda-ku, Tokyo 102
Japan

Printed in the United States of America

10 9 8 7 6 5 4 3

Library of Congress Cataloging-in-Publication Data

Spiegler, Michael D.
    Contemporary behavior therapy/Michael D. Spiegler, David C. Guevremont.—3rd ed.
        p.   cm.
    Includes bibliographical references and index.
    ISBN 0-534-33893-3
    1. Behavior therapy.   I. Guevremont, David C., 1959-   .
II. Title.
[DNLM: 1. Behavior Therapy.   WM 425 S755c 1998.]
RC489.B4S68   1998
616.89'142—dc21
DNLM/DLC
for Library of Congress
                                                      97-28203
                                                          CIP

Michael D. Spiegler (Ph.D., clinical psychology, Vanderbilt University) is Professor of Psychology at Providence College. He has been involved with behavior therapy as a teacher, scholar, and clinician for 25 years. He was a pioneer in developing film modeling therapy and skills training for chronic psychiatric disorders. His other areas of research include observational learning, anxiety, the treatment of obesity, and active learning. Professor Spiegler is coauthor of *Personality: Strategies and Issues* and *The Community Training Center*. He also can be found running, flying, skiing, listening to early music, savoring wine, and spending time with his daughter.

David C. Guevremont (Ph.D., child clinical psychology, West Virginia University) is Director of the Attention Deficit Hyperactivity Disorder Clinic at Blackstone Valley Psychological Institute. His clinical activities primarily involve the behavioral assessment and treatment of children with attention deficit disorders and aggressive behaviors. He has published widely in the areas of hyperactivity, attention deficits, children's social skills, and behavioral interventions. His avocational interests include sports, contemporary music, and film.

Thank you for reading this preface. Few people read prefaces, and so we want to reinforce your exceptional behavior by answering one of the questions you are likely to ask: How is this book different from other introductions to behavior therapy?

Contemporary Behavior Therapy is simultaneously an introduction for beginning students and a comprehensive, scholarly review and resource for advanced students and professionals. To make this a "teaching book"—one from which students can easily learn—we have written in a casual, inviting style and employed many pedagogical features including

- ◆ *unifying principles and themes* that are initially presented in brief, introductory chapters and then drawn on throughout the book;
- ◆ *a consistent behavioral perspective,* including using behavioral principles—such as prompting, shaping, reinforcement, modeling, and behavior rehearsal—to teach behavioral principles and procedures, as well as using behavioral rather than trait descriptions in describing disorders;
- ◆ *unique conceptual schemes* that organize the currently diverse field of behavior therapy;
- ◆ *Participation Exercises* that provide students with hands-on experience with behavior therapy principles and procedures and promote active learning;
- ◆ *many illustrations* that are functional rather than decorative;
- ◆ *numerous Cases* that provide rich detail about the application of behavior therapy to a wide array of problems and disorders; and
- ◆ *integration of clinical, research, and professional facets* of the practice of behavior therapy.

Contemporary Behavior Therapy is written for readers in a variety of disciplines. Applications and examples are drawn from diverse fields, and no previous background is needed because all the basic concepts are presented in Chapters 3 and 4. Readers can skip over the sections in these chapters that cover concepts with which they are familiar. Similarly, theoretical issues in behavior therapy are set off in In Theory "boxes" so that they can be omitted in courses that do not cover theory.

What makes this book a scholarly review of behavior therapy is its comprehensiveness and critical evaluation. All of the major behavior therapy procedures are covered. The amount of coverage given each procedure, disorder, and client population is based on actual clinical practice, which was determined through a survey of 2,300 behavior therapists. The latest research findings are presented (some 2,000 references are cited), and they are synthesized and evaluated. Further, the effectiveness, role, and status of each of the major treatment procedures are discussed in All Things Considered sections.

What is new to the Third Edition of *Contemporary Behavior Therapy?* Besides its being thoroughly updated to reflect the field of behavior therapy at the turn of the century, here is a sample of the numerous changes in this edition.

◆ A unique overview of the process of behavior therapy and its interrelationship with behavioral assessment.
◆ Expanded coverage of cognitive-behavioral therapy, including assessment of cognitions; use of cognitive therapy for schizophrenic delusions; detailed analyses of the content and functions of self-instructions; and critical analysis of and suggestions for enhancing the effectiveness of problem-solving therapy/training.
◆ A second chapter on behavioral medicine that includes child and adult insomnia, eating disorders, addictive disorders, and a full discussion of relapse prevention.
◆ Expanded discussion of modeling and skills training that includes a broad overview of skills training approaches in behavior therapy and their applications to skills deficits associated with schizophrenia, as well as the most recent work on video self-modeling.
◆ Description and critique of recent novel and controversial applications, including the use of virtual reality and EMDR in treating anxiety-related disorders.
◆ New coverage of behavioral child management training.
◆ New coverage of contemporary issues in behavior therapy, including cultural diversity, preventing HIV infection, technological advances, and the role of behavior therapy in the era of managed health care.
◆ All the Participation Exercises have been revised (based on student feedback) and 11 new Participation Exercises have been added, including a series of 4 Exercises that guide students through the process of behavior therapy by their changing one of their own behaviors in an analogous way to which behavior therapy is used for clinical problems.
◆ More than 600 new references.

The book is divided into four parts. Part I presents the fundamental principles of behavior therapy, which are repeatedly illustrated and drawn on in subsequent chapters. Part II covers all of the major behavior therapy procedures used today. Part III illustrates complex applications: to behavioral medicine, to psychological disorders with primary physical characteristics, and to behavioral community psychology. Finally, Part IV discusses ethical issues and provides a final evaluation of and commentary on the present status and future of behavior therapy.

The decision to use reference notes rather than traditional APA-style referencing was not taken lightly. When we consulted with colleagues and adopters of the previous edition, the majority indicated that reference notes were preferable or acceptable. The primary consideration was that students find APA-style parenthetical citations burdensome; they are hurdles to be jumped, literally and figuratively. Interested students can easily find the names and dates of references at the end of each chapter in Reference Notes.

We have written *Contemporary Behavior Therapy*, Third Edition, as teachers, researchers, and clinicians. As teachers, we have incorporated many features to enhance learning, such as stressing general principles and providing numerous examples, including everyday illustrations to which students can relate. As researchers, we appreciate the importance of empirically validating treatment procedures. Thus, we have not only presented the evidence for the efficacy of behavior therapy procedures by describing studies, but we also have evaluated their limitations critically. As clinicians, we find the practice of behavior therapy to be challenging, stimulating, and rewarding, and we have tried to impart this in our writing.

Acknowledgments

We are indebted to many people who have contributed in various ways to the book you are currently holding in your hands.

We want to acknowledge and thank our students/assistants who have contributed to writing and documenting the book: Kevin Byrne, Dawn Couto, Jon Edwards, Joan Long, Gloria Pacheco, and Meghan Wrona. Monica Ripa played a major role in getting references in order (a tall order given the number of references in this edition). We are especially grateful to Danielle Santorelli who was our most competent and dedicated assistant during the production phase. She prepared the name index and contributed to the quality of the book in many ways. Thanks, Danielle, for being there when we needed you and for your cheerfulness, which made a difference in the book and our lives.

We want to thank our reviewers for their helpful suggestions: Marvin R. Goldfried, Peter A. Holmes, Karin Lifter, David I. Mostofsky, William O'Donohue, and Michael J. Selby.

The book has benefited from the consultation of our colleagues and friends Haig Agigian, Vincent Calia, John Marquis, and George Raymond, and the expert services and advice of Paul Bienvenue and Roger Desautels regarding original figures and photographs. Annmarie Mullen performed myriad secretarial tasks with remarkable accuracy and speed. Our thanks to Jenny Kendler for Moogkey, and Julie Spiegler for donating his intrinsic talents as a proof reader and catching a few that almost got in.

Special thanks to Tim Gillison for shepherding the book through its production. His expertise, competence, and ingenuity have made a "clinically significant" difference in the overall quality of the final product. Moreover, Tim's dedication, dependability, and good humor were stress-inoculation for us as we coped with the stressors inherent in a tight production schedule.

We appreciate the wise counsel and personal support of Phil Curson and Frank Graham. Finally, we want to express our gratitude for the efforts of Rob and Dorothy, which made the publication of the Third Edition of *Contemporary Behavior Therapy* possible and eliminated any loose bricks on the road to its completion.

I (M.D.S.) am grateful for the continued perspective on "matters of consequence" provided by a little princess (who is no longer very little), my daughter Heather. She is wise beyond her years, and she is a source of abundant joy in my life. I am indebted to Margi Waller for initially urging me to follow my vision for *Contemporary Behavior Therapy* and for continuing to support my work on it. I appreciate Mary O'Keeffe's consultation and her just being there for me. Last and first, I am forever grateful to Lillian and Julie Spiegler who have provided originating and maintaining conditions in the form of abundant social reinforcement and unconditional positive regard (if you'll pardon the expression!).

I (D.C.G.) am grateful to my family and colleagues at Blackstone Valley Psychological Institute for their support during the process of writing the Third Edition.

Writing *Contemporary Behavior Therapy,* Third Edition, has consumed much of our lives during the past few years. Fortunately, our collaboration continues to be a most satisfying professional enterprise. Accordingly, once again, we want to acknowledge the debt we owe to each other for making the process of conceptualizing and writing *Contemporary Behavior Therapy* highly reinforcing.

Michael D. Spiegler
David C. Guevremont

Contents

Case Studies, Participation Exercises, and In Theory Boxes

Case Studies

Participation Exercises

In Theory Boxes

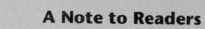

A Note to Readers

To aid your journey through this book, you should be aware of several topographical features we've included to help you learn about behavior therapy and to facilitate your reading. Each chapter begins with an outline of its content, and we suggest you look it over before starting to read. All major behavior therapy terms are printed in **boldface type** at the point where they are first defined. These terms also are defined succinctly in a comprehensive Glossary at the end of the book. References are designated by superscript numbers in the text that correspond to reference notes at the end of each chapter.

Three features are set off from the main text by grey bars. *Cases* are a continuous part of the text, so you should read them as you come to them. *Participation Exercises* give you direct experience with behavior therapy principles and procedures. Instructions for when to read and carry out the Participation Exercises are provided in the text or in a footnote for each Exercise. Some of the Participation Exercises have work sheets that you can remove from Appendix C. *In Theory* boxes describe theoretical issues related to behavior therapy, and you should read each one as soon as you have come to a logical pause in the text (usually at the end of a section).

We have written *Contemporary Behavior Therapy,* Third Edition, specifically for students and have incorporated many suggestions from students who have used the previous two editions. We'd appreciate *your* comments and feedback on the book. Tell us what you liked and didn't like and your ideas for improving the book. You can communicate with us by post at: Michael D. Spiegler, Department of Psychology, Providence College, Providence, RI 02918-0001; or by e-mail at: <spiegler@providence.edu>. We'll reinforce your efforts with a response.

Happy reading and learning.

BASIC PRINCIPLES

Imagine that you are about to partake of an elaborate four-course dinner. You can think of each of the four parts of this book as one of the courses. In Part I, we serve the appetizers, the ideas that will prepare your palate for the rest of the dinner. We begin with an overview of the field of behavior therapy in Chapter 1, followed by a look at the historical events that shaped contemporary behavior therapy in Chapter 2. Next, Chapter 3 introduces the behavioral model, the principles that underlie behavior therapy. Chapter 4 explains how the behavioral model is applied to behavior therapy, describes the basic processes involved in implementing behavior therapy, and discusses how the effectiveness of behavior therapy is evaluated. Finally, Chapter 5 describes behavioral assessment, the procedures for gathering information about clients' problems and measuring clients' progress in therapy.

Dinner is served. Please join us.

Chapter 1

Introduction

Opening a textbook for the first time is like walking into a psychotherapist's office for the initial visit. Both student and client (patient) come with general expectations for what is about to transpire. Students assume that they will be taught by the author, just as new clients in psychotherapy expect that they will be cured of their problems by the therapist.

Being taught and being cured are passive processes, and therein lies a common misconception about reading textbooks and being in psychotherapy, especially behavior therapy. As teachers and behavior therapists, we believe that for education and psychotherapy to be maximally effective, students and clients must be active participants in the process. In behavior therapy, clients are actively engaged in therapy procedures. In education, students learn best when they are actively engaged in learning, and we have written this book with that goal in mind.

One way you will actively learn about behavior therapy is through Participation Exercises that will give you hands-on experience with the ideas, concepts, and procedures used in behavior therapy. Some Participation Exercises take a very brief time to complete and should be done when you come to them in the chapter. Others require a bit more time; it would be optimal to do them before continuing your reading, but you can do them later. Finally, there are Exercises that will be carried out over a number of days or that require the assistance of another person and therefore must be done after reading the chapter. We will indicate our suggestion as to when to do each Participation Exercise, either in the text or in a footnote. The first Participation Exercise is an example of one you should do right now.

◆ ▨▨▨▨▨▨▨▨▨▨▨▨▨▨▨▨▨▨▨▨▨▨▨▨▨▨▨▨▨▨▨▨▨▨

Participation Exercise 1-1

ASSESSING YOUR INITIAL IDEAS ABOUT BEHAVIOR THERAPY

You have no doubt heard about behavior therapy. How accurate is your picture of behavior therapy? This Exercise will help answer that question. Read each of the following statements and write down whether you think it is primarily true or primarily false.

1. Behavior therapy is the application of well-established laws of learning.
2. Behavior therapy directly changes symptoms.
3. A trusting relationship between client and therapist is not important in behavior therapy.
4. Behavior therapy does not deal with problems of feelings, such as depression and low self-esteem.
5. Generally, little verbal interchange takes place between the therapist and client in behavior therapy.
6. The client's cooperation is not necessary for behavior therapy to be maximally successful.
7. Most clients in behavior therapy can be successfully treated in fewer than five sessions.

8. Behavior therapy is not applicable to changing mental processes such as thoughts.
9. Positive reinforcement works better with children than with adults.
10. Many behavior therapy procedures use painful or aversive treatments.
11. Behavior therapy primarily deals with relatively simple problems, such as phobias (for example, fear of snakes) or undesirable habits (for instance, smoking).
12. Behavior therapy uses biological treatments such as drugs and psycho-surgery (for example, lobotomies).
13. The behavior therapist determines the goals for the client.
14. The behavior therapist is directly responsible for the success of therapy.

You may have recognized that many of the statements are false. In fact, *all* of these statements are predominantly false. They are all myths or misconceptions about behavior therapy.

TERMINOLOGY AND SCOPE

Behavior therapy also is referred to as *behavior modification* and *cognitive-behavioral therapy*. Generally, the terms are interchangeable. Behavior therapists occasionally make distinctions among them, but the distinctions are not standard.[1] *Behavior modification* is a generic term that sometimes is confused with *any* procedure that modifies behaviors, including some rather radical procedures ranging from lobotomies to wilderness survival courses,[2] which are totally unrelated to behavior therapy. The term **cognitive-behavioral therapy** refers specifically to treatments that change cognitions (thoughts, beliefs) that are influencing psychological problems. Thus, *behavior therapy* is the "purest" term.

The major goal of behavior therapy is to help clients deal with psychological problems, a goal shared with many other forms of psychotherapy. *Psychological problems* are referred to with many different terms, including *mental illness, psychiatric disorder, psychopathology, emotional disturbance*, and *abnormal behavior*. We will primarily use the terms *psychological* or *psychiatric disorder, psychological problem, problem behavior*, and *problem*. Examples of psychological problems include feeling anxious, feeling depressed, having interpersonal difficulties, experiencing problems with sexual adjustment, being overwhelmed by upsetting recurrent thoughts, engaging in bizarre behaviors (such as urinating in public), and, in general, being unable to cope with the everyday demands of living. Psychological problems may be personally distressing to clients and disturbing to other people (for example, parents may be upset by their child's aggressive acts).

In addition to treating psychological disorders, the principles and procedures of behavior therapy also have been adapted to improve everyday (normal) behaviors, such as work productivity and child rearing. We will describe a variety of these applications as well.

WHAT IS BEHAVIOR THERAPY? DEFINING THEMES AND CHARACTERISTICS

If the statements in Participation Exercise 1-1 reveal something of what behavior therapy is *not,* then just what *is* behavior therapy? Unfortunately, no single, agreed-upon definition exists.[3] Behavior therapy is both diverse and evolving, and thus it is difficult to define it concisely.

In lieu of a general definition, we believe that five defining themes are at the core of behavior therapy: scientific, active, present focus, self-control, and learning focus.[4] The themes are interrelated and overlap in their influence on the practice of behavior therapy. We will briefly explain the themes here. Their meanings and implications will be expanded on in Chapters 3, 4, and 5 and then repeatedly illustrated in the applications of behavior therapy described throughout the book.

Scientific

At the core of behavior therapy is a commitment to a scientific approach that involves *precision* and *empirical evaluation.* All aspects of behavior therapy are defined precisely, including the behaviors targeted for change, treatment goals, and assessment and therapy procedures. Treatment protocols or manuals that spell out the details of particular therapy procedures have been developed for a number of behavior therapies.[5] Using such manuals assures that different therapists are employing the same procedures that have been shown to be effective. Another example of precision is that clients' progress is continuously monitored by quantitative measurements of the behaviors to be changed—before, during, and after therapy.

Behavior therapy employs procedures that have been empirically evaluated.[6] This means that conclusions about the effectiveness of therapies are based on research—involving controlled studies that can be independently repeated by other researchers—rather than on personal beliefs, authority, or testimony.[7]

Active

In behavior therapy, clients engage in specific actions to alleviate their problems. In other words, clients *do* something about their difficulties, rather than *just* talk about them. Behavior therapy is an *action therapy,* in contrast to a *verbal therapy* (such as psychoanalysis or client-centered therapy). In verbal psychotherapies, the dialogue between the client and therapist is the major mode through which therapy techniques are implemented. In action therapies, the therapy techniques involve tasks the client does, and the conversation between client and therapist is primarily for exchanging information. For example, clients in behavior therapy monitor their behaviors during the course of their daily lives, learn and practice coping skills, and role play problem situations in therapy sessions. Specific therapeutic tasks that clients perform in their everyday environments, called **homework assignments,** are an integral part of behavior therapy.[8]

Behavior therapy is frequently carried out, at least in part, in the client's natural environment. The logic is simple. The client's problem is treated where it is occurring, which obviously is not in the therapist's office. "Taking therapy home" makes it more likely that the changes achieved in therapy will generalize to the client's life and continue after therapy has ended.[9]

The term **in vivo** (Latin for "in life") is used to designate therapy procedures that are implemented in the client's natural environment. In vivo therapy is implemented in one of three ways. First, the therapist may work directly with the client in the client's natural environment. This approach is costly in terms of the therapist's time and is therefore only used occasionally. Second, the therapist can train people in the client's life, such as parents, spouses, and teachers, to act as nonprofessional change agents.[10] Third, clients can serve as their own change agents by carrying out therapy procedures by themselves.

Present Focus

The focus of behavior therapy is in the present. Clients' problems are assumed to be influenced by present conditions. Behavioral assessment procedures focus on the client's current, rather than past, circumstances to find factors that are responsible for the person's problems. Behavior therapy techniques then are employed to change the relevant current factors that are influencing the client's behaviors. This emphasis contrasts with other types of psychotherapy, such as psychoanalytic therapy, in which the major influences on clients' problems are assumed to lie in the past.

Self-Control

Behavior therapy clients frequently are trained to initiate, conduct, and evaluate their own treatment, with the guidance of a behavior therapist.[11] This **self-control approach** has three important advantages. First, clients who are instrumental in changing their own behaviors are more likely to maintain the change. Second, being responsible for the change is personally empowering.[12] Third, clients become skilled in dealing with their problems and thus may be able to cope with future problems on their own.[13] Thus, in the long run, the self-control approach can be highly efficient.

Learning Focus

The emphasis on learning is a final theme that distinguishes behavior therapy from other schools of psychotherapy. Learning is important in three different respects. First, the behavioral model holds that most of our problem behaviors develop, are maintained, and change primarily through learning. Behavior therapists do not believe that all behaviors come about through learning, as some are strongly influenced by heredity and biology.

Nonetheless, virtually all of our behaviors can be influenced by learning, even if they have biological components.

Second, behavior therapy provides clients with learning experiences in which old (maladaptive) behaviors are replaced by new (adaptive) behaviors. Indeed, there is a strong *educational* component in behavior therapy, and behavior therapists often serve as teachers.

Third, theories of learning (such as classical conditioning) are used to explain why behavior therapy procedures work. You will read about such explanations in the In Theory sections in later chapters.

Other Common Characteristics of Behavior Therapy

Behavior therapy also is defined by five characteristics that often are present, although they are less central than the defining themes. As with the themes, you will see numerous illustrations of the common characteristics in later chapters.

COLLABORATIVE

Behavior therapy involves collaboration between the therapist and client. In general, behavior therapists share their expertise so that clients become knowledgeable partners in their therapy. (In contrast to this all-cards-on-the-table approach, in some forms of psychotherapy the therapist creates a professional mystique, which sets the therapist apart from the client by virtue of the therapist's special knowledge.) Decisions about therapy goals and treatment procedures are made jointly. For example, behavior therapists provide information about treatment options. They describe what each of the appropriate therapies entails and the effectiveness of each (based on research findings). Clients then can decide on the type of treatment that is best suited to their needs and preferences.

INDIVIDUALIZED

The specific behavior therapy procedures for each client are individualized. Although standard therapy and assessment procedures are used, they are tailored to each client's unique problem, the specific circumstances in which the problem occurs, and the client's personal characteristics. For instance, reinforcement is used to motivate adaptive behaviors with people of all ages, but the specific reinforcer (such as playing a game versus attending a concert) is likely to be different for clients of different ages.

STEPWISE PROGRESSION

Behavior therapy often proceeds in a stepwise progression, moving from simple to complex, from easier to harder, or from less threatening to more threatening. For example, a child who was socially withdrawn was taught—through modeling and reinforcement procedures—to interact with peers in steps: initially playing by herself in the presence of peers, then playing with peers, and finally initiating play with peers.

BREVITY

Behavior therapy is relatively brief, often involving fewer therapy sessions and less overall time than many other types of therapy. This is due, in part, to the self-control approach.

TREATMENT PACKAGE

Two or more behavior therapy procedures frequently are combined in a **treatment package** in an attempt to increase the effectiveness and efficiency of the therapy.[14] This practice is analogous to the treatment of many medical problems, such as the use of medication, diet, and exercise for cardiovascular disease.

THERAPIST-CLIENT RELATIONSHIP IN BEHAVIOR THERAPY

The relationship between the therapist and the client is important in all forms of psychotherapy.[15] This is no less true for behavior therapy, even though the relationship is considered a necessary but not a sufficient condition for successful treatment.[16] In other words, clients in behavior therapy are presumed to be helped by the specific change techniques used rather than by their relationship with the therapist. Interestingly, clients in behavior therapy may attribute their improvement more to the therapist-client relationship than to the therapy procedures.[17] From the behavior therapist's perspective, the role played by the client-therapist relationship is analogous to the role of anesthesia in surgery.

> Somebody goes . . . for surgery because there are certain procedures that need to be implemented. In order for these procedures to take place, the person must be under anesthesia; the anesthesia facilitates what is really important. However, if anything goes wrong with the anesthesia during the surgery, then *that* becomes the priority. Similarly . . . a good . . . [therapist-client relationship] is necessary and often crucial. Without it you just can't proceed.[18]

In behavior therapy, the therapist-client relationship facilitates the implementation of specific therapy procedures in a variety of ways, including increasing the client's positive expectations and hope for success; encouraging the client to complete homework assignments that may involve risk taking; overcoming obstacles that arise in therapy, including noncompliance; and increasing the reinforcement value of therapists' praise and approval.[19]

MANY VARIETIES OF BEHAVIOR THERAPY

Behavior therapy is not a single technique. There are many different forms of behavior therapy—in other words, many behavior therapies. They are unified by the defining themes and characteristics you read about earlier. The following examples illustrate the variety of behavior therapy procedures. (The chapters in which they are introduced are in parentheses.)

Positive Reinforcement (Chapter 6): A sixth-grade boy was doing poorly in 4 subjects because he was spending an average of only 10 minutes a day doing homework. The therapist suggested that his parents have him earn privileges by doing appropriate amounts of homework. The boy was able to play with friends, have an evening snack, and watch television only after doing predetermined amounts of homework.

Modeling and Behavior Rehearsal (Chapter 11): A woman was intimidated by her boss and consequently was unable to speak to him about work problems. She learned to express her desires appropriately to her boss by observing the therapist demonstrate effective ways to tell superiors politely yet forcefully about dissatisfactions and personal preferences. Then the woman practiced these behaviors—initially with the therapist, later with less threatening people than her boss, and finally with her boss.

Response Cost (Chapter 7): A seven-year-old boy, who was big for his age, frequently bullied smaller children. To decrease the boy's bullying, a rule was instituted specifying that he would miss recess or gym, his favorite school activities, each time he was caught fighting.

Cognitive Restructuring (Chapter 12): In order to increase her self-esteem, a woman was taught to substitute positive, self-enhancing thoughts (such as "I look nice today" or "I'm doing a great job") for her habitual negative, self-effacing ideas (such as "I look a mess today" or "I can't do anything right").

Stress Inoculation (Chapter 13): A business executive drank excessively when he arrived home each evening after a frustrating day at the office. To deal with his frustration, the man was taught appropriate coping skills, including relaxation and cognitive restructuring. In therapy, he role played being in various frustrating situations and practiced applying the coping skills. Then he used the skills in his everyday life whenever he felt frustrated and had the urge to drink.

Prompting and Reinforcement (Chapters 6 and 16): At a local zoo, children's littering became a problem. The director set up procedures to increase cleanup behaviors. First, signs (prompts) depicting animals disposing of garbage in trash cans were posted throughout the zoo. Second, zoo attendants handed out small rewards (such as animal stickers and balloons) to children who were observed properly disposing of trash.

Systematic Desensitization (Chapter 9): A student was doing poorly in school because she panicked during examinations. To overcome her test anxiety, the student first was taught muscle relaxation. While relaxed, she repeatedly visualized increasingly more anxiety-evoking situations (for example, beginning with hearing the announcement that an exam would be given in two weeks and ending with being handed the exam). The objective was to substitute relaxation for the anxiety associated with test situations.

Extinction and Differential Reinforcement of Other Behaviors (Chapter 7): A young mother had severely beaten her three-year-old son on several occasions when he had a temper tantrum. The more the mother tried to get her son to stop crying, the angrier she got; eventually she beat the child. The mother was taught to ignore her son during a temper tantrum (extinction) and to reinforce him with attention when he began engaging in any other behaviors (differential reinforcement of other behaviors). This treatment package not only reduced the frequency and duration of her son's temper tantrums, but it also helped the mother cope with her frustration and eliminate her child abuse.

Token Economy and Shaping (Chapters 8 and 6): A 36-year-old man who was hospitalized with a diagnosis of schizophrenia was extremely socially withdrawn. He was placed in a token economy program in which he earned points first for engaging in minimal social contacts (such as asking a nurse for something he wanted) and later for extended social interactions (for example, having a conversation with another patient while they worked on a project together). The man was able to exchange the points he earned for a variety of reinforcers (such as watching TV and playing pool).

Behavioral Couple Therapy and Problem-Solving Therapy (Chapter 13): A married couple sought help because they no longer found pleasure in each other's company. They were continually finding themselves at a dead end when it came to making even the simplest decisions. They were taught problem-solving strategies for dealing with conflicts. These strategies involved learning to generate a variety of potential solutions to disagreements and then evaluating them in order to select the optimal solution.

Even from the small sample of behavior therapy procedures just presented, it is clear that many diverse behavior therapies are used to treat a wide array of problems, including some very serious and complex psychological disorders.

Purpose of This Book

We wrote this book to introduce you to contemporary behavior therapy. We first will present its general principles and then illustrate how they are applied to treat clients' problems. You can expect to learn what is done in behavior therapy, but not how to do it. It is true that you may be able to apply many of the principles and some of the procedures to deal with minor problems in your everyday life. However, if a major problem in your life should arise—one that seriously affects your life and does not resolve itself quickly—you should consult with a professional. Appendix A contains guidelines for choosing a behavior therapist.

Summary

1. The basic aim of behavior therapy is to help clients deal with psychological problems. Behavior therapy principles and procedures also are employed to modify everyday (normal) problems.

2. There is no single, agreed-upon definition of behavior therapy. Behavior therapy can be characterized by five defining themes: scientific, active, present focus, self-control, and learning focus.
3. The scientific approach refers to the following: precisely defining treatment goals, assessment procedures, and therapy procedures; continuously monitoring clients' progress using quantitative measurements; and evaluating the effectiveness of procedures using controlled research.
4. Behavior therapy is an action therapy in which clients engage in specific actions, often in the client's natural environment.
5. Behavior therapy is present-focused. The conditions influencing the clients' present problems are assumed to exist in the present, and therapy procedures deal with these current maintaining conditions.
6. The self-control approach teaches clients to initiate, conduct, and evaluate their own treatment.
7. Behavior therapy is learning-focused in that problem behaviors are assumed to be learned and/or can be changed through learning. Also, theories of learning often are used to explain why behavior therapies work.
8. Five common characteristics further define behavior therapy. Behavior therapy is collaborative and individualized. It proceeds in a stepwise progression, tends to be relatively brief, and often involves treatment packages.
9. Behavior therapy consists of a wide variety of different treatment procedures.

REFERENCE NOTES

1. Martin & Pear, 1996; Wilson, 1978.
2. For example, Krakauer, 1995, p. 75.
3. Kazdin & Wilson, 1978.
4. Compare with Cottraux, 1993.
5. For example, Dobson & Shaw, 1989; Meichenbaum, 1994; compare with Addis & Carpenter, 1997; Chorpita, 1995; Raw, 1993.
6. Spiegler & Guevremont, 1994.
7. Date, 1996; Persons, 1994.
8. For example, Burns & Nolen-Hoeksema, 1992; Edelman & Chambless, 1995; Mahrer, Nordin, & Miller, 1995; Startup & Edmonds, 1994.
9. For example, Edelman & Chambless, 1993; Risley, 1995.
10. Petronko, Harris, & Kormann, 1994.
11. For example, Israel, Guile, Baker, & Silverman, 1994; Silverman, Ginsburg, & Kurtines, 1995; Watson & Tharp, 1989.
12. For example, Israel, Guile, Baker, & Silverman, 1994; Suarez, Peters, Crowe, Easterling, & Adams, 1988.
13. For example, Otto & Gould, 1995; Otto & Pollack, 1994; Otto, Pollack, Meltzer-Brody, & Rosenbaum, 1992; Otto, Pollack, Sachs, Reiter, Meltzer-Brody, & Rosenbaum, 1993.
14. For example, Carr & Carlson, 1993; Gould & Otto, 1995; Otto & Gould, 1995; Otto, Pava, & Sprich-Buckminster, 1995.
15. Gaston, Goldfried, Greenberg, Horvath, Raue, & Watson, 1995.
16. Fleece, 1995; Raue, Castonguay, & Goldfried, 1993; Raue & Goldfried, 1994; Schapp, Bennun, Schindler, & Hoogduin, 1993.
17. Raue & Goldfried, 1994.
18. Gaston, Goldfried, Greenberg, Horvath, Raue, & Watson, 1995, p. 5, italics in original.
19. Gaston, Goldfried, Greenberg, Horvath, Raue, & Watson, 1995; Kohlenberg & Tsai, 1991, 1994, 1995; Raue & Goldfried, 1994.

Chapter 2

Antecedents of Contemporary Behavior Therapy

Behavior therapy has "a long past but a short history."[1] In rudimentary forms, behavior therapy is very old. Humans have been employing behavioral principles to modify people's behaviors for thousands of years, such as parents rewarding children for doing chores. Such individual applications to everyday behaviors are haphazard, but they can be effective. To treat more serious problems, a systematic approach is necessary. The formal, systematic application of behavioral principles to treat psychological disorders—that is, behavior therapy—is just about 50 years old.

HISTORICAL PRECURSORS

A number of historical cases of treatment of psychological disorders closely resemble contemporary behavior therapies. For example, Pliny the Elder, a 1st-century C.E. Roman scholar, treated drinking problems with a precursor to aversion therapy. He created an aversion to alcohol by putting putrid spiders at the bottom of the problem drinker's glass.[2] An early account of a cognitive therapy strategy in treating depression is portrayed in a 10th-century Icelandic saga, written down in the 13th century.[3] In Egil's saga, a daughter helps her grieving father overcome his severe depression by getting him to engage in sequentially more active behaviors, including writing a poem, which leads him to feel better about himself.

   At the close of the 18th century, Jean-Marc-Gaspard Itard attempted to socialize the "Wild Boy of Aveyron," a child who grew up without human contact.[4] To teach the boy language and other social behaviors, Itard employed procedures similar to contemporary behavior therapies used to treat children with autistic disorder, such as modeling, prompting, shaping, and time out from positive reinforcement.[5]

   In the early 19th century, Alexander Maconochie, a captain in the Royal Navy, had the dubious distinction of being in charge of one of the worst British penal colonies, located on Norfolk Island, Australia.[6] To rehabilitate the prisoners, Maconochie established a point system that allowed each prisoner to redeem himself by performing appropriate tasks and social behaviors. In Maconochie's words, "When a man keeps the key of his own prison, he is soon persuaded to fit it into the lock." Despite the apparent success of this early token economy, Maconochie's superiors disapproved of his innovative methods and denigrated their effectiveness.[7]

   An 1845 paper presented to the Royal Academy of Medicine in Paris reported that François Leuret, a physician, treated a 30-year-old wine merchant for his obsessional thoughts. Leuret had the man recite song lyrics, behaviors that competed with his disturbing, repetitive thoughts.[8] This procedure is similar to some present-day cognitive-behavioral interventions.

   These early harbingers of behavior therapy procedures have only historical significance and interest. They have had no real influence on the development of contemporary behavior therapy.[9]

EARLY EXPERIMENTAL WORK

The inspiration for contemporary behavior therapy came from experimental work on learning carried out at the beginning of the 20th century. Russian physiologist Ivan Pavlov is credited with the first systematic account of what has come to be called *classical* (or *Pavlovian*) *conditioning*.[10] In this form of learning, a neutral stimulus (one that elicits no particular response) is repeatedly paired with a stimulus that naturally elicits a particular response. The result is that eventually the neutral stimulus alone elicits the response. In Pavlov's well-known experiments with dogs, a neutral stimulus, such as a light or a tone, was paired with food, a stimulus that reflexively produces salivation in the dog. After repeated pairings of these two stimuli, the light alone began to elicit salivation. This classical conditioning process is shown in Figure 2-1.

In addition to his important laboratory experiments with animals, Pavlov wrote about the application of learning procedures to treat psychological disorders.[11] Pavlov's critical contribution to behavior therapy, however, was the influence his work had on John B. Watson, an experimental psychologist at Johns Hopkins University. Watson is the father of *behaviorism*, the school of thought on which behavior therapy is largely based. Behaviorism emphasizes the importance of objectively studying behaviors by dealing only with directly observable stimuli and responses. Watson's behaviorism rejected mentalistic concepts such as consciousness, thought, and imagery.[12]

In 1924, Mary Cover Jones, one of Watson's students, successfully treated a three-year-old boy named Peter who had an intense fear of rabbits.[13] The therapy consisted of two basic procedures. First, Peter watched other children happily playing with a rabbit, which may have led Peter to realize that rabbits

John B. Watson

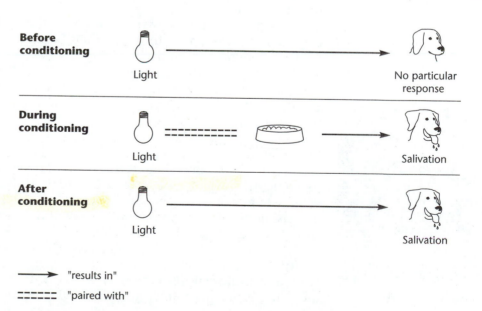

Figure 2-1   The classical conditioning process recognized by Pavlov

Before conditioning

Light → No particular response

During conditioning

Light ===== 🍲 → Salivation

After conditioning

Light → Salivation

→   "results in"

=====   "paired with"

Ivan Pavlov (center) in his laboratory

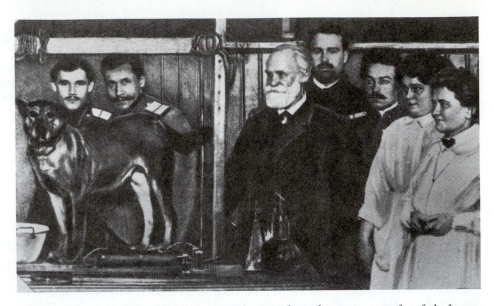

Mary Cover Jones

Edward Thorndike

were not necessarily frightening. Then, when he was not fearful, Jones exposed Peter to the rabbit. She placed a caged rabbit in the room while Peter was eating a favorite food. The cage was at a sufficient distance so that its presence did not interfere with Peter's eating and did not upset him. Gradually, over a period of days, Jones brought the rabbit closer to Peter, always keeping it at a distance with which Peter was comfortable. Jones eventually took the rabbit out of the cage and gradually brought it closer to Peter. After this treatment, Peter was able to comfortably hold and play with the rabbit. Years later, Jones's two therapy procedures—modeling and in vivo exposure—were refined and now are widely used behavior therapies for the treatment of fears.

Hobart and Willie Mowrer also were influenced by Pavlov's classical conditioning principles. In 1935, they began a treatment program for nocturnal enuresis (bedwetting) at the New Haven Children's Center.[14] The program involved placing a special pad under the child's bedsheet; when the child began to urinate at night, a buzzer sounded and awakened the child.[15] Eventually, the child came to associate a full bladder with awakening. After repeatedly pairing these two events, a full bladder would awaken the child, thereby eliminating the need for the buzzer. The technique proved to be highly successful and still is used today.

At the same time that Pavlov was studying classical conditioning, psychologist Edward Thorndike at Columbia University was investigating what would come to be called *operant* (or *instrumental*) *conditioning*,[16] increasing or decreasing a person's behavior by systematically changing its consequences, such as by reinforcing it.

In a different arena, Edmund Jacobson, a physiologist at the University of Chicago in the 1920s and 1930s, was experimenting with muscle relaxation as a treatment for tension associated with a wide array of disorders, including generalized anxiety, phobias, depression, hypertension, colitis,

Willie Mowrer and Hobart
Mowrer

tics, and stuttering.[17] Jacobson's *progressive relaxation* is the basis for the
extensive use of muscle relaxation in behavior therapy.

GROWING DISCONTENT WITH PSYCHOANALYSIS

Despite the effectiveness of some early behavior therapies,[18] contemporary
behavior therapy did not begin in earnest until the 1950s.[19] The events that
occurred at that time must be understood in relation to the nature and status
of psychoanalysis, the prevailing model of psychotherapy.

Psychoanalysis, originally developed by Sigmund Freud, focuses on
exploring clients' early childhood experiences and attempting to uncover
unconscious conflicts and desires. The objective is for clients to gain insight
about the origin of their problems—that is, to understand what has caused
their psychological disorders. Insight is believed to be the key to change; for
this reason, psychoanalysis and similar therapies are called *insight therapies*.

Psychoanalysis was the only major approach to psychotherapy during
the first half of the 20th century. However, following World War II, doubts
about the effectiveness of psychoanalysis as a general treatment method
began to mount. It had become increasingly clear that because psychoanalysis is such a lengthy process—frequently taking several years—it was
unsuitable for treating the large number of returning veterans who required
psychological treatment as a result of the war.

This growing discontent with traditional psychoanalytic psychotherapy
received a major impetus from a retrospective study by British psychologist

Hans Eysenck

Hans Eysenck (pronounced EYE-zink) published in 1952.[20] Eysenck investigated the effectiveness of insight therapies by examining records from hospitals and insurance companies. He concluded that people treated by traditional insight psychotherapy were no more likely to improve than those who received no treatment at all. Subsequent reanalysis of Eysenck's data showed that his conclusion was exaggerated.[21] Nonetheless, Eysenck's original conclusions did serve as an impetus for psychotherapists to seriously question the benefits of traditional psychotherapy and to seek more effective alternatives. One of those alternatives was behavior therapy.

FORMAL BEGINNINGS OF CONTEMPORARY BEHAVIOR THERAPY

Contemporary behavior therapy had its formal beginnings in the 1950s, simultaneously in the United States and Canada, South Africa, and Great Britain.

Developments in North America

B. F. Skinner

Beginning in the 1930s, psychologist B. F. Skinner at Harvard University began his extensive investigation of operant conditioning, using pigeons and rats as subjects. Like Pavlov, Skinner speculated about the therapeutic uses of learning principles,[22] but he did not carry his ideas to fruition. It remained for his students and followers to apply operant principles to therapy.

In the early 1950s, Ogden Lindsley, then a graduate student working with Skinner at Harvard, directed a series of studies to determine the feasibility of using operant conditioning procedures with adults with psychiatric disorders.[23] His initial research demonstrated that people with psychiatric disorders whose behaviors seemed aimless would consistently perform simple tasks when given meaningful reinforcers. Lindsley's investigations could not legitimately be considered therapy, but they led to the development of sophisticated procedures, derived from operant conditioning principles, to treat complex human problems. Incidentally, Lindsley may have been the first person to formally use the term *behavior therapy* to describe the systematic use of learning procedures to treat psychological disorders.[24]

In the late 1950s, Teodoro Ayllon (pronounced eye-YONE) at the Saskatchewan Hospital in Canada performed classic demonstrations of the effectiveness of operant principles in modifying severely disturbed behaviors of patients with psychiatric disorders.[25] Ayllon's demonstrations were critical in overcoming the widespread resistance to the behavioral model. According to psychoanalysis, the model still prevailing at the time, psychological disorders are the result of deep-seated, unconscious conflicts. This implied that successful treatment had to delve into those conflicts.[26] One of Ayllon's demonstration studies indirectly challenged these psychoanalytic notions. Using reinforcement procedures, Ayllon had taught a 54-year-old patient to hold a broom while standing in an upright position (Figure 2-2).[27] Ayllon then asked two psychoanalysts to observe this behavior and comment on it. One of them gave the following explanation.

Ogden Lindsley

Figure 2-2 Sketch of the patient's stance that Ayllon reinforced in his demonstration study
SOURCE: Haughton & Ayllon, 1965, p. 96.

Teodoro Ayllon

Nathan Azrin

Her constant and compulsive pacing holding a broom . . . could be seen as a ritualistic procedure, a magical action. When regression conquers the associative process, primitive and archaic forms of thinking control the behavior. Symbolism is a predominant mode of expression of deep seated unfulfilled desires and instinctual impulses. . . .

Her broom could then be:

1. a child that gives her love and she gives him in return her devotion;
2. a phallic symbol;
3. the sceptre of an omnipotent queen.[28]

In 1961, Ayllon teamed up with Nathan Azrin, another of Skinner's former students, to design the first comprehensive token economy at Anna State Hospital in Illinois.[29] A token economy provides clients with token reinforcers (such as poker chips or points) to motivate them to perform desired behaviors; the tokens then can be exchanged for actual reinforcers (for instance, a snack or time watching TV). The Anna State Hospital token economy paved the way for the widespread application of this treatment method.

In setting up their token economy, Ayllon and Azrin, like most other early behavior therapists, encountered considerable resistance from the hospital staff. Most of the staff did not believe that the new behavioral treatment methods could be effective and were reluctant to support Ayllon and Azrin's attempts. As was typical of behavior therapy efforts at the time, the Anna State Hospital token economy was set up as an experimental program largely funded by a research grant, which separated it from the mainstream hospital programs. Resisting the insurgence of a new treatment model, the staffs of other hospital programs were reluctant to provide patients for the new token economy, especially patients with whom they were having some success. So the patients who were referred to Ayllon and Azrin's experimental program were those who had not responded to traditional treatments and were considered incurable. Naturally, this "stacked the deck" against the new behavior therapy program. Ironically, these unfavorable conditions turned out to be a blessing in disguise. The token economy resulted in remarkable changes in the so-called incurable patients, which only strengthened the case for the effectiveness of behavior therapy procedures. This cycle of facing *skepticism* from traditional professionals, having to work under *adverse conditions,* and nonetheless *demonstrating effectiveness* was a common experience for early behavior therapists through at least the mid-1970s.

Developments in South Africa

Meanwhile, in South Africa, psychiatrist Joseph Wolpe had become disenchanted with psychoanalytic methods of treatment. In the 1950s, he developed several keystone behavior therapies, most notably systematic desensitization and assertion training, for treating problems such as irrational

Joseph Wolpe

Arnold Lazarus

Stanley Rachman

fears and social inhibitions. Wolpe's treatment approach involved replacing debilitating anxiety with more adaptive reactions such as deep muscle relaxation and assertive behavior. Wolpe explained his procedures in terms of classical conditioning and neurophysiological concepts.[30] Wolpe's work has had a major influence on behavior therapy, and he deserves the distinction of being called the first behavior therapist.[31]

Prominent among the people whom Wolpe trained in South Africa were Arnold Lazarus and Stanley Rachman. Lazarus initially made important contributions by adapting systematic desensitization to groups of clients and to children.[32] Throughout his career, Lazarus has strongly advocated extending the boundaries of behavior therapy. He has developed innovative therapy techniques on the basis of their effectiveness rather than their theoretical explanation—in contrast to Wolpe, whose work always has been tightly bound to learning theory.[33] Since 1966, Lazarus has practiced and taught in the United States. Rachman, who had collaborated with Lazarus in South Africa, emigrated to Great Britain in 1959 to work closely with Eysenck. Rachman introduced desensitization to British behavior therapists, and he became one of behavior therapy's major advocates and researchers in Great Britain.[34]

Developments in Great Britain

Great Britain was the third major seat of contemporary behavior therapy's origins in the 1950s. The development of behavior therapy in Great Britain was spearheaded by Eysenck at the Institute of Psychiatry at the University of London. This work was facilitated by M. B. Shapiro,[35] who, as director of the Clinical-Teaching Section, championed the intensive study of individual cases, as did Skinner and his associates.[36] This emphasis is but one commonality among the early behavior therapists in North America, South Africa, and Great Britain. As is often the case in the history of science, the simultaneous development of similar approaches apparently occurred independently. Nonetheless, behavior therapy in North America, South Africa, and Great Britain in the 1950s presented a strong and moderately unified alternative to traditional psychoanalytic therapy.

ACCEPTANCE AND GROWTH OF BEHAVIOR THERAPY

In the 1960s, there were few behavior therapists in private practice, and those working in psychiatric hospitals and outpatient facilities still were encountering resistance from traditional psychotherapists. Even in academic settings, which are among the most accepting and nurturing atmospheres for new ideas, behavior therapists often were isolated because their colleagues viewed behavior therapy as a radical departure from mainstream psychology.

To overcome these barriers to acceptance and growth, behavior therapists in the late 1950s and early 1960s spent considerable time gathering evidence that behavior therapy was a viable alternative to traditional psychotherapy. This effort included publication of demonstration projects, such as Ayllon's studies. These studies showed that a wide array of clinical problems could be successfully treated in a relatively brief period with behavior therapy techniques.[37]

In the 1960s, while already established behavior therapy procedures (such as systematic desensitization) were being refined, another major approach to behavior therapy was born. Psychologist Albert Bandura at Stanford University developed a social learning theory that included not only principles of classical and operant conditioning but also *observational learning,*[38] the process of changing one's own behaviors by observing the behaviors of another person (a model). In addition, Bandura's social learning theory emphasized the critical role that cognitions (thoughts, images, and expectations) play in psychological functioning, including their role in the development and treatment of psychological disorders.

Making cognitions a legitimate focus of behavior therapy was antithetical to Watson's behaviorism because cognitions are not directly observable by others. Watson's behaviorism may have been a useful position for early behavior therapists to adopt; it countered the deeply entrenched psychoanalytic perspective emphasizing unconscious forces that, of course, cannot be directly observed. Today, most behavior therapists believe that dealing only with directly observable behaviors is too restrictive.[39] After all, humans *do* think, expect, plan, and imagine, and these cognitive processes clearly influence how people act.

During the 1960s, cognitive-behavioral therapy—which changes clients' maladaptive cognitions that contribute to psychological disorders—was created by several prominent behavior therapists. Independently, Aaron Beck at the University of Pennsylvania developed *cognitive therapy,*[40] and Albert Ellis in private practice in New York City designed *rational emotive behavior therapy.*[41] Both therapies are aimed at modifying the negative and illogical thoughts associated with many psychological disorders, such as depression and anxiety. Donald Meichenbaum (pronounced MIKE-en-baum) at the University of Waterloo in Ontario developed cognitive-behavioral treatment packages. These packages— notably *self-instructional training* and *stress inoculation*—are used to treat a wide range of psychological problems, including impulsive behaviors, anxiety, anger, pain, and schizophrenic behaviors.[42] Meichenbaum was among the first to apply cognitive-behavioral interventions with children. Initially, cognitive-behavioral therapies served as supplements to existing behavior therapy procedures, but they rapidly evolved as a major approach in the field.

In 1966, the Association for Advancement of Behavior Therapy was established in the United States. Cyril Franks, who previously had worked with Eysenck and Rachman at the Institute of Psychiatry in London, was its first president. It has become the major professional organization that advocates for behavior therapy and facilitates the field's further development. Additionally, by 1970, four major professional journals were devoted exclusively to behavior therapy (see Table 2-1).

Albert Bandura

Table 2-1 Examples of behavior therapy journals

Title	Year Began
Advances in Behaviour Research and Therapy	1977
Behavior Modification	1977
the Behavior Therapist	1978
Behavior Therapy	1970
Behaviour Research and Therapy	1963
Behavioural and Cognitive Psychotherapy	1976
Behavioural Interventions	1986
Cognitive and Behavioral Practice	1994
Cognitive Therapy and Research	1977
Child and Family Behavior Therapy	1982
Clinical Behavior Therapy Review	1979
Corrective and Social Psychiatry and Journal of Behavior Technology Methods and Therapy	1974
Journal of Applied Behavior Analysis	1968
Journal of Behavior Therapy and Experimental Psychiatry	1970
Journal of Behavioral Assessment and Psychopathology	1979
Journal of Rational-Emotive & Cognitive-Behavior Therapy	1983
Revista Mexicana de Analisis de la Conducta (Mexican Journal of Behaviour Analysis)	1975

Still, some critics voiced the opinion that behavior therapy would soon fade into oblivion, along with a host of other "faddish" therapies that arose in the 1960s, such as encounter groups. However, developments in the 1970s clearly showed that behavior therapy was much more than a passing fancy. Behavior therapy was beginning to be acknowledged as an acceptable form of treatment, and even the *treatment of choice* (that is, the optimal treatment) for certain psychological problems.

Cyril Franks

Emergence of Behavior Therapy

In the 1970s, behavior therapy emerged as a major force in psychology and made a significant impact on psychiatry, social work, and education. The principles and techniques of behavior therapy also were adapted to enhance the everyday functioning of people in areas as diverse as business and industry,[43] child rearing,[44] ecology,[45] and the arts.[46] Applications include improving athletic performance,[47] increasing people's willingness to take prescribed medications,[48] enhancing the quality of life of nursing home residents and geriatric patients,[49] and more efficiently teaching young children to play musical instruments.[50] Examples of larger-scale behavioral interventions include promoting energy conservation,[51] preventing crimes,[52] providing individual instruction for large college classes,[53] and influencing entire communities to engage in behaviors that lower the risk of cardiovascular disease.[54]

During the 1980s, two important developments in the field of behavior therapy increased its applicability and acceptance. First, cognitive-behavioral therapy emerged as a major force (see Chapters 12 and 13). Second, behavior therapy began to make significant contributions to the field of *behavioral medicine*, which involves the treatment and prevention of medical problems (see Chapter 14).[55]

By 1990, the Association for Advancement of Behavior Therapy was a quarter of a century old, having grown in membership from 18 (in 1966) to approximately 4,000. Other influential behavior therapy societies had been founded in other countries, including Argentina, France, Germany, Great Britain, Israel, Japan, Mexico, the Netherlands, and Sweden.[56] More than 20 major journals devoted solely to behavior therapy had been established (see Table 2-1), and empirical research on behavior therapy filled the leading clinical psychology journals as well as many prestigious publications in social work, education, and psychiatry.

One indication of the increasing maturity of the field of behavior therapy is the fact that, for the past 20 years, its strongest critics have been its proponents rather than its opponents. In effect, the field of behavior therapy had reached the point where convincing skeptical outsiders was no longer a priority.[57] Instead, behavior therapists began to scrutinize their own therapy methods and the impact they were having on clients and on the broad field of psychotherapy.[58]

Summary

1. Behavioral principles have been employed for thousands of years to change people's problematic behaviors. However, only in the past 50 years have they been applied systematically and been called behavior therapy.
2. There are a number of historical accounts of treatment procedures that resemble those of contemporary behavior therapy. However, the immediate impetus for the development of behavior therapy came from

experimental research on learning conducted in the early part of the 20th century. This included the work of Pavlov, who conceptualized classical conditioning; Watson, who founded behaviorism, an approach that only dealt with observable behaviors; Jones, whose early treatment of fear in a young child became a classic study; and the Mowrers, who designed the bell-and-pad treatment for bedwetting based on classical conditioning.

3. Contemporary behavior therapy began in the 1950s, in part because of a growing discontent with psychoanalysis. It started simultaneously in North America, South Africa, and Great Britain. In the United States, Lindsley used the operant conditioning principles developed by Thorndike and Skinner to influence the behaviors of patients with psychiatric disorders, and Ayllon and Azrin developed the first token economy. In South Africa, Wolpe developed systematic desensitization and assertion training, and Lazarus broadened the application of these procedures. Rachman brought behavior therapy from South Africa to England and collaborated with Eysenck, an advocate for behavior therapy and critic of psychoanalytic therapy.

4. Early behavior therapy efforts were met with strong criticism and resistance from traditional psychotherapists. Initially, behavior therapists had to focus on demonstrating that behavior therapy could be effective.

5. In the 1960s, Bandura developed a social learning theory that combined observational learning with classical and operant conditioning. The theory emphasized the critical role that cognition (thinking) plays in psychological functioning—a drastic departure from Watson's behaviorism.

6. Cognitive-behavioral therapy changes clients' cognitions that maintain psychological disorders. Originally developed by Ellis, Beck, and Meichenbaum, cognitive-behavioral therapy began as a supplement to existing behavior therapy procedures but rapidly evolved into a major behavior therapy approach.

7. In the 1970s, behavior therapy emerged as a major force among psychotherapy approaches.

8. The Association for Advancement of Behavior Therapy was established in 1966 in the United States to advocate for behavior therapy and has served as its major professional organization.

Reference Notes

1. Franks & Wilson, 1973.
2. Franks, 1963.
3. Arnarson, 1994; Fell, 1975.
4. Itard, 1962.
5. Lovaas, 1977.
6. Kazdin, 1978.
7. Pitts, 1976.
8. Stewart, 1961.
9. Franks, 1969.
10. Pavlov, 1927.
11. Kazdin, 1978.
12. Watson, 1914.
13. Jones, 1924; compare with Kornfeld, 1989.
14. Kazdin, 1978.
15. Mowrer & Mowrer, 1938.
16. Thorndike, 1911, 1931, 1933.

17. Jacobson, 1929, 1934.
18. Yates, 1970.
19. Sobell, 1994.
20. Eysenck, 1952.
21. For example, Cartwright, 1955; Luborsky, 1954; Smith & Glass, 1977.
22. Skinner, 1953.
23. Lindsley, 1956, 1960, 1963; Skinner, 1954; Skinner, Solomon, & Lindsley, 1953; Skinner, Solomon, Lindsley, & Richards, 1954.
24. Skinner, Solomon, & Lindsley, 1953.
25. For example, Ayllon, 1963, 1965; Ayllon & Michael, 1959.
26. Freud, 1955.
27. Haughton & Ayllon, 1965.
28. Haughton & Ayllon, 1965, pp. 97-98.
29. Ayllon & Azrin, 1968.
30. Wolpe, 1958.
31. Wolpe, 1990.
32. Lazarus, 1959, 1961; Lazarus & Abramovitz, 1962.
33. Lazarus, 1966, 1967, 1971, 1976.
34. Rachman, 1959, 1967, 1972, 1990; Rachman & Eysenck, 1966.
35. For example, Shapiro, 1951, 1952, 1957, 1961a, 1961b, 1966.
36. Skinner, 1953.
37. Ullmann & Krasner, 1965.
38. Bandura, 1969, 1977b, 1986b; Bandura & Walters, 1963.
39. For example, Cloitre, 1995.
40. Beck, 1963, 1972, 1976.
41. Ellis, 1962, 1970.
42. Meichenbaum, 1974, 1975, 1977; Meichenbaum & Cameron, 1972, 1973.
43. Hermann, De Montes, Dominguez, Montes, & Hopkins, 1973; New tool, 1971; Pedalino & Gamboa, 1974.
44. For example, Becker, 1971; Christophersen, 1977; Patterson, 1975; Patterson & Gullion, 1976.
45. Kazdin, 1977b.
46. Madsen, Greer, & Madsen, 1975.
47. For example, Rushall & Siedentop, 1972; Rachman & Hodgson, 1980; Rachman & Teasdale, 1969.
48. For example, Epstein & Masek, 1978; Lowe & Lutzker, 1979.
49. For example, Libb & Clements, 1969; Sachs, 1975.
50. Madsen, Greer, & Madsen, 1975.
51. Kazdin, 1977b.
52. For example, McNees, Egli, Marshall, Schnelle, Schnelle, & Risley, 1976; Schnelle, Kirchner, Macrae, McNees, Eck, Snodgrass, Casey, & Uselton, 1978; Schnelle, Kirchner, McNees, & Lawler, 1975.
53. For example, Keller, 1968.
54. Maccoby, Farquhar, Wood, & Alexander, 1977.
55. Arnkoff & Glass, 1992; Glass & Arnkoff, 1992.
56. Kazdin, 1978.
57. Nezu, 1996.
58. For example, Baer, Hurley, Minichiello, Ott, Penzel, & Ricciardi, 1992; Kazdin & Wilson, 1978; Krasner, 1976; Stolz & Associates, 1978.

Chapter 3

The Behavioral Model

Behavior therapy is much more than the sum of its specific therapeutic procedures. To appreciate the nature of behavior therapy, you must understand the model on which it is based. In this chapter we will describe the general model of human behavior that forms the basis of behavior therapy. Then, in Chapter 4, we will outline the principles of behavior therapy derived from the model. Thus, Chapters 3 and 4 present the core of behavior therapy.

PEOPLE ARE WHAT THEY DO: PREEMINENCE OF BEHAVIOR

How do we define who a person is? What makes us unique? According to the behavioral model, each of us is defined by our behaviors. *We are what we do.* Some people find this concept strange because we do not typically define ourselves and others in terms of behaviors.

Before reading any further, take a few minutes to do a simple demonstration. Think of someone you know well. Write a brief description of that person so that someone who doesn't know the person could get a feel for what he or she is like. When you have finished, continue reading.

Behavioral Versus Trait Descriptions of Behavior

People are more commonly described in terms of their traits than in terms of their behaviors. *Traits* are relatively stable and enduring personality characteristics. In response to the question "What is your roommate June like?" Tonya might reply:

> Oh, she's really *nice.* She's *friendly, considerate,* and *helpful.* June is very *smart* and *conscientious.* She's a lot of *fun,* too. I think she's *interesting.* She's really *straightforward* and *honest.*

In Tonya's description of June, the italicized words are traits. When you wrote the description of the person you know well a moment ago, the odds are that much of it involved her or his traits.

Traits are convenient ways of describing people, but they have a number of drawbacks. Because traits are not observable—they exist only in our minds—they leave much room for individual interpretation. Consider the following illustration. John may frequently telephone his friends, drop them notes, and invite them to his house. Would you conclude that John is friendly? Might it be equally valid to say that John is lonely, given the same observations? As this example shows, trait descriptions of people often are imprecise.

Trait descriptions present an additional problem: they provide no information about when the trait will influence the person's behaviors. Tonya described June as conscientious. Surely June is not always conscientious; thus, we do not know *when* she will be conscientious. For example, is June likely to be more conscientious in some situations (for example, when doing her schoolwork) than in others (for instance, in returning phone calls promptly)? To answer such a question, Tonya could describe situations in which she has seen June act conscientiously. Tonya might observe that June studies at least four hours a day, plans her work carefully, and usually finishes her assignments ahead of time.

To clarify June's conscientiousness, Tonya has done a curious thing. She has described June's *behaviors,* the same behaviors that she had observed in order to describe her as conscientious. Let's look at the process Tonya went through to conclude that June is conscientious. After observing June's actions, Tonya summarized June's behaviors with the term *conscientious* and inferred that June's behaviors were the result of a general trait of conscientiousness.

We typically use the three-step process illustrated in Figure 3-1 to describe and explain people's behaviors. First, we observe someone's behaviors. Second, we attempt to summarize and explain the behaviors by a personality trait. Third, we go back to the initial behaviors to clarify the meaning of the personality trait. The problem with this three step process is that it is circular—in other words, it begins and ends with the same observations of a person's behaviors. Thus, traits provide only a pseudo-explanation of why people act the way they do. Moreover, traits are superfluous, according to the behavioral model, because they provide no more information than behavioral observations do.

Now let's contrast trait descriptions with behavioral descriptions. In the behavioral model, people are described by their behaviors. This is a direct, one-step process. Behavioral descriptions are more specific and detailed than trait descriptions. On the downside, they are lengthier. Compare the inference "June is conscientious" with the observation "June studies at least four hours a day, plans her work carefully, and usually finishes her assignments ahead of time." The accuracy and therefore the usefulness of the behavioral description may outweigh its being lengthier.

There are two major advantages of looking at behaviors rather than traits for the practice of behavior therapy. First, because descriptions of a client's behaviors are more precise, assessment and treatment can be more precise as well. Second, behavioral descriptions promote individuality, whereas trait descriptions classify clients' problems into broad categories (such as depression, anxiety, and schizophrenia).

Figure 3-1 The relationship of behaviors and traits

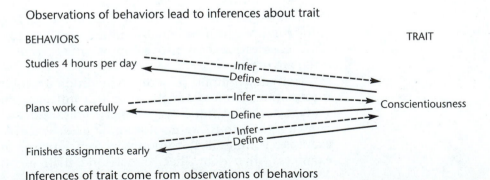

Observations of behaviors lead to inferences about trait

BEHAVIORS   TRAIT

Studies 4 hours per day   ----Infer----
                          ----Define----

Plans work carefully   ----Infer----   Conscientiousness
                          ----Define----

Finishes assignments early ----Infer----
                           ----Define----

Inferences of trait come from observations of behaviors

Being able to distinguish behaviors from traits is important for understanding the behavioral model. Descriptions that concern what a person *does* refer to behaviors, whereas descriptions that concern what the person *is* or characteristics that he or she *has* refer to traits. Participation Exercise 3-1 provides a check of your understanding of this distinction.

Participation Exercise 3-1

DISTINGUISHING BETWEEN TRAITS AND BEHAVIORS*

See if you can differentiate between trait and behavioral descriptions in the following paragraph. On a sheet of paper, number from 1 to 20, and write the letter *T* for trait or *B* for behavior for each of the numbered statements.

(1) Ramon is extremely perceptive. (2) He notices even small changes in others' emotions and (3) accurately tells them how they are feeling. (4) He reads a great deal and (5) is very knowledgeable about many topics. (6) He is very intelligent, and (7) he can recall facts he learned years ago. (8) Ramon is a warm, sincere, good-natured person. (9) He is a good friend, (10) goes out of his way to help other people, and (11) is generous with his friends. (12) He always dresses neatly. (13) Ramon works hard, and (14) he is dedicated to his work. (15) He is a good athlete. (16) He swims during the summer and ice skates during the winter. (17) He is an active person (18) who is very energetic. (19) Although he is gregarious, (20) Ramon frequently spends time alone.

Now check your answers in Appendix B. Look at the descriptions you mislabeled and apply the following rule: what a person *does* is a behavior; what a person *is* or *has* is a trait.

Behavior therapists deal with clients' behaviors, not their traits. However, clients often describe themselves and their problems by using traits (for example, "I'm shy and withdrawn"). Thus, behavior therapists must "translate" traits into behaviors. This involves identifying the *behaviors* that are associated with clients' trait descriptions. The key question the therapist asks is: "What specific things do you do that lead you to describe yourself as [the trait]?"

The process of identifying the behaviors that result in a trait description was illustrated earlier with Tonya's trait description of June. As you can see from the additional examples in Table 3-1, there is some overlap among behaviors that indicate different traits. This lack of exclusivity is one reason that trait descriptions are imprecise. It also is a reason why describing the specific behaviors that led to the inference of a trait is necessary to grasp the meaning of the trait. Participation Exercise 3-2 will give you experience in translating traits into behaviors.

* You should do this Participation Exercise before you continue.

Trait	Behaviors That Might Indicate the Trait
Happy	Smiling; laughing; talking about feelings of joy
Depressed	Crying; sitting alone; moving slowly; saying that one is depressed ("down" or unhappy)
Friendly	Greeting people; smiling at others
Trustworthy	Arriving on time to appointments; carrying out assigned tasks; keeping secrets
Generous	Volunteering to help others; frequently paying for the check when dining with others

Table 3-1 Examples of behaviors that might indicate particular traits

---

Participation Exercise 3-2

TRANSLATING TRAITS INTO BEHAVIORS*

Translating trait descriptions into behavioral descriptions involves finding behaviors that could be indicative of particular traits. On a sheet of paper, list several behaviors that might help describe individuals with the following traits:

1. Sociable
2. Hostile
3. Helpful
4. Thrifty
5. Dependable
6. Smart
7. Patient
8. Healthy

Examples of behaviors you might have listed for each trait are given in Appendix B. Your behaviors need not be the same, but they should be activities individuals *do* (in other words, behaviors) that most people would agree indicate the particular trait.

OVERT AND COVERT BEHAVIORS

Behavior is anything a person *does*. There are two broad categories of behavior: overt and covert. **Overt behaviors** are *actions* that other people can directly observe; in a sense, they are public behaviors. Examples include eating, walking, talking, kissing, driving a car, writing a sentence, hanging up one's coat, cooking, laughing, and singing—all behaviors we can "see" others engaging in.

   Covert behaviors are things we do that others cannot directly observe—in other words, private behaviors. (*Covert behaviors* do not refer to secretive actions, such as cheating on an exam or hiding an object, which are overt behaviors that can be observed.) Covert behaviors include *thinking* (and other cognitive processes such as remembering), *feeling* (emotions), and *physiological responses* (for example, decreasing blood pressure and relaxing muscles). Cognitions, emotions, and physiological responses, together with overt actions, constitute the four **modes of behavior** assessed and treated

* You should do this Participation Exercise before you continue.

in behavior therapy. Participation Exercise 3-3 will help you distinguish between overt and covert behaviors.

Participation Exercise 3-3

DISTINGUISHING BETWEEN OVERT AND COVERT BEHAVIORS*

Distinguishing between overt (public) and covert (private) behaviors is easy. You need only ask yourself whether you can *directly observe* the behavior. If you can directly observe the behavior, it is overt. If you cannot directly observe the behavior, it is covert.

For each of the behaviors listed, write *O* next to the overt behaviors and *C* next to the covert behaviors (or write the letters on a sheet of paper). Then check the answers in Appendix B.

1. Singing	11. Listening
2. Thinking	12. Observing
3. Smiling	13. Speaking
4. Learning	14. Dreaming
5. Eating	15. Drinking
6. Remembering	16. Smoking
7. Liking	17. Hoping
8. Staring	18. Touching
9. Enjoying	19. Concentrating
10. Writing	20. Sighing

Covert Behaviors: Special Considerations

Covert behaviors are no less important than overt behaviors. Indeed, many behaviors that supposedly set us apart from our relatives in the animal kingdom are covert, including complex thinking and reasoning. Although behavior therapists deal with both overt and covert behaviors, this was not always the case. Early behavior therapists followed the tradition of Watson's behaviorism and dealt only with overt behaviors (see Chapter 2).

Assessing overt behaviors is relatively straightforward because they are directly observable. In contrast, covert behaviors are private, which makes assessing them more complicated. Each of us has direct knowledge of our own covert behaviors, but we have only indirect knowledge of other people's covert behaviors.

Other people's covert behaviors are inferred from their overt behaviors. (An exception is physiological responses that can be measured directly by instruments, such as a stethoscope and a polygraph.) Most often we learn of others' covert behaviors when they tell us about their thoughts and feelings.

* You should do this Participation Exercise before you continue.

Table 3-2 Examples of
overt behaviors that serve
as anchors for covert
behaviors

Overt Behaviors	Covert Behaviors
Telling others what's "on your mind"	Thinking
Missing an appointment	Forgetting
Staring, wrinkling one's brow, remaining motionless	Concentrating
Trembling, pacing, biting one's nails	Feeling frightened
Hugging, kissing, saying "I love you"	Feeling in love
Applauding, thanking	Appreciating

Talking about one's private experiences is an overt behavior. The other way
we learn about someone's covert behaviors is to observe what the person does
and infer from their overt actions what is "going on inside of them." For
instance, if you see someone smiling and laughing, you are likely to conclude
that the individual is feeling happy. You could say that you have "anchored"
covert behavior with overt behavior.[1] Examples of overt behaviors that serve
as anchors for common covert behaviors are found in Table 3-2. Participation
Exercise 3-4 will give you practice in the anchoring process that behavior
therapists employ.

**Participation
Exercise 3-4**

FINDING OVERT BEHAVIORAL ANCHORS FOR COVERT BEHAVIORS*

In this Participation Exercise, you will think of one or more overt behavioral
anchors for each of six common covert behaviors. In other words, think of
observable behaviors that most people would agree are likely to indicate that the
covert behavior is occurring. As an example, note that you've been asked to
perform a covert behavior, namely to *think* of overt behavioral anchors. If you
want other people, such as your course instructor, to know that you've done this
Exercise, you'll have to perform some overt behavior that indicates that you have
thought of overt behavioral anchors. *Writing down* overt behavioral anchors for
each of the following covert behaviors is an overt behavior.

1. Silent reading
2. Worrying
3. Feeling happy
4. Being interested (in a particular topic)
5. Listening (to a speaker)
6. Liking (a particular person)

Now, compare the overt behavioral anchors you have written with those in
Appendix B.

* You should do this Participation Exercise before you continue.

Why Do We Behave the Way We Do?

How often have you asked, "Why did I do that?" or "Why did so-and-so act that way?" People are fascinated with "why questions" about human behavior. Many theories have been developed to explain human behavior. According to the behavioral model, *a person's behaviors are caused by present events that occur before and after the behaviors have been performed*. **Antecedents** are events that occur or are present *before* the behavior is performed. **Consequences** are events that occur *after* and as a result of the behavior. For example, feeling tired is an antecedent for sleeping, and feeling rested the next day is a consequence of sleeping.

ABC Model

The **ABC model** describes the temporal sequence of antecedents, behavior, and consequences. The specific antecedents and consequences that cause an individual to perform a behavior are called its **maintaining conditions.**[2] However, not all antecedents and consequences of a behavior are its maintaining conditions. Only a relatively small number of antecedents and consequences *maintain* (influence) a behavior, and we will refer to these as **maintaining antecedents** and **maintaining consequences.**

MAINTAINING ANTECEDENTS

Maintaining antecedents serve two functions: they are (1) *prerequisites* and (2) *situational cues* for performing a behavior. In order to engage in a behavior, one must have the requisite knowledge, skills, and resources. For example, *going to the movies* requires knowing where the theater is located and what time the movie starts, being able to get to the theater, and having enough money to pay for a ticket. If these antecedents appear trivial, consider whether you could go to a movie without them.

Situational cues are maintaining antecedents that "set the stage" for the behavior to occur. Situational cues indicate that the time, place, and circumstances are appropriate for performing a particular behavior. Consider the cues that signal you to stop for a traffic light or to pay attention in class. In each case, situational cues play a critical role in determining whether you perform these behaviors. You are not likely to stop at a green light or to daydream when a professor says, "For the next exam, be sure you study. . . ." Behaviors that are influenced by situational cues are said to be under **stimulus control**.[3] Stimulus control has a strong influence on many of our everyday behaviors.

MAINTAINING CONSEQUENCES

Whereas maintaining antecedents are responsible for the behavior being performed in the first place, *maintaining consequences determine whether the behavior will occur again* (see Figure 3-2). In general, when the consequences

◆   **In Theory 3-1**

IT'S *WHERE* YOU ARE (NOT WHO YOU ARE) THAT COUNTS: BEHAVIOR IS SITUATION-SPECIFIC

Our predictions about how people in our lives will act often are correct because people generally behave *consistently*. Many theories have been developed to explain the source of this consistency.

According to the behavioral model, the consistency is determined by the situation in which the behavior is performed. *Situation* refers to the context, including where we are, whom we are with, and what is happening. Situational cues indicate what behaviors are expected in the particular circumstances and are likely to meet with positive consequences. The cues also may tell us which behaviors are inappropriate in the setting and are likely to result in negative consequences. Our personal views about what is expected or appropriate behavior in the situation, based on our previous experiences with similar situations, also are important.

Because our behavior is influenced by the cues in each situation in which we find ourselves, how we act is likely to be consistent in the same or similar situations. The most reliable information we have to predict another person's behaviors is the context in which those behaviors occur. Thus, we say that behavior is **situation-specific.**[4]

A simple example will illustrate what is meant by situation-specific behaviors. Carl is a college student who typically sits quietly in each of his lecture classes, usually talks at a moderate volume whenever he eats with friends at the cafeteria, and often yells himself hoarse at basketball games. In each instance, how loudly Carl speaks is influenced by the social expectations and restrictions associated with the specific context. Carl's speech volume is consistent in similar situations, but it varies in different situations. For example, although Carl sits quietly in all of his lecture classes, he often speaks up in seminars and discussion sections where the demands are different than in lectures.

By way of contrast, the major alternative to the situation-specificity explanation of the consistency of behavior is to attribute the consistency to a person's traits. We might call Carl quiet or loud. Both these descriptions would be inaccurate, however, because *quiet* would not predict Carl's behavior at basketball games and *loud* would not predict Carl's behavior in lecture classes. A description of Carl's behavior in different situations would be more accurate.

---

of performing a behavior are favorable, the individual is more likely to engage in the behavior again. Unfavorable consequences make it less likely that the person will engage in the behavior in the future.

Consequences include what happens directly to the person, to other people, and to the physical environment as a result of the behavior. Consequences can be immediate or delayed.

CALVIN AND HOBBES copyright 1990 Walterson. Dist. by UNIVERSAL PRESS SYNDICATE. Reprinted with permission. All rights reserved.

You may be wondering how events that occur *after* a behavior has been performed can influence that behavior. In fact, the actual consequences of a behavior can influence only the future occurrence of the behavior. However, *expectations* about the probable consequences, which are *antecedents,* influence whether a person will perform a behavior in the present (see Figure 3-2). In other words, a person's prediction about what is likely to happen as a result of performing a particular behavior is one factor that determines whether the conditions are right for performing the behavior. Our expectations about the maintaining consequences of our actions are largely a product of the consequences we have experienced for similar behaviors in the past. *Maintaining consequences for today's actions are the maintaining antecedents of tomorrow's actions.* For example, if Julius's dinner guests praised his Caesar salad last week, he will be tempted to make one this week. The guests' praise was a consequence of making a Caesar salad last week, but it becomes an antecedent of the same behavior this week.

Figure 3-2   The ABC model

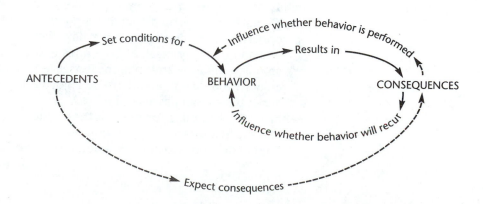

IDENTIFYING MAINTAINING ANTECEDENTS
AND MAINTAINING CONSEQUENCES

Contrary to the popular misconception, behavior therapy does not *directly* change symptoms or behaviors. *Behavior therapy treats problem behaviors by changing their maintaining conditions.* The process of identifying and changing the maintaining conditions of behaviors is central to the behavior therapy process.[5]

◆ ▨▨

Participation Exercise 3-5

IDENTIFYING ANTECEDENTS AND CONSEQUENCES*

This Exercise contains a list of six behaviors and the details surrounding each. From the details, list the antecedents and consequences for each behavior on Work Sheet 3-1.† Include all of the antecedents and consequences that are actually contained in the scenario, but do not assume any that are not mentioned. When you have finished, check your answers with those in Appendix B.

Behavior 1: Calling the police. One hot summer evening, Mrs. Kriegel was sitting in her second-floor apartment. As she looked out the window, she saw two young men attack an elderly woman and then run off with the woman's purse. She immediately called the police. The police thanked her and then rushed to the scene of the crime. Mrs. Kriegel realized she had done the right thing.

Behavior 2: Going to a play. Juanita read about a new play in town. It had received especially good reviews. She knew she could get a student pass to see it and that she could earn extra credit for her English class if she saw the play. As it turned out, she was disappointed in the play and felt it was a waste of time. The extra credit, however, did boost her grade.

Behavior 3: Getting up late. Al did not go to bed until after 3 A.M. He was so drunk that he forgot to set his alarm clock. He awoke two hours late the next morning and missed the last bus to the office. When he finally arrived at his office, he discovered that he had missed two important appointments with clients.

Behavior 4: Cooking a fancy meal. Brendan's parents were coming for a visit, and he wanted to make a good impression. It was the perfect opportunity for him to try out a new recipe, and besides, he enjoyed preparing a fancy meal. Although his efforts turned the kitchen into a complete disaster area, the meal itself was a success, and his parents enjoyed the dinner. Brendan also enjoyed the dinner and felt satisfied about the evening as a whole.

Behavior 5: Shopping for new clothes. Jane badly needed new clothes, and she had saved enough money during the summer to go shopping. She got directions to the new shopping mall and borrowed the family car.

* This Participation Exercise can be done before you continue or later.
† You will find this work sheet in Appendix C.

Jane came home with a comfortable and stylish new wardrobe. She felt good about her new clothes, and her mother and friends commented on how good she looked in the clothes.

Behavior 6: Pulling a fire alarm. Tom spotted a fire alarm box at the corner. He wanted to impress his friends and thought of all the excitement that would occur if he pulled the alarm. After reading the instructions and looking to see that no one was around, he pulled the alarm. Fire trucks raced to the scene within minutes. A crowd quickly gathered. The angry fire chief announced that it was a false alarm. The fire marshal began an investigation, while the crowd slowly dispersed and the fire trucks returned to the station.

◆

As we have said, all of the antecedents and consequences of a behavior are not its maintaining conditions. In behavior therapy, the therapist and client must select from among the antecedents and consequences those that appear to have the most influence on the behavior. In other words, the *probable* maintaining conditions of a behavior are identified and changed.

An example will help to clarify the concept of maintaining antecedents and maintaining consequences and their roles in determining behaviors. Consider the behavior you are engaging in right now—namely, reading a chapter in your textbook. What are the prerequisites and situational cues that have led to your reading the chapter? What are the likely consequences of reading the chapter? Take a moment to write down these antecedents and consequences and then look at the examples in Figure 3-3.

Present Maintaining Conditions Versus Past Originating Conditions: A Critical Distinction

According to the behavioral approach, our behavior is caused by *present* conditions. What role do our past experiences play in determining our current behaviors? The answer is that past events have only an indirect influence on our present behaviors. The factors that directly cause our present behaviors are occurring now.

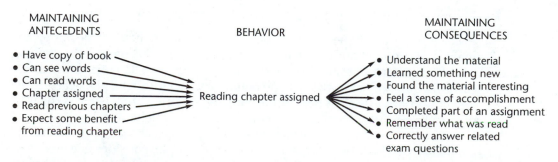

MAINTAINING ANTECEDENTS	BEHAVIOR	MAINTAINING CONSEQUENCES
• Have copy of book • Can see words • Can read words • Chapter assigned • Read previous chapters • Expect some benefit from reading chapter	Reading chapter assigned	• Understand the material • Learned something new • Found the material interesting • Feel a sense of accomplishment • Completed part of an assignment • Remember what was read • Correctly answer related exam questions

Figure 3-3   Some of the possible maintaining antecedents and maintaining consequences of performing a specific behavior: reading an assigned chapter

Let's look at a personal example. When was the last time you dressed yourself? Unless you are lounging at home in your sleeping attire, the answer probably is sometime earlier today. In fact, you dress yourself one or more times a day, every day. What are the maintaining conditions of *dressing yourself*? The maintaining antecedents may include knowing how to dress yourself, having clothes, waking up in the morning, and anticipating going somewhere outside your home. The maintaining consequences may include feeling properly dressed, being complimented on your attire, and not getting arrested for indecent exposure.

Do you recall your first attempts to dress yourself? You may have resisted dressing yourself initially. After all, you had been used to having others dress you, and dressing yourself was difficult and frustrating. Nonetheless, you learned to dress yourself. What were the conditions that resulted in your learning to dress yourself? The major maintaining antecedent probably was being told to get dressed by your parents. The maintaining consequences probably included being praised by your parents and being permitted to engage in some desirable activity (such as going outside to play) that required being dressed.

This example illustrates that the same behavior—dressing yourself—is maintained today by one set of conditions that is very different from the set of conditions under which it originated. This is the essence of a critical distinction between present maintaining conditions and past originating conditions.

Past events can have an *indirect* influence on current behaviors, as when the memory of previous events affects your current behaviors.[6] For instance, *recalling* how pleasant it was to be comforted by your mother when you were crying can help maintain crying years after you received the sympathy. However, note that it is not Mom's actual comfort that is influencing your current behavior. Rather, it is a *memory* of being comforted that serves as a maintaining condition—and memories are *present* events.

Behavior therapists assume that behaviors occurring in the present are directly influenced by present conditions. In other words, *present behaviors are maintained by present maintaining conditions*. Thus, the way to change a present behavior is to change its present maintaining conditions.

Learning and Environment Versus Heredity and Biology

According to the behavioral model, most of our behaviors develop, are maintained, and change primarily through learning. *Learning* is the process by which environmental factors influence behaviors. The **environment** comprises all external influences on behaviors, including the physical setting and conditions as well as the people who are present. What, then, is the role of hereditary and biological factors in determining behaviors?

Hereditary and biological factors are thought to set broad upper limits on a person's psychological characteristics. For example, considerable evidence shows that intelligence has a definite genetic component.[7] Within the broad limits established by one's genetic endowment, however, intelligence can be substantially increased (as by an enriched intellectual environment) or

DON'T LOOK BACK: THE ROLE OF PAST EVENTS ON CURRENT BEHAVIORS

The idea that past events have only a weak influence on our present behaviors may seem contrary to the widely held notion that our past, especially early childhood, has a profound effect on our current lives. The idea that the child is parent to the adult is rooted in psychoanalysis, and like other psychoanalytic concepts, it has become part of our popular common belief system.

The behavioral and psychoanalytic views are not completely contradictory. Both hold that adults are products of their previous experiences. The two perspectives differ, however, in how they view the nature of that influence. Psychoanalysis postulates that early experiences have a direct and permanent influence on later behaviors, implying that current circumstances have little or no influence on adult (or later childhood) behaviors. The behavioral model holds that the behaviors that result from early experiences can, with appropriate learning, be changed so that these early experiences exert little or no influence on later behaviors.

Looking to the past for the determinants of present behaviors can be problematic. Examining past events involves gathering retrospective information, which may be inaccurate. Not only do we forget the specifics of past events, but also we inevitably reconstruct history, as when we fill in missing details or adjust apparent inconsistencies in our recollections. Moreover, even if it were possible to collect reliable accounts of past events, there is no way to test the validity of hypotheses we generate about the causes of the past events since we cannot go back in time.

In contrast, the *current* factors that are influencing the way we behave are considerably easier to assess. First, they are occurring in the present, so obtaining the needed information is more feasible. Second, because the factors are currently active, it is possible to systematically alter them and observe the effects on behaviors. This makes it possible to validate hypotheses about the current maintaining conditions of behaviors.

Viewing the past from the present has its limitations.
PEANUTS Reprinted by permission of UFS, Inc.

decreased (as by minimal intellectual stimulation).[8] Similarly, one's level of activity at birth tends to correspond to the degree to which one engages in active behaviors as an adult.[9] Nevertheless, environmental factors also contribute to activity level, as the following hypothetical example illustrates.

At birth, Hyman exhibited a high activity level, whereas Lois exhibited a low activity level. When Hyman grows up, we would expect to see him doing things quickly, involved in many activities, and usually on the go with abundant energy. In contrast, we would anticipate that as an adult Lois would generally move slowly, engage in only a few activities, and spend much time in sedentary behaviors.

However, suppose in adulthood Hyman's wife models and encourages a slow-paced life, and Lois's husband displays and rewards a fast-paced life. Under these circumstances, it is possible that Lois and Hyman might exhibit similar levels of activity as adults. Hyman's activity would be below his "biological" level, and Lois's activity would be above hers. However, Lois is

---

◆   **In Theory 3-3**

FREEDOM IN TRIADIC RECIPROCAL DETERMINISM

What is the relationship among our (1) environment, (2) covert behaviors (how we think and feel), and (3) overt behaviors? In practice, each of these factors influences and is influenced by the two other factors, as Figure 3-4 depicts. In other words, they are *reciprocally determined*. Bandura describes such a relationship as *triadic reciprocal determinism*.[10] As an example, consider how the environment, covert behaviors, and overt behaviors might reciprocally influence one another in the case of writing a paper. The various combinations of determinism are illustrated in Table 3-3.

The notion of triadic reciprocal determinism has important implications for personal freedom. How we behave is not rigidly determined by external forces. We can alter or create the factors that influence our behaviors. For instance, a woman who overeats when socializing with friends in restaurants can set up social engagements where food is not served. Likewise, a man who thinks poorly of himself because he is unsuccessful in his work can select a job at which he can succeed, which, in turn, will influence his self-concept. The key to personal freedom lies in understanding the factors that influence our behaviors and accepting responsibility for controlling them.

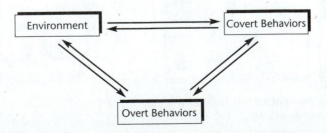

Figure 3-4 According to the principle of triadic reciprocal determinism, the environment, overt behaviors, and covert behaviors each influence and are influenced by the two other factors (In Theory 3-3)

Table 3-3 Examples of how the environment, covert behaviors, and overt behaviors might reciprocally determine one another in the case of writing a paper (In Theory 3-3)

ENVIRONMENT influences OVERT BEHAVIOR

When Chung writes in a quiet place, he gets more writing done.

OVERT BEHAVIOR influences ENVIRONMENT

Sally doesn't get much writing done in her dorm because of too many distractions; next time, she writes at the library.

COVERT BEHAVIOR influences OVERT BEHAVIOR

When Joan thinks that a particular topic is interesting, she spends more time writing about it.

OVERT BEHAVIOR influences COVERT BEHAVIOR

When Carlos successfully completes a difficult paper, he feels competent as a student.

ENVIRONMENT influences COVERT BEHAVIOR

When Manny waits until the night before to write a paper, he gets anxious.

COVERT BEHAVIOR influences ENVIRONMENT

If Lena is having difficulty concentrating while writing a paper, she does her writing in the writing study hall, where she can get help from a teaching assistant.

---

not likely to engage in the very high level of activity that Hyman could potentially engage in.

Many behaviors can be influenced by learning, even if they have hereditable or biological components.[11] Thus, some psychological disorders that appear to have substantial hereditable or biological origins can be changed through learning (for example, autistic behaviors and developmental disabilities of children, and schizophrenic behaviors and some types of depressive behaviors of adults[12]). It also is possible that behavior therapy procedures that teach clients more adaptive ways of behaving can change biological functioning, such as central nervous system activity.[13] To summarize, heredity and biology set wide boundaries for behaviors; within these limits, learning and environmental factors play a significant role in influencing behaviors.

SUMMARY

1. The behavioral model defines people in terms of their behaviors.
2. In contrast, the most common way of describing people is in terms of their traits. The problems with trait descriptions are that they are open to alternative interpretations; they provide no information about when the trait will influence a person's behaviors; and they are based on circular reasoning.
3. Behavioral descriptions are more precise than trait descriptions, and they preserve individuality.
4. Behavior is anything a person does. Overt behaviors are actions that other people can directly observe. Covert behaviors are private behaviors, consisting of thoughts, feelings, and physiological responses.

Covert behaviors are inferred from overt behaviors, with the exception of physiological responses, which can be measured directly by instruments.

5. The ABC model describes the temporal sequence of antecedents, behavior, and consequences. The specific antecedents and consequences that cause an individual to perform a behavior are its maintaining conditions. Maintaining antecedents serve two functions: they are both prerequisites and situational cues for performing a behavior. Maintaining consequences determine whether the behavior will occur again.

6. Behavior therapy treats problem behaviors by directly changing their maintaining conditions.

7. The past originating conditions of a behavior—those conditions that account for its initial development—have only an indirect influence on our present behaviors.

8. Our behaviors are situation-specific. They are consistent in the same or a similar situation and vary in different situations.

9. Most of our behaviors develop, are maintained, and change primarily through learning. Heredity and biology set broad upper limits for some behaviors, but learning and environmental factors still play a significant role in influencing them.

10. Triadic reciprocal determinism indicates that the environment, covert behaviors, and overt behaviors are interrelated, each influencing and being influenced by the others.

REFERENCE NOTES

1. Craighead, Kazdin, & Mahoney, 1976.
2. For example, Mace, 1994.
3. For example, Kennedy & Itkonen, 1993.
4. Mischel, 1968, 1973.
5. Compare with Cautela, 1993.
6. For example, Sahakian & Charlesworth, 1994.
7. Willerman, 1979.
8. For example, Lee, 1951; Skeels, 1966.
9. For example, Buss, Plomin, & Willerman, 1973; Torgersen, 1985.
10. Bandura, 1986a, 1986b; compare with Tryon, 1995.
11. For example, Iwata, 1994; Otto & Pollack, 1994.
12. O'Leary & Wilson, 1975.
13. For example, Baxter, Schwartz, Bergman, Szuba, Guze, Mazziotta, Akazraju, Selin, Ferng, Munford, & Phelps, 1992.

Chapter 4

The Practice of Behavior Therapy

The behavioral model described in Chapter 3 is the basis for behavior therapy. In this chapter, you'll get an overview of how that model is applied in the practice of behavior therapy.

We begin with a classic case published in 1965. The senior therapist was Arnold Lazarus, one of the founders of behavior therapy. The case illustrates many of the principles of the behavioral model presented in Chapter 3. It also provides examples of the defining themes and characteristics of behavior therapy described in Chapter 1. As you read through the case, see if you can identify the themes and characteristics.

Case 4-1

THE BEHAVIORAL ANALYSIS OF A PHOBIA IN A NINE-YEAR-OLD BOY[1]*

Background

When he was referred for therapy, Paul, age nine, had been absent from school for three weeks. The summer vacation had ended six weeks previously, and on entering the fourth grade, Paul avoided the classroom situation. He was often found hiding in the cloakroom and subsequently began spending less time at school each day. Thereafter, neither threats, bribes, nor punishments could induce him to reenter school.

Paul's history revealed a series of similar episodes. During his first day of kindergarten, he succeeded in climbing over an extremely high wall and fled home. His first-grade teacher considered him to be "disturbed." Serious difficulties regarding school attendance were first exhibited when Paul entered the second grade of a parochial school. It was alleged that the second-grade teacher . . . generally intimidated the children and was very free with physical punishment. . . . At this stage he became progressively more reluctant to enter the school and finally refused entirely. A psychiatrist was consulted and is reported to have advised the parents to use coercion, whereupon Paul was literally dragged screaming to school by a truant officer. Paul was especially bitter about his experience with the psychiatrist. In the third grade Paul was transferred to the neighborhood public school where he spent a trouble-free year at the hands of an exceedingly kind teacher.

A series of specific traumatic events commenced with [Paul's] near-drowning when five years old. Toward the end of his third grade, he underwent a serious appendectomy with critical complications, which was followed by painful postoperative experiences in a doctor's consulting room. During one of these examinations, as Paul bitterly recounted, he had been left alone by his parents. Shortly after his recovery from surgery, he witnessed a drowning [that] upset

---

* The title we have given this case is intended to be a humorous counterpoint to Freud's (1955) classic case, "The Analysis of a Phobia in a Five-Year-Old Boy." The similarity between the two cases, especially with respect to the treatment, ends with the titles.

him considerably. Following his entry into the fourth grade, the sudden death of a 12-year-old girl, who had been a close friend of his elder sister, profoundly affected the entire family. It is also noteworthy that Paul's father experienced personal stress in his work situation during the child's turbulent second grade, as well as immediately preceding fourth grade. Finally, Paul seemed to have been intimidated by a warning from his eldest sister that fourth-grade schoolwork was particularly difficult. . . .

Treatment Plan

After the initial interview, it was evident that Paul's school phobia was the most disruptive response pattern of a generally bewildered and intimidated child. Although subsequent interviews revealed the plethora of familial tensions, situational crises, and [a history of] . . . specific traumatic events [described earlier] . . . the initial therapeutic objective was to reinstate normal school attendance. . . .

The school was situated two and one-half blocks away from the home. The routine was for Paul to leave for school at 8:30 A.M. in order to arrive by 8:40. The first recess was from 10:00–10:30, lunch break from 12:00–1:00, and classes ended at 3:30 P.M. At the time when therapy was initiated, the boy was extremely surly and dejected in the mornings (as reported by the parents), refused breakfast, rarely dressed himself, and became noticeably more fearful toward 8:30. Parental attempts at reassurance, coaxing, or coercion elicited only sobbing and further withdrawal.

Accordingly, the boy was exposed to the following increasingly [more] difficult steps along the main dimensions of his school phobia:

1. On a Sunday afternoon, accompanied by the therapists, he walked from his house to the school. The therapists were able to allay Paul's anxiety by means of distraction and humor, so that his initial exposure was relatively pleasant.

2. On the next two days at 8:30 A.M., accompanied by one of the therapists, he walked from his house into the schoolyard. Again, Paul's feelings of anxiety were reduced by means of coaxing, encouragement, relaxation, and the use of "emotive imagery" (i.e., the deliberate picturing of subjectively pleasant images such as Christmas and a visit to Disneyland while relating them to the school situation). . . . Approximately 15 minutes were spent roaming around the school grounds, after which Paul returned home.

3. After school was over for the day, the therapist was able to persuade the boy to enter the classroom and sit down at his desk. Part of the normal school routine was then playfully enacted.

4. On the following three mornings, the therapist accompanied the boy into the classroom with the other children. They chatted with the teacher, and left immediately after the opening exercises.

5. A week after beginning this program, Paul spent the entire morning in class. The therapist sat in the classroom and smiled approvingly at Paul whenever he interacted with his classmates or the teacher.

6. Two days later when Paul and the therapist arrived at school, the boy lined up with the other children and allowed the therapist to wait for him inside the classroom. This was the first time that Paul had not insisted on having the therapist in constant view.

7. Thereafter, the therapist sat in the school library adjoining the classroom.

8. It was then agreed that the therapist would leave at 2:30 P.M. while Paul remained for the last hour of school.

9. On the following day, Paul remained alone at school from 1:45 P.M. until 2:45 P.M. (Earlier that day, the therapist had unsuccessfully attempted to leave the boy alone from 10 until noon.)

10. Instead of fetching the boy at his home, the therapist arranged to meet him at the school gate at 8:30 A.M. Paul also agreed to remain alone at school from 10:45 A.M. until noon provided that the therapist return to eat lunch with him. At 1:45 P.M. the therapist left again with the promise that if the boy remained until school ended (3:30 P.M.) he would visit Paul that evening and play the guitar for him.

11. Occasional setbacks made it necessary to instruct the lad's mother not to allow the boy into the house during school hours. In addition, the teacher was asked to provide special jobs for the boy so as to increase his active participation and make school more attractive. . . .

12. After meeting the boy in the mornings, the therapist gradually left him alone at school for progressively longer periods of time. After six days of this procedure, the therapist was able to leave at 10 A.M.

13. The boy was assured that the therapist would be in the faculty room until 10 A.M., if needed. Thus, he came to school knowing the therapist was present, but not actually seeing him.

14. With Paul's consent the therapist arrived at school shortly *after* the boy entered the classroom at 8:40 A.M.

15. School attendance independent of the therapist's presence was achieved by means of specific rewards (a comic book, and variously colored tokens [that] would eventually procure a baseball glove) contingent upon his entering school and remaining there alone. He was at liberty to telephone the therapist in the morning if he wanted him at school, in which event he would forfeit his rewards for that day.

16. Since the therapist's presence seemed to have at least as much reward value as the comic books and tokens, it was necessary to enlist the mother's cooperation to effect the therapist's final withdrawal. The overall diminution of the boy's anxieties, together

with the general gains [that] had accrued to his home situation, made it therapeutically feasible for the mother to emphasize the fact that school attendance was compulsory, and that social agencies beyond the control of both therapists and parents would enforce this requirement eventually.

17. Approximately three weeks later, Paul had accumulated enough tokens to procure his baseball glove. He then agreed with his parents that rewards of this kind were no longer necessary.

Outcome

Paul's therapy was carried out over 4½ months, during which there were a number of setbacks. At the end of treatment, Paul was not only attending school regularly but, according to his mother's reports, his behavior had improved outside of school. For example, Paul had become less moody, more willing to participate in household chores, more congenial in his relationships with his peers, and more self-sufficient. Ten months after the termination of therapy, Paul's mother reported that Paul had not only maintained the positive changes but he also had progressed further.

DEFINING THEMES AND COMMON CHARACTERISTICS OF BEHAVIOR THERAPY IN CASE 4-1

Many features of the treatment for Paul's school-phobic behaviors are typical of behavior therapy. The *scientific approach* taken in Paul's case is evident in the precision used in the assessment and treatment. For example, highly specific details regarding the circumstances surrounding the problem behaviors, such as precise times, were gathered. The targets of treatment were specific, clearly defined overt behaviors: staying away from school and going to school.

Paul was encouraged to engage in *active* procedures that helped reduce his fear and increase his school attendance and his positive feelings about being in school. This approach contrasts with verbal psychotherapy, in which Paul would only have talked about his problems with the therapist. Further, Paul's therapy took place in vivo. The therapists worked directly with Paul in the school setting, where the problem was occurring. Because a therapist had to be at school with Paul for many hours, multiple therapists were employed. It is not typical to use multiple therapists in behavior therapy. However, it is common, especially with children, to enlist the aid of nonprofessional change agents, like Paul's mother and teacher, to implement specific aspects of the treatment.

The focus of therapy was clearly in the *present*. The maintaining conditions of Paul's problem that were identified were occurring at present—namely, fear of going to school and lack of positive consequences for attending school. Although the therapists had abundant information about previous problems indirectly related to Paul's difficulties, the therapists concentrated on current factors.

No clear-cut examples of the *self-control approach* appear in Case 4-1. In the 1960s, when this case occurred, the self-control approach was not an integral part of behavior therapy.

Four common characteristics of behavior therapy also are part of Case 4-1. Consistent with the *collaborative nature* of behavior therapy, Paul was consulted about a variety of treatment decisions even though he was only nine. Although standard therapy procedures were employed, they were *individualized* to fit Paul's unique case (for example, the reinforcers for school attendance, such as a baseball glove, were matched to Paul's interests). Paul's treatment involved *a stepwise progression* in which Paul was gradually exposed to increasingly more anxiety-evoking events. Finally, a variety of behavior therapy procedures were combined in *a treatment package* (including emotive imagery, in vivo exposure, shaping, and reinforcement).

PROCESS OF BEHAVIOR THERAPY: AN OVERVIEW

The process of behavior therapy involves a series of interrelated steps, which are shown schematically in Figure 4-1. The steps are as follows:

1. Clarifying the client's problem
2. Designing a target behavior
3. Formulating goals for therapy
4. Identifying the maintaining conditions of the target behavior
5. Designing a plan to change the maintaining conditions
6. Implementing the change plan (treatment procedures)
7. Evaluating the success of the change plan
8. Conducting follow-up assessment

Additionally, measurement of the target behavior begins immediately after the target behavior has been defined (step 2), and continues through the evaluation of therapy (step 7). Steps 1 to 4, 7, and 8 will be discussed in this chapter, and steps 5 and 6 will be covered in later chapters.

If the therapy procedures have successfully changed the target behavior, then the therapy is either (1) terminated or (2) the process is started again with another target behavior. If the therapy procedures have not been successful, the therapist and client return to the step where the process broke down. For instance, the target behavior may not have been defined precisely enough or the therapy procedures may not have been implemented correctly.

CLARIFYING THE PROBLEM

Clients often describe their problems in broad, vague terms (for example, "I'm unhappy much of the time"; "I can't seem to cope with my job"). The

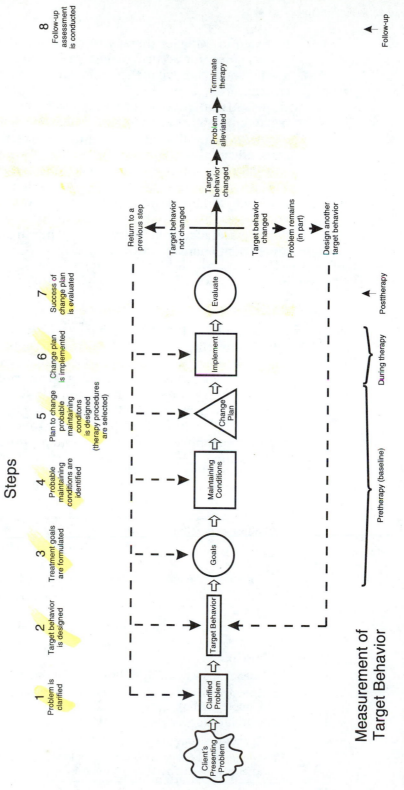

Figure 4-1 The process of behavior therapy

SOURCE: © Michael D. Spiegler and David C. Guevremont

first step in behavior therapy is to clarify the client's presenting problem. For instance, for a client whose presenting problem is "I'm stressed out a lot," specifying what the client means by "stressed out" and "a lot" is critical.

Clients often come to therapy with multiple problems. Accordingly, behavior therapy begins by narrowing the client's complaints to one or two problems that will be worked on initially. Treating one problem at a time has three advantages. First, clients can focus their attention more easily on one task than on multiple tasks. Second, concentrating on a single problem often results in change relatively quickly, which may motivate the client to continue working on other problems. Third, problems may be related to one another, so that alleviating one problem may reduce or even eliminate other problems (as with Paul in Case 4-1).[2] Thus, treating one problem at a time is an efficient approach in the long run.

DESIGNING A TARGET BEHAVIOR

The second step in behavior therapy—designing a target behavior—further refines the client's problem. A **target behavior** is a narrow, discrete aspect of the problem that can be clearly defined and easily measured. A series of target behaviors was developed for Paul's fear of going to school (see Table 4-1). The target behaviors were arranged in order of increasing difficulty, and each of the 11 target behaviors was dealt with in sequence, starting with the easiest and least anxiety-provoking. The same advantages of focusing on one or two problems hold for treating one or two target behaviors at a time.

Table 4-1 Target behaviors selected for Paul (Case 4-1), in order of increasing difficulty

1. Walking from the house to the school with the therapist on a nonschool day
2. Walking from the house to the schoolyard with the therapist at an appropriate time (that is, 8:30 A.M.) on a school day
3. Spending 15 minutes in the schoolyard with the therapist
4. Entering the classroom and sitting at a desk with the therapist present after school hours
5. "Playing school" in the classroom with the therapist after school hours
6. Entering the classroom and talking with the teacher in the presence of the therapist
7. Spending the morning in the classroom with the therapist present
8. Spending the day at school without the therapist in sight (but available in the school building)
9. Walking to school alone
10. Spending all day in school with the therapist unavailable part of the day
11. Spending all day in school with the therapist unavailable (that is, normal school attendance—the total target behavior)

Characteristics of Good Target Behaviors

Target behaviors should meet four requirements.

1. *Narrow in scope.* The target behavior usually addresses one part of the problem rather than the entire problem. Further, the definition of the target behavior may include a specific time when and place where it is appropriate to engage in it (for example, "making one's bed before leaving the house").

2. *Unambiguously defined.* When a target behavior is defined precisely, it can be assessed reliably. In the case of an overt behavior, knowing the definition of the target behavior should allow anyone observing the client to tell whether the client is engaging in the target behavior.

3. *Measurable.* The target behavior should be quantified whenever possible. Numbers are more precise than qualitative categories (such as improved versus unimproved). The measurements can be of (1) *frequency* (how often), (2) *duration* (length of time), (3) *intensity* (strength), or (4) *amount of by-product* of the target behavior (for example, the amount of liquid soap remaining in a soap dispenser as an indication of hand washing[3]). Table 4-2 describes these measures and provides examples. The type of measure employed depends on such factors as the nature of the target behavior, the client's goals, and practical considerations. As you will note in Table 4-2, not all of the measures are relevant to all target behaviors.

4. *Appropriate for the problem and client.* The target behavior must fit the problem and be adaptive. This includes not causing other problems (for instance, in the treatment of obesity, smoking as a substitute for snacking

Table 4-2 Types of measures used to assess target behaviors

Type	Description	Examples
FREQUENCY	Number of times the behavior occurs	1. Number of days child attends school 2. Number of cigarettes smoked
TIME	a. Length of time spent engaging in target behavior b. Latency (length of time to begin a target behavior)	1. Hours child spends in school 2. Minutes spent smoking 1. Minutes to enter school after being dropped off by parents 2. Minutes to light up after sitting down at desk
	c. Interval between responses (length of time between the occurrence of instances of the target behavior)	1. *Not relevant to school attendance* 2. Minutes between cigarettes smoked
INTENSITY	Strength of the target behavior	1. How anxious (on scale of 1–10) child feels while in school 2. *Not relevant to cigarette smoking*
AMOUNT OF BY-PRODUCT	Number of by-products of engaging in the target behavior	1. Number of punches in lunch meal ticket 2. Number of cigarette butts left in ashtray

between meals results in its own health hazards). The target behavior also must suit the particular client's circumstances and abilities. For example, a visually impaired client would not be asked to read cue cards as reminders to eat healthy snacks.

Acceleration and Deceleration Target Behaviors

There are two categories of target behaviors. **Acceleration target behaviors** are increased, and **deceleration target behaviors** are decreased. Acceleration target behaviors are set up for **behavioral deficits,** which are adaptive behaviors that clients are not performing often enough, long enough, or strongly enough (such as paying attention in class and standing up for one's rights). Deceleration target behaviors are established for **behavioral excesses,** which are maladaptive behaviors that clients are performing too often, for too long a time, or too strongly (for example, fighting and smoking).

Dealing with acceleration target behaviors is simple and straightforward. Behavior therapy procedures are used to increase the acceleration target behavior directly. For example, if social interaction was the acceleration

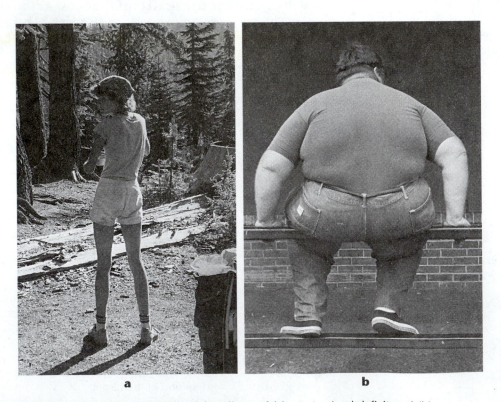

| a | b |

Photos 4-1a and b   Examples of the effects of (a) a behavioral deficit and (b) a behavioral excess in eating

target behavior for a hospitalized client who was depressed, the nurses might praise the client each time they saw her interacting with someone. Dealing with deceleration target behaviors is more complicated.

SPECIAL CONSIDERATIONS FOR DECELERATION TARGET BEHAVIORS

Two basic strategies are used to treat deceleration target behaviors. One is to decrease the deceleration target behavior directly, as parents often try to do by punishing a child's misbehavior. This strategy is simple, but it often provides an incomplete solution. When a problem behavior is eliminated or substantially decreased, a void is created in the person's life. No matter how disruptive the problem behavior was, it served a function and accounted for periods of time in the person's life.

The preferred strategy for treating deceleration target behaviors fills the functional and temporal void with an appropriate adaptive behavior. This is done by increasing an acceleration target behavior that substitutes for the deceleration target behavior. For instance, if the deceleration target behavior is criticizing friends, complimenting friends would be a suitable substitute behavior. Often both strategies are implemented simultaneously. In other words, the deceleration target behavior is decreased at the same time that an appropriate substitute acceleration target behavior is increased.

An acceleration target behavior that is used as a substitute for a deceleration target behavior must meet three requirements. First, it must serve the same general function; compliments and criticisms, for example, are both ways of communicating feedback. Second, it should be adaptive; nothing is gained by substituting one maladaptive behavior for another. Third, the acceleration and deceleration target behaviors should be **competing responses;** that is, it should be difficult to perform both at the same time (as is true of complimenting and criticizing). The more the client performs the acceleration target behavior, the fewer opportunities the client has to engage in the deceleration target behavior. It is standard practice in behavior therapy to include an acceleration target behavior in treatment plans that involve a deceleration target behavior. Table 4-3 has examples of deceleration target behaviors and suitable competing acceleration target behaviors.

Table 4-3 Examples of acceleration target behaviors that compete with deceleration target behaviors

Deceleration Target Behavior	Competing Acceleration Target Behavior
Studying in front of the television	Studying in the library
Biting fingernails	Keeping hands in pockets or at sides
Driving home from parties drunk	Taking a taxi home
Staying up until 3 A.M.	Getting into bed and turning out the lights at 1 A.M.
Talking to "voices" (that is, hallucinating)	Talking to other people
Criticizing others	Praising others

Participation Exercise 4-1

FINDING COMPETING ACCELERATION TARGET BEHAVIORS TO SUBSTITUTE FOR UNDESIRABLE BEHAVIORS*

In this Participation Exercise, you will devise acceleration target behaviors that compete with undesirable behaviors. For each undesirable behavior, write one or more acceleration target behaviors (behaviors that are to be increased) that, when performed, make it unlikely that the undesirable behavior will occur. Be sure that each of your acceleration target behaviors meets the requirements for a good target behavior that we described earlier in the chapter.

1. Eating junk food between meals
2. Cramming for exams
3. Blowing an entire paycheck
4. Using foul language
5. Leaving lights on that are not in use
6. Wasting time
7. Being late for classes
8. Procrastinating in paying bills
9. Littering

Examples of appropriate competing acceleration target behaviors are given in Appendix B.

DEAD PERSON RULE

One problem with deceleration target behaviors is that they indicate only what clients should *not* do. In contrast, acceleration target behaviors tell clients what to do. Consider a typical scene in an elementary school classroom. Toni is disrupting the class by talking to Heather when the class is supposed to be reading silently. If the teacher tells Toni, "Don't talk to Heather" (a deceleration target behavior), all Toni knows is what she is *not* allowed to do. She could obey her teacher by talking to Jessica or by dancing in the aisle. It would be more useful if the teacher told Toni, "Read your book" (an acceleration target behavior).

In practice, it is easier but less beneficial to deal with behavioral excesses by specifying what a client should not do than what the client should do. To avoid making this mistake, behavior therapists follow the **dead person rule**: *Never ask a client to do something a dead person can do.* Only dead people are capable of *not* behaving! "Don't talk" violates the dead person rule because dead people "can" not talk. Applying the dead person rule means that the client is asked to do something *active.* "Read your book" follows the dead person rule because dead people can't read books.

Ironically, the dead person rule violates itself. "Never asking a client to do something a dead person can do" is itself something a dead person *could* do. The general principle could be rephrased as a *live person rule:* Always ask a client to do something that only a live person can do. However, the purpose of the dead person rule is to remind therapists to formulate target behaviors

* You should do this Participation Exercise before you continue.

that clients can perform actively. This function is better served by the catchy nature of the dead person rule. Participation Exercise 4-2 gives you a chance to apply the dead person rule to common violations of the rule.

| Participation Exercise 4-2 | RESURRECTING THE DEAD: IDENTIFYING AND CORRECTING DEAD PERSON BEHAVIORS* |

The dead person rule is violated often in everyday life. This Participation Exercise will make you aware of common violations of the dead person rule and give you practice in rephrasing dead person behaviors as live person behaviors.

Part I: Changing Dead Person Behaviors to Live Person Behaviors

A series of frequently heard or seen instructions are listed in Table 4-4. Each instruction requests someone to perform a dead person behavior. For each instruction, write a *live person behavior* that is appropriate for the situation. Put the live person behavior in the third column of Work Sheet 4-1, Part I.† When you have finished, compare your answers to those in Appendix B.

* You should do Part I of the Participation Exercise before you continue, but you will need to do Part II later.
† You will find this work sheet in Appendix C.

Table 4-4 Common instructions that violate the dead person rule (Participation Exercise 4-2)

Situation/Context	Instruction
Parent to child	"Don't be impolite."
Sign in park	DO NOT LITTER
Teacher to student	"No running in the hallway."
Sign on one of two side-by-side doors	DO NOT ENTER
Parent to young boy having trouble tying his shoe	"Don't cry; big boys don't cry."
Parent to child at dinner table	"Don't eat with your fingers."
Sign at petting zoo	DO NOT FEED THE ANIMALS
Parent to child being put to bed	"I don't want to hear another word out of you."
Traffic sign at fork in road	NO LEFT TURN
Teacher to student	"Don't look at other students' tests."
Instructions on a written form	DO NOT WRITE BELOW THE RED LINE
Lifeguard to swimmer	"No diving off the side."
Parent to child	"Don't hit your sister when she takes your toy."

Part II: Identifying Common Dead Person Behaviors

Over the next few days, look for violations of the dead person rule you hear in people's instructions to others and see in written instructions. Record five of these instances in Part II of Work Sheet 4-1 in the blank spaces provided. Briefly note the situation or context (following the models in Table 4-4), then write the dead person instruction, and finally rephrase the instruction so that it refers to a live person behavior.

◆

Measuring the Target Behavior

Measurement of the target behavior begins as soon as it has been defined and before therapy begins. This initial measurement provides a **baseline,** which consists of the repeated measurement of the natural occurrence of a target behavior prior to the introduction of a treatment. A baseline provides a standard by which to evaluate if and how much a target behavior changes after a treatment has been introduced.[4] Measurement of the target behavior continues throughout the remainder of the therapy process, thereby affording an ongoing progress check.

Formulating Treatment Goals

Clients' goals are formulated, reevaluated, and changed at various points in the course of therapy. (Thus, designating "formulating goals" as the third step in the process of behavior therapy is arbitrary.) Clients always enter therapy with some goals, although they may be implicit and very general (for instance, "getting help with my problem" or "feeling better"). More specific goals can be formulated once the client's problem is clarified and a target behavior has been designed. Sometimes clients change their goals during the course of the therapy procedures. For example, they may raise or lower their expectations about the degree to which the target behavior might change, based on its ongoing assessment.

The client is given the major responsibility for deciding on the therapy goals, and the goals always are individualized. However, the therapist assists the client in clarifying expectations about the outcome of treatment and making goals realistic. The therapist takes a more active role in goal setting when the client's goals are either (1) clearly unrealistic (for example, parents want their child to comply with 100% of their instructions) or (2) likely to result in negative consequences for the client or others (for instance, a high school senior wants to lose 20 pounds in the two weeks before her prom).

IDENTIFYING MAINTAINING CONDITIONS

Identifying the maintaining conditions of the target behavior is a critical step because it is those conditions that will be changed in order to change the target behavior.[5] A variety of behavioral assessment procedures are employed to pinpoint maintaining antecedents and maintaining consequences.

The assessment typically begins with an interview in which the therapist questions the client in detail about the antecedents and consequences of the target behavior.[6] The questions would include: "In what situations do you engage in the target behavior most frequently and least frequently?"; "What are you thinking and how are you feeling right before you perform the target behavior?"; "What happens right after you perform the target behavior?"; and "What are the long-term effects of engaging in the target behavior?"

The retrospective information gathered in interviews may be checked out with other assessment procedures.[7] The client may be asked to keep a record of when the target behavior occurs during the week and to note the antecedents and consequences in each case. Parents may be instructed to observe the circumstances in which their child engages in the target behavior. Sometimes a simulated situation is set up in which possible maintaining conditions are systematically presented and removed, and the effects on the target behavior are noted.[8] For example, a child who has trouble concentrating on schoolwork might be asked to work on an assignment with and without an adult present.

Participation Exercise 4-3   DESIGNING AN ANALOGUE TARGET BEHAVIOR AND IDENTIFYING ITS MAINTAINING CONDITIONS*

To enhance your appreciation of the process of behavior therapy, you will have an opportunity to engage in analogues of its major steps in a series of four Participation Exercises. In this Participation Exercise, you will choose a simple behavior you might like to change, define it as a target behavior, and identify its probable maintaining conditions. Next, you will measure the target behavior (Participation Exercise 5-4). Then, after learning about different ways to change the maintaining conditions of target behaviors, you will design change plans based on consequential behavior therapies (Participation Exercise 8-2), and cognitive-behavioral therapies (Participation Exercise 13-3).

Part I: Choosing a Behavior to Change

Clients enter behavior therapy with a "real" problem. However, for this and the other analogue Participation Exercises, you will select a simple behavior that you *might* like to change or would be willing to change. You also should be willing to discuss the behavior with classmates, as you will benefit from their feedback in doing this Exercise.

Examples of behaviors students have chosen for this purpose include making one's bed before leaving the house each morning, exercising daily, writing home regularly, keeping one's car neat, and cutting down on TV time. The behavior can be either a behavioral deficit (which you want to increase) or a behavioral excess (which you want to decrease). The behavior should occur routinely so that it can easily be assessed.

It is important that you do *not* select a behavior that is a true problem for you (for example, any behavior related to anxiety or fear). The behavior definitely should *not* be one for which you would ever seek help from a therapist. Further, the behavior should play a minor role in your life. If the behavior does not change, your life should not be affected in any significant way.

Part II: Designing a Target Behavior

The next step is to design a precise target behavior for the behavior you have selected. Be sure the target behavior has the characteristics of a good target behavior (see page 51). You may find it helpful to ask one or two classmates to read the definition of your target behavior. They may see ambiguities in the definition and may be able to point out ways to make the definition more precise.

Part III: Identifying Maintaining Conditions

Once you have a target behavior, you must identify its maintaining conditions. Make a list of the probable maintaining antecedents, both prerequisites and situational cues, and the probable maintaining consequences; in other words,

* You will need to do this Participation Exercise later, but you should read it now.

identify the antecedents and consequences that are most likely to be influencing your engaging in the behavior. Remember that not all antecedents and consequences of a behavior are its maintaining conditions.

When you have listed all the probable maintaining antecedents and consequences you can think of, show your list to one or two classmates. Have them question you about the relevance and importance of the antecedents and consequences you listed and suggest other *possible* maintaining conditions you may not have considered.

Save the written definition of the target behavior and the list of maintaining conditions. You will need them for later analogue Participation Exercises.

CHANGING MAINTAINING CONDITIONS

A target behavior is changed indirectly by directly changing its maintaining conditions. In Case 4-1, for example, Paul's acceleration target behavior—school attendance—occurred infrequently because its consequences (anxiety) were negative. Accordingly, school attendance was increased by changing the maintaining consequences. Specifically, Paul was given positive consequences for attending school, such as the support and friendship of the therapists and specific tangible reinforcers.

Most behaviors are maintained by multiple antecedents and consequences. For example, among the common maintaining consequences of self-injurious behaviors (such as head banging) associated with severe developmental disorders are social attention, direct sensory stimulation, and removal of clients from a frustrating task.[9] Generally, it is not feasible or necessary to change all of the maintaining conditions in order to change the behavior because the maintaining conditions of a behavior tend to be interrelated. Behavior therapists select for change those maintaining conditions (1) that appear to exert the greatest control over the target behavior and (2) that are most likely to be modified by available behavior therapy procedures.

BEHAVIOR THERAPY RESEARCH

Research is an integral part of behavior therapy. *Process research* involves discovering the effective components of a therapy procedure—in other words, what makes it work.[10] *Outcome research*, used to evaluate the effectiveness of therapy procedures, is the major type of research done by behavior therapists. Outcome research is used both to evaluate the effectiveness of a specific treatment for a particular client and to validate the effectiveness of a therapy procedure in general. We will describe the three strategies most commonly used to evaluate treatment effectiveness: case studies, single subject studies, and experiments.

Case Studies

Case studies, such as Case 4-1 at the beginning of this chapter, provide detailed descriptions of what transpires during the treatment of a specific client.[11] Besides documenting the success of therapy for individuals, case studies also are useful for describing new therapy procedures and presenting unusual applications.[12] The case studies in this book will give you a behind-the-scenes look at the practice of behavior therapy. (Be aware that the sections in this book designated *Case*, such as Case 4-1, contain single subject studies and experiments as well as case studies.)

The inability to generalize to other clients from the findings of a case study is a major limitation of this research method. A single case cannot be considered representative of all or even most people. Sometimes, however, a series of case studies that replicates a therapy procedure with a number of clients is used to document the effectiveness of the procedure.[13] Another limitation of case studies is that they do not provide definitive information about the causes of changes in clients' problem behaviors. The reason is that case studies cannot rule out the possibility that factors other than the treatment might have contributed to improvement. For example, variations in a client's life circumstances—such as gaining a new job—that occur concurrently with therapy may be responsible for changes in the client's problems.

Single Subject Studies

Single subject studies systematically compare what happens when target behaviors are treated and when they are not treated. When a target behavior changes only after the therapy is introduced, this effect provides evidence that the changes were due to the therapy.[14] Thus, single subject studies allow more definitive conclusions to be drawn about the effects of a treatment than do case studies.

Single subject studies are especially useful in clinical practice to evaluate the effectiveness of therapy procedures for a particular client. They also may be a viable alternative to experiments involving groups of clients for demonstrating the efficacy of therapies when a limited number of clients are available for research.[15] The two most common types of single subject studies are reversal studies and multiple baseline studies.

REVERSAL STUDIES

Reversal studies systematically introduce and withdraw the therapy and examine what happens to the target behavior. Reversal studies always involve a minimum of three phases: baseline, treatment, and reversal. In the first phase, a *baseline* level of the target behavior is obtained to provide a basis for comparison.

In the second phase, the *treatment* is begun, and the target behavior continues to be assessed. If the therapy is effective, the client's target behavior will change from the baseline level. An acceleration target behavior

Figure 4-2 Hypothetical data in a reversal study indicating typical changes that would be expected in an acceleration target behavior if the treatment was effective

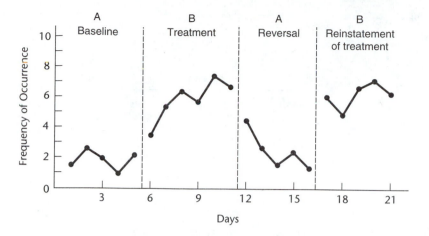

will increase, and a deceleration target behavior will decrease. Figure 4-2 shows the expected change for an acceleration target behavior.

Change that occurs in the target behavior from the baseline to the treatment phase is not necessarily due to the therapy. Some unaccounted-for factors in the client's life may have caused the change. To determine whether the therapy was influencing the change in the target behavior, a third phase of the study is introduced. The therapy is terminated, but the target behavior continues to be assessed. This is called a **reversal phase** because the conditions are reversed to their former state; that is, the target behavior is only being assessed as during baseline. If the therapy is responsible for the change in the target behavior, then the target behavior will return to baseline levels when the therapy is withdrawn (as depicted in Figure 4-2).

These three phases—baseline, treatment, and reversal—make up an **ABA study**. *A* stands for no therapy (assessment only)—in the baseline and reversal phases—and *B* stands for treatment. An ABA study provides evidence that the therapy was responsible for changes in the target behavior. However, ending with the reversal phase leaves clients back where they started—that is, at the baseline level. Thus, a fourth phase, *reinstatement of treatment,* is added so that the client can continue to benefit from the therapy. The study thus becomes an **ABAB study,** with the second *B* standing for the reinstatement of treatment. If the therapy is effective, the target behavior will again change in the desired direction (see Figure 4-2). The second B phase provides additional evidence that the therapy is responsible for the change in the target behavior. Compared with an ABA study, an ABAB study provides greater confidence in attributing the change to the therapy. Table 4-5 summarizes an ABAB reversal study.

Reversal studies have three major limitations. First, they cannot be used with all target behaviors. Reversal studies are appropriate for target behaviors that are maintained by external factors, such as a teenage girl who does her homework only as long as she earns special privileges. In contrast, target behaviors that are learned in therapy and that become relatively permanent

Table 4-5 Phases of a reversal study

	PHASES			
	A **Baseline**	**B** **Treatment**	**A** **Reversal**	**B** **Reinstatement** **of Treatment**
Procedure	Measure target behavior	Introduce treatment; measure target behavior	Withdraw treatment; measure target behavior	Reinstate treatment; measure target behavior
Purpose	Assess normal level of target behavior	Change target behavior	Check whether treatment is responsible for change in target behavior	Reinstate change in target behavior
Expectation	None	Target behavior will change in desired direction	Target behavior will return to baseline level	Target behavior will change in desired direction

behaviors in the clients' repertoire, such as social skills, are unlikely to change when the therapy is withdrawn.

Second, it is not legitimate to generalize from the results of an individual client's treatment to clients in general. As with case studies, this limitation can be circumvented in part by conducting a series of single subject studies with the same therapy for a number of clients with the same problem.[16]

A third limitation of reversal studies is that withdrawing therapy may be unethical. Consider the situation in which introducing a therapy procedure reduces a client's self-injurious behaviors (for instance, head banging). In such cases, it may not be ethical to employ a reversal period even though it is important to assess the effectiveness of the therapy. Multiple baseline studies solve this dilemma.

MULTIPLE BASELINE STUDIES

In a **multiple baseline study,** the same therapy procedure is introduced sequentially for two or more target behaviors. (In variations, a therapy procedure may be introduced sequentially for several clients or in several settings.)

The rationale underlying the multiple baseline study is simple. If the therapy is responsible for changes in the client's target behaviors, then each target behavior should change *only* when the therapy is applied specifically to it. The target behaviors that have not yet been treated serve as comparison conditions.

Let's look at a hypothetical example of a multiple baseline study that examined the effectiveness of Therapy X on three different acceleration target behaviors. As you can see in Figure 4-3, baseline levels of the three target behaviors were recorded for five days. On Day 6, the therapy was introduced for Behavior 1 only. As the first target behavior was being treated, the remaining two target behaviors were just assessed; that is, baseline

Figure 4-3 Hypothetical data in a multiple baseline study indicating typical changes that would be expected in three different acceleration target behaviors if the therapy was effective

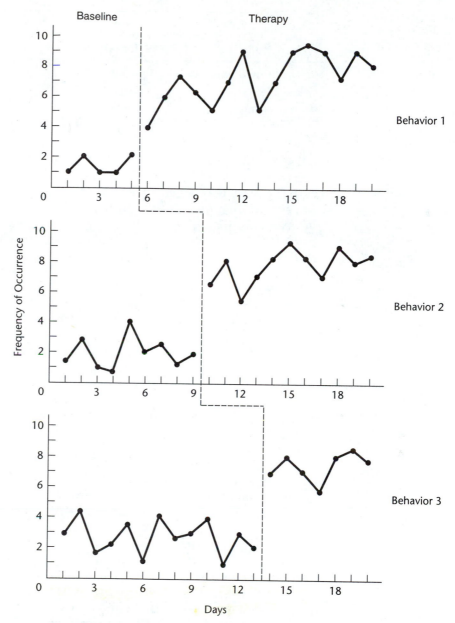

measures were continued. Notice in Figure 4-3 that only the target behavior being treated (Behavior 1) increased (presumably because of the therapy). The remaining target behaviors remained at their baseline levels (presumably because they received no treatment). After the first target behavior had changed in the desired direction, the therapy was introduced on Day 10 for Behavior 2. Behavior 2 then increased from its baseline rate, which provided additional evidence of the therapy's effectiveness. In contrast, Behavior 3 remained at its baseline level, which is what would be expected if the therapy

Table 4-6 Variables that change and remain constant in multiple baseline studies

Type of Study	VARIABLES		
	Target Behaviors	Clients	Settings
Across target behaviors	Different	Same	Same
Across clients	Same	Different	Same
Across settings	Same	Same	Different

was responsible for the changes in the target behaviors. Finally, after Behavior 2 increased, the therapy was applied to Behavior 3 on Day 14. As with the other two target behaviors, Behavior 3 increased when the therapy was introduced, further substantiating the claim that the therapy was responsible for the changes in the target behaviors. Because each target behavior changed *only* after the therapy was applied to it, it is reasonable to conclude that the changes were due to the therapy and not to other factors.

Table 4-6 indicates the variables that change and remain constant in each of the three basic multiple baseline studies. In a multiple baseline *across target behaviors* study (as in our hypothetical example), the therapy is implemented for different target behaviors with the same client and in the same setting. By holding the client and the setting constant, changes in the target behaviors cannot be attributed to differences in people or environmental conditions. In a multiple baseline *across clients* study, the therapy is implemented with different clients for the same target behavior and in the same setting. Finally, in a multiple baseline *across settings* study, the therapy is implemented in different settings with the same client and the same target behavior.

Multiple baseline studies, like reversal studies, have limited generalizability. Experiments with groups of clients most legitimately allow findings to be generalized to other clients. Experiments also allow the effects of factors other than the therapy to be ruled out with the greatest confidence.

Experiments

In evaluating the effects of therapy, it is important to *control* for *extraneous factors*—that is, any factors other than the therapy that are likely to affect clients' problems (such as clients' motivation to change and life circumstances that might help with problems). Researchers use the term *control* to mean "account for the effects of an extraneous factor."

In the simplest experiment, clients are *randomly* assigned to two groups. *Random assignment* means that each client has an equal chance of being assigned to each group. One group is given the therapy. The other group is not given the therapy and serves as a comparison or **control group.** Table 4-7 has examples of the types of control groups commonly used in therapy outcome experiments.

The object in an experiment is to make the two groups equivalent, *except* that one group receives therapy and the other does not. If clients

Table 4-7 Types of control groups commonly used in behavior therapy outcome experiments

CONTROL GROUP	DESCRIPTION	PURPOSE	EXAMPLE
NO TREATMENT	Clients receive no therapy. Target behaviors are assessed at the same time that clients in the therapy group receive pre- and posttherapy assessments.	To control for improvements in clients' problems that are due to factors other than the specific therapy procedures.	A young child was referred for therapy because of aggressive behaviors. The child's aggressive behaviors were assessed and then reassessed 10 weeks later.
WAIT-LIST	Clients initially receive no therapy. Target behaviors are assessed at the same time that clients in the therapy group receive pre- and posttherapy assessments. After the therapy group's final assessment, clients receive therapy.	To control for the influence of clients' expectations that they will receive therapy.	Couples seeking help for their marital conflict had their marital relationship assessed and then reassessed two months later. They then participated in two months of marital therapy, after which their marital relationship was assessed again.
NO CONTACT	Clients receive no therapy. Target behaviors are assessed without the clients' being aware that they are part of a therapy study and without direct contact with the therapist or researcher.	To control for improvements in clients' problems that are due to being participants in a therapy study rather than to the specific therapy procedures.	All people between the ages of 21 and 35 in a community were mailed a questionnaire to complete about their anxiety three days after an earthquake struck and then again five months later.
ATTENTION	Clients meet with a therapist for the same amount of time as clients in the therapy condition but receive no therapy.	To control for improvements in clients' problems that are due to the therapists' attention rather than to the specific therapy procedures.	College students with severe test anxiety met with a therapist once a week for 12 sessions and discussed theories of the development and course of test anxiety.
PLACEBO	Clients receive a therapy-like procedure that they are led to believe is highly effective but in fact has no proven efficacy.	To control for improvements in clients' problems that are due to clients' expectations that the therapy they are receiving will be effective rather than to the specific therapy procedures.	Clients who were depressed were told that listening to a specially prepared audiotape of rhythmic clicking sounds before they went to sleep for three weeks would result in dramatic improvements in their mood.

in the therapy group improve and clients in the control group do not improve (or at least do not improve as much), then we can confidently conclude that the improvement is due to the therapy and not other (extraneous) factors.

The groups are made equivalent with respect to extraneous factors in two ways. First, random assignment makes it unlikely that the overall composition of each group will differ in terms of preexisting differences among the clients. Second, the two groups are dealt with in the same way (for instance, they are given the same assessment measures), except for the presence or absence of therapy.

The findings of experiments are more generalizable than the findings of case studies or single subject studies. The reason is that therapy outcome experiments are based on a number of clients rather than on a single case. However, because the results of experiments always represent averages for a group of clients, the influence on individual clients is lost. Thus, experiments cannot be used to evaluate the effectiveness of an individual client's treatment.

ANALOGUE EXPERIMENTS

Ideally, the effectiveness of therapy procedures should be evaluated in clinical practice. This goal cannot always be met because of practical and ethical constraints. Practically, for example, it may be difficult to recruit clients with similar problems; to obtain measures of clients' target behaviors in the clients' natural environments; to assure that therapists follow treatment guidelines (so that all clients receive identical therapy procedures); and to monitor extraneous factors that could influence clients' target behaviors. Independent of practical problems, ethical issues exist. For instance, it may be unethical to use new, untested therapies with clients who are in serious need of treatment or to assign such clients to control groups.

Analogue experiments can circumvent the practical and ethical dilemmas associated with clinical experiments.[17] In **analogue experiments, the conditions of the study are similar (analogous), but not identical, to the conditions that exist in actual clinical practice.** Analogue experiments differ from clinical experiments in terms of (1) the problems treated, (2) the people treated, (3) how the treatment is administered, or (4) some combination of these factors. For instance, the target behavior in the study might be a mild form of a psychological problem. An example would be social anxiety that is inconvenient because it makes the person feel uneasy around others but that is not debilitating so as to prevent social interactions. The participants in an analogue experiment may be people who are not actively seeking therapy, such as individuals who respond to a newspaper advertisement asking for volunteers for a therapy study. Finally, the participants may receive an abbreviated version of the therapy or the treatment may be automated (for example, the treatment might use recorded instructions to ensure that all participants receive identical therapy procedures).

Analogue experiments are easier to carry out than actual clinical studies, and they do not pose some of the ethical problems associated with clinical research. The major disadvantage of analogue experiments is that the generalizability of findings to actual clinical conditions may be limited. Accordingly, analogue research is most useful as an initial step in evaluating therapy—before it is used with actual clients. If such preliminary testing indicates that the therapy is effective, actual clinical research is more justified.[18]

◆   **In Theory 4-1**

BEHAVIOR THERAPY AS AN EXPERIMENT

The process of behavior therapy is similar to the process of performing an experiment. An experiment begins with a hypothesis that a particular *independent variable* (a condition that is directly varied) influences a particular *dependent variable* (the behavior being studied). To test the hypothesis, the independent variable is varied, and measurements are made of the dependent variable to see if it changes. This is done while extraneous factors that might affect the dependent variable are controlled so that they cannot influence the dependent variable. If the dependent variable changes along with changes in the independent variable, then the hypothesis is supported. In other words, there is evidence that the independent variable has a causative effect on the dependent variable.

You can see the parallels between an experiment and the process of behavior therapy if you substitute *maintaining conditions* for independent variable and *target behavior* for dependent variable. The behavior therapist hypothesizes that certain conditions are maintaining the target behavior. The hypothesis is tested in therapy by changing the maintaining conditions and observing whether the target behavior changes. If the target behavior changes in the desired direction,

then the hypothesis is supported and the therapy is successful. If the target behavior does not change in the desired direction, the hypothesis is not supported and the treatment is not successful. The parallels between behavior therapy and an experiment are detailed in Table 4-8.

One major difference exists between behavior therapy and an experiment. In an experiment, factors other than the independent variable are prevented, through control procedures, from influencing the dependent variable. Accordingly, cause-and-effect relationships can be established with a high degree of certainty. This is less true for behavior therapy. If the hypothesized maintaining conditions are changed and the target behavior changes, then therapy is successful. However, generally it is not possible to know definitively that changing the hypothesized maintaining conditions resulted in the change. The reason is that in the therapy situation it usually is not possible to control for the effects of all extraneous variables, such as beneficial changes in a client's life that occur while the person is in therapy. Not knowing definitively what accounts for the success of therapy usually is acceptable in clinical work because the goal of behavior therapy is to alleviate a client's problem.

Table 4-8 Parallels between behavior therapy and an experiment

Step	Behavior Therapy	Experiment
1. *Define what is to be changed*	Target behavior	Dependent variable*
2. *Assess baseline level*	Pretherapy measurement of target behavior	Preexperiment measurement of dependent variable
3. *Search for influential factors*	Identify maintaining antecedents and maintaining consequences of target behavior	Decide on independent variable*
4. *Formulate hypothesis*	"If correct maintaining conditions have been identified, then modifying them will change the target behavior."	"If independent variable does influence dependent variable, then varying the independent variable will result in the dependent variable changing."
5. *Test hypothesis*	Implement therapy (that is, modify maintaining conditions)	Carry out experiment (that is, vary independent variable)
6. *Examine outcome*	Posttherapy measurement of target behavior	Postexperiment measurement of dependent variable
7. *Draw conclusions when*		
a. *Change is in expected direction*	Therapy successful	Hypothesis confirmed
b. *No change or change is in unexpected direction*	Reassess maintaining conditions (that is, return to Step 3)	Find other independent variable (that is, return to Step 3)

* In an experiment, the condition that is directly varied is called the *independent variable.* The object of an experiment is to observe the influence of the independent variable on subjects' behaviors. The specific behavior under investigation is called the *dependent variable* because it is hypothesized to depend on or be influenced by the condition varied by the experimenter (that is, the independent variable).

WHAT CONSTITUTES EFFECTIVE BEHAVIOR THERAPY?

Four general *outcome measures*—or criteria of therapy effectiveness—are used to evaluate behavior therapy. First, the changes in the problem behaviors must occur in clients' everyday lives. Second, the changes should be meaningful (that is, not trivial). Third, the changes should endure over time. Fourth, the therapy procedures should be acceptable or palatable to clients.

Generalization Beyond Therapy

For therapy to be considered effective, the changes that occur in therapy also must occur in the client's everyday life. In other words, the therapy's effects must *generalize* or transfer from the therapy setting to the client's natural environment, which usually includes a variety of situations.[19] For example, it is important for children who are socially withdrawn to learn to develop social interaction with a variety of peers (such as friends, siblings, and new acquaintances) in different settings (for instance, at home and at a playground).[20]

Meaningfulness of Change

Effective therapy should result in a change that is clearly meaningful for the client, which is known as **clinical significance.**[21]* Clinical significance is based primarily on one or both of two criteria. First, clinical significance is evaluated with reference to norms relevant to the particular client.[22] Consider the case of a 5-year-old girl who interacts with her peers only 5% of the time. Suppose that after therapy the girl is spending 25% of her time at school interacting with her classmates. Although 25% clearly represents a change, this level of interaction is compared with the normal level for 5-year-old girls. If the norm were 55%, then the therapy outcome would not be considered clinically significant.

Second, clinical significance can be evaluated in terms of general standards for adaptive or acceptable functioning, which is referred to as **social validity.**[23] Social validity usually is assessed by having knowledgeable people judge whether the client's behaviors following therapy are adaptive or acceptable.[24] For example, social embarrassment is a major reason that people seek treatment for *tics*, which involve recurring, sudden, rapid movements, such as facial grimacing and muscle twitches. In one study evaluating the effectiveness of behavior therapy for tics, teachers and graduate students viewed videotapes of clients before and after treatment and rated how distracting the clients' movements were to others and how potentially embarrassing they were to the clients.[25]

Durability of Change

The third critical therapy outcome measure is durability, which typically is called **long-term maintenance** (of treatment gains). The changes that occur as a result of therapy should continue long after therapy has ended. Durability of treatment effects is determined by assessing the client's functioning at various time intervals after therapy has been terminated—optimally several years later.[26] Such **follow-up assessment** (or **follow-up,** for short) has become a standard measure in behavior therapy outcome research. The major practical obstacle to obtaining follow-up assessments is keeping track of clients' whereabouts and getting clients to undergo additional assessment procedures.[27]

---

* *Clinical significance* is independent of *statistical significance*, which refers only to the reliability of a finding. A statistically significant finding has a high probability of being repeated, but it implies nothing about the meaningfulness of the finding. For example, an outcome study may demonstrate that a therapy for smoking cessation, compared with a no-treatment control condition, leads to a statistically significant reduction in cigarettes smoked, say an average of 33 versus 36 cigarettes per day. However, because 3 fewer cigarettes per day would not improve the clients' health, the therapy has no *clinical significance*.

Acceptability of Therapy to the Client

A final outcome measure concerns the **acceptability** of the treatment procedures to the client and sometimes to significant others, as in the case of young children.[28] In this context, *acceptability* refers to how palatable the therapy procedures are. It does not refer to whether the client is pleased with the *results* of therapy or to the actual *effectiveness* of the treatment.[29]

Some forms of behavior therapy are more likely to be acceptable than others. As with many treatments for medical problems, effective behavior therapy sometimes involves discomfort and may be intrusive (for example, getting in the way of the client's normal activities). How much discomfort and intrusion clients are willing to tolerate in order to alleviate their problems is a matter of individual preference.[30] However, all other things being equal, therapy procedures that are more acceptable to clients in general are more useful because clients are more likely to seek therapy and remain in treatment.[31] Conversely, clients tend to drop out of treatments that have low acceptability.[32]

SUMMARY

1. The process of behavior therapy involves eight basic procedures: clarifying the client's problem, designing a target behavior, formulating goals, identifying maintaining conditions, designing a plan to change the maintaining conditions, implementing therapy procedures, evaluating their effectiveness, and conducting follow-up assessment. Assessment begins after the target behavior is designed and continues through the course of therapy and after therapy is terminated.

2. Only one or two problems are treated simultaneously. Each problem is defined as a target behavior, an aspect of the problem that is relatively small, discrete, and measurable.

3. A good target behavior is narrow in scope, unambiguously defined, measurable, and appropriate for the problem and the client.

4. Acceleration target behaviors are increased and are designed for behavioral deficits, which refer to adaptive behaviors clients are not performing enough. Deceleration target behaviors are decreased and are designed for behavioral excesses, which refer to maladaptive behaviors clients are performing too much.

5. An acceleration target behavior is treated by directly increasing it. A deceleration target behavior can be directly decreased. However, the preferred strategy is to indirectly decrease it by increasing an acceleration target behavior that competes with the deceleration target behavior; this strategy replaces the maladaptive behavior with an adaptive behavior.

6. The dead person rule states: Never ask a client to do something a dead person can do.

7. The client, with the assistance of the therapist, formulates therapy goals that the client may reevaluate and change over the course of therapy.

8. Once a target behavior has been selected, its probable maintaining conditions are identified, and then these conditions are changed in order to modify the target behaviors.

9. Outcome research evaluates whether therapy is effective, both for individual clients and for a therapy procedure in general.

10. Case studies are detailed, descriptive accounts of what transpired in the treatment of individual clients. Case studies are limited in terms of the generalizability of their findings to other clients and in terms of determining whether the therapy caused the changes in the target behavior.

11. Single subject studies systematically compare what happens when target behaviors are treated and when they are not treated. Reversal designs systematically introduce and withdraw the therapy to assess its effects on the target behavior. In multiple baseline studies, the same therapy procedure is introduced sequentially for two or more target behaviors. Single subject studies are limited in terms of the generalizability of their findings.

12. Experiments employ groups of clients and control for the effects of extraneous variables. In a simple experiment, clients are randomly assigned to two groups: one receives therapy and the other does not receive therapy (and serves as a control group). Experiments provide results that can be generalized and that most definitively indicate whether the therapy itself has resulted in the changes in clients' target behaviors.

13. Analogue experiments set up conditions that are similar but not identical to the conditions that exist in actual clinical practice and thereby circumvent some practical and ethical problems of clinical research.

14. Behavior therapy can be usefully viewed as a scientific experiment in which hypotheses about the causes of the client's target behaviors are tested.

15. Four outcome measures are used to evaluate the effectiveness of behavior therapy: generalization beyond therapy, meaningfulness of change, durability of change, and acceptability to the client.

REFERENCE NOTES

1. Lazarus, Davison, & Polefka, 1965, pp. 225-227, 229.
2. Voeltz & Evans, 1982.
3. Finney, Miller, & Adler, 1993.
4. Barlow & Hersen, 1984.
5. For example, Derby, Wacker, Sasso, Steege, Northup, Cigland, & Asinus, 1992; Iwata, Vollmer, & Zarcone, 1990.
6. O'Neill, Horner, Albin, Storey, & Sprague, 1990.
7. For example, Storey, Lawry, Ashworth, Danko, & Strain, 1994.
8. For example, Chapman, Fisher, Piazza, & Kurtz, 1993.
9. For example, Smith, Iwata, Vollmer, & Zarcone, 1993.
10. Whisman, 1993.

11. For example, Campbell & Lutzker, 1993.

12. For example, Cautela & Kearney, 1993; Davison & Lazarus, 1995.

13. For example, Mathews, Teasdale, Munby, Johnston, & Shaw, 1977; Wolpe, 1958.

14. Haynes, Spain, & Oliveira, 1993; Kazdin, 1993.

15. Hilliard, 1993; Peterson & Bell-Dolan, 1995.

16. Baer, Osnes, & Stokes, 1983; Baer, Williams, Osnes, & Stokes, 1983; Guevremont, Osnes, & Stokes, 1986a, 1986b.

17. For example, McGlynn, Moore, Rose, & Lazarte, 1995.

18. For example, Paul, 1969a.

19. Risley, 1995.

20. Belchic & Harris, 1994.

21. For example, Jacobson, 1988; Jacobson, Follette, & Revenstorf, 1984; Kazdin, 1977a; Kendall & Norton-Ford, 1982; Wolf, 1978.

22. Jacobson, 1988.

23. Carr & Carlson, 1993; Kazdin, 1977a; Wolf, 1978.

24. For example, Finney, Rapoff, Hall, & Christopherson, 1983; Frisch & Froberg, 1987; Jones, Kazdin, & Haney, 1981; Minkin, Braukmann, Minkin, Timbers, Timbers, Fixsen, Phillips, & Wolf, 1976; Romano & Bellack, 1980.

25. Finney, Rapoff, Hall, & Christopherson, 1983.

26. For example, Foxx & Faw, 1990.

27. For example, Heimberg, Salzman, Holt, & Blendell, 1993.

28. Smith & Linscheid, 1994.

29. For example, Cox, Fergus, & Swinson, 1994; Newton, Hartley, & Sturmey, 1993.

30. Renfrey, 1992; Tarnowski, Simonian, Bekeny, & Park, 1992.

31. Meichenbaum, 1991.

32. For example, Callahan & Leitenberg, 1973; Smith, Marcus, & Eldredge, 1994; Wilson & Tracey, 1976.

Chapter 5

Behavioral Assessment

Behavioral assessment is to behavior therapy what a banana is to a banana split—in other words, indispensable. Behavioral assessment procedures provide the data that guide the development of a unique treatment plan for the client and that measure its effectiveness.

The goals of behavioral assessment are to gather information to (1) select and define target behaviors precisely, (2) identify the maintaining conditions of the target behaviors, and (3) measure changes in the target behaviors over the course of therapy and after therapy has ended. In sum, it is the elements of the ABC model—antecedents, behavior, and consequences—that are assessed. Our discussion will focus on the eight most frequently used behavioral assessment methods: interview, direct self-report inventory, self-recording, checklist and rating scale, systematic naturalistic observation, simulated observation, role playing, and physiological measurement (see Table 5-1).[1]

MULTIMODAL AND MULTIMETHOD ASSESSMENT

Behavioral assessment typically is **multimodal** in that measurements are made of two or more modes of behavior.[2] Multimodal assessment is necessary because psychological disorders generally involve more than one mode of behavior.[3] For example, depression may consist of reduced activity, hopeless thoughts, sadness, and weight loss.

Additionally, behavior therapists usually use two or more methods to gather information—that is, **multimethod assessment.** When information obtained from one method also is found with other methods, therapists have more confidence that the information is valid. Table 5-2 gives examples of how anger and aggressive behaviors might be assessed using each of the eight most common behavioral assessment methods for each of the four modes of behavior.

The particular modes of behavior assessed and the methods used depend on the nature of the problem and practical considerations. As Table 5-2

Table 5-1 Most frequently used methods of behavioral assessment
SOURCE: Based on data from Guevremont & Spiegler, 1990.

Rank	Method	% of Behavior Therapists Using Frequently*
1	Interview	90
2	Direct self-report inventory	63
3	Self-recording	56
4	Checklist or rating scale	51
5	Systematic naturalistic observation	30
6	Simulated observation	23
7	Role playing	20
8	Physiological measurement	19

* Percentage of behavior therapists indicating that they used the method with six or more clients in the past year.

Table 5-2 Behavioral assessment methods used to assess *anger* and *aggressive behaviors* (commonly used methods are printed in **bold face**)

Method	Modes of Behavior			
	Overt Behaviors	Cognitions	Emotions	Physiological Responses
Interview	"Describe what you do when you get angry at your wife."	"What thoughts go through your mind when you get angry at your wife?"	"How are you feeling when you hit your wife?"	"What specific bodily reactions do you have when you get angry at your wife?"
Direct self-report inventory	True or false: "I often use physical violence to get my way."	True or false: "When I get angry, I think about attacking someone."	True or false: "When I am angry, I feel like I am going to explode."	True or false: "When I get angry, I start to sweat."
Checklist & rating scale	**Parents check off all the specific aggressive acts a teenager engaged in last week.**	Not used.	Teacher rates the severity of a student's anger using a five-point scale.	Mother checks off possible physiological responses (such as sweating and shaking) she observes in her son that may indicate anger.
Self-recording	**Client keeps diary of incidents of aggressive acts.**	**Client keeps diary of thoughts before, during, and after incidents of anger and aggressive behaviors.**	**Client records occurrences of angry feelings during the day.**	**Client records pulse when provoked to anger.**
Systematic naturalistic observation	**Therapist observes parent-child interactions at home, coding examples of parental verbally and physically aggressive behaviors.**	Not used.	Therapist observes overt behaviors (such as shaking fist or making threatening remarks) that may indicate client feels angry.	In client's home, therapist observes overt signs of physiological reactions (for example, face flushing and rapid breathing).
Simulated observation	**Therapist deliberately provokes client and notes client's overt responses.**	Not used.	Therapist deliberately provokes client and notes client's overt behaviors (such as shaking fist or making threatening remarks) that may indicate client feels angry.	Therapist deliberately provokes client and notes overt signs of physiological reactions (for example, face flushed and rapid breathing).

(continued)

Table 5-2 *(continued)*

	Modes of Behavior			
Method	Overt Behaviors	Cognitions	Emotions	Physiological Responses
Role playing	**Scenario is presented of client's boss' criticizing client for being late. Therapist role plays boss, and client responds to boss's criticism. Therapist observes what client says.**	Scenario is presented of client's boss' criticizing client for being late. Therapist role plays boss and client responds to boss's criticism. Client describes thoughts while responding to criticism.	Scenario is presented of client's boss' criticizing client for being late. Therapist role plays boss, and client responds to boss's criticism. Therapist observes client's overt responses (such as grimaces) that may indicate anger.	Scenario is presented of client's boss' criticizing client for being late. Therapist role plays boss, and client responds to boss's criticism. Therapist observes client's overt signs of physiological reactions (such as face flushing).
Physiological measurement	Not used.	Not used.	Heart rate and blood pressure, signs of arousal that may indicate anger, are measured while client thinks about frustrating situations.	**A father's heart rate, blood pressure, and galvanic skin response are measured before, during, and after he watches a video of his children's misbehaving.**

indicates, certain methods of assessment are optimal for each mode of behavior, and some of the methods are not appropriate for some modes. In assessing a client's thoughts, for example, interviews, self-report inventories, and self-recordings are the optimal methods, and role playing is a potential method; the remaining four assessment methods are not applicable. In practice, the most efficient and least costly methods of assessment typically are chosen, which is the reason behavioral interviews are used most frequently.

Case 5-1 describes behavioral assessment procedures used with a woman who was being treated for excessive anger and violent behaviors. It previews some of the behavioral assessment methods and issues that we will cover later in the chapter.

BEHAVIORAL ASSESSMENT IN A CASE OF DOMESTIC VIOLENCE

Case 5-1 Tina T. was a 36-year-old college graduate who worked as a computer sales representative. She had a 5-year history of violence toward her husband and 10-year-old daughter. Tina contacted a behavior therapist when her husband threatened to move to another city with their daughter if she did not seek help.

In the initial interview, Tina admitted that she had a serious problem, which she described as "uncontrollable fits of anger." The therapist asked Tina a series of questions to elucidate the nature of her problem and its maintaining conditions. The questions included the following:

1. When you have an uncontrollable "fit of anger," what do you do? How do you feel? What are you thinking? What bodily reactions do you experience?

2. What seems to precipitate your "anger fits"? Are they associated with something your husband or daughter says or does? Are there any situations that make you more prone to have a "fit"? Where do your "fits" usually occur? Who is there at the time? At what time of day and on which days of the week? What feelings and thoughts do you have right before an "anger fit"?

3. What happens after your "anger fits"? How do your husband and daughter react to your "fits"? What do they do and say? How long do their reactions last? What do you do after your "fits"? How do you feel? What thoughts run through your mind?

4. What strategies have you used to deal with your problem and how successful have they been?

The interview revealed that Tina's "anger fits" initially involved yelling and cursing, then throwing objects at her daughter and husband, and finally beating them with her fists and household objects. She became angry whenever she was frustrated about a situation she believed she could not handle (such as unreasonable demands from others). Her "fits" most often occurred shortly after returning home from work. A fit (which rarely lasted more than five minutes) gradually subsided and became less violent as she "vented her anger." At that point, she started to cry and beg for her family's forgiveness, which was usually forthcoming.

Other assessment procedures were instituted to confirm the accuracy of the information Tina gave in the interview and to provide additional data.

1. Tina filled out the Novaco Anger Inventory, a questionnaire that assesses anger reactions in a wide array of situations.[4] The inventory contains descriptions of 80 situations, and clients rate the degree of anger they would expect to feel if the situation actually occurred.

2. Tina started an *anger diary* in which she (1) described each instance when she was provoked to anger, (2) rated the intensity of the anger (using a scale ranging from "no anger" to "rage"), (3) noted how she reacted (including overt and covert behaviors), and (4) described the consequences of her reactions.[5] The anger diary provided the therapist with information about the situations that elicited Tina's anger and the ways in which she typically responded. It also helped Tina become more aware of her anger and her reactions to it. Tina used the anger diary throughout her treatment as an ongoing measure of her progress.

3. The therapist visited Tina's house on 3 consecutive Tuesdays, shortly after she arrived home from work, to directly observe her behaviors. Besides assessing Tina's aggressive acts toward her daughter and husband (for example, yelling and hitting), the therapist recorded positive behaviors (such as praising and physical affection). A data sheet, based on a modified Patterson Coding System,[6] was prepared that listed 18 different aggressive and positive behaviors. Over the course of 30 minutes, the therapist recorded each of these behaviors he observed Tina perform.

4. In the third therapy session, Tina and her therapist role played several troublesome situations revealed in her anger diary and Anger Inventory. The therapist played the role of either husband or daughter and observed Tina's reactions to provocations. Tina's heart rate and blood pressure were monitored during the role playing and compared with baseline recordings taken when Tina was calm and not at all angry.

Based on the information gathered from these assessment procedures, the therapist designed a treatment plan for two related behaviors: positive interactions with family members and adaptive reactions to frustration. Among the findings of the behavioral assessment, the home observations revealed that Tina rarely had positive interactions with her husband and daughter. Thus, one component of Tina's therapy involved teaching Tina specific ways to engage positively with her family. In both the home observations and role playing, the therapist observed that Tina reacted to provocation immediately. Accordingly, another component of Tina's treatment was self-instructional training, in which she reminded herself to pause and think before reacting. From the interview, anger diary, and home observations, it became clear that a critical maintaining consequence of her anger and aggression was the sympathetic responses from her family to the remorse Tina expressed after one of her "fits." Consequently, part of the therapy involved training family members to withhold their sympathy when Tina indicated that she was sorry about an "anger fit."

Tina's anger diary provided a continuous measure of her progress over the course of the five-and-a-half months of her therapy. The diary revealed steady improvement. Two home observations in the last weeks of therapy indicated that Tina now handled frustration and other potential provocations with restraint and often with prosocial responses. At the end of therapy, Tina again filled out the Anger Inventory; both the number of different situations that evoked anger and the intensity of the anger she experienced had decreased significantly. Additionally, role playing with concurrent physiological recording during the last therapy session showed that Tina became less aroused in potentially provocative situations and that she responded in more socially appropriate ways than she had at the beginning of therapy. Two long-term follow-up telephone interviews with Tina, six months and one year after treatment, indicated that her anger and violence were no longer problematic for her or for her family.

Case 5-1 highlights some of the essentials of behavioral assessment. Behavior therapy and assessment are closely linked; assessment procedures initially supply information to identify maintaining conditions, to design a treatment plan, and to monitor progress. The assessment proceeds in a stepwise fashion, by cumulatively gathering and substantiating data. Finally, employing a multimodal and multimethod approach provides the most comprehensive assessment.

CHARACTERISTICS OF BEHAVIORAL ASSESSMENT

In a sense, behavioral assessment is defined independently of the methods used. What is critical is *how* the assessment procedures are used. For example, the interview is the most common method of psychological assessment, so it is hardly unique to behavioral assessment. However, the emphases in a behavioral interview (such as focusing on current circumstances) distinguish it from interviews in other types of therapy. Some of the general differences between behavioral and nonbehavioral (traditional) approaches to assessment are summarized in Table 5-3.

Behavioral assessment procedures share five characteristics that are consistent with the behavioral model and overlap with the defining themes and common characteristics of behavior therapy (see Chapter 1).

Individualized. Behavioral assessment is used to gather unique and detailed information about a client's problem and its maintaining conditions.[7] Thus, *diagnosis*—assigning a problem behavior to a general category of disorders (for example, borderline personality disorder)—is not a goal of behavioral assessment. Diagnostic categories provide trait descriptions of a client's problems, lumping the client with many other people diagnosed as having the same disorder. Moreover, a diagnosis does not supply the behavior therapist with the specific details of the client's problem needed to proceed with therapy.

Table 5-3 Comparison of behavioral and traditional assessment
SOURCE: Adapted from Barios, 1988.

	Behavioral	Traditional
AIMS	To identify target behaviors	To describe personality functioning
	To identify maintaining conditions	To identify etiology (origin)
	To select appropriate treatment	To diagnose or classify
	To evaluate and revise treatment	
ASSUMPTIONS		
1. Role of behavior	Sample of client's typical behaviors in specific situations	Sign of client's personality (for example, traits and intrapsychic dynamics)
2. Role of past	Unimportant (present behavior caused by present events)	Crucial (present behavior caused by past events)
3. Consistency of behavior	Consistent in the same situation	Consistent in different situations
INTERPRETATION		
1. Direct or indirect	Direct (sample)	Indirect (sign)
2. Degree of inference	Low (behavior to behavior)	High (behavior to personality)

◆ **In Theory 5-1**

IS THERE A PLACE
FOR DIAGNOSIS
IN BEHAVIOR
THERAPY?

Diagnosis involves classifying client's problems into discrete categories of disorders. The standard diagnostic categories used today to classify psychological disorders were developed by the American Psychiatric Association. They were published in 1994 in *Diagnostic and Statistical Manual of Mental Disorders* (4th edition),[8] which is referred to as *DSM-IV*.

Philosophically, diagnosis is antithetical to the fundamental premises of behavior therapy and behavioral assessment. Unlike the individualistic approach of behavior therapy, diagnosis groups clients' problems into single categories.[9] For example, rather than dealing with a client's particular anxiety-related behaviors, DSM-IV views the client as having an *anxiety disorder*. The client's individual problem now is indistinguishable from the problems of all people with the same diagnosis. This often results in two false assumptions: (1) that all individuals with the same disorder display the same behaviors and impairments and (2) that an individual who has a particular diagnosis displays all, or even most of, the symptoms that are supposed to be characteristic of the diagnosis. Thus, based on a diagnosis, one may attribute characteristics to a client that the client does not possess.

Diagnosis is a trait concept, which is another basic way in which diagnosis runs counter to the behavioral approach. Strictly speaking, a diagnosis refers to people's behaviors rather than to people themselves. Unfortunately, this fact frequently is forgotten. The client

becomes the diagnosis, which leads to viewing the client as a *schizophrenic* rather than an *individual with schizophrenia,* for example. This unfortunate error results in people being stigmatized and discriminated against. Further, in the case of some disorders, it is assumed that, once diagnosed, the person always has the disorder, although the symptoms may not always be present.[10] This undocumented assumption accounts for such well-known expressions as "Once an alcoholic, always an alcoholic." That expression, incidently, embodies our earlier point regarding the regrettable common practice of equating the person with the diagnosis.

Diagnosis often does not provide information critical to a meaningful behavioral assessment of an individual client's problem and to designing behavior therapy procedures for treating the problem. Diagnosis does not specify (1) the specific behaviors that are problematic for an individual client; (2) under what conditions they are problematic; (3) their frequency, intensity, or duration; and (4) the maintaining conditions of the problem behaviors.

Does this mean that behavior therapists do not use diagnostic labels in referring to their clients' problems? No, it does not. In fact, most behavior therapists do assign DSM-IV diagnoses. In clinical practice, the major reason for doing so is that official diagnoses are required by clinics, hospitals, schools, and social service agencies before treatment and services can be offered and by health insurance and health care providers before the treatment will be paid for.

Another reason for diagnosis is that in some cases—but certainly not in all—it provides information that is helpful for comprehensive planning of clients' treatment (for example, considering medication for a client with major depressive disorder). However, even in cases where useful information comes from a diagnosis, it is never sufficient to design a comprehensive treatment plan. The unique aspects of each client's problem must be considered, which requires a thorough behavioral assessment of its particular maintaining conditions.

One other reason for diagnosis is that it may be necessary for research, so that different researchers can be assured that they are studying the same *basic* clinical phenomena.

The behavioral alternative to diagnosis is a detailed description of a client's unique problem and the antecedents and consequences that are maintaining it. On the one hand, the end product of a thorough behavioral assessment is much lengthier and makes comparisons between clients (such as for research) much more difficult. On the other hand, behavioral assessment provides the necessary information for designing individualized treatment that is most likely to be effective.

Present-focus.   The focus of behavioral assessment, like behavior therapy, is on relevant information about the client's current functioning and life conditions. Details about the client's past, especially early childhood, are considered relatively unimportant.

Directly samples relevant behaviors.   Behavioral assessment procedures take *samples* of a client's behaviors to provide information about how the client typically functions in particular situations. For example, to predict a teenage girl's typical ability to remain focused on schoolwork, the therapist might give the girl several different classroom assignments and observe her on-task behaviors (such as writing down answers) and her off-task behaviors (such as looking around the room). This is a direct approach, in which behaviors are used to predict other behaviors.

In contrast, nonbehavioral, traditional assessment is *indirect*. Behaviors are used as *signs,* rather than samples, of something other than behavior, such as a trait or psychological state. For example, seeing blood in Rorschach inkblots might be considered a sign of underlying aggressiveness.

Narrow-focus.   Behavioral assessment deals with discrete behaviors and specific circumstances rather than a client's total personality or lifestyle. This tactic is consistent with the fact that behavior therapy focuses on target behaviors.

Integrated with therapy.   Behavioral assessment is an integral and continuous part of therapy. Assessment of the client's problem and its maintaining conditions is the first step in behavior therapy, and assessment continues throughout therapy to evaluate changes in the client's target behavior. In fact, it often is difficult to distinguish between behavior therapy and assessment.[11] For example, maintaining records of all the food clients eat is important in the treatment of obesity. Besides providing the therapist with valuable information, food records make clients aware of the food they consume and their eating habits. Such awareness is a critical part of the treatment.

BEHAVIORAL INTERVIEWS

An interview is usually the first assessment method used in behavior therapy.[12] Initial interviews have four major goals: (1) establishing rapport with the client, (2) understanding the client's problem and selecting target behaviors, (3) gathering data about maintaining conditions,[13] and (4) educating the client about the behavioral approach to treatment. The first and fourth goals—establishing rapport and informing clients about the behavioral approach—are not assessment procedures themselves, but they are essential parts of initial interviews with clients.

Building *rapport,* the first goal, involves developing a relationship of mutual trust.[14] Listening attentively and nonjudgmentally and letting clients know that they are understood are among the ways in which the therapist builds rapport with the client.

The second goal is for the therapist to begin to understand the client's problem thoroughly. Clients often describe their problems in vague, trait terms. They may say, for example, that they are "shy" or "hot-headed." The therapist questions the client to elicit the specific details of the client's unique problem. It is not enough to know that the client "has trouble in relationships with men," for example. Does "trouble" mean that she cannot approach men or that she feels uneasy in their company? Is the client referring to casual or intimate "relationships"? Once the specifics of the problem are delineated, the client and therapist can select a target behavior.

The third goal of the initial interview is to begin assessing the maintaining conditions of the target behavior. The therapist asks about the antecedents and consequences of the behavior. Specifically, *when* and *where* (under what circumstances) does the client get anxious with men? What happens, to the client and to the interaction with the man, when the client experiences anxiety, immediately and later on?

The fourth goal is to provide clients with information about the behavioral model of psychological problems and the general nature of behavior therapy—that is, what the client can expect to happen in behavior therapy. Clients need to know what they are getting into and to decide whether the behavioral approach is right for them. For example, a client who believes that his or her problems can be alleviated only by working through early childhood conflicts might need to be referred to a psychoanalyst.

The standard questions asked in a behavioral interview (as well as by other behavioral assessment methods) are *what, when, where, how,* and *how*

Table 5-4 Examples of information typically gathered in initial behavioral interviews

1. What brings you here today?
2. When did the problem begin?
3. How often does it occur?
4. When (in what situations) does it occur?
5. What tends to occur before the problem (antecedents)?
6. What tends to occur after the problem, and how does the problem affect your life (consequences)?
7. What do you think about when the problem is occurring?
8. What do you feel when the problem is occurring?
9. What steps have you already taken to alleviate the problem, and with what results?

often questions. They provide information concerning the specific nature of the problem as well as its maintaining conditions. In contrast, traditional assessment emphasizes why questions to gather information about the causes of the client's problem. One problem with why questions is that often clients are not aware of the causes of their behaviors (which is a reason they have come to therapy). Further, from a behavioral point of view, the causes of behaviors are their maintaining conditions, which are assessed by the standard behavioral questions.

The focus in the behavioral interview is on the present rather than the past. You can see these emphases in the examples in Table 5-4 of questions typically asked in an initial behavioral interview. Besides the client, significant people in the client's life (such as a parent or spouse) may be interviewed to provide additional as well as corroborating information.

◆ ▬▬▬▬▬▬▬▬▬▬▬▬▬▬▬▬▬▬▬▬▬▬▬▬▬▬▬▬▬

Participation Exercise 5-1

BEHAVIORAL QUESTIONING: WHAT, WHEN, WHERE, HOW, AND HOW OFTEN?*

Clients typically describe their problems in vague, general terms. Through behavioral interviewing, the nature of the problem is clarified, so that goals for therapy can be established, target behaviors can be selected and defined, and probable maintaining conditions can be identified.

Here you will find brief problem descriptions given by a client or a client's advocate in the first therapy session. For each description, write five questions that you think would be helpful for a behavior therapist to ask the client or the client's advocate. The questions should be directed at clarifying goals, selecting target behaviors, and identifying probable maintaining conditions. Be sure that the format of your questions is appropriate for a *behavioral* interview (refer to the title of the Participation Exercise for a reminder). When you have finished, look at the sample questions in Appendix B to get an idea of the *type* of questions that would be appropriate.

* This Participation Exercise can be done before you continue or later.

1. The father of a nine-year-old girl reports: "My daughter's self-concept is so poor and she has so little self-confidence that she fails at most things she tries."

2. A 37-year-old business executive says: "There has been so much pressure on me lately. Between work and family responsibilities, I feel like I'm just going to explode."

3. The mother of a five-year-old boy reports: "My son can be an absolute monster. He has no respect for authority and always has to have things his way or else he acts up."

4. Two college juniors, boyfriend and girlfriend, report: "We are either best friends or at each others' throats. We seem to have a Jekyll and Hyde relationship."

5. A 22-year-old woman says: "I have this habit of avoiding responsibility, and it makes me feel like a coward. I lost two jobs in the past 6 months because of my stupid attitude."

DIRECT SELF-REPORT INVENTORIES

Direct self-report inventories are questionnaires containing brief statements or questions that require a simple response from the client, such as answering "yes" or "no" or rating how true a statement is on a five-point scale. Behavioral self-report inventories are *direct,* in that the information obtained is taken at face value. For instance, a client who responds "yes" or "often" to the item "I avoid going to parties" provides information about a specific situation the client avoids. In contrast, the same answer might be used in traditional assessment to *indirectly infer* a trait of shyness.[15] This contrast illustrates how behavioral assessment is defined by the way in which assessment procedures are applied rather than by the methods themselves.

Many direct self-report inventories have been developed to assess an array of problem behaviors, including fear and anxiety;[16] depressive behaviors;[17] social skills, including assertive behaviors;[18] health-related disorders, such as premenstrual syndrome, Type A behavior, and eating

Table 5-5 Examples of items used in direct self-report inventories

Problem	Sample Item
UNASSERTIVE BEHAVIOR	When the food you are served at a restaurant is not done to your satisfaction, you complain about it to the waiter or waitress. (Agree or Disagree)
DEPRESSION	I cry often. (True or False)
ANXIETY/FEAR	Enclosed spaces (Rate on scale from 1-5, with 1 being no discomfort and 5 being extreme discomfort in the situation.)
OBESITY	I have one or more between-meal snacks each day. (True or False)
SEXUAL DYSFUNCTION	I become aroused by sexual fantasies. (Agree or Disagree)
SOCIAL SKILLS	I often share my toys with other kids. (Yes or No)
MARITAL DISCORD	My partner does not understand me. (Usually, Sometimes, or Never)

disorders;[19] sexual dysfunctions;[20] and marital problems.[21] Table 5-5 gives examples of items that might appear on direct self-report inventories for different problem behaviors.

Direct self-report inventories are highly efficient, which is the major reason behavior therapists use them frequently. Clients complete them on their own, and the inventories can be scored quickly. Self-report inventories that focus on a particular problem, such as the Beck Depression Inventory, often are used as simple measures of changes in target behaviors. However, most self-report inventories do not supply the specific details required to assess the unique nature of a client's problem. Accordingly, they are most useful for initial screening.

The validity of self-report inventories depends on clients' ability and willingness to provide accurate and honest answers. Clients may not do this for various reasons, including the inclination to present oneself in a favorable light; the tendency to overestimate or underestimate one's own behaviors; and the frequent discrepancy between what people say and what they do.

Participation Exercise 5-2	**ARE YOU IN THE HABIT OF GOOD STUDY HABITS? FIND OUT WITH A DIRECT SELF-REPORT INVENTORY***

Next to each of the 15 statements describing study habits, write the number in the following scale that is most appropriate for you.

3 = Consistently
2 = Usually
1 = Occasionally
0 = Rarely or never

1. I review my class notes each evening.
2. I study in a setting free of distractions.
3. I read assigned material before class but do not study or learn it until shortly before the exam on the material.
4. I look up the meaning of words I do not know while I am reading.
5. I get a good night's sleep before important exams.
6. I use background music to relax me while studying.
7. I start studying for exams at least three days before the exam.
8. Before reading course material, I survey (skim) the reading to get an idea of what it includes.
9. While reading course material, I underline or highlight as many important points as possible rather than make brief notes as I read.
10. I take practice tests (such as in a study guide) when they are available.
11. When I get back an exam, I make sure I know the correct answers to the questions that I got wrong.
12. If I don't understand something a teacher says in class, I write it in my notes and try to figure it out later.

* This Participation Exercise can be done before you continue or later.

13. I read the chapter summary before and after I read the chapter.
14. After completing a reading assignment, I write down the key ideas.
15. I read all my assignments at the same speed.

The major purpose of this Participation Exercise was to give you the experience of completing a direct self-report inventory. So, before checking "how you did," think about the experience. To what extent do you think the inventory adequately assessed your study skills? Were you completely honest in your responses? For instance, did you note any tendency to respond as you think you *should* study rather than how you *do* study? What advantages of self-report inventories emerged? What limitations did you become aware of?

If you'd like to score the inventory, first reverse the scoring of the items that describe poor study habits. For items 3, 6, 9, 12, and 15: change *3* to *0*, change *2* to *1*, change *1* to *2*, and change *0* to *3*. Now add the scores for all 15 items. Obviously, the higher the sum (the closer to 45), the better your study habits. You may find it helpful to consider changing the study habits that you assigned a *0* or a *1* (after reversing scores). Also, if you are unsure about why a particular study habit is good or bad, consult with a teacher, your learning assistance center, or a book on study skills.

BEHAVIORAL CHECKLISTS AND RATING SCALES

Checklists and rating scales are similar in format to self-report inventories, but they are completed by someone other than the client, such as a parent, teacher, or spouse. Checklists and rating scales list potential problem behaviors. With a **checklist,** the informant checks off those behaviors that are problematic for the client. With a **rating scale,** the informant evaluates each behavior by indicating how frequently it occurs or how severe it is. Thus, rating scales provide more information than checklists.[22] Checklists and rating scales are completed retrospectively; that is, they are based on the informant's recollections of the client's behaviors. For example, after school hours a teacher might complete a checklist of a student's behaviors that day.

Although checklists and rating scales typically are used to assess target behaviors, they can be used to identify maintaining conditions. For example, using the Children's Headache Assessment Scale, parents rate environmental antecedents associated with their child's headaches.[23]

Many checklists and rating scales have been developed for both adults and children.[24] Some are broad, measuring problem behaviors in general; others are narrow, assessing specific problem areas. For example, the Child Behavior Checklist includes 113 common problem areas associated with childhood.[25] In contrast, the Children's Attention Profile is a rating scale designed specifically to assess inattention and hyperactivity in children within a classroom setting (see Figure 5-1).[26]

Many of the same advantages and limitations that were described for self-report inventories also apply to checklists and rating scales. They are

Figure 5-1 The Children's Attention Profile
SOURCE: © 1986 Craig Edelbrock

CAP Rating Scale

Child's Name:	FOR OFFICE USE ONLY
Today's Date:	
Filled Out By:	

Below is a list of items that describes pupils. For each item that describes the pupil *now* or *within the past week*, check whether the item is Not True, Somewhat or Sometimes True, or Very or Often True. Please check all items as well as you can, even if some do not seem to apply to this pupil.

	Not True	Somewhat or Sometimes True	Very or Often True
1. Fails to finish things he/she starts	☐	☐	☐
2. Can't concentrate, can't pay attention for long	☐	☐	☐
3. Can't sit still, restless, or hyperactive	☐	☐	☐
4. Fidgets	☐	☐	☐
5. Daydreams or gets lost in his/her thoughts	☐	☐	☐
6. Impulsive or acts without thinking	☐	☐	☐
7. Difficulty following directions	☐	☐	☐
8. Talks out of turn	☐	☐	☐
9. Messy work	☐	☐	☐
10. Inattentive, easily distracted	☐	☐	☐
11. Talks too much	☐	☐	☐
12. Fails to carry out assigned tasks	☐	☐	☐

Please feel free to write any comments about the pupil's work or behavior in the last week.

efficient; most can be completed in 15 minutes or less. Generally, they are used for initial screening purposes and as global measures of change. Sometimes they are used to select target behaviors.[27]

The utility of checklists and rating scales depends on informants' accurately observing the client's behaviors and making reliable ratings. *Reliability,* in general, refers to the consistency or dependability of observations. The specific type of reliability germane to checklists and rating scales is **interrater reliability,** which is the degree to which two or more raters agree. It is measured by comparing the responses of the raters and calculating the percentage of agreement.

Participation Exercise 5-3 will give you a chance to use a behavioral checklist—and probably have fun in the process.

Participation Exercise 5-3

CHECKING OUT A PROFESSOR*

Behavioral checklists, like the checklist in this Participation Exercise, usually require only a few minutes to complete. Table 5-6 contains a list of 40 behaviors in which professors might engage. Choose one of your current or past professors whose class you have been in for at least a month. Using Work Sheet 5-1,† place a check mark next to each of the behaviors that the professor performed on *at least one occasion.* Complete the checklist anytime you are not in the professor's class; this is analogous to how checklists are used in behavioral assessment.

To ascertain how reliable your responses to the checklist are, you will need the help of another student who has been in the professor's class. Ask this student to fill out the checklist using the duplicate copy of Work Sheet 5-1.‡ Then compare your two checklists to obtain your interrater reliability. Count the number of times you and the other student agree—that is, the items for which you both either have a check mark or do not have a check mark. (If you agree most of the time, it will be easier to count the number of disagreements and subtract that from 40.) Divide the number of agreements by 40 and multiply by 100 to get the *percentage of agreement.*

Table 5-6 Behaviors in which professors might engage (Participation Exercise 5-3)

Paces	Strokes beard
Fumbles with notes	Tells jokes
Arrives late	Stutters
Speaks in monotone	Loses train of thought
Talks with hands	Argues with students
Smiles	Reads notes
Taps pen on desk	Fiddles with clothing
Pauses for long time	Repeats self
Plays with hair	Drinks coffee in class
Talks rapidly	Ridicules students
Hums	Listens attentively to students
Dismisses class early	Gives hard exams
Checks watch	Tells personal stories
Sits on desk	Falls asleep
Coughs	Cracks knuckles
Makes eye contact	Uses blackboard
Speaks softly	Talks to students before class
Keeps class late	Talks to students after class
Picks nose	Cancels class
Rubs eyes	Takes attendance

* You should complete the checklist before you continue, but you will need to check your interrater reliability later.
† You will find this work sheet in Appendix C.
‡ You will find this duplicate work sheet in Appendix C.

Doing this Participation Exercise should give you some insight into the checklist method. Obviously, it can be done quickly. Did you have any problems completing the checklist? Were you clear about what each behavior referred to so that you could easily say whether you've noticed the professor engaging in each behavior? How reliable were your observations? Any ambiguity in what was meant by the behaviors on the checklist would lower interrater reliability. What other factors might account for your having less than 100% agreement?

◆

SELF-RECORDING

Self-recording (or **self-monitoring**) involves clients' observing and recording their own behaviors. Self-recording capitalizes on the fact that clients almost always are available to observe and record their own behaviors. Compared with observations made by others, self-recording is time-efficient, especially for infrequent behaviors (such as seizures) that would necessitate constant observation by an outsider.[28] Self-recordings can be made of both overt and covert behaviors and also of the antecedents and consequences of the target behaviors. Clients' privacy is protected with self-recording, which is not the case when others make the observations.

In the simplest form of self-recording, clients record the number of times they perform a target behavior. This can be done, for example, by making tally marks on a small card or by using an inexpensive golf or knitting counter (see Photos 5-1a, b, and c).[29] Clients can record their observations in diaries (such as the anger diary used by Tina in Case 5-1) or on simple forms, such as the one in Figure 5-2. Elaborate recording devices also have been developed,[30] such as a cigarette pack that indicates the number of cigarettes removed.[31]

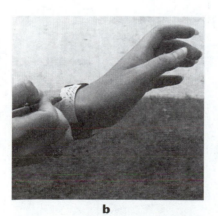

a   b   c

Photos 5-1a, b, and c   Examples of simple, inexpensive self-recording devices

Three potential problems are associated with self-recording. First, its usefulness depends on the client's ability and willingness to make careful and candid recordings. There are three ways to increase the accuracy and honesty of self-recording: (1) by simplifying recording procedures, (2) by recording as soon after the observation as possible, and (3) by having independent observers make occasional spot checks.

Second, self-recording tends to interrupt ongoing activities. Clients usually must stop whatever they are doing, at least briefly, to make recordings. If the target behavior occurs often, frequent interruptions will occur. Not surprisingly, clients may find self-recording irritating, which can result in their failing to record.

The third potential problem with self-recording is that the behavior may change *because* it is being recorded.

Reactivity

When clients are aware that their behaviors are being assessed, they may behave atypically. This phenomenon, known as **reactivity,** results in an inaccurate picture of the client's typical behaviors.[32] For example, when children self-monitor remaining at an assigned task in the classroom, their on-task behaviors increase substantially.[33] Likewise, when clients with

Figure 5-2 Sample form used to record binge eating, including relevant environmental circumstances, thoughts, and feelings

Date	Time	Place	Activity	Thoughts	Feelings
9/6	2:45 PM	home	watching TV	I'm wasting time. I'm lazy.	depressed helpless lonely
9/8	10:00 AM	work	on break	I'm going to have to stay late again to finish my work.	upset mad frustrated
9/13	7:30 PM	home	getting ready for a date	Will I look good enough? Will I say stupid things? What's going to happen at the end of the evening?	nervous anxious

serious hair-pulling habits (called *trichotillomania*) self-monitor hair-pulling, their hair-pulling decreases dramatically.[34] Reactivity can occur whenever clients are aware that they are being assessed, which means that it is a potential problem with any direct observational assessment procedure, but not with retrospective observational procedures, such as checklists and rating scales.

Self-recording may alter the behavior being recorded for at least two reasons.[35] First, in the case of deceleration target behaviors, the client may find it annoying and bothersome to record each instance of the target behavior; the result is that self-recording serves as an aversive consequence for performing the target behavior. Second, self-recording acceleration target behaviors may serve as positive feedback, which reinforces the behaviors.

The ideal safeguard against reactivity is to use assessment procedures that minimize the client's awareness of them. When other people observe the client's behavior—as in naturalistic observation, simulated observation, and role playing—the observers are made as unobtrusive as possible, as by placing them behind a one-way observation mirror (glass that allows observers on

"Anthropologists! Anthropologists!"
THE FAR SIDE copyright 1984 UNIVERSAL PRESS SYNDICATE. Reprinted with permission. All rights reserved.

one side to see through but acts as a mirror from the client's side; see Photo 5-3, p. 97).

However, unobtrusive observation often is not possible, and it is never possible with self-recording. In such cases, reactivity may be minimized by allowing clients to get used to the observation procedures before actual observations begin. During an **adaptation period,** observations are made but the data are not used (in other words, a "practice period").[36] If sufficient time is allowed for adaptation to the observation procedures, clients usually become accustomed to them, and reactivity is insignificant.

Observational assessment procedures are not always reactive, and some procedures tend to be more reactive than others. For instance, merely self-recording caloric intake may result in weight loss for some clients, but self-recording of eating habits is not likely to be associated with weight loss.[37]

So far, we have been talking about reactivity as a problem. On the one hand, reactivity is a problem when accurate information about the current status of a client's target behavior is required, such as to establish a baseline level. On the other hand, if the client's self-recording the target behavior changes it in the desired direction, why not harness reactivity in the service of therapy? Self-recording occasionally is used as a therapy procedure.[38] However, the changes produced through self-recording tend to be relatively small and short-lived.[39] Accordingly, self-recording as a therapy procedure generally is employed as one component of a treatment package rather than as the only treatment.[40]

Participation Exercise 5-4 provides an experience analogous to clients' self-recording target behaviors. Because this Participation Exercise must be done over a number of days, you will not be able to do it now. However, you should read through it now (and carry it out in the coming week) because some of the procedures involved in self-recording are discussed in the instructions.

Participation Exercise 5-4

SELF-RECORDING YOUR ANALOGUE TARGET BEHAVIOR

This is the second part of the behavior therapy analogue you began in Participation Exercise 4-3. Now you will measure with a self-recording procedure the target behavior you chose.

Part I: Selecting Measurement Units

Choose an appropriate *unit of behavior* (such as pages read or minutes watching TV) and a *unit of time* (for example, an hour or a day) for your target behavior. You will be observing and recording a unit of behavior per unit of time (for instance, number of minutes of TV watched per day). Table 5-7 gives examples of units of behavior and time appropriate for various behaviors.

Table 5-7 Examples of units of behavior and time appropriate for various behaviors (Participation Exercise 5-4)

SOURCE: Based on Liebert & Spiegler (1994).

Behavior	Unit of Behavior	Unit of Time
Reading	Pages	Day or hour
Writing	Lines	Day or hour
Jogging	Quarter-miles	Day
Swimming	Laps in a pool	Day
Being late	Times late	Day
Daydreaming	Minutes spent	Day or hour
Talking on the telephone	Minutes spent	Day or hour
Swearing	Curse words	Day or hour
Studying	Minutes spent	Day
Drinking		Day or hour
Coffee	Cups	
Beer	Ounces	
Smoking	Cigarettes	Day or hour

Part II: Setting Up the Measurement

Now decide how you will record the behavior. The simplest procedure is to divide an index card into time intervals and record each time you perform the behavior, as was done with tally marks in Figure 5-3. At the end of each day (or whatever unit of time you are using), calculate the sum of the behaviors; this number becomes your rate for the unit of time (for example, 56 ounces of diet soda drunk per day).

Figure 5-3 Example of an index card record of pages read in a week (Participation Exercise 5-4)

		Total Per Day
Mon.	||||| ||||| ||||| ||||| |||||		26
Tues.	||||| ||||| ||||| ||||| ||||| |||		28
Wed.	||||| ||||| ||||| ||||| ||||| |||		28
Thurs.	||||| ||||| ||||| ||||| ||||| ||||| ||||| ||||| ||||| ||||| |||||			56
Fri.	||||| ||||| ||||| ||||| ||||| ||||| ||||| ||||| ||||| ||||| ||||| ||		57
Sat.	||||| ||||| ||||| ||||| ||||| |||||		30
Sun.		0

Sat. night big date

Sunday slept till 1:30 PM

Figure 5-4 Graph of a week's reading (Participation Exercise 5-4)

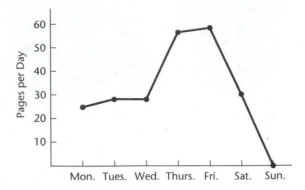

Part III: Observing and Recording

Now you are ready to observe and record your target behavior. Be sure that you carry your recording device (such as an index card) with you whenever you might be engaging in your target behavior. Make your observations over the course of two weeks so that you can observe the behavior under various conditions. Plot your observations on a graph on which the horizontal axis represents units of time and the vertical axis represents units of behavior (see Figure 5-4). *Be sure to save the graph;* it will be used as a baseline of your target behavior in Participation Exercise 8-2.

Your experiences in doing this Participation Exercise may have been similar to those of clients who are asked to self-record target behaviors. For example, you may have found it inconvenient to record the behavior, especially when you were engaged in other activities. Accordingly, you may have put off recording until later, which may have led to inaccurate recording or forgetting to record altogether. You may have found your behavior changing as a result of self-recording (reactivity). Additionally, you may have learned something about your target behavior, such as how often it actually occurs and the circumstances in which you engage in the behavior more frequently and less frequently.

SYSTEMATIC NATURALISTIC OBSERVATION

Systematic naturalistic observation consists of someone observing and recording the client's specific, predefined overt behaviors as they are naturally occurring.[41] Precise definitions of the behaviors, including criteria for differentiating each target behavior from similar behaviors, are essential. Table 5-8 gives examples of such definitions.

The type of measure used—such as frequency, time, or strength—is based on the nature of the target behavior and the purpose of the assessment.[42] When observations are made *continuously* over a relatively brief time, such as an hour or two, considerable observer time is required. A more efficient procedure is *time sampling* in which observations are restricted to specific

Table 5-8 Examples of definitions used for behavioral observations

---

PHYSICALLY AGGRESSIVE BEHAVIORS

Definition: The client physically strikes another person with any part of his or her body or with an object, with potential for inflicting pain on the other person.

Examples: Hitting, slapping, punching, tripping, tackling, pushing, biting, kicking, throwing an object at another person, hitting another person with a stick.

Nonexamples: Spitting, making faces, calling another person names, making verbal threats or threatening gestures at another person.

VERBALLY EXPRESSING ADMIRATION

Definition: The client verbally praises, compliments, expresses a liking or admiration for another person, or expresses a sense of awe about another person's behavior or accomplishment.

Examples: "You did a nice job, " "I really like you," "You look very handsome," "How did you get that done so quickly?" "I enjoy talking with you very much," "Your fast ball is incredible."

Nonexamples: "Would you like to have dinner with me?" "How about a kiss?" "What do you know, he finally got a good grade" (a backhanded compliment), hugging, kissing, embracing, or any other physical show of affection without concomitant verbal affection.

INITIATING SOCIAL CONTACT

Definition: (1) The client initiates social contact by verbally greeting or *starting* an interaction with another person, (2) uses a neutral or pleasant tone of voice when talking to the person, (3) directly looks at the person when initiating contact, and (4) is within 15 feet of the other person at the time the social contact is begun.

Examples: Introducing oneself to another person, asking another person a question (for example, "Can you please tell me where the exit is?"), calling another person by name, or starting a conversation with another person through a comment (for instance, "The team played well today").

Nonexamples: Yelling at or otherwise using an unpleasant tone of voice, talking to another person *only* after that person initiated the contact, talking to someone without looking at the person, or initiating social contact from a distance of greater than 15 feet.

---

time intervals, such as the first five minutes of each hour.[43] Devices used to make recordings range from simple to complex, including paper and pencil; clocks and counters; electromechanical devices, such as event recorders and keyboards; and audio and video recordings.

Training observers, often nonprofessionals such as parents and teachers, is essential.[44] Observers first study the definitions of the behaviors and familiarize themselves with the recording system. Then, they practice making observations until their observations are highly accurate, which is determined by **interobserver reliability** (the equivalent of interrater reliability). The minimum level of acceptable agreement among observers is usually between 80% and 90%.[45]

Systematic naturalistic observation has three potential problems: reactivity, observer error or bias, and impracticality. To minimize reactivity, observers spend time in the natural environment and make practice observations before the actual observations begin. During this adaptation period, clients become accustomed to the observer's presence, and often they

Photo 5-2 Systematic naturalistic observation of a four-year-old child interacting with her peers in a preschool playground. Following an adaptation period, the children have become accustomed to the observer's presence.

"forget" that the observer is there (the observer blends into the background, so to speak). The result is that clients do not alter their normal behaviors much when the observer is present.

Most observational errors are attributable to ambiguously defined target behaviors. Even when the behaviors to be observed are clearly defined, observers' personal biases may make the observations unreliable. Observers' expectations about how the target behaviors will change are a major source of bias.[46] Failure to take into account the cultural context of behaviors is another source of bias. Consider the following interaction observed in an African-American family.[47]

ADOLESCENT: I thought you were my friend.
PARENT: I am no pal to you.

European-American observers recorded this interaction as "harsh discipline." However, African-American observers, who were more familiar with the cultural context in which the interaction took place, recorded it as "constructive discipline." Cultural issues must be considered when designing observational codes, and codes developed for one population may not be applicable to other populations.[48]

Systematic naturalistic observations often are impractical.[49] Considerable observer time is required, such as for training, travel to the client's natural environment, and the actual observing. If the client performs the target behavior infrequently, an observer may spend an inordinate amount of time waiting for it to occur. Further, naturalistic observation may not be possible because it invades a client's privacy, as would be the case in a client's bedroom or professional office. When these practical limitations make systematic naturalistic observation impractical, simulated observation provides an alternative.

SIMULATED OBSERVATION

Simulated observation involves setting up conditions that closely resemble the natural environment in which the client's problem is occurring. Simulated observation often is conducted by using observation rooms that allow observers to see and hear the client through a one-way mirror and microphone. Simulated observation is more efficient than systematic naturalistic observation in terms of saving therapists' time.[50]

Simulated observations make it possible to test hypotheses concerning external maintaining conditions by systematically varying them and observing changes in the client's target behavior.[51] For example, suppose the therapist suspects that a wife and husband's ability to communicate is least effective when they talk about financial matters. To test this hypothesis, the therapist can observe the couple interacting while they attempt to solve problems concerning money and a variety of other topics.[52]

Simulated observation procedures that have been previously developed and validated for particular problems often are used. An example is the Restricted Academic Situations Test, which assesses children's ability to pay attention while working independently on written assignments in the classroom.[53] The child is seated at a desk in the observation room and told to complete a written assignment while remaining seated at the desk. From behind a one-way mirror, the therapist records the child's behaviors in 30-second intervals for 20 minutes (see Figure 5-5). The specific behaviors

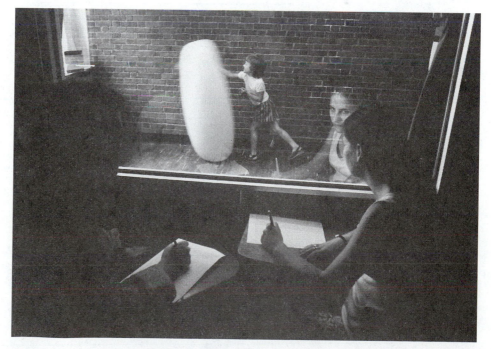

Photo 5-3 Observing a child's aggressive behaviors from behind a one-way mirror

Figure 5-5 Sample recording sheet used for the Restricted Academic Situations Test

Restricted Academic Situation Coding Sheet

Interval Number:	1	2	3	4	5	6	7	8	9	10	11	12	13	14	15
Off task															
Fidgeting															
Vocalizing															
Plays with object															
Out of seat															

Interval Number:	16	17	18	19	20	21	22	23	24	25	26	27	28	29	30
Off task															
Fidgeting															
Vocalizing															
Plays with object															
Out of seat															

Interval Number:	31	32	33	34	35	36	37	38	39	40	Total
Off task											/40
Fidgeting											/40
Vocalizing											/40
Plays with object											/40
Out of seat											/40

TOTAL: /200

Child's name: _____   Coder initials: _____

Date: _____

Week #	Initial	Wk 1	Wk 2	Wk 3	Wk 4

Comments:

recorded are leaving the seat, playing with objects around the desk, fidgeting in the seat, talking out loud, and looking away from the written work. The observer simply places a check mark in the appropriate behavior category anytime the behavior occurs during the 30-second interval. The percentage of time the child engages in each behavior provides data that can be used to pinpoint target behaviors and assess progress during and after therapy.

The primary limitation of simulated observation is the ability to generalize from observations made under a simulated condition to the client's natural environment. The more closely the simulated setting approximates the natural conditions, the greater will be the generalizability.[54]

ROLE PLAYING

In **role playing,** clients enact problem situations to provide the therapist with samples of how they typically behave in those situations. Role playing is especially useful in assessing social skills, such as assertive behaviors.[55] Role playing is an efficient form of simulated observation. No special physical arrangements are needed because the relevant environmental conditions are imagined—clients act *as if* they were in the problem situation. With interpersonal difficulties, the therapist plays the roles of other people. For example, a client who reported difficulty in giving her secretary work was asked to make work-related requests of the therapist, who played the role of the secretary.

Generalizability is a potential limitation of role playing. The more clients are able to behave *as if* they were in the actual situations, the more likely the behaviors observed will be valid indications of how they typically act. Many clients initially feel uneasy or awkward engaging in role playing. With practice, however, most clients are able to "get into" role playing. The therapist also must be able to play roles realistically, which requires *specific* knowledge of how people react to the client. This includes avoiding stereotypic concepts of role relationships, such as how fathers "typically" deal with sons. Reactivity is a potential problem in role playing, such as when clients act more appropriately during role playing than they typically do in actual situations.

PHYSIOLOGICAL MEASUREMENTS

When physiological components of a target behavior are relevant, direct measurements of physiological responses are made. The most frequent measures are heart rate, blood pressure, respiration, muscle tension, and skin electrical conductivity.[56] These responses are used to assess complex behaviors, such as feeling anxious[57] and sexual arousal.[58] Physiological responses can be the sole target behavior, as when biofeedback is used to treat high blood pressure.

Physiological measurements most often are carried out in specially equipped research laboratories. The high cost of the instrumentation required to obtain accurate physiological measures precludes general application in most clinics or private offices. Ideally, physiological recordings would be made in clients' natural environments where their problems are occurring. However, portable measurement devices tend to be less reliable than stationary laboratory apparatus. In the future, technological advances may make in vivo physiological recording more feasible.[59] Even then, they may be too expensive for widespread use.

Physiological measurements are no more or less valid than other assessment methods, although people sometimes give them more credence either because they seem like "pure" measures or because of the technology involved. Physiological measurements are relevant for assessing some behaviors and not for others.

Pulse rate is a simple measure of anxiety that clients can easily use in their natural environments. If you'd like to see how your heart rate changes in various situations, do Participation Exercise 5-5 over the course of the next few days.

◆

Participation Exercise 5-5

GETTING AT THE HEART OF THE MATTER: MEASURING YOUR PULSE*

This Participation Exercise will expose you to the procedures clients use to take their own pulse rate while engaging in everyday behaviors. You will compare your heart rate at rest with your heart rate in situations likely to increase the rate considerably and in situations likely to increase the rate only slightly. Because people's normal heart rates can differ widely, *changes* in heart rate from the individual's resting base rate are used, rather than the absolute rate.

Part I: Taking Your Pulse

Your pulse can be counted easily from the radial artery or carotid artery. The radial artery is located on the thumb side of the wrist. To locate it, turn your right palm upward. Place your index and middle fingers of your left hand (not your thumb, which has a pulse of its own) over the artery, as shown in Photo 5-4. You should not be wearing a watch or bracelet on the wrist from which you are taking your pulse. If you typically wear your watch on your right wrist, you should use your right hand to take your left radial pulse.

The carotid artery runs parallel to your esophagus (windpipe) in your neck. Gently place the index and middle fingers of your right hand along the left side of your esophagus, as shown in Photo 5-5. Do not exert too much pressure on the carotid artery, which can reflexively decrease your heart rate.

* You will need to do this Participation Exercise later.

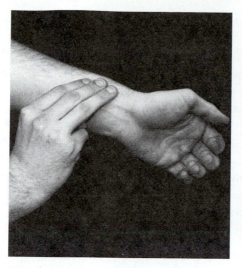

Photo 5-4   Placement of fingers for taking the radial pulse

Photo 5-5   Placement of fingers for taking the carotid pulse

Once you have learned to locate your pulse using either the radial or carotid artery (whichever is easiest for you), you are ready to measure your heart rate. You'll need a watch or clock that displays seconds. Although you will be measuring *heartbeats per minute,* you do not have to count your pulse for a full minute. You can count for 15 seconds and multiply by 4.

Part II: Assessing Your Resting Heart Rate

To measure your resting heart rate, you should lie down or sit in a very comfortable chair (such as a recliner) for about 5 minutes. Listen to some relaxing music; imagine calm, pleasant scenes; think calming thoughts; or otherwise relax. When you feel very relaxed, count your pulse for 15 seconds; then continue to relax for another minute. Again, count your pulse for 15 seconds. Add these 2 counts and multiply by 2 to get your resting heart rate. Record this resting rate on Work Sheet 5-2,* first line, last column.

Part III: Assessing Your Heart Rate In Vivo

To provide you with an analogue of how clients assess their heart rate in actual situations that cause them anxiety, you will take your pulse in six situations that are likely to result in different heart rates. Refer to Table 5-9 for a list of situations from which you can choose. Select three from column A and three from column B; write these in the first column ("Activity") of the work sheet. Then, complete the following steps the next time each of these situations arises.

* You will find this work sheet in Appendix C.

Table 5-9 Situations for counting your pulse (Participation Exercise 5-5)

Instructions: Choose three situations from column A and three situations from column B.

A	B
Reading for pleasure	Watching an exciting TV show
Listening to quiet music	Dancing
Writing a letter	Engaging in an aerobic sport
Eating a meal	Asking for a date
Chatting with friends	Five minutes before an exam
Taking notes in class	Five minutes before an oral report
Waiting in a line	Waiting to be called on in class when not prepared
Sitting in your favorite class	Right after rushing into class
Talking to a friend on the phone	Seeing someone you want to date but are too nervous to ask
Just before going to sleep	Walking in late to class
	Running up three or more flights of stairs
	Five minutes before meeting a date
	Waiting in class for a paper or exam to be passed back
	Right before meeting with a teacher to discuss a grade

1. Take your pulse for 15 seconds, multiply by 4, and record your heart rate in the last column ("Heart rate") of the work sheet.

2. In the second column ("Subjective feeling"), write a number from 1 through 5 to indicate how you were feeling when you took your pulse, using the following scale.

1	2	3	4	5
Calm				Anxious
Relaxed				Tense
Peaceful				Agitated

3. In the third column ("Activity level"), write a number from 1 through 5 to indicate your level of physical activity before you took your pulse, using the following scale.

1	2	3	4	5
At rest				Rigorous exercise

4. Multiply the numbers in the second and third columns and place the product in the fourth column ("Combined rating").

Part IV: Evaluation

Looking at your completed work sheet, you are likely to see that (1) your heart rate in A situations was higher than your resting rate but lower than your heart rate in B situations; (2) a positive correlation exists between your activity level and your heart rate (that is, the more active you were, the higher your heart rate); and (3) a positive correlation exists between how anxious you feel and your heart rate (that is, the more anxious you were, the higher your heart rate). Although this last general expectation occurs for a majority of people, some individuals experience a *decrease* in heart rate when they feel anxious. The critical indication of anxiety, then, is *change from resting pulse.*

◆

◆ ALL THINGS CONSIDERED: BEHAVIORAL ASSESSMENT

If we liken behavior therapy to a pilot, behavioral assessment is the navigator. Behavioral assessment determines the direction in which therapy will proceed, provides the necessary course corrections along the way, and indicates when the destination has been reached.

Multimodal and multimethod assessment are essential ingredients of behavioral assessment. Assessing more than one mode of a problem behavior can result in more effective treatment. For example, anxiety may involve a client's thoughts, feelings, and actions. To assess only one of these modes might result in incomplete treatment. Different modes of a problem behavior may be optimally assessed by different methods because assessment methods vary in their ability to tap each of the modes of behavior[60] (as you saw in Table 5-2, pages 75-76). In addition, information gathered by one assessment method may be verified with other methods.

In this chapter, we have sketched a picture of behavioral assessment circa 1997. Behavioral assessment has evolved over the past 40 years, and its basic nature continues to change. For example, historically the focus of behavioral assessment (and therapy) was overt behaviors. Systematic naturalistic observation was considered the optimal method of assessment, and self-report measures were viewed as less valid.

Today, systematic naturalistic observation is no longer considered the sine qua non of behavioral assessment.[61] However, naturalistic observation remains a highly desirable method for many target behaviors,[62] and it is frequently used in research.[63] Self-report methods, such as direct self-report inventories and self-recording, have become more popular both for their efficiency and their ability to directly tap cognitive and emotional modes of behavior, something that is not possible with naturalistic observation.[64]

Although assessment has always been recognized as important in the practice of behavior therapy, developments in behavioral assessment have escalated in recent years. Literally hundreds of behavioral assessment procedures and instruments have been developed, with the aim of providing behavior therapists with more reliable, valid, and practical methods. Still, the developments in behavioral assessment are not of the same magnitude as in behavioral treatment procedures. Given current trends in the field, we would predict that behavioral assessment in the future will continue to be refined; will address the need for specialized techniques for clients from diverse cultures (see Chapter 18); and will be increasingly integrated with traditional methods of assessment (consistent with the trend toward integration of behavior therapy discussed in Chapter 18).[65]

SUMMARY

1. Behavioral assessment is an indispensable part of behavior therapy. Its goals are to gather information to precisely define target behaviors, identify their maintaining conditions, and measure changes in target behaviors over the course of therapy.
2. Behavioral assessment is multimodal (assessing more than one mode of behavior) and multimethod (using more than one method of assessment).
3. Behavioral assessment procedures share five characteristics: individualized, present-focus, directly samples relevant behaviors, narrow-focus, and integrated with therapy.
4. An interview is usually the first assessment method used. The four goals of initial behavioral interviews are to establish rapport with the client; to gather information about the client's problem; to obtain data about its maintaining conditions; and to educate the client about the behavioral approach. The interview focuses on the present and asks what, when, where, and how often questions, rather than why questions.
5. Direct self-report inventories are questionnaires containing brief statements or questions about behaviors and maintaining conditions that require a simple response or rating. They are highly efficient and most often used for initial screening. Their validity depends on truthful answers.
6. Behavioral checklists and rating scales contain lists of potential problem behaviors, to which someone who knows the client well responds. With checklists, the informant indicates all the behaviors the client performs. With rating scales, the informant uses a scale of frequency or severity to evaluate the client on each behavior. Checklists and rating scales are efficient.
7. Self-recording involves clients' observing and keeping records of their own behaviors. It is time-efficient and can be used to assess covert as well as overt behaviors. Clients must be motivated to self-record and must make truthful recordings. Reactivity—a change in the client's behaviors because the behaviors are being recorded—is a potential problem.
8. Systematic naturalistic observations are made in the situations in which the target behavior normally occurs. These observations are most

accurate when the target behaviors are defined clearly and observers are well trained. The reliability of the observations is assessed by comparing the observations of two or more independent observers. Three potential problems with systematic naturalistic observations are observer error and bias, reactivity, and impracticality.

9. Simulated observations are made under conditions set up to resemble the client's natural environment. A one-way observation mirror often is used. A potential limitation is the ability to generalize what is observed in the simulation to the client's natural environment.

10. In role playing, a form of simulated observation, clients enact problem situations to provide the therapist with samples of how they typically behave. Generalization to the natural environment may be limited because clients may perform differently from the way they typically behave.

11. Physiological measurements directly assess physiological responses associated with the target behavior. They can be costly and usually take place in specially equipped laboratories.

12. Each behavioral assessment method has its strengths and limitations. Multimethod and multimodal assessment helps overcome the limitations of single methods and provides more complete information about clients' problems.

13. Initially, behavioral assessment focused on overt behaviors and systematic naturalistic observations. Today, self-report methods that tap cognitive and emotional modes of behavior frequently are employed.

REFERENCE NOTES

1. Guevremont & Spiegler, 1990; compare with Swan & MacDonald, 1978.
2. Eifert & Wilson, 1991; Kazdin, 1992; Peterson & Bell-Dolan, 1995.
3. Compare with Jorgensen & Carey, 1994; Lazarus, 1989a.
4. Novaco, 1975.
5. Bornstein, Hamilton, & Bornstein, 1986; Nomellini & Katz, 1983; Novaco, 1975.
6. Patterson, Ray, Shaw, & Cobb, 1969.
7. Goldfried & Sprafkin, 1974.
8. American Psychiatric Association, 1994.
9. Compare with Kutchins & Kirk, 1995.
10. For example, Rosenhan, 1973.
11. Goldfried & Sprafkin, 1974.
12. Morganstern, 1976.
13. For example, Storey, Lawry, Ashworth, Danko, & Strain, 1994.
14. Marquis, 1972; Peterson, 1968; Rimm & Masters, 1979.
15. Liebert & Spiegler, 1994.

16. Beidel, Turner, & Morris, 1995; Glass & Arnkoff, 1994; Nietzel, Bernstein, & Russell, 1988.
17. Rehm, 1988.
18. Becker & Heimberg, 1988.
19. Williamson, Davis, & Prather, 1988.
20. McConaghy, 1988.
21. Margolin, Michelli, & Jacobson, 1988.
22. Aiken, 1996.
23. Budd, Workman, Lemsky, & Quick, 1994.
24. Gross & Wixted, 1988; Morrison, 1988.
25. Achenbach, 1978.
26. For example, Guevremont, DuPaul, & Barkley, 1990.
27. Gross & Wixted, 1988.
28. Aiken, 1996.
29. Lindsley, 1968.
30. Schwitzgebel & Schwitzgebel, 1973.
31. Azrin & Powell, 1968.
32. For example, Kirby, Fowler, & Bear, 1991; Johnson & Bolstad, 1973.
33. Reid, 1996.

34. Rothbaum, 1992.
35. Kazdin, 1974e.
36. Haynes, 1978.
37. Green, 1978.
38. For example, Clees, 1994-95; Critchfield & Vargas, 1991; Maletzky, 1974; Spiegler, 1983, pp. 294-295.
39. Thoresen & Mahoney, 1974.
40. For example, Azrin & Peterson, 1990; Kazdin, 1994.
41. For example, Heiman, 1995; Messer & Gross, 1995.
42. Foster, Bell-Dolan, & Burge, 1988.
43. For example, Davis & Chittum, 1994.
44. For example, Barton & Ascione, 1984; Hartmann & Wood, 1982.
45. Hartmann, 1982.
46. Kent & Foster, 1977; Rosenthal, 1969.
47. Cauce, 1995.
48. Markman, Leber, Cordova, & St. Peters, 1995.
49. Wade, Baker, & Hartmann, 1979.
50. Foster, Bell-Dolan, & Burge, 1988.
51. For example, Guevremont & Dumas, 1996.
52. For example, Burman, Margolin, & John, 1993.
53. Guevremont, DuPaul, & Barkley, 1990.
54. Bellack, Hersen, & Turner, 1979; Foster & Cone, 1980; Reisinger & Ora, 1977.
55. For example, Eisler, Hersen, Miller, & Blanchard, 1975; McFall & Marston, 1970; Prince, 1975.
56. Sturgis & Gramling, 1988.
57. Nietzel, Bernstein, & Russell, 1988.
58. Gordon & Carey, 1995; McConaghy, 1988.
59. For example, Holden & Barlow, 1986.
60. Tryon & Pinto, 1994.
61. Guevremont & Spiegler, 1990; Jacobson, 1985.
62. Cone, in press; Foster & Cone, 1986.
63. Cone, 1993.
64. Jensen & Hayes, 1986; Kendall, 1987b.
65. Barrios, 1988; Bellack & Hersen, 1988; Kendall, 1987a.

PART II

BEHAVIOR THERAPY

Now that we've whetted your appetite, you are ready for the elaborate main course: behavior therapy with all the trimmings. In this section, you will get to sink your teeth into a variety of behavior therapies. We'll begin with relatively simple therapy procedures and proceed to more complex ones. The presentation is cumulative, so that an appreciation of previously discussed therapies is necessary for you to fully appreciate the therapies described later.

Chapter 6 deals with reinforcement therapy that increases clients' adaptive behaviors, and Chapter 7 with deceleration behavior therapy that decreases clients' maladaptive behaviors. The token economy, contingency contract, and behavioral child management training, the topics of Chapter 8, are consequential behavior therapy treatment packages. Exposure therapy, covered in Chapters 9 and 10, treats anxiety and other exaggerated negative emotions by safely exposing clients to situations that make them anxious. Modeling therapy and skills training are the topics of Chapter 11. Finally, cognitive-behavioral therapy, which changes clients' cognitions that maintain their psychological disorders, is discussed in Chapters 12 and 13.

Chapter 6

Reinforcement Therapy

Teachers motivate students to learn by awarding high grades for good test performance. Parents get children to do chores by allowing them to watch TV if they complete their chores. Employers ensure continued work output by paying employees. These are common examples of the use of reinforcement in everyday life. People have always reinforced other people's behaviors (and their own) to get others (and themselves) to act in particular ways. Clearly, the concept of reinforcement was not invented by behavior therapists. What behavior therapists have done, however, is to uncover the basic principles of reinforcement, which allow them to use reinforcement to change behaviors effectively and reliably.

WHAT IS REINFORCEMENT?

To reinforce is to strengthen. The term *reinforcement* refers to strengthening a behavior so that it will continue to be performed. Formally, **reinforcement** occurs whenever the consequences of a behavior increase the likelihood that the behavior will be repeated. This is an *empirical definition* because it is based on the *observation* that the behavior occurs again. The reinforcing consequence is known as a **reinforcer.** The person receives the reinforcer only if he or she engages in the behavior. Another way of saying this is that the reinforcer is *contingent* on the behavior being performed.

Reinforcers usually are pleasant or desirable. However, whether a consequence is a reinforcer depends on its effects on the behavior and not on its subjective properties for the person. In other words, reinforcers are defined by their accelerating effects on the behaviors they follow. Reinforcers differ from rewards. *Rewards* are pleasant consequences of a behavior that do not necessarily make it more likely that the person will perform the behavior again.[1] Receiving your driver's license is a common example.

Behavior therapists do not assume that a consequence will be a reinforcer. A *potential* reinforcer is identified and then made contingent on the client's engaging in the target behavior. If the behavior accelerates, then the therapist knows the consequence was a reinforcer.

Besides increasing the likelihood that the behavior will recur, reinforcers provide positive feedback.[2] Reinforcers indicate that people are engaging in an appropriate behavior and are performing it properly. When you receive an *A* for a poem in a writing class, the grade tells you that you've written a good poem as well as increases the chances of your continuing to write poetry.

Information that serves as feedback can come from many different sources. For example, **biofeedback** gives clients highly specific information about their physiological processes (such as heart rate and skin temperature), which enables them to modify the physiological processes to treat various physical disorders (see Chapter 14).[3]

Positive and Negative Reinforcement

Reinforcement always *increases* the frequency of a behavior. This accelerating effect can come about in two ways. One way occurs when an event—usually a pleasant one—is *presented* (added) as a consequence of a person's performing a behavior. This is known as **positive reinforcement,** and the consequence is a **positive reinforcer.** For instance, you hold the door for the person behind you, and the person says, "Thank you." If hearing "thank you" makes you more likely to hold the door for people in the future, then "thank you" is a positive reinforcer and positive reinforcement has occurred.

The other way that a behavior is accelerated occurs when an event—usually an unpleasant one—is *removed* or *avoided* (subtracted) as a consequence of a person's performing a behavior. This is **negative reinforcement,** and the consequence is a **negative reinforcer.** Many everyday behaviors are maintained by negative reinforcement. For example, taking aspirin is reinforced by relief from pain, napping is reinforced by decreasing fatigue, dieting is reinforced by avoiding weight gain, and driving below the speed limit is reinforced by avoiding a ticket. In each instance, we avoid or escape from something undesirable. Such was the case with a 19-year-old man suffering from autistic disorder who had been stealing and ingesting pills whenever and wherever he could find them.[4] In searching for the maintaining conditions of this hazardous behavior, the therapist learned that when the man ingested pills, he immediately was taken away from work that he disliked. Apparently, leaving work was negatively reinforcing his potentially life-threatening behavior.

Although negative reinforcement plays an important role in maintaining people's behaviors, it rarely is used as a therapy procedure.[5] For this reason, this chapter deals almost exclusively with positive reinforcement.

Many people, including professionals, mistakenly use the term *negative reinforcement* to refer to procedures that decelerate a behavior, often erroneously equating it with *punishment* (see Chapter 7).[6] Remember: reinforcement, positive or negative, always refers to the *acceleration* of a behavior. It may help to think of the terms *positive* and *negative* as mathematical signs that merely indicate whether the consequence is *added* (positive) or *subtracted* (negative) to increase the frequency of the behavior.[7]

Before reading any further, take two minutes to list specific things that you believe can serve as reinforcers for your behaviors—in other words, things that will get you to perform various behaviors. Save this list; you will use it later in Participation Exercise 6-2.

CATEGORIES OF POSITIVE REINFORCERS

Positive reinforcers can be grouped into four major categories: tangible reinforcers, social reinforcers, token reinforcers, and reinforcing activities. Some reinforcers fit into more than one category.

Tangible Reinforcers

Many of the reinforcers you just listed were probably **tangible reinforcers,** which are material objects that have personal value. Food, clothes, toys, music CDs, books, and recreational equipment are examples of tangible items that are reinforcers for many people.[8] Tangible reinforcers are concrete and substantive; in other words, you can literally hold on to them. Although it is common to associate reinforcers exclusively with tangible reinforcers, they are only one type of reinforcer.

Social Reinforcers

Social reinforcers consist of attention, praise, approval, and acknowledgment from other people. These reinforcers are administered verbally (for example, "Great job!"), in writing (for instance, a thank you note), physically (as with a pat on the back), and through gestures (such as smiling).[9]

Social reinforcers have four advantages. First, they are easy to administer. All that is needed is another person. Second, people have a limitless supply of social reinforcers to give to others. Third, social reinforcers generally can be administered immediately after the target behavior has been performed, which increases the effectiveness of a reinforcer. Fourth, social reinforcers are **natural reinforcers**—that is, consequences that people receive as a regular part of their daily lives. Using social reinforcers during therapy increases the chances that the target behavior will be maintained after therapy has ended because the reinforcers will continue to be available.[10]

Social reinforcers are among the most powerful consequences for initiating and maintaining behaviors. People of all ages, including very young children, actively seek positive attention and praise from others for engaging in desirable behaviors.[11] For example, think about how your daily behaviors (such as the way you dress) are influenced by other people's approval and attention. Social reinforcement was the major component used in Case 6-1 to treat a patient whose legs were paralyzed due to psychological rather than physical causes, which is called *conversion disorder*.

Case 6-1

TREATMENT OF A CONVERSION DISORDER BY SOCIAL REINFORCEMENT[12]

On admission to a psychiatric hospital, a 42-year-old married man was bent forward at the waist (at a 45-degree angle), unable to straighten his body or move his legs. For 15 years, he had complained of lower back pain. Despite two orthopedic surgeries, his complaints continued. Every 4 to 6 weeks, he had 10- to 14-day episodes of being totally unable to walk, which he referred to as "drawing over." The patient had been hospitalized many times and treated with heat and muscle relaxants. He had been retired for 5 years and had taken on household duties while his wife went to work to support the family.

Orthopedic and neurological evaluations revealed no abnormalities. Behavioral assessment, however, indicated that the patient received considerable reinforcement for his physical complaints, such as being served breakfast in bed and not having to do household chores. Moreover, a number of stressors in his life coincided with the onset of his recent "drawing over" episodes. These included being discharged from the National Guard after 20 years of service, problems with his children, and difficulty adjusting to the role reversal with his wife.

Treatment began in the hospital. Each therapy session started with 10 minutes of conversation with an attractive young female assistant. Following the conversation, the assistant asked the patient to leave his wheelchair and to stand and walk as far as possible, and she praised his efforts (for example, "You're standing very well today" and "I'm very proud of you").

In Phase 1, only standing was reinforced. As Figure 6-1 shows, this resulted in minimal walking. When both standing and walking were reinforced in Phase 2, walking increased. To check whether social reinforcement specifically for walking was responsible for the increase, a five-day reversal period, in which only standing was reinforced, was instituted in Phase 3. The patient did not increase his walking distance, except on Day 11. When reinforcement for both standing and walking was reinstated in Phase 4A, walking increased further. The social reinforcement for both standing and walking led to additional increases when a walker was substituted for the wheelchair (Phase 4B) and then when the walker was taken away (Phase 4C). By Day 18, the patient was walking normally and was discharged from the hospital. Four weeks later, the patient had increased his walking to an average of 350 yards a day.

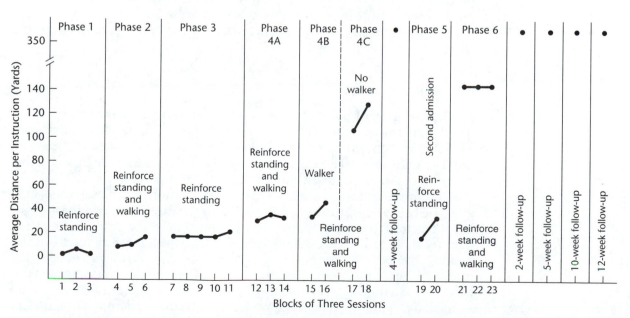

Figure 6-1   Average distance that the patient walked during all phases of treatment and follow-up (Case 6-1)
SOURCE: Kallman, Hersen, & O'Toole, 1975, p. 412.

Immediately after the follow-up assessment, the patient had a severe "drawing over" episode and was readmitted to the hospital, unable to walk. The therapist learned that the patient's family had reinforced his "sick-role" behaviors with social attention. Accordingly, family retraining was made part of the treatment.

The patient began walking again when social reinforcers were reintroduced for standing (Phase 5 in Figure 6-1). His walking dramatically increased when the social reinforcers were administered for both standing and walking (Phase 6). During this last phase of therapy, the family members were videotaped while interacting with the patient. Analysis of the tape revealed that they generally ignored his "well-role" behaviors. Accordingly, the family was taught to socially reinforce the patient's attempts to stand and walk and to ignore his physical complaints. The social reinforcement procedures previously used by the assistant in the hospital were modeled for family members. After his second hospital discharge, the patient again increased his daily walking to an average of 350 yards. Follow-up assessments over the next 12 weeks indicated that he continued to walk normally.

Case 6-1 illustrates the potency of social reinforcement. Initially, it appeared that the client's physical complaints were exacerbated by the attention he received at home from family members. Later, the client's walking was accelerated through the attention and praise of a hospital assistant. The case also points out that changes achieved in therapy do not automatically continue in the client's natural environment. Usually, specific procedures must be implemented to ensure that the treatment effects are maintained outside therapy. This was accomplished in Case 6-1 by ensuring that the reinforcement contingencies used in therapy continued in the client's home environment.

Token Reinforcers

A third category of positive reinforcers are **token reinforcers,** symbolic items that have value because of what they can be exchanged for or stand for. Money is a token reinforcer because it can be exchanged for valued goods and services. Other everyday examples of token reinforcers include a good grade, a trophy or award, a varsity letter, and a college diploma.

Reinforcement is most effective when the reinforcer comes immediately after the behavior is performed. However, in the case of many reinforcers, it is not practical to provide the reinforcer immediately. For instance, Kavitha's parents want to use bike riding after school as a reinforcer for Kavitha's making her bed in the morning. When Kavitha makes her bed in the morning, her parents say, "Because you made your bed, you can ride your bike this afternoon." This *promise of a delayed reinforcer* (an IOU) is an immediate, symbolic token reinforcer. It serves the important function of bridging the time between the behavior and the substantive reinforcer. (The parents' IOU also may provide social reinforcement.)

Examples of token reinforcers used to increase adaptive behaviors of clients in behavior therapy include points used to purchase retail items[13] and food and gas coupons[14] to promote abstinence in clients with drug addictions, stickers to increase school attendance in children with severe anxiety,[15] and fast food coupons (such as a free pizza) to promote cooperation among disruptive adolescents in an inner city school.[16] In behavior therapy, token reinforcers are used most extensively in token economies (see Chapter 8).

Reinforcing Activities

Engaging in activities is the fourth category of positive reinforcers. Examples of activities that serve as reinforcers for many people are listening to music, shopping, playing sports, watching TV, playing computer games, socializing with friends, talking on the telephone, eating, and attending special weekend events.[17]

Reinforcing activities are usually pleasurable. However, activities in which a person frequently engages—but does not necessarily enjoy—can serve as reinforcers. This is the basis of the Premack principle.

PREMACK PRINCIPLE

Mary-Lynne, like many of us, turns on the radio every time she starts her car. She does not fasten her seat belt, however. What do you think would happen if Mary-Lynne could turn on her car radio only *after* she had put on her seat belt? Most likely, Mary-Lynne would start to wear her seat belt.

More than 30 years ago, David Premack discovered that higher-probability behaviors—whether they are considered enjoyable or not—can serve as reinforcers for lower-probability behaviors. This has come to be called the **Premack principle.**[18]

The Premack principle lends itself to creative applications in behavior therapy.[19] Typically, *probability* is measured by *frequency of occurrence*.* Acceleration target behaviors often are low-probability behaviors—that is, they occur infrequently, which is the reason they need to be accelerated. Thus, high-probability behaviors can be used as reinforcers for many acceleration target behaviors.[20] Although the high-probability behaviors need not be pleasurable to serve as reinforcers, high-probability behaviors that are distinctly *aversive* to the individual generally do not function as reinforcers.[21] Another qualification concerning high-probability behaviors used as reinforcers is that they must not be occurring so often that they lose their effectiveness in motivating clients to engage in the low-probability target behavior. As the familiar adage tells us, too much of a good thing can be bad.[22]

* According to Premack's (1965) original formulation, frequency and probability are not equivalent. Thus, the use of higher-frequency behaviors to reinforce lower-frequency behaviors is not strictly the Premack principle. However, the term *Premack principle* is generally used in behavior therapy to indicate using higher-frequency behaviors as reinforcers, and we are following that convention.

Employing high-probability behaviors as reinforcers is especially useful with clients for whom other reinforcers are difficult to identify. A prime example is hospitalized patients with chronic psychiatric disorders for whom tangible and social reinforcers may be ineffective.[23] If we observe their daily activities, we note such typical behaviors as standing, staring out the window, pacing, and sleeping in a chair. These simple, mundane activities (that might erroneously be labeled "doing nothing") are high-probability behaviors. Thus, they can serve as reinforcers according to the Premack principle, as Case 6-2 illustrates.

Case 6-2

SOCIAL INTERACTION INCREASED THROUGH THE PREMACK PRINCIPLE[24]

B. H. was a 44-year-old female patient in a psychiatric hospital who rarely interacted with other patients or staff members. She responded to questions by nodding or with one-word answers. The staff reported that they had never observed B. H. enjoying anything. She spent almost all her waking hours sitting in a specific chair in the day room. It was decided to use this high-probability behavior to reinforce social interactions, which were decidedly low-probability behaviors for B. H.

The ward psychologist informed B. H. that she would be permitted to sit in her favorite chair only after she had interacted with another patient or staff member. Initially 2 minutes of social interaction was required for 30 minutes of sitting. B. H. nodded that she understood, at which point the psychologist immediately reinforced their interchange by permitting her to sit in her chair for 30 minutes. The psychologist made the contingency explicit by telling B. H. that she had just earned sitting time by listening and communicating that she understood.

At the end of the first 30-minute period, a staff member approached B. H. and suggested that they have a cup of coffee together, reminding B. H. that she had to spend 2 minutes interacting with others in order to sit in her chair. B. H. reluctantly accepted the invitation. For the rest of the day, one of the ward staff approached B. H. after each 30-minute period of sitting and suggested some minimal social activity that would allow her to continue to sit.

On each successive day, 1 minute of social interaction was added to the criterion required for 30 minutes of sitting. By the end of the second week, B. H. had to spend 15 minutes interacting with others for every 30 minutes that she spent sitting. As B. H. progressed, the staff gave her fewer and fewer suggestions about how she might socialize. They left B. H. to choose how she wanted to spend time with others from the examples the staff had initially provided. By the 12th day, B. H. was getting up from her chair after 30 minutes without having to be reminded by a staff member.

Within 3 weeks, B. H. was spending more than the required time with others and less than 30 minutes sitting in her chair. For example, she often played dominoes with a particular patient. Initially, she would get up in the middle of the game as soon as she had accumulated enough socializing time to sit in her chair. After a while, she would first finish a game, which took more than 30 minutes. Eventually B. H. was spending the majority of each day in some social activity.

In using the Premack principle to accelerate B. H.'s social behaviors, the ward staff did not assume that she enjoyed sitting in her chair. All they knew was that sitting in the chair had a higher probability of occurring than social interaction. From the increases observed in B. H.'s social behaviors, it appeared that sitting in the chair was a reinforcer. The Premack principle will work for you as well, as you'll find out by doing Participation Exercise 6-1 over the course of the next couple of weeks.

Participation Exercise 6-1

DOING WHAT COMES UNNATURALLY: APPLYING THE PREMACK PRINCIPLE

You can easily see how well the Premack principle works by using it to accelerate one of your own low-probability behaviors. Choose a behavior that *you "should" be doing at least once a day but that you rarely do.* For many people, examples would be washing dishes right after meals, flossing their teeth, making the bed, and exercising (although these might not be examples for you). Keep a record for a week of the number of times each day you perform the low-probability behavior you have chosen. This record will provide a baseline.

Next, make a list of your routine high-probability behaviors, those you perform at least once a day without fail. These will be routine behaviors such as taking a shower, shaving, putting on makeup, combing your hair, eating breakfast, and checking the mail (or whatever your routine behaviors are). You do not have to consider the routine behaviors enjoyable.

Select one of these high-probability behaviors as a reinforcer. It must generally occur some time *after* you engage in the low-probability behavior. For example, if your low-probability behavior were making your bed before leaving the house in the morning, then you could reinforce it with any high-probability behavior that you do after leaving the house in the morning, such as listening to the car radio or stopping for a cup of coffee.

After a week of recording a baseline, implement the Premack principle by following the rule: *engage in the high-probability behavior only after you have performed the low-probability behavior.* Continue to record the number of times you perform the low-probability behavior each day. You should observe an increase in the frequency of your low-probability behavior.

IDENTIFYING REINFORCERS

Reinforcers are most effective when they are individualized for each client. Behavior therapists do not assume that consequences that are reinforcers for one person will be reinforcers for all people. *Potential* reinforcers are first identified and then tested to see if they indeed accelerate the target behavior. Behavior therapists use a variety of methods for identifying potential reinforcers for clients, including directly questioning the client, selecting from generalized reinforcers, and observing the clients' routine behaviors.

Questioning Clients

Asking clients about potential reinforcers is the easiest and most frequently used procedure. The therapist might start with a general question, such as "What things do you find enjoyable or rewarding?" Then the questions would get more specific, asking about narrow categories of reinforcers (for example, "What do you like to do in the evenings?"; "If you had some extra money, what would you buy with it?"; "Where would you like to go if you had a day off?").

Direct questioning has its limitations. It does not work for clients with severely limited intellectual and verbal abilities. Clients who are suffering from depression cannot think of reinforcers because nothing seems rewarding or worthwhile to them. In such cases, the therapist can question people who know the client.

Exposing Clients to Generalized Reinforcers

Consequences that are reinforcing for many people are called **generalized reinforcers.**[25] Common examples include food, money, and praise. Generalized reinforcers vary with demographic characteristics, such as age, gender, and cultural background. For example, food and music are generalized reinforcers for most people. However, the specific food and music are likely to be different for young children and adults, as well as for Hispanic and Japanese individuals. Similarly, generalized reinforcers are likely to vary with specialized clinical populations. For instance, the privilege of taking methadone at home rather than at a clinic is a generalized reinforcer for clients addicted to heroin.[26]

One method of identifying potential reinforcers is to expose clients to an array of generalized reinforcers. Clients select those that they think will be reinforcers for them. For example, children can be taken to a toy store and asked to pick out toys they would like to have. Adults might make selections from a merchandise catalog or the entertainment section of the Sunday newspaper. Special procedures have been developed for clients with very limited intellectual and verbal capacities.[27] For instance, clients with severe mental impairments spent time in a room containing 16 potential reinforcers, such as a fan, juice, and a swing.[28] Reinforcer preference was determined by the frequency with which clients approached each of the objects. Whether these preferred items were reinforcers was tested empirically by seeing if they accelerated target behaviors.

Standardized lists of generalized reinforcers have been developed to aid in finding potential reinforcers for clients. The Reinforcement Survey Schedule is a direct self-report inventory. Clients rate the degree to which they enjoy common tangible reinforcers and reinforcing activities listed (see Table 6-1).[29] The Children's Reinforcement Survey Schedule contains generalized reinforcers for children (see Table 6-2).[30] An adult checks off valued generalized reinforcers for the child. With the Pleasant Events Schedule, the client rates an extensive list of behaviors on two dimensions: (1) the frequency of engaging in each behavior and (2) the amount of pleasure derived from engaging in each behavior.[31] Reinforcement menus, like the one in Figure 6-2, allow children to point to pictures of generalized reinforcers they like.[32]

Table 6-1   Sample items on the Reinforcement Survey Schedule

SOURCE: Cautela & Kastenbaum, 1967.

	Not at All	A Little	A Fair Amount	Much	Very Much
Eating					
Ice cream	___	___	___	___	___
Fruit	___	___	___	___	___
Cookies	___	___	___	___	___
Solving problems					
Crossword puzzles	___	___	___	___	___
Figuring out how something works	___	___	___	___	___
Nude men	___	___	___	___	___
Nude women	___	___	___	___	___
Watching sports					
Football	___	___	___	___	___
Baseball	___	___	___	___	___
Golf	___	___	___	___	___
Reading					
Adventure	___	___	___	___	___
Mystery	___	___	___	___	___
Sexy	___	___	___	___	___
Looking at beautiful scenery	___	___	___	___	___
Television, movies, or radio	___	___	___	___	___
Shopping					
Clothes	___	___	___	___	___
Auto parts and supplies	___	___	___	___	___
Gardening	___	___	___	___	___
Sleeping	___	___	___	___	___
Being right					
In an argument	___	___	___	___	___
About your work	___	___	___	___	___
Being praised					
About your appearance	___	___	___	___	___
About your work	___	___	___	___	___
Being in church or temple	___	___	___	___	___
Peace and quiet	___	___	___	___	___

Table 6-2 Examples of generalized reinforcers appearing on the Children's Reinforcement Survey Schedule
source: Phillips, Fischer, and Singh, 1977, pp. 131-132.

Instructions: Check off valued reinforcers according to child's report.

Food
    Candy (what kind?)
    Ice cream (favorite flavor?)
    Potato chips

Toys
    Racing cars
    Dolls

Entertainment
    Television (favorite program?)
    Movies (what kind?)

Sports and games
    Playing football
        with other kids
        with your father
    Swimming
    Tennis
    Checkers
    Fishing

Music, arts, and crafts
    Playing a musical instrument (what kind?)
    Building models
    Working with clay
    Singing

Excursions
    Ride in the car
    Visit to the seashore
    A family picnic
    An airplane ride
    Visiting a friend

Social
    Playing with friends
    Being praised (by whom?)
    Being hugged or kissed
    Girl Scouts, Boy Scouts, or other clubs

Learning
    A new language
    Piano lessons

School work
    Reading
    Science
    Gym

Helping around the house
    Setting the table
    Making the bed
    Going on errands

Personal appearance
    Getting new clothes
    Getting a haircut
    Dressing up in a costume

Figure 6-2 Part of a reinforcement menu
source: Adapted from Daley, 1969, p. 44.

Observing Clients' Routine Behaviors

A third method of identifying reinforcers is to observe clients in their natural environments and note the behaviors that they engage in most frequently and spend the most time doing. These high-probability behaviors can serve as reinforcing activities according to the Premack principle.

◆ ▬▬▬▬▬▬▬▬▬▬▬▬▬▬▬▬▬▬▬▬▬▬▬▬▬▬▬▬▬▬▬▬▬▬▬▬▬

Participation Exercise 6-2

IDENTIFYING YOUR OWN POTENTIAL REINFORCERS*

Earlier, you made a list of your potential reinforcers. Now, you can compile a more complete list, using two of the methods you have just read about for identifying potential reinforcers.

Part I: Direct Questioning

As you answer the following questions, keep a running list of potential reinforcers that are elicited by the questions, eliminating duplicates. Some of the questions directly identify reinforcers, while others are designed to cue areas in your life in which you may find potential reinforcers.

1. What things do you like to use? Buy? Consume (for example, what kind of food)?
2. What would you like as a gift?
3. What is being sold in stores, ads, or catalogs that draws your attention?
4. What activities do you enjoy?
5. What do you like to do in your spare time?
6. What do you like to do most in your work?
7. What do you consider a fun night out? Night at home? Weekend? Vacation?
8. What accomplishments give you satisfaction?
9. What are you doing when you feel happy? Alive? Useful? Important?
10. What types of social interactions do you enjoy? Do you engage in?
11. What types of social events do you like? Do you go to?
12. What do you like other people to do for you? Say to you?
13. With whom do you like to spend your time?
14. What do you like to happen when you finish doing something well?
15. What allows you to persevere at difficult and long tasks?

Part II: Identifying Pleasant Activities

Table 6-3 contains 50 activities that are potential reinforcers. You will rate each item twice. First, answer the question *"How often have you engaged in the activity during the past 30 days?"* for each item, using the following scale.

* You will need to do this Participation Exercise later, but you should read it now.

Table 6-3 Common activities that are potential reinforcers (Participation Exercise 6-2)
SOURCE: Adapted from MacPhillamy & Lewinsohn, 1971.

Attending a concert	Playing videogames
Attending a club meeting	Playing sports
Being with my parents	Playing a musical instrument
Being alone	Playing with a pet
Complimenting or praising someone	Playing board games
Cooking	Reading the newspaper
Dancing	Reading fiction
Dating	Riding a bike
Daydreaming	Staying up late
Doing volunteer work	Saying prayers
Doing art work	Shopping
Driving	Skating
Eating out	Sleeping late
Eating snacks	Straightening up (house or car)
Exercising	Taking a walk
Getting up early in the morning	Taking a nap
Getting dressed up	Taking a shower
Getting or giving a massage or back rub	Talking on the telephone
Going to a mall	Teaching someone
Going to the movies	Telling stories and jokes
Going to a party	Watching a TV program
Helping someone	Watching a video
Listening to or watching the news	Watching sports events
Listening to music	Watching people
Listening to radio talk shows	Writing letters

1 = *Not at all* in the past 30 days.
2 = *A few times* (1-6) in the past 30 days.
3 = *Often* (7 or more) in the past 30 days.

Write the number in the *Frequency* column of Work Sheet 6-1.*

After rating the frequency of the 50 activities, read each item again and answer the question, "*How pleasant, enjoyable, or rewarding was the activity during the past month?*" using the following scale.

1 = This activity was *not* pleasant. (It was either unpleasant or neutral.)
2 = This activity was *somewhat* pleasant. (It was mildly or moderately pleasant.)
3 = This activity was *very* pleasant. (It was strongly or extremely pleasant.)

Write the number in the *Pleasantness* column of your work sheet. If you've engaged in an activity more than once in the past month, make an average pleasantness rating. If you have not engaged in an activity during the past month, rate it according to how enjoyable you think it would have been.

* You will find this work sheet in Appendix C.

When you've rated the activities twice, multiply the frequency and pleasantness ratings for each activity and write the product in the *Frequency × Pleasantness* column. Higher products indicate more frequent and more pleasant activities and thus potential reinforcers. Add the activities with the highest products to your list of potential reinforcers that you compiled in Part A, eliminating duplicates.

At this point you should have a sizable list of potential reinforcers (which you should save because you may need it for Participation Exercise 8-2). Remember that an activity is an *actual* reinforcer only if it accelerates a behavior that it follows.

Photo 6-1   Providing customers with free samples of products is analogous to reinforcer sampling.

Alternatives to Identifying Reinforcers

Sometimes it is difficult to identify reinforcers—especially ones that are practical as well as potent. In such instances, generalized reinforcers can be tried, drawing from generalized reinforcers that are appropriate for the particular client's demographic characteristics (such as gender and age). The odds are good that one or more will work for the client.

It also is possible to create a reinforcer by making a generalized reinforcer desirable and valuable to the client. **Reinforcer sampling** is a procedure in which clients are first given a generalized reinforcer noncontingently—that is, without having to do anything to obtain it.[33] The aim is to "hook" the client on the generalized reinforcer. When the client begins to enjoy the reinforcer and wants more of it, the client is required to perform a target behavior to obtain the reinforcer. For example, to get him to clean his room, a mother taught her son a new game that they played together each night for a week. The boy came to enjoy the game and to look forward to playing it. At this point, the mother made playing the game contingent on the boy's cleaning his room. Reinforcer sampling had established the game as a reinforcer, as evidenced by the fact that the boy began to clean his room. Businesses use an analogous strategy when they give customers free samples in order to induce them to buy a product.

Another way to create reinforcers is to expose the client to other people (models) who are partaking of the reinforcer and who clearly are enjoying themselves. What we find enjoyable or valuable is determined in part by what we observe others enjoying and valuing. Humor is a good example. The next time you watch a comedy show on TV, check to see if your laughter coincides with the laugh track (an indispensable feature of TV comedy).

ADMINISTERING REINFORCERS

After identifying a client's potential reinforcers, the next step is to design procedures for administering them after the client performs the target behavior.

Sources of Reinforcers

Reinforcers can be administered (1) by other people and (2) by clients themselves, and reinforcers also can be (3) a natural consequence of the behavior. In behavior therapy, other people most often dispense reinforcers for a client. These **reinforcing agents** include therapists,[34] parents,[35] teachers,[36] spouses,[37] siblings,[38] and peers.[39] Adults usually reinforce children's behaviors, but sometimes children reinforce adults' behaviors.[40]

Clients can reinforce their own behaviors, which is called **self-reinforcement.**[41] Self-reinforcement has a number of advantages over reinforcement provided by others. Because the reinforcing agent is always present, reinforcement can occur immediately after the target behavior is performed. Self-reinforcement is likely to increase generalization beyond therapy and to increase long-term maintenance of the target behavior. Additionally, self-reinforcement makes clients responsible for their behavior changes. The major limitation of self-reinforcement is that clients may be less reliable in administering reinforcers than are other people who are specifically charged with that responsibility.

Reinforcers do not come only from reinforcing agents—that is, other people or oneself. They also can be a natural result of engaging in the target behavior. For instance, increased endurance and energy are a natural result of regular aerobic exercise and are likely to reinforce such exercise. The increased endurance and energy are examples of natural reinforcers. Besides being naturally occurring consequences of the behavior, as in the previous example, natural reinforcers also can come from reinforcing agents, as when saying "good morning" to someone is likely to be reinforced by receiving a similar greeting in return.

Continuous Versus Intermittent Reinforcement

Reinforcers are administered on two basic schedules. A *schedule of reinforcement* is a rule that specifies which occurrences of a target behavior will be reinforced. With a **continuous reinforcement schedule** people are reinforced *every time* they engage in the target behavior. With an **intermittent reinforcement schedule** only *some* of the occurrences of the target behavior are reinforced. When an intermittent schedule of reinforcement is based on a specified interval of *time* (for instance, a reinforcer is given after every five-minute interval in which the individual performs the behavior one or more times), it is known as an *interval schedule*. When it is based on the *number* of times the behavior must be performed for it to be reinforced (for example, a reinforcer is given after every five times the person engages in the target behavior), it is called a *ratio schedule*.

Continuous reinforcement is most useful when the client is first learning to perform a target behavior. Once the behavior is established, the client is usually switched to an intermittent schedule. Intermittent reinforcement is more economical, and it increases the chances that the client will continue to engage in the target behavior in the long run. It simulates what occurs in clients' natural environments, where behaviors are reinforced some but not all of the time. Thus, intermittent reinforcement is one way to promote long-term maintenance of target behaviors. To appreciate just how powerful intermittent reinforcement can be in maintaining behaviors, consider what happens with compulsive gambling. Although gamblers are reinforced (that is, win) only occasionally, they will continue to place many bets following their last payoff.

Individual Versus Group Contingencies

Reinforcers most often are administered through **individual contingencies**, so that the consequences a person receives (or fails to receive) depend only on his or her behavior. An example in a classroom is when any student who scores at least 80% on a quiz gets 5 extra minutes of recess. In contrast, with a **group contingency**, all members of a group receive (or fail to receive) the same consequences, depending on the performance of the group.

In one type of group contingency, each group member must meet a specified performance criterion for all the group members to receive the reinforcer. For instance, if all students get 80% or better on a quiz, then the whole class receives 5 extra minutes of recess. Another type of group contingency depends on the total or average performance of all the group members to determine if the reinforcer is administered to the entire group.[42] For example, if the average of all the students' quizzes is 80%, the entire class gets extra recess.

The decision to use individual versus group contingencies when a group of clients is being treated varies with the particular application.[43] Among the considerations is whether group pressure, which enhances the effectiveness of a group contingency, could be detrimental to the clients (as by fostering excessive coercive power).[44]

Guidelines for Administering Reinforcers

Behavior therapists have developed guidelines for administering reinforcers. The following are seven important guidelines.

1. *Reinforcers should be contingent on the client's performing the target behavior.* The reinforcer is administered only *after* the client has performed the target behavior. Providing a potentially reinforcing item or activity before the client engages in the target behavior will not accelerate it.

2. *The reinforcer should be administered immediately after the client performs the target behavior.* Immediate reinforcement is more effective than delayed reinforcement, especially when a target behavior is being learned initially.

3. *The client should be aware that the reinforcer is a consequence of the target behavior.* Knowledge of the contingency will enhance the reinforcement effect. The simplest way is to tell the client the reason for the reinforcer as it is administered (for example, "You did a good job on your homework, so now you can ride your bike.").

4. *Continuous reinforcement should be used initially, followed by intermittent reinforcement.* Continuous reinforcement is optimal for initially accelerating a target behavior, and intermittent reinforcement helps to maintain it.

5. *Reinforcers should be kept potent.* Reinforcers can lose their potency with repeated use (the idea that too much of a good thing can be bad). Procedures for maintaining the incentive value of reinforcers include (1) dispensing reinforcers in small amounts, (2) using reinforcers that are less likely to lead to satiation (for example, praise rather than food), and (3) switching reinforcers periodically.

6. *Natural reinforcers should be used in therapy.* Employing reinforcers that the client is likely to receive outside therapy enhances generalization and long-term maintenance.

7. *Reinforcers should be administered consistently.* All reinforcing agents for a client should use the same criteria for administering reinforcers.

INITIATING BEHAVIORS: PROMPTING AND SHAPING

A client must perform a behavior in order for it to be reinforced. This obvious fact becomes salient when a client is engaging in the desired target behavior infrequently or not at all. Three procedures are employed in behavior therapy to initiate behaviors: prompting, shaping, and modeling. We'll discuss prompting and shaping here and modeling in Chapter 11.

HAGAR reprinted with special permission of King Features Syndicate, Inc.

Prompting

Prompting provides people with cues, or **prompts,** that remind or instruct them to perform a behavior. Every day we rely on prompts to guide our behavior, such as when we stop at a red light, write appointments on a calendar, and remind friends to call us. There are four types of prompts: verbal, environmental, physical, and behavioral.

Verbal prompts involve telling clients what they are expected to do. In an unusual application of prompting, children were taught to prompt their teacher to praise their good behaviors.[45] For instance, children would approach the teacher with a completed assignment and say "I finished all my math problems" to remind the teacher to praise them.

Environmental prompts are cues in the environment that remind clients to perform behaviors, such as a posted note. In one application to help prevent AIDS, signs in a bar about the risk of AIDS and the benefits of using condoms increased men's taking free condoms.[46] Other examples of environmental prompts used in behavior therapy are alarms to remind elderly people to take their medications;[47] written cue cards to prompt adults with mild handicaps to perform home maintenance tasks;[48] and pictorial signs to remind children with autistic disorder to perform daily living skills (such as getting dressed).[49]

Physical prompts (also called *physical guidance*) involve someone physically directing a client through a behavior—for example, teaching a child to write by holding the child's hand and making the required movements. Physical prompts are used extensively to teach self-care skills to individuals with developmental disabilities, such as training self-feeding skills to children who are both deaf and blind.[50]

Behavioral prompts involve one behavior cuing another. For example, a husband in marital therapy learned to use his wife's crying as a signal to respond with sympathy rather than to become upset. An individual's own behavior can serve as a prompt to engage in another behavior. For instance, parents may learn to use their feeling angry at their child as a cue to leave the room to "cool off."

Prompting usually is a temporary measure. As the client performs the behavior more frequently due to reinforcement, the prompts become less

Photo 6-2   How many environmental prompts can you identify in this picture?

necessary and they are gradually withdrawn—a process known as **fading**. Prompting (in conjunction with modeling and shaping) is a standard procedure for eliciting very low-frequency behaviors. Teaching language to children with autistic disorder is a prime example.[51] To teach the names of objects, for instance, the therapist will point to the object and say, "What is this? *Pencil.*" (The therapist's saying the word *pencil* is the prompt.) As the child begins to imitate the prompt, the therapist fades the prompt by saying it at successively lower volumes. Eventually the therapist whispers the prompt, then merely mouths it, and finally asks the child, "What is this?" without any prompt.

Shaping involves reinforcing successive steps required for a complex behavior.
Reprinted with permission of Mal Hancock.

Shaping

Shaping is a procedure in which the components of a target behavior are reinforced, rather than the complete target behavior. Successively closer approximations of the total behavior are reinforced so that finally it is the complete behavior that is reinforced. This process is shown schematically in Figure 6-3. The children's game of "hot and cold" is a variation of shaping.[52] One child has to locate a particular object while a playmate directs the child toward the object by saying "hot" when the child gets closer and "cold" when the child starts to move farther away.

Shaping is used to accelerate target behaviors that a client is performing infrequently or that are difficult or complex for a client, such as teaching fire-exiting emergency skills to a nine-year-old girl with autistic disorder.[53] The total behavior is broken down into its logical component parts or steps, and then each is reinforced as it occurs. The process is cumulative in that each component plus all preceding components are reinforced. For instance, suppose a therapist were teaching a child to say the sentence "I want milk." The therapist would first reinforce "I," then "I want," and finally "I want milk."

Shaping generally is part of a treatment package. Case 6-3 illustrates the use of shaping and prompting to accelerate talking in a man who had not spoken in 19 years.

Figure 6-3 Schematic diagram representing the principle of shaping
SOURCE: © Michael D. Spiegler and David C. Guevremont

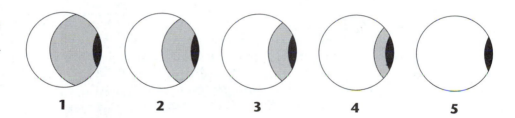

| 1 | 2 | 3 | 4 | 5 |

Target behavior: reinforced

Approximations of target behavior: reinforced

Behaviors not close enough to target behavior to be reinforced

Case 6-3

INSTITUTING SPEECH IN A PATIENT WITH LONG-STANDING MUTISM BY PROMPTING AND SHAPING[54]

A 40-year-old male patient in a psychiatric hospital had been completely mute and virtually unresponsive during 19 years of hospitalization. For example, in group therapy he remained impassive, staring straight ahead even when he was offered a cigarette, which other patients accepted. During one group therapy session, the therapist accidentally dropped a package of chewing gum, and the patient momentarily moved his eyes toward it. This response was chosen as a starting point to shape the patient's speaking.

Individual therapy sessions were held three times a week. The therapist began by holding a stick of gum in front of the patient's face and waited until he looked at it, at which point the patient was given the gum. When the patient consistently looked at the gum, the therapist waited for any lip movement before reinforcing the patient with gum. Then, looking, lip movements, and any sound were required for the reinforcer. Next, the therapist used the prompt "Say gum, gum," and the reinforcer was made contingent on closer and closer approximations of "gum."

At the end of the 18th session, the patient spontaneously said, "Gum, please." This breakthrough was accompanied by other verbal responses, such as answering questions about his name and age. Thereafter, the patient responded to other questions the therapist asked, but he did not respond to other staff members. To generalize his responding to other people, a nurse was brought in to the therapy sessions. After a month, the patient was responding to the nurse's questions. Finally, the patient's verbal requests were shaped. All the staff members with whom the patient had contact did things for the patient only when he specifically asked for them.

The use of prompting and shaping to initiate speaking in a person who had been mute for essentially all his adult life is impressive. As Case 6-3 illustrates, shaping requires careful observation of the client's actions in order to make fine discriminations between the components of the target behavior. Participation Exercise 6-3 will help you appreciate the subtle skills required for effective shaping.

Participation Exercise 6-3

SHAPING YOUR SHAPING SKILLS*

To do this exercise, you will need the help of a friend for about 20 minutes.

Choose a behavior that is (1) simple, (2) brief (taking less than a minute), and (3) easily broken down into components or steps. Examples of suitable behaviors are opening and closing a book, removing the top of a pen and replacing it, standing up and sitting down, opening and closing a window, and talking about a particular topic (such as schoolwork or the weather).

List the major components of the behavior ahead of time and keep them in mind. (The major components of two simple behaviors are listed in Table 6-4 as examples.) However, your friend may not perform each of the components.

---

* You will need to do this Participation Exercise later, but you should read it now.

Table 6-4 Major components of two simple behaviors (Participation Exercise 6-3)

Opening and closing a book
  1. Movement of either hand
  2. Movement of either hand in the direction of the book
  3. Touching the book with the hand
  4. Opening the book partially
  5. Opening the book fully
  6. Closing the book partially
  7. Closing the book fully

Criticizing
  1. Any verbal utterance
  2. Any statement (as opposed to a question)
  3. Any negative statement
  4. Any negative statement that is a criticism

Further, he or she is likely to perform some steps between the major components you've identified. The key to effective shaping is to be able to notice differences between responses so that you are *always reinforcing closer approximations to the behavior.*

When your friend arrives, say something like the following:

> I am going to try to get you to perform a simple behavior—nothing embarrassing. I'll do this by saying "good" every time you get closer to performing the behavior. I can't give you any hints about what I want you to do. I will give you feedback as you get closer to the behavior by saying "good."

Your friend may appear quizzical or skeptical ("You want me to do something but you won't tell me what?"). Just be sure she or he understands the instructions. If at any time your friend asks a question like "What do you want me to do?" answer "Just get me to say 'good.' "

At first, your friend may remain motionless and speechless for several minutes (as he or she tries to figure out what to do or say). To get started, reinforce—by saying "good"—the first movement (or utterance, in the case of a verbal behavior) your friend makes (as the therapist did in Case 6-3). Then reinforce behaviors that are closer and closer to the target behavior. It is critical that you say "good" *immediately* after the component response is made. Otherwise, your friend may associate the reinforcer with some other response that he or she made at about the same time.

When your friend finally performs the behavior, congratulate her or him, describe the shaping procedure you were using, and ask your friend to comment on the process. Your friend may raise questions and issues that will enhance your understanding of shaping.

◆ ALL THINGS CONSIDERED: REINFORCEMENT THERAPY

Reinforcement therapy is consistently effective in accelerating many different target behaviors for clients of all ages and intellectual and physical capabilities.[55] For example, reinforcement procedures are indispensable in promoting socially adaptive behaviors of clients with schizophrenia, brain damage, and mental retardation.[56]

The key to effective application of reinforcement is *consistently administering potent reinforcers, which have been specifically identified for the client, immediately after the behavior occurs.* After a client is successfully performing the target behavior, specific steps must be taken to ensure that the client will perform the behavior in his or her natural environment and will continue to do so over the long run. Four procedures are employed to promote generalization and long-term maintenance: (1) using natural reinforcers, (2) using self-reinforcement, (3) training people in the client's home environment as reinforcing agents, and (4) administering reinforcers intermittently. The first three assure that the target behavior will continue to be reinforced. The fourth procedure increases the chances that the client will continue to perform the behavior even when it is reinforced only occasionally in the client's natural environment, which often occurs.

Behaviors will be maintained only if they are reinforced. While this principle may appear obvious, many people harbor the illusion that once a person is engaging in a behavior, the behavior should magically continue—that is, without further reinforcement. In other words, reinforcement is mistakenly viewed as a quick cure—like taking an aspirin to relieve a headache. Behaviors must be reinforced occasionally (intermittently) if they are to continue.

Reinforcement therapy is used to accelerate socially adaptive and desirable behaviors. Some critics have argued that clients should perform socially desirable behaviors without their having to be reinforced because the natural consequences of the behaviors are intrinsically worthwhile. If this were so, then why don't the clients engage in these "intrinsically worthwhile" behaviors? Apparently, they do not have intrinsic worth to the clients, which is the reason that *extrinsic* reinforcers are required to initiate and maintain socially desirable behaviors.

Another common criticism of reinforcement is that it is a form of bribery. *Bribery* is offering something valuable, such as money or a favor, in order to influence someone to act, usually dishonestly or illegally. Bribes are given *before* the behavior is performed, while reinforcers are always given after the behavior occurs. Receiving reinforcers for engaging in appropriate or adaptive behaviors is no more a form of bribery than being paid a salary for a day's work. Further, reinforcers are not used in behavior therapy to accelerate dishonest or illegal behaviors.

Although reinforcement therapy is not a panacea, it is unquestionably the most widely applicable therapy, and its effectiveness has been demonstrated by a large body of empirical research. Accelerating desirable behaviors with reinforcement has no major negative side effects. Reinforcement therapy provides clients with new, adaptive behaviors that are alternatives to their maladaptive problem behaviors. In doing so, reinforcement therapy increases clients' freedom by giving them more options for how to behave and enhances clients' dignity as human beings.

Summary

1. Reinforcement occurs whenever the consequences of a behavior increase the likelihood that the behavior will be repeated. Reinforcers usually are pleasant or desirable consequences, but whether a consequence is a reinforcer depends on its effects.
2. Reinforcers provide feedback about whether a behavior is being performed properly.
3. Reinforcement can be positive or negative, depending on whether the consequence is added or removed, respectively.
4. The four major categories of positive reinforcers are tangible reinforcers, social reinforcers, token reinforcers, and reinforcing activities.
5. Social reinforcers are versatile because they are easy to administer, they usually can be administered immediately, and they are natural reinforcers.
6. The Premack principle uses high-probability behaviors as reinforcers for low-probability behaviors.
7. Reinforcers are identified by questioning clients, exposing them to generalized reinforcers, and observing their frequent activities.
8. Reinforcer sampling and exposure to models enjoying potential reinforcers are ways of creating reinforcers.
9. Reinforcers are administered by other people and by clients themselves, and they can occur as a natural consequence of the behavior.
10. Continuous reinforcement is used to teach behaviors initially; intermittent reinforcement helps to maintain behaviors.
11. With groups of clients, reinforcers can be administered in a group contingency. All members of the group receive or fail to receive the reinforcers, depending on the performance of the group.
12. Prompting provides the cues that remind or instruct clients to perform target behaviors. Prompts can be verbal, environmental, physical, or behavioral. After the client is performing the behavior, prompts are faded (gradually withdrawn).
13. Shaping involves reinforcing components of a target behavior in sequence until the full target behavior is performed. Shaping is used to accelerate difficult or complex target behaviors or behaviors that occur infrequently.
14. Reinforcement therapy consistently has been effective in accelerating many different target behaviors for clients of all ages and intellectual and physical capabilities.
15. Behavior will be maintained only if it is reinforced. Procedures for enhancing long-term maintenance employ natural reinforcers, self-reinforcement, natural reinforcing agents, and intermittent reinforcement.

REFERENCE NOTES

1. Kazdin, 1989.
2. For example, Babcock, Sulzer-Azaroff, Sanderson, & Scibak, 1992; Pollack, Fleming, & Sulzer-Azaroff, 1994.
3. For example, Utz, 1994; Watson, Allen, & Allen, 1993.
4. Chapman, Fisher, Piazza, & Kurtz, 1993.
5. Compare with Bloxham, Long, Alderman, & Hollin, 1993; Iwata, 1987; Marcus & Vollmer, 1995.
6. Guevremont & Spiegler, 1990; McConnell, 1990.
7. Compare with Michael, 1975.
8. For example, McCain & Kelley, 1993; Williamson, Williamson, Watkins, & Hughes, 1992.
9. For example, Luiselli, 1993.
10. For example, Stark, Knapp, Bowen, Powers, Jelalian, Evans, Passero, Mulvihill, & Hovell, 1993.
11. For example, Connell, Carta, & Baer, 1993.
12. Kallman, Hersen, & O'Toole, 1975.
13. Higgins, Budney, Bickel, Hughes, Foerg, & Badger, 1993.
14. Rowan-Szal, Joe, Chatham, & Simpson, 1994.
15. Hagopian & Slifer, 1993.
16. Brigham, Bakken, Scruggs, & Mastropiere, 1992.
17. For example, Davis & Chittum, 1994.
18. Premack, 1965.
19. Danaher, 1974.
20. For example, Homme, C'de Baca, Devine, Steinhorst, & Rickert, 1963; Horan & Johnson, 1971; Roberts, 1969; Wasik, 1970.
21. Watson & Tharp, 1972.
22. Timberlake & Farmer-Dougan, 1991.
23. Spiegler & Agigian, 1977.
24. From the author's (MDS) case files.
25. Bandura, 1969.
26. Schmitz, Rhoades, & Grabowski, 1994.
27. For example, Bigelow, Huynen, & Lutzker, 1993; Fox & DeShaw, 1993a, 1993b.
28. Pace, Ivancic, Edwards, Iwata, & Page, 1985.
29. Cautela & Kastenbaum, 1967.
30. Phillips, Fischer, & Singh, 1977.
31. MacPhillamy & Lewinsohn, 1971.
32. Daley, 1969; Homme, 1971.
33. For example, Bigelow, Huynen, & Lutzker, 1993; Steed, Bigelow, Huynen, & Lutzker, 1995.
34. For example, Kallman, Hersen, & O'Toole, 1975.
35. For example, Wahler, 1969.
36. For example, Stark, Collins, Osnes, & Stokes, 1986; Thomas, Becker, & Armstrong, 1968.
37. For example, Stuart, 1969, 1980.
38. For example, James & Egel, 1986.
39. For example, Solomon & Wahler, 1973; Strain, 1981.
40. For example, Graubard, Rosenberg, & Miller, 1974.
41. For example, Ajibola & Clement, 1995.
42. For example, Brigham, Bakken, Scruggs, & Mastropiere, 1992; Davis & Chittum, 1994.
43. For example, Pigott & Heggie, 1986; Shapiro, Albright, & Ager, 1986.
44. For example, Kazdin & Geesey, 1977.
45. Hrydowy, Stokes, & Martin, 1984.
46. Honnen & Kleinke, 1990.
47. Lemsky, 1996.
48. McAdam & Cuvo, 1994.
49. Pierce & Schreibman, 1994.
50. Luiselli, 1993.
51. Lovaas, 1977.
52. Morgan, 1974.
53. Bigelow, Huynen, & Lutzker, 1993.
54. Isaacs, Thomas, & Goldiamond, 1960.
55. Kazdin & Wilson, 1978.
56. Rachman & Wilson, 1980.

Chapter 7

Deceleration Behavior Therapy

Reinforcement therapy, as you have just seen, is used to *directly* increase desirable behaviors. However, reinforcement therapy also can be used to decrease undesirable behaviors, albeit *indirectly*. **Differential reinforcement** involves reinforcing an acceleration target behavior that is an alternative to the deceleration target behavior. An example would be reinforcing complimenting to reduce criticizing.

DIFFERENTIAL REINFORCEMENT

Differential reinforcement works because *the more the client engages in the alternative behavior, the less the client will be engaging in the deceleration target behavior.* Consider the case of a young girl with severe mental retardation who frequently hit herself.[1] To reduce her self-destructive behavior, she was reinforced for using her hands to play with a puzzle. Differential reinforcement was effective because while her hands were engaged in playing with the puzzle, she could not use them to hit herself.

Four strategies of differential reinforcement are used to indirectly decelerate undesirable behaviors. In order of most to least optimal, they are differential reinforcement of (1) incompatible behaviors; (2) competing behaviors; (3) any other behaviors; and (4) a lowered frequency of the undesirable behavior.

Differential Reinforcement of Incompatible Behaviors

The best strategy is to reinforce an acceleration target behavior that is *incompatible* with the deceleration target behavior—that is, **differential reinforcement of incompatible behaviors.** *Incompatible* means that the acceleration and deceleration target behaviors cannot occur simultaneously. Thus, while performing the acceleration target behavior, it is *impossible* to perform the deceleration behavior. For example, differential reinforcement of incompatible behavior was used as part of a treatment package to reduce excessive crying associated with infantile colic.[2] The parents played music and attended to the infant (for example, made eye contact, talked softly, and gently touched) whenever the infant was quiet and alert for 30 seconds or more. The infant's crying was reduced by 75%.

◆

| Participation Exercise 7-1 | FINDING INCOMPATIBLE ACCELERATION TARGET BEHAVIORS TO SUBSTITUTE FOR UNDESIRABLE BEHAVIORS* |

Designing target behaviors that are incompatible with undesirable behaviors involves ingenuity and is even more challenging than devising competing acceleration target behaviors, which you did in Participation Exercise 4-1.

* You should do this Participation Exercise before you continue.

For each undesirable behavior that follows, write an *incompatible* acceleration target behavior. Be sure that the acceleration target behavior meets the standards for a good target behavior as described in Chapter 4 (pp. 51-52), including making the target behavior appropriate and realistic. You will know that you have designed an incompatible behavior if it is *impossible* for someone to engage in the behavior you have devised and the undesirable behavior *simultaneously.*

1. Biting one's nails
2. Interrupting others during conversations
3. Sleeping in class
4. Making self-deprecating statements (such as "I'm just no good")
5. Leaving clothes on the floor

Differential Reinforcement of Competing Behaviors

Although reinforcement of incompatible behaviors is the optimal strategy for reducing undesirable behaviors, in practice, finding appropriate incompatible behaviors for the client is not always possible. In such cases, the next best strategy is **differential reinforcement of competing behaviors.** Engaging in a competing acceleration target behavior reduces, but does not eliminate, the opportunity to engage simultaneously in the undesirable behavior.[3] "Doing math problems" competes with "wandering around the classroom," but it is still possible to do math problems while wandering!

Differential Reinforcement of Other Behaviors

Reinforcing an incompatible or competing behavior has the advantage that an adaptive behavior is substituted for a maladaptive behavior. However, this is not always possible, as when an alternative acceleration target behavior cannot be identified easily. When a target behavior is seriously maladaptive, it may be necessary to reinforce *any other* behavior in order to decrease the target behavior quickly.

Differential reinforcement of other behaviors is employed primarily for high-frequency behaviors that are either dangerous to others (such as hitting people)[4] or self-injurious (such as head banging).[5] In such cases, engaging in virtually any other behavior is preferable to engaging in the deceleration target behavior. For example, a child who frequently hurled objects at other people was reinforced for throwing objects at anything but a person. Although throwing things at inanimate objects is undesirable, it is *less* undesirable than injuring people (being the lesser of two evils). Differential reinforcement of other behaviors occasionally is used for less severe maladaptive behaviors, such as noncompliance in preschoolers,[6] sibling conflict, and repetitive habits, such as vocal tics.[7]

Differential Reinforcement of Low Response Rates

Reinforcing *low rates* of the undesirable behavior is the least advantageous differential reinforcement strategy.[8] Sometimes, it may be unreasonable to expect that the client can go "cold turkey" and completely stop engaging in the maladaptive behavior, such as when the rate of performing the behavior is very high. In such cases, the client can be reinforced for performing the deceleration target behavior less often, which is called **differential reinforcement of low response rates.** This strategy was used with an adolescent boy who frequently talked out inappropriately in a special education class.[9] The teacher told the boy that she would spend extra time with him if he talked out three times or less during a class period. This contingency lowered the boy's talking-out rate from an average of more than 30 times a class period to an average of less than 3 times a period.

Differential reinforcement of low response rates can eliminate a behavior completely if the criterion for reinforcement is gradually decreased to zero. For example, first the client might be reinforced for 10 or fewer responses, then 5 or fewer, next 2 or fewer, and finally, no responses.[10]

DECELERATION BEHAVIOR THERAPY: DIRECTLY DECREASING UNDESIRABLE BEHAVIORS

In some cases, differential reinforcement may not reduce the undesirable behavior sufficiently or fast enough. This is likely to happen in three circumstances.

First, it may be difficult to find a suitable acceleration target behavior. In the case of substance abuse, for example, few alternative behaviors are as immediately satisfying as the physical effects of some drugs.

Second, increasing the acceleration target behavior may result in only a partial decrease of the maladaptive target behavior because the acceleration target behavior does not sufficiently substitute for the deceleration target behavior. For instance, it is possible for a person to compliment and criticize someone virtually in the same breath (such as "I love your suit, but that tie just doesn't make it").

Third, differential reinforcement typically decreases the deceleration target behavior *gradually*, which may not be fast enough. This would be the case with behaviors (1) that are potentially dangerous to the client (for instance, self-mutilation) or to other people (such as physically aggressive acts) and (2) that infringe on others' rights (for example, destroying someone's property).

Two forms of deceleration behavior therapy are used to reduce undesirable behaviors directly. **Consequential deceleration therapy** *changes the consequences* of the maladaptive target behavior. **Aversion therapy** *associates the maladaptive target behavior with something unpleasant.* Consequential deceleration therapy is more broadly applicable than aversion therapy, and we will describe it first.

Both forms of deceleration therapy can be used in conjunction with procedures, such as differential reinforcement, that accelerate alternative, desirable behavior. Indeed, treating an acceleration target behavior along with a deceleration target behavior is standard practice in behavior therapy.

CONSEQUENTIAL DECELERATION THERAPY

Consequential deceleration therapy involves two basic operations: (1) *eliminating reinforcement for the target behavior* and (2) *making the consequences of the behavior undesirable.* Two therapy procedures—extinction and time out from positive reinforcement—decelerate maladaptive behaviors by directly removing or withholding the reinforcers that maintain them.

Extinction

All behaviors are maintained by reinforcement. When the reinforcers that are maintaining a behavior are no longer available, the person eventually stops engaging in the behavior. The process of eliminating (withdrawing or withholding) reinforcers is called **extinction.** Case 7-1 is a classic example of extinction.

ELIMINATING BEDTIME TEMPER TANTRUMS BY EXTINCTION[11]

Case 7-1   The client was a 21-month-old boy who had prolonged temper tantrums at bedtime. When his parents put the boy to bed, he screamed and cried when they left the room. The parents responded by remaining in the room until the child fell asleep (from a ½ hour to 2 hours). Thus, it appeared that the child's temper tantrums were being reinforced by his parents' attention.

The therapist suggested an extinction procedure. The child was placed in his bed as usual each night. However, shortly thereafter the parents left the room and did not return even when the child cried. As Figure 7-1 shows, after the boy cried for 45 minutes the first night of extinction, the length of crying quickly declined to zero. By the tenth night the child even smiled when the parents left his bedroom, and he continued to go to sleep without incident for the next week.

At this point, an unfortunate event occurred. When the child's aunt put the boy to bed, he cried as she began to leave the room, and so she stayed in the bedroom until he went to sleep. This negatively reinforced the tantrum behavior that had been eliminated. In fact, this single reinforcer increased the child's crying to its pretreatment level.

The parents instituted the extinction procedures again. The broken line in Figure 7-1 shows that the child's crying reached zero by the seventh night of the second extinction attempt, indicating that the procedures were

Figure 7-1 Results of two attempts to eliminate, through extinction, bedtime temper tantrums in a 21-month-old child (Case 7-1)

SOURCE: Adapted from Williams, 1959, p. 269.

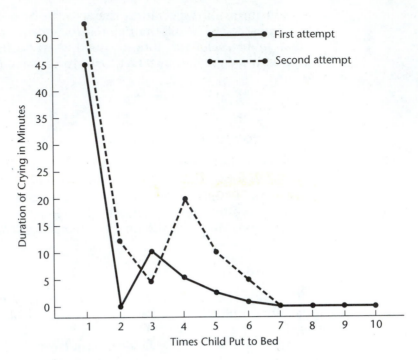

successful. The parents reported that no additional bedtime temper tantrums occurred during the following two-year period.

Correctly identifying the reinforcer that is maintaining the deceleration target behavior is critical for extinction to work.[12] In Case 7-1, the child's bedtime temper tantrums were reinforced by social attention, so extinction appropriately involved ignoring the behavior. Extinction often is used for behaviors that are reinforced by social attention. (You are likely to have used extinction in social situations, such as by ignoring a friend's obnoxious bragging at a party.)

Some people make the mistake of equating ignoring and extinction. Ignoring as an extinction procedure is appropriate *only* when the deceleration target behavior is being maintained by social attention. Consider the example of a nine-year-old boy who regularly stole money from his mother's purse. The boy's mother decided to pretend not to see her son taking money from her purse and to say nothing to him about it. She believed that she was using extinction. However, not surprisingly, her son's stealing did not decline because the behavior was not being reinforced by social attention.

Extinction can be effective as the sole treatment, as in Case 7-1. Generally, however, it is more effective when it is combined with other therapies, such as differential reinforcement.[13]

Extinction has four potential problems. First, in some but certainly not all cases, extinction may work relatively slowly. This is a problem with target behaviors that must be decelerated rapidly, such as self-injurious behaviors.[14]

Second, in one of every four cases, extinction results in an initial intensification of the target behavior before it begins to decrease.[15] This intensification, known as an *extinction burst*, is especially undesirable with dangerous behaviors.[16] Extinction bursts are reduced when extinction is combined with other deceleration procedures, such as differential reinforcement.[17]

Third, the effects of extinction may not generalize to circumstances other than the specific one in which the extinction was carried out. This may have occurred in Case 7-1. The boy had not cried for a week and a half with his parents, who had administered the extinction procedure. However, when his aunt put him to bed, the circumstances changed and he cried. This incident illustrates the importance of avoiding inadvertent reinforcement of the deceleration target behavior during extinction.

The fourth potential problem with extinction is that the target behavior may recur temporarily after it has been eliminated, which is known as *spontaneous recovery*. Spontaneous recovery is another factor that may have accounted for the return of the boy's crying in Case 7-1. Spontaneous recovery is *not* an indication that extinction has been ineffective. In fact, the intensity of the deceleration target behavior generally is weaker during spontaneous recovery than it was before extinction, and the target behavior soon begins to decline again. Nonetheless, when using extinction, change agents must be prepared to expect that the deceleration target behavior may recur temporarily.[18]

Extinction also has two practical limitations. First, the reinforcer maintaining the target behavior must be identified, which is not always possible. Second, the reinforcer must be *completely* withheld for extinction to be most effective.[19] As you saw in Case 7-1, even a single, isolated exception can reinstate the target behavior and, moreover, can maintain it for a considerable time thereafter. In effect, the behavior has been placed on an intermittent reinforcement schedule, which increases the durability of the behavior.

Time Out from Positive Reinforcement

Time out from positive reinforcement (or **time out,** for short) involves *temporarily* withdrawing a client's access to generalized reinforcers immediately after the client performs the deceleration target behavior. Parents are using time out when they have their child stand in a corner for several minutes following a misbehavior. Time out can be thought of as time-limited extinction. However, in contrast to extinction, the actual reinforcers for the deceleration target behavior are not identified. In fact, it is access to a range of potential generalized reinforcers that is temporarily denied.[20] However, there is no evidence that the generalized reinforcers are actually reinforcers for the client (in other words, that they will increase behaviors). Technically, then, the term *time out from positive reinforcement* is a misnomer, and the procedure should be called *time out from generalized reinforcers*.

Photo 7-1   A child spending a few minutes in a corner is a common way that time out from positive reinforcement is implemented.

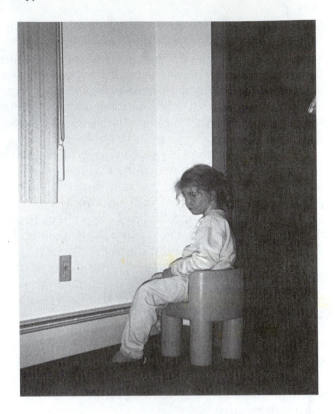

Typically, time out requires the client, usually a child, to leave the situation in which the undesirable behavior occurs and spend a specified amount of time in a designated time-out area. This may be an isolated corner or a special **time-out room** that does not allow access to generalized reinforcers (such as windows to look out of or objects to play with).[21]

Practical considerations often make it impossible to completely elimi-nate reinforcers during the time-out period. For example, in a school setting, a time-out room may not be available, and so children are put in a remote corner of the classroom for time out. Although many of the previously available generalized reinforcers have been removed (such as interacting with other children), the child still has access to some generalized reinforcers (such as observing other children, albeit from a distance).[22] Such "partial" time out tends to be less effective than "total" time out in which all generalized reinforcers are removed.[23]

Effective time out requires that six conditions be met.

1. *The client should be aware of the reason for time out and its duration.* This can be done most easily by telling the client the reason for the time out and how long it will be (for instance, "For speaking disrespectfully, you have a three-minute time out").

2. *The duration of time out should be brief.* Usually 5 minutes or less is sufficient. Time-out periods as short as 15 seconds have reduced inappropri-ate eating behaviors and table manners in institutionalized children with

mental retardation.[24] For children up to age 5, a rule of thumb is that the duration of time out should not exceed approximately 1 minute for each year of the child's age.[25] Relatively short periods are effective; moreover, lengthening the time period does not necessarily increase the effectiveness of time out.[26] Incidentally, time out from positive reinforcement is not simply isolation (seclusion).[27] Isolation is not a behavior therapy procedure. The duration of time out is brief and specified ahead of time, whereas isolation often is for a long, indeterminate period.

3. *No reinforcers should be present or introduced during the time-out period.* For example, the adult should not respond to the child's questions (such as "Is the time up yet?"), thereby giving the child social attention.

4. *Time out should be terminated only when the specified time has elapsed.* If the child is taken out of time out beforehand, the time out procedure may be less effective in the future.

5. *Time out also should be terminated only when the child is behaving appropriately,* which means not engaging in any maladaptive behaviors. This provision ensures that a maladaptive behavior, such as screaming, is not inadvertently negatively reinforced by termination of time out or positively reinforced by gaining access to reinforcers.

6. *Time out should not allow clients to escape or avoid situations they find unpleasant, including responsibilities.* If a child dislikes school work, for example, then removing the student from the classroom allows the student to avoid school work.

Time out has been used to decelerate a variety of maladaptive behaviors of children, adolescents, and, occasionally, adults. Target behaviors have included self-injurious behaviors of children with autistic disorder,[28] inappropriate table manners and eating habits of institutionalized children with mental retardation,[29] verbal and physical aggression of children and adolescents,[30] disruptive social behaviors of adults with psychiatric disorders,[31] and alcohol consumption of chronic abusers.[32]

Many parents apply time out when their young children do not comply with instructions or rules,[33] and elementary school teachers use time out as a standard discipline procedure. When applied correctly, time out is highly effective and efficient. Children learn the time-out routine easily and generally comply with it. Further, just the threat of time out can serve as a deterrent for future misbehavior (for example, "The next time you eat with your fingers, you'll have a time out").

An interesting positive side effect of time out used in the home or school is that it gives adults a "time out" of sorts—not from positive reinforcement but from aversive elements of the child's misbehavior. The brief respite may lessen the chances that the adults will become overly upset and even abusive.

The widespread use of time out by parents and teachers who have little or no training in its correct implementation often results in misapplication. For example, many parents send their children to their room for misbehavior, which, given the contents of most children's rooms, hardly constitutes time out from positive reinforcement.

Although correctly applied time out from positive reinforcement is effective with most children, it does not work well with all clients. Some clients, such as children with attention deficit hyperactivity disorder, experience difficulty remaining in time out for even a minute or two.[34] In such cases, undesirable consequences for failure to stay in time out may be added to the time-out procedure.

The second category of consequential deceleration therapy makes the consequences of the maladaptive behavior undesirable. Both extinction and time out from positive reinforcement also may involve undesirable consequences, in that clients are likely to experience removal of reinforcers as unpleasant. But this is a side effect of the primary operation of extinction and time out, which is removing reinforcers. The three therapies that use undesirable consequences—response cost, overcorrection, and physically aversive consequences—do not specifically eliminate the reinforcers maintaining the maladaptive behavior. Rather, they make the consequences of performing the target behavior unpleasant.

Response Cost

Response cost involves removing a valued item or privilege, which the client possesses or is entitled to, when an undesirable behavior is performed.[35] Response cost is common in our daily lives in the form of fines, such as for illegal parking and failure to return library books, the loss of points

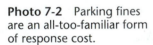

Photo 7-2 Parking fines are an all-too-familiar form of response cost.

for turning in assignments late, and the loss of TV time or a favorite dessert for misbehavior. In each case, there is a *cost* for performing a particular behavior.

In behavior therapy, one way of implementing response cost is for the client to deposit valuables with the therapist (for example, favorite articles of clothing). If the client performs the target behavior, the therapist disposes of one of the items by donating it to the client's least favorite cause or charity. Sometimes clients may dispose of items themselves.

An alternative procedure involves the client's making out bank checks to his or her least favorite cause or charity. If the client performs the deceleration target behavior, the therapist automatically mails one of the checks. In one case, an African-American client who was abusing amphetamines gave his therapist $50 checks made out to the Ku Klux Klan, which were to be mailed to the Klan if the client used the drug. The client forfeited $50 on a single occasion. At a 15-month follow-up, the client had not taken the drug once.[36] In practice, clients usually forfeit very few valuables because the mere threat of response cost often is sufficient incentive to eliminate the maladaptive behavior.[37]

Ogden Lindsley developed a response cost procedure for reducing the number of personal items that his family left lying around the house.[38] Whoever found an item in an inappropriate place (such as a jacket on the piano bench) put it in a large box, called the Sunday Box. The owner was not permitted to retrieve the item until the following Sunday. Lindsley discovered the power of his response cost procedure the day he left his briefcase on the coffee table. He had to live without the briefcase and its contents until the beginning of the next week. You can discover for yourself how well the Sunday Box works—without necessarily repeating Lindsley's experience—by doing Participation Exercise 7-2 over the course of the next few weeks.

◆ ▬▬▬▬▬▬▬▬▬▬▬▬▬▬▬▬▬▬▬▬▬▬▬▬▬▬▬▬▬▬▬▬

Participation Exercise 7-2

BOXING YOUR WAY TO A NEATER ROOM[39]

If you are a member of the Messy Room Club, this Participation Exercise is for you. It is a variation of the Sunday Box technique, and it is easy to do.

1. Make a list of the items that are frequently out of place in one room in your house. Knowing the possible fate of the items you list, you may be reluctant to include items that you "cannot do without." However, remember that the more valuable the items, the more likely it is that the procedures will help you keep them in their proper places.

2. Next to each item on your list, write the precise location in which it belongs (for example, books on shelf, hair dryer on hook in bathroom, and socks in top drawer).

3. Find a cardboard box or other suitable container large enough to hold all of the items on your list.

4. Specify a particular time each day for inspecting the room. A good time is when you return home in the afternoon or evening.

5. Every day at the inspection time, place all the items on your list that are out of their designated locations in the box, and *leave them there until the predetermined retrieval time* (see step 6). An alternative procedure is to have a friend inspect the room each day and put out-of-place items in the box. (Roommates who would like your common living space to be neater may be delighted to help.) Be sure your list of items and their designated locations is written explicitly so that your helper can identify them easily.

6. Every fourth day, at the designated inspection time, count the number of items in the box and record this number. Then remove all the items. They are yours to keep—for at least the next 24 hours!

You should follow these steps for at least 4 cycles (16 days). A declining number of items in your box in successive 4-day cycles will indicate that the response cost is working. You may even have your Messy Room Club membership revoked.

Response cost has been used extensively with children in school.[40] In one program for children with learning and conduct problems, response cost (loss of recess time) was compared to reinforcement (extra recess time).[41] Both procedures increased students' attention and good work habits in the classroom. However, after the treatment procedures were stopped, only children who had received the response cost maintained their improvements. Similar procedures have been taught to parents to decrease children's misbehaviors at home.[42]

A battery-operated device has been developed for administering response cost combined with reinforcement.[43] It was designed to treat problems with paying attention in the classroom. A small box on the student's desk displays the cumulative points the student has earned. The points are exchanged at

a later time for desired reinforcers. The teacher visually monitors the child's behavior from anywhere in the classroom. A point is earned automatically, once per minute, as long as the student continues to pay attention to his or her work. The teacher deducts points using a hand-held, remote-control device whenever the child is not paying attention to the task. When a point is deducted, a red light on top of the box on the student's desk comes on for 15 seconds. These procedures have been effective in significantly improving attention to school work in boys with attention deficit hyperactivity disorder.[44] One reason the procedures have been effective is that they simultaneously decelerate an undesirable behavior (off-task behavior) and accelerate a desirable behavior (on-task behavior).

Response cost can be a highly effective procedure for decelerating a variety of target behaviors with children, adolescents, and adults. Its effects may endure when the response cost contingency is no longer operative.[45] Additionally, most people view response cost as an acceptable deceleration therapy, which facilitates its application.[46]

Overcorrection

Overcorrection decelerates maladaptive behaviors by having clients correct the effects of their actions and then intensively practice an appropriate alternative behavior.[47] Richard Foxx and Nathan Azrin originally developed overcorrection to treat behaviors that harm and annoy others or that are destructive.[48] Overcorrection also is used for behaviors that have negative consequences primarily for the client, including self-injurious behaviors,[49] bedwetting,[50] and excessive and stereotypic behaviors.[51]

Overcorrection has two phases: (1) *restitution,* in which the client makes amends for the damage done, and (2) *positive practice,* in which the client performs an appropriate adaptive behavior in an exaggerated fashion (usually repeatedly). Case 7-2 illustrates both phases of overcorrection.

REDUCING OBJECT THROWING BY OVERCORRECTION[52]

Case 7-2   A 62-year-old woman, who had been a patient in a psychiatric hospital for 43 years, engaged in a number of inappropriate and dangerous behaviors, including throwing objects from the floor at other people. Overcorrection was instituted to decelerate object throwing.

In the restitution phase, the patient was instructed by a staff member to apologize to individuals who had been hit. If the patient refused, the staff member apologized in the patient's behalf and prompted her to nod in agreement.

Positive practice consisted of five minutes of picking up trash on the floor and putting it into a garbage can. Initially the patient refused to do the positive practice, so the staff member physically guided her through the clean-up activity. The physical prompting was discontinued when, after several sessions, the patient began to perform the positive practice voluntarily.

Before the overcorrection procedure was instituted, the patient threw objects at other people an average of 13 times a day. After two weeks of overcorrection, the frequency of the target behavior decreased to an average of less than one incident per day. The frequency remained at or below that level for four months, at which point observations were terminated.

Sometimes only one phase of overcorrection is employed. When restitution alone is used, it involves an exaggerated or augmented form of making amends. This procedure was instituted for 34 hospitalized adults with mental retardation who frequently stole from one another, especially food at meal or snack times.[53] Initially, staff members had the clients return the food (or what was left of it) to its owner. This procedure was not potent enough, and the stealing continued at a high rate (see Figure 7-2). The staff then used an exaggerated restitution procedure called **theft reversal,** in which the offender not only returned the stolen food but also purchased additional food for the victim. As Figure 7-2 shows, theft reversal dramatically reduced the number of thefts.

Positive practice is used without restitution when the maladaptive behavior results in a consequence that cannot easily be corrected, which may be the case with behaviors that do not affect others or the environment. For example, children in a classroom had problems with talking out and leaving their seats at inappropriate times.[54] During recess, the children were asked to practice appropriate classroom behaviors, such as raising their hands and asking permission to leave their seats. These behaviors were practiced repeatedly for five minutes. This positive practice markedly improved classroom behaviors compared to response cost (losing recess time). Generally, overcorrection is applied immediately after the target behavior is performed,[55] but it also appears to be effective when it is delayed, as in the example just described.[56]

Figure 7-2 Daily stealing episodes for 34 institutionalized adults with mental retardation during simple correction and theft reversal (exaggerated restitution) source: Azrin & Wesolowski, 1974.

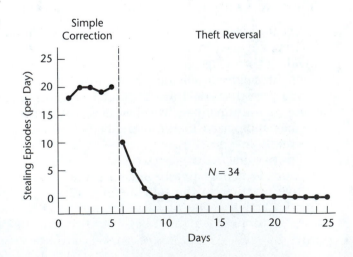

Overcorrection has been compared to time out in treating conflicts between siblings.[57] Overcorrection consisted of making an apology as restitution for the undesirable behavior and then positively practicing a prosocial alternative, such as giving toys to the sibling or making complimentary statements about the sibling. Positive practice was continued for a time comparable to time-out durations, which was set at one minute per age of the child. Time out and overcorrection were *equally* effective in reducing sibling conflicts, and both were rated as acceptable deceleration strategies by the children's parents.

Overcorrection can augment other deceleration strategies. For instance, with a group of clients who were developmentally disabled and deaf and blind, differential reinforcement of other behaviors alone was ineffective in reducing maladaptive behaviors such as self-injurious behaviors and hitting others. The addition of overcorrection to the reinforcement procedures resulted in rapid reductions in the maladaptive behaviors.[58] In contrast to other consequential decelerating therapies that only decelerate the maladaptive behaviors, overcorrection has the distinct advantage of providing for and emphasizing alternative adaptive behaviors.[59]

Overcorrection is more limited in its range of applications than other consequential deceleration therapies. It is appropriate primarily for behaviors that have a correctable adverse effect. For such problems, overcorrection procedures have been demonstrated to be quite effective in decelerating a variety of maladaptive behaviors, especially when both phases are employed.[60]

Overcorrection has potential uses outside therapy, many of which are as yet untapped. For example, some consumer protection laws mandate automatic payment of several times the amount of loss or damage incurred by the consumer when businesses are found negligent. Community service as an alternative to fines or incarceration for convicted criminals is a form of overcorrection. Ecological problems, such as littering or wasting energy, also seem to be suitable targets for overcorrection.

Participation Exercise 7-3

DESIGNING NOVEL OVERCORRECTIONS*

In this Participation Exercise, you will design procedures for novel applications of overcorrection to everyday undesirable behaviors. You may discover some useful ideas for reducing some of your own unwanted behaviors. At the very least, you will check your understanding of overcorrection.

A list of behaviors that potentially could be decelerated by overcorrection follows. For each, describe one or more procedures for restitution and for positive practice. Then compare your procedures with the samples in Appendix B.

1. Littering in a park
2. Misspelling words in a paper

* This Participation Exercise can be done before you continue or later.

3. Leaving clothes in inappropriate places
4. Being late for classes or appointments
5. Trashing the neighbor's lawn
6. Leaving unnecessary lights on in the house
7. Putting dishes in the sink without washing them

Physically Aversive Consequences

Physically aversive consequences refer to stimuli that hurt or result in unpleasant physical sensations. Most people associate techniques that decelerate maladaptive behaviors with applying physically aversive consequences, as when a parent spanks a child. In fact, physically aversive consequences are used infrequently in behavior therapy.[61] A number of potential undesirable side effects as well as ethical and humanitarian objections are associated with their use, and these will be discussed later in the chapter. Although time out, response cost, and overcorrection are effective and do not use physically aversive consequences, these therapy procedures often take longer to work than physically aversive consequences. Thus, when rapid deceleration of a maladaptive behavior is required, physically aversive consequences may be the treatment of choice.

Self-injurious behaviors (such as hitting or scratching oneself) are the major target behaviors treated by physically aversive consequences. These behaviors can result in serious physical harm and, in extreme cases, death. They occur most frequently with clients who have severe psychological problems, such as autistic disorder. Ironically, mild electric shock often is an effective and efficient means of significantly reducing self-injurious behaviors.[62] The shock itself lasts only a second or two. It results in a sharp, stinging sensation that lasts for no more than a few minutes, and no permanent tissue damage occurs. (The shock used in deceleration therapies is *not* the same as electroconvulsive shock treatment [ECT]).* The use of shock may be justified by a cost-benefit analysis, as you will see in Case 7-3.

Case 7-3

ELIMINATING SELF-DESTRUCTIVE BEHAVIOR USING CONTINGENT SHOCK[63]

The client was a six-year-old girl with diffuse brain damage and no verbal communication skills. She frequently climbed in high places (for instance, on furniture and window sills), which posed a serious threat to her physical well-being. "Her body bore multiple scars from past falls, her front teeth were missing, having been imbedded in molding from which she had fallen while climbing outside the second story of her house."

* Electroconvulsive shock treatment is a medical treatment primarily used for severe depression that has not responded to psychotherapy and medication. It involves passing electricity through the brain while the patient is sedated; this leads to a convulsion, temporary unconsciousness, and amnesia for the experience. Electroconvulsive shock therapy is *not* a behavior therapy.

Figure 7-3 The client dangerously climbing in the room in which the therapy was administered (Case 7-3; tracings from photographs taken through a one-way mirror) SOURCE: Risley, 1968, p. 23.

The initial behavioral assessment revealed that the child's climbing was probably maintained by her mother's attention. Time out from positive reinforcement, extinction, and differential reinforcement of competing behaviors (such as sitting at a table) were tried to no avail. At this point, the therapist, in consultation with the child's parents, decided to use contingent electric shock because of the seriousness of the problem.

Therapy was carried out in a room with an 11-foot ceiling. In the center was a small table with chairs. Above a bookcase next to the door was a 5-inch ledge, 6 feet from the floor. The child could climb up the bookcase, onto the ledge, and then onto the door (as shown in Figure 7-3).

Each therapy session began with the therapist and child seated at the table. Whenever the child climbed on the bookcase, the therapist shouted "No!" and immediately applied a one-second shock to the child's calf or lower thigh. The therapist then returned to his chair. The shock was delivered by a hand-held, battery-powered device resembling a long flashlight. The pain lasted only for the one-second duration of the shock, and there were no aftereffects (such as redness, swelling, tingling, or aching).

The contingent shock rapidly reduced the girl's climbing, as can be seen in Figure 7-4. In the first session, the child climbed 9 times, in the second 3 times, and thereafter only twice in the next 18 sessions.

Although the climbing had been eliminated in the therapy sessions, it had not decreased at home (as indicated by the mother's record of climbing at home). The treatment effects were specific to the therapy room and especially to the therapist. Accordingly, the girl's mother—who had observed the therapy sessions from behind a one-way mirror—began to implement the therapy at home. When her daughter began to climb, the mother shouted "No!" and applied the shock as the therapist had done. She

Figure 7-4 Rapid decline of the child's climbing when the therapist administered mild shock contingent on climbing (Case 7-3)
SOURCE: Data from Risley, 1968.

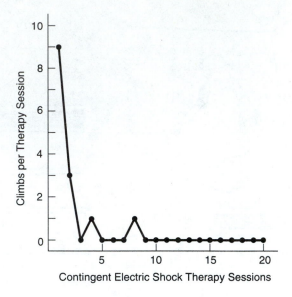

Figure 7-5 Gradual decline of the child's climbing at home, before and after the child's mother administered mild shock contingent on climbing (Case 7-3). Dotted lines indicate the days on which the shock apparatus was malfunctioning, and the arrow indicates the day on which it was operative again.
SOURCE: Adapted from Risley, 1968, p. 29.

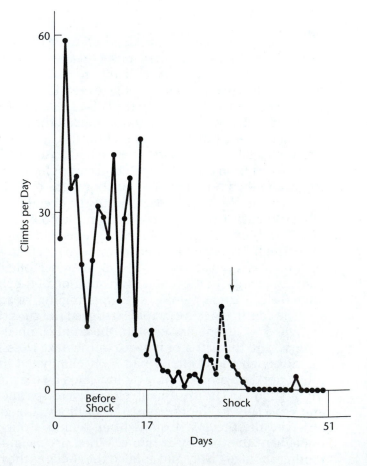

then resumed whatever she had been doing without further interaction with the child.

In the 16 days before the therapy was instituted at home, the mother observed the child climbing an average of 29 times per day (see Figure 7-5). Within 4 days after the mother began the therapy at home, the rate of climbing was reduced to an average of twice a day. The shock device malfunctioned for 4 days (Days 29-32), but after it was repaired (Day 33) the number of climbing incidents rapidly decreased to zero, and, with one exception, did not recur in the next 15 days.

Sophisticated and precise means of monitoring self-injurious behaviors and administering electric shock have been developed. The Self-Injurious Behavior Inhibiting System (SIBIS; pronounced SEYE-biss), for example, is a lightweight device that a client wears on the part of the body that is subject to injury (see Photo 7-3).[64] The device measures the impact of the blow and automatically delivers a mild electric shock whenever the force of the impact exceeds a preprogrammed level (based on the intensity that will cause physical damage). The strength of the shock delivered by the device is like that of a rubber band snapped on the arm. The SIBIS can detect self-injurious behaviors and administer contingent electric shock more precisely and consistently than a therapist can. Additionally, the client does not develop negative associations with the person who directly administers the shock.

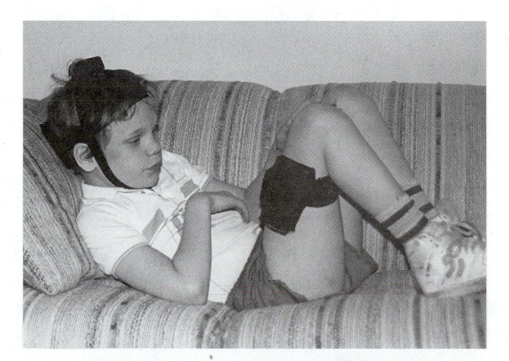

Photo 7-3   A child with autistic disorder wearing the Self-Injurious Behavior Inhibiting System (SIBIS).

The effectiveness of the SIBIS has been evaluated in a small number of studies. It appears to be capable of rapid and dramatic decreases in self-injurious behaviors. One study, for example, reported that five clients with long-standing histories of severe self-injurious behaviors experienced immediate and almost complete elimination of the behaviors.[65] The effectiveness of the SIBIS varies considerably with individual clients, including being ineffective with some clients. Studies that have followed clients for up to six years indicate that with some clients the use of the SIBIS can be faded; in some cases periodically reinstituting the SIBIS is required; and in other cases continuous use of the SIBIS is necessary to maintain low rates of self-injurious behavior.[66] Besides reducing self-injurious behaviors, the use of the SIBIS has resulted in increases in clients' positive emotions, such as smiling and laughing.[67]

Electric shock is a good aversive stimulus for four reasons. First, it is easily administered. Second, it can be activated instantaneously (at the press of a switch). Third, its intensity can be controlled precisely. Ease and precision of administration are important because physically aversive consequences are most potent when they are delivered immediately after the target behavior is performed. Fourth, most people experience electric shock as aversive.

Many people, including some behavior therapists, consider electric shock an unacceptable treatment (for example, because they think it is too harsh).[68] A number of less innocuous physically aversive stimuli have been employed to treat a wide variety of problem behaviors, and some of these are listed in Table 7-1.

Effective Use of Consequential Deceleration Therapy

Guidelines have been developed for the effective application of consequential deceleration therapy, and six of the most common are given in Table 7-2. To use consequential deceleration therapy effectively, behavior therapists also must recognize and minimize potential negative side effects.

Table 7-1 Examples of "more acceptable" physically aversive consequences

Aversive Consequence	Problem Behavior
Rubber band snapped on wrist	Trichotillomania (pulling out hair)
Noxious odor	Self-stimulating behaviors
Cigarette smoke	Compulsive eating
Lemon juice	Head banging
Bitter substance	Nail biting
Mild mouthwash	Biting other children
Water mist sprayed in face	Face slapping
Loud noise	Bruxism (teeth grinding)
Bright light	Dangerous nocturnal rocking

NOTE: References in order are Mastellone, 1974, Clark & Thomason, 1983; Morganstern, 1974; Sajwaj, Libet, & Agras, 1974; Vargas & Adesso, 1976; Matson & Ollendick, 1976; Clark & Thomason, 1983; Heller & Strang, 1973; Martin & Conway, 1976.

Table 7-2 Guidelines for the effective use of consequential deceleration therapies

1. The consequence (removal of reinforcers or introduction of undesirable consequences) should occur immediately after the target behavior.

   The closer in time the consequence is to the target behavior, the greater is its effectiveness because the client is more likely to associate the consequence with the target behavior.

2. The consequence should be administered each time the target behavior occurs.

   Greater suppression results from the continuous (that is, for each occurrence) and consistent (for example, by both parents) administration of the consequence, especially at the beginning of treatment.

3. The client should be made aware of the target behavior for which the consequence will be administered.

   The client should be told and reminded about the contingency between the target behavior and the consequence (for example, reminding a student, "When you turn in an assignment late, you will lose one letter grade").

4. Reinforcement should not closely follow the delivery of the consequence.

   The consequence should not be a signal to the client that a reinforcer is forthcoming (for example, comforting a child who is crying because of a reprimand for a misbehavior). This may lead to an *increase* in the deceleration target behavior.

5. The consequence should be preceded by a warning cue.

   After the cue (for example, "No!") becomes associated with the negative consequence, the cue alone may serve to decelerate the target behavior.

6. An adaptive behavior that competes with the undesirable target behavior should be reinforced in conjunction with decelerating the maladaptive behavior.

   Engaging in a competing adaptive behavior decreases the opportunities to engage in the maladaptive target behavior.

Potential Negative Side Effects

Negative side effects of consequential deceleration therapy actually are infrequent. In general, they occur less often when deceleration procedures are combined with procedures that accelerate alternative adaptive behaviors than when deceleration procedures are used alone.[69] Additionally, the milder the undesirable consequences are, the fewer are the undesirable side effects observed.[70] Most negative side effects fall into three categories: avoidance behaviors, emotional responses, and perpetuation effects.

AVOIDANCE BEHAVIORS

Deceleration therapy may lead clients to develop a negative attitude toward the therapy situation—including the therapist and anyone else administering the treatment (such as parents and teachers)—and subsequently to avoid it.[71] Children may run away when they are being taken to the therapist's office; adults may fail to show up for therapy sessions. The negative association and avoidance may extend to "innocent bystanders." For example, an adolescent who must forfeit a privilege for fighting with a sibling may stop interacting with the sibling altogether.

Avoidance behaviors can be minimized by having more than one person administer the therapy (for example, both parents) and by varying the setting in which the treatment takes place. The people administering the undesirable consequences also should provide positive consequences for alternative behaviors (so that these individuals are not seen solely as "bearers of bad news"). This is especially important when these people have ongoing relationships with the client (such as the client's parents).

EMOTIONAL RESPONSES

Clients treated by consequential deceleration therapy sometimes exhibit disruptive emotional responses, such as crying, tantrums, soiling and wetting their pants, and fear.[72] Occasionally, clients become physically aggressive toward the therapist or others carrying out the procedures[73] and toward themselves.[74] These emotional responses interfere with the therapy process by making the procedure more difficult to use. They also may add to clients' negative associations to the therapy situation.

PERPETUATION EFFECTS

Despite their legitimate application in behavior therapy, using undesirable consequences—especially physically aversive consequences—is never a preferred strategy. Thus, it is regrettable that one of the possible side effects of consequential deceleration therapy is that clients may learn this strategy as a means of controlling other people's behaviors. One revealing finding, for example, is that children whose parents use physically aversive consequences are more likely to behave aggressively.[75]

A related side effect is that the use of undesirable consequences may be reinforced in the change agent, especially in nonprofessionals such as parents.[76] Undesirable consequences often lead to a rapid reduction of the deceleration target behavior. Thus, their use is negatively reinforced because of the relief experienced by the change agent when the client stops performing the target behavior. The unfortunate result is that nonprofessionals may be more likely to use undesirable consequences in the future when their behavior change efforts are no longer being supervised by a professional.

AVERSION THERAPY

Consequential deceleration therapy delivers an undesirable stimulus immediately *after* the client performs the maladaptive behavior. In contrast, in *aversion therapy* an aversive stimulus is introduced *while* the client is engaging in the maladaptive behavior. The stimulus is terminated as soon as the client stops performing the behavior. The objective is for the client to *associate* performing the maladaptive behavior with the aversive stimulus so that performing the behavior becomes aversive.

The same kind of association between a behavior and an aversive stimulus sometimes inadvertently occurs in our lives. For example, a person may get airsick when a plane encounters turbulence. Subsequently, the person may avoid traveling by plane, which is associated with getting sick.

◆ **In Theory 7-1**

PUNISHMENT: WHAT'S IN A NAME?

You may have noticed the conspicuous absence of the word *punishment* when you were reading about physically aversive consequences and perhaps even earlier in this chapter. Technically, **punishment** occurs whenever a consequence of a behavior results in that behavior being performed less frequently in the future. (This empirical definition directly parallels the empirical definition of reinforcement.) Not surprisingly, then, using physically aversive consequences is a form of punishment. However, you may not have realized that *all* consequential deceleration therapies are types of punishment. We deliberately have avoided using the term *punishment* so as not to prejudice you against these therapies.

Most people think that punishment is synonymous with physically aversive consequences. Humanitarian objections to inflicting physical pain or discomfort have merit, and the use of physically aversive conse-quences, even when justified, has a bad public reputation. Since the term *punishment* is primarily associated with physically aversive consequences, all punishment procedures become guilty by association.

What we call something strongly affects how we view it. Shakespeare's Juliet was wrong when she said that "a rose by any other name would smell as sweet." Similarly, punishment by any other name would not smell as sour. Because this book is an introduction to behavior therapy, we did not want to bias you before you had learned about how consequential deceleration therapies operate and how effective they can be. We wanted you to draw your own conclusions about their merits. Although we have chosen not to use the term *punishment,* you will encounter it in the behavior therapy literature as the generic name for all consequential deceleration therapies.

Aversion therapy has been used to treat two classes of maladaptive behaviors: addictive behaviors (such as to alcohol) and sexually deviant behaviors (such as exhibiting oneself), which are known as *paraphilias.*

Basic Procedures

Maladaptive behaviors can be paired with any stimulus that the client finds aversive (unpleasant, distasteful, or painful). Shock and nausea-producing drugs are the most frequently used physically aversive stimuli, and occasionally noxious odors, and hot air and smoke (to decelerate cigarette smoking) are employed. The electric shock in aversion therapy is the same as that used in consequential deceleration therapy and shares the same advantages described earlier (page 154). Psychologically aversive stimuli include feelings of humiliation and unpleasant thoughts.

The aversive stimulus employed may depend on the target behavior. For example, nausea is generally more effective than shock in treating alcohol abuse.[77] The strength of the stimulus is determined by the client. For the therapy to be effective, the client must tell the therapist honestly the intensity at which the stimulus becomes aversive. This requirement is one reason that high motivation to change is necessary with aversion therapy.

The aversive stimulus is associated with the target behavior in one of three ways. Ideally, the association is created as the client is (1) *actually engaging* in the target behavior. Because this is not always possible or efficient, the client can be (2) *symbolically exposed* to the target behavior, as by viewing pictures of the target behavior or listening to a verbal description of it, or by (3) *imagining performing* the target behavior. The first method is illustrated in Case 7-4, and you will see examples of the other two later in the chapter.

Case 7-4

ELIMINATING CHRONIC RUMINATIVE VOMITING BY AVERSION THERAPY[78]

Nine-month-old Mark was hospitalized for malnutrition and weight loss caused by *ruminative vomiting,* a potentially fatal condition characterized by regurgitating, chewing, and reswallowing food. Mark had begun vomiting after meals when he was six months old, and medical and psychological treatments over the next three and a half months were unsuccessful. The critical nature of Mark's condition warranted the use of aversion therapy. Figure 7-6 shows Mark's weight during a three-week baseline.

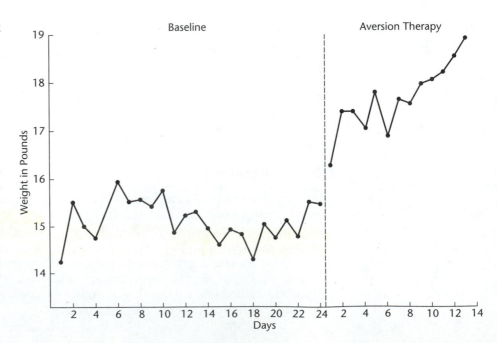

Figure 7-6 Mark's weight during baseline and aversion therapy (Case 7-4)
SOURCE: Adapted from Cunningham & Linscheid, 1976.

Mild shocks were administered for half-second intervals as Mark vomited and were terminated as soon as he stopped vomiting. The electrodes were strapped lightly to his calf, and the shock was activated by a remote switch. This arrangement made it possible for Mark to move about freely. The therapy was initially conducted in Mark's hospital room with Mark in various locations (for example, in his bed, in a highchair, and playing on the floor) and with several observers present. Sometimes Mark was left alone and observed via a closed circuit TV system. Later, the therapy was conducted in the ward day room and in a simulated home environment. Finally, to facilitate generalization, Mark and his mother were monitored alone under circumstances approximating those in their home.

After two weeks of aversion therapy, Mark's ruminative vomiting had ceased completely. He had gained almost three pounds (see Figure 7-6), and there were improvements in his behaviors such as his crying less frequently and starting to babble again. At a six-month follow-up assessment, ruminative vomiting had not recurred, Mark continued to gain weight, and his parents reported no further problems.

One limitation of aversion therapy (as well as many other therapies) is that the treatment effects may remain specific to the therapy situation—in other words, not generalize to other situations. One way to build in generalization is to conduct the therapy in a variety of settings, especially those where the client is likely to be after treatment. Such generalization procedures were part of Mark's therapy and may have been one of the factors contributing to its success.

Whereas Mark's behavior was self-injurious, Case 7-5 provides an example of an adult who wanted to change a sexual habit that was harmless to himself and others. The case illustrates how clients can be exposed symbolically to the target behavior and the use of drug-induced nausea as the aversive stimulus.

Treatment of Transvestic (Cross-Dressing) Behaviors by Aversion Therapy[79]

Case 7-5

A 22-year-old married truck driver reported that he had experienced the desire to dress as a woman since he was 8 years old. From the age of 15 and through his military service and marriage, he had derived erotic satisfaction from dressing in female clothes and viewing himself in the mirror. At the same time, he maintained a good sexual relationship with his wife. He was strongly motivated to seek therapy because of his fear of being detected wearing women's clothes and because of the urging of his wife, who had just recently learned of her husband's cross-dressing.

The therapist prepared slides of the client in various stages of female dress and had the client prepare an audiotape that described these activities. The client was then exposed to the slides and tape to confirm that they induced sexual excitement.

The treatment involved pairing the transvestic experience with nausea, produced by injection of the drug apomorphine. As soon as the injection began to take effect, the slides and tape were presented, and they were terminated only after the client began to vomit. The treatment was administered several times a day for six days, which was sufficient to completely eliminate the client's desire to wear female attire. Follow-up over a six-month period, including interviews with both the client and his wife, indicated that the client no longer cross-dressed.

Covert Sensitization

In **covert sensitization,** the target behavior and the aversive stimulus are associated completely in the client's imagination. Developed by Joseph Cautela,[80] covert sensitization has been used most frequently to treat sexually deviant behaviors,[81] overeating,[82] alcohol addiction,[83] and smoking.[84] Other target behaviors have included incestuous behaviors,[85] shoplifting,[86] nail biting,[87] and self-injurious behaviors.[88] Covert sensitization is used almost exclusively with adults.[89]

The therapist verbally describes both the client's engaging in the deceleration target behavior and the aversive stimulus. Nausea is the most common aversive stimulus employed. If you have any doubt about the aversiveness of nausea induced through a verbal description, you probably won't after reading the following narrative for a college professor who wanted to stop smoking cigarettes.

> You are sitting at your desk in the office preparing your lectures for class. . . . While you are writing, you put down your pencil and start to reach for a cigarette. As soon as you start reaching for the cigarette, you get a nauseated feeling in your stomach. You begin to feel sick to your stomach, like you are about to vomit. You touch the pack of cigarettes and bitter spit comes into your mouth; when you take the cigarette out of the pack some pieces of food come into your throat. Now you feel sick and your stomach cramps. As you are about to put the cigarette in your mouth, you puke all over the pack of cigarettes. The cigarette in your hand is very soggy and full of green vomit. There is a stink coming from the vomit. Snot is coming from your nose. Your hands feel all slimy and full of vomit. The whole desk is a mess. Your clothes are all full of puke. You get up from your desk and turn away from the vomit and cigarettes. You immediately begin to feel better being away from the vomit and cigarettes.[90]

Covert sensitization has several advantages over other aversion therapies. First, no equipment, such as a shock apparatus, is required. Second, unlike some drug-induced aversion, covert sensitization can be safely carried out without any medical supervision. Third, an aversive *image* is portable, making it possible for the client to self-administer covert sensitization in vivo. Whenever and wherever a client engages in the maladaptive behavior (or even thinks about it), the client can "switch on" the aversive imagery to inhibit the undesirable behavior. A final advantage of covert sensitization over some other aversion therapies is that clients may consider it more acceptable, because imagining an aversive event is viewed as less distasteful than actually experiencing it. Accordingly, clients may be more motivated to continue in therapy. Clients' motivation is an important consideration because of the high dropout rate with aversion therapy.[91]

Evidence for the efficacy of covert sensitization comes primarily from case studies.[92] Relatively few controlled experiments have been conducted, and some of the existing studies have yielded equivocal findings.[93] Thus, behavior therapists use covert sensitization because of its practical advantages rather than its proven effectiveness. Covert sensitization appears to be more effective with deviant sexual behaviors[94] than with addictive behaviors such as alcohol abuse, overeating, and smoking.[95]

Aversion-Relief Therapy

When an unpleasant experience ends, you feel relief, which is a pleasant experience. In aversion therapy, exposure to the aversive stimulus is unpleasant, and the client experiences a brief, pleasant relief when it is terminated. **Aversion-relief therapy** associates this relief with a competing adaptive behavior in order to accelerate the adaptive behavior.[96] This is accomplished by adding a relief phase to the standard aversion therapy procedures, as illustrated in Figure 7-7. When the aversive stimulus is terminated, the client focuses on an alternative adaptive behavior. Clients can actually perform the adaptive behavior or can be exposed to it symbolically or in their imaginations. Aversion-relief therapy has been employed primarily to treat deviant sexual practices.[97] It also has been used with substance abuse. Case 7-6 provides an example that is noteworthy because it is one of the few attempts to control heroin abuse with behavior therapy.

Figure 7-7 Comparison of aversion therapy and aversion-relief therapy

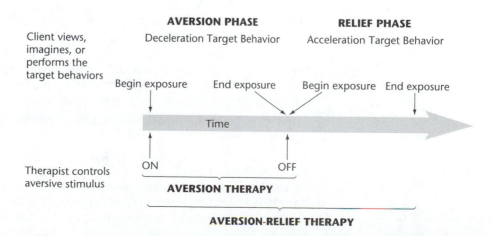

Chronic Heroin Use Treated by Aversion-Relief Therapy[98]

Case 7-6

For approximately three years before seeking treatment, Mr. M. [a 23-year-old married graduate student] had been taking heroin . . . an average of two to three times per week. Periodically he abstained for as long as seven or eight days, but would invariably return to the two- to three-day pattern. By never using heroin on more than two successive days, he maintained some tenuous control over the habit. However, tolerance for the drug had been increasing steadily, requiring more frequent administrations at higher dosage. His drug usage had put his marriage in danger of dissolution, and his academic productiveness had fallen.

Because of the gravity of his situation, he volunteered for electric [shock] aversion treatment. The procedures were described to him in detail, and he was given the option of terminating whenever he desired.

Aversion treatment was carried out in twenty 20-minute sessions over approximately 2½ months. The client was seated comfortably in a Barca Lounger Chair. The shock intensity was set at a level described as painful but not unbearable. . . . The client was asked to imagine and verbally describe the behavior sequence leading up to and including heroin intake. . . .

Throughout these verbalizations, he was encouraged to imagine the situations as clearly as possible and to try to capture the feelings involved. Randomly, during these descriptions the therapist would deliver a shock to his arm and simultaneously say, "Stop." Mr. M. was asked to continue his description until the shock became intolerable and then . . . to alter his fantasy and describe a socially adaptive and drug-free situation. Usually the client switched to a scene where he and his wife were on an outing, planning a trip, or conversing. At the indication of scene change, the therapist immediately terminated the shock.

Throughout treatment Mr. M. abstained from heroin except that after the fifteenth . . . session he reported sniffing a small amount of the drug. He stated that he was "curious" about its effects after having abstained. However, his experience with it was negative.

As treatment progressed, Mr. M. reported . . . increasing ambivalence in his attitude toward heroin. . . . His relationship with his wife improved markedly, as did his academic performance. He was offered and accepted an opportunity to pursue advanced graduate work at another institution. An eight-month follow-up by correspondence, corroborated by his wife, confirmed that Mr. M. had remained drug-free.

Case 7-6 illustrates two general characteristics of behavior therapy. First, before therapy begins, the therapist explains the treatment procedures. This explanation is especially important with aversion therapy because of its

---

◆   **In Theory 7-2**

CONSEQUENTIAL DECELERATION THERAPY VERSUS AVERSION THERAPY: BASIC DIFFERENCES

The two broad approaches to decelerating maladaptive behaviors directly—consequential deceleration therapy and aversion therapy—are similar in some ways and differ significantly in other ways.

Procedurally, the two approaches differ in the timing of the undesirable event that decelerates the target behavior. With consequential therapy, the event occurs *after* the target behavior has been performed; in aversion therapy, the event occurs *while* the target behavior is being performed. The two temporal sequences are consistent with two different models of learning.

Consequential deceleration therapy fits the operant conditioning model. The undesirable consequences decrease the likelihood that the target behavior will recur (just as desirable consequences—reinforcers—increase the chances of the behavior being repeated). If the consequences are sufficiently undesirable, the person will stop performing the target behavior.

In contrast, aversion therapy fits the classical conditioning model. The target behavior is associated with a stimulus that results in discomfort or pain. Before treatment, the target behavior did not result in unpleasant feelings. With repeated pairings of the target behavior (conditioned stimulus) and the aversive stimulus (unconditioned stimulus), the target behavior comes to elicit unpleasant feelings (conditioned response). After aversion therapy, performing the target behavior (and sometimes even thinking about it) results in an *automatic* negative emotional response, which makes it less likely that the client will perform the target behavior.

Another important difference between the two approaches lies in their requirements for implementation. With consequential therapy, the therapist usually has to wait for the client to perform the target behavior in order to change its consequences. With aversion therapy, the therapist usually elicits the target behavior directly (as by asking the client to imagine performing the behavior) in order to associate it with an aversive stimulus. Moreover, with aversion therapy the target behavior often is presented symbolically rather than having the client actually engage in it.

---

unpleasant nature. Second, the case illustrates how treating one central target behavior is likely to have positive carryover effects to other problem behaviors (in this case, Mr. M.'s failing marriage and poor academic performance).[99]

◆   ## ALL THINGS CONSIDERED: DECELERATION BEHAVIOR THERAPY

Deceleration behavior therapy is an important part of the behavior therapist's armamentarium. It can be highly effective and efficient in treating maladaptive behaviors. In general, success rates of consequential deceleration therapy have been higher than success rates of aversion therapy. This difference is due, at least in part, to the fact that the primary targets of aversion therapy—addictive and sexually deviant behaviors—are highly resistant to treatment of any kind.[100]

With both consequential deceleration therapy and aversion therapy, the reduction of the target behavior may be only temporary, which can be a major limitation of these treatments.[101] However, in some cases, as with self-injurious and highly disruptive behaviors, even a temporary suppression of the target behavior is desirable, especially when no other treatments have been effective. Moreover, temporary suppression provides the opportunity to reinforce alternative adaptive behaviors.

The optimal strategy for creating durable changes is to accelerate adaptive competing behaviors. Another strategy frequently used in aversion therapy is to have clients return periodically (for instance, every couple of months) for additional therapy sessions called **booster treatments**.[102] Reexposing the client to the target behavior and the aversive stimulus keeps that association "active." For example, booster treatments for alcohol abuse greatly increase the chances of continued abstinence.[103]

Despite the proven efficacy of deceleration behavior therapy, three issues militate against its application: ethical and humanitarian objections, undesirable side effects, and practical problems.

Some people believe that it is unethical or immoral to subject clients to pain or discomfort, particularly if alternative treatments are available. One counterargument is that using deceleration behavior therapy may result in a favorable cost-benefit analysis—namely, a small cost for a large gain. Another rebuttal is that it is unethical to use alternative therapies that take considerably more time to work than deceleration behavior therapy procedures do. To protect the client's rights, the pros and cons of using deceleration therapy procedures are discussed with the client, and informed consent always is required. These are just two of the strict guidelines followed by behavior therapists for the ethical use of deceleration therapy,[104] which we will discuss further in Chapter 17.

In some cases, objections to deceleration behavior therapy are based on erroneous ideas about its procedures and effects. A prime example is the myth that aversion therapy can force an involuntary client to develop an aversion to something (as portrayed, for example, in the popular science fiction novel and film, *A Clockwork Orange*). In fact, it is highly unlikely that an aversion would develop without the person's cooperation (see Chapter 17 for an extended discussion of this issue).

Deceleration therapy procedures do have potentially undesirable side effects. They were discussed earlier for consequential deceleration therapy (pages 155-156), and the same side effects hold for aversion therapy. To put this concern in perspective, the undesirable side effects are not inevitable. In fact, they are the exception rather than the rule; when they do occur, they are usually temporary, declining over the course of therapy.[105] Nonetheless, behavior therapists must be alert to their occurrence.

There also are practical problems associated with deceleration therapy procedures. They are less acceptable to both clients and therapists than other behavior therapies. Clients generally do not want to subject themselves to pain or discomfort, or even to the loss of reinforcers. Further, some therapists find it distasteful to administer aversive stimuli.

A related problem concerns the client's motivation to change. High motivation is necessary to enter and remain in treatment that has distinctly negative aspects. Clients who are not highly motivated to change are less likely to cooperate with the therapy procedures and more likely to drop out of therapy altogether.[106]

In sum, deceleration behavior therapy procedures can be effective means of treating maladaptive behaviors, especially when time is of the essence. Otherwise, deceleration therapy should be used after more acceptable therapies have been tried and have not been effective. Finally, deceleration therapy techniques always should be part of a treatment package that includes procedures for providing alternative adaptive behaviors.

SUMMARY

1. Reinforcement therapy is used indirectly to decelerate maladaptive behaviors through differential reinforcement, which involves reinforcing an acceleration target behavior that is an alternative to the deceleration target behavior. Differential reinforcement can be of incompatible behaviors, of competing behaviors, of any other behaviors, and of low response rates of the target behavior.

2. The two strategies used to decrease maladaptive behaviors directly are consequential deceleration therapy, which changes the consequences of maladaptive behaviors, and aversion therapy, which associates unpleasant events with maladaptive behaviors.

3. Extinction and time out from positive reinforcement remove the reinforcers maintaining the deceleration target behavior. Extinction does this by permanently removing or withholding the reinforcers that maintain the behavior.

4. Time out from positive reinforcement involves immediately and temporarily removing the client's access to generalized reinforcers in the situation in which the maladaptive behavior occurs. Time out always is brief and often is implemented in a special area, such as a time-out room.

5. Response cost, overcorrection, and physically aversive consequences introduce undesirable consequences to decelerate maladaptive behaviors. Response cost involves removing a valued item or privilege when a maladaptive behavior is performed.

6. Overcorrection decelerates maladaptive behaviors by having clients correct the effects of their actions (restitution) and then intensively practice an appropriate alternative behavior (positive practice).

7. Physically aversive consequences can quickly decelerate undesirable behaviors, which is the reason self-injurious behaviors are the major

problems treated. Painful but harmless electric shock frequently is used as the aversive consequence.

8. Physically aversive consequences are used infrequently in behavior therapy because they have potential negative side effects, including avoidance behaviors, emotional responses, and perpetuation effects. There also are ethical and humanitarian objections to the use of physically aversive consequences.

9. Technically, punishment refers to any procedure that decelerates a behavior by changing its consequences. All consequential deceleration therapies are examples of punishment.

10. Aversion therapy introduces an unpleasant or painful stimulus while the client is engaging in the maladaptive behavior. The aim is for the client to associate the target behavior with the unpleasant stimulus so that the client experiences performing the target behavior as unpleasant. The association is created in one of three ways: as the client is actually engaging in the target behavior, as the client is symbolically exposed to the behavior, or as the client is imagining performing the behavior. Electric shock and nausea are the most common aversive stimuli used.

11. In covert sensitization, the client imagines both the target behavior and the aversive stimulus, which is usually nausea created by the therapist's vivid descriptions of disgusting events.

12. Aversion-relief therapy associates the pleasant relief that occurs when an aversive stimulus is terminated with an alternative, adaptive behavior in order to accelerate the adaptive behavior.

13. Consequential deceleration therapy fits the operant model of learning, and aversion therapy fits the classical conditioning model.

14. Success rates of consequential deceleration therapy have been higher than success rates of aversion therapy. A major limitation of both is that the decrease of the target behavior may be only temporary. Three issues that militate against the use of deceleration behavior therapy are ethical and humanitarian objections, undesirable side effects, and practical problemzs.

REFERENCE NOTES

1. For example, Nunes, Murphy, & Ruprecht, 1977.
2. Larson & Ayllon, 1990.
3. For example, Ayllon, Layman, & Kandel, 1975; Deitz, Repp, & Deitz, 1976; Shafto & Sulzbacher, 1977.
4. Luiselli & Greenridge, 1982.
5. For example, Conrin, Pennypacker, Johnston, & Rast, 1982; Vollmer, Iwata, Zarcone, Smith, & Mazaleski, 1993.
6. Goetz, Holmberg, & LeBlanc, 1975.
7. Leitenberg, Burchard, Burchard, Fuller, & Lysaght, 1977; Wagaman, Miltenberger, & Williams, 1995.

8. For example, Deitz, 1977; Lennox, Miltenberger, & Donnelly, 1987; Poling & Ryan, 1982; Singh, Dawson, & Manning, 1981.
9. Deitz & Repp, 1973.
10. Deitz, 1977.
11. Williams, 1959.
12. For example, Ducharme & Van Houten, 1994.
13. For example, Mazaleski, Iwata, Vollmer, Zarcone, & Smith, 1993.
14. For example, Allen, Turner, & Everett, 1970; Lerman & Iwata, 1996; Neisworth & Moore, 1972.

15. Cooper, Heron, & Heward, 1987; Lerman & Iwata, 1996.
16. For example, LaVigna & Donnellan, 1986.
17. Ducharme & Van Houten, 1994; Kazdin, 1994; Lerman & Iwata, 1995.
18. Ducharme & Van Houten, 1994.
19. For example, Lawton, France, & Blampied, 1991.
20. Ducharme & Van Houten, 1994.
21. For example, Bloxham, Long, Alderman, & Hollin, 1993.
22. Kazdin, 1994.
23. Costenbader & Reading-Brown, 1995; Twyman, Johnson, Buie, & Nelson, 1994.
24. Barton, Guess, Garcia, & Baer, 1970.
25. Barkley, 1987.
26. For example, White, Nielson, & Johnson, 1972.
27. Compare with Williams & Williams, 1995.
28. For example, Tate & Baroff, 1966.
29. Barton, Guess, Garcia, & Baer, 1970.
30. For example, Kendall, Nay, & Jeffers, 1975.
31. Cayner & Kiland, 1974.
32. For example, Bigelow, Liebson, & Griffiths, 1974; Griffiths, Bigelow, & Liebson, 1974.
33. For example, Forehand & McMahon, 1981; Rortvedt & Miltenberger, 1994.
34. For example, McNeil, Clemens-Mowrer, Gurwitch, & Funderburk, 1994.
35. Kazdin, 1972.
36. Boudin, 1972.
37. For example, Mann, 1972, 1976.
38. Lindsley, 1966.
39. Spiegler, 1989.
40. For example, McCain & Kelley, 1994.
41. For example, Sullivan & O'Leary, 1990.
42. Barkley, 1987.
43. Rapport, Murphy, & Bailey, 1982.
44. DuPaul, Guevremont, & Barkley, 1992; Evans, Ferre, Ford, & Green, 1995.
45. Sullivan & O'Leary, 1990.
46. Blampied & Kahan, 1992.
47. MacKenzie-Keating & McDonald, 1990.
48. Foxx & Azrin, 1972.
49. For example, Harris & Romanczyk, 1976.
50. Azrin, Sneed, & Foxx, 1973.
51. Rollings, Baumeister, & Baumeister, 1977.
52. Foxx & Azrin, 1972.
53. Azrin & Wesolowski, 1974.
54. Azrin & Powers, 1975.
55. Axelrod, Brantner, & Meddock, 1978; Ollendick & Matson, 1978.
56. Azrin & Powers, 1975.
57. Adams & Kelley, 1992.
58. Sisson, Van Hasselt, & Hersen, 1993.
59. Carey & Bucher, 1981, 1986.
60. Axelrod, Brantner, & Meddock, 1978; Ollendick & Matson, 1978.
61. Guevremont & Spiegler, 1990.
62. For example, Bucher & Lovaas, 1968; Prochaska, Smith, Marzilli, Colby, & Donovan, 1974.
63. Risley, 1968; quotation from p. 22.
64. Linscheid, Iwata, Ricketts, Williams, & Griffin, 1990.
65. Linscheid, Iwata, Ricketts, Williams, & Griffin, 1990.
66. Linscheid, Hartel, & Cooley, 1993; Williams, Kirkpatrick-Sanchez, & Crocker, 1994.
67. Linscheid, Pejeau, Cohen, & Footo-Lenz, 1994.
68. Kazdin, 1980.
69. For example, Carey & Bucher, 1986.
70. Kazdin, 1989.
71. For example, Azrin & Holz, 1966.
72. For example, Azrin & Wesolowski, 1975; Carey & Bucher, 1981.
73. For example, Foxx & Azrin, 1972; Knight & McKenzie, 1974; Mayhew & Harris, 1978.
74. For example, Azrin, Gottlieb, Hughart, Wesolowski, & Rahn, 1975; Rollings, Baumeister, & Baumeister, 1977.
75. Kazdin, 1987; Timberlake, 1981.
76. Kazdin, 1989.
77. Nathan, 1976.
78. Cunningham & Linscheid, 1976.
79. Lavin, Thorpe, Barker, Blakemore, & Conway, 1961.
80. Cautela, 1966, 1967.
81. For example, Barlow, 1993; Dougher, 1993; Krop & Burgess, 1993a; Maletzky, 1993.
82. For example, Cautela, 1966; Janda & Rimm, 1972; Stuart, 1967.
83. For example, Anant, 1968; Ashem & Donner, 1968; Cautela, 1967, 1970, 1971; Cautela & Wisocki, 1969; Hedberg & Campbell, 1974; Smith & Gregory, 1976.
84. For example, Lawson & May, 1970; Sipich, Russell, & Tobias, 1974; Tooley & Pratt, 1967; Wagner & Bragg, 1970.
85. Harbert, Barlow, Hersen, & Austin, 1974.
86. Gauthier & Pellerin, 1982.
87. Daniels, 1974; Paquin, 1977.
88. Cautela & Baron, 1969.
89. Compare with Cautela, 1982.
90. Cautela, 1972, pp. 88-89.
91. For example, Callahan & Leitenberg, 1973; Wilson & Tracey, 1976.

92. For example, Cautela & Kearney, 1993.

93. Rachman & Wilson, 1980.

94. For example, Barlow, Leitenberg, & Agras, 1969; Callahan & Leitenberg, 1973; Harbert, Barlow, Hersen, & Austin, 1974.

95. For example, Diament & Wilson, 1975; Foreyt & Hagen, 1973; Lichtenstein & Danaher, 1976.

96. Thorpe, Schmidt, Brown, & Castell, 1964.

97. Feldman & MacCulloch, 1971.

98. Lubetkin & Fishman, 1974, pp. 193-194.

99. Voeltz & Evans, 1982.

100. Kazdin & Wilson, 1978.

101. Compare with Linscheid, Hartel, & Cooley, 1993.

102. Rachman & Teasdale, 1969.

103. Voegtlin, Lemere, Broz, & O'Hollaren, 1941.

104. For example, Risley & Twardosz, 1974.

105. Kazdin, 1989.

106. For example, Callahan & Leitenberg, 1973; Wilson & Tracey, 1976.

Chapter 8

Token Economy, Contingency Contract, and Behavioral Child Management Training

Now that you are familiar with the basic principles and procedures of consequential behavior therapy, we can explore their application in three standard treatment packages: token economy, contingency contract, and behavioral child management training. Each of these treatment packages makes explicit the relationship between a client's target behavior and its specific consequences. A wide array of acceleration and deceleration behaviors have been modified with these treatment packages, including promoting independent living skills of clients with handicaps, decreasing delinquent behaviors, and increasing young children's compliance with parental instructions.

TOKEN ECONOMY

Even if you are unfamiliar with the term *token economy,* you are familiar with the concept. Every day you participate in an elaborate token economy—our monetary system.

What Is a Token Economy?

A **token economy** is a system for motivating clients to perform desirable behaviors and to refrain from performing undesirable behaviors.[1] Clients earn **tokens**—token reinforcers such as poker chips or points—for adaptive behaviors and lose tokens for maladaptive behaviors. The tokens then are exchanged for actual reinforcers called **backup reinforcers.** The token economy includes detailed, explicit procedures for clients' earning and spending tokens. Token economies are used more often for groups of clients than for individuals, and most of our discussion will deal with group programs.

Modern token economies have some highly innovative historical precursors. In Chapter 2, you read about Maconochie's point system for prisoners in Australia at the beginning of the 19th century.[2] At about the same time in England, Joseph Lancaster set up an elaborate token reinforcement system to motivate students' learning.[3] Because the school had a large number of students and few teachers, superior students tutored other students in small groups. The students, as well as their tutors, received token reinforcers based on the students' performance. By the late 19th century, a number of school systems in the United States were using token reinforcement to promote learning and foster appropriate classroom conduct (such as being prompt and orderly).[4] The token economy as we know it today began with a program for hospitalized patients with chronic psychiatric disorders developed by Teodoro Ayllon and Nathan Azrin in 1961 at Anna State Hospital in southern Illinois.[5]

Basic Elements

A token economy consists of four basic elements:

1. *A list of acceleration and deceleration target behaviors and the number of tokens that clients can earn or lose for performing each.* Token economies primarily deal with acceleration target behaviors. Target behaviors vary with clients' problems. For individuals with mental retardation, dressing might be a target behavior, whereas for students a target behavior might be completing an assignment.

2. *A list of backup reinforcers and the token cost of each.* The list of backup reinforcers is general to all the clients in the program and includes some reinforcers that will motivate each of the clients.

3. *The type of token.* The tokens can be concrete or symbolic. Tangible tokens include poker chips (different colors for different values), metal washers, specially designed paper currency, trading stamps, and money itself. Points are symbolic tokens.

4. *Specific procedures and rules for the operation of the token economy* (for example, deciding when tokens can be exchanged for backup reinforcers). Such rules are essential when a small number of staff members must administer the program with a large number of clients.

Token economies are used to treat diverse problem behaviors and client populations.[6] To see how token economies function, we will describe two token economies in detail: the Community Training Center—a program for patients with chronic psychiatric disorders—and Achievement Place—a home-style program for juveniles who have been arrested for minor offenses. We also will briefly review the application of token economies to persons with mental retardation, children in classrooms, and individuals and families.

The Community Training Center: A Token Economy for Patients with Chronic Psychiatric Disorders

The Community Training Center, a daytime treatment program for individuals previously hospitalized for chronic psychiatric disorders, was developed by Michael Spiegler and Haig Agigian at the Palo Alto (California) Veterans Administration Hospital.[7] The goal of the program was to prepare the patients, called *trainees,* for independent living in the community. The trainees had been hospitalized for an average of more than 8 years. Most trainees were male, and their average age was 45. They lacked the self-care, home management, interpersonal, and community interaction skills necessary to live independent lives. To treat these behavioral deficits, the Community Training Center was run as a school. Trainees attended classes that directly taught the skills. Table 8-1 gives examples of these classes.

For the most part, trainees had little desire to learn the skills taught. They were frightened of independent living and had grown accustomed, through

Table 8-1 Examples of classes at the Community Training Center
SOURCE: Spiegler & Agigian, 1977, pp. 37-38.

Interpersonal and Cognitive Skills	Health-related Skills
Social communication	Relaxation
Advanced social communication	Exercise
Assertion training	Health and hygiene
Social relations	Self-medication
Advanced social relations	
Sexual information and desensitization	
Thinking straight	
Problem solving	

Community Survival Skills	Socialization Skills
Community interaction	Humor
Money management	Social customs
Driving	Current events
Cooking	Social dancing
Volunteer and vocational placement	Discussion
Telephone usage	

Miscellaneous
Academic subjects
Graduate seminar

years of hospitalization, to acting dependently. A token economy, called the *credit system*, was designed to motivate the trainees to develop independent living skills.

CREDITS AND CREDIT CARDS

The units of exchange in the credit system were points called *credits*. Each day, trainees were given a new *credit card*, on which all credit transactions were recorded (see Figure 8-1). Trainees filled out their own credit cards. For example, they recorded what they had done to earn credits (such as attending a class) and the number of credits they had earned. Trainees' recording transactions themselves made the contingency between their behaviors and the reinforcers salient. It also gave the trainees practice in self-reinforcement, which is important for independent living. Staff members validated transactions to prevent cheating (see Figure 8-1).

EARNING CREDITS

Trainees earned credits for learning skills, which were assessed by written and oral quizzes and behavioral tests (such as role playing). Trainees also earned credits for doing homework, which was an integral part of many classes. Most homework assignments involved practicing skills in the community (for instance, taking a friend out to lunch).

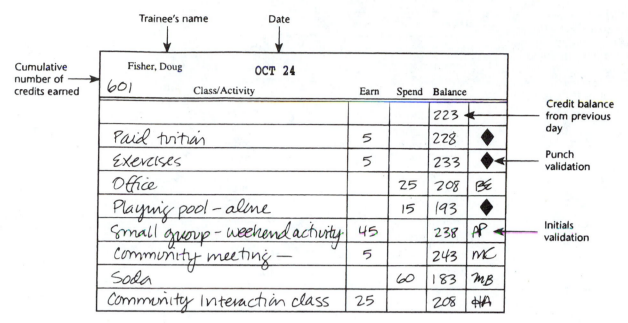

Figure 8-1   Example of a credit card used by trainees in the Community Training Center credit system (token economy)

SOURCE: Adapted from Spiegler & Agigian, 1977, p. 119.

The procedures for administering credits during classes were based on four principles, which are important in all token economies. First, the criteria for earning credits were clearly defined. Second, trainees were made aware of the criteria (as by posting them in the classroom). Third, credits were awarded as soon as possible after a target behavior was performed. Fourth, earning credits was paired with social reinforcers (such as praise from the instructor and other class members).

Generally, each target behavior resulted in earning a specified number of credits. Occasionally, however, the credit values were individualized for trainees, depending on the relative difficulty of that behavior for the trainee. For example, trainees who rarely spoke to other people received substantially more credits for commenting on another trainee's performance in class than did trainees who had little difficulty conversing with others.

BACKUP REINFORCERS

Trainees spent their credits on a variety of backup reinforcers that fell into two categories: reinforcing activities and tangible reinforcers. In designing the credit system, trainees were interviewed to determine potential reinforcers. Trainees also were observed for several weeks to assess how they spent their time during the day. Activities in which they engaged frequently became potential backup reinforcers, consistent with the Premack principle.

Table 8-2 Examples of reinforcing activities and their credit costs at the Community Training Center

SOURCE: Adapted from Spiegler & Agigian, 1977, p. 127.

Activity	Credit Cost
Travel club	10/hour
Photography	10/hour
Short films	10/hour
Feature films	50/film
Pool	
Playing alone	15/game
Playing with 1 or 2 others	10/game
Playing with 3 others	5/game
Ping-pong	
Singles	10/game
Doubles	5/game
Bowling	10/hour
Table games	10/hour
Ceramics	10/hour
Cooking	10/hour
Reading	15/hour
Sitting	25/hour

Examples of reinforcing activities that could be purchased with credits, along with their costs, are listed in Table 8-2. Notice that the credit costs reflect the relative therapeutic benefit of activities. The more beneficial an activity, the lower its cost was, which encouraged trainees to spend credits on more beneficial activities. For example, activities with other people (such as playing table games) provide opportunities to practice social communication skills, and trainees paid less for social activities than for solitary activities. For instance, table games cost 10 credits per hour while reading cost 15 credits per hour and just sitting cost 25 credits per hour.

The *Reinforcement Room* was a large area in which trainees could engage in a variety of pleasurable activities, such as playing pool, darts, and pinball; watching television; listening to music; and reading magazines. These reinforcers could be purchased in two ways. Trainees could spend their credits for specific activities ("à la carte"), or they could purchase a block of time in the Reinforcement Room and engage in whatever activities they chose during that period ("smorgasbord").

Trainees also spent their credits at the *Crediteria,* a store where a variety of items could be purchased with credits (see Table 8-3). Posters advertising items sold in the Crediteria were displayed around the Community Training Center to encourage trainees to spend their credits. Exchanging tokens for backup reinforcers is important because this is the primary way in which clients' adaptive behaviors are reinforced.

DECELERATING MALADAPTIVE BEHAVIORS

The major function of the credit system was to accelerate adaptive social and daily living skills by reinforcing them, initially with credits and later with

Table 8-3 Examples of items sold at the Community Training Center Crediteria and their credit costs
SOURCE: Spiegler & Agigian, 1977, p. 129.

Item	Credit Cost
Coffee	20/6 oz.
First paper cup each day	5
Additional paper cups	50
Sugar	5
Cream	5
Soft drink	60/can
Sandwich	50
Candy	
Small	30
Large	60
Cookies	40/package
Potato chips	40/bag
Popcorn	40/bag
Ice cream	50
Juice	20/cup
Canned dessert	50/can
Small notebook	100
Pen	50
Toothpaste	300
Razor blades	100
Toothbrush	200
After-shave lotion	300
Soap	200
Bubble bath	300
Model kit	400

backup reinforcers. Trainees' maladaptive behaviors were treated primarily by reinforcing competing adaptive behaviors.

Maladaptive behaviors also were decelerated directly by having trainees pay credits for engaging in them (in other words, response cost). Examples of undesirable behaviors for which trainees paid credits are listed in Table 8-4. Notice that the credit costs for engaging in maladaptive behaviors are considerably higher than the credit costs for reinforcing activities listed in Table 8-2 (page 174). The high credit cost for the undesirable behaviors discouraged trainees from engaging in them. For example, missing class and sleeping in class, which were the most expensive undesirable behaviors, were rarely purchased—which means that trainees rarely engaged in these behaviors.

EVALUATION OF THE COMMUNITY TRAINING CENTER PROGRAM

The effectiveness of the Community Training Center program has been demonstrated in a number of studies.[8] One experiment compared a sample of graduates from the program with a sample of patients not in the program. The two groups were matched for age, diagnosis, length of hospitalization,

Table 8-4 Examples of undesirable behaviors and the average number of credits trainees at the Community Training Center paid to engage in them

SOURCE: Adapted from Spiegler & Agigian, 1977, p. 132.

Undesirable Behavior	Average Credit Cost
Sleeping in class	75
Smoking in class	50
Leaving class early (unexcused)	50
Cutting class	100
Being late to class	15
Coming to class without having done the homework	50
Pacing in class	20
Having an unbalanced credit card	10
Making a mess (for example, flicking ashes on the floor)	25
Begging	20

NOTE: The credits charged for performing a maladaptive behavior varied with individual trainees' particular problems with the maladaptive behavior.

type of hospital treatment, and time spent in the community. The groups were compared on eight different indices of personal adjustment. As Figure 8-2 shows, the Community Training Center graduates had significantly higher functioning on all but one of the outcome variables.

Rehospitalization is a critical measure of the effectiveness of treatment for previously hospitalized patients. The Community Training Center

Figure 8-2 Comparison of personal adjustment between Community Training Center graduates and a comparable sample of outpatients. The Community Training Center graduates showed higher functioning than the comparison outpatients on all but the last index of personal adjustment.

SOURCE: Data from Spiegler & Agigian, 1977.

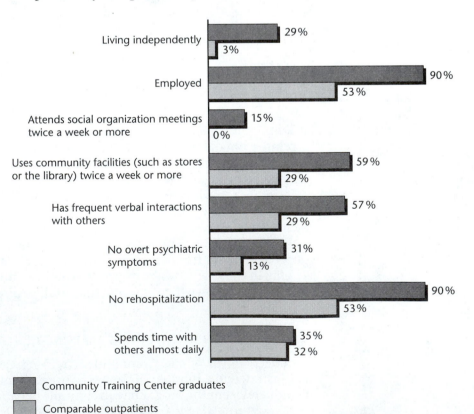

program resulted in consistently lower rehospitalization rates than comparable programs. For example, during the first two years of the Community Training Center, the rehospitalization rate was 11%; during the comparable period for the previous daytime treatment program, the rate was 73%. In another comparison, during a 6-month period, the Community Training Center rehospitalization rate was 5%, in contrast to 22% and 31% for two programs using different forms of treatment.

Achievement Place: A Token Economy for Juveniles in Trouble with the Law

Achievement Place is the prototype of the *teaching-family model* for rehabilitating juvenile offenders. It was established in 1967 in Lawrence, Kansas, under the direction of Elery Phillips, Montrose Wolf, and Dean Fixsen,[9] and it has inspired more than 200 other programs.[10] A token economy is central to the operation of Achievement Place. To illustrate its use, we will describe the original program for boys. (Most of the teaching-family programs have been for boys.[11])

Achievement Place served as a residence for 6 to 8 boys, 10 to 16 years of age, from lower socioeconomic backgrounds. The boys had been referred by the courts for committing minor crimes, such as petty theft and fighting. Achievement Place was set up in a large house in the boys' local community. It was run by two *teaching parents,* a married couple who were trained in behavior therapy.[12]

At Achievement Place, points were earned for appropriate social behaviors (such as proper manners), academic performance (for example, good study behaviors), and daily living skills (for instance, personal hygiene). Points were lost for inappropriate behaviors in these areas. Table 8-5 lists some of the behaviors for which points were earned or lost. Backup reinforcers were primarily privileges that were naturally available at Achievement Place (see Table 8-6).

The token economy was divided into three levels or systems. At first, a boy was placed on a *daily system,* in which the points he earned were exchangeable each day for backup reinforcers. This arrangement helped the boys learn how the token economy worked. After a boy became familiar with the token economy, he was switched to a *weekly system,* in which the points earned were exchanged for backup reinforcers once a week. For example, a boy could purchase a week's worth of snacks and television time. Table 8-6 shows a comparison of the points needed to purchase different privileges on the daily and weekly systems. Most boys were on the weekly system for the 9 to 12 months they typically resided at Achievement Place. Because ample opportunities to earn points existed, the boys usually were able to buy all the privileges they desired.

The final level in the token economy, the *merit system,* was reserved for boys who were ready to leave Achievement Place in the near future. Under the merit system, the use of points to motivate appropriate behaviors was eliminated. A boy would not earn or lose points, and he would not have to

Table 8-5 Examples of behaviors for which boys at Achievement Place earned or lost points
SOURCE: Phillips, 1968, p. 215.

Behaviors That Earned Points	Points
Watching news on television or reading the newspaper	300 per day
Cleaning and maintaining neatness in one's room	500 per day
Keeping neat and clean	500 per day
Reading books	5 to 10 per page
Aiding houseparents in various household tasks	20 to 1000 per task
Doing dishes	500 to 1000 per meal
Being well dressed for an evening meal	100 to 500 per meal
Doing homework	500 per day
Obtaining desirable grades on school report cards	500 to 1000 per grade
Turning out lights when not in use	25 per light

Behaviors That Lost Points	Points
Failing grades on the report card	500 to 1000 per grade
Speaking aggressively	20 to 50 per response
Forgetting to wash hands before meals	100 to 300 per meal
Arguing	300 per response
Disobeying	100 to 1000 per response
Being late	10 per minute
Displaying poor manners	50 to 100 per response
Engaging in poor posture	50 to 100 per response
Using poor grammar	20 to 50 per response
Stealing, lying, or cheating	10,000 per response

pay points for any backup reinforcers—as long as he continued to demonstrate a high level of appropriate social, academic, and daily living behaviors. Instead, the teaching parents merely praised the boy for appropriate behaviors. The merit system prepared boys for returning to their home environments, where no point system existed.[13]

Table 8-6 Privileges that could be earned with points on the daily and weekly point systems at Achievement Place
SOURCE: Phillips, Phillips, Fixsen, & Wolf, 1971, p. 46.

Privilege	Price in Points	
	Weekly System	Daily System
Hobbies and games	3000	400
Snacks	1000	150
Television	1000	50
Allowance (per $1)	2000	300
Permission to leave Achievement Place (home, downtown, sports events)	3000	NA
Bonds (savings for gifts, special clothing, etc.)	1000	150
Special privileges	Variable	NA

NA = not available.

A DAY AT ACHIEVEMENT PLACE

A typical weekday at Achievement Place began when the boys arose at about 6:30 A.M., washed and dressed, and cleaned their rooms. Morning chores were followed by breakfast, and then the boys were off to school.

Each day one boy served as *manager,* and he paid points to hold this prestigious position. The manager assigned cleanup jobs, supervised their completion, and awarded points to other boys for doing the jobs. The manager earned points according to how well the boys performed the household chores.[14]

Academic achievement was a major goal of the program. Each boy attended the same school in which he had been enrolled before coming to Achievement Place. The teachers and school administrators worked closely with the teaching parents, providing them with systematic feedback about each boy's school performance through daily or weekly report cards. The boys earned or lost points at Achievement Place based on how well they were doing at school.[15]

After school, the boys returned to Achievement Place, had a snack (purchased with points), and then began their homework or other point-earning activities, such as chores around the house. Later they spent time in various recreational activities (such as bike riding or playing games) for which they paid points.

After dinner, a "family conference" was held. The boys and the teaching parents discussed the events of the day, evaluated the manager's performance, discussed problems with the program, and decided on consequences for specific rule violations. The conferences allowed the boys to be active collaborators in their treatment program. The boys spent the rest of the evening, until bedtime at about 10:30 P.M., in group or individual activities.

EVALUATION OF ACHIEVEMENT PLACE
AND OTHER TEACHING-FAMILY PROGRAMS

The effectiveness of Achievement Place and other teaching-family programs has been evaluated in numerous controlled studies.[16] The programs have been shown to be effective in reducing delinquent and other inappropriate behaviors (such as acting aggressively and using poor grammar) and increasing appropriate prosocial behaviors (such as being on time, completing homework, and saving money). Favorable changes in attitudes also have been found, including increased self-esteem and optimism about having control over one's life.[17]

Unfortunately, the behavioral changes occur only while boys are in the program and for a year or so afterward.[18] This poor long-term maintenance of treatment gains is not surprising, however. The environment at teaching-family group homes is very different from that of the home environments from which the boys came and—most importantly—to which they returned. Most of the boys were from home environments where they received little reinforcement for prosocial behaviors and ample reinforcement for antisocial behaviors from some of their peers—just the opposite of the contingencies in the teaching-family homes.[19] Thus, when the boys left the teaching-family home, the contingencies changed—that is, prosocial behaviors were no longer reinforced, which resulted in their eventual decline. Given the poor home environments from which most youths in teaching-family programs come, specific procedures must be used to promote long-term maintenance of treatment gains. One approach is to provide aftercare in specially developed foster homes.[20] Another approach is to give parents behavioral child management training (which we will describe later in this chapter).[21]

Token Economies for Training Individuals with Mental Retardation

Individuals institutionalized because of mental retardation display many of the same behavioral deficits as patients hospitalized for psychiatric disorders. For example, they frequently lack basic self-care and daily living skills (such as dressing appropriately and preparing simple meals). Token economies are effective in teaching such skills and motivating their consistent practice.[22] In addition to accelerating target behaviors, token economies can decelerate various socially inappropriate behaviors (such as eating with one's fingers) and personally maladaptive behaviors (such as refusing to brush one's teeth) among institutionalized persons with mental retardation.[23]

Language skills often are target behaviors for children, adolescents, and sometimes adults with mental retardation.[24] Because of the complexity of language and speech skills, token reinforcement programs usually are administered individually and are likely to be part of a treatment package that includes modeling, prompting, and shaping.

Token economies are effective in increasing the quantity and quality of job-related tasks performed by individuals with mental retardation.[25] In one sophisticated token economy program, young adults with moderate mental retardation earned tokens for jobs on three levels.[26] The lowest level involved janitorial-type tasks; the middle level consisted of jobs with more responsibility, such as using machines and checking attendance; the highest level required more skill, responsibility, and independence, such as sorting and distributing mail and serving as a teacher's aide. The clients advanced through the levels by meeting specified performance criteria. The tokens were exchangeable for a variety of backup reinforcers, including favorite snacks, money, and access to pleasurable activities. The program successfully placed some of the third-level clients into jobs in the community.

In another program, residents of a group home for adults with mental retardation received tokens for various tasks involved in running the home and for socializing with other residents and staff.[27] They also earned tokens for attending recreational activities in the community and for behaviors leading to gainful employment, such as contacting prospective employers and going on job interviews. Once residents were working in the community, their employers were asked to participate in the token economy program. The employers provided the staff with feedback about residents' performance on the job so that the residents could receive tokens for appropriate on-the-job behaviors.[28]

Token Economies in the Classroom

Token economies have been successfully applied in preschool, elementary, and secondary classrooms at various educational levels (including special education, remedial, and mainstream). These programs have focused on classroom conduct and academic performance.

CLASSROOM CONDUCT

A variety of undesirable behaviors that interfere with classroom learning have been modified by token economies. Examples include aggressive behaviors toward other students, talking out of turn, being out of one's seat, disregarding teachers' instructions, throwing objects, destroying property, and disturbing other students. Three basic strategies are used to treat classroom conduct problems: (1) earning tokens for engaging in competing acceleration target behaviors, (2) losing tokens for performing inappropriate behaviors, and (3) both earning and losing tokens. Earning and losing tokens appear to be equally effective in modifying classroom conduct and academic behaviors.[29] Backup reinforcers in classroom token economies have included tangible reinforcers (such as toys, snacks, and school supplies) and attractive activities (for example, extended recess time and field trips). As children get older, in-class backup reinforcers become less potent than reinforcers available at home (such as playing video games or talking on the telephone). When this occurs, tokens earned at school can be exchanged for backup reinforcers at home.[30]

ACADEMIC PERFORMANCE

The ultimate purpose of decreasing disruptive classroom behaviors is to enhance clients' academic performance. Attention and proper conduct in the classroom alone often are not sufficient.[31] Thus, token economies also are used to increase learning of academic skills *directly*. The same basic strategies used to treat classroom conduct problems are employed to promote academic skills.

Token economies have successfully increased children's academic performance in basic subject areas, such as arithmetic, reading, and spelling[32] as well as in more complex skills, such as creative writing. These programs not only have increased students' skill levels, but they also have been associated with higher grades and fewer suspensions from school.[33]

One illustrative program was designed to increase writing skills. Elementary school students earned points for the number of different adjectives,

Figure 8-3 Average number of different adjectives, verbs, and sentence beginnings used during baseline and token reinforcement phases in a class designed to increase elementary school students' writing skills
SOURCE: Adapted from Maloney & Hopkins, 1973, p. 429.

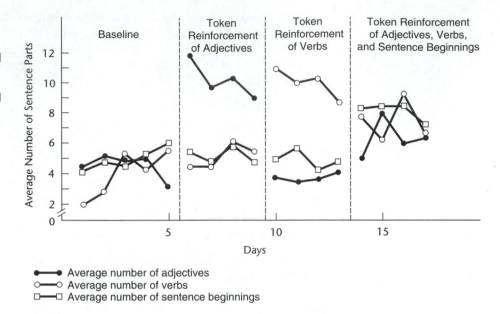

verbs, and beginnings of sentences they wrote in stories.[34] The class was divided into two teams, and a group contingency was employed. Backup reinforcers included candy and early recess. As Figure 8-3 shows, an increase in the number of different sentence parts (such as adjectives) occurred when, and only when, points were given for the specific sentence parts. For example, the average number of adjectives used increased during the four days that adjectives were reinforced with points, but not on the following four days when only verbs were reinforced. When all three sentence parts were reinforced, an increase in each part was observed. Moreover, people who were unfamiliar with the procedures used in the class rated the stories written during the token reinforcement days as more creative than those written during the baseline period, when no token reinforcers were administered.

Token Economies for Individuals

Token economies are used for individuals and small groups (such as families) as well as with large groups of clients. Individual token economies most often are employed with children for such problems as stuttering, excessive television watching, using inappropriate table manners, and reading difficulties.[35] In one case, a divorced father used a token economy to increase his 14-year-old son's completion of household chores, which had been an area of constant conflict between them.[36] The simple token economy reduced conflict and helped improve the relationship between the father and son. In another application, a home token economy was set up for a 6-year-old boy to treat three persistent problems: getting out of bed at night; eating only certain foods (such as pizza); and disobeying his parents' instructions.[37] The boy's parents gave stars to the boy for proper behaviors, and he exchanged them for tangible reinforcers and privileges listed on a reinforcement menu. The token economy resulted in immediate and substantial improvement of each of the problem behaviors.

Individual token economies can be more comprehensive and complex than the two examples you just read about. Table 8-7 shows the details of one such token economy for a nine-year-old boy with serious behavioral problems. Individual token economies occasionally are used with adults—in particular, adults with mental retardation and with senior citizens.

Table 8-7   Details of a home token economy for a 9-year-old boy with significant behavioral problems

Your Responsibilities	Points Earned
Get dressed for school (socks, pants, shirt, and shoes on by 7:45 A.M.)	10 points
Bring home homework assignment notebook and appropriate homework materials	25 points
Feed the dog (by 5:30 P.M.)	15 points
Take a bath (by 7 P.M. with no more than one reminder)	15 points
Go to bed (by 8:30 P.M. with no more than one reminder)	10 points
Clean room (bed made, dirty clothes in hamper, toys in box)	30 points
Total possible points per day	105 points
Total possible points per week	735 points

Backup Reinforcers	Cost
Daily	
Special snack	10 points
TV time (30 minutes)	15 points
Use of Nintendo (30 minutes)	25 points
Stay up later (15 minutes)	15 points
Weekly	
Choice of restaurant (McDonald's, Burger King, Pizza Hut, or Domino's)	60 points
Allowance ($1, maximum of $5)	80 points
Have friend stay overnight	70 points
Rent a video of your choice (with parents' approval of the movie)	40 points
Three packs of baseball cards	50 points
Go rollerskating	70 points
Go to movie	70 points
Longer-term	
A day at the amusement park and rides	150 points
New CD	175 points
New skateboard	250 points
_____	____ points

Photo 8-1 Parents can be trained to administer simple token economy programs for their children at home. Stickers, which are placed on charts, may be used as tokens and exchanged for backup reinforcers.

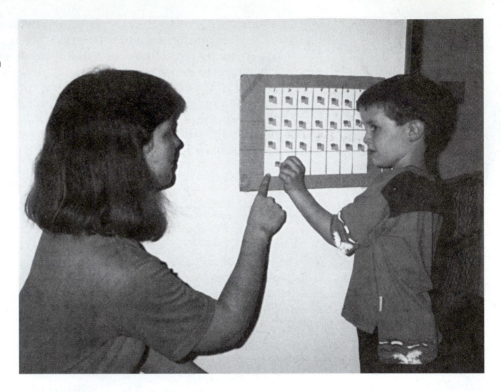

Case 8-1

INCREASING ADHERENCE TO A MEDICAL REGIMEN WITH AN INDIVIDUAL TOKEN ECONOMY[38]

Mr. A. was an 82-year-old retired longshoreman who had suffered a massive heart attack. His physician told him to exercise, to eat foods high in potassium, and to take his medication, but he failed to follow these instructions. Mr. A.'s granddaughter, who lived with him, agreed to administer a token economy in which Mr. A. earned poker chips for walking, drinking orange juice (which is high in potassium), and taking his medication. He exchanged the poker chips for the privilege of choosing his dinner menu at home or going out to a restaurant of his choice. The effectiveness of the token economy was evaluated with a combined multiple baseline–reversal study (see Figure 8-4). Token reinforcement was first introduced for walking, then for drinking juice, and finally for taking his medication. As Figure 8-4 shows, each target behavior increased with token reinforcement but not before tokens were given. When the tokens were temporarily withdrawn for all three target behaviors in a reversal period, all three behaviors declined to baseline levels. Reinstating the tokens immediately brought the behaviors back to the treatment level. Clearly, Mr. A.'s health-maintenance behaviors were influenced by the token economy. Additionally, instituting the token economy appeared to improve Mr. A.'s relation-

Figure 8-4 Number of adherence behaviors (walking, drinking orange juice, and taking pills) per day Mr. A performed under baseline and token reinforcement conditions (Case 8-1)
SOURCE: Dapcich-Miura & Hovell, 1979.

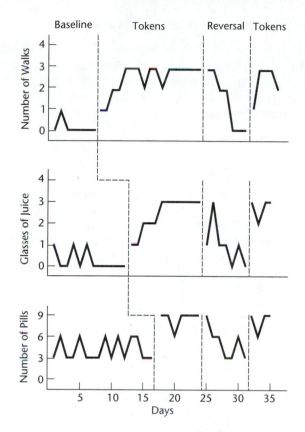

ship with his family by reducing arguments, especially about Mr. A.'s adherence to his medical regimen.

If you'd like to experience the process of setting up and being motivated by a token economy (and also receive some personal benefits), do Participation Exercise 8-1 over the next couple of weeks.

**Participation
Exercise 8-1**

DESIGNING AND IMPLEMENTING A TOKEN ECONOMY

A good way to learn how token economies work is to design and participate in one yourself. This Participation Exercise provides directions for setting up a simple token economy to motivate you to do those everyday chores that you'd rather not do.

Part I: Selecting Behaviors to Change

Step 1: Make a list of four chores that you "must" do but dislike doing. Depending on your tastes and tolerances, such chores might include doing laundry, ironing, making your bed, cleaning the bathroom, paying bills, shopping for food, taking out the garbage, and writing letters. Write the four chores you have chosen in the first column on Work Sheets 8-1, 8-3, and 8-4.*

Part II: Establishing a Baseline

Step 2: In order to assess whether the token economy increases the chores you do, you will need to know how often you did the chores before the token economy was instituted. In other words, you'll need to record a baseline. Over five consecutive days, place a check mark in the middle column on Work Sheet 8-1 each time you do one of the chores. At the end of the five days, add the number of check marks for each chore and write the sum in the last column of Work Sheet 8-1.

Part III: Setting Up the Token Economy

Now you are ready to set up your token economy.

Step 3: Rank order the four chores from most unpleasant to least unpleasant for you.

Step 4: On Work Sheet 8-2,† write the four chores, in rank order, in column A. Column B contains the points you will receive for doing each of the chores. Note that the more unpleasant a chore, the higher the number of points you will earn for doing it (from most to least unpleasant: 40, 30, 20, and 10).

Part IV: Identifying Backup Reinforcers

You will exchange the points you earn for backup reinforcers, which will be simple activities that meet the following three requirements.

1. Engaging in the activity for relatively brief periods of time is enjoyable.
2. You engage in the activity frequently (at least several times per week).
3. *Include as backup reinforcers only activities that you are willing to give up temporarily* (if you do not earn them). The reason is that during the time your token economy is in effect, you will be able to engage in the backup reinforcing activities only when you have performed your chores. (For example, if you consider jogging an essential part of your life and won't give it up for any reason, do not make jogging a backup reinforcer.)

Your backup reinforcing activities might include listening to music, talking on the telephone, watching TV, reading for pleasure, having a cup of coffee with friends, and exercising.

* You will find these work sheets in Appendix C.
† You will find this work sheet in Appendix C.

Step 5: Choose four activities that meet the three requirements just described.

Step 6: Rank order the four activities from most enjoyable to least enjoyable.

Step 7: Write the four activities, in rank order, on Work Sheet 8-2, column C. Column D lists the points that each backup reinforcer will cost you. Note that the more enjoyable an activity is, the higher is the cost (from most to least enjoyable: 25, 20, 10, and 5).

Part V: Implementing the Token Economy

You now are ready to start your token economy. Begin on the same day of the week on which you started your baseline and continue the token economy for five consecutive days.

Step 8: Each time you complete one of your chores, place a check mark in the second column of Work Sheet 8-3 next to the chore. Then, write the number of points earned for doing that chore (refer to Work Sheet 8-2, column B) in the *Points Earned* column of Work Sheet 8-5.*

Step 9: Each time you engage in one of the backup reinforcing activities, record the number of points spent in the *Points Spent* column of Work Sheet 8-5. Then calculate your balance by subtracting the number of points you just spent from your previous balance and record the new balance in the *Point Balance* column.

While your token economy is in effect, you may engage in the reinforcing activities *only* after purchasing them with points. If you violate this rule, the token economy will not accelerate your doing the chores.

Part VI: Evaluating the Token Economy

Step 10: At the end of the five days in which your token economy was in effect, add up the number of check marks for each chore in the middle column of Work Sheet 8-3. Record the sums in the last column of Work Sheet 8-3.

Now you can compare the frequency of doing chores during the baseline period with the frequency of doing chores during the token economy period. If the token economy was effective, you should have done more chores during the token economy period than during the baseline period. If this did not occur, you may have to increase the point values earned for each chore or select more enjoyable backup reinforcers.

If your token economy appears to have been effective in increasing the chores you do, you may want to provide further evidence for its efficacy by introducing a reversal period. For another five-day period (beginning on the same day of the week), discontinue the token economy. However, continue to record the number of times you do each chore by placing check marks in the middle column on Work Sheet 8-4. At the end of the five-day reversal period, add up the number of times you did each chore. Record the sums in the last column on Work Sheet 8-4. Because the token economy was not in effect during the reversal period, your

---

* You will find this work sheet in Appendix C.

frequency of doing chores would be expected to be lower during the reversal period than during the token economy period.

◆

Token Economy in Perspective

Since the first major token economy was developed more than 35 years ago,[39] numerous token economies have been implemented to treat diverse target behaviors, ranging from simple self-care skills to complex problems that develop in marital relations. Clients of all ages—from children to the elderly—with a wide range of intellectual capacities have been treated. Token economies have been used in many different settings—in homes, class-rooms, group living situations, hospitals, outpatient facilities, and work environments. The token economy is one of the most well-validated be-havioral treatments.[40]

The effectiveness of token economies has been systematically evaluated with reversal and multiple baseline studies. Typically, clients perform target behaviors at high rates only when they are receiving tokens for engaging in the target behaviors. These consistent findings provide impressive evidence that the token economy is responsible for changes in clients' target be-haviors.

The rapid loss of treatment gains typically observed when token rein-forcement is discontinued is a measure of the effectiveness of token econ-omies. It also is a major limitation of token economies. The problem is this: clients enter a token economy program because they have a deficit of adaptive behaviors and/or an excess of maladaptive behaviors. Often this is because, in their present natural environments, adaptive behaviors are not being reinforced, or maladaptive behaviors are being reinforced. The token economy reverses these contingencies. Moreover, it does so very effectively, resulting in impressive (sometimes immediate) changes. When clients leave the token economy and return to their previous home environments, another reversal of the contingencies often occurs. In other words, the clients' behaviors once again are maintained by the contingencies that initially led to the clients' problems.

The most obvious solution to this dilemma is to keep clients in the token program. Occasionally, this solution is a viable one, as when a token economy is instituted in a client's natural environment. For example, two token economies were continued for more than 11 years to promote safety in open-pit mines (see Chapter 16 for more details).[41]

In most cases, however, token economies are only temporary treatment procedures. The key to long-term maintenance of treatment gains is for clients to be reinforced in their natural environments for the same behaviors that were reinforced in the token economy. Sometimes it is possible to change the environment to which clients return after leaving a token program. For instance, parents can be trained to reinforce their child's adaptive behaviors. Alternatively, clients can go to a different environment, such as a specialized foster home in which the foster parents are trained in behavior therapy procedures.

The reinforcers typically used in token economies are different from those the clients usually receive. Accordingly, provisions must be made to shift to reinforcers that are naturally available in the client's home environment. Toward this end, social reinforcers such as praise are generally administered along with tokens. Further, the use of tokens may be gradually withdrawn while clients are still in the token economy. This allows natural reinforcers (such as feeling good after completing a task) to assume an increasingly important role in maintaining the adaptive behaviors. Tokens can be withdrawn gradually by having clients move through levels within the token economy, such as the daily, weekly, and merit systems at Achievement Place.[42] Clients also may be reinforced with tokens on an intermittent reinforcement schedule.[43]

Critics have voiced ethical and humanitarian objections to token economies. For example, token economies have been described as demeaning, especially for adults. The argument is that token reinforcement is appropriate for children but not for adults, who are supposed to be "above" receiving tokens for behaving appropriately. Interestingly, the same people who think token reinforcement is inappropriate for adults often forget that they participate in a large-scale token economy every time they make a monetary transaction. The token economy also has been mistakenly viewed as a form of bribery (an argument we rebutted in Chapter 6, page 132).

In fact, the evidence indicates that token economies enhance clients' dignity by increasing their self-esteem, self-respect, pride, and sense of worth. Consider the following evaluation of an early token economy at a psychiatric hospital: "The program's most notable contribution to patient life is the lessening of staff control and putting the burden of responsibility, and thus more self-respect, on the patient."[44] Or consider the comment of a highly intelligent, 40-year-old trainee at the Community Training Center. The man approached the program director and, with obvious pride in what

CALVIN AND HOBBES copyright 1986 Watterson. Dist. by UNIVERSAL PRESS SYNDICATE. Reprinted with permission. All rights reserved.

he had accomplished in his classes, said, "Doctor, I earned 120 credits today."[45] These words sound very much like a sales executive telling her husband at dinner, "I earned a bonus today for closing the deal," or a college student telling his roommate, "I got an *A* on the paper I worked so hard on."

CONTINGENCY CONTRACT

A **contingency contract** is a written agreement between a client and one or more other people that specifies the relationship between a target behavior and its consequences. The essential components of a contingency contract are clear, unambiguous statements of (1) the target behavior; (2) the con-

Figure 8-5 Contingency contract for a seven-year-old boy

Date: January 21, 1997

Mrs. Perez (teacher) will sign Paul's daily behavior report card after lunch and then again after school is over each day if Paul:

1. Stays in his seat unless he gets permission to leave his seat.

2. Raises his hand when he wants to ask a question.

3. Completes his classwork satisfactorily.

When Paul has received ten of Mrs. Perez's signatures he may choose one of the following rewards:

> Get 10 minutes of extra recess time
> Go to the library for 20 minutes of free reading
> Collect lunch money from other students on Friday
> Feed the class goldfish
> Bring a toy from home to show his classmates
> Get a special snack from his teacher
> Bring a treat from home for his classmates
> Go to McDonald's for lunch with Mr. Kregg (gym teacher)
> Choose a book for Mrs. Perez to read to the class
> Be first in line to go to lunch

I, Paul, agree to the terms of the above agreement.

_____

I, Mrs. Perez, agree to provide Paul with the rewards specified above if Paul keeps his part of the agreement. I also agree not to provide Paul with any of the above rewards while the agreement is in effect if he does not earn the necessary ten signatures.

_____

I, Paul's mother, agree to review Paul's behavior report card each day and to keep track of the number of signatures he has earned. At home, I agree to give Paul 15 minutes of extra television time or 15 minutes of extra time playing Nintendo each time he earns three signatures from his teacher.

_____

Figure 8-6 Pictorial contingency contract showing the target behavior and the reinforcer

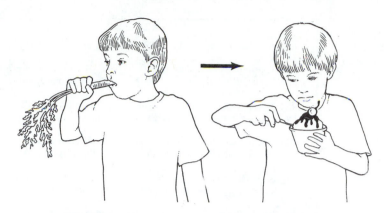

sequences for performing (or failing to perform) the target behavior; and (3) the precise contingency between the target behavior and the consequences (for example, "If the client does X for three consecutive days, then the client will receive Y").

The contract in Figure 8-5 illustrates other features of contingency contracts. They specify the responsibilities of the client and the other people involved in the therapy, each of whom signs the contract. For clients who cannot read, the contract can consist of pictures as shown in Figure 8-6. With deceleration target behaviors, contracts can include both reinforcement and response cost contingencies, as the one in Figure 8-7.

A contingency contract frequently is one component in a behavior therapy treatment package. For example, contingency contracts were part of an effective substance abuse treatment program for adolescents and young adults.[46] Clients contracted to engage in specific overt behaviors that competed with drug abuse, such as attending school, complying with an early curfew, and notifying their families of their whereabouts when they were not at home, school, or work. The contracts—which involved participation of the client, family members, and the therapist—were reviewed on a weekly basis. Daily and long-term reinforcers were administered by family members (for example, a parent's driving the client to a friend's house).

Using contingency contracts to formalize treatment plans has a number of benefits. Contingency contracts minimize disagreements about the conditions of the plan, with the contract's being the final authority—which underscores the importance of stating the terms of the contract unambiguously. Signing the contract increases the commitment of the people involved to fulfill their roles in complying with the contract. The process of designing a contingency contract makes clients active participants in therapy. When the people participating in the contract are having difficulty in their relationship (for example, child and parents, or spouses), jointly developing a contingency contract may benefit the relationship by providing structure to their interactions and fostering practice in negotiating and cooperating.

Contingency contracts are easy to write and implement,[47] and they are used as part of treatment plans for clients of all ages.[48] Examples of problems treated are disruptive classroom behaviors,[49] attending school,[50] homework performance,[51] antisocial behaviors,[52] sibling cooperation,[53] studying,[54]

Figure 8-7 Contingency contract with individual contingencies for each target behavior used with a 15-year-old boy

Effective dates: From: <u>11/1/97</u>   To: <u>11/8/97</u>

1. If Curtis goes to school each day and attends *all* his classes,

1. His parents will give Curtis $10 spending money per week (on Fridays).

2. If Curtis comes home after school by 4 P.M. to check in with his parents,

2. His parents will allow Curtis to stay out until 10 P.M. on Saturday night.

3. If Curtis comes home no later than 6 P.M. to have dinner with the family,

3. His parents will let Curtis keep his bedroom as neat or messy as he likes.

<u>Bonus</u>: Each time Curtis goes four weeks with fewer than six infractions, his parents will give him money to purchase one compact disc (maximum of $17 per purchase).

<u>Penalty</u>: Each time Curtis has more than six infractions, he will be grounded (remain in the house and not be able to watch television) for the full day on Saturday.

By signing below, I agree to follow each of the terms of this agreement.

_____
Curtis Williams

_____
Mrs. Williams

_____
Mr. Williams

This contract will be reviewed weekly.

physical exercise,[55] smoking,[56] overeating,[57] problem drinking,[58] and marital harmony.[59] Contingency contracts sometimes are used to increase compliance with behavior therapy homework assignments, such as getting parents who physically abuse their children to practice using positive reinforcement procedures with their children.[60] Relatively few studies have examined the essential features of contingency contracts.[61] It is clear, however, that specifying the contingency between the behavior and the consequence is necessary.[62]

BEHAVIORAL CHILD MANAGEMENT TRAINING

One-third of all referrals of children for psychotherapy involve so-called "misbehavior" and "discipline" problems.[63] They include noncompliance with parental requests and rules, and disruptive behaviors (such as aggressive acts, oppositional behaviors, and temper tantrums). When these behaviors occur occasionally, as they do with most children, they are considered normal—"just a stage" or "growing pains." However, when the noncompliant and disruptive behaviors are frequent, long-lasting, or intense, parents appropriately may seek professional assistance.

One approach to dealing with children's noncompliant and disruptive behaviors is for the child to receive individual psychotherapy. However, around 1960 it became clear that traditional psychotherapy with children exhibiting such problems was largely ineffective.[64] The reason may have been because the problem did not reside within the child, as was assumed in traditional psychotherapy, but rather it resided in the parent-child interactions. In fact, parents who seek help for their child's noncompliant and disruptive behaviors interact differently with their child than parents who are not reporting such problems. Specifically, extensive observations have revealed that parents who are experiencing difficulty with their children's problem behaviors (1) give more vague and inconsistent instructions; (2) use more negative, threatening, and angry warnings in an attempt to modify the child's behaviors; (3) administer inconsistent and ineffective consequences for undesirable behaviors; and (4) provide fewer positive consequences for their children's prosocial, desirable behaviors.[65]

These observations led two prominent behavior therapists—Gerald Patterson[66] at the Oregon Social Learning Center and Rex Forehand[67] at the University of Georgia—to develop *behavioral child management training* (also known as *behavioral parent training*).[68] **Behavioral child management training** involves teaching parents behavior therapy procedures to manage their children's behavioral problems effectively.

The primary goals of behavioral child management training are to increase parents' use of (1) clear, direct, and age-appropriate instructions to their children; (2) positive consequences for prosocial, desirable child behaviors; and (3) consistent, effective, and appropriate negative consequences for children's noncompliant and disruptive behaviors. Positive reinforcement, including differential reinforcement, and time out from positive reinforcement are the major therapy procedures that are taught to parents. The use of contingency contracts, home token economies, and response cost also may be taught.[69]

Parents initially learn to notice and reinforce their children's desirable behaviors. They are taught to use a variety of reinforcers, including enthusiastic praise (for instance, "What a great job. You came the first time I asked!"); physical affection (a hug, for example); and the provision of privileges (such as staying up 15 minutes later). Next, parents are taught how to differentially reinforce behaviors that compete with serious undesirable behaviors, such as hitting siblings, and to ignore minor undesirable behaviors, such as whining. Parents learn to give clear-cut instructions calmly and to refrain from angry, indirect negative instructions (such as "Wait until your father gets home"). They also learn to use time out in a consistent manner.

Behavioral child management training is conducted with a single family or in small groups containing 4 to 10 sets of parents. Parents rehearse the behavior therapy procedures in the training sessions and receive feedback from the therapist. The practice involves role playing, with the therapist or another parent playing the role of the child. Occasionally, the parents practice with their own child during training sessions. Homework between sessions is an integral part of the training.[70] For example, parents may be asked to self-monitor and self-reinforce their use of the behavioral skills they have learned.

Behavioral child management training is effective in modifying parents' interactions with their children[71] and, most importantly, in changing children's noncompliant and disruptive behaviors. Specifically, the children become more compliant with their parents' instructions and show even better compliance than children who had no significant behavioral problems.[72] In one study, for example, children whose parents received the behavioral training showed a 63% reduction in problem behaviors in comparison to a 17% reduction for children whose parents received a nonbehavioral (control) treatment.[73]

Behavioral child management training has been applied effectively to a variety of child behavior problems, including noncompliance with instructions and rules,[74] oppositional behaviors,[75] disruptive behaviors,[76] aggressive behaviors,[77] fighting and stealing,[78] childhood sleep problems,[79] eating behavior of undernourished children with cystic fibrosis,[80] and doing homework.[81] The training also has been effective for parents who physically abuse their children[82] and parents with mild mental retardation.[83]

Behavioral child management training sometimes results in improvements in the problem behaviors of untreated siblings.[84] However, positive changes in children's behaviors that occur in the home do not generalize spontaneously to school,[85] suggesting that additional interventions are needed to address problem behaviors in other settings.

The positive effects of behavioral child management training are consistently maintained over time, as demonstrated in follow-up studies ranging from 4½ to 10½ years after the training.[86] The major exception to this impressive long-term maintenance occurs when parents have significant problems of their own, such as a major psychiatric disorder (such as depression) or harsh economic constraints and unsafe living conditions. Such difficulties are likely to interfere with parents' effectively learning and implementing behavioral child management skills.[87]

Participation Exercise 8-2

CHANGING YOUR ANALOGUE TARGET BEHAVIOR THROUGH CONSEQUENTIAL BEHAVIOR THERAPY*

Consequential behavior therapies are potent means of changing the maintaining conditions of target behaviors. In this Participation Exercise, you will develop a change plan using one of these therapies for your analogue target behavior. You'll need to refer to the preparation you did in Participation Exercises 4-3, 5-4, and possibly 6-20.

Part I: Designing a Change Plan

If you are dealing with an acceleration target behavior, reinforcement procedures (Chapters 6 and 8) will be appropriate. If reinforcers are delayed, an individual

---

* You will need to do this Participation Exercise later.

token system might be appropriate. If you are dealing with a deceleration target behavior, you can use differential reinforcement and/or one of the consequential therapies that directly decelerate behavioral excesses (Chapter 7). Response cost and overcorrection probably are your best bets. (Do *not* use aversion therapy procedures, as aversion therapy is not a consequential behavior therapy.) You may want to include a contingency contract to formalize your change plan, even if you are the only one signing it.

Look over your list of maintaining consequences (which you compiled for Participation Exercise 4-3), and decide which you will change in order to modify your target behavior. Refer to the guidelines for deciding on which maintaining conditions to change (page 59).

The change plan should consist of a detailed description of the specific procedures you will use to change the maintaining conditions. For example, spell out the specific consequences for performing (or not performing) the target behavior and decide when they will be administered and by whom. You may self-administer the consequences, or enlist the assistance of a friend.

Make your change plan simple. Generally, the simpler the change plan, the more likely you (and clients in behavior therapy) will be to adhere to it, which is critical for its success. When you have completed a written change plan, show it to classmates to get their reactions and suggestions for improving it.

Part II: Implementing the Change Plan

You can see how effective your change plan is by implementing it. Continue the change plan for at least two weeks. As you begin to implement the plan, resume the self-recording procedures you used in Participation Exercise 5-4. Graph your self-recordings every few days. To see if your change plan is effective, compare your present graph (while your change plan is in effect) with your baseline graph (which you made in Participation Exercise 5-4). If your target behavior is changing in the desired direction, you have some evidence that the change plan is working.

◆

Summary

1. A token economy is a system for motivating clients to perform desirable behaviors and to refrain from performing undesirable behaviors. Clients earn token reinforcers for adaptive behaviors and lose them for maladaptive behaviors. Tokens can be tangible, such as poker chips, or symbolic, such as points. The tokens are exchanged for backup reinforcers. Token economies are most often used for groups of clients.
2. The basic elements of a token economy are (1) a list of target behaviors and the number of tokens clients can earn for performing each; (2) a list of backup reinforcers and the token cost of each; (3) the type of token used; and (4) specific procedures and rules for running the token economy.
3. The Community Training Center, a daytime treatment program for

individuals previously hospitalized for chronic psychiatric disorders, employed a token economy to motivate learning social and daily living skills needed for independent living. The program was shown to be superior to other comparable daytime treatment programs.

4. Achievement Place was a home-style, residential rehabilitation program for juvenile offenders that employed a token economy. Points were earned for appropriate social behaviors, academic performance, and daily living skills, and points were lost for inappropriate behaviors. The program was effective while the clients were in treatment and up to a year afterwards. Often, however, the gains were not maintained on a longer-term basis.

5. Token economies have been successfully applied to teach clients with mental retardation self-care and daily living skills and to modify classroom conduct and academic performance.

6. Token economies have been used with both individuals and small groups, such as families.

7. Evidence from reversal and multiple baseline studies clearly shows that token economies can modify clients' behaviors. However, treatment gains often decline rapidly when token reinforcement is discontinued unless specific procedures to foster durability of change are instituted. Such procedures include gradually withdrawing tokens and increasing natural reinforcers, such as social reinforcers, and establishing the same reinforcement contingencies used in the token program in the environment to which clients return.

8. A contingency contract is a written agreement between a client and others that specifies the relationship between a target behavior and its consequences.

9. Behavioral child management training involves teaching parents consequential behavior therapy procedures to manage their children's behavior problems effectively. The major therapy procedures taught are positive reinforcement, differential reinforcement, and time out from positive reinforcement.

REFERENCE NOTES

1. For example, Franco, Galanter, Castañeda, & Paterson, 1995.
2. Barry, 1958; Maconochie, 1848.
3. Kaestle, 1973; Lancaster, 1805.
4. For example, Ulman & Klem, 1975.
5. Ayllon & Azrin, 1968.
6. Kazdin, 1977c; Milan, 1987.
7. Spiegler & Agigian, 1977.
8. Spiegler & Agigian, 1977.
9. Phillips, 1968.
10. Braukmann & Wolf, 1987.
11. Compare with Minkin, Braukmann, Minkin, Timbers, Timbers, Fixsen, Phillips, & Wolf, 1976; Timbers, Timbers, Fixsen, Phillips, & Wolf, 1973.
12. Fixsen, Phillips, Phillips, & Wolf, 1976; Phillips, Phillips, Fixsen, & Wolf, 1971.
13. Phillips, Phillips, Fixsen, & Wolf, 1971.
14. Phillips, Phillips, Wolf, & Fixsen, 1973.
15. Bailey, Wolf, & Phillips, 1970.
16. Braukmann, Wolf, & Kirigin Ramp, 1985; Fixsen, Phillips, Phillips, & Wolf, 1976; Kirigin, Braukmann, Atwater, & Wolf, 1982; Maloney, Fixsen, & Phillips, 1981.
17. Eitzen, 1975.
18. For example, Bailey, Timbers, Phillips, & Wolf, 1971; Phillips, 1968.

19. Compare with Wilson & Herrnstein, 1985.
20. For example, Jones & Timbers, 1983; Meadowcroft, Hawkins, Trout, Grealish, & Stark, 1982.
21. Reid, Eddy, Bank, & Fetrow, 1994.
22. For example, Girardeau & Spradlin, 1964; Horner & Keilitz, 1975; Hunt, Fitzhugh, & Fitzhugh, 1968; Spradlin & Girardeau, 1966.
23. For example, Peniston, 1975.
24. For example, Baer & Guess, 1971, 1973; Brickes & Brickes, 1970; Guess, 1969; Guess & Baer, 1973; MacCubrey, 1971; Schumaker & Sherman, 1970.
25. For example, Hunt & Zimmerman, 1969; Zimmerman, Stuckey, Garlick, & Miller, 1969.
26. Welch & Gist, 1974.
27. Asylum on the front porch, 1974; Clark, Bussone, & Kivitz, 1974; Clark, Kivitz, & Rosen, 1972; Wilkie, Kivitz, Clark, Byer, & Cohen, 1968.
28. Clark, Bussone, & Kivitz, 1974.
29. Sullivan & O'Leary, 1990.
30. Kelley, 1990.
31. For example, Ferritor, Buckholdt, Hamblin, & Smith, 1972; Harris & Sherman, 1974. See also O'Leary, 1972; Winett & Winkler, 1972.
32. For example, Ayllon & Roberts, 1974; Chadwick & Day, 1971; Dalton, Rubino, & Hislop, 1973; Glynn, 1970; Knapczyk & Livingston, 1973; Lahey & Drabman, 1974; McLaughlin, 1982; Wilson & McReynolds, 1973.
33. For example, Bushell, 1978; Heaton & Safer, 1982.
34. Maloney & Hopkins, 1973.
35. Heward, Dardig, & Rossett, 1979; Ingham & Andrews, 1973; Jason, 1985; Moore & Callias, 1987.
36. Strauss, 1986.
37. Heward, Dardig, & Rossett, 1979.
38. Dapcich-Miura & Hovell, 1979.
39. Ayllon & Azrin, 1965, 1968.
40. For example, Glynn, 1990.
41. Fox, Hopkins, & Anger, 1987.
42. For example, Paul & Lentz, 1977; Phillips, Phillips, Fixsen, & Wolf, 1971.
43. For example, Rosen & Rosen, 1983.
44. Atthowe & Krasner, 1968, p. 41.
45. Spiegler, 1983.
46. Azrin, McMahon, Donohue, Besalel, Lapinski, Kogan, Acierno, & Galloway, 1994.
47. See DeRisi & Butz, 1975; Hall & Hall, 1982; O'Banion & Whaley, 1981.
48. Kazdin, 1994.
49. White-Blackburn, Semb, & Semb, 1977.
50. Vaal, 1973.
51. Kahle & Kelley, 1994.
52. Stuart, 1971; Stuart & Lott, 1972.
53. Guevremont, 1987.
54. Bristol & Sloane, 1974.
55. Wysocki, Hall, Iwata, & Riordan, 1979.
56. Spring, Sipich, Trimble, & Goeckner, 1978.
57. Mann, 1972.
58. Miller, 1972.
59. Jacobson & Margolin, 1979; Stuart, 1969.
60. Wolfe & Sandler, 1981.
61. Kazdin, 1994.
62. Spring, Sipich, Trimble, & Goechner, 1978.
63. Forehand & McMahon, 1981.
64. Levitt, 1957, 1963.
65. For example, Patterson, 1982; Patterson, Reid, & Dishion, 1992.
66. Patterson, 1982.
67. Forehand & McMahon, 1981.
68. Wells, 1994.
69. Barkley, Guevremont, Anastopolous, & Fletcher, 1992; Robin & Foster, 1989.
70. For example, Barkley, 1989; Wells, Griest, & Forehand, 1980.
71. For example, Peed, Roberts, & Forehand, 1977.
72. Forehand & King, 1977; Wells & Egan, 1988.
73. Patterson, Chamberlain, & Reid, 1982.
74. For example, Long, Forehand, Wierson, & Morgan, 1993.
75. For example Powers & Roberts, 1995; Webster-Statton, Kolpacoff, & Hollingsworth, 1988.
76. For example, Powers, Singer, Stevens, & Sowers, 1992.
77. For example, Patterson, Chamberlain, & Reid, 1982.
78. For example, Reid, Hinjosa-Rivera, & Loeber, 1980.
79. For example, Wolfson, Lacks, & Futterman, 1992.
80. For example, Stark, Knapp, Bowen, Powers, Jelalian, Evans, Passero, Mulvihill, & Hovell, 1993; Stark, Powers, Jelalian, Rape, & Miller, 1994.
81. For example, Anesko & O'Leary, 1982.
82. Wolfe & Wekerle, 1993.
83. Bakken, Miltenberger, & Schauss, 1993.
84. For example, Humphreys, Forehand, McMahon, & Roberts, 1978; Patterson, 1974.
85. For example, Breiner & Forehand, 1981.
86. For example, Baum & Forehand, 1981; Forehand & Long, 1988; Patterson & Reid, 1973.
87. Forehand & Long, 1988; Wahler & Graves, 1983; Wells, 1994.

Chapter 9

Brief/Graduated Exposure Therapy: Systematic Desensitization and In Vivo Exposure

Exposure therapies are used to treat anxiety, fear, and other intense negative emotional reactions by exposing clients—under carefully controlled conditions—to the situations or events that create the negative emotion. In a sense, exposure therapies are refined applications of the common wisdom that you should get back on the horse that has just thrown you. Exposure therapies provide clients with safe encounters with events that they perceive as unsafe.

We will use the terms *anxiety* and *fear* interchangeably to refer to intense, inappropriate, and maladaptive reactions that are characterized by uneasiness, dread about future events, a variety of physical responses (such as muscle tension, increased heart rate, and sweating), and avoidance of the feared events.* Anxiety is *inappropriate* when its intensity is disproportionate to the actual situation. Intense anxiety interferes with normal, everyday functioning. For example, a person who is extremely frightened of venturing outside, even though doing so would involve little objective danger, might become a recluse. Anxiety-related disorders are the most prevalent psychological problem in the United States, affecting an estimated 24 million adults[1] and 5 million children and adolescents.[2]

Some strong fears are realistic and adaptive, such as the fear of walking alone at night in high-crime neighborhoods. Further, mild anxiety can be adaptive when it motivates us to act. For example, most students require some anxiety about an upcoming exam to get them to study. The goal of exposure therapies is to reduce the client's anxiety to a level that allows the client to function effectively and to feel comfortable.

There are two basic models of exposure therapy. **Brief/graduated exposure therapy** exposes the client to a threatening event (1) for a short period of time (usually ranging from a few seconds to a few minutes), and (2) the exposure is incremental, beginning with aspects of the event that produce minimal anxiety and progressing to more anxiety-evoking aspects. Graduated exposure is a prime example of the stepwise progression that characterizes behavior therapy procedures. **Prolonged/intense exposure therapy** exposes the client to the threatening event (1) for a lengthy period of time (10 to 15 minutes at a minimum and sometimes more than an hour), and (2) from the outset, the client is exposed to aspects of the event that elicit intense anxiety.

Both models can be implemented in an in vivo or imaginal mode. *Exposure in vivo* involves actually encountering the event (such as taking a flight in the case of fear of flying). *Imaginal exposure* involves vividly imagining the event, as one does in a daydream (for example, visualizing taking a flight). The specific exposure therapies that comprise each model

---

* Early theorists made a distinction between fear and anxiety. *Fear* referred to apprehension concerning a tangible or realistic event, whereas *anxiety* referred to apprehension about something intangible or unrealistic. Some theorists have considered fear to be emotional and anxiety to be cognitive in nature (for example, Beck & Emery, 1985). In general, behavior therapists have not found it useful to distinguish between the two concepts (for example, Rachman, 1990), which is the position we have adopted in this book.

Table 9-1 Exposure therapies categorized by model of exposure and type of exposure

		TYPE OF EXPOSURE	
		In vivo	*Imaginal*
MODEL OF EXPOSURE	*Brief/graduated*	In vivo exposure therapy	Systematic desensitization
	Prolonged/intense	In vivo flooding	Imaginal flooding Implosive therapy

are listed in Table 9-1. In this chapter we will describe brief/graduated exposure therapies (systematic desensitization and in vivo exposure therapy), and in Chapter 10 we will cover prolonged/intense exposure therapies (in vivo flooding, imaginal flooding, and implosive therapy).

SYSTEMATIC DESENSITIZATION: BASIC PROCEDURES

Joseph Wolpe, one of the founders of behavior therapy, developed systematic desensitization some 50 years ago.[3] In **systematic desensitization**, the client imagines successively more anxiety-arousing situations while engaging in a behavior that competes with anxiety (such as relaxing). The client gradually (systematically) becomes less sensitive (desensitized) to the situations.

Systematic desensitization involves three steps.

1. The client is taught a response that competes with anxiety.
2. The specific events that cause anxiety are ordered in terms of the amount of anxiety they engender.
3. The client repeatedly visualizes the anxiety-evoking events, in order of increasing anxiety, while performing the competing response.

Relaxation as a Competing Response to Anxiety

People do not report feeling anxious and relaxed at the same time. Muscle relaxation competes with some of the physiological components of anxiety. Deeply relaxed skeletal muscles are associated with slower heart rate, lower blood pressure, and slower and more regular breathing. Wolpe capitalized on this phenomenon by countering anxiety with deep muscle relaxation, which is a shortened version of Edmund Jacobson's progressive relaxation, which can take up to 200 hours to learn.[4]

Training in **deep muscle relaxation** involves relaxing various skeletal muscle groups: arms, face, neck, shoulders, chest, abdomen, and legs. Clients first learn to differentiate between relaxation and tension by initially tensing and then relaxing each set of muscles. Later, clients create deeper and deeper states of relaxation in their muscles without first tensing them.[5]

Photo 9-1   Client being taught deep muscle relaxation. The client (reclining) is tensing his lower arm muscles before relaxing them.

Clients usually sit in a comfortable armchair, such as a recliner, close their eyes, and follow the therapist's relaxation instructions (see Photo 9-1). The following is an excerpt from relaxation instructions:

> Close your eyes, settle back comfortably, and we'll begin. Let's start with your left hand. I want you to clench your left hand into a fist, clench it very tightly and study those tensions, hold it . . . (5-second pause) and now relax. Relax your left hand and let it rest comfortably. Just let it relax . . . (15-second pause). Once again now, clench your left hand . . . clench it very tightly, study those tensions . . . (5-second pause) and now relax. Relax your hand and once again note the very pleasant contrast between tension and relaxation.

For highly anxious clients, relaxation training can serve as a prerequisite for systematic desensitization. Without initially having some control over their anxiety—which deep muscle relaxation provides—some clients are unwilling to expose themselves to feared situations, which is an essential part of systematic desensitization.[6] Deep muscle relaxation training alone can be effective in the treatment of anxiety disorders and in some cases is as effective as exposure therapy.[7] Deep muscle relaxation training also is used to treat a host of psychological and physical disorders other than anxiety (as you will see in Chapters 14 and 15).[8] Table 9-2 lists examples of the problems for which relaxation training has been used.

Constructing an Anxiety Hierarchy

An **anxiety hierarchy** is a list of events that elicit anxiety, ordered in terms of increasing levels of anxiety. The first step in constructing an anxiety

Table 9-2 Examples of problems treated by relaxation training

Medical Problems	Psychological Problems
Asthma	Anxiety
Headaches	Insomnia
Hypertension	Nightmares
Pain (acute and chronic)	Temper tantrums
Postpartum distress	
Postsurgical distress	
Raynaud's disease	
Side effects of chemotherapy for cancer	

hierarchy is to identify the events that make the client anxious. The therapist questions the client in detail to discover the specific situations that elicit anxiety. Clients also may complete a **fear survey schedule,** which contains a lengthy list of stimuli that evoke anxiety; clients indicate how anxious each event makes them.[9] Table 9-3 contains a portion of a fear survey schedule for adults. Fear survey schedules for children include events

Table 9-3 Portion of a fear survey schedule
SOURCE: Developed by Spiegler & Liebert, 1970.

Instructions: The items in this questionnaire are objects, experiences, or ideas that may cause fear, anxiety, or other unpleasant feelings. Using the scale below, write the appropriate number after each item to describe the degree to which the item causes you to feel fear, anxiety, or other unpleasant feelings.

1 = Not at all
2 = A little
3 = A moderate amount
4 = Much
5 = Very much

1. Open wounds	18. Cats	34. Going blind
2. Being alone	19. Being watched while working	35. Drowning
3. Speaking in public	20. Dirt	36. Examinations
4. Falling	21. Dogs	37. Cancer
5. Automobiles	22. Sick people	38. Fog
6. Being teased	23. Fire	39. Being lost
7. Dentists	24. Mice	40. Police
8. Thunder	25. Blood	41. Talking on the telephone
9. Failure	26. Enclosed places	42. Death of a loved one
10. High places	27. Flying in airplanes	43. Pain
11. Receiving injections	28. Darkness	44. Suicide
12. Strangers	29. Lightning	45. War
13. Feeling angry	30. Doctors	46. Going insane
14. Insects	31. Losing control	47. Violence
15. Sudden noises	32. Making mistakes	48. Psychologists
16. Crowds	33. Older people	
17. Large open spaces		

youngsters often find fear-provoking, such as being in the dark and being in a fight.[10]

The events that have been identified as evoking anxiety are ordered from least to most anxiety-evoking. Often this process makes use of the **Subjective Units of Discomfort scale**. The units of this scale are called **SUDs** and range from 0 to 100 (sometimes the scale is 0 to 10). Zero represents no anxiety; 100 represents the highest level of anxiety the client can imagine.[11] Assigning SUDs levels (numbers) to each anxiety-evoking event is one way to create an anxiety hierarchy, as you will see later in Participation Exercise 9-2.

As the word *subjective* implies, SUDs are specific to each individual. People who report experiencing the same SUDs levels are not necessarily experiencing equivalent degrees of discomfort. Thus, it is not possible to compare people's anxiety by using SUDs. However, the same individual's SUDs levels can be compared at various times and in different situations. For example, if a client reported experiencing 60 SUDs last week and 40 SUDs today in the same situation, then it is safe to conclude that the client is less anxious today. Comparisons of a client's SUDs levels are used as measures of change in therapy. You can use SUDs to assess your own changing levels of anxiety or discomfort in your daily life, as you'll see by doing Participation Exercise 9-1 during the next few days.

Participation Exercise 9-1

DAILY SUDSING

In this Participation Exercise, you will use the Subjective Units of Discomfort scale to evaluate your degree of discomfort in a variety of situations in your daily life.

Choose a regularly occurring situation or experience in your life in which you generally feel uncomfortable. A situation that occurs daily is ideal. Whenever the situation occurs, rate your SUDs level. Record the SUDs on Work Sheet 9-1* along with a brief description of (1) your feelings and thoughts and (2) what is happening in the situation. The description should be detailed enough so that you can identify the events and feelings and thoughts that were occurring each time you recorded your SUDs level. Record a minimum of 10 instances of the situation you have chosen. Figure 9-1 (page 204) shows a portion of a work sheet for a student named Ellen, as an example. She monitored her SUDs levels when she spoke up in her history class over the course of the semester.

When you have collected your series of SUDs ratings, make a simple graph of the ratings. Divide the vertical axis into 100 units (by 10s) and the horizontal axis into as many ratings as you have made. (See the example of Ellen's graph in Figure 9-2, p. 204.) The graph will give you an overall picture of how your level of discomfort varied over the recording period. To account for the variations, consult your work sheet for particular circumstances that may have changed your level of discomfort.

* You will find this work sheet in Appendix C.

Figure 9-1 Portion of Ellen's work sheet of SUDs levels, feelings and thoughts, and descriptions of what was happening each time she spoke in history class (Participation Exercise 9-1)

		Situation: Speaking up in history class	
Date	**SUDs**	**Feelings and thoughts**	**What is happening**
9/4	80	Scared to death; I'm going to sound dumb	Professor asks our reasons for taking course
9/6	—		Didn't do anything
9/9	75	This is hard; butterflies	Answering questions from reading
9/11	70	Nervous; here I go again—better say something worthwhile	Joining discussion

Figure 9-2 Ellen's SUDs levels each time she spoke in her history class (Participation Exercise 9-1)

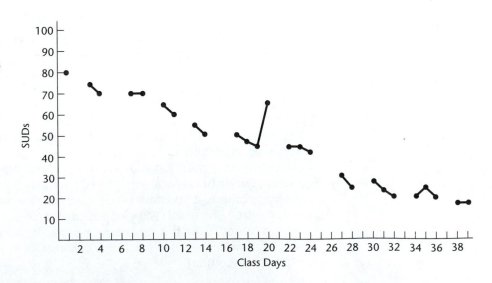

Anxiety hierarchies often include events that share a common theme. For instance, fear of evaluation might include fear of speaking in public, of being interviewed, and of taking tests. If a client is anxious about more than one class of situations, multiple anxiety hierarchies are constructed.

The rank ordering in anxiety hierarchies is specific to individual clients. Look carefully at the three hierarchies in Table 9-4 (p. 207). If you were to order the items, you might do so differently.

◆ ▨▨

Participation Exercise 9-2

CONSTRUCTING AN ANXIETY HIERARCHY*

This Participation Exercise will give you experience with two different procedures that are used in systematic desensitization to construct anxiety hierarchies. Begin by reading the situations in Table 9-5; they describe circumstances that might make people anxious. From Table 9-5, choose two situations in which you can imagine yourself being anxious. Alternatively, you can make up one or two of your own situations that actually make you anxious.

Part I: Constructing an Anxiety Hierarchy Using SUDs

1. Assume the role of a person who is experiencing the anxiety described in one of the situations you chose.

2. Write 8 brief descriptions of circumstances or scenes related to the situation that would cause you to experience varying levels of anxiety.

3. Assign SUDs to each scene (using a scale of 1 to 100).

4. Write the numbers 1 through 8 on a sheet of paper. List the events from lowest anxiety (SUDs) to highest anxiety (SUDs), with number 1 being lowest.

Table 9-5   Situations to be role played for constructing anxiety hierarchies (Participation Exercise 9-2)

1. You receive a letter in your mailbox instructing you to make an appointment with the dean before the end of the week to discuss "concerns" about your academic standing. You know that you have not been doing as well as you would like in your classes, but you didn't know your academic standing was in jeopardy.

2. You have a dentist appointment next week to have several cavities filled. You always have hated going to the dentist, and you have put off this visit for months.

3. You got into an automobile accident with your parents' car after borrowing it for the weekend. The accident was your fault, and the damages are estimated at $2800. You have not yet told your parents, but you are supposed to return the car in an hour.

4. You have a final exam in two days. The exam is in your most difficult subject this semester. You need a high grade on the exam to pass the course. You haven't started studying for the exam yet, and you have two other final exams before the one you are dreading most.

5. You have to give an oral presentation in one of your classes in two days. You have always had difficulty speaking in public, and this is a particularly large class. One-third of your grade is based on this oral presentation.

* This Participation Exercise can be done before you continue or later.

Part II: Constructing an Anxiety Hierarchy by Interpolation

1. Now assume the role of a person who is experiencing the anxiety described in the other situation you chose.

2. Write the numbers 9 through 1 on a sheet of paper. Put 9 at the top and leave several spaces between numbers. Follow the instructions for each number in the following order.

> For *9,* write a scene related to the situation that would cause "you" to feel *extremely anxious.*
>
> For *1,* write a scene that would cause "you" virtually *no anxiety.*
>
> For *5,* write a scene that would cause "you" to experience a level of anxiety that is approximately midway between scene 1 and scene 9.
>
> For *7,* write a scene that would cause "you" to experience a level of anxiety that is approximately midway between scene 5 and scene 9.
>
> For *3,* write a scene that would cause "you" to experience a level of anxiety that is approximately midway between number 1 and number 5.
>
> For *8,* write a scene that would cause "you" to experience a level of anxiety that is approximately midway between scene 7 and scene 9.
>
> For *2,* write a scene that would cause "you" to experience a level of anxiety that is approximately midway between scene 1 and scene 3.
>
> For *6,* write a scene that would cause "you" to experience a level of anxiety that is approximately midway between scene 5 and scene 7.
>
> For *4,* write a scene that would cause "you" to experience a level of anxiety that is approximately midway between scene 3 and scene 5.

After you have constructed both anxiety hierarchies, consider what you have learned about the process. Did you find one procedure easier? What made it easier? Do you think one procedure resulted in a more valid hierarchy than the other? Why? Based on your experience in making up the two anxiety hierarchies, what difficulties do you think clients might have in constructing anxiety hierarchies?

◆

The Desensitization Process

Desensitizing the events associated with anxiety begins as soon as the client has learned deep muscle relaxation (or another competing response) and has constructed an anxiety hierarchy. The desensitization starts with the client seated in a comfortable chair. The therapist instructs the client to relax all of his or her muscles. Then, the therapist describes scenes from the anxiety hierarchy for the client to imagine, starting with the lowest item on the hierarchy.

The description must contain sufficient details to enable the client to vividly and realistically imagine being in the situation. For example, based on details provided by the client, the therapist might elaborate on the top item in the dating hierarchy in Table 9-4, "initially greeting date," as follows:

Table 9-4 Examples of anxiety hierarchies

Item	SUDs	Item	SUDs
DATING		**FLYING**	
10. Initially greeting date	95	20. Plane is flying in rough weather	100
9. Saying goodnight	85	19. Plane touching down on runway	95
8. Being on the date	75	18. Pilot turns on seatbelt sign and announces turbulence ahead	90
7. Driving to pick up date	65		
6. Getting ready to go on date	55		
5. Calling someone for date	45	17. Plane is banking	85
4. Asking for potential date's telephone number	35	16. Plane is descending for landing	80
3. Talking to potential date in class	30	15. Announcement of preparation for final descent and landing	75
2. Meeting an attractive member of the opposite sex	20		
1. Thinking about going on date next weekend	10	14. Plane is taking off	65
DEATH		13. Plane is taxiing to the runway	60
19. Death of a close friend or loved one	100	12. Plane is climbing to cruising altitude	55
18. Death of strangers in a dramatic fashion	85	11. Plane is cruising in good weather	50
17. Watching horror movies	80	10. Sitting down and fastening seatbelt	45
16. Seeing others in dangerous situations	75	9. Announcement that the plane is ready for boarding	40
15. Hearing about a fatal and especially gruesome disease	70	8. Boarding the plane	35
14. Being around guns	60	7. Waiting to be boarded	30
13. Swimming in the ocean at night	55	6. Checking in at the airport	25
12. Riding as a passenger in a car on the highway	50	5. Driving to the airport	22
11. Flying in an airplane	48	4. Calling the airport to find out if the flight is on time	20
10. Driving a car on the highway	45	3. Packing for the trip	15
9. Thoughts of fire	43	2. Purchasing ticket 10 days before flight	10
8. Climbing on high objects	40	1. Making reservations 3 weeks before flight	5
7. Being alone in a house at night	38		
6. Thinking about auto crashes	35		
5. Thoughts of earthquakes	25		
4. Thinking of witches and ghosts	20		
3. Swimming in a pool at night	15		
2. Seeing a snake	10		
1. Hearing a siren	5		

You arrive at your date's apartment and knock on the door. There is no immediate answer and waiting seems endless. Finally, your date opens the door, smiles, and says, "Hi!"

For many clients, visualizing an anxiety-evoking scene results in the same emotional responses that they experience when they are actually in the situation. If clients have difficulty imagining scenes vividly enough, visualization training can be provided.

The client imagines each scene for about 15 seconds at a time. Whenever the client experiences any anxiety or discomfort, the client signals the therapist, usually by raising a finger. When this occurs, the therapist instructs the client to "stop visualizing the scene and just continue relaxing." The result is that the client visualizes anxiety-evoking scenes *only when relaxed*. The aim is for relaxation to replace the tension previously associated with the scene. Each scene in the hierarchy is repeatedly presented until the client reports experiencing virtually no discomfort while visualizing it. Then, the next highest scene in the hierarchy is visualized. Case 9-1 presents a verbatim excerpt from the first session of the desensitization process.

"Now relax. . . . Just like last week, I'm going to hold the cape up for the count of 10. . . . When you start getting angry, I'll put it down."

<table>
<tr><td>

Case 9-1

</td><td>

EXCERPT FROM AN INITIAL SESSION OF SYSTEMATIC DESENSITIZATION FOR SEVERE TEST ANXIETY[12]

</td></tr>
</table>

A 24-year-old female art student suffered from severe test anxiety, which had caused her to fail a number of tests. When she discussed her anxiety with the therapist, it was discovered that other situations also made her anxious. Accordingly, four different anxiety hierarchies were constructed: taking tests; discord between other people; being scrutinized by others; and being devalued by others.

The desensitization process began with the therapist instructing the client to become deeply relaxed. Then the therapist said:

> I am now going to ask you to imagine a number of scenes. You will imagine them clearly and they will generally interfere little, if at all, with your state of relaxation. If, however, at any time you feel disturbed or worried and want to attract my attention, you will be able to do so by raising your left index finger. First I want you to imagine that you are standing at a familiar street corner on a pleasant morning watching the traffic go by. You see cars, motorcycles, trucks, bicycles, people, and traffic lights; and you can hear the sounds associated with all these things. (*Pause about 15 sec.*) Now stop imagining that scene and give all your attention once again to relaxing. If the scene you imagined disturbed you even in the slightest degree, I want you to raise your left index finger *now*. (*Client does not raise finger.*) Now imagine that you are at home studying in the evening. It is the 20th of May, exactly a month before your examination. (*Pause of 5 sec.*) Now stop imagining the scene. Go on relaxing. (*Pause of 10 sec.*) Now imagine the same scene again—a month before your examination. (*Pause of 5 sec.*) Stop imagining the scene and just think of your muscles. Let go, and enjoy your state of calm. (*Pause of 15 sec.*) Now again imagine that you are studying at home a month before your examination. (*Pause of 5 sec.*) Stop the scene, and now think of nothing but your own body. (*Pause of 5 sec.*) If you felt any disturbance whatsoever to the last scene raise your finger. (*Client does not raise finger.*) If the amount of disturbance decreased from the first presentation to the third, do nothing, otherwise again raise your finger. (*Client does not raise finger.*) Just keep on relaxing. (*Pause of 15 sec.*) Imagine that you are sitting on a bench at a bus stop and across the road are two strange men whose voices are raised in an argument. (*Pause of 10 sec.*) Stop imagining the scene and just relax. (*Pause of 10 sec.*) Now again imagine the scene of these two men arguing across the road. (*Pause of 10 sec.*) Stop the scene and relax. Now I am going to count up to 5 and you will open your eyes, feeling very calm and refreshed.

A total of 17 desensitization sessions were required for the client to report no anxiety while visualizing the highest scene in each anxiety hierarchy. Afterward, the client successfully passed a series of examinations, which demonstrated that the anxiety reduction generalized from the imagined scenes to the actual situations.

Three features of Case 9-1 are typical of systematic desensitization. First, before presenting scenes, the therapist checked to see that the client was deeply relaxed. This was done by presenting a neutral scene—one that was not expected to elicit any anxiety—and observing if the client experienced anxiety. Second, scenes from more than one hierarchy were visualized in the same session. Third, the therapy was relatively brief.

Essential and Facilitative Components of Systematic Desensitization

Therapies usually have both essential and facilitative components. An *essential component* is an element that is necessary for the therapy to be effective—in other words, the therapy will not work without it. A *facilitative component* is an element that is not always necessary for the therapy to be effective but that may enhance its effectiveness and efficiency. Researchers isolate the essential components of a therapy by systematically omitting components and then comparing the abbreviated treatment with the full treatment.[13] If an abbreviated treatment is shown to be as effective as the complete one, then the missing component is not essential.

The three major components of systematic desensitization are (1) *repeated safe exposure* to anxiety-evoking situations (2) in a *gradual manner* (3) while engaging in a *competing response*. Which of these components is essential? A number of studies have shown that it is not necessary to expose clients to the anxiety scene gradually. In fact, desensitization can be effective when the client is exposed to the highest items in the hierarchy first[14] or just to the highest items.[15] Research also has demonstrated that desensitization with and without relaxation training can be equally effective.[16] The essential component in systematic desensitization, then, is *repeated exposure to anxiety-evoking situations without the client experiencing any negative consequences.*[17] For example, a man who is afraid to ride in a car imagines himself safely riding in a car and reaching his destination.*

The facilitative components—gradual exposure and a competing response—are more likely to be beneficial when the client's anxiety is severe. In one study with cancer patients, for example, both gradual exposure and relaxation were necessary to alleviate nausea that patients experienced in anticipation of chemotherapy.[18] One effect of the facilitative components of desensitization may be to render the therapy more acceptable to clients (less "painful"), which in turn may motivate clients to remain in therapy.

---

* The studies that isolated the essential and facilitative components of systematic desensitization were carried out with mild to moderately anxious volunteers rather than actual clients and in research rather than clinical settings. Accordingly, it is important to exercise caution in generalizing from these analogue studies to clinical practice.

VARIATIONS OF SYSTEMATIC DESENSITIZATION

The standard systematic desensitization procedures originated by Wolpe are still widely used. In a nutshell, these procedures involve gradually having an individual client imagine anxiety-evoking events only while remaining relaxed. Additionally, a number of variations of standard systematic desensitization have been devised. We shall look at four examples that involve competing responses other than muscle relaxation; target behaviors other than anxiety; groups of clients; and a coping model of systematic desensitization.

Other Competing Responses

Deep muscle relaxation is the most frequently used competing response for anxiety and other negative emotional reactions treated by systematic desensitization. In some cases, other responses may be more appropriate. For example, some clients—especially young children but also some adults—have difficulty learning deep muscle relaxation. Alternative competing responses include sexual arousal, assertive behaviors, eating, pleasant thoughts, and humor.

Emotive imagery refers to pleasant thoughts that compete with anxiety.[19] It was part of the treatment of Paul's school-phobic behavior in Case 4-1 (see page 45). Humor and laughter are particularly well-suited as competing responses to anxiety.[20] Research in psychology and medicine has demonstrated the effectiveness of humor and laughter in treating a wide array of problems,[21] including coping with AIDS.[22] One advantage that humor and laughter have over deep muscle relaxation is that the client does not have to learn the response. Thus, humor as the competing response, makes it possible to carry out "crisis" desensitization in a single session, as Case 9-2 illustrates.

Case 9-2

ONE-SESSION SYSTEMATIC DESENSITIZATION FOR FEAR OF HUMILIATION[23]

A 20-year-old woman contacted a behavior therapist with a pressing problem. She was distressed about having to attend a banquet that same evening because she feared that she might be embarrassed by her former male friend and his new woman friend. The client and the therapist constructed an anxiety hierarchy of potentially humiliating situations that might arise at the banquet. The scenes were presented to the woman with details that elicited laughter. In one scene, for example, the woman pictured herself sitting at the banquet and seeing her old flame enter the room. In describing the scene, the therapist added that the man was dressed in tights. The woman found the recast scenes quite humorous, and she completed the hierarchy in the single therapy session. Several hours later, she attended the banquet and experienced only minor discomfort.

Other Target Behaviors

Anxiety or fear is, by far, the most frequent problem treated by systematic desensitization. However, systematic desensitization as a general model of treatment—substituting a positive emotional reaction for a negative emotional reaction—is applicable to a variety of problems. Examples include anger,[24] asthmatic attacks,[25] insomnia,[26] motion sickness,[27] nightmares,[28] problem drinking,[29] sleepwalking,[30] speech disorders,[31] and even racial prejudice.[32] Case 9-3 illustrates the application of systematic desensitization to the treatment of anger, using humor as a competing response. The woman's anger was intense and sometimes resulted in her physically abusing her child and husband.

Case 9-3

SUBSTITUTING HUMOR FOR ANGER THROUGH SYSTEMATIC DESENSITIZATION[33]

The patient was a 22-year-old female who referred herself for treatment because of a reported lack of ability to control extreme anger responses within her relationships with her husband and with her three-year-old son. The latter was described as a very active child whose almost constant misbehavior appeared to be attempts to antagonize his mother and gain her attention. Behavioral observations of the mother interacting with her child supported her description of the situation. The patient reported that she generally reacted to the child's misbehavior with extreme rage responses which consisted of screaming at the top of her voice, jumping up and down, smashing things, and physically attacking her child. She described her rage responses as so "automatic" as to be beyond her control. Her relationship with her husband was also marked by interpersonal strife. The patient reported that when she became angry with her husband she screamed at and berated him, and he occasionally became the target of thrown objects and physical assaults. Acquaintances and relatives attributed [her] family problems to a "violent temper" which had been a disruptive factor in her relationships since childhood. At the time she referred herself for treatment, the patient reported that she had been contemplating suicide because "my temper makes everyone, including me, miserable."

After seven sessions of desensitization with relaxation, negligible progress had been made. The strength and explosive quality of the patient's anger responses rendered her incapable of imagining any but the most innocuous scenes involving her husband or son without experiencing anger. The lack of success with relaxation resulted in the search for another potential competing response. [Accordingly, the hierarchy items were] . . . embellished with as much humorous content as possible. The insertion of humorous content into the items generally took the form of . . . slapstick comedy. For example, an item concerned with her son's engaging in mischievous behavior while the patient is driving was presented in the following form:

> As you're driving to the supermarket, little Pascal the Rascal begins to get restless. Suddenly he drops from his position on the ceiling and trampolines off the rear seat onto the rear view mirror. From this precarious position, he amuses himself by flashing obscene gestures at shocked pedestrians. As you begin to turn into the supermarket parking lot, Pascal alights from his perch and lands with both feet on the accelerator. As the car careens through the parking lot, you hear Pascal observe, "Hmm, . . . 25-80 in 2 sec . . . not bad." But right now your main concern is the two elderly . . . women that you're bearing down upon. You can see them very clearly, limping toward the door of the supermarket clutching their little bargain coupons. One, who is clutching a prayer book in the other hand, turns and, upon seeing your car approaching at 70 mph, utters a string of profanities, throws her coupons into the air, and lays a strip of Neolite as she sprints out of the way and does a swan dive into a nearby [ditch]. The other, moving equally as fast, nimbly eludes your car and takes refuge in a nearby shopping cart, which picks up speed as it rolls downhill across the parking lot . . . .

The patient was asked to signal the therapist if a scene evoked anger. [When this occurred, the therapist introduced and emphasized] some humorous aspect of the situation being described. . . .

Whereas no visible progress was achieved during the relaxation phase of treatment, the introduction of humor proved to be highly effective. During the first humor session, it was possible to present all of the scenes . . . without the patient's experiencing anger. During the eight treatment sessions which followed, she generally reacted to the scenes with laughter and amusement, and seldom reported anger arousal. As the treatment continued, she began to report major reductions in the frequency and intensity of her anger responses in her interactions with her son and husband. After three sessions, she reported that relatives had noted a marked improvement in her "temper." . . . Behavioral observations of playroom interactions before and after treatment were consistent with the patient's reports of positive changes in her response to noxious behaviors on [her son's] part. She likewise reported that her anger responses to her husband had markedly decreased and that she was able to remain calm in the face of situations which had previously infuriated her. The patient stated that her depressive episodes and suicidal ideation had ceased.

Group Systematic Desensitization

Groups of clients can be treated using systematic desensitization by making slight modifications in the standard procedures.[34] Deep muscle relaxation is simultaneously taught to the entire group. When the clients share a common problem, a **group hierarchy** is constructed, which combines information from each client.[35] When a group hierarchy is not appropriate, individual hierarchies are used. The hierarchy items are written on cards to which each client refers during desensitization. When one or more clients signal anxiety for a scene, all the group members are asked to visualize the scene again. Although this may be inefficient for some group members, it does not decrease the effectiveness of the treatment.

Group desensitization has some advantages over individually administered desensitization. It requires less therapist time, and sharing similar problems and solutions can be therapeutically beneficial for clients.

Coping Desensitization

In standard desensitization, anxiety associated with specific events is replaced with a competing response. In **coping desensitization**, a variation developed by Marvin Goldfried, clients use specific anxiety-related *bodily sensations to actively cope* with anxiety.[36] Typically, relaxation is used to cope with the muscle tension experienced while visualizing scenes. When a client signals the therapist that a scene is producing anxiety, the therapist instructs the client to "stay with the scene and use relaxation to cope with the anxiety" (rather than to stop imagining the scene and continue to relax as in standard desensitization). Another way clients can cope with anxiety is to use appropriate self-instructions, such as "I'm handling things; I don't have to be anxious." (The use of self-instructions will be described in detail in Chapter 13.)

In addition to the difference in the desensitization process, minor differences between coping and standard desensitization exist and are summarized in Table 9-6. For example, hierarchy items need not have a common theme, as they often do in standard desensitization. Because sensations associated with anxiety are desensitized, rather than specific anxiety-producing events, the hierarchy items only must result in increasing levels of anxiety. This feature makes coping desensitization applicable to nonspecific anxiety (generalized anxiety disorder).[37]

Coping desensitization is a prime example of a self-control procedure.[38] First, clients practice reducing their anxiety while visualizing anxiety-evoking scenes by imagining themselves actively coping with the situation and their emotional reaction to it. Second, clients learn to use anxiety sensations as reminders to use the coping skills, which they can do whenever they experience sensations of anxiety in their lives.

Although few studies have evaluated the effectiveness of coping desensitization, it appears to be at least as effective as standard desensitization in reducing anxiety.[39] Some evidence also exists that the coping skills generalize to unrelated anxiety-evoking situations other than the ones specifically treated in therapy.[40]

Table 9-6 Comparison of coping and standard desensitization (with major differences in coping desensitization in **bold** print)

	Coping Desensitization	*Standard Desensitization*
Relaxation training	**Learn to use tension as a cue to relax** and learn deep muscle relaxation	Learn deep muscle relaxation only
Hierarchy construction	**No common theme necessary**—just items eliciting increasing levels of anxiety	Common theme usual among items eliciting increasing levels of anxiety
Dealing with anxiety experienced during scene presentation	**Continue visualizing scene and use muscle tension as a cue to cope using relaxation**	Stop visualizing scene and focus on relaxing muscles
Homework	**Practice relaxing muscles whenever anxiety sensations are experienced** and practice deep muscle relaxation	Practice deep muscle relaxation only

Systematic Desensitization in Perspective

Systematic desensitization was the first major behavior therapy for anxiety-related disorders. It is a highly effective and efficient treatment that still is widely practiced[41] and still is being put to new uses, such as for the treatment of body image disturbances.[42] The general model of treatment provided by systematic desensitization also is useful for treating a variety of problems that are maintained by other maladaptive emotional reactions, such as anger.

Systematic desensitization is not applicable to all clients or types of anxiety. Generally, it is not used for young children because they often experience difficulty carrying out the procedures.[43] Techniques more suitable for children include emotive imagery, in vivo exposure (covered later in this chapter), flooding (Chapter 10), and modeling therapy (Chapter 11).

When anxiety is maintained by a skill deficit, making the client feel more comfortable in the situation is not sufficient.[44] For example, people who experience dating anxiety often do not know how to act appropriately while on a date. In such cases, anxiety may be a by-product of the skill deficit rather than the primary maintaining condition of the problem. Thus, the appropriate treatment is skills training (Chapter 11). When both a skill deficit and anxiety are maintaining conditions of a problem, both need to be treated.

Systematic desensitization is an acceptable treatment to clients. It is relatively "painless" because clients are gradually and symbolically exposed to anxiety-evoking situations. Further, clients control the process by proceeding at their own pace and terminating exposure when they begin to feel anxious.

◆ In Theory 9-1

WHY DOES BRIEF/ GRADUATED EXPOSURE THERAPY WORK?

Why does systematic desensitization reduce anxiety? A number of theoretical explanations have been advanced, and we will describe the five most common. These explanations hold for in vivo exposure as well.

Counterconditioning

Wolpe's original theory involved a *counterconditioning process* in which an adaptive response (feeling relaxed, for example) is substituted for a maladaptive response (such as anxiety) to a threatening stimulus.[45] To understand this process, it is helpful to first see how anxiety may develop according to a classical conditioning model of learning. Anxiety or fear develops when a neutral event (a conditioned stimulus), one that does not elicit anxiety, is associated with an event that naturally causes anxiety (an unconditioned stimulus). Consider the simple example diagrammed in Figure 9-3. You *speak up in class* (conditioned stimulus) and *students laugh at you* (unconditioned stimulus). This establishes an association between speaking in class and feeling embarrassed or humiliated. Being laughed at is a stimulus that "naturally" makes you anxious. Subsequently, speaking in class may make you anxious.

Desensitization counters this conditioning by associating the anxiety-evoking event with relaxation or another anxiety-competing response (see Figure 9-4). One problem with the counterconditioning explanation is that desensitization without a competing response can be effective.

Reciprocal Inhibition

Wolpe's theory included a more basic, neurophysiological explanation. Our physical emotional responses (for example, increased heart rate and sweating) are largely controlled by the autonomic nervous system,

Figure 9-3 Development of anxiety through classical conditioning (In Theory 9-1)

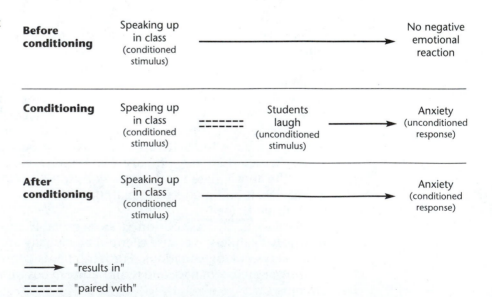

Before conditioning	Speaking up in class (conditioned stimulus)	⟶		No negative emotional reaction
Conditioning	Speaking up in class (conditioned stimulus)	≡≡≡≡≡	Students laugh (unconditioned stimulus) ⟶	Anxiety (unconditioned response)
After conditioning	Speaking up in class (conditioned stimulus)	⟶		Anxiety (conditioned response)

⟶ "results in"

≡≡≡≡≡ "paired with"

Figure 9-4 Reduction of anxiety through counterconditioning via systematic desensitization (In Theory 9-1)

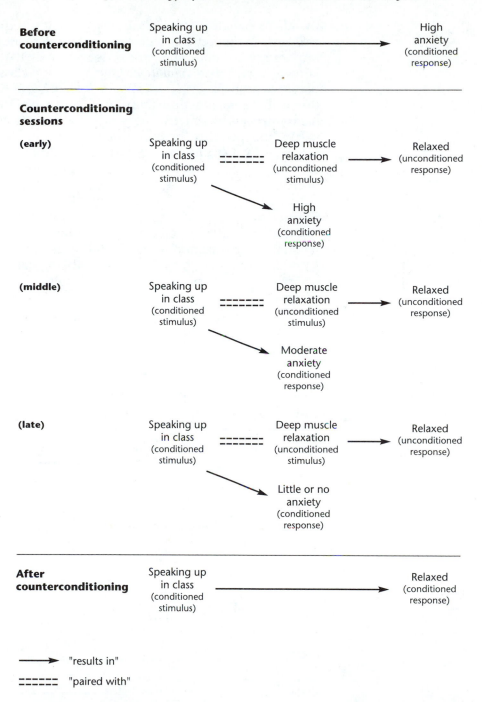

Before counterconditioning

Speaking up in class (conditioned stimulus) ⟶ High anxiety (conditioned response)

Counterconditioning sessions

(early)

Speaking up in class (conditioned stimulus) ======= Deep muscle relaxation (unconditioned stimulus) ⟶ Relaxed (unconditioned response)

↘ High anxiety (conditioned response)

(middle)

Speaking up in class (conditioned stimulus) ======= Deep muscle relaxation (unconditioned stimulus) ⟶ Relaxed (unconditioned response)

↘ Moderate anxiety (conditioned response)

(late)

Speaking up in class (conditioned stimulus) ======= Deep muscle relaxation (unconditioned stimulus) ⟶ Relaxed (unconditioned response)

↘ Little or no anxiety (conditioned response)

After counterconditioning

Speaking up in class (conditioned stimulus) ⟶ Relaxed (conditioned response)

⟶ "results in"

====== "paired with"

which is divided into two branches: sympathetic and parasympathetic. The physical symptoms of anxiety are primarily sympathetic functions, while relaxation generally is asso- ciated with parasympathetic functions. At any given moment, either the sympathetic or the parasympathetic system predominates. Thus, during systematic desensitization, the client's anxiety is *inhibited* by a *reciprocal* or opposite physiological response, relaxation. This process is known as *reciprocal inhibition*. One potential problem with this explanation is that sympathetic activity and parasympathetic activity are only partly independent because both branches of the autonomic nervous system always are active to some degree.

Extinction

Another explanation of how systematic desensitization works suggests that extinction is the basic underlying mechanism.[46] The ex-

tinction explanation, like Wolpe's counterconditioning explanation, assumes that anxiety or fear develops by classical conditioning (see Figure 9-5). Extinction involves terminating reinforcement. In classical conditioning, reinforcement specifically refers to the pairing of the conditioned stimulus and the unconditioned stimulus. This pairing is broken in systematic desensitization when the client is repeatedly exposed to the conditioned stimulus (speaking in class) *in the absence* of the unconditioned stimulus (being laughed at), as Figure 9-5 shows.

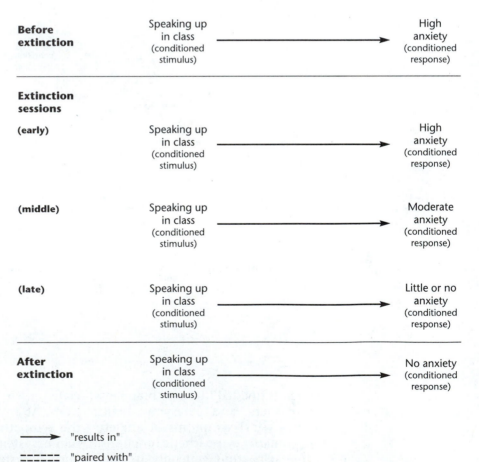

Figure 9-5 Reduction of anxiety through extinction via systematic desensitization (In Theory 9-1)

Before extinction   Speaking up in class (conditioned stimulus) ⟶ High anxiety (conditioned response)

Extinction sessions

(early)   Speaking up in class (conditioned stimulus) ⟶ High anxiety (conditioned response)

(middle)   Speaking up in class (conditioned stimulus) ⟶ Moderate anxiety (conditioned response)

(late)   Speaking up in class (conditioned stimulus) ⟶ Little or no anxiety (conditioned response)

After extinction   Speaking up in class (conditioned stimulus) ⟶ No anxiety (conditioned response)

⟶ "results in"

====== "paired with"

Cognitive Factors

Besides conditioning explanations, cognitive theories have been proposed. They all involve changes in the client's thinking, which may occur in at least three different ways.

One explanation is that the safe exposure to anxiety-arousing situations during systematic desensitization may result in clients' *thinking about the situations more realistically.*[47] Realistic thinking renders the situations less threatening. Desensitization is used to treat anxiety that is unrealistic in the sense of being inappropriate and exaggerated for the situation. Relaxation may help clients focus and think more objectively about their anxiety, which allows them to see it is as unrealistic.[48]

A second explanation suggests that desensitization leads clients to *expect that they will be less fearful* than they had assumed they would be when exposed to anxiety-evoking events. This change in expectation occurs because clients' levels of anxiety are reduced during desensitization. Explaining systematic desensitization in terms of changing expectations is consistent with the finding that when people are led to believe that they are less afraid (as through false feedback), they actually feel less afraid.[49]

A third explanation holds that desensitization may *strengthen clients' beliefs that they are capable of coping with their anxiety.*[50] This belief would be expected to develop from clients' repeated successes during desensitization—that is, they repeatedly imagine themselves in anxiety-provoking situations without experiencing negative consequences, including feeling anxious.

Nonspecific Factors

Finally, it has been suggested that the effects of desensitization can be explained by *nonspecific factors,* which are elements that are part of therapy in general but not part of the specific therapy itself. The attention a therapist gives the client is a generic nonspecific factor. Research studies have controlled for therapist attention in order to assess its impact on therapy outcome. This is done by comparing clients who receive desensitization with clients in an attention-control condition, in which clients spend time with the therapist but receive no therapy itself. These studies indicate that nonspecific factors such as therapist attention can play a role in the success of systematic desensitization.[51] However, the studies also show that nonspecific factors alone do not account for the effectiveness of desensitization.[52]

Obviously, there are many answers to the question: Why does systematic desensitization work? We have presented the most prominent theoretical explanations; a variety of other explanations have been proposed, including those based on shaping and modeling.[53]

EFFICIENCY OF SYSTEMATIC DESENSITIZATION

Systematic desensitization is efficient in three ways. First, exposure to problematic situations in one's imagination is less time-consuming (for both client and therapist) than in vivo exposure, which involves venturing to the actual anxiety-provoking situations. Clients do generalize the anxiety reduction they experience with imagined scenes to the real-life situations. Second, compared with traditional psychotherapies that treat anxiety-related problems, systematic desensitization requires relatively few sessions. Third, the procedures can be adapted for groups of clients.

Additionally, desensitization can be automated by using tape-recorded instructions,[54] written instructions,[55] or computer programs.[56] Self-administered desensitization obviously reduces the amount of time therapists need to spend with clients. In some instances, such procedures can be as effective as therapist-directed treatment.[57] However, self-administered desensitization is used infrequently because it has limitations, especially for clients who are extremely anxious or who present particular problems for treatment (such as difficulty in relaxing).[58] A therapist can modify standard procedures to handle unexpected problems that arise (as in Case 9-3, in which the therapist introduced humorous scenes) and can provide support and encouragement.[59]

EFFECTIVENESS OF SYSTEMATIC DESENSITIZATION

There is no doubt that systematic desensitization is an effective procedure for treating a wide variety of anxiety-related problems. The findings of hundreds of studies assessing the effectiveness of systematic desensitization over the past 40 years are overwhelmingly positive.[60] As early as 1969, a review of the controlled outcome studies of systematic desensitization concluded that, "for the first time in the history of psychological treatments, a specific treatment . . . reliably produced measurable benefits for clients across a broad range of distressing problems in which anxiety was of fundamental importance."[61] Seven years and many studies later, another comprehensive review concluded: "Systematic desensitization is demonstrably more effective than both no treatment and every psychotherapy variant with which it has so far been compared."[62]

The primary source of evidence for the effectiveness of systematic desensitization comes from experiments. Recent studies have examined the durability of treatment effects, which appears to be good. For example, one study found that 70% of clients with dental phobias still were maintaining regular dental checkups between 1 and 4 years after being treated by systematic desensitization.[63] Case 9-4 presents a classic analogue experiment by Gordon Paul illustrating the type of study that has provided evidence for the efficacy of systematic desensitization.

Case 9-4

EFFECTIVENESS OF SYSTEMATIC DESENSITIZATION IN TREATING PUBLIC SPEAKING ANXIETY: A CLASSIC EXPERIMENTAL TEST[64]

Students often enroll in public speaking classes because they are anxious about talking in front of groups. The participants in this experiment were volunteers from one such class. They were first given a comprehensive pretreatment assessment consisting of self-report, physiological, and overt behavioral measures of public speaking anxiety. The self-report measures asked the students to rate the amount of anxiety they experienced in various situations related to public speaking. The physiological measures were pulse rate and palmar sweat. As the participants gave 4-minute impromptu speeches, trained observers in the audience rated their overt indications of anxiety on a checklist (see Figure 9-6). The observers rated whether each of 20 overt indications of speech anxiety was present or absent in each 30-second interval.

Figure 9-6 Checklist observers used to rate participants' overt indications of anxiety while giving a speech (Case 9-4)

SOURCE: Adapted from Paul, 1966, p. 109.

TIMED BEHAVIORAL CHECKLIST FOR PERFORMANCE ANXIETY

Rater _____ Name _____

Date _____ Speech No. _____ I.D. _____

Behavior observed	1	2	3	4	5	6	7	8	Sum
1. Paces									
2. Sways									
3. Shuffles feet									
4. Knees tremble									
5. Extraneous arm and hand movement (swings, scratches, toys, etc.)									
6. Arms rigid									
7. Hands restrained (in pockets, behind back, clasped)									
8. Hand tremors									
9. No eye contact									
10. Face muscles tense (drawn, tics, grimaces)									
11. Face "deadpan"									
12. Face pale									
13. Face flushed (blushes)									
14. Moistens lips									
15. Swallows									
16. Clears throat									
17. Breathes heavily									
18. Perspires (face, hands, armpits)									
19. Voice quivers									
20. Speech blocks or stammers									

Comments: Grand total [ ]

Figure 9-7 Percentage of participants showing a decrease in anxiety immediately after treatment (Case 9-4)
SOURCE: Data from Paul, 1966.

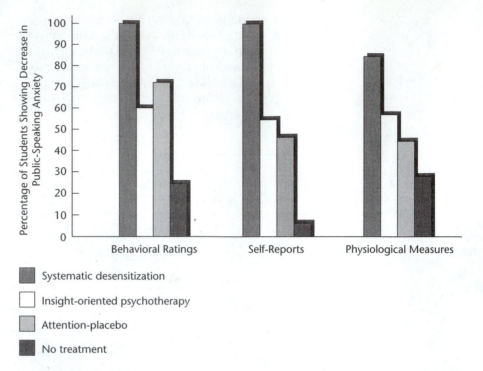

Systematic desensitization

Insight-oriented psychotherapy

Attention-placebo

No treatment

The participants were randomly assigned to one of four conditions: standard systematic desensitization, insight-oriented psychotherapy, attention-placebo, or no treatment. Insight-oriented psychotherapy involved a dialogue between therapist and participant which emphasized gaining self-understanding about the origins of the participant's speech anxiety. Participants in the attention-placebo control condition were given what they thought was a fast-acting tranquilizer; actually it was a capsule containing sodium bicarbonate, which is an inactive substance. This group was included to control for the possible beneficial effects of interacting with the therapist and participants' positive expectations of improvement. Treatment and attention-placebo participants attended five sessions over a six-week period. Participants in the no-treatment control condition just had their public-speaking anxiety assessed at the same time as the participants in the other conditions. The purpose of the no-treatment control condition was to determine whether changes would take place without any treatment or therapist contact.

After the last session, the self-report, physiological, and behavioral measures were administered again. The results, shown in Figure 9-7, revealed a clear superiority of systematic desensitization over insight-oriented therapy and the two control conditions. Follow-up assessments based on the participants' self-reports six weeks[65] and two years[66] after therapy indicated the same pattern of results.

This classic experiment has been criticized on two counts. One criticism is that five sessions is hardly enough time for insight-oriented therapy to be effective. An adequate therapist-client relationship, which is critical in insight-oriented therapy, cannot be built in five sessions.[67] Still, the greater efficiency of systematic desensitization may be sufficient grounds for concluding that it is a superior treatment for specific anxieties.

The other criticism of Paul's research concerned symptom substitution, a general criticism of behavior therapy made by psychoanalysts in the 1950s and 1960s.[68] *Symptom substitution* refers to the notion that treating only behaviors, and not their "underlying causes," will result in another maladaptive behavior (symptom) replacing (substituting for) the treated behavior. A hypothetical example would be a client's developing a fear of undressing in locker rooms after successfully being desensitized to a fear of public speaking. A psychoanalyst might argue that this occurred because the underlying cause of the public speaking, such as an unconscious conflict about exposing oneself in public places, was not treated. Although the client no longer was afraid of speaking in public, an underlying unconscious conflict still existed, and it manifested itself in another symptom, fear of undressing in locker rooms.

The symptom substitution criticism of behavior therapy is fallacious for two reasons. First, it is based on the *mistaken* premise that behavior therapy treats symptoms (problem behaviors).[69] As you know, behavior therapy directly changes the maintaining conditions—which are the *causes*—of problem behaviors (symptoms).

Second, and most importantly, there is no empirical support for symptom substitution's occurring in behavior therapy.[70]* For example, Case 9-4 was carried out in the mid-1960s when the symptom substitution criticism was prevalent. Accordingly, evidence for symptom substitution was specifically sought. In fact, none of the participants treated developed any maladaptive substitute behaviors.

In Vivo Exposure Therapy

In vivo exposure therapy (or **in vivo exposure,** for short) essentially is systematic desensitization in which the client is exposed to the actual feared event (rather than imagining it). The exposure is brief and graduated, and the client has the option of terminating the exposure if it becomes too uncomfortable. For example, a six-year old girl who was afraid to remain at school without her mother very gradually increased the amount of time she spent in class alone until she could remain in the classroom without her mother for the entire school day.[71]

Muscle relaxation often is used to compete with anxiety, although complete deep muscle relaxation is not possible because the client is using a variety of muscles during the in vivo exposure.[72] However, it is possible for clients to relax all muscles that are not essential to the behaviors being performed and to tense the required muscles only as much as is needed. This procedure is known as **differential relaxation**.[73] For example, standing

---

* Symptom substitution is different than negative side effects, which may pose potential problems for all types of therapy (Kazdin & Wilson, 1978).

requires some tension in the neck, back, and leg muscles, but facial, arm, chest, and abdominal muscles do not have to be tensed. (Participation Exercise 14-1, which begins on page 382, will teach you differential relaxation to reduce muscle tension associated with your everyday activities.) Other competing responses used for in vivo exposure therapy include pleasant images, humor, and sexual arousal. Sometimes simply the *therapist's presence*—which is reassuring and calming to the client—is effective. The basic procedures of in vivo exposure using differential relaxation are illustrated in Case 9-5.

Case 9-5

TREATMENT OF FEAR OF LEAVING HOSPITAL GROUNDS BY IN VIVO EXPOSURE[74]

A 36-year-old man, who had been hospitalized for 7 years for a serious psychiatric disorder, was intensely afraid of venturing outside the hospital. Spending increasing amounts of time outside the hospital was established as an acceleration target behavior.

> After several relaxation sessions in the office, the relaxation sessions were continued while the patient was seated in an automobile. Each week the automobile was driven by the therapist closer to the gate of the hospital grounds, and then farther and farther away from the hospital, until a five-mile drive took place during the third session in the car. During each trip outside the hospital, the patient was let out of the car for increasing lengths of time, going from one minute to a half-hour in three weeks. Concomitant with therapy sessions outside the hospital grounds, the patient was encouraged to go on trips with other patients. By the seventh week, the patient had been to a country fair in the neighboring state, an art show across the river, a local fireman's carnival, and a fishing trip. The art show was the only trip on which the therapist accompanied the patient, and even then, he was alone for half the two-hour show. After the seventh session it was no longer necessary to encourage the patient to go out on day passes, since he signed up for passes and outside activities on his own. At the end of seven in vivo [exposure] . . . sessions, the patient felt comfortable enough to venture outside the hospital without the support of the therapist [or other patients].

The principle of graduated exposure is seen clearly in this case. Exposure was graduated both *spatially,* by increasing the distance the patient ventured from the hospital, and *temporally,* by increasing the time he spent outside the car.

Self-Managed In Vivo Exposure

Case 9-5 illustrates two forms of in vivo exposure. Initially, the therapist was present to guide the client through the exposure, which is **therapist-**

assisted exposure.[75] Later, the client engaged in the exposure procedures on his own, following the therapist's directions, which is **self-managed exposure**.[76] Clients typically take notes on their self-managed exposure to help the therapist monitor their progress (see Figure 9-8). Because self-managed exposure involves structured tasks that clients directly control, some clients find the self-managed exposure less threatening than therapist-assisted exposure.

Self-managed in vivo exposure was part of a treatment package used with a 28-year-old teacher suffering from *body dysmorphic disorder*[77] (preoccupation with a perceived physical defect that is not noticeable to others[78]). The teacher was convinced that she had a "bad" complexion. Her repeated checking of her face in the mirror for blemishes significantly interfered with her work and home life. Self-managed in vivo exposure involved the client's gradually applying less makeup and getting physically closer to people at work when she talked to them. After the 11th session, the therapist instructed her to wear no makeup at all and to expose herself to a broader range of people by going to stores and restaurants. By the end of the treatment, she was spending no time checking for physical defects (in contrast to 4 hours a day prior to treatment).

Self-managed exposure clearly is more efficient than therapist-assisted exposure. Additionally, clients may be less likely to drop out of therapy when they fully control their own exposure.[79] Self-managed treatment at home can be implemented through the use of treatment manuals written for clients and with the assistance of family members.[80] The therapist may make occasional home visits to ensure that the client is carrying out the exposure correctly.[81] It even is possible to initiate self-managed in vivo exposure

Figure 9-8 Example of a form clients complete during self-managed exposure assignments

Client's name: _____ Date: _____
Therapist's name:_____
Describe your location and task:_____
_____
_____
Exact starting time: _____
Heart rate before exposure (2 x 30 sec. sample):_____
Respiration rate before exposure (2 x 30 sec. sample):_____
SUDs rating before the exposure:_____
Exposure YES/NO
Exposure duration:_____
Exact ending time:_____
Describe fear behaviors observed during the task:_____
_____
_____
Describe reasons for terminating the exposure:_____
_____
_____

completely through telephone calls.[82] Telephone-administered therapy has obvious advantages for clients who are housebound or who live far from available therapists. Case 9-6 is an unusual example of self-managed in vivo exposure that illustrates the flexibility of the procedure.

Self-Managed In Vivo Exposure for Fear of Dogs[83]

Case 9-6   A man sought the help of a behavior therapist to deal with his overwhelming fear of dogs. Between the first and second therapy sessions, a fortuitous incident occurred. A friend told the client that his dog had just had puppies, and he jokingly asked the client if he wanted one of them. After consulting with his therapist, the client decided to take one of the puppies because he believed he could tolerate a *puppy* in his home.

The situation contained all the essential ingredients for self-managed in vivo exposure. The client would be exposed to a dog that gradually became larger. Moreover, his exposure to the dog would be in the context of happy interactions with his children and the accompanying pleasure would serve as a competing response to his anxiety about dogs. After six months of raising the puppy, the client reported no more fear of dogs.

In Case 9-6, the client initiated in vivo exposure with a therapist's advice. Sometimes, people successfully deal with their fears completely on their own by engaging in an *informal* self-managed in vivo exposure process. Case 9-7 is an example.

Self-Initiated and Self-Managed In Vivo Exposure for Separation Anxiety in a Five-Year-Old Girl[84]

Case 9-7   During the first week of school, five-year-old Hadar was having difficulty leaving the parent who dropped her off at school. Hadar insisted that the parent come into the room and remain with her. Each time the parent prepared to leave, Hadar clung to the parent and cried. Eventually, the teacher, Mrs. Mort, had to help physically separate Hadar from her parent and urge the parent to exit the room quickly.

Mrs. Mort suggested to Hadar's parents that they attempt to leave her just inside the classroom door, where the children signed in each morning. On Monday of the second week of classes, Hadar's father walked Hadar into the classroom and told her that he was going to leave after she signed in. Hadar asked her father to stay, but he said he had to go to work and would see her after school. Hadar protested, but not as much as in the previous week. This procedure was carried out for the next two days.

A week and a half after school had begun, Hadar spontaneously "took charge" of the in vivo exposure. On Thursday of the second week, Hadar told her father, "You don't have to come into the room with me. You can just walk me to the door." Several days later, Hadar told her mother that she could leave her just inside the entrance to the school, which was a short distance from her classroom. After another few days, Hadar indicated that she would say goodbye right before entering the school. Finally, in the middle of the third week of school, Hadar said that it was "okay" to drop her off at the end of the walk that led to the front door of the school, which is the point where most parents left their children. Thereafter, Hadar was able to leave her parent each morning with little or no visible signs of distress. Four years later, the problem had not recurred.

After some initial interventions made by her teacher and parents, Hadar apparently assumed responsibility for overcoming her fear of leaving her parents at school each morning. She progressed through her spontaneously created anxiety hierarchy at a pace that was comfortable for her. Hadar also may have benefited from other children's modeling being dropped off for school without their parents' remaining with them. The case is noteworthy because the self-initiated and self-managed therapy was done by a five-year-old child.

IN VIVO EXPOSURE IN THE TREATMENT OF SEXUAL DYSFUNCTIONS

Self-managed in vivo exposure is especially useful when the therapist's presence is inappropriate, such as in the treatment of sexual dysfunctions.[85] *Sexual dysfunctions* include diminished sexual desire, problems achieving orgasm, and pain during intercourse. Couples, rather than individuals, are treated because sexual dysfunctions are viewed in the context of a sexual relationship and not as a problem of one of the partners.[86]

Anxiety often is a primary maintaining condition of sexual dysfunctions. Thus, at home, the couple is instructed to engage in physical intimacies gradually. Increasingly more anxiety-producing sexual behaviors form an anxiety hierarchy. For example, at the bottom of the hierarchy might be holding hands, and at the top might be sexual intercourse. The physical contact produces sexual arousal (often mild at first), which competes with the anxiety. The couple proceeds up the hierarchy, stopping whenever anxiety begins and sexual arousal starts to diminish. Only when both partners feel comfortable engaging in a particular sexual behavior is the next step in the hierarchy attempted. Sexual performance, including intercourse and orgasm, is not a goal during in vivo exposure. Couples are instructed to follow the rule that pleasurable physical contact alone is the goal of each in vivo exposure session. In such a *nondemand situation*, couples learn to enjoy sexual activity by gradually coming to feel comfortable and sexually aroused.

In Vivo Exposure Therapy in Perspective

In vivo exposure, like systematic desensitization, is a versatile procedure that can be applied to many different anxiety-related disorders.[87] For example, in vivo exposure is at least as effective as medication in treating clients with panic attacks.*[88] It is superior to other psychological interventions and behavior therapies (including educational information-based approaches, social support, cognitive restructuring, and relaxation training) in reducing anxiety associated with social phobias.†[89]

In vivo exposure can reduce both overt behavioral and cognitive components of anxiety. For example, clients treated by in vivo exposure therapy for public speaking anxiety showed fewer overt behavioral components of anxiety (such as pacing while talking) and reported fewer cognitive components of anxiety (such as worrying about others' negative evaluations of them).[90]

In vivo exposure has three advantages over systematic desensitization. First, in some instances, in vivo exposure is more effective than systematic desensitization; because the therapy takes place directly in the anxiety-evoking situation, the need to generalize from the imagined to the actual situation is eliminated. Second, in vivo exposure can be effective for clients who have difficulty imagining scenes, which occasionally occurs with adults and often with young children.[91] Third, avoidance behaviors can be monitored directly with in vivo exposure; this is not possible with systematic desensitization, in which the client only imagines being in the threatening situation.[92]

In vivo exposure has three limitations. First, because in vivo exposure involves going to the actual environment where the client's anxiety occurs, considerable therapist time is required. For example, two therapists were required to implement the in vivo exposure with Paul in Case 4-1. Self-managed in vivo exposure is one way to deal with the problem of inordinate demands on therapist time. A second limitation is that in vivo exposure is not feasible with certain anxiety-evoking events, such as earthquakes or lightning. Third, some clients cannot tolerate being in the actual threatening situation, even when exposure is graduated and the client is engaging in a competing response. Imaginal exposure in systematic desensitization may be all that the client can tolerate, at least initially.

Exposure Through Virtual Reality

Reaping the advantages of in vivo exposure without its disadvantages may seem like having one's cake and eating it too. However, this may be possible by exposing clients to anxiety-producing stimuli through computer-generated virtual reality technology.[93] Clients wear a head-mounted display that provides a computer-generated view of a virtual reality environment (see Photo 9-2).[94] Electromagnetic sensors placed on the head and arm monitor the client's movements so that the client is able to "interact" with objects in

---

* *Panic attacks* are sudden episodic periods of intense fear that are accompanied by physical symptoms—such as difficulty breathing, heart palpitations, and dizziness—and thoughts of losing control or dying.
† A *social phobia* refers to marked and persistent fear of social or performance situations that involve possible scrutiny, criticism, or embarrassment.

Photo 9-2 Client with a fear of heights undergoing exposure therapy using virtual reality technology.

the virtual environment. As is implied by the term *virtual reality*, what the client views is about as real as if the client were in the actual situation.[95] When the procedures were used to treat fear of heights, one of the virtual reality scenes was an open elevator door with only space below. Not even the therapists, who were exposed to this virtual reality scene, were willing to "walk off the elevator into midair" without being prompted to do so and being reassured that it was perfectly safe.[96]

In the only test of the effectiveness of virtual reality exposure to date, clients with a fear of heights were exposed to visual imagery that conveyed the sensation of being in situations of gradually increasing heights—for example, standing on an outdoor balcony that was on the ground, on the 2nd floor, on the 10th floor, and finally on the 20th floor.[97] Clients were exposed to the feared stimuli at their own pace. The treatment, conducted in 7 weekly 35- to 45-minute sessions, resulted in significant reductions in fear of heights, compared with clients in a wait-list control group.

At present, virtual reality exposure therapy is just barely a reality, but its potential benefits are exciting to consider. These include the ability to expose clients to anxiety-evoking situations that they could not be exposed to in vivo (such as earthquakes) and the savings in time compared with in vivo exposure.

SUMMARY

1. Exposure therapies are used to treat anxiety, fear, and other intense negative emotional responses by exposing clients to the events that create negative emotions.

2. There are two models of exposure therapy. With brief/graduated exposure, the client is gradually exposed to increasingly threatening events for a short period. With prolonged/intense exposure, the client is exposed all at once to highly threatening events for a lengthy period. In both models, the client can be exposed to the threatening events imaginally or in vivo.

3. In systematic desensitization, the prototype of brief/graduated exposure, the client is exposed imaginally to successively more anxiety-arousing situations while engaging in a response that competes with anxiety.

4. Systematic desensitization involves three steps. First, the client learns a response that competes with anxiety, most often muscle relaxation. Second, the client and therapist construct an anxiety hierarchy, which is a list of events ranked in terms of increasing levels of anxiety they elicit. Clients use the Subjective Units of Discomfort (SUDs) scale to rate the level of discomfort they experience. Third, the client visualizes the anxiety-evoking events in the hierarchy, beginning at the low end, while performing the competing response. If the client experiences anxiety while visualizing a scene, the client stops visualizing it and relaxes.

5. The essential component of systematic desensitization is repeated exposure to anxiety-evoking situations without experiencing any negative consequences. The facilitative components are gradual exposure and a competing response.

6. In group desensitization, a number of clients simultaneously undergo the procedures, visualizing scenes from either a group hierarchy or individual hierarchies.

7. In coping desensitization, clients become aware of the specific bodily sensations associated with their anxiety. Then they use the sensations as cues to relax, first while visualizing anxiety-evoking scenes and later in the actual anxiety-evoking situations.

8. Systematic desensitization and in vivo exposure can be explained in terms of learning (counterconditioning and extinction), physiological processes (reciprocal inhibition), cognitive variables, and nonspecific factors. The learning explanations are predicated on anxiety being developed and maintained through classical conditioning.

9. Systematic desensitization is an effective and efficient treatment for anxiety-related disorders. When problem behaviors are maintained by both anxiety and skills deficits, skills training must be added to systematic desensitization.

10. With in vivo exposure therapy, clients are exposed to the actual feared events. The competing response is usually differential relaxation, which involves clients' relaxing all nonessential muscles. The exposure is brief and graduated, and clients may terminate the exposure if they experience anxiety. In vivo exposure can be therapist-assisted or self-managed. Self-managed in vivo exposure is useful especially when it is impractical or inappropriate for the therapist to be present.

11. A major component of therapy for sexual dysfunctions involves self-managed in vivo exposure. The couple gradually engages in increasingly more anxiety-producing sexual behaviors.

12. In vivo exposure is a versatile procedure that sometimes is superior to systematic desensitization. Its limitations include the extensive amount of therapist time required; its not being applicable to some anxiety-evoking events; and the inability of some clients to tolerate being in the actual threatening situation.

13. Exposing clients to anxiety-producing stimuli through computer-generated virtual reality technology is a promising new method of treatment.

REFERENCE NOTES

1. Landers, 1990.
2. Wilson, O'Leary, & Nathan, 1992.
3. Wolpe, 1958.
4. Jacobson, 1929.
5. Compare with Lucic, Steffen, Harrigan, & Stuebing, 1991.
6. McGlynn, Moore, Rose, & Lazarte, 1995.
7. Öst, Westling, & Hellström, 1993.
8. For example, Jorgensen & Carey, 1994; Spector, Carey, Jorgensen, Meisler, & Carnrike, 1993.
9. For example, Geer, 1965; Spiegler & Liebert, 1970; Wolpe & Lang, 1964.
10. McCathie & Spence, 1991; Ramirez & Kratochwill, 1990; Ollendick, 1983; Scherer & Nakamura, 1968.
11. Wolpe & Lazarus, 1966; see also Spiegler & Agigian, 1977, p. 100.
12. Wolpe & Lazarus, 1966, quotation from p. 81.
13. Lang, 1969.
14. For example, Krapfl, 1967; Richardson & Suinn, 1973.
15. For example, Goldfried & Davison, 1994; Walker, Hedberg, Clement, & Wright, 1981.
16. For example, Miller & Nawas, 1970; Nawas, Welsch, & Fishman, 1970.
17. Bandura, 1969; Lang, 1969.
18. Morrow, 1986.
19. Lazarus & Abramovitz, 1962.
20. Nevo & Shapira, 1988.
21. Cousins, 1979, 1989.
22. Seligson & Peterson, 1992.
23. Ventis, 1973.
24. For example, Rimm, DeGroot, Boord, Heiman, & Dillow, 1971.
25. For example, Moore, 1965.
26. For example, Steinmark & Borkovec, 1974.
27. Saunders, 1976.
28. For example, Shorkey & Himle, 1974.
29. For example, Hedberg & Campbell, 1974.
30. For example, Meyer, 1975.
31. For example, Walton & Mather, 1963.
32. For example, Cotharin & Mikulas, 1975.
33. Smith, 1973, pp. 577-578.
34. For example, Anton, 1976; Lazarus, 1961; Paul & Shannon, 1966; Taylor, 1971.
35. For example, Spiegler, Cooley, Marshall, Prince, Puckett, & Skenazy, 1976.
36. Goldfried, 1971.
37. Borkovec & Costello, 1993; Borkovec & Mathews, 1988; Borkovec & Whisman, 1996.
38. For example, Borkovec & Costello, 1993; Borkovec & Whisman, 1996.
39. Spiegler, Cooley, Marshall, Prince, Puckett, & Skenazy, 1976.
40. Borkovec & Mathews, 1988.
41. Guevremont & Spiegler, 1990.
42. Fisher & Thompson, 1994.
43. For example, Silverman & Rabian, 1994.
44. Compare with Kirkland & Hollandsworth, 1980.
45. Wolpe, 1958.
46. Kazdin & Wilcoxon, 1976.
47. For example, Borkovec & Whisman, 1996.
48. Beck, 1976.
49. Lick, 1975; Valins & Ray, 1967
50. Bandura, 1977a, 1978, 1984.
51. Compare with Strupp, 1995.
52. Kazdin & Wilcoxon, 1976.
53. Kazdin & Wilcoxon, 1976.
54. For example, Donner & Guerney, 1969; Evans & Kellam, 1973; Lang, Melamed, & Hart, 1970.
55. For example, Rosen, Glasgow, & Barrera, 1976.
56. For example, Chandler, Burck, & Sampson, 1986.
57. For example, Evans & Kellam, 1973; Rosen, Glasgow, & Barrera, 1976.
58. For example, Bernstein & Borkovec, 1973; Carlson & Bernstein, 1995; Marquis, Morgan, & Piaget, 1971.
59. For example, Goldfried & Davison, 1994; Walker, Hedberg, Clement, & Wright, 1981.

60. For example, Kazdin & Wilcoxon, 1976; Kazdin & Wilson, 1978; Masters, Burish, Hollon, & Rimm, 1987.
61. Paul, 1969b, p. 159.
62. Leitenberg, 1976, p. 131.
63. Liddell, DiFazio, Blackwood, & Ackerman, 1994.
64. Paul, 1966.
65. Paul, 1966.
66. Paul, 1967.
67. Strupp, 1966.
68. Cahoon, 1968; Ullmann & Krasner, 1965.
69. For example, Sahakian & Charlesworth, 1994.
70. For example, Bandura, 1969; Kazdin & Wilson, 1978; Sloane, Staples, Cristol, Yorkston, & Whipple, 1975.
71. Hagopian & Slifer, 1993.
72. For example, McCarthy & Craig, 1995; McGlynn, Moore, Rose, & Lazarte, 1995.
73. Goldfried & Davison, 1994.
74. Weidner, 1970; quotation from p. 80.
75. Williams, Dooseman, & Kleifield, 1984.
76. For example, Marks, 1978.
77. Neziroglu & Yaryura-Tobias, 1993.
78. Thompson, 1992.
79. For example, Barlow, O'Brien, & Last, 1984; Jannoun, Munby, Catalan, & Gelder, 1980.
80. Barlow, O'Brien, & Last, 1984; Mathews, Teasdale, Munby, Johnston, & Shaw, 1977; Munby & Johnston, 1980.
81. For example, Mathews, Gelder, & Johnston, 1981; Mathews, Teasdale, Munby, Johnston, & Shaw, 1977.
82. McNamee, O'Sullivan, Lelliott, & Marks, 1989; Swinson, Fergus, Cox, & Wickwire, 1995.
83. Goldfried & Davison, 1994.
84. From the author's (MDS) clinical files.
85. Masters & Johnson, 1970.
86. For example, Kaplan, 1974, 1975; Masters & Johnson, 1970; Wolpe & Lazarus, 1966.
87. For example, Chambless, 1985; Hill, 1989; McGlynn & Cornell, 1985; Marks, 1978, 1987; Menzies & Clarke, 1993.
88. Clum, Clum, & Surls, 1993.
89. Donohue, Van Hasselt, & Hersen, 1994.
90. Newman, Hofmann, Trabert, Roth, & Taylor, 1994.
91. Hill, 1989; Morris & Kratochwill, 1983; Ollendick & Cerny, 1981.
92. Chambless, 1985.
93. Rothbaum, Hodges, Kooper, Opdyke, Williford, & North, 1995a, 1995b.
94. Hodges, Rothbaum, Kooper, Opdyke, Meyer, De Graff, & Williford, 1994.
95. Hodges, Rothbaum, Kooper, Opdyke, Meyer, De Graff, & Williford, 1994; Kalawsky, 1993.
96. Rothbaum, Hodges, Kooper, Opdyke, Williford, & North, 1995b.
97. Rothbaum, Hodges, Kooper, Opdyke, Williford, & North, 1995b.

Chapter 10

Prolonged/Intense Exposure Therapy: Flooding and Implosive Therapy

You have just read about the brief/graduated model of exposure in Chapter 9. Now we turn to the other model of exposure therapy, prolonged/intense exposure, which includes in vivo flooding, imaginal flooding, and implosive therapy. These therapies share with systematic desensitization and in vivo exposure therapy the fundamental process of reducing anxiety by confronting the client with the source of the anxiety. Brief/graduated exposure minimizes clients' anxiety during treatment by presenting clients with small doses of anxiety-evoking stimuli that gradually become more intense. In contrast, prolonged/intense exposure *maximizes* clients' anxiety with large doses of anxiety-evoking stimuli that, from the outset, are intense. Prolonged/intense exposure therapies reduce anxiety by initially increasing it. Accordingly, they are sometimes called **anxiety-induction therapies**. In a sense, these therapies fight anxiety with anxiety.

FLOODING

Flooding refers to in vivo or imaginal exposure to highly anxiety-evoking stimuli for a prolonged period of time (sometimes for more than an hour).[1] Although the client experiences anxiety during exposure, the feared negative consequences do not actually occur—a characteristic of all exposure therapies.

Basic Procedures

Flooding consists of two basic procedures. First, the client is exposed to stimuli that elicit high levels of anxiety.[2] Second, the client remains exposed to the threatening stimuli for a prolonged period without engaging in any anxiety-reducing behaviors. The behaviors that highly anxious clients use to reduce their anxiety often are maladaptive. Consider *bulimia,* a disorder in which the person first binges (consumes large quantities of food) and then purges the food, usually by vomiting. The purging reduces the client's anxiety about binge eating and gaining weight, but it also is unhealthy. In flooding, clients are prevented from engaging in their typical maladaptive anxiety-reducing responses, a procedure known as **response prevention.** (Flooding itself sometimes is referred to as *response prevention.*) In treating bulimia with flooding, the client is instructed to binge eat (exposure) but is not allowed to vomit (response prevention).[3]

Although successful flooding usually requires prolonged exposure, occasionally very brief exposure that is highly intense and includes response prevention can be effective. This possibility is illustrated by Case 10-1, an example of how a phobic reaction was eliminated by a real-life experience that directly parallels flooding.

Professor Gallagher and his controversial technique of simultaneously confronting the fear of heights, snakes and the dark.
THE FAR SIDE copyright 1986 UNIVERSAL PRESS SYNDICATE.
Reprinted with permission. All rights reserved.

DEBUGGING A COCKROACH PHOBIA BY NATURALISTIC FLOODING[4]

Case 10-1   When a world-famous entomologist (insect specialist), B. G., was a graduate student, he was given a lab assignment to draw blood from a cockroach. This seemingly innocuous task for someone who was about to embark on a career studying insects created tremendous anxiety for B. G. Although he had been fascinated with insects from an early age, he detested cockroaches. His aversion to cockroaches began when he first encountered them in his home as a child. Although his repulsion to and avoidance of cockroaches had persisted into adulthood, it had not generalized to other insects.

To complete his lab assignment, B. G. had to go with other students from his class to an underground passageway and secure a specimen from the thousands of cockroaches that could be found there. He went to the passageway feeling intensely anxious. As his classmates nonchalantly picked up cockroaches and returned to the lab, B. G. stood there frozen, not knowing what he would do. At that moment, B. G. realized that if he could not complete this lab assignment, he would have to drop out of his graduate

program. Although he was terrified, he reached out and grabbed a cockroach. Almost immediately his anxiety began to diminish. By the time he reached the lab holding his cockroach, the anxiety was completely gone. Fifty years later, B. G. has remained free of his intense aversion to cockroaches.

In Vivo Flooding

In vivo flooding involves prolonged/intense exposure to the *actual* anxiety-producing stimuli. Case 10-2 illustrates the basic procedures of in vivo flooding, including the essential component: *exposure to a highly aversive situation long enough for the client's discomfort to peak and then start to decline.*[5] In the case description, note that before the therapy began, the therapist explained in vivo flooding, which included telling the client that the treatment would cause some discomfort.

FEAR OF RIDING ON ESCALATORS TREATED BY IN VIVO FLOODING[6]

Case 10-2

The patient was a 24-year-old female student with an intense fear and aversion of escalators. She had developed this phobia about 7 years previously. She had ascended an escalator with some of her immediate family with relative ease, but had expressed fear of descending because of the apparent height. The relatives had jokingly forced her on to the escalator, and ever since she had experienced an aversion toward escalators, always taking the stairs or the elevator. . . . On one occasion she had unexpectedly come upon an escalator while shopping, and had become so overwhelmed with anxiety that it was only with great difficulty that she had prevented herself from vomiting. Whenever she was in the company of anyone who proposed riding an escalator to another floor, she would experience a quickening of the pulse and would bluntly refuse. Before the therapeutic session, she had made some unsuccessful attempts to overcome the fear by attempting, in the company of friends, to get on to an escalator. On those occasions when she could bring herself to stand at the foot of the escalator, she would not step on [because she feared] . . . that by holding on to the hand rail she would be pulled downward and so miss her step.

At the single session during which the history of the disorder was obtained, the in vivo flooding procedure was explained to the patient. She was told that the technique had been successfully employed in the treatment of numerous phobias and was almost certain to work in her case. She was also informed that she would experience some emotional distress but was assured that [the therapist] would be with her throughout the experience to ensure no resulting adverse effects. [The therapist] then arranged to meet her at a large department store with four levels of escalators.

Initially, the patient manifested an intense anxiety reaction when requested to approach the escalator, and it was only through much coaxing, reassurance, and [mild] physical [prompting] from [the therapist] that she finally stepped on to it. She then threatened to vomit and seemed at the verge of tears, all the time clinging tightly to [the therapist's] shirt. Getting on to the second flight of the escalator was much easier, but she still manifested the same signs of anxiety. After 27 minutes of riding up and down the escalator, she was approaching it with increasing readiness and reported a dramatic decrease in anxiety. She was then instructed to ride the escalator alone, and did so with relative ease. When she felt that there was no need for further treatment the session was terminated, after 29 minutes. Six months later the patient reported that she still experienced no anxiety on escalators except on rare occasions when descending.

The woman in Case 10-2 clearly was motivated to rid herself of her intense fear. Before seeking therapy, she had attempted unsuccessfully to overcome her fear on her own (unlike B. G. in Case 10-1). The woman experienced considerable initial anxiety during the flooding procedure, followed by a rapid decrease in anxiety. Response prevention involved the therapist's using verbal and physical prompts to prevent the woman's typical response to escalators—namely, avoiding them. Although flooding can be a very efficient treatment involving one or two sessions of intense exposure, as in Case 10-2, typically more sessions are required.

Case 10-2 described the development and maintenance of the patient's fear of riding on escalators. Her intense fear began with a single, traumatic experience. From that time on, she avoided going on escalators, which reduced her fear and reinforced her avoidance behaviors. This sequence of events is consistent with the two-factor learning theory described in In Theory 10-1.

◆   In Theory 10-1

WHY DOES PROLONGED/ INTENSE EXPOSURE THERAPY WORK?

The predominant theoretical explanation of prolonged/intense exposure therapy[7] is based on a two-factor learning theory of how debilitating anxiety develops and is maintained.[8] First, anxiety develops by classical conditioning (see In Theory 9-1, pages 216-219). An initially neutral event that does not elicit anxiety is associated with a threat; subsequently the previously neutral event causes the person to feel anxious. For instance, a person who previously had no fear of being in an automobile may develop an intense fear of driving in cars after being in an automobile accident.

Second, through operant conditioning, the person learns to engage in an anxiety-reducing response whenever the person is faced with the anxiety-evoking event. Usually this response involves avoiding the anxiety-evoking event. The response continues and is strengthened because it is negatively reinforced— that is, it terminates the unpleasant experience of anxiety. For example, when a person who is afraid of driving in cars refuses an offer of a ride, the person's anxiety declines because the threatening situation is avoided. On the one hand, the avoidance behavior is adaptive because it keeps the individual from feeling anxious. On the other hand, the behavior is maladaptive because the person never learns that driving in a car can be safe; also, in our car-dependent world, such an avoidance response limits one's mobility.

The aim of prolonged/intense exposure therapy is for the client to *experience the threatening situation and concomitant high anxiety without engaging in the maladaptive anxiety-reducing response* (that is, avoidance). When the client experiences the anxiety without the anticipated negative consequences (for example, a car accident), the client learns that the situation is not necessarily threatening, which diminishes the client's anxiety.

What accounts for this learning experience? The simplest theoretical explanation is *extinction* in the classical conditioning model. The association between the threatening situation (for example, riding in a car) and negative consequences (an accident) is broken because the negative consequences do not occur. (See In Theory 9-1, page 218, for more details.)

Other explanations of prolonged/intense exposure involve cognitive factors. Based on their experience during therapeutic exposure, clients may come to view threatening situations differently.[9] For instance, a client may change the belief that being in a car is dangerous to the belief that being in a car is usually safe. Success in coping with the threatening situation during exposure—that is, becoming less anxious and no longer avoiding the threatening situation— heightens clients' beliefs that they are capable of dealing with anxiety-evoking situations.[10] As a result, clients will be more likely to expose themselves to situations in their everyday environments that were previously threatening to them.[11]

The learning and cognitive explanations just described also are applicable to brief/graduated exposure therapy, which reflects the commonalities among exposure therapies (see In Theory 10-2, pages 255-256).

Besides phobic behaviors, in vivo flooding also is used to treat *obsessive-compulsive disorder,* which involves being preoccupied (obsessed) with particular anxiety-evoking events and alleviating the resulting anxiety by performing maladaptive ritualistic behaviors (compulsions).[12] Case 10-3 illustrates how in vivo flooding is applied to obsessive-compulsive behaviors.

Case 10-3
HOME TREATMENT OF OBSESSIVE-COMPULSIVE BEHAVIORS BY IN VIVO FLOODING[13]

A 45-year-old divorced woman suffered from obsessive-compulsive disorder that consisted of washing and cleaning rituals whenever she came in contact with objects that she thought might be even remotely associated with death. For example, holding a newspaper article about someone who had been killed would make her intensely anxious. The disorder first occurred when the woman was 15 years old, at the time of her mother's death.

When the client entered treatment, she was to be remarried in two weeks. She did not feel that she could deal with the marriage in her present condition. She was experiencing panic attacks and heart palpitations related to her fear of contamination almost daily. As time passed, the number of objects she considered potentially contaminated increased.

In vivo flooding was indicated because the client wanted to alleviate her problem within two weeks, and she was highly motivated to deal with her problem. Although most of the treatment took place in her home in the evening, in vivo flooding began in a hospital mortuary. There the client and the therapist became "contaminated" by handling a corpse, which made the client intensely anxious. Later, the therapist and the client completely "contaminated" the client's apartment. The therapist instructed her to refrain from engaging in her typical rituals of washing and cleansing to reduce the anxiety she was experiencing during the flooding. That evening and the next morning, she successfully resisted engaging in her rituals. During daily hour-long therapy sessions, the therapist gave her various "contaminated" objects while encouraging her not to resort to her rituals and praising her for complying. By the third day of flooding, she had not performed the rituals. However, when the client's fiancé brought some groceries from his house to her apartment, the client was unable to touch them, fearing that they were contaminated by association with his deceased wife. She called the therapist, and over the phone, the therapist guided her through a flooding session that consisted of "contaminating" her entire apartment by placing the groceries throughout the apartment.

After 12 days of therapy, the client reported that she had made considerable progress with her problem, and she was married the next day. Although she continued to have periodic episodes of tension over the next 8 months, she no longer felt the urge to engage in her compulsive rituals.

In Case 10-3, the therapist directed each of the in vivo flooding sessions, including one by telephone. The therapist's presence and guidance no doubt make it easier for clients to undergo in vivo flooding. In contrast to self-directed in vivo exposure, which is brief and gradual, self-directed in vivo flooding is especially difficult for clients. Nonetheless, it is occasionally employed successfully, such as in the treatment of social phobias where the therapist's presence in the client's actual social circumstances is impractical.[14]

Case 10-3 provides an example of a relatively severe obsessive-compulsive disorder. The woman's anxiety was intense, as evidenced by her panic attacks. Moreover, her obsession was extensive because virtually any object she touched in the course of the day could potentially be associated with death. Given the level of her anxiety, it is not hard to understand how difficult the prolonged/intense exposure of flooding might have been for the woman. Like most clients who decide to undergo flooding, she was highly motivated to alleviate her problem behaviors.

Medication frequently is prescribed for obsessive-compulsive disorder. However, in vivo flooding appears to be a superior treatment for several reasons. In vivo flooding can be as effective as antidepressant medication (for example, Prozac), which is used to treat obsessive-compulsive disorder, and clients may view it as more effective than medication.[15] The findings of one study, for example, showed that when clients received both medication (Luvox) and flooding, they were less likely to need medication one year after treatment had ended than when clients were treated with medication alone.[16] Interestingly, both a lower relapse rate and a lower drop-out rate have been reported for in vivo flooding in comparison with medication-based treatments.[17]

Recent studies have shown actual changes in brain chemistry for clients with obsessive-compulsive disorder treated with in vivo flooding.[18] Specifically, clients underwent PET (positron emission tomography) scanning before and after 10 weeks of in vivo flooding. Changes in glucose metabolic rates (which are reliable indicators of neural activity) were assessed in the brain regions (caudate nucleus) believed to be involved in obsessive-compulsive disorder. Only clients who showed significant reductions in obsessive-compulsive behaviors following in vivo flooding showed significant changes in glucose metabolic rates. These results are comparable to brain activity changes associated with successful treatment of obsessive-compulsive disorder with medication (such as Prozac).

Imaginal Flooding

Imaginal flooding follows the same basic principles and procedures used with in vivo flooding except that exposure occurs in the client's imagination. One advantage of imaginal exposure is that there are no restrictions on the nature of the anxiety-evoking situations that can be treated. This feature has proved useful in the application of imaginal flooding to help victims of traumatic experiences, such as natural disasters and physical assault. Such people may suffer from *posttraumatic stress disorder,* which is characterized by (1) upsetting recurrent recollections of the event (such as nightmares and flashbacks); (2) avoiding any stimuli associated with the event (for example, refusing to drive in a car after being in a serious automobile accident); and

(3) a variety of distressing symptoms, including anxiety, depression, and an inability to concentrate.

In vivo exposure to the actual traumatic events (such as rape or an earthquake) generally is not appropriate for practical and ethical reasons. Imaginal flooding is well-suited for re-creating the circumstances of the trauma safely—that is, without the actual aversive consequences occurring.[19] Imaginal flooding was first used to treat posttraumatic stress disorders in Vietnam veterans.[20] It now is being applied to other traumas, such as rape[21] and war-related traumas in civilians,[22] as Case 10-4 illustrates.

Case 10-4

TREATMENT OF AN ADOLESCENT'S POSTTRAUMATIC STRESS DISORDER BY IMAGINAL FLOODING[23]

A 14-year-old Lebanese boy was referred for evaluation by his school principal because of academic and behavioral problems. Six months earlier, the client had been abducted in Beirut by the Lebanese militia for 2 days. At the time of the evaluation, the boy was suffering from anxiety related to recollections of his traumatic experience. He also complained about the following: avoiding the area where he had been abducted; having difficulty concentrating and remembering information; and being depressed. The boy had not experienced these problems before he was abducted.

The therapist described the pros and cons of imaginal flooding and systematic desensitization, and the boy and his parents chose flooding. Before therapy began, a number of self-report inventories (of general anxiety and depression) and cognitive measures (of memory and concentration) were administered. The client also was given a 12-step behavioral avoidance test that involved leaving his home, walking to the area of his abduction, entering a store, making a purchase, and walking home by another route. During the behavioral avoidance test, 2 assistants unobtrusively observed the client through a store window and by following the client at a distance. Finally, during flooding, the client reported his level of discomfort using a 10-point SUDs scale.

The client was asked to imagine the 4 different scenes described in Table 10-1. Flooding was applied to each scene in succession—in other

Table 10-1 Scenes used in imaginal flooding for a 14-year-old boy with posttraumatic stress disorder (Case 10-4)
SOURCE: Saigh, 1987, p. 148.

Scene Number	Content
1	Approaching the area where the abduction occurred, being stopped, forced into a car at gunpoint, blindfolded, and driven away
2	Walking into a building while blindfolded, being questioned and accused, and listening to the militia argue over the merits of his execution
3	Being interrogated, responding, receiving repeated blows to the head and body, and experiencing intermittent periods of isolation
4	Learning that he was going to be released and not trusting the militia to keep its word

words, after one scene no longer induced anxiety, the client was exposed to the next scene. The client was asked to imagine the scenes in detail, including the visual, auditory, and physical components of the stimuli associated with the scenes (such as the location of the abduction, voices of the abductors, and discomfort caused by the blindfold). Also, the auditory, physical, and cognitive cues associated with how the client responded were introduced into the scenes (such as verbal replies to his interrogators, physical pain experienced, and thoughts of being executed). Each of the 6 therapy sessions involved 60 minutes of flooding, which was preceded and followed by 10 minutes of relaxation exercises.

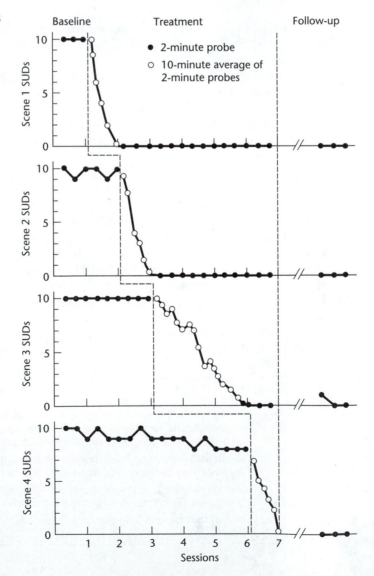

Figure 10-1 SUDs ratings across flooding sessions for a 14-year-old boy with posttraumatic stress disorder (Case 10-4)
SOURCE: Adapted from Saigh, 1987.

There were multiple indications that the flooding was successful in reducing the client's discomfort about his traumatic abduction. Because the four scenes were treated in succession, a multiple baseline was created. For example, during exposure to the first scene, the other three scenes remained untreated. It would be expected that the untreated scenes would continue to produce anxiety until they were treated. To test this hypothesis, the client's reaction to the as yet untreated scenes was assessed periodically. The client was asked to imagine the untreated scenes and indicate his SUDs level for each. As expected, the client continued to rate the anxiety produced by the untreated scenes as high (see Figure 10-1).

As Figure 10-1 shows, scenes 1, 2, and 4 were each successfully treated (reduced to zero SUDs) in the course of a single therapy session, while scene 3 required three sessions for successful treatment. The client's anxiety and depression decreased, and his memory and concentration increased. This improvement was evident immediately after treatment and was maintained at a 4-month follow-up. Immediately after treatment and 4 months later, the boy completed all 12 steps of the behavioral avoidance test, compared with only 4 steps prior to therapy.

Because the area in Beirut where the client had been abducted remained a dangerous locale, he generally continued to avoid going there. However, after the termination of therapy, he did visit the area several times out of necessity. He reported that he experienced no abnormal anxiety on these occasions. Finally, the client expressed satisfaction with the flooding treatment, and he commented that the success of the therapy was adequate compensation for the discomfort he experienced during the flooding sessions.

Case 10-4 illustrates all the basic elements of imaginal flooding. The vividness of the scenes the client imagines is a critical factor in making imaginal flooding effective. Accordingly, the client was asked to use multiple senses to experience both the stimuli surrounding the anxiety-evoking situations and his responses to the situations. Exposure to these cues was both prolonged (60 minutes) and intense (highly anxiety-inducing).

Deep muscle relaxation sometimes is induced before and after a flooding session. This practice may at first seem paradoxical, given that the purpose of flooding is to induce high levels of anxiety. The relaxation is *not* a competing response to anxiety, as in systematic desensitization. Rather, relaxation is used before flooding, to enhance the vividness of the imagery, and after flooding, to allow the client to return quickly to a normal level of arousal (that is, low anxiety). Additionally, relaxation training teaches clients that they have control over their feelings and provides a coping skill they can use outside therapy.[24]

Eye Movement Desensitization and Reprocessing

Eye movement desensitization and reprocessing (EMDR) is a new and controversial exposure-based treatment aimed at alleviating upsetting memories and thoughts about traumatic experiences (such as sexual assaults, accidents, and combat-related traumas).[25] EMDR consists of three basic phases that involve (1) assessment and preparation, (2) imaginal flooding, and (3) cognitive restructuring.

In the *assessment and preparation* phase, clients (1) identify a traumatic image (memory) that results in anxiety or distress; (2) identify the physical sensations associated with the anxiety; (3) assess the level of anxiety using a 0 to 10 SUDs scale; (4) identify a maladaptive belief that is strongly associated with the event (for example, in the case of a rape image, "I should have run away" or "I am totally powerless"); and (5) think of an adaptive belief that would alleviate the distress associated with the traumatic event (for example, "I did the best I could" or "I have options") and rate how personally believable the adaptive belief is on a 1 to 7 scale.

Next, in the *imaginal flooding* phase, the client visualizes the traumatic image while verbalizing the maladaptive belief and concentrating on the physical sensations of the associated anxiety. During this process, the client is told to visually track the therapist's index finger as it is moved rapidly and rhythmically back and forth across the client's line of vision (from left to right, twice per second, 12 to 24 times). Then, the client is told (1) to block out the experience momentarily and take a deep breath and (2) to report what he or she is imagining, thinking, and feeling and rate the experience using SUDs.

Francine Shapiro, the psychologist who developed EMDR, theorizes that the eye movements produce a neurological effect that facilitates the processing of emotionally charged, stress-related material.[26] Shapiro likens EMDR eye movements to the rapid eye movements in sleep, which are associated with intense dreaming.

When the client's SUDs rating has been reduced to 0 or 1, the client is ready for the final phase of treatment that involves *cognitive restructuring* (which we'll describe in detail in Chapter 12). The client again is asked to imagine the traumatic image (which now elicits little, if any, anxiety) but this time while thinking of the adaptive belief. The objective is to associate the traumatic image with the adaptive belief so that the image no longer results in tension and maladaptive thinking. The believability of the adaptive belief is reassessed at this time; it is expected that the client now will find it highly believable.

Following Shapiro's first published account of EMDR in 1989,[27] a slew of reports and testimonials appeared in both the professional and popular literature.[28] Many of them have suggested that EMDR results in rapid (for example, a single session) and dramatic (such as complete elimination of symptoms) improvement in trauma-based anxiety problems.[29] This appeared to be the case, for example, with a four-year-old boy who experienced repeated nightmares, sleep disturbance, bed wetting, and flashbacks after his home was invaded by armed, masked men. The boy's symptoms were completely eliminated in a single session of EMDR, and he was symptom-free at a three-month follow-up.[30]

Unfortunately, these claims are misleading because much of the evidence for the effectiveness of EMDR comes from studies that have serious methodological flaws, including drawing broad conclusions on the efficacy of EMDR on the basis of case study findings; using poorly specified and vaguely defined treatment procedures; using multiple treatments without isolating the specific contribution of EMDR; and conducting outcome studies without appropriate control groups.[31] Moreover, the vast majority of outcome studies attesting to EMDR's efficacy have relied on subjective impressions of the therapist and client as the measure of clients' improvement.[32]

When appropriate control conditions and objective measures of treatment outcomes have been employed, the results have been far less favorable.[33] For example, there is little evidence that the treatment effects generalize and are maintained outside therapy. When EMDR is compared directly with EMDR without the eye movement component or to standard imaginal flooding (also without eye movements), there is no evidence that eye movements are necessary.[34]* In general, controlled outcome studies have failed to support the efficacy of the techniques beyond that of its imaginal flooding component.[35]

Thus, except for the addition of eye movements, EMDR is a treatment package consisting of variants of imaginal flooding and cognitive restructuring. In contrast to the documented efficacy of these two therapy components, at the present time the effectiveness of EMDR has not been demonstrated according to the standards of empirical validation typically required of behavior therapy procedures.[36]

Flooding in Perspective

Flooding is a commonly used behavior therapy for anxiety-related disorders, including phobias,[37] obsessive-compulsive disorder,[38] posttraumatic stress disorder,[39] and agoraphobia[40] (which is the nonspecific fear of being in situations from which escape might be difficult if the person should become highly anxious). Other problems treated by flooding include bulimia,[41] physical complaints,[42] psychogenic urinary retention,[43] and agitated depression.[44]

Outcome studies indicate that flooding, in vivo and imaginal, is an effective treatment. Although some studies have found in vivo flooding to have more striking results,[45] no general statement can be made about the superiority of one variant over the other.[46] In specific cases, one form of presentation may be superior (for example, imaginal flooding when the threatening event cannot be reproduced).[47] In vivo and imaginal flooding occasionally are combined, as for clients with intense social phobias[48] and with severe trauma-based anxiety.[49] The use of imaginal flooding prior to in

---

* It is possible that eye movements might be a *facilitative* component, serving to make the flooding more effective or efficient for some clients (just as gradual exposure and a competing response are facilitative components of systematic desensitization; see Chapter 9). For example, following the therapist's hand movements may help clients focus their attention on the scenes they are imagining. Further, a therapist may be able to detect a client's wandering attention by noting that the client is not tracking hand movements (Agigian, 1996). This and other possible functions of the eye movement component of EMDR will, we hope, be elucidated by future empirical research.

vivo flooding may actually facilitate subsequent in vivo exposure for some clients who are initially unable to tolerate in vivo exposure to feared situations.[50] Studies comparing the efficacy of flooding with that of systematic desensitization also have not found either of these two exposure therapies to be clearly superior.[51]

One major drawback of flooding is the discomfort it produces. In one study, clients were treated for test anxiety with modeling, systematic desensitization, or flooding.[52] Nearly all the clients who had received modeling and about half who had received desensitization indicated satisfaction with their treatments. In contrast, clients who had undergone flooding said they would not recommend the treatment because of the discomfort they had experienced—even though the flooding had led to a significant reduction in their anxiety! Moreover, clients may be more likely to refuse to enter therapy or drop out of therapy that involves flooding, compared with less upsetting exposure therapies.[53]

In an effort to make flooding more comfortable for clients, occasionally prolonged exposure that includes response prevention is presented *gradually*.[54] In other words, the client is exposed to increasingly more anxiety-evoking stimuli (rather than the very highest anxiety-evoking stimuli initially). However, the exposure is for a prolonged period and is terminated only when the client's anxiety begins to diminish.

Some therapists have considered the possibility that flooding might be made less aversive for clients if the exposure occurred in the presence of and assisted by a family member.[55] Three studies have systematically examined this possibility. Two have reported no additional benefits of family-assisted exposure beyond those achieved with therapist-assisted exposure or self-exposure.[56] Moreover, when the relationship between the client and the relative is marked by conflict or overdependence, the relative's assistance may diminish the effectiveness of the therapy.[57]

Implosive Therapy

Implosive therapy is an imaginal prolonged/intense exposure therapy in which the scenes the client visualizes (1) are exaggerated and (2) include hypothesized stimuli related to the fear. As in flooding, response prevention is an integral part of the procedure. Implosive therapy was developed by Thomas Stampfl in the mid-1950s as a treatment for anxiety-related disorders and other negative emotional responses, such as anger.[58] The treatment procedures have remained relatively unchanged since 1967, when Stampfl and Donald Levis first described them and their rationale.[59]

Three features concerning scene presentation in implosive therapy differentiate it from imaginal flooding: (1) the use of hypothesized anxiety-producing cues; (2) the exaggeration of scenes to heighten anxiety; and (3) the elaboration of scenes as they are presented. These differences are highlighted in Table 10-2.

As with imaginal flooding, the actual cues the client reports in the threatening situation are used in the scenes. These cues include where the

Thomas Stampfl

Donald Levis

Table 10-2 Differences between the scenes in implosive therapy and imaginal flooding

	Implosive Therapy	Imaginal Flooding
CUES INCORPORATED IN SCENE	Client-reported cues and therapist-hypothesized cues	Client-reported cues only
DESCRIPTION OF SCENE	Exaggeration of reported scenes	Actual reported scenes (unexaggerated)
CONSTRUCTION OF SCENE	Scenes evolve as they are presented	Scenes constructed before they are presented

client is, who is there, what is going on, and what the client is thinking and feeling. To these actual cues, the therapist adds hypothesized cues.[60] The hypothesized cues are inferred from the therapist's knowledge of the client and the client's problem. With bulimia, for example, the therapist will incorporate cues typically associated with the disorder, such as striving for perfection and fear of failure, rejection, abandonment, and loss of love.[61] Other hypothesized cues are derived from the therapist's *psychoanalytic* interpretations. For instance, the therapist might speculate that a man who was afraid of going to the dentist also would fear castration (tooth extraction is a psychoanalytic symbol for castration), which in turn would suggest an unresolved Oedipal complex. (The appropriateness of using psychoanalytic interpretations in behavior therapy will be addressed later, when we evaluate implosive therapy.)

Because hypothesized cues are speculative, it is critical to determine whether they fit for the client. The cues are assumed to be relevant for the client if the client shows strong emotional responses when the therapist introduces the cues into a scene. Emotional responses are assessed by the therapist's observations of the client's overt indications (such as a flushed face or increased body movements) and reports of being upset.[62]

In addition to the use of hypothesized cues, descriptions of the anxiety-arousing scenes are embellished with exaggerated and sometimes fantasy-like details to heighten the client's anxiety. The exaggerated scenes sometimes help clients realize that their worst fears are absurd and could not actually occur. The following is an example of an exaggerated scene used with a client who was afraid of flying insects.

> Insects are flying around your head. First there is one, then a few, then dozens. They just keep flying around you, more and more of them, until you are surrounded by hundreds of flying insects. They are getting bigger and bigger by the moment. Huge bugs, the size of birds, are flying so close to you that you can feel the vibrations of their wings against your skin. And now they begin to touch your skin, to bite you while moving up from your ankles and legs to your groin. At the same time, more insects are moving up your hands and arms to your face, biting into your skin. And now they are boring into you, from all directions, all over your body. They are flying into your mouth and down your esophagus. You can feel them flying

inside your stomach, bouncing off the walls of your stomach and tearing up your insides.

The third characteristic of implosive therapy that differentiates it from imaginal flooding is the way in which scenes are elaborated and evolve with successive presentations. For each scene, the therapist begins by describing what appear to be the salient cues (actual and hypothesized) that make the client anxious. Then the therapist questions the client about his or her reactions (for instance, "How does that make you feel?" or "What are you thinking?"). Using the client's feedback, the therapist can further refine and embellish the scene. Additionally, the therapist and client may engage in role playing as part of the scene presentation. Case 10-5 illustrates how hypothesized cues are presented and their validity is assessed as well as how role playing is used during scene presentation.

Case 10-5

ANXIETY ATTACKS TREATED BY IMPLOSIVE THERAPY: EXCERPT FROM A THERAPY SESSION[63]

A young college professor reported first experiencing anxiety attacks shortly after she and her husband moved to another city. Although the move furthered her husband's career, it interfered with the client's professional development. Her anxiety appeared to be elicited by the situational cues of being in the presence of other people and the imagined cues of being unable to speak, losing control, and fainting. In addition, the therapist hypothesized that the client was afraid of unexpressed anger toward her husband. To test this hypothesis, the therapist presented a relevant scene for the client to imagine and assessed her reaction to it.

THERAPIST: . . . See yourself getting up in the morning. Your husband has gone to work. Another day faces you sitting around the apartment doing nothing but wasting time. You really feel bored, unproductive. What is going through your mind?

CLIENT: I need to find a job. I have to do something with my life.

THERAPIST: That's right. You don't want to waste your time. This morning you set out to find a job. You go down to the employment bureau. See yourself there. You're filling out forms. But no jobs are available for you. Next, you look through the want ad section of the newspaper, but nothing in your area is advertised. You already tried the colleges in the area but they are not hiring. How do you feel?

CLIENT: Depressed.

THERAPIST: That's right. Feel the depression. You had a good teaching job. People liked you. You had friends. But you moved and your life has become worthless, empty, and unproductive. You now think about your husband. He likes his job. He is moving up the ladder of success. How do you feel?

CLIENT: I feel angry.

THERAPIST: Try to feel the anger toward your husband.

CLIENT: No, it is not his fault. We both agreed to the move.

THERAPIST: Whether it is his fault or not, try to imagine that all he is really concerned about is his work and his needs. Your needs and aspirations are not important. See him, get a clear image. Ask him to go back to his former job so you can return to your old job. Verbalize it.

CLIENT: "Can we go back to [couple's former residence]?"

THERAPIST: Put some feeling into the request.

CLIENT: "Can we?"

THERAPIST: He looks at you in a cold, rejecting manner. "No. You agreed to come here. I am making more money. You will find something here. Stop feeling sorry for yourself." Feel that concern. Try and communicate to him so he will understand.

CLIENT: "Please. I can't stand it here."

THERAPIST: "Stop acting like a baby. Grow up." How do you feel?

CLIENT: Mad.

THERAPIST: Tell him off, express your anger. Tell him you hate him.

CLIENT: "I hate you."

THERAPIST: Say it with feeling.

CLIENT: "I hate you. I hate you. I hate you."

Following this scene, the client was asked to imagine being back in high school, a period when she had felt alone and rejected. At that time, she had not felt any anger toward her peers who rejected her. A series of scenes involving rejection in high school were described to the client. The therapist augmented successive scenes with new material provided by the client. Eventually, the client was able to feel considerable anger and hostility toward the people who had rejected her. The therapist continued to present each scene, with embellishments, until the client experienced a high degree of upset (anxiety, anger, and depression) and then the negative feelings began to diminish.

As homework assignments in implosive therapy, clients are asked to spend at least 20 minutes each day imagining the scenes presented in the previous session, which gives the client additional exposure to the threatening scenes. Clients are encouraged to vary the content of the scenes to increase generalization.

Clients can be taught to use implosive therapy on their own to deal with daily anxiety. They learn to analyze the cues that make them anxious. Then they construct scenes incorporating these cues with the goal of engendering as much anxiety as possible, such as by including worst-case scenarios.[64]

Like imaginal flooding, implosive therapy frequently is used to treat victims of trauma. Often the therapy is relatively brief, as the following case illustrates.

	TREATMENT OF INTRUSIVE MEMORIES OF INCEST WITH IMPLOSIVE THERAPY[65]
Case 10-6	

A 22-year-old woman reported that between the ages of 12 and 15 her father repeatedly forced her to have sexual relations with him (fondling, fellatio, and intercourse). She believed that her mother had known about this and had done nothing to stop it. After being discharged from an alcohol treatment program, she increasingly became bothered by thoughts about the incest. (Presumably her drinking had served to dull her memories.) She reported having headaches and difficulty sleeping. She also was worried that her fiancé and foster family would reject her if they knew about the incest.

The client was given five hour-and-a-half sessions of implosive therapy on consecutive days. The scenes were based on the first time her father forced her to have sexual relations and dealt with three bothersome themes: (1) intrusive thoughts of the incest; (2) anger and confusion about her mother's failure to intercede; and (3) fears of rejection if people learned of the incest. In describing the scenes, the therapist embellished these themes with real and hypothesized thoughts and events. For example, one scene involved the following hypothesized cues.

> The client was caught with her father by a succession of people, including her mother, other family members, and her fiancé. They reacted with astonishment, disgust, and eventual rejection.

Three different outcome measures were used to assess the efficacy of the treatment: (1) a physiological measure of anxiety (skin conductance); (2) observations of overt behaviors indicative of anxiety (such as audible, rapid respiration); and (3) the client's self-recordings of the number of incest-related thoughts and dreams she had. Significant decreases occurred on all three measures at the six-week follow-up. Because the patient moved to another city, only the self-report measure was used at the six-month follow-up, and it indicated that the treatment effects were maintained. A year after therapy, the patient reported that her thoughts about incest were no longer problematic.

Implosive Therapy in Perspective

Although implosive therapy was developed almost 40 years ago, much of the evidence for its effectiveness comes from case studies rather than controlled experiments.[66] Although some research shows that implosive therapy can reduce anxiety,[67] many of the studies contain methodological flaws.[68] Some studies indicate that implosive therapy is not more effective than control conditions.[69] Moreover, implosive therapy has generally not been shown to be superior to other therapies, such as systematic desensitization.[70] In sum, no definitive statements about the effectiveness of implosive therapy can be made.

Much of the published work on implosive therapy concerns the classical conditioning model presumed to underlie the process of the therapy, which is the same as that used to explain flooding (see In Theory 10-1, pages 237-238).[71] Many of the studies cited as evidence for this theory are based on analogue research with laboratory animals.[72] In a typical study, an animal, such as a rat, is given an electric shock on one side of a cage.[73] After a number of shocks, the rat will avoid the side of the cage where it was shocked. This avoidance behavior is eliminated by repeated trials in which the rat is placed on the threatening side (1) without shock occurring and (2) with the opportunity for escape blocked by a physical barrier (response prevention). In our view, eliminating a rat's escape behavior is too far removed from treating human anxiety and avoidance to be considered appropriate evidence.[74]

Incorporating psychoanalytic themes in implosive therapy scenes is, not surprisingly, highly controversial.[75] Stampfl originally presented implosive therapy as an integration of psychoanalytic and behavioral principles,[76] although it has always been considered a behavior therapy.[77] Clearly, the assessment of early childhood experiences and the use of interpretations based on psychoanalytic theory are inconsistent with behavior therapy practices. Moreover, the relevance of the psychoanalytic component of implosive therapy is questionable. There is no evidence that the use of hypothesized cues based on psychoanalysis is necessary for implosive therapy to be effective. In fact, implosive therapy with little or no psychoanalytic imagery can be successful.[78] Further, the demonstrated effectiveness of imaginal flooding—which is essentially implosive therapy without hypothesized and exaggerated cues—is indirect evidence that the psychoanalytic component is unnecessary. Unfortunately, there are no studies comparing implosive therapy and imaginal flooding, which might provide direct evidence for this contention.

There also has been no examination of the role of exaggerating elements of the implosive scenes, the other major procedural difference between implosive therapy and imaginal flooding. One possibility is that exaggerated images may be more useful when clients' fears are less severe, since the purpose of the exaggeration is to increase clients' anxiety. When implosive therapy was first developed, it was used to treat relatively mild phobic reactions.[79] In such cases, increasing the client's level of anxiety through exaggerated images might be beneficial. More recently, however, implosive therapy has been applied to severe problems, most notably posttraumatic stress disorder.[80] Clients with such disorders typically experience very high levels of anxiety, which may eliminate the need for presenting exaggerated images.[81]

◆ ## ALL THINGS CONSIDERED: PROLONGED/INTENSE EXPOSURE THERAPY

Prolonged/intense exposure therapies clearly have their place in the treatment of anxiety-related disorders. These therapies can be both effective and highly efficient means of reducing clients' anxiety. Group treatment using imaginal flooding for anxiety-based problems, for example, is an effective and efficient alternative to individual treatment.[82]

At the same time, there is no doubt that clients perceive prolonged/intense exposure therapies as "bitter medicine,"[83] a factor that limits their usefulness. (You will gain *some* empathic understanding of the experience clients have in prolonged/intense exposure by thinking of a situation you would find extremely uncomfortable; then, imagine being in the situation or even thinking about it for an hour.)

Because of the discomfort associated with prolonged/intense exposure, clients may not elect such treatment, even though prolonged/intense exposure therapy may be the treatment of choice for their problems. Further, some therapists may decide not to administer prolonged/intense exposure therapy because of the discomfort clients experience.

A *potential* danger of flooding and implosive therapy is that the prolonged and intense exposure to the feared situation will make clients even more anxious or fearful than before therapy. This possibility exists because both flooding and implosive therapy induce anxiety in order to reduce it. Fortunately, there is no evidence that serious negative side effects occur. In a survey of behavior therapists who had used flooding or implosive therapy, serious negative side effects were reported in only 0.26% of the clients treated (9 out of 3,493).[84] The major exception to this general finding is the use of prolonged/intense exposure therapy for posttraumatic stress disorder with clients who have a history of other serious psychiatric disorders.[85] In such cases, the chances of being retraumatized, of increased anxiety, and of other adverse reactions to the treatment are substantially increased.[86]

The major ethical or humanitarian objection to prolonged/intense exposure therapy is that it increases clients' anxiety. The question is: Should already traumatized clients, such as victims of rape or incest, be subjected to therapy procedures that further disturb them?[87] Such treatment runs counter to the ethical principle: "First, do no harm." However, the following two caveats should be kept in mind. First, clients have prior knowledge about the process of prolonged/intense exposure therapy, and they consent to undergo the temporarily stressful treatment. Second, discomfort often is a necessary part of psychotherapy; for example, many psychotherapies require clients to confront disturbing events in their lives.

Ultimately, the decision to use prolonged/intense exposure therapy should be based on a cost-benefit analysis of the objections and the practical advantages. For example, sometimes prolonged/intense exposure can bring about a marked reduction in anxiety in a few sessions and occasionally in a single session, which is generally quicker than brief/graduated exposure.[88] More rapid treatment has obvious advantages (including ethical and humanitarian ones) for distressed clients. In some cases, only a limited time may be available for treatment (such as in Case 10-3, where the woman wanted to overcome her obsessive-compulsive disorder before getting married in two weeks).[89]

Another factor that enters into the choice of therapy is that clients differ in their tolerance for discomfort. Some clients find that getting the treatment over with quickly compensates for the brief distress they experience. For example, the teenage boy who was treated for recurring disturbing thoughts about his abduction (Case 10-4) reported that the success of his treatment was adequate compensation for the unpleasantness he experienced during the flooding sessions.

◆   ## ALL THINGS CONSIDERED: EXPOSURE THERAPY

A variety of exposure therapies exists. All share the common procedural element of *exposure to the anxiety-evoking stimulus without actual negative consequences occurring*. Exposure therapies differ in the specific ways in which the exposure occurs: imaginal or in vivo and brief/graduated or prolonged/ intense (see Table 9-1, page 200). It appears that each of the exposure therapies is useful and that no one exposure therapy is optimal for all cases.

Systematic desensitization, the grandparent of exposure therapies, is a tried-and-true treatment that is broadly applicable. Because exposure is imaginal, the nature of the anxiety-evoking stimuli is limited only by the client's imagination. Because the exposure is brief, graduated, and imaginal, systematic desensitization is the least distressing exposure therapy. Systematic desensitization also has the practical advantage that it can be implemented in a therapist's office.

In vivo exposure shares with systematic desensitization the advantages associated with brief/graduated exposure without the potential limitation of clients' inability to imagine scenes clearly. Exposure to the actual situations is likely to be more upsetting, but the treatment may be quicker and may generalize better to actual situations. Therapist-assisted in vivo exposure is costly in terms of therapists' time, but self-managed treatment, when viable, is highly cost-effective.[90] In vivo exposure now is recognized as one of the critical components in the treatment of agoraphobia, which is the most debilitating phobic disorder.

In vivo flooding can rapidly reduce fear. It is the treatment of choice for obsessive-compulsive disorder and is often used for agoraphobia. In vivo flooding is applicable to a wide range of clients, including the elderly.[91] Two potential limitations of in vivo flooding are that clients must be willing to subject themselves to the discomfort of prolonged/intense exposure to the actual feared stimulus and that therapist assistance generally is necessary, which is not always practical.

Imaginal flooding and implosive therapy also can result in rapid reduction of fear, and implosive therapy may prove to be especially effective in alleviating the arousal symptoms of posttraumatic stress disorder, including intrusive thoughts and flashbacks, hypervigilance, and sleep disturbances.[92] Both imaginal flooding and implosive therapy share with systematic desensitization the advantages of imaginal exposure. Imaginal flooding and implosive therapy do involve discomfort for the client, although usually to a lesser degree than in vivo flooding.

As these brief evaluations of specific exposure therapies indicate, each is a viable treatment for some clients and some anxiety-related disorders. None, however, is useful in all cases. A similar conclusion can be drawn if we examine the relative merits of the two basic dimensions of exposure: imaginal versus in vivo and brief/graduated versus prolonged/intense.

Although some behavior therapists believe that exposure in vivo generally is superior to imaginal exposure,[93] there is reason to question this broad conclusion.[94] Many of the investigations that indicate that exposure in vivo is more effective than imaginal exposure are analogue studies in which the problems treated are mild.[95] When studies using only clinical samples (actual clients with serious anxiety-related problems) are examined, it appears that exposure in vivo has no clear-cut, general superiority. This is true when in vivo exposure is compared with systematic desensitization[96] and when in vivo flooding is compared with imaginal flooding.[97]

In cases where the actual feared stimuli cannot be reproduced, imaginal exposure must be used. For instance, a client who repeatedly checks to see that the front door is locked may fear that an intruder will enter the house. Although such a scenario can be created easily in the client's imagination, actually producing these events would be impractical and unethical. Not surprisingly, then, imaginal flooding has been shown to be superior to in vivo flooding in preventing relapse with clients who compulsively check.[98] The safest conclusion that can be drawn about imaginal versus in vivo exposure is that both are useful and effective procedures.

The decision to employ brief/graduated or prolonged/intense exposure may depend on the psychological disorder being treated. For instance, in vivo exposure (brief/graduated) is particularly useful with agoraphobia, while imaginal flooding (prolonged/intense) appears well-suited for post-traumatic stress disorder.[99] In the case of obsessive-compulsive disorder, both types of exposure may be warranted because they affect different aspects of the disorder. Brief/graduated exposure reduces anxiety and avoidance behaviors, whereas prolonged/intense exposure reduces ritualistic acts.[100] Other factors likely to influence the decision about the optimal model of exposure include the severity of the complaint and the client's preference.

The actual decision about which of the five major exposure therapies to employ is a joint one, drawing on the behavior therapist's knowledge and experience and the client's personal preference. In some cases, the therapist clearly can recommend one exposure therapy based on research findings regarding its relative effectiveness with the particular disorder. The therapist describes to the client the procedures of each potentially beneficial therapy, as well as its pros and cons. With exposure therapies, the issue of how much discomfort the client is willing to endure must be considered in addition to factors of effectiveness and efficiency.

As a group, exposure therapies appear to be the single most potent behavior therapy for anxiety-related disorders[101] and can have long-lasting effects. This conclusion does not mean that exposure alone always is sufficient. Indeed, with severe and multifaceted disorders, the use of more than one type of therapy often is required. When a client's anxiety is maintained by more than one maintaining condition, separate therapies may be required to deal with each. For example, social anxiety often is maintained by a combination of subjective feelings of anxiety, avoidance of social situations, negative attitudes about social interactions, and social skills deficits. Subjective feelings and avoidance behaviors are treated optimally by exposure therapy, negative attitudes by cognitive restructuring (see Chapter 12), and skills deficits by social skills training (see Chapter 11).

◆   **In Theory 10-2**

EXPOSURE THERAPIES OR THERAPY?

Behavior therapists have been notoriously inconsistent in their use of terms to describe exposure therapies, with the exception of systematic desensitization. In some cases the same term is used to designate more than one therapy, as Table 10-3 shows. The inconsistency leads to confusion about the specific therapy procedures being employed. Further, it may reflect the current state of affairs—namely, a genuine overlap among exposure therapies.

To begin with, all of the exposure therapies share common theoretical explanations (see In Theory 9-1, pages 216-219, and In Theory 10-1, pages 237-238). Additionally, although the five major exposure therapies we have described seem to differ in a variety of procedural aspects, in fact, they may have more similarities than differences.

A simple example is that implosive therapy actually is a specialized form of imaginal flooding. Implosive therapy always involves flooding, which may account for the frequent use of the term *implosive (flooding) therapy* to indicate implosive therapy.[102]

A more complex example of overlapping procedures involves the fact that whichever form of flooding clients receive—in vivo or imaginal—they often also receive the other form. With in vivo flooding, clients know about the nature of the exposure in advance. Thus, it is likely that before an in vivo session, they think about (imagine) the exposure procedure, including the stimuli to be presented; this process approximates imaginal flooding.[103] Likewise, imaginal flooding may involve in vivo flooding. Therapists may recommend that clients engage in self-initiated in vivo flooding at home.[104] Even without this suggestion, clients may naturally engage in flooding

Table 10-3 Common terms used to designate exposure therapies

Most Common Term	Other Terms
Systematic desensitization	Desensitization
In vivo exposure	In vivo desensitization Graduated exposure Graded exposure Exposure
In vivo flooding	Flooding In vivo exposure Exposure Response prevention In vivo exposure with response prevention Rapid exposure
Imaginal flooding	Flooding In vitro flooding Fantasy flooding
Implosive therapy	Implosion Implosive (flooding) therapy Flooding

as they encounter the threatening events during the course of their daily activities.[105]

Another instance of procedural overlap is the use of competing responses. Only in brief/graduated exposure therapies do clients specifically engage in behaviors that compete with anxiety (often muscle relaxation). In prolonged/intense exposure therapies, however, the presence of a supportive therapist may serve a similar function. It also is possible that clients spontaneously employ coping responses (such as using reassuring self-instructions) that compete with the high levels of anxiety encountered in prolonged/intense exposure.

The similarities among exposure therapies raise the question of whether it would be more fruitful to classify such procedures as *exposure therapy with variations* than as different *exposure therapies*. Uncovering the similarities may increase our understanding of the fundamental nature of exposure therapy and help account for the effectiveness of seemingly differing therapies. Such efforts are consistent with the trend toward integrating psychotherapies (about which we will comment further in Chapter 18).[106]

Summary

1. Prolonged/intense exposure therapies reduce anxiety by exposing clients to anxiety-evoking stimuli that, from the outset, are intense and for extended periods. The exposure is continued until the client's anxiety peaks and then begins to decline. Although the client experiences anxiety during exposure, the feared negative consequences do not actually occur.
2. Flooding requires that the client remain exposed, in vivo or imaginally, to the anxiety-evoking stimuli for a prolonged period without engaging in anxiety-reducing behaviors, which is known as response prevention.
3. Imaginal flooding makes it possible to expose the client to any anxiety-evoking stimulus. The procedure can be used to treat posttraumatic stress disorder, for which it would be impractical and unethical to use in vivo exposure.
4. Both in vivo and imaginal flooding are effective treatments, although some studies have found in vivo flooding to be superior. The major drawback of flooding is the discomfort it produces.
5. Extinction is the major theoretical explanation for the effectiveness of prolonged/intense exposure. The explanation rests on a two-factor theory of the development and maintenance of anxiety. Anxiety is initially learned by classical conditioning; the anxiety-reducing responses (avoidance) that follow are maintained by operant conditioning (negative reinforcement). The effectiveness of prolonged/intense exposure therapy also can be explained by clients' changing their negative beliefs about their anxiety.
6. Eye movement desensitization and reprocessing (EMDR) is a new and controversial variant of exposure-based therapy that essentially involves

imaginal flooding (including rapid, rhythmic eye movements) and cognitive restructuring. Currently, the effectiveness of EMDR has not been demonstrated according to the standards of empirical validation typically required of behavior therapy procedures.

7. Implosive therapy involves imaginal prolonged/intense exposure in which the scenes the client visualizes are exaggerated and elaborated with hypothesized cues (often psychoanalytically based) related to the client's fear. Implosive therapy generally has not proved superior to other therapies, such as systematic desensitization. It is questionable whether the hypothesized cues add to the effectiveness of implosive therapy.

8. Because of the discomfort caused by prolonged/intense exposure therapies, clients may not choose these treatments, despite their effectiveness.

9. Although exposure therapies differ in a variety of procedural aspects, they overlap sufficiently to raise the question of whether they should be considered variations of a single therapy.

REFERENCE NOTES

1. Malleson, 1959.
2. For example, Agras, Kazdin, & Wilson, 1979; Chambless, Foa, Groves, & Goldstein, 1982.
3. Leitenberg, 1993; Leitenberg, Gross, Peterson, & Rosen, 1984; Wilson, Rossiter, Kliefield, & Lindholm, 1986.
4. Greenberg, 1992.
5. For example, Kozak, Foa, & Steketee, 1988.
6. Nesbitt, 1973, pp. 405-406.
7. For example, Stampfl & Levis, 1967.
8. Mowrer, 1960; Solomon, 1964.
9. For example, Goldfried & Robins, 1983.
10. Bandura, 1986b, 1988.
11. Compare with Barlow, 1988; Wilson, 1990.
12. For example, Abramowitz, 1996; Calamari, Faber, Hitsman, & Poppe, 1994; Steketee, 1994; Van Oppen, De Hann, Van Balkom, Spinhoven, Hoogduin, & Van Dyck, 1995; Walker, Freeman, & Christensen, 1994.
13. Meyer, Robertson, & Tatlow, 1975.
14. Scholing & Emmelkamp, 1993a, 1993b.
15. For example, Van Balkom, Van Oppen, Vermeulen, Van Dyck, Nauta, & Vorst, 1994.
16. Cottraux, Mollard, Bouvard, & Marks, 1993.
17. Stanley & Turner, 1995.
18. Baxter, Schwartz, Bergman, Szuba, Guze, Mazziotta, Akazraju, Selin, Ferng, Munford, & Phelps, 1992; Schwartz, Stoessel, Baxter, Martin, & Phelps, 1996.
19. For example, Frueh, 1995.
20. Foa & Rothbaum, 1989; Frueh, Turner, & Beidel, 1995.
21. For example, Foa, Rothbaum, Riggs, & Murdock, 1991.
22. For example, Saigh, 1986, 1987.
23. Saigh, 1987.
24. Keane, Fairbank, Caddell, & Zimering, 1989.
25. Shapiro, 1989a, 1989b, 1995.
26. Shapiro, 1995; compare with Rosen, 1995.
27. Shapiro, 1989a, 1989b.
28. Cowley, 1994; Oldenburg, 1994; Stone, 1994.
29. For example, Kleinknecht, 1993; Forbes, Creamer, & Rycroft, 1994; Sanderson & Carpenter, 1992; compare with Jacobson, Mulick, & Schwartz, 1995.
30. Cocco & Sharpe, 1993.
31. For example, Herbert & Mueser, 1992; Kleinknecht & Morgan, 1992; Lohr, Kleinknecht, Conley, Dal Cerro, Schmidt, & Sonntag, 1992; Marquis, 1991.
32. For example, Kleinknecht & Morgan, 1992; Lipke & Botkin, 1992; McCann, 1992; Marquis, 1991; Puk, 1991; Shapiro, 1989a; Wolpe & Abrams, 1991.
33. For example, Acierno, Hersen, Van Hasselt, Tremont, & Meuser, 1994; Acierno, Tremont, Last, & Montgomery, 1994; Boudewyns, Stwerka, Hyer, Albrecht, & Sperr, 1993; Montgomery, 1993; Renfrey & Spates, 1994.
34. For example, Acierno, Tremont, Last, & Mont-

gomery, 1994; Boudewyns, Stwerka, Hyer, Albrecht, & Sperr, 1993; Pitman, Orr, Altman, Longpre, Poire, & Lasko, 1993; Renfrey & Spates, 1994; Rosen, 1996; Sanderson & Carpenter, 1992.

35. For example, Acierno, Hersen, Van Hasselt, & Meuser, 1994; Marafiote, 1993; Page & Crino, 1993; Vaughan, Armstrong, Gold, O'Connor, Jenneke, & Tarrier, 1994.

36. For example, Acierno, Hersen, Van Hasselt, Tremont, & Meuser, 1994; Lohr, Tolin, & Montgomery, 1996; Meichenbaum, 1994.

37. For example, Butler, 1985; Stravynski & Greenberg, 1989; Yule, Sacks, & Hersov, 1974.

38. Abramowitz, 1996; Steketee, 1994; Van Balkom, Van Oppen, Vermeulen, Van Dyck, Nauta, & Vorst, 1994.

39. For example, Meichenbaum, 1994; Otto, Penava, Pollock, & Smoller, 1995.

40. Chambless, 1985; Swinson & Kuch, 1989; Trull, Nietzel, & Main, 1988.

41. For example, Leitenberg, Gross, Peterson, & Rosen, 1984; Schmidt, 1989.

42. For example, Stambaugh, 1977.

43. Glasgow, 1975; Lamontagne & Marks, 1973.

44. Hannie & Adams, 1974.

45. For example, Emmelkamp & Wessels, 1975; Watson, Mullet, & Pillay, 1973.

46. James, 1986.

47. For example, Saigh, 1986, 1987.

48. For example, Turner, Beidel, & Jacob, 1994.

49. Richards, Lovell, & Marks, 1994.

50. Steketee, 1994.

51. For example, Boulougouris, Marks, & Marset, 1971; De Moor, 1970; Horne & Matson, 1977; Strahley, 1965; Suarez, McCutcheon, & Adams, 1976.

52. Horne & Matson, 1977.

53. For example, Greyson, Foa, & Steketee, 1985; Richard, 1995; Smith, Marcus, & Eldredge, 1994.

54. For example, Öst, Westling, & Hellström, 1993.

55. For example, Emmelkamp, De Haan, & Hoogduin, 1990; Mehta, 1990.

56. Steketee & Lam, 1993.

57. Emmelkamp, De Haan, & Hoogduin, 1990.

58. Stampfl, 1961.

59. Levis, 1980; Stampfl & Levis, 1967, 1973.

60. Stampfl, 1970.

61. Johnson, Corrigan, & Mayo, 1987.

62. Levis, 1980; Levis & Malloy, 1982.

63. Levis, 1980; quoted therapeutic dialogue from pp. 125-126.

64. Levis, 1980.

65. Rychtarik, Silverman, Landingham, & Prue, 1984.

66. Saper, Blank, & Chapman, 1995.

67. Hogan & Kirchner, 1967; Levis & Carrera, 1967; Stampfl, 1966.

68. Morganstern, 1973.

69. For example, Hodgson & Rachman, 1970; Willis & Edwards, 1969.

70. For example, Borkovec, 1970, 1972; Mealiea & Nawas, 1971.

71. For example, Levis, 1985.

72. For example, Levis, 1979, 1991, 1993.

73. For example, Bankart & Elliott, 1974; Schiff, Smith, & Prochaska, 1972; Shipley, Mock, & Levis, 1971.

74. Compare with Levis, 1991, 1993; Mineka, 1985; Mineka & Zinbarg, 1991.

75. Levis, 1988.

76. Stampfl & Levis, 1967.

77. For example, Levis, 1980; Stampfl & Levis, 1967.

78. Hogan, 1968, 1969.

79. For example, Hogan & Kirchner, 1967.

80. Sharpe, Tarrier, & Rotundo, 1994.

81. McCaffrey & Fairbank, 1985; Keane, Fairbank, Caddell, Zimering, & Bender, 1985; Rychtarik, Silverman, Landingham, & Prue, 1984.

82. Fals-Stewart, Marks, & Schafer, 1993; Steketee, 1994.

83. Cox, Fergus, & Swinson, 1994.

84. Shipley & Boudewyns, 1980.

85. Meichenbaum, 1994.

86. For example, Allen & Bloom, 1994; Pitman, Altman, Greenwald, Longpre, Macklin, Poire, & Steketee, 1991.

87. Kilpatrick & Best, 1984.

88. For example, Marshall, Gauthier, Christie, Currie, & Gordon, 1977; Rychtarik, Silverman, Landingham, & Prue, 1984; Nesbitt, 1973; Yule, Sacks, & Hersov, 1974.

89. For example, Rychtarik, Silverman, Landingham, & Prue, 1984.

90. For example, Van Oppen, De Hann, Van Balkom, Spinhoven, Hoogduin, & Van Dyck, 1995.

91. Calamari, Faber, Hitsman, & Poppe, 1994.

92. Sharpe, Tarrier, & Rotundo, 1994.

93. Emmelkamp, 1982; Jansson & Öst, 1982; Mavissakalian & Barlow, 1981; Wilson, 1982.

94. James, 1985, 1986.

95. For example, Emmelkamp & Wessels, 1975; Rabavilas, Boulougouris, & Stefanis, 1976.

96. James, 1985.

97. James, 1986.
98. Foa, Steketee, Turner, & Fischer, 1980.
99. For example, Chambless, Foa, Groves, & Goldstein, 1982; Keane, Fairbank, Caddell, & Zimering, 1989.
100. Foa, Rothbaum, & Kozak, 1989.
101. Trull, Nietzel, & Main, 1988.
102. For example, Keane, Fairbank, Caddell, & Zimering, 1989; Levis, 1993; Levis & Hare, 1977.
103. Marshall, Gauthier, & Gordon, 1979.
104. Barlow, O'Brien, & Last, 1984; Mathews, Teasdale, Munby, Johnston, & Shaw, 1977.
105. For example, Mathews, Johnston, Lancashire, Munby, Shaw, & Gelder, 1976.
106. For example, Arkowitz, 1992a, 1992b, 1995; Goldfried, 1995; Goldfried, Castonguay, & Safran, 1992; Goldfried, Wiser, & Raue, 1992.

Chapter 11

Modeling Therapy and Skills Training

When you hear the word *modeling,* what is your first association? Many people think of a fashion model. Clothing designers and manufacturers would like us to buy their new fashions. They want us to *imitate* the models' behavior, which means wearing the new clothing. Most people find fashion models attractive and wouldn't mind looking like them. Further, people implicitly assume that by wearing a model's clothing, they will be attractive also. This chapter is not about fashion modeling, of course. But some of the same principles of modeling used by the fashion industry are employed by behavior therapists to help clients with their problems. In behavior therapy, **modeling** refers to therapy procedures in which a client observes a person demonstrating some behavior from which the client can benefit.

Learning by observing other people's behaviors is a pervasive part of our lives. We learn language, attitudes and preferences, standards for how to act, mannerisms, and countless skills by observing others. Many of our habits, such as verbal expressions and body language, are borrowed from others with whom we identify, such as our parents. On a grander scale, the course of world history has been influenced by the people who were imitated. Christopher Columbus usually is credited with being the first European to discover America because it was after his voyage that other people followed. In fact, Norse explorers had found America some 600 years before Columbus. However, because the Norse were not imitated, their place in history is diminished.

Modeling can play a role in the development and maintenance of psychological and physical disorders. For example, the aggression people have observed in their families-of-origin influences the amount and type of aggression in their own marriages.[1] Similarly, how people experience pain seems to be influenced by how significant people in their lives have dealt with pain.[2] There is even evidence that observing mass media depictions of suicide, actual or fictional, may lead to imitation; suicide rates typically rise following such media presentations.[3]

Do What I Do: Basics of Modeling

The basic ingredients of modeling are simple: a **model** who demonstrates some behavior and an **observer** who attends to what the model does. A model who is actually present ("in the flesh") is known as a **live model,** and a model who is observed indirectly is called a **symbolic model.**

Symbolic models are observed on television, in books, and through oral description. Mythology and fairy tales are rich, time-honored sources of culturally shared symbolic models.[4] Hansel and Gretel are models of courage, while Beauty (of "Beauty and the Beast") is a model of compassion. A common form of symbolic modeling is **covert modeling,** in which people *imagine* a model engaging in a behavior they want to be able to perform.[5] For instance, before getting up to make a class presentation, a student might visualize a popular teacher giving an interesting lecture.

Observing a model provides information about (1) what the model does and (2) what happens to the model as a result of the model's actions. The consequences of a model's behaviors—known as **vicarious consequences**—are important because they indicate the consequences observers may receive for imitating the model. **Vicarious reinforcement** occurs when the consequences of the model's behaviors *increase* the likelihood that observers will imitate the model. With **vicarious negative consequences**, the consequences of the model's acts *decrease* the likelihood that observers will imitate the model. Consider whether you'd be more or less likely to speak up in class if your professor praised (vicarious reinforcement) or ridiculed (vicarious negative consequences) other students who spoke up in class.[6]

Modeling serves five functions for observers—teaching, prompting, motivating, reducing anxiety, and discouraging—which are described in Table 11-1.[7] Behavior therapies involving modeling often serve multiple functions. Social skills training, for example, generally involves instructing, prompting, and motivating clients to engage in socially adaptive behaviors. Although the discouraging function of modeling has potential for treating deceleration target behaviors in behavior therapy,[8] it is rarely used.[9]

Table 11-1 Five functions of modeling

Function	Description	Example
Teach	Observer learns a new behavior by observing model	Children's learning language by hearing adults speak
Prompt	Observer is cued (reminded) to perform a behavior after observing a model engage in the behavior	People's laughing when they hear other people laugh, as with laugh tracks on TV sitcoms
Motivate	Observing a model's behavior and the favorable consequences it receives (vicarious reinforcement) serves as an incentive for an observer to engage in the same behavior	Students' volunteering to read aloud when they observe other students' reading aloud and the teacher's responding favorably
Reduce anxiety	Observing a model safely engage in an anxiety-evoking behavior reduces an observer's anxiety	Children's overcoming their fear of getting on a swing by watching other children who are enjoying swinging
Discourage	Observing a model's behavior and the unfavorable consequences it receives (vicarious negative consequences) decreases the likelihood that the observer will imitate the model's behavior	Children's seeing peers punished for hitting others are less likely to engage in the same or even a similar behavior

◆   **In Theory 11-1**

THREE STAGES OF OBSERVATIONAL LEARNING

Observational learning is the process by which people are influenced by observing someone's behaviors. The process involves three sequential stages, illustrated in Figure 11-1.[10] The first stage is *exposure* to (observation of) the model's behaviors. The second stage is *acquisition* of (learning) the model's behaviors. Acquisition requires the observer to pay attention to and remember what the model does. The

third and final stage of observational learning is *acceptance* of the model's behaviors as a guide for one's own actions.

Four types of acceptance are possible. Table 11-2 contains everyday examples of the possible outcomes in the acceptance stage. Acceptance can involve imitation or counterimitation, and it can be either specific or general. *Imitation* involves behaving *like* the model, and *counterimitation*

Figure 11-1   Three stages of observational learning and the possible outcomes in each stage (In Theory 11-1)

First Stage: EXPOSURE   Second Stage: ACQUISITION   Third Stage: ACCEPTANCE

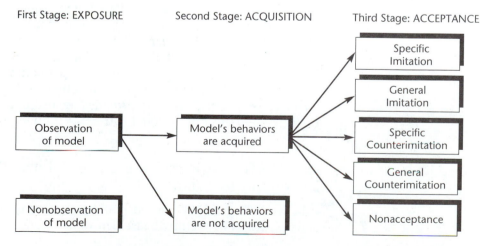

Table 11-2 Examples of the five possible outcomes in the acceptance stage of observational learning (In Theory 11-1)

Modeled Behavior: A parent puts dishes away in the kitchen cabinet	
Acceptance Outcome	Example of Child's Behavior
SPECIFIC IMITATION	Child puts dishes away in the kitchen cabinet.
GENERAL IMITATION	Child puts books away on the bookshelves.
SPECIFIC COUNTERIMITATION	Child takes dishes out of the cabinet.
GENERAL COUNTERIMITATION	Child takes books off the bookshelves.
NONACCEPTANCE	Child does nothing with the dishes or comparable objects.

involves behaving *differently* than the model. In *specific imitation,* the observer engages in the *same* behavior as the model; in other words, the observer *copies* the model. In *specific counterimitation,* the observer does *exactly the opposite* of what the model did. In *general imitation,* the observer behaves *similarly* (but not in precisely the same way) to the model. In *general counterimitation,* the observer behaves *differently* (but not in the directly opposite manner) than the model. Finally, an observer may be exposed to a model and remember what the model did but may not be influenced by the model; this is called *nonacceptance.*

Exposure and acquisition are necessary but not sufficient conditions for modeling to influence an observer. The observer also must accept the model's behaviors as a guide for his or her own behaviors. The form of acceptance is largely determined by the vicarious consequences that occur. Vicarious reinforcement is most likely to result in imitation, whereas vicarious negative consequences are most likely to result in counterimitation.

Nature of Modeling Therapy

Modeling therapies are based on the simple principle that clients can benefit from other people's experiences. Behavior therapists employ a variety of modeling procedures that are frequently combined with other behavior therapies, such as reinforcement, prompting, shaping, and in vivo exposure. Modeling procedures often are supplemented with **behavior rehearsal,** which involves clients' practicing the target behavior.

Although modeling often is part of a treatment package, it can be highly effective by itself. Case 11-1 provides an example of how powerful even casual observation of a model can be in influencing a person's behaviors.

Case 11-1

ACCELERATING A PRESCRIBED ORAL HYGIENE PRACTICE THROUGH MODELING[11]

Julie was a 25-year-old married woman who had recently had oral surgery for serious, progressive gum disease. The dentist reminded Julie to use her Water

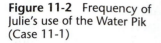

Figure 11-2 Frequency of Julie's use of the Water Pik (Case 11-1)

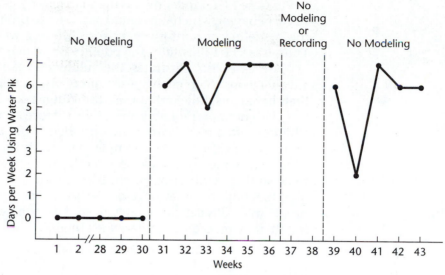

Pik, a device that squirts water to clean between the teeth. She had bought a Water Pik months before her surgery, but had never used it. The dentist warned that if she did not use the Water Pik daily, her gum condition would regress.

Several months after Julie's surgery, her husband, Art, became concerned because Julie was not using the Water Pik and mentioned this to her. Julie said that she would start using it. Another month passed, and the Water Pik remained unused. Art became increasingly concerned and began to remind her to use the Water Pik. Julie became annoyed at Art's "playing parent" and told him to stop worrying about *her* teeth.

At this point Art called the dentist. The dentist suggested that Art use the Water Pik himself on a daily basis and record the times that his wife used it to see if his modeling made a difference.

The results of Art's modeling were striking. As Figure 11-2 shows, Julie had not used the Water Pik once in the 30 weeks prior to Art's modeling. During the first week of modeling, Julie used the Water Pik 6 out of 7 days; the next week she used it every day; after a drop to 5 times per week in the third week, she used the Water Pik every day for the next 3 weeks.

No modeling or recording took place during the next two weeks because Art was out of town on business. The day he returned from his trip, he called the dentist to report on the success of the dentist's advice. The dentist suggested that Art discontinue his modeling and just continue to record how often Julie used the Water Pik. During the next five weeks Julie used the Water Pik an average of 5½ times per week (see Figure 11-2). This was a vast improvement from her baseline rate (zero). Moreover, the outcome of the informal modeling therapy was clinically significant because 5½ times a week was sufficient to keep her gums healthy.

In Case 11-1, modeling was the sole treatment. Art merely performed the target behavior, which Julie could observe. No prompting to pay attention to the modeling or reinforcement for imitating was used, as often is done. Thus, Case 11-1 illustrates the potency of modeling alone.

The case also illustrates the subtleness of modeling, which can be advantageous when clients resist direct instructions from others to change their behaviors. Julie did not use the Water Pik when Art reminded her; in fact, Art's prompts probably made Julie more resistant to using the Water Pik. Children often resist parents' telling them what to do but will respond to more subtle prompts. For example, parents' bringing their own plates and silverware to the sink after a meal may be more effective in getting their child to do so than reminding the child each time.

Modeling therapies have been used primarily for two broad classes of problems—skills deficits and fears—and we will describe a variety of modeling therapy procedures to deal with them.

Skills Training

Skills deficits often are maintaining conditions of clients' problems. In order to perform a skill, a person must (1) know what to do; (2) be proficient at the skill; (3) be adequately motivated to perform the skill; and (4) know when it is appropriate to use the skill. Skills deficits, then, consist of deficits in one or more of these four components, which are described in Table 11-3.

Skills training refers to treatment packages designed to overcome clients' skills deficits.[12] Along with modeling, skills training may entail direct instruction, prompting, shaping, reinforcement, behavior rehearsal, role playing, and corrective feedback.[13] Modeling is a key component of skills training because direct instruction often is insufficient to communicate the subtleties of performing complex skills, and prompting and shaping alone may be inadequate.[14] The client may need to "see" the behavior performed.[15] The major components of skills training are illustrated in the

Table 11-3 Types of skills deficits

Deficit in	Description	Example
KNOWLEDGE	Client does not know how to perform the skill	Young child with profound mental retardation has never learned to talk
PROFICIENCY	Client is not competent at performing the skill because of inadequate practice	Psychiatric patient who has been hospitalized for many years is out of practice managing money
MOTIVATION	Client does not have adequate incentives to perform the skill	Nursing home resident who has no desire or reason to engage in self-care skills
DISCRIMINATION	Client does not know the conditions (time and place) in which it is appropriate to perform the skill	Student who initiates conversations with classmates while the professor is lecturing

Not all clients need skills training.

following excerpt from a social skills training session with a high school student who was having difficulty calling for dates.

THERAPIST: Suppose you wanted to ask Cornelia to attend a dance at school. What might you say?

CLIENT: Well, I'm not exactly sure. I guess I'd just ask her if she wanted to go.

THERAPIST: Why don't you pretend that you are calling Cornelia and actually say what you might say on the phone to her?

CLIENT: OK, but don't expect much.

THERAPIST: Remember, we are only practicing. Just give it a try. [prompting]

CLIENT: "Hello, Cornelia, this is Clint. How y'all doin'? Listen, if you've got nothing better to do, would you want to go to the dance with me?" [role playing]

THERAPIST: That's a reasonable start. [feedback, shaping] Let's see if you can do even better. For one thing, you don't want to make it sound like going to the dance with you is a last resort. [direct instruction] Let me demonstrate one possible way you might continue the conversation after you've said hello. Listen and see if you can hear a difference. [prompting] "There's a dance at school next Saturday, and I'd like to take you if you're not busy." [modeling]

CLIENT: Yeah, I can hear the difference.

THERAPIST: Why don't you try to say something like that.

CLIENT: "I saw the sign about the dance next weekend at the gym, and I was wondering if you'd like to go with me." [behavior rehearsal]

THERAPIST: Very good. That's much better. No apologies; just a straightforward statement of what you'd like. [feedback]

The general procedures for skills training are presented in a flowchart in Figure 11-3. The sequence begins with an assessment of the problem, which often includes behavioral observations in the client's natural environment or in a role-playing situation. Once it is determined that the problem is being maintained by a skills deficit and the type of skills deficit has been assessed, skills training is instituted. When further assessment reveals that the client can perform the relevant skills successfully, training ends. Additionally, both follow-up assessments and booster treatments may be necessary.[16]

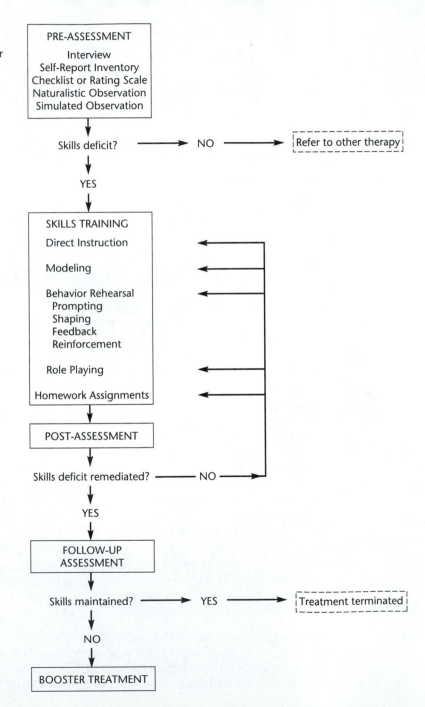

Figure 11-3 Process of skills training
SOURCE: © Michael D. Spiegler and David C. Guevremont

One of the earliest applications of skills training was to treat language skills deficits associated with autistic disorder,[17] mental retardation,[18] and learning disabilities;[19] recently, similar training has been offered to patients with head injuries.[20] Other uses of skills training include alleviating deficits in cognitive skills,[21] problem-solving skills,[22] self-appraisal skills,[23] stress management skills,[24] academic skills,[25] consumer skills,[26] employment skills,[27] and child management skills[28] (as you read about in Chapter 8).

A major application of skills training is to alleviate social skills deficits in children[29] and adults,[30] including specific social interaction skills related to social isolation,[31] couple relationships,[32] and sexual behaviors.[33] We will illustrate the nature of skills training by focusing on basic social skills training, including assertion training.[34]

SOCIAL SKILLS TRAINING

Social skills, the interpersonal competencies necessary to successfully interact with others, are essential for normal living. Their absence is correlated with a host of adjustment problems throughout the life span.[35] For example, in childhood and adolescence, social skills deficits are associated with social isolation, poor academic achievement, and delinquency;[36] in adulthood, social skills deficits are associated with depression, social anxiety,

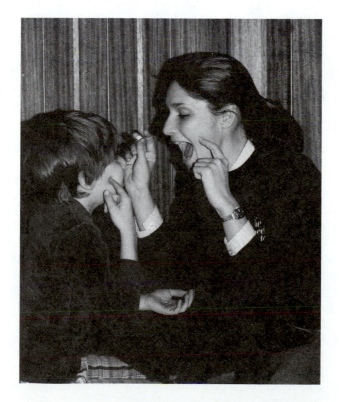

Photo 11-1 Modeling is a key component in language training for children with autistic disorder. The therapist models the correct mouth and tongue positions and the sound for the child to imitate.

and schizophrenia.[37] Not surprisingly, a majority of clients in psychotherapy have social skills deficits.

Social Skills Training for Specific Social Skills Deficits

Children who exhibit low levels of social interaction with peers are prime candidates for social skills training. Film modeling has proved effective with nursery school children who rarely interact with their peers.[38] One such modeling film, 23 minutes in length,

> portrayed a sequence of 11 scenes in which children interacted in a nursery school setting. In each of these episodes, a child is shown first observing the interaction of others and then joining in the social activities, with reinforcing consequences ensuing. The other children, for example, offer him play material, talk to him, smile, and generally respond in a positive manner to his advances into the activity. The scenes [are] graduated on a dimension of threat in terms of the vigor of the social activity and the size of the group. The initial scenes involve very calm activities such as sharing a book or toy while two children are seated at a table. In the terminal scenes, as many as six children are shown gleefully tossing play equipment around the room.[39]

Viewing such modeling films once or twice has been sufficient to increase children's social interactions to a normal level, and these gains have been maintained over time.[40] Film modeling is highly efficient, compared with other procedures such as shaping.[41] Live peer modeling also is effective in increasing social interaction with children.[42]

Poor social interaction skills are a serious handicap for adolescents, for whom socializing is so important. Case 11-2 illustrates the use of social skills training for this problem.

SOCIAL SKILLS TRAINING WITH A YOUNG ADOLESCENT[43]

Case 11-2   A 14-year-old boy, whom we will call Sherman, primarily interacted with children who were 5 to 8 years younger. He had no friends his own age and was especially reluctant to interact with his classmates. He had difficulty engaging in even simple conversations with peers.

Social skills training for Sherman was conducted twice weekly for 20 to 30 minutes. The training focused on 4 conversational skills: (1) asking appropriate questions; (2) making positive or acknowledging comments; (3) maintaining appropriate eye contact; and (4) acting warmly and friendly.

For each skill, the therapist provided Sherman with a rationale for learning it and modeled each of the components of the behaviors. Then, Sherman rehearsed each of the skills with the therapist. After demonstrating proficiency in each of the conversational skills with the therapist, Sherman practiced them with peer "conversational partners" of both genders. Each 10-minute conversation began with the therapist prompting Sherman to use the conversational skills and ended with the therapist providing Sherman with feedback concerning each of the 4 target skills. Sherman was assigned homework that involved practicing the new conversational skills with others at home and at school.

The social skills training was evaluated using a multiple-baseline design across the four conversational skills. As can be seen in Figure 11-4, the performance of each targeted social skill was extremely low during baseline assessments of conversations with different peer partners. Significant increases in each conversational skill occurred after Sherman was trained in that specific skill.

Figure 11-4 Sherman's performance of the four conversational skills taught in social skills training evaluated by a multiple-baseline study (Case 11-2) SOURCE: Franco, Christoff, Crimmins, & Kelly, 1983.

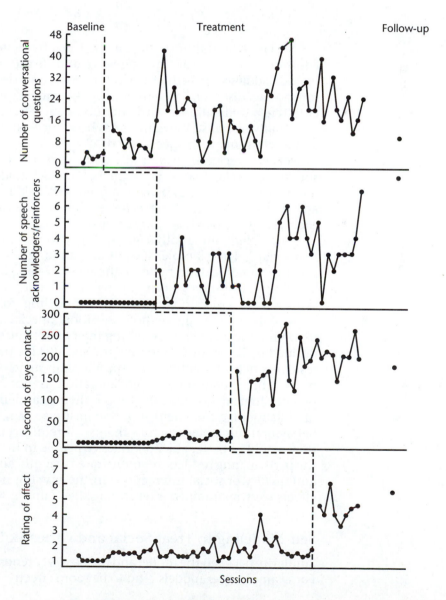

To assess the social validity of Sherman's behavior changes, 10 peers who attended a different school rated videos of Sherman's conversations before and after training. The peer ratings consistently indicated that Sherman's social skills had improved considerably. Further, ratings by Sherman's parents and teachers showed significant improvements in Sherman's overall social adjustment, ability to make friends, ease of interacting with peers, and involvement in extracurricular activities following training. In a telephone call 16 months after treatment, the therapist learned that Sherman's improved social skills and peer relations had been maintained. Sherman now had classmates come to his house, he had begun to date, and he was trying out for a school athletic team.

Social skills training also has had positive effects with children and adolescents who engage in aggressive and disruptive behaviors. Examples include adolescents being treated for sexual offenses,[44] youths hospitalized for conduct disorder,[45] juveniles who are incarcerated,[46] inner-city minority children,[47] and children with attention deficit hyperactivity disorder.[48]

Finally, social skills training has been successfully extended to children and adolescents with special needs. For example, children diagnosed with cancer who received social skills training reported receiving greater social support from classmates and teachers.[49] Likewise, adolescents with language and hearing disabilities benefited from social skills training and then were able to use self-control strategies (such as self-reinforcement) to maintain their use of the newly acquired skills.[50]

The elderly are another group for whom social skills training can be beneficial.[51] For example, social skills training was employed with female nursing home residents between the ages of 74 and 89 who increasingly were avoiding social interactions and reported feeling lonely.[52] Conversational skills were taught through discussion, modeling, role playing, and feedback in 5 to 8 individual one-hour sessions. Special attention was given to involving the women in designing their own treatment. First, each resident decided if she wanted to receive the social skills training. Then, interested residents helped identify their specific skills deficits and problematic situations. This therapist-client collaboration is noteworthy because elderly people often are not consulted about their treatment.[53] As another example of collaborative treatment, the therapist also taught the residents general behavioral principles (such as the use of reinforcement and extinction) so they would be better able to influence people in their environment. Each of the participating residents demonstrated a significant increase in the number and quality of social interactions in the nursing home, and these positive effects were maintained after social skills training was completed.

Self-Modeling to Treat Social and Other Skills Deficits

Similarity between the model and the observer tends to enhance imitation.[54] For example, peer models tend to be more effective than adult models with children.[55] Similarity is maximized by **self-modeling,** in which clients serve as their own models of adaptive functioning.[56] Usually, a video is made of the client's performing the target behavior, and then the client views the video. Self-modeling also can be covert; that is, clients imagine themselves performing the target behavior.

Self-modeling motivates novices by providing evidence that they can successfully perform required skills. As one student pilot commented while watching a video of his landing: "I can see what I did right and what I did wrong, but mostly I can see that I *did* it."[57] The standard procedures used in self-modeling therapy are illustrated in Case 11-3.

Case 11-3

MODIFYING INAPPROPRIATE SOCIAL BEHAVIORS BY SELF-MODELING[58]

Ten-year-old Chuck, a resident of a treatment center for patients with bronchial asthma, spent most of his time alone. His peers rebuffed his attempts to interact with them by calling him "boob" and "baby." Chuck would respond by retreating to his room and having a temper tantrum. He also displayed inappropriate behaviors with adults, such as giggling constantly, attempting to tickle them, and jumping into their laps during interviews.

To deal with these problems, a self-modeling video was prepared. Chuck and two other boys were asked to take part in a "television film." In one self-modeling sequence, Chuck appropriately approached the two boys who were playing a game and asked if he could play with them; in another sequence, Chuck came into an adult's office and seated himself in a chair (rather than on the adult's lap).

During the two weeks after the video was made, Chuck's behaviors did not change. (Change could have resulted from the behavior rehearsal involved in making the video, but in this case it did not.) At this point Chuck was taught to operate the video recorder, and he viewed the appropriate self-modeling tape daily for four weeks. The frequency of Chuck's socially appropriate behaviors in his daily interactions increased substantially. After treatment ended, Chuck maintained his appropriate social behaviors for the remaining six months that he was at the center. It is noteworthy that many of the reports of Chuck's improved behaviors came from staff members who were unaware that Chuck had undergone the self-modeling treatment.

To make a self-modeling video the client must be able to perform either (1) the target behavior under *some* conditions or (2) each of the components of the target behavior. In Case 11-3, Chuck knew how to behave appropriately, but he needed an incentive to do so. The attraction of making a "television film" provided the incentive for Chuck. When a client has difficulty performing the target behavior in a particular problematic situation, it is possible to film the client in a nonproblematic situation. By inserting scenes of the problematic situation, the final edited version can be made to appear as if the client was performing the target behavior in the problematic situation.[59] When the client can perform only the individual components of the behavior, a video is made of the client performing each component separately. Then, the video is edited to make it appear that the client is performing the components in sequence.[60] This could be done, for example, for a girl who cannot put on her shoes by herself but is capable of putting her foot in a shoe, tightening the laces, tying an overhand knot, and tying a bow.

Photos 11-2a and b
(a) Example of self-modeling for teaching a woman (on the right) sign language. First the woman is videotaped performing the behavior, which the therapist (center) prompts. (b) Then the woman watches her own modeling on a monitor.

a

b

Another example of self-modeling to increase socially appropriate behaviors involved a four-year-old boy who most often engaged in play behaviors that are considered stereotypic for girls (such as playing with an ironing board and dolls). The boy observed himself and a peer on a video engaging in play behaviors that were more typical of boys (such as playing with trucks).[61] The goal of the treatment was to expand the boy's repertoire of play behaviors so that he would be able to engage in *both* "masculine" and "feminine" behaviors. Viewing the self-modeling tapes effectively modified his gender-stereotypic behaviors. The changes generalized to other settings and were maintained at a one-year follow-up assessment.

Peter Dowrick has been the leader in the development of video self-modeling therapy.[62] Among his recent innovations is a technique he calls *video futures*. The self-modeling video shows the client acting adaptively in a challenging situation that the client will encounter in the future. As an example, children who are anxious about going to a new school would view a video of themselves enjoying being in their future classrooms. *Futures planning* is a broader technique in which clients' future life goals are depicted in a video that motivates them to initiate and sustain behaviors aimed at achieving their long-term goals.[63] For example, as a result of viewing a video of herself working in a restaurant kitchen, a woman might enroll in cooking classes.[64]

Self-modeling therapy has been applied to clients across the age spectrum. For example, self-modeling was the major intervention used to increase exercise with a group of women (aged 57 to 70) with mental retardation.[65] The women were videotaped while performing 25-minute exercise programs developed specifically for each client. The video included a narration describing the exercises being performed and encouraging the woman's performance. To counter potential embarrassment about seeing themselves on the video,[66] the women had their hair styled and cosmetics applied before taping so that they would be more pleased with their appearance. The final videos were edited so that only sequences in which the women were exercising appropriately remained, which is a standard practice in self-modeling therapy.[67] Clients were given the opportunity to exercise for 25 minutes, 3 days per week, using their self-modeling videos. This intervention resulted in all of the women maintaining high levels of independent exercising for up to 6 months.

Besides being useful for teaching skills,[68] self-modeling has been successful in treating such problems as elective mutism,[69] stuttering,[70] aggressive behaviors,[71] hyperactivity,[72] depression,[73] sexual responsiveness,[74] and hearing impairment among the elderly.[75] Self-modeling can lead to rapid changes in a target behavior, sometimes requiring as little as 12 minutes of self-observation to achieve clinically significant effects.[76]

Social Skills Training for Pervasive Social Skills Deficits

Social skills deficits associated with serious problems such as autistic disorder and mental retardation[77] and severe social phobias[78] may require live modeling and intensive individual treatment. In a small number of cases, children with extreme social skills deficits may actually lack the ability to imitate. The ability to imitate is a social skill called **generalized imitation.**[79] Most children learn generalized imitation in the course of normal development by being reinforced for imitating the behaviors of adults and peers. However, a small percentage of children do not learn to imitate. Generalized imitation can be taught by prompting and shaping. The process begins by reinforcing any imitative response, whether or not the behavior is socially relevant.

The need to first establish generalized imitation is illustrated in the case of a 6-year-old boy who was enrolled in a preschool because he interacted with peers only 5% of the time (compared with 55% of the time for children judged socially competent).[80] Moreover, he became noticeably upset whenever he had to interact with his peers. Because the boy would not attend to potential peer models, modeling could not be used to teach him basic social skills.

Accordingly, training in generalized imitation was the first step in the treatment. The therapist befriended the boy and responded immediately to any of the boy's overtures for attention, help, or approval. The therapist reinforced the boy whenever the boy imitated him, no matter what behavior was imitated. The boy became attached to the therapist, and he often talked about the therapist and eagerly waited for him at the school door. Moreover, the boy began to imitate many of the therapist's characteristic behaviors. At this point, the boy had acquired generalized imitation and could benefit from modeling procedures to increase his social interactions.

Social Skills Training for Clients with Schizophrenia

Social skills deficits and social withdrawal are hallmarks of schizophrenia.[81] Even when disabling symptoms such as hallucinations and delusions are absent (usually as a result of medication), significant social impairment often continues to be a problem.[82] Moreover, the rate of relapse and rehospitalization is higher for clients who are socially isolated and who cannot function effectively within the community.[83]

The goals of social skills training for clients with schizophrenia are (1) to increase social interactions; (2) to teach the types of social skills needed to function in the community (such as talking to neighbors); and (3) to reduce stress by teaching clients to cope with problematic social situations that arise in their daily lives.[84]

The specific skills taught depend on the severity of the client's social deficits. For clients with the most severe deficits, social communication skills might include basic nonverbal behaviors, such as appropriate eye contact, facial expressions, posture, and proximity to others. Clients who are able to perform basic skills are trained in holding conversations, making assertive responses, interviewing for a job, asking for a date, and general social problem solving that can be applied to any interpersonal problem in daily community living.[85] As with other applications of social skills training, the primary components are modeling, behavior rehearsal, feedback, and reinforcement.

Social skills training has been effective in teaching clients with schizophrenia social skills, as assessed through role playing. Although clients often generalize the skills from therapy sessions to their hospital living setting, generalization outside the hospital is a major challenge.[86] This is illustrated by the findings of a study evaluating an intensive social skills training program for clients with schizophrenia.[87] The clients were taught conversational skills 4 days a week in 20- to 30-minute sessions. The clients' rehearsal of these skills was videotaped, and while they watched themselves on the video, they received feedback from the therapist about their performance. Additionally, the clients, who were in an ongoing token economy, earned tokens for participating in the training. The social skills training resulted in significant increases in appropriate conversational skills during the training sessions. However, the skills did not generalize spontaneously to other situations or people.

To promote generalization, the clients were given (1) homework assignments to practice the conversational skills on the hospital unit; (2) prompts to do the homework assignments; and (3) positive reinforcers when the target behaviors were performed. These procedures led to significant increases in clients' use of the conversational skills in different settings and with people other than the trainers, and the skills were maintained three months after the training had ended.

Acquiring social skills appears to improve social competence and reduce social anxiety, according to clients' self-reports, and to improve hospital discharge rates.[88] Social skills training also has a moderate influence on reducing the probability of relapse in comparison with other forms of psychological treatment (such as family education and family therapy), particularly within the first 3 to 6 months after treatment is terminated.[89] Long-term maintenance (for example, 12 to 24 months) of the positive effects of social skills training compared with other therapies has not yet been established.[90]

One strategy that may enhance the durability of behavior changes following social skills training is to teach clients general problem-solving skills that can be applied to diverse social situations. Clients first learn to identify when they are experiencing stress due to interpersonal problems; then to generate and evaluate potential solutions; and finally to select an active and socially acceptable plan to alleviate the problem. In one intensive 6-month social problem-solving training program, clients with schizophrenia received 12 hours of training a week.[91] After the training, the clients showed better social functioning, lower relapse rates, and a greater subjective quality of life than clients in a comparison treatment program who were given occupational therapy.

Skills training relying heavily on modeling also has been used to teach clients with schizophrenia daily living skills, such as personal hygiene, self-care, job finding, self-administration of medication, personal recreation,

Many people have deficits in appropriate assertive behaviors.
HAGAR reprinted with special permission of King Features Syndicate, Inc.

food preparation, vocational skills, home maintenance, use of public transportation, and management of personal finances.[92]

The ability to behave in an assertive manner—that is, to secure and protect what one is entitled to—is a general social skill that often underlies successful performance of many social skills that clients with schizophrenia are taught. Further, acting assertively is especially important for clients with schizophrenia because their rights are particularly vulnerable to abuse by others.

Deficits in assertive behaviors clearly are not restricted to clients with schizophrenia. Indeed, the ability to act assertively is an essential basic social skill that many people lack.[93]

ASSERTION TRAINING

Assertive behaviors are actions that secure and maintain what one is entitled to in an interpersonal situation without infringing on the rights of others.* Deficits in assertive behaviors are extremely common. The importance of assertive behaviors is illustrated by their potential role in preventing AIDS.[94] For example, a program to reduce high-risk sexual practices among gay men taught participants to act assertively with respect to their sexual behaviors.[95] Participants learned to hold frank discussions with potential partners about a commitment to low-risk sexual behaviors and to refuse to engage in high-risk sexual behaviors.

Nature of Assertive Behaviors

Assertive behaviors fall into several categories that are relatively distinct[96] (see Table 11-4). Assertive behaviors are, for the most part, situation-specific,

---

* *Assertive behavior* has been variously and vaguely defined (for example, it has been equated with socially adaptive behavior). Our definition is an attempt to combine widely accepted but restrictive definitions (for example, Alberti & Emmons, 1995; Lazarus, 1971; Wolpe, 1990).

Table 11-4 Five relatively distinct forms of assertive behavior

Type of Assertive Behavior	Example
Asking for what you are entitled to	Correcting the mistake when you receive incorrect change
Standing up for your rights	Objecting when a person steps ahead of you in line
Refusing unreasonable requests	Saying no when a friend asks to borrow money you can't spare
Expressing opinions and feelings (even when they are unpopular or negative)	Voicing your conservative views in a group of liberals
Expressing desires and requests	Telling your sexual partner what you enjoy

which has three important implications.[97] First, we cannot characterize a *person* as assertive or unassertive. We can, however, say that a person's *behavior* in a particular situation is assertive or unassertive. Second, training in one form of assertive behavior may not generalize to other forms.[98] Third, assertive behaviors are not always appropriate or adaptive.[99] How appropriate they are is determined by the consequences, for oneself and others, of being assertive in the particular situation.[100] For example, if a waiter overcharges you by a small amount, you can act assertively and bring it to the waiter's attention. If you are in a rush, however, you may decide to pay the higher amount. This would be an unassertive but appropriate response under the circumstances.

It is important to distinguish between assertive and aggressive behaviors, which are distinctly different.[101] The difference lies in the *means* by which one's desires are secured. Assertive behaviors accomplish this end without violating others' rights. In contrast, aggressive behaviors achieve the same goal, but at someone else's expense. Table 11-5 describes differences between assertive, aggressive, and unassertive responses.

Assessing Assertive Behavior Deficits

Clients' deficits in assertive behaviors are assessed by a variety of methods, including interviews, direct self-report inventories, role playing, self-monitoring, and systematic naturalistic observations.[102] As always, a multi-method approach is preferable to only one assessment method. Identifying the type(s) of skills deficit the client has is essential in selecting the most appropriate treatment method(s).

Self-report inventories are efficient means of providing initial information about a client's deficits in assertive behavior. Two types of self-report inventories are used. With one type, clients rate the degree to which they engage in various assertive behaviors.[103] An example of this type of inventory appears in Participation Exercise 11-1.

Table 11-5 Comparison of assertive, aggressive, and unassertive responses to common situations

Situation	Assertive Response	Aggressive Response	Unassertive Response
You don't drink alcoholic beverages, and at a party someone offers you a mixed drink.	"No, thank you."	"No! I don't want any alcohol; just get it away from me."	"Oh . . . thanks but . . . I guess it won't hurt me."
You come to a professor to get help with an assignment you don't understand. The professor tells you that she doesn't have time to help you.	"I realize you are busy, but the assignment is due soon and I don't want to turn it in late. Might you have a few minutes later today or early tomorrow?"	"How do you expect me to do the assignment when I don't understand it? You could find the time if you wanted to. You just don't give a damn."	"Oh, OK. I guess I'll just do the best I can."
You are rushing off to class and don't want to be late. A friend stops you to ask you to help him move some furniture in his room right then.	"Sorry, I'm on my way to class. If you still need help this evening, let me know."	"You must be kidding! I'm on my way to class. Find someone else."	"Well, I'm on my way to class, but I guess I could give you a hand for just a few minutes."
You have just parked your car next to a car that has a dented fender. As you get out of your car, the owner of the other car comes up to you and accuses you of denting the fender.	"I just pulled in, and I am sure that I didn't hit your car."	"Hey, watch who you are accusing! I didn't touch your car, buddy."	"I didn't do that. I didn't hit your car, honest. Why do you think I did it?"

◆ ▬▬

Participation Exercise 11-1

ASSESSING YOUR ASSERTIVE BEHAVIORS BY A SELF-REPORT INVENTORY*

Below is an example of a self-report inventory for assessing assertive behaviors.[104] There are no right or wrong answers. List the numbers 1 to 14 on a sheet of paper.

* You should do this Participation Exercise before you continue.

Read each item, and write the number in the following scale that is most appropriate for each.

0 = Never
1 = Rarely
2 = Sometimes
3 = Usually
4 = Always

1. When someone is unfair to me, I call it to the person's attention.
2. I make decisions easily.
3. I speak up when someone steps ahead of me in line.
4. When a salesperson tries to sell me something that I do not want or need, I tell the salesperson I am not interested.
5. I freely speak up when I am in a group.
6. If a person has borrowed something from me (such as money or a book) and is late in returning it, I say something to the person.
7. I express my positive feelings to others.
8. I express my negative feelings to others.
9. If food I have ordered in a restaurant is served improperly, I ask to have it corrected.
10. I return merchandise that I find to be defective.
11. I refuse unreasonable requests made of me.
12. I compliment and praise others.
13. If someone is disturbing me, I say something to the person.
14. When I am not receiving service to which I am entitled, I ask for it.

Your responses to this inventory may make you aware of how you deal with various situations that call for assertive behaviors. The higher the scale score for an item, the more assertive you tend to be in the particular situation described. However, it is not appropriate to add the scores to obtain a total assertiveness score because the items are related to different situations and assertive behaviors are situation-specific.

The second common type of self-report inventory has clients indicate how they would respond to a situation (described in writing) by choosing one of several responses. An item from the Conflict Resolution Inventory[105] that measures one type of assertive behavior, refusing unreasonable requests, is shown in Figure 11-5.

Complete assessment of assertive behavior deficits usually requires behavioral observations. If feasible, systematic naturalistic observations are made of the client in the situations in which the client is having difficulty behaving assertively. Simulated observations are more typical, however, because they are easier to arrange. Generally, the simulated observations involve the client's role playing responses to hypothetical situations that call for assertive behaviors.

Figure 11-5 Item on the Conflict Resolution Inventory

SOURCE: McFall & Lillesand, 1971, p. 315.

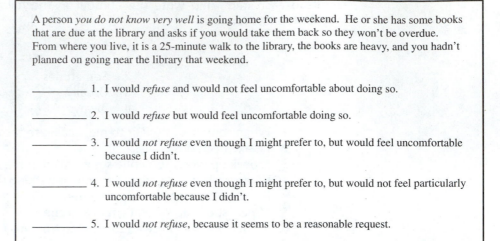

A person *you do not know very well* is going home for the weekend. He or she has some books that are due at the library and asks if you would take them back so they won't be overdue. From where you live, it is a 25-minute walk to the library, the books are heavy, and you hadn't planned on going near the library that weekend.

_____ 1. I would *refuse* and would not feel uncomfortable about doing so.

_____ 2. I would *refuse* but would feel uncomfortable doing so.

_____ 3. I would *not refuse* even though I might prefer to, but would feel uncomfortable because I didn't.

_____ 4. I would *not refuse* even though I might prefer to, but would not feel particularly uncomfortable because I didn't.

_____ 5. I would *not refuse*, because it seems to be a reasonable request.

Behavioral observations make it possible to assess the stylistic components of the client's attempts to act assertively, such as voice tone and body posture. *How* a person acts may be more critical than *what* the person does or says. Rating scales have been developed for assessing assertive styles.[106] Examples of stylistic components of assertive behaviors are described in Table 11-6 and compared with their unassertive and aggressive counterparts.

Table 11-6 Physical and verbal stylistic components of assertive, unassertive, and aggressive behaviors

	Assertive	*Unassertive*	*Aggressive*
EYE CONTACT	**Looking at person while talking**	Looking away from person while talking	Intently staring at person while talking
FACIAL EXPRESSION	**Appropriate to message**	Sheepish or expressionless	Hostile no matter what the message is
GESTURES	**Moderate; appropriate to message**	None or inappropriate to message	Excessive; overenthusiastic
BODY POSTURE	**Erect; at an appropriate distance; leaning slightly toward the person**	Slouched; a bit too far from the person; leaning away from the person	Erect; either too close or too far from person; exaggerated leaning in either direction
VOICE QUALITY	**Firm (confident); appropriate volume; appropriate expression**	Apologetic; whisper; monotone	Overzealous; shouting; "soapbox" speech

Assertion Training Procedures

Assertion training refers to the specific social skills training procedures used to teach clients how and when to behave assertively. Modeling is especially valuable in teaching assertive behaviors because stylistic components that are difficult to describe verbally can be demonstrated (for example, appropriate volume and expression to show confidence).

Homework assignments are routinely used in assertion training and proceed in a stepwise progression. They begin with simple interactions that are relatively nonthreatening for the client, such as making simple requests of a sales clerk. As the client becomes more proficient and confident, the interactions become more challenging, such as asking one's boss for a day off. Table 11-7 contains an example of a hierarchy for practicing assertive behaviors.

Feedback on the client's performance both in the therapy sessions and for homework assignments is an important aspect of the training. The therapist reinforces the client for acting assertively but not for obtaining a favorable outcome. The reason is that the outcome of an assertive behavior rarely is totally in the client's control (for instance, securing a day off from work may depend on the availability of other workers).

Assertion training includes preparation for failure because assertive behaviors do not always get people what they desire. Using hypothetical situations in which assertive responses fail to achieve the desired outcome, the therapist models alternative responses that the client can use in such situations. Then, the client rehearses similar responses while role playing the situation with the therapist.

Table 11-7 Hierarchy of assertive behaviors practiced by a client having difficulty with refusing unreasonable requests (in descending order)

9. Refusing an unreasonable request from a close friend when the request is very important to the friend

8. Refusing an unreasonable request from a close friend when the request is moderately important to the friend

7. Refusing an unreasonable request from an acquaintance when the request is very important to the acquaintance

6. Refusing an unreasonable request from an acquaintance when the request is moderately important to the acquaintance

5. Refusing an unreasonable request from a close friend when the request is unimportant to the friend

4. Refusing an unreasonable request from an acquaintance when the request is unimportant to the acquaintance

3. Refusing an unreasonable request from a stranger when the request is very important to the stranger

2. Refusing an unreasonable request from a stranger when the request is moderately important to the stranger

1. Refusing an unreasonable request from a stranger when the request is unimportant to the stranger

NOTE: The rank ordering is an individual matter and will vary from client to client.

Table 11-8 Covert modeling scenes used to accelerate assertive behaviors

Situation	Modeled Assertive Behavior	Vicarious Reinforcement
1. A woman is eating in a restaurant with friends. She orders a salad and tells the waiter to put the dressing on the side. When the salad arrives, it has the dressing directly on it.	The woman immediately turns to the waiter and says, "I asked for my salad with the dressing on the side. Please bring me another salad without dressing and the dressing in a separate dish."	A few minutes later the waiter returns with the salad correctly prepared and says that he is very sorry for the error and hopes that the woman enjoys the salad.
2. A man who has a drinking problem is at a party where drinks are being served. The host offers him a cocktail.	The man says to the host, "No, thank you, but I would like a soft drink if you have one."	The host replies, "I sure do. I'll be right back with it."

Symbolic modeling also is used in assertion training. For example, covert modeling was part of the treatment of a sexually abused seven-year-old girl who responded with emotional outbursts and sexually inappropriate behaviors when she felt taken advantage of.[107] The girl was asked to visualize scenes in which a similar peer model constructively dealt with her negative feelings, such as by talking to a teacher who treated her unfairly.

Some examples of typical scenes used with covert modeling in assertion training appear in Table 11-8. Covert modeling can be an effective form of assertion training[108] and in some cases it is as effective as live modeling.[109] Covert modeling may be supplemented with **covert behavior rehearsal,** which involves clients' imagining themselves performing target behaviors. Informal covert behavior rehearsal is a common technique we use to prepare ourselves for potentially difficult interpersonal interactions. For example, right before going to see a professor about getting an extension on a paper, a student might mentally rehearse making the request.

Literally hundreds of studies have demonstrated the effectiveness of assertion training for clients with diverse problems and across the age spectrum.[110]* Another line of research has identified the most effective ways of acting assertively. For example, when people act assertively, they are considered competent and likable if they include an empathic statement as part of an assertive response[111] and they give compliments to others.[112] Although assertion training clearly is a behavior therapy, it has been incorporated into many different kinds of psychotherapy (such as Gestalt therapy). Assertion training also has been a hot topic in "pop" psychology for

---

* Research on assertion training has decreased significantly over the past 15 years. This may be due, in part, to deficits' in assertive behavior not being classified as a disorder in the *Diagnostic and Statistical Manual of Mental Disorders* (American Psychiatric Association, 1987, 1994), which generally is necessary for research funding.

many years. Consider the large number of books on the subject written for the general public, including "treatises . . . on the technique of how, when and why to say no; what to say no to; and why you should not feel guilty in saying no."[113]

◆ ▬▬▬▬▬▬▬▬▬▬▬▬▬▬▬▬▬▬▬▬▬▬▬▬▬▬▬▬▬▬

Participation   **APPLYING ASSERTION TRAINING FOR REFUSING**
Exercise 11-2   **UNREASONABLE REQUESTS***

You can experience assertion training with a procedure that uses symbolic modeling, behavior rehearsal, and feedback to teach appropriate refusal of unreasonable requests. Table 11-9 contains six hypothetical situations in which requests are made in a letter. For each, read the letter, keeping in mind the particular situation. Assume that you have received the letter and write an appropriate reply. If the request is unreasonable, refuse the request; if the request is reasonable, agree to it.

Here are some general guidelines for writing an *appropriate* refusal to an unreasonable request.

1. Be polite.
2. Be direct; say what you mean. If you mean that you *don't want* to do something, say that directly (and politely) instead of saying that you are not sure whether you can do it. The former reply would be honest and unambiguous, while the latter would be dishonest and ambiguous.
3. Do not apologize excessively. It might, however, be appropriate to wish the writer luck in obtaining a positive response from others.
4. Tailor the letter to the degree of unreasonableness of the request. For example, a mildly unreasonable request should be responded to with mild refusal, such as "Sorry, but I won't be able to help you out," rather than a very strong reply, such as "There's just no way that I will help you."
5. Consider your relationship, present and future, with the writer. If it is important to you, you may want to tone down your reply.
6. In *some* cases, it may be appropriate to compromise, which, in effect, would render the request more reasonable so that you feel comfortable doing part of what the writer requested.
7. Remember: You are entitled to refuse others' unreasonable requests—and even reasonable ones.

After you have replied to the first letter, look at Table 11-10 (page 287) and read the modeled reply along with the explanation, which will give you feedback on what you have written. Your reply need not match the modeled reply, but it should contain the same basic elements. Repeat the process for each situation and letter. To benefit from the feedback provided in Table 11-10, refer to the modeled reply after writing each letter and before writing the next letter.

* This Participation Exercise can be done before you continue or later.

Table 11-9 Hypothetical situations and letters requiring responses (Participation Exercise 11-2)

Situation	Letter to Respond to

1. You are invited to a party by a student you met briefly in a class you took during the summer. She asks you to pick up someone whom you hardly know, which will mean your driving 30 miles out of your way.	Dear Classmate,
	  How's it going? We're having a little party at my house next Thursday, and I'd like you to come. My cousin was coming but he's having trouble getting a ride down. Do you think you can give him a lift? He lives about 45 minutes out of town so I've enclosed a map. See you on Thursday.
	      Regards,
	      Classmate

2. You have plans to go away for the weekend, and you will need your car. You receive a letter from a close relative.	Dear Cousin,
	  I am coming into town next weekend and am looking forward to seeing you. I am coming by bus so I'll need transportation to get around. I realize that it's short notice, but do you think I might borrow your car for the weekend? I'll have it back to you first thing Monday morning.
	      Thanks,
	      Cousin Avis

3. A record company you recently joined has sent you four tapes you never ordered. In fact, you have promptly returned the order card stating that you didn't want any tapes sent to you.	Dear Record Club Member,
	  We have, up to this time, sent you four tapes for a total of $39.80. We have not received any payment, however. Please send full payment immediately, including shipping and handling costs, as indicated on the enclosed bill.
	      Thank you,
	      President,
	      Ripoff Records, Inc.

4. You are taking a course in the spring semester, and you receive a letter during the winter break from the professor who will be teaching the course.	Dear Student,
	  You are registered for Psychology 988 this coming semester. Due to the extensive background required to understand the material, I am asking students to return four days early for brief introductory sessions. I will be expecting you unless I hear from you before then.
	      Sincerely,
	      Professor Broozer

5. You receive a letter asking for a contribution to a religious organization you have never heard of and know nothing about.	Dear Neighbor,
	  In order for our organization to grow and to build new places of worship, it is essential that we receive financial backing from people like you. Please open up your heart and send your check today. Return this card with your contribution so that we can continue sending you news and information.
	      Most sincerely,
	      President,
	      United Affluent Church

6. A close friend of yours writes to you asking if you would pick up an important package for him at the local post office and pay the delivery charge. You pass the post office daily on your way to work.	Dear Friend,
	  I won't be in the city until some time next week, but I'm expecting an important package to arrive at the main post office. I would really appreciate it if you could pick it up for me and pay the delivery charge. It should only be a few dollars. I'll pay you when I get back.
	      Thanks,
	      Your friend

Table 11-10 Model letters for refusing unreasonable requests, with explanations (Participation Exercise 11-2)

Model Letter	Explanatory Note
1. Dear Classmate, Thanks for the invitation to the party. I'll sure be there, but I really won't be able to pick up your cousin. Thirty miles is just too far for me to go out of my way. I'm looking forward to seeing you at the party.	Polite and friendly; states what you will and will not do; ends on an upbeat note
2. Dear Cousin Avis, Nice to hear from you. I am going away this weekend, so I won't be able to lend you my car for the weekend. Sorry that I'll miss your visit and that I can't help with transportation. Hope you have a pleasant visit.	Clearly says no; explains reasons (briefly, without *unnecessary* details or elaboration), which is appropriate for someone you are close to; genuine expression of regret is sometimes desirable (note that it is brief and to the point); pleasant wishes close the polite refusal
3. Dear President: I did not order any of the four tapes you have sent me. In each case, I promptly returned the order card and checked off that I did not want the tape. Therefore, I refuse to pay for them, although I will return them at your company's expense.	Clearly explains situation; categorically says no; adds a compromise that demonstrates good faith
4. Dear Professor Broozer: I'm sorry, but I will not be able to return to school four days early as you requested. I have made plans for those days. I would be willing to make up the class sessions I miss when I return.	Clearly says it will not be possible to do what has been requested; gives a simple explanation (without elaboration); demonstrates an appreciation of the problem by proposing an alternative means of handling it, which may be prudent, given your future relationship with the professor
5. Dear President, I am not interested in your organization or in receiving any further news or information.	Very brief, formal reply, appropriate for the impersonal form letter received; unequivocally states your position
6. Dear Friend, I'll be glad to pick up the package for you. Give me a call when you get back in town, and we'll arrange for you to pick it up.	Request is *reasonable* in this case

VICARIOUS EXTINCTION: REDUCING FEAR BY MODELING

Fear or anxiety is maintained by the anticipation of negative consequences (such as expecting to be turned down when asking for a date) and by skills deficits (such as not knowing how to ask for a date). Modeling can treat both of these maintaining conditions simultaneously when a model demonstrates the anxiety-evoking behaviors without incurring negative consequences, a process known as **vicarious extinction.**

Vicarious extinction typically employs a **coping model**—a model who is initially fearful and incompetent and who gradually becomes more comfortable and competent performing an anxiety-evoking behavior.[114] Coping models are appropriate for clients who are fearful and incompetent themselves. In contrast, a **mastery model** is an expert who shows no fear and is competent from the outset.[115] Mastery models are more suitable for precise skill development, such as learning to physically defend oneself from sexual assault.[116]

Live Modeling to Reduce Fear

Live models have been used to treat a variety of fear and anxiety-related disorders, such as specific phobias (for example, fear of small animals),[117] test anxiety,[118] social phobia,[119] and obsessive-compulsive disorder.[120] Case 11-4 is an unusual application of parental modeling and in vivo exposure to reduce a child's fear of dental treatment.

Case 11-4

PLANNED AND UNPLANNED TREATMENT OF DENTAL FEAR WITH PARENTAL MODELING AND IN VIVO EXPOSURE[121]

Four-year-old S. Z. needed major restorative dental work, but she was intensely afraid of the dentist. In the six attempted visits to the dentist, S. Z. would "scream, cry, shake violently as [she] walked to the dentist, was short of breath and would adamantly refuse to cooperate." S. Z.'s mother reported that she too was terrified of dentists, and she believed that her daughter had learned to fear dentists from her.[122] Although S. Z.'s mother did not want to be treated for her own fear, she did agree to serve as a model for her daughter.

In the first five weekly visits to the dentist's office, S. Z. and her mother viewed a video depicting various dental procedures and spent time in the office with no dental procedures being performed (in vivo exposure). During the sixth visit, the therapist and the mother both modeled experiencing a one-minute dental checkup. Playing the role of coping models, they exhibited initial hesitance, cooperated with the procedures, and then said that it "wasn't that bad at all." The mother had been instructed to act as if she were unafraid and cooperate with the dentist, which she was able to do despite her own fear of dental treatment. During the seventh treatment session, S. Z. received dental treatment while her mother provided reassurance.

The eighth and final session served as a posttherapy assessment. The dentist performed two procedures on S. Z. under local anesthesia. S. Z. sat by herself in the chair and showed no overt signs of fear. Before therapy and during the final session, the mother used a 100-point SUDs scale to rate S. Z. on 10 dental-related behaviors, ranging from "telling S. Z. about an appointment" to "dentist using drill." During the final session the average SUDs rating was 6, compared with 78 before therapy. Over the next 6 months, S. Z. received considerable dental treatment. At a 6-month follow-up, S. Z.'s average SUDs rating was 3. A 1-year telephone follow-up with both the mother and the dentist indicated that S. Z. continued to display little or no fear of dental procedures.

S. Z.'s mother was not specifically treated for her fear of dental procedures. However, she had participated in S. Z.'s in vivo exposure procedures and her modeling for S. Z. involved both self-modeling and behavior rehearsal. Apparently, this indirect therapy was sufficient to almost eliminate her own fear. Her own pretherapy, posttherapy, and 6-month follow-up average SUDs ratings were 54, 3, and 7, respectively. A year later, the mother and her dentist reported that she was experiencing very little fear about dental visits.

Participant Modeling to Reduce Fear

In **participant modeling**, the therapist models the anxiety-evoking behavior for the client and then encourages and guides the client's practicing the behavior. Developed by Brunhilde Ritter,[123] participant modeling combines modeling, prompting, behavior rehearsal, and in vivo exposure. Participant modeling also is known as *contact desensitization*[124] and as *guided participation*,[125] for reasons that will become apparent shortly. The three basic steps in participant modeling are as follows:

1. *Modeling.* The therapist first models the anxiety-evoking behavior for the client.
2. *Prompting, Behavior Rehearsal,* and *In Vivo Exposure.* The therapist asks (verbally prompts) the client to imitate the behavior she or he has just modeled. The therapist physically prompts the client to perform the behavior (such as by actually holding a client's hand while petting a dog). The physical contact between the therapist and client also reassures and calms the client, and these feelings compete with anxiety.
3. *Fading of Prompts.* The therapist gradually fades the verbal and physical prompts. The client begins to perform the behavior with the therapist present but without physical contact. Finally, the client performs the behavior without the therapist present.

The behaviors that are modeled and practiced are arranged in a hierarchy. The treatment proceeds from the least to the most threatening behaviors. The rate of exposure is determined by the client's fear level, as in in vivo exposure therapy. Case 11-5 illustrates the basic steps in participant modeling.

Photo 11-3 Therapist helping a client overcome her fear of crossing streets through participant modeling

Case 11-5

SEVERE FEAR OF CROSSING STREETS TREATED BY PARTICIPANT MODELING[126]

Mrs. S. was a 49-year-old widow who had been intensely afraid of crossing streets for 10 years. Her fear had caused her to withdraw from social contacts almost completely, and her resulting despair had led her to attempt suicide. Participant modeling proceeded as follows:

A low-traffic location in which a narrow street intersected with a moderately wide street was chosen. The counselor walked across the narrow street for about one minute while Mrs. S. watched. Then the counselor firmly placed her arm around Mrs. S.'s waist and walked across with her. This was repeated . . . until Mrs. S. reported she was fairly comfortable at performing the task. . . . Street crossing was then continued while physical contact between counselor and Mrs. S. was gradually reduced until the counselor only lightly touched the back of Mrs. S.'s arm . . . [and] walked slightly behind her. Contact was then eliminated completely, with the counselor first walking alongside Mrs. S. as the street was crossed and then slightly behind her. The counselor subsequently followed Mrs. S. approximately three-fourths of the way across the street and allowed her to go the remaining distance alone. Gradually the counselor reduced the distance she accompanied Mrs. S. until eventually Mrs. S. was able to cross the street entirely alone.

These procedures then were applied on increasingly wider and busier streets. Mrs. S. was given increased responsibility for her therapy, including planning and carrying out her own homework assignments. She had set four specific goals for therapy, including independently crossing the four streets of a busy intersection. She accomplished all four goals in less than seven weeks.

Participant modeling has been used to treat a variety of anxiety-related problems, including specific phobias,[127] dental fear,[128] speech anxiety,[129] fear of water,[130] and agoraphobia.[131] Participant modeling has been shown to be superior to live modeling,[132] film modeling,[133] and in vivo exposure.[134] The potency of participant modeling may be due to the integration of modeling, behavior rehearsal, and in vivo exposure. Clients' fears are reduced both by what they "see" and by what they do. The latter process, called *enactive learning,* is a powerful teaching method.[135]

Film/Video Modeling to Reduce Fear

Fear of medical and dental procedures can have far-reaching consequences because it can keep people from seeking regular health checkups and obtaining necessary treatment. Film/video modeling has been highly successful in reducing such fear and avoidance behaviors. One survey indicated that 37% of all pediatric hospitals in the United States used film/video modeling to prepare children for hospitalization and surgery.[136] In this section, we will describe film/video modeling therapies for reducing fear of surgery and related medical procedures. Parallel modeling therapies have proven effective in reducing fear of dentistry in children and adults.[137]

◆ **In Theory 11-2**

SELF-EFFICACY
AS A GENERAL
EXPLANATION OF
THE EFFECTS OF
BEHAVIOR THERAPY

When we are confronted with a difficult or frightening task, we usually have a "sense" of the chances of successfully performing it. **Perceived self-efficacy** refers to the belief that one can be successful at a task. The self-efficacy is *perceived* because it depends on how the individual views his or her chances of success, independent of the external odds. A person can have high perceived self-efficacy for an impossible task, such as swimming across the Pacific Ocean, and low self-efficacy for a relatively easy task, such as swimming across a pool.

According to Albert Bandura's theory of perceived self-efficacy, people's levels of self-efficacy determine (1) whether they will attempt a task; (2) the effort they will put into completing the task; and (3) the time they will spend on the task.[138] The stronger one's perceived self-efficacy, the more vigorous and persistent one tends to be in the face of obstacles and setbacks.[139] Self-efficacy is situation-specific; it varies with the particular task.[140] For example, an individual's self-efficacy expectations about his or her ability to stop smoking predicts success in smoking cessation but not in remaining on a diet.[141]

Bandura has speculated that modeling and other behavior therapies (as well as other forms of psychotherapy) are effective because they create and strengthen a client's perceived self-efficacy.[142] In other words, Bandura is proposing a single concept to explain how behavior therapies work. Recall that one of the proposed theoretical explanations of exposure therapies is that they heighten clients' beliefs that they are capable of handling their anxiety (see In Theory 9-1 and 10-1, pages 219 and 238, respectively).

Self-efficacy is strengthened by information provided by the following four sources.

1. *Performance accomplishments.* Direct experience in succeeding at a task may be the most powerful source of self-efficacy.

2. *Vicarious experience.* Observing models succeed at tasks helps clients believe that they themselves can succeed.

3. *Verbal persuasion.* Telling or logically proving to clients that they can succeed is the most common source of self-efficacy in verbal psychotherapies and also plays a role in behavior therapies, especially cognitive-behavioral therapies (as you will see in Chapters 12 and 13).

4. *Emotional arousal.* Level of emotional arousal (as evidenced by one's heart rate, breathing, sweating, and so on) is one factor that people use to judge their self-efficacy. Generally, high arousal is associated with anxiety and hence low self-efficacy; low arousal tends to be associated with calm and confidence and hence high self-efficacy. Therapies that lower clients' arousal levels (such as relaxation training) can enhance clients' perceived self-efficacy.

Table 11-11 presents examples of behavior therapies that provide clients with each of the four sources of self-efficacy.

Table 11-11 Examples of behavior therapies that provide clients with each of the four sources of self-efficacy (numbers in parentheses refer to chapters in which the therapies are discussed) (In Theory 11-2)

Self-Efficacy Source	Behavior Therapies
Performance accomplishments	In vivo exposure therapy (9) In vivo flooding (10) Reinforcement therapy (6) Behavior rehearsal (11) Participant modeling (11) Stress inoculation training (13) Problem-solving therapy (13)
Vicarious experience	Modeling therapy (11)
Verbal persuasion	Rational emotive behavior therapy (12) Cognitive therapy (12) Self-instructional training (13)
Emotional arousal	Systematic desensitization (9) Relaxation training (9) Imaginal flooding (10) Implosive therapy (10)

NOTE: The sources of self-efficacy categories are not mutually exclusive; for a given therapy, self-efficacy may come from more than one source.

Barbara Melamed spearheaded the use of films to reduce children's anxiety about hospitalization and medical procedures with *Ethan Has an Operation*, a 16-minute modeling film depicting the experiences of a 7-year-old boy who has been hospitalized for a hernia operation (see Photo 11-4).[143]

Photo 11-4 Scene from the film *Ethan Has an Operation* showing Ethan in the operating room as the surgeon inserts an intravenous needle

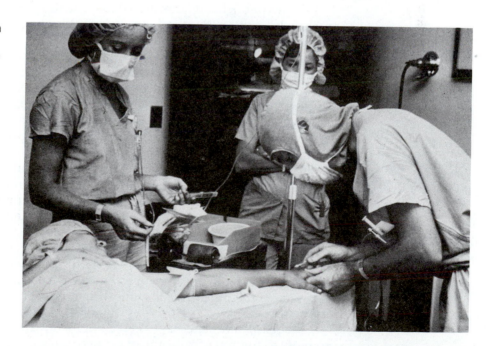

This film . . . consists of 15 scenes showing various events that most children encounter when hospitalized for elective surgery from the time of admission to the time of discharge including a child's orientation to the hospital ward and medical personnel such as the surgeon and anesthesiologist; having a blood test and exposure to standard hospital equipment; separation from the mother; and scenes in the operating and recovery rooms. In addition to explanations of the hospital procedures provided by the medical staff, various scenes are narrated by the child, who describes his feelings and concerns that he had at each stage of the hospital experience. Both the child's behavior and verbal remarks exemplify the behavior of a coping model so that while he exhibits some anxiety and apprehension, he is able to overcome his initial fears and complete each event in a successful and nonanxious manner.[144]

To test the effectiveness of the film, it was shown to children (ages 4 through 12) who were being hospitalized for elective surgery and who had never been in the hospital before. Their anxiety was assessed by self-report inventories, systematic naturalistic observations, and a physiological measure; the assessments were made the night before surgery and 3 to 4 weeks after surgery. The children who saw the modeling film exhibited significantly less anxiety after their operations than children who saw a control film (which depicted a boy on a nature trip). Further, parents' reports indicated that, after leaving the hospital, children who had seen the modeling film presented fewer problems with their conduct than children who had seen the control film.[145]

Related work has demonstrated that a realistic modeling film depicting a child receiving an injection can reduce the pain experienced from injections.[146] The 18-minute film shows a series of boys and girls receiving injections from a nurse. Each child is first shown playing or reading in a hospital bed. A nurse then enters the room carrying a syringe. After talking to the child for a short time, the nurse gives the child the injection. At the moment of the injection, a close-up of the child's upper body and face shows the child's wincing, exclaiming "Ouch," and frowning, which is an example of a moderate and realistic reaction to the injection. Then, the nurse puts a Band-Aid on the injection site, says goodbye, and leaves the room.

Children (ages 4 to 9) viewed the film in their homes 36 hours before receiving their preoperative injections. These children, who had seen realistic coping models, were compared with two other groups of children. One group saw the same basic film, except that the patient-models did not show any signs of pain or discomfort. Such behavior is unrealistic because injections do hurt, at least slightly. Another group of children saw no movie at all. Children who had seen the realistic film showing some pain indicated experiencing the least pain when they received their injections; those who had viewed the unrealistic film showing no pain reported experiencing the most pain.[147]

Modeling films also have been combined with other behavior therapies to reduce children's fears of medical procedures. For example, a 12-minute

© BORN LOSER reprinted by permission of NEA, Inc.

modeling film (*Joy Gets a Bone Marrow and Spinal Tap*) was part of a treatment package to reduce the distress of young cancer patients (ages 3 to 7) undergoing two very painful treatments, bone-marrow aspirations and spinal taps.[148] (The other major components of the treatment package were breathing exercises, attention diversion strategies, emotive imagery, behavior rehearsal, and reinforcement.) The model in the film, Joy, is a 6-year-old leukemia patient who comes to the clinic for treatment.

> She describes her thoughts and feelings. . . . As a coping model, Joy admits she is scared about the procedures, exhibits some signs of distress, but then copes effectively. . . . Joy explains *why* she has to have the procedures and she illustrates *what* happens at each point in the procedures.[149]

The treatment package successfully reduced the distress for each of the children in the study.

Modeling films to treat adults' fear and distress *during* medical procedures also are beneficial.[150] For example, hyperbaric oxygen therapy (HBO) is a highly intrusive medical procedure in which patients must remain enclosed in a narrow chamber for as long as two hours.[151] To reduce distress and increase compliance with HBO, adult patients viewed a nine-minute coping modeling video before their first HBO session and a feature film (to distract patients) during the first HBO session. No therapy was provided in subsequent sessions. The brief intervention was highly successful and long-lasting. Each of the five therapy patients completed all of their HBO sessions, whereas two of the five control patients refused any HBO and three terminated HBO early.

Sexual anxiety in women is yet another target behavior that has been treated with video modeling.[152] While relaxed and with the option to turn off the modeling videos if they became too anxious, women viewed videos of couples engaging in increasingly more intimate sexual behaviors. In the small number of cases where this treatment has been used, it has been effective in lowering clients' sexual anxiety, and one-year and two-year follow-ups indicate that the changes were maintained.

Storytelling to Reduce Fear and Other Negative Emotions

Storytelling is another form of symbolic modeling used to treat fear. For example, a puppet show depicting a teddy bear going through a typical hospital visit has been shown to be as effective as films, including *Ethan Has an Operation*, which is considered a benchmark.[153] Many commercially available books and pamphlets describing various diagnostic and treatment procedures, such as those found in physicians' offices, have been produced. They usually include modeling in that they describe the experiences of actual or hypothetical patients. For instance, *My Tonsillectomy Coloring Book* presents pictures with rhyming captions that tell the story of a young boy, Cowboy Tim, who goes to the hospital to have his tonsils removed (see Figure 11-6).

Uncle Lightfoot is an 85-page book designed to reduce children's fear of the dark.[154] The book presents the story of a young boy, Michael, who is afraid of the dark. Michael visits his adopted uncle, Lightfoot, who is a Native

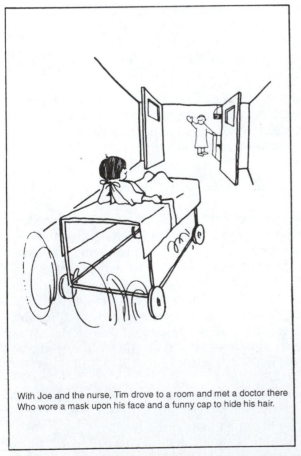

With Joe and the nurse, Tim drove to a room and met a doctor there
Who wore a mask upon his face and a funny cap to hide his hair.

The doctor let him breathe through it and that was quite a treat,
He felt just like an astronaut and drifted off to sleep.

Figure 11-6 Pages from *My Tonsillectomy Coloring Book* that uses modeling to reduce children's anxiety about their impending tonsillectomies
SOURCE: Bob Knight and Associates, 1969.

Figure 11-7 Picture from *Uncle Lightfoot*, a story book that uses modeling to reduce children's fear of the dark
SOURCE: Coffman, 1980.

American living on a farm. Uncle Lightfoot teaches Michael games to play in the dark, which makes being in the dark fun (see Figure 11-7). Michael is a coping model, and the games he learns put him in progressively more threatening situations (depicted, in part, by the pictures in the book becoming darker). Games based on the ones Michael plays have been developed, allowing children to engage in behavior rehearsal with their parents after reading the book.

Folktale characters serve as models of adaptive functioning in a given culture. Because members of the culture are familiar with the characters, they easily can identify with them. Folktales have been used to enhance the psychological functioning of Puerto Rican children (ages 5 to 11) living in the United States who have a high risk of developing psychological disorders.[155] The children were read two types of folktales: original Puerto Rican folktales and Puerto Rican folktales that were adapted to include settings and values indigenous to the United States. The children and their mothers discussed the stories and acted out the prominent behaviors portrayed. This modeling therapy significantly reduced the children's general level of anxiety and aggressive behaviors and improved their social judgment, as compared both with traditional art/play therapy and with no treatment. The reductions in anxiety were maintained 1 year later. In general, the adapted folktales, which bridged the children's bicultural identification, were more effective than the original folktales that were based solely on Puerto Rican culture. This finding is consistent with the general principle of maximizing observer-model similarity.

Covert modeling, in which clients imagine modeling sequences, can be used to treat anxiety-related problems, such as social anxiety,[156] phobias,[157] anxiety anticipatory to surgery,[158] and obsessive-compulsive disorder.[159] Covert modeling implicitly is part of storytelling because the observer imagines the character's actions. Parents and teachers frequently use stories, rather than direct instructions, to influence children's behaviors and emotions.[160] Modeling can be more effective than instructions because modeling provides *suggestions* rather than directives, which puts children "in charge" of their own behaviors. For instance, a father discovered that it was more effective to tell his eight-year-old daughter a story about the way he handled a bully when he was a child than to give her explicit instructions about how to deal with a bully.[161]

◆ ALL THINGS CONSIDERED: MODELING THERAPY AND SKILLS TRAINING

Modeling is effective in reducing skills deficits and treating fear and anxiety-related disorders.[162] Although early research consisted mostly of analogue studies (for example, studies of college students afraid of snakes),[163] recent controlled experiments have dealt with clinical populations and serious problems. Overall, modeling therapies have been found to be at least as effective as other behavior therapies with which they have been compared. For a number of specific applications, such as in reducing children's fears,[164] modeling procedures have been shown to be more effective.[165]

Modeling therapies are very efficient. Significant changes sometimes are obtained in one or two brief sessions.[166] The reason for this efficiency may be that modeling simultaneously teaches clients adaptive behaviors, prompts their performance, motivates their practice, and reduces anxiety about performing the behaviors. Symbolic modeling is highly cost-effective. Modeling videos and books can be used by many clients simultaneously and do not require therapists' time. For example, modeling videos to reduce fear of dental procedures now are routinely shown in some dentists' offices. The major limitation of standard symbolic modeling presentations is that they are aimed at the "average" client, which means that they are not individualized. Symbolic modeling can be supplemented with individualized live modeling, in which case the live modeling may not have to be as extensive and time-consuming because the client has already been exposed to symbolic modeling. Further, present technology makes it possible to customize symbolic modeling relatively easily. For instance, individualized modeling videos can be made using camcorders,[167] and written stories can be customized with a word processor by changing a few significant phrases (such as names of people and locations).

Modeling therapies can be carried out easily in naturalistic settings by nonprofessional behavior change agents, which is another way in which they are efficient. In one application, social skills training for preschoolers with low levels of peer social interactions consisted of modeling and prompting by teachers' aides, followed by behavior rehearsal.[168] The training significantly increased the children's levels of social interactions in a short time.

Modeling can be highly cost-effective in another way. **Natural models**—people in the everyday environment who exhibit behaviors that clients need to learn and practice—are abundantly available, and clients can observe them on their own.[169] For example, a client who is fearful of speaking to people at social gatherings could go to a large party and observe how people speak to one another and what happens when they do (vicarious consequences). Although the use of natural models is a potentially potent and efficient form of modeling therapy, the extent to which behavior therapists instruct clients to observe natural models is unknown.

Modeling appears to be an inherently acceptable therapy to clients. It is a subtle and unintrusive treatment. Modeling indirectly influences clients merely by presenting an example of how one might behave. Thus, clients may feel freer, more in control, and more responsible for their behavior changes with modeling than with other types of behavior therapy that operate directly "on them," such as reinforcement. This is important because behavior change is more effective when people believe that they are personally responsible for the change.

Modeling is a component of many behavior therapies. For example, modeling becomes part of in vivo exposure and in vivo flooding when the therapist demonstrates the desired behavior for the client (such as walking out of the house in the case of agoraphobia).[170] The therapist's modeling not only prompts the target behavior but also shows the client that no harm comes from performing it. Modeling also is a component of many cognitive-behavioral therapies, which you will read about in Chapters 12 and 13.

Besides being a treatment modality, modeling is used to teach therapy skills to therapists and nonprofessional change agents, including clients themselves.[171] For example, modeling is an essential component in behavioral child management training (as you saw in Chapter 8).[172] The therapist first models a behavior management procedure, such as shaping. Then parents practice shaping their children's behaviors and receive feedback from the therapist. Similar procedures are used to teach family members to care for elderly relatives with physical and psychological impairments.[173] Modeling also has potential for encouraging clients to seek therapy[174] and in preparing clients for psychotherapy.[175]

SUMMARY

1. Modeling requires two people: a model who demonstrates a behavior and an observer who attends to what the model does. Live models are actually present, and symbolic models are observed indirectly, as on TV.
2. Observing a model provides information about what the model does as well as the consequences of the model's actions, which are called vicarious consequences (vicarious reinforcement or vicarious negative consequences).

3. Modeling serves five functions for observers: teaching, prompting, motivating, reducing anxiety, and discouraging.

4. Observational learning is the process by which people are influenced by observing a model's behaviors. It involves three stages: exposure to the model, acquisition of the model's behaviors, and acceptance of the model's behaviors as guides for one's own actions. The observer can be influenced by the model in four ways: specific imitation, specific counterimitation, general imitation, and general counterimitation.

5. Modeling procedures often are supplemented with behavior rehearsal, which involves systematic practice. Modeling often is part of a treatment package, but modeling can be effective by itself.

6. Modeling therapies have been used primarily for two broad classes of target behaviors: skills deficits and fears. Skills deficits can involve deficiencies in knowledge, proficiency, motivation, and discrimination. Skills training is a treatment package that may include modeling, direct instruction, prompting, shaping, reinforcement, behavior rehearsal, role playing, and corrective feedback.

7. Modeling films/videos are an effective means of increasing social interactions of young children, adolescents, and elderly clients.

8. Self-modeling, in which clients serve as their own models (usually on a video), can be effective in alleviating social skills deficits. Video futures have clients view self-modeling sequences of their acting adaptively in challenging situations they will encounter in the future.

9. Pervasive social skills deficits may require live modeling and intensive individual treatment. In some cases, clients may have to be taught generalized imitation—the ability to imitate—before modeling can be used to treat other behaviors.

10. Social skills training is an important component in the treatment of clients with schizophrenia. The major goals are to increase social interactions, to teach skills needed for functioning in the community, and to reduce stress by teaching clients to cope with problematic social situations.

11. Assertive behaviors are actions that secure and maintain what one is entitled to in an interpersonal situation without impinging on the rights of others. Assertive behaviors are situation-specific.

12. Assertion training begins by assessing the nature and extent of the client's deficits in assertive behaviors. Live or symbolic modeling and behavior rehearsal are the primary components of assertion training. In covert modeling and covert behavior rehearsal, clients imagine a model who acts assertively and imagine themselves imitating the model. The effectiveness of assertion training treatment packages has been well documented.

13. Vicarious extinction involves reducing fear or anxiety by having a client observe a model performing the feared behavior without the model incurring negative consequences. A coping model is initially fearful and incompetent and then gradually becomes comfortable and competent performing the feared behavior. A mastery model shows no fear and is

competent from the outset. Coping models are more appropriate for reducing fear.

14. In participant modeling, the therapist models the anxiety-evoking behaviors for the client, then verbally and physically prompts the client to perform the behaviors, and finally fades the prompts.

15. Perceived self-efficacy is the belief that one will be successful at a task. Modeling and other therapies may be effective because they increase clients' self-efficacy through performance accomplishments, vicarious experiences, verbal persuasion, and emotional arousal.

16. Film/video modeling has been used to treat fear of medical procedures in both children and adults. Storytelling is another form of symbolic modeling used to reduce fear and other negative emotions in children.

17. Modeling therapies are effective and efficient treatments for skills deficits and for anxiety-related disorders. They simultaneously teach clients adaptive behaviors, prompt performance, motivate practice, and reduce anxiety about performing the threatening behaviors. Modeling is a subtle and unintrusive therapy and is acceptable to clients. Modeling is a component of many behavior therapies because therapists often model adaptive behaviors. Modeling also is used to train therapists and other change agents in therapy procedures.

REFERENCE NOTES

1. Kalmuss, 1984.
2. Craig, 1986.
3. Gould & Shaffer, 1986; Lester, 1987; Ostroff & Boyd, 1987; compare with Wasserman, 1984.
4. For example, Bly, 1990; Campbell, 1988; Constantino, Malgady, & Rogler, 1986.
5. Kazdin, 1973, 1974a, 1974b, 1974c.
6. Compare with Strain, Shores, & Kerr, 1976; Wilson, Robertson, Herlong, & Haynes, 1979.
7. Bandura, 1971, 1977b.
8. Kazdin, 1979; Rosenthal & Steffek, 1991.
9. Compare with Kellam, 1969; Maeda, 1985; Olson & Roberts, 1987; Owusu-Bempah & Howitt, 1985; Rosenthal, Linehan, Kelley, Rosenthal, Theobald, & Davis, 1978; Rosenthal, Rosenthal, & Chang, 1977; Wickramasekera, 1976.
10. Liebert & Spiegler, 1994.
11. From the author's (MDS) clinical files.
12. O'Donohue & Krasner, 1995a, 1995b.
13. For example, Corrigan, Schade, & Liberman, 1992; Hansen, MacMillan, & Shawchuck, 1990; Taras, Matson, & Leary, 1988.
14. For example, Charlop & Milstein, 1989; Gambrill, 1995a.
15. For example, Star, 1986.
16. For example, Baggs & Spence, 1990.
17. For example, Charlop & Milstein, 1989; Charlop, Schreibman, & Tryon, 1983; Egel, Richman, & Koegel, 1981; Lovaas, 1977, 1987.
18. For example, Goldstein & Mousetis, 1989; Rietveld, 1983.
19. For example, Rivera & Smith, 1988; Smith & Lovitt, 1975.
20. For example, Foxx, Martella, & Marchand-Martella, 1989.
21. Newman & Haaga, 1995.
22. O'Donohue & Noll, 1995.
23. Szymanski & O'Donohue, 1995.
24. Pierce, 1995.
25. Vargas & Shanley, 1995.
26. Haring, Breen, Weiner, Kennedy, & Bednerah, 1995.
27. Rusch, Hughes, & Wilson, 1995.
28. Barclay & Houts, 1995.
29. Matson, Sevin, & Box, 1995.
30. Trower, 1995.
31. Gambrill, 1995b.
32. Gottman & Rushe, 1995.

33. Gold, Letourneau, & O'Donohue, 1995.
34. Gambrill 1995a.
35. Frame & Matson, 1987.
36. Matson, Sevin, & Box, 1995.
37. Gambrill, 1995b; Trower, 1995.
38. Ballard & Crooks, 1984; O'Connor, 1969; Rao, Moely, & Lockman, 1987.
39. O'Connor, 1969, p. 18.
40. O'Connor, 1969; Rao, Moely, & Lockman, 1987.
41. O'Connor, 1969.
42. For example, Star, 1986.
43. Franco, Christoff, Crimmins, & Kelly, 1983.
44. For example, Graves, Openshaw, & Adams, 1992.
45. For example, Foxx, Faw, & Weber, 1991.
46. For example, Cunliffe, 1992.
47. For example, Middleton & Cartledge, 1995.
48. For example, Guevremont, 1990.
49. Varni, Katz, Colegrove, & Dolgin, 1993.
50. Rasing, Coninx, Duker, & Van Den Hurk, 1994.
51. Gambrill, 1985; Garland, 1985.
52. Carstensen & Fisher, 1991.
53. O'Donohue, Fisher, & Krasner, 1986.
54. Bandura, 1986b.
55. For example, Barry & Overmann, 1977; Hicks, 1965; Kazdin, 1974b; Kornhaber & Schroeder, 1975; Rosekrans, 1967.
56. Meharg & Woltersdorf, 1990.
57. Simmons, 1993, p. 161, emphasis in original.
58. Creer & Miklich, 1970.
59. For example, Dowrick, 1991; Dowrick & Hood, 1978; Dowrick & Raeburn, 1977.
60. Dowrick, 1994.
61. Dowrick, 1983.
62. Dowrick, 1991, 1994.
63. Dowrick, Ben, & Wiedle, 1995.
64. Dowrick, 1996.
65. Neef, Bill-Harvey, Shade, Iezzi, & DeLorenzo, 1995.
66. Raymond, Dowrick, & Kleinke, 1993.
67. Dowrick & Raeburn, 1995.
68. Dowrick, 1979, 1986.
69. Dowrick & Hood, 1978; Kehle, Owen, & Cressy, 1990; Pigott & Gonzales, 1987.
70. Hosford, 1974.
71. Dowrick, 1978.
72. Davis, 1979; Dowrick & Raeburn, 1977; Kehle, Clark, Jenson, & Wampold, 1986.
73. Kahn, Kehle, Jenson, & Clark, 1990; Prince & Dowrick, 1984.
74. Hosford & Brown, 1975.
75. Andersson, Melin, Scott, & Lindberg, 1995.
76. Dowrick & Raeburn, 1995.
77. For example, James & Egel, 1986; Taras, Matson, & Leary, 1988; Valenti-Hein, Yarnold, & Mueser, 1994.
78. Stravynski, Belisle, Marcouiller, Lavellee, & Elie, 1994.
79. Metz, 1965.
80. Ross, Ross, & Evans, 1971; quotations from p. 277.
81. Bellack, Morrison, Wixted, & Mueser, 1990; Spiegler & Agigian, 1977; Trower, 1995.
82. Emmelkamp, 1994.
83. For example, Bellack & Mueser, 1994.
84. For example, Liberman, Vaccaro, & Corrigan, in press.
85. For example, Liberman, Wallace, Blackwell, Eckman, Vaccaro, & Kuehnel, 1993.
86. Emmelkamp, 1994.
87. Wong, Martinez-Diaz, Massel, Edelstein, Wiegand, Bowen, & Liberman, 1993.
88. For example, Benton & Schroeder, 1990.
89. For example, Bellack & Mueser, 1994; Benton & Schroeder, 1990.
90. For example, Bellack & Mueser, 1994; Benton & Schroeder, 1990; Emmelkamp, 1994.
91. Liberman, Wallace, Blackwell, & Vaccaro, 1993.
92. For example, Bellack & Mueser, 1994; Liberman, Kopelowicz, & Young, 1994; Spiegler & Agigian, 1977.
93. Alberti & Emmons, 1995.
94. Powell, 1996.
95. Kelly, St. Lawrence, Hood, & Brasfield, 1989.
96. For example, Bucell, 1979.
97. For example, Frisch & Froberg, 1987; Gambrill, 1995a; Lazarus, 1973.
98. Lazarus, 1973; Schroeder & Black, 1985.
99. Gambrill, 1995a.
100. Wilson & Gallois, 1993.
101. Alberti & Emmons, 1995; Gambrill, 1995a.
102. Gambrill, 1995a; St. Lawrence, 1987.
103. For example, Gambrill & Richey, 1975; Rathus, 1973.
104. Alberti & Emmons, 1995.
105. McFall & Lillesand, 1971.
106. For example, Eisler, Hersen, & Miller, 1973; Hersen, Eisler, Miller, Johnson, & Pinkston, 1973; McFall & Lillesand, 1971; Prince, 1975.
107. Krop & Burgess, 1993b.
108. For example, Hersen, Kazdin, Bellack, & Turner, 1979; Kazdin, 1974d, 1976; Maeda, 1985; Rosenthal & Reese, 1976.
109. For example, Hersen, Kazdin, Bellack, & Turner, 1979; Rosenthal & Reese, 1976.
110. Gambrill, 1995a.

111. Kern, 1982; Kern, Cavell, & Beck, 1985; Romano & Bellack, 1980; Woolfolk & Dever, 1979.
112. Levin & Gross, 1984; St. Lawrence, Hansen, Cutts, Tisdelle, & Irish, 1985.
113. Franks & Wilson, 1976, p. 148.
114. Meichenbaum, 1971.
115. Bandura, 1986b.
116. Ozer & Bandura, 1990.
117. For example, Öst, 1989.
118. For example, Sarason, 1975.
119. For example, Mattick & Peters, 1988.
120. For example, Silverman, 1986; Thyer, 1985.
121. Klesges, Malott, & Ugland, 1984; quotation from p. 161.
122. Milgrom, Mancl, King, & Weinstein, 1995.
123. Ritter, 1968a, 1968b.
124. Ritter, 1968a, 1968b, 1969a, 1969b, 1969c.
125. Bandura, 1976; Bandura, Jeffery, & Gajdos, 1975; Bandura, Jeffery, & Wright, 1974; Blanchard, 1970.
126. Ritter, 1969a; quotation from pp. 170-171.
127. For example, Ladouceur, 1983; Minor, Leone, & Baldwin, 1984.
128. Klingman, Melamed, Cuthbert, & Hermecz, 1984.
129. Altmaier, Leary, Halpern, & Sellers, 1985.
130. Downs, Rosenthal, & Lichstein, 1988; Menzies & Clarke, 1993; Osborn, 1986.
131. For example, Williams & Zane, 1989.
132. Menzies & Clarke, 1993.
133. For example, Downs, Rosenthal, & Lichstein, 1988; Klingman, Melamed, Cuthbert, & Hermecz, 1984.
134. Williams, Dooseman, & Kleifield, 1984; Williams, Turner, & Peer, 1985; Williams & Zane, 1989.
135. Bandura, 1986b.
136. Peterson & Ridley-Johnson, 1980.
137. Kleinknecht & Bernstein, 1979; Klorman, Hilpert, Michael, LaGana, & Sveen, 1980; Melamed, 1979; Melamed, Hawes, Helby, & Glick, 1975; Melamed, Weinstein, Hawes, & Katkin-Borland, 1975.
138. Bandura, 1977a, 1986b, 1989, 1997; Schwarzer, 1992.
139. Cervone & Peake, 1986.
140. Cervone & Scott, 1995.
141. For example, Haaga, 1990.
142. Bandura, 1984.
143. Melamed & Siegel, 1975.
144. Melamed & Siegel, 1975, p. 514.
145. Melamed & Siegel, 1975.
146. Vernon, 1974.
147. Vernon, 1974.
148. Jay, Elliott, Ozolins, Olson, & Pruitt, 1985.
149. Jay, Elliott, Ozolins, Olson, & Pruitt, 1985, p. 516.
150. Shipley, Butt, & Horwitz, 1979; Shipley, Butt, Horwitz, & Farbry, 1978.
151. Allen, Danforth, & Drabman, 1989.
152. Nemetz, Craig, & Reith, 1978; Wincze & Caird, 1976.
153. Peterson, Schultheis, Ridley-Johnson, Miller, & Tracy, 1984.
154. Mikulas & Coffman, 1989; Mikulas, Coffman, Dayton, Frayne, & Maier, 1985.
155. Constantino, Malgady, & Rogler, 1986.
156. Dawe & Hart, 1986.
157. Cautela, 1993; Jackson & Francey, 1985.
158. A. J. Kearney, 1993.
159. Hay, Hay, & Nelson, 1977.
160. Compare with Swaggart, Gagnon, Bock, Earles, Quinn, Myles, & Simpson, 1995.
161. Author's (MDS) clinical files.
162. Bandura, 1986b; Rachman & Wilson, 1980.
163. For example, Thelen, Fry, Fehrenbach, & Frautschi, 1979.
164. Graziano, DeGiovanni, & Garcia, 1979; Ollendick, 1979.
165. Rachman & Wilson, 1980.
166. For example, Allen, Danforth, & Drabman, 1989; Dowrick & Raeburn, 1995; Rao, Moely, & Lockman, 1987; Spiegler, Liebert, McMains, & Fernandez, 1969.
167. For example, Charlop & Milstein, 1989; Dowrick, 1991.
168. Storey, Danko, Ashworth, & Strain, 1994.
169. Spiegler, 1970.
170. For example, Mattick & Peters, 1988; Silverman, 1986; Thyer, 1985.
171. Altmaier & Bernstein, 1981; Brown, Kratochwill, & Bergan, 1982; Duley, Cancelli, Kratochwill, Bergan, & Meredith, 1983.
172. For example, Ducharme, Pontes, Guger, Crozier, Lucas, & Popynick, 1994; Ducharme & Popynick, 1993; Minor, Minor, & Williams, 1983; Webster-Stratton, 1981a, 1981b, 1982a, 1982b, 1984.
173. Pinkston, Linsk, & Young, 1988.
174. Park & Williams, 1986.
175. For example, Day & Reznikoff, 1980; Doster, 1972; Truax, Shapiro, & Wargo, 1968; Weinstein, 1988.

Chapter 12

Cognitive-Behavioral Therapy: Cognitive Restructuring

Michael stood at the top of the expert ski slope contemplating his fate. "Do you think I can make it?" Michael asked Daryl, his ski instructor. Daryl smiled and matter-of-factly said, *"Whether you think you can, or whether you think you can't, you're right."*

The way we think about events in our lives exerts a powerful and pervasive influence on how we act and feel.[1] *Cognitions* are thoughts—including beliefs, assumptions, expectations, attributions, and attitudes. *Cognitive-behavioral therapy* changes cognitions that are the maintaining conditions of a wide array of psychological disorders and problems. Cognitive-behavioral therapy has proliferated during the past 15 years. In a 1987 survey of more than 3,000 behavior therapists, 69% of the respondents identified their approach to therapy as cognitive-behavioral.[2] Clearly, cognitive-behavioral interventions are at the forefront of behavior therapy.[3]

NATURE OF COGNITIVE-BEHAVIORAL THERAPY

The nature of cognitive-behavioral therapy is revealed by its hyphenated name. Clients' cognitions are modified in two ways: cognitively and behaviorally. Cognitions are modified *directly* by teaching clients to change their maladaptive thoughts and *indirectly* by helping clients change their overt actions. Changing what people do overtly in order to change what they think is the time-honored strategy for attitude change.[4] For example, arguing *for* a political position with which you *disagree* is likely to make you more favorably disposed toward the position. Although the emphasis on cognitive (direct) versus overt behavioral (indirect) change varies in different cognitive-behavioral therapies, most include both cognitive and behavioral components.[5]

Cognitive-behavioral therapies fit into two basic models.* **Cognitive restructuring therapy,** the first model, teaches clients to change distorted and erroneous cognitions that are maintaining their problem behaviors. **Cognitive restructuring** involves recognizing maladaptive cognitions and substituting more adaptive cognitions for them. Cognitive restructuring is used when clients' problems are maintained by an *excess* of *maladaptive* thoughts. The other model is **cognitive-behavioral coping skills therapy,** which teaches clients adaptive responses—both cognitive and overt behavioral—to deal effectively with difficult situations they encounter. This model is appropriate for problems that are maintained by a *deficit* in *adaptive* cognitions. The two models are summarized in Table 12-1. Cognitive restructuring therapy is covered in this chapter, and cognitive-behavioral coping skills therapy is described in Chapter 13.

* Our conceptualization of two models of cognitive-behavioral therapy is consistent with Kendall and Braswell's (1985) distinction between cognitive distortions and deficits, and it shares commonalities with the categories of mechanisms used to change cognitions proposed by Ross (1977) and Hollon and Beck (1986).

Table 12-1 Two models of cognitive-behavioral therapy

	Cognitive Restructuring	Cognitive-Behavioral Coping Skills
USED TO TREAT	Excess of maladaptive cognitions	Deficit of adaptive cognitions
GOAL OF THERAPY	Substituting adaptive cognitions for maladaptive cognitions	Using cognitive-behavioral coping skills
EXAMPLES OF THERAPIES	Thought stopping Rational emotive behavior therapy Cognitive therapy	Self-instructional training Problem-solving therapy/training Stress inoculation training Cognitive-behavioral couple therapy

Operationalizing Cognitions: Making Private Thoughts Public

Behavior therapists pride themselves on dealing with concrete, observable phenomena. How, then, do they handle such abstract, amorphous phenomena as thoughts, beliefs, and attitudes? You may discover the answer to this dilemma by taking just two minutes to complete Participation Exercise 12-1 before reading any further.

Participation Exercise 12-1

THINKING ABOUT THINKING

Identify a problem that you must solve or deal with in the near future. The problem can be a major one, such as having to make a decision that will influence your future in a significant way; or the problem can be a minor one, such as deciding what you should do this weekend. The only requirement is that the problem be detailed enough so that you can easily spend several minutes thinking about it.

Once you have chosen a problem, think about it for one minute. As you think about the problem, *be aware of your thoughts, particularly the form they take.* "Listen" to yourself thinking. After doing this for a minute, continue reading.

What form did your thoughts take? They probably included words, phrases, and perhaps full sentences. Much of our thinking involves the explicit use of language (as you will see in In Theory 12-1). Capitalizing on this fact, behavior therapists operationally define cognitions as **self-talk,** or what people say to themselves when they are thinking. If you want to know what someone is thinking, the question that is likely to be most productive is: *"What are you saying to yourself?"* Cognitions also consist of sensory images (including visual, auditory, and tactile), but the focus in cognitive-behavioral therapy is on inner, verbal language.[6]

We often are not aware of our inner speech. In other words, we do not think about our thinking (as you just did in Participation Exercise 12-1). Thinking is a habitual, automatic process that goes on even when we are not specifically engaged in mental endeavors, such as when we are exercising and eating.

Only after clients can identify what they are telling themselves can they change the cognitions that are maintaining their problems. Thus, the first step in cognitive-behavioral therapy is for clients to become aware of their self-talk—especially before, during, and after their problem behaviors occur.

This chapter is devoted primarily to two cognitive-behavioral therapies that make extensive use of cognitive restructuring: *rational emotive behavior therapy* and *cognitive therapy.* We also will briefly describe *thought stopping,* a simple technique that employs cognitive restructuring to reduce upsetting thoughts. However, first things first—that is, assessing cognitions, the initial step in cognitive restructuring therapy.

◆   **In Theory 12-1**

TALKING TO YOURSELF ISN'T NECESSARILY CRAZY

The world is such and such or so-and-so only because we tell ourselves that is the way it is. . . . You talk to yourself. You're not unique at that. Every one of us does that. We carry on internal talk. . . . In fact we maintain our world with our internal talk.[7]

Thus does Carlos Castaneda's Don Juan suggest the salience of "inner speech" in our lives. More specifically, inner speech has been described as the

soundless, mental speech, arising at the instant we think about something, plan or solve problems in our mind, recall books read or conversations heard, read and write silently. In all such instances, we think and remember with the aid of words which we articulate to ourselves. Inner speech is nothing but speech to oneself, or concealed verbalization, which is instrumental in the logical processing of sensory data, in their realization and comprehension within a definite system of concepts and judgments. The elements of inner speech are found in all our conscious perceptions, actions, and emotional experiences, where they manifest themselves as verbal sets, instructions to oneself, or as verbal interpretations of sensations and perceptions. This renders inner speech a rather important and universal mechanism.[8]

Assessing Cognitions

Four basic methods are used by behavior therapists to assess clients' cognitions: interview, self-recording, direct self-report inventory, and think-aloud procedures. Each method elicits clients' self-reports of their cognitions, which is the only way to gain direct information about another's thoughts. The application of interview techniques and self-recording will be illustrated later in the chapter. Here, we will describe the use of self-report inventories and think-aloud procedures.

Direct self-report inventories contain a list of common self-statements related to a particular problem area. Clients indicate the extent to which they make each self-statement.[9] For example, the Social Interaction Self-Statement Test, developed by Carol Glass, lists 15 positive and 15 negative self-statements about problematic heterosocial dating interactions (see Table 12-2).[10] Adults rate each statement on a 5-point scale to indicate how frequently they have had each thought. Children's cognitions also can be assessed with self-report inventories. For instance, the Children's Negative Affectivity Self-Statement Questionnaire assesses maladaptive thoughts associated with anxiety.[11] Standardized self-report inventories are efficient methods for initial screening purposes. They give the therapist a general idea about the type of thoughts the client is having. Specific, individualized assessment requires other methods of assessing cognitions.

Think-aloud approaches have clients verbalize their thoughts (usually by talking into a tape recorder) while engaging in a simulated task or role-playing situation.[12] Because think-aloud methods assess cognitions as they are occurring, they may be better suited to tapping actual thoughts than other methods, such as self-report inventories.[13]

The Articulated Thoughts in Simulated Situations method, developed by Gerald Davison, is an example of a think-aloud procedure.[14] Clients listen to audiotape scenarios designed to elicit different cognitions. A social criticism scenario, for instance, describes a person at a social function who overhears two acquaintances talking about him or her in highly negative terms (such as by ridiculing the person's behaviors and manner of dress). Clients are asked to imagine themselves in the situation and to "tune in" to their thoughts. Every 30 seconds, a tone prompts clients to say their thoughts aloud into a microphone. Clients are assured that there are no right or wrong

Table 12-2 Examples of items on the Social Interaction Self-Statement Test (rated on a five-point scale from "Hardly Ever" to "Very Often")

I hope I don't make a fool of myself.

She/he probably won't be interested in me.

This will be a good opportunity.

It would crush me if she/he didn't respond to me.

This is an awkward situation but I can handle it.

Maybe we'll hit it off real well.

What I say will probably sound stupid.

thoughts, and they are encouraged to verbalize their thoughts without concern about whether they seem appropriate.

Think-aloud procedures are designed for simulated situations rather than actual situations. Talking into a tape recorder while engaging in everyday activities usually is not practical. Thus, highly relevant but low-frequency thoughts that are likely to occur only in vivo may be missed with think-aloud methods.

Thought Stopping

Thought stopping is designed to decrease the frequency and duration of disturbing thoughts by interrupting them and substituting pleasant thoughts for them.[15] Examples of the target behaviors treated with thought stopping are obsessive ruminations (such as constantly worrying about being contaminated by germs), depressive ideas (for example, "Nothing seems to go right"), and self-deprecating thoughts (for instance, "I'm just not good at anything").

Thought stopping involves two phases: (1) first interrupting the disturbing thoughts and (2) then focusing on pleasant thoughts.* Whenever disturbing thoughts occur, the client says, "Stop!" The word is said with a sharp, jolting expression, as if warning of imminent danger. Initially, clients say "Stop!" aloud and later silently to themselves. Although saying "Stop!" usually is the interrupting stimulus, another appropriate stimulus could be used, such as a loud noise or an image of a stop sign.[16]

Therapists sometimes introduce thought stopping to clients with a dramatic demonstration of its effect. The therapist asks the client to concentrate on the disturbing thought and to signal the therapist (such as by raising a finger) when the thought is clear. At that moment, the therapist shouts, "Stop!" The client is then asked, "What happened?" Typically, clients report that they were startled and that the disturbing thought vanished. (You can experience the impact of the procedure for yourself by asking a friend to sharply shout "Stop!" when you are thinking about something intensely.)

Although "Stop!" momentarily eliminates intrusive thoughts, the thoughts may reappear quickly if the person does not start thinking about something else. (As you know, trying *not to think* about something "guarantees" your thinking about it.) Thus, in the second phase of thought stopping, immediately after saying "Stop!" the client focuses on a thought that competes with the disturbing thought (for example, thoughts of succeeding can be substituted for thoughts of failing). The client rehearses appropriate competing thoughts ahead of time so that they will be available at the instant they are needed. The two-phase thought stopping procedure

---

* Thought stopping should not be confused with *thought suppression* that involves deliberate attempts *not* to think about something. Unlike thought stopping, thought suppression can result in either an immediate or delayed increase of the thoughts (Zeitlin, Netten, & Hodder, 1995).

is similar to aversion-relief therapy (discussed in Chapter 7) because it simultaneously decelerates an undesirable target behavior (disturbing thoughts) and accelerates an alternative desirable target behavior (pleasant thoughts). Case 12-1 illustrates thought stopping for intrusive thoughts of jealousy.

ELIMINATING JEALOUSY BY THOUGHT STOPPING[17]

Case 12-1   A 27-year-old unmarried man, K. F., discovered that the woman he was living with had had a brief affair with another man a few weeks before. After an initial period of feeling intensely hurt and angry, K. F. resolved to forget the incident. He wanted the relationship to continue, and he believed that the woman's feelings for him had not changed. However, he frequently thought about the woman's affair and became extremely upset whenever he imagined her being sexually intimate with the other man. These thoughts not only were disturbing, but they also prevented him from concentrating on whatever he was doing at the time.

Several years previously, K. F. had learned thought stopping as part of the treatment for another problem. Recalling the procedure, he applied thought stopping to his jealous thoughts. Whenever he began ruminating about the woman's affair, he yelled "Stop!" to himself and then imagined one of two prearranged pleasant thoughts. One involved the woman acting lovingly toward him. The other was completely unrelated to the woman or the relationship; it concerned his playing a good game of tennis, which was a source of personal satisfaction. Both pleasant thoughts successfully kept him from thinking of the woman's affair.

Before thought stopping, the distressing thoughts had lasted from several minutes to as long as an hour and had occurred on the average of 10 times a day. Thought stopping immediately reduced the duration of the intrusive thoughts to only a few seconds, and the frequency of the intrusive thoughts gradually declined. By the end of the second week, the thoughts occurred about 5 times per week; after a month, they occurred no more than once a week. Three months after K. F. initiated thought stopping, he was completely free of the disturbing thoughts, and they did not return during the 2-year span of his relationship with the woman.

Thought Stopping in Perspective

Thought stopping is a simple, straightforward procedure that is used to treat intrusive, disturbing thoughts. Such thoughts not only are upsetting to the individual, but they also result in a variety of serious problems that thought stopping has been successful in treating, including anxiety,[18] compulsive behaviors,[19] headaches,[20] excessive masturbation,[21] physical aggression,[22] and self-injurious behaviors.[23]

Clients can quickly learn and easily apply thought stopping on their own with little or no supervision from a therapist. As illustrated in Case 12-1, thought stopping, like other cognitive-behavioral therapies, provides clients with self-control skills that they can generalize to other problems.[24]

Thought stopping usually is part of a treatment package. It is used relatively frequently, which seems to indicate that it is effective.[25] However, little controlled research has been done to validate its effectiveness.[26] Further, it is difficult to draw conclusions from the few existing outcome studies because they contain methodological weaknesses.[27] Despite the lack of definitive evidence for its efficacy, there appear to be no risks associated with clients' using thought stopping.

RATIONAL EMOTIVE BEHAVIOR THERAPY

Albert Ellis

Rational emotive behavior therapy[28] (REBT) is a well-known treatment that employs cognitive restructuring to change the irrational thoughts that cause psychological problems such as anxiety, depression, anger, and guilt.[29] REBT was designed by Albert Ellis 40 years ago.[30] The procedures follow logically from Ellis's theory of how psychological disorders develop and are maintained. Before reading about his theory, take two minutes to complete Participation Exercise 12-2. It will provide an experience that will help you understand Ellis's theory.

Participation Exercise 12-2

WHAT ARE YOU MAD ABOUT?

First, take out a paper and pen. Then, read the following scenario and picture yourself in the situation described—in other words, role play it in your mind as if it was happening to you.

> You are taking out a special friend for a birthday celebration that you want to be especially nice. You have made a reservation at a fancy restaurant and have dressed up for the occasion. When you arrive at the restaurant, you give your name to the hostess, who goes to check the reservation book to see which table you've been assigned. As you are waiting, your friend remarks, with obvious appreciation, how elegant the restaurant is. When the hostess returns, she tells you that she cannot find your reservation and that it will not be possible to seat you that evening. Not surprisingly, you are mad!

Now write brief answers to the following two questions.

1. What has made you angry?
2. What are you saying to yourself?

Now continue reading.

Rational Emotive Theory of Psychological Disorders

According to Ellis's rational emotive theory, psychological problems—negative emotions and maladaptive behaviors—are maintained by the *interpretations* people give to events in their lives. This is the fundamental assumption on which REBT and other cognitive restructuring therapies are based. It was succinctly stated almost 2000 years ago by the Greek Stoic philosopher Epictetus, who said that *people are disturbed not by things but by the views they take of them.*

What is striking about this simple idea is that most people would disagree with it. Generally, people believe that "things" cause negative emotions. When someone takes the parking spot we are about to pull into, we get angry *because* someone took "our" spot. In contrast, Ellis's theory holds that our *beliefs* about the event, not the event itself, are what make us angry. The sequence always is the same: (1) some event activates (2) an irrational belief that results in (3) negative consequences (negative emotions as well as maladaptive behaviors). In the parking spot example, our anger is likely to be the *direct* result of irrational beliefs such as: "That was *my* parking spot"; "It's not fair"; "That so-and-so *made* me late for my appointment." Why are these beliefs irrational?

The beliefs that maintain psychological problems are irrational because they have arisen from faulty reasoning or logical errors, such as absolute thinking, overgeneralizing, and catastrophizing.[31] *Absolute thinking* is viewing an event in an all-or-none, black-or-white fashion, such as "I must *always* do well" and "Others should treat me considerately and precisely in the manner I would like to be treated." *Overgeneralization* is drawing the conclusion that all instances of a situation will turn out a particular way because one or two did. For example, after having delivered one poor lecture, a professor told himself, "I'll never be a good lecturer." *Catastrophizing* involves seeing minor situations as disastrous. For instance, a woman who received a low grade on a quiz told herself, "This is the end of my college career."

Ellis has found that two themes often run through the irrational ideas that lead to psychological problems: personal worthlessness and a sense of duty. *Personal worthlessness* is a specific form of overgeneralization associated with failure. For example, a business executive decides that she is "a total failure" because she was unable to get all her work done by the end of the day.

To appreciate the second theme, *before* you continue reading, write down three things you *have* to do this week.

A *sense of duty*, the second theme in irrational ideas, is evident in the use of *must, have to, should,* and *ought to* in speech and thoughts. Ellis colorfully has called the use of these words *musturbation*.[32] Musturbatory statements are irrational because, in fact, there are only a few behaviors that people *must* do (to stay alive). Consider what happens when you are physically ill and unable to attend to normal activities, such as the three things you *have* to do this week. At such times, all the tasks you *had* to get done do not, in fact, get done—yet somehow you survive, and the consequences rarely are catastrophic.

Insisting that you *must* do something is abdicating personal choice. It often may be convenient to blame an external source for what is actually a personal choice. When Juanita responds, "I *have* to study" to her friends' invitation to go out for the evening, her friends readily accept her reason. However, they are likely to find it difficult to accept "I *want* to study." How can Juanita want to study and not want to go out with her friends? Something must be wrong with her! In fact, Juanita may want to go out with her friends, but she wants to study more—most likely because of the negative consequences of not studying, such as failing an exam the next day. Yet, however disagreeable those consequences, she still has the choice to study or go out with her friends.

Although irrational beliefs play an important role in maintaining psychological disorders, they are not the only maintaining conditions. Psychological disorders also are influenced by a complex interaction of innate, biological, developmental, and environmental factors.[33] By changing clients' irrational beliefs, cognitive restructuring therapies modify an important—albeit not the only—class of maintaining conditions.

◆ ▰▰▰▰▰▰▰▰▰▰▰▰▰▰▰▰▰▰▰▰▰▰▰▰▰

Participation Exercise 12-3

KICKING THE MUSTURBATION HABIT*

Most people are unaware that they frequently use the words *must, have to, should,* and *ought to*. For example, students tell teachers, "I can't take the exam on Friday because I *have* to go home for a wedding"; teachers inform students, "You *must* turn in your papers on time." And countless times each day people speak as if the world would end if they do not do one thing or another.

The purpose of this Participation Exercise is to make you aware of your own musturbation and to give you practice in the REBT technique of disputing irrational thoughts and substituting rational thoughts for them.

Over the course of the next few days, write down examples of your use of the words *must, should, have to,* and *ought to* in your speech and thoughts. Record them in the first column of Work Sheet 12-1.† Because we generally are oblivious to our musturbating, ask friends to point out your use of must-type words.

When you have a minimum of 10 musturbatory statements, write a brief rebuttal of each in the second column of the work sheet. The rebuttal should explain why the statement is irrational. Finally, write a rational statement in the third column of the work sheet as an alternative to the irrational, musturbatory statement. The rational statement should reflect your taking responsibility for directing your actions. It should state what you want or choose to do rather than what you believe you must do. Part of a student's work sheet is shown in Figure 12-1 to give you examples of possible rebuttals and rational thoughts.

* You will need to do this Participation Exercise later.
† You will find this work sheet in Appendix C.

Figure 12-1 Excerpts from a student's work sheet used in Participation Exercise 12-3

Musturbatory Thoughts	Rational Rebuttal	Rational Thoughts
I can't go to class because I have to study for next period.	I could go to class if I chose to. I just feel it's important to be well prepared for the exam.	I would rather miss class than risk not being prepared.
I must clean up my room before my parents visit this weekend.	My parents are going to be upset with a messy room, but they won't disown me if my room is a mess.	I'd like to get my room neat before my parents get here.
I have to get home in time to see my favorite TV program.	I sure do enjoy my favorite TV show, but my life won't end if I miss an episode.	I hope I can get home in time for my favorite TV show.

Process of Rational Emotive Behavior Therapy

If irrational beliefs are responsible for the development and maintenance of clients' problems, it follows that the aim of therapy would be to modify these beliefs. This modification is accomplished through three major procedures: (1) identifying thoughts based on irrational beliefs; (2) challenging the irrational beliefs; and (3) replacing thoughts based on irrational beliefs with thoughts based on rational beliefs.

First, to identify thoughts based on irrational beliefs, clients are asked about the specific self-statements they make when they feel upset (for example, depressed) or when they are engaging in maladaptive behaviors. As with other cognitive restructuring therapies, clients may have to learn to attend to their self-talk. Clients may be asked to write down their self-talk whenever their problems occur. Once the client's self-talk associated with the problem has been identified, the therapist points out the self-statements that are based on irrational beliefs and explains why the beliefs are irrational.[34]

Next, the therapist teaches the client to challenge irrational statements by stating why they are irrational. For example:

CLIENT: I feel awful because Tanya wouldn't go out with me. I don't seem to attract women that I am attracted to.

Table 12-3 Example of how the client's understanding of (self-talk about) the causal sequence of events leads to emotional reactions and how the resulting emotional reactions change in REBT

	Real-Life Situation	Client's Self-Talk About Situation	Client's Emotional Reaction
BEFORE THERAPY	Failed course	(Unaware of or not focusing on self-talk)	Angry, depressed
DURING THERAPY	Failed course	1. "This is horrible." 2. "My parents will hit the roof." 3. "I am just plain stupid."	Angry, depressed
AFTER THERAPY	Failed course	1. "This sure won't help my average." 2. "My parents aren't going to be pleased, but they'll get over it." 3. "It's not the end of the world; I can make up the course."	Upset, disappointed

THERAPIST: That doesn't make any sense. You are blowing up the situation, overgeneralizing. I'm sure you don't feel great being turned down, but it's not the end of the world. And it certainly does not follow that just because Tanya isn't interested in going out with you that you are not attractive to other women you like.

Active disputing of irrational beliefs is the key element that distinguishes REBT from other cognitive restructuring therapies.[35] As much as 90% of the therapy session may involve the therapist's challenging the rationality of the client's thoughts and debunking the client's myths about how the world "should be."[36]

Finally, the client learns to substitute rational thoughts for irrational thoughts. In the previous example, the therapist might suggest that the client tell himself, "I'm disappointed that Tanya wouldn't go out with me, but she is not the last woman in the world." Table 12-3 presents an example of the changes in clients' thinking and emotional reactions that are expected over the course of REBT.

Case 12-2 presents part of an initial REBT session and illustrates many of the principles and procedures employed in REBT.

Case 12-2

TREATMENT OF DEPRESSION BY RATIONAL EMOTIVE BEHAVIOR THERAPY[37]

The client was a college student in his second semester at a highly competitive university. He had not found high school particularly challenging, and he earned high grades with little effort. He described himself as apathetic and depressed. The dialogue that follows is an excerpt from the first REBT session. It is annotated with comments about the process and procedures.

THERAPIST: How long have you had these feelings of depression?

CLIENT: Ever since the beginning of this quarter, I think.

THERAPIST: Can you tell me what is bothering you?

CLIENT: Everything is . . . I don't know . . . a bunch of shit. I don't seem to care about anything anymore. I don't even care about school anymore, and that used to mean a lot to me.

THERAPIST: How are you doing in school, gradewise?

T (therapist) asks about possible activating events.

CLIENT: Lousy. This quarter I've studied a total of two hours.

THERAPIST: Let's see. Fall quarter was your first at Stanford? How were your grades then?

CLIENT: Shitty; had a 2.3 average. *C* average. And I worked hard, too. I feel like shoving the whole thing.

THERAPIST: Maybe this is part of what is getting you down. . . . What does that make you, in your eyes?

T inquires about interpretations of external events.

CLIENT: I'm a failure. . . . I'll never get accepted to a decent medical school with grades like that. I'll probably end up pumping gas in Salinas . . . that's all I'm good for. I feel worthless.

C (client) draws an illogical conclusion.

THERAPIST: Sounds like you've been saying to yourself, "I'm a failure . . . I'm worthless" on account of your *C* average last quarter. That would be enough to depress anybody.

T introduces idea of self-talk.

CLIENT: It's true. I've got to do well and I'm not.

Musturbation and absolute thinking.

THERAPIST: So, you believe that in order for you to consider yourself a worthwhile person, you've got to succeed at something . . . like making *A*'s at Stanford?

T makes C's irrational belief explicit.

CLIENT: A person's got to be good at something to be worth a damn. School was the only thing I was ever much good at in the first place.

C confirms the irrational belief.

THERAPIST: I'd like to point out that you're competing against some of the best students in the country, and they don't care very much about grading on a curve there. An average performance among outstanding people isn't really average, after all, is it?

T introduces rational ideas to counter C's irrational ideas.

CLIENT: I know what you are getting at, but that doesn't help too much. Any decent medical school requires at least a *B+* average, and I've got to get into medical school. That's been my goal ever since I was a kid.

More musturbation.

THERAPIST: Now, wait a minute! You say you *have* to go to medical school. Sounds like you think not going to medical school is against the law. Is that so?

CLIENT: Well, not exactly. You know what I mean.

THERAPIST: I'm not sure. Do you really mean that you want very much to go to medical school? Because that is very different from believing that you *must* go to medical school. If you think you have to go to medical school, you are going to treat it like it's a life-or-death thing, which it isn't. But you believe that it is, and that is likely to be a major reason why you're depressed.

T challenges the irrationality of C's "have to" and suggests the rational alternative "want to."

T explains that irrational beliefs maintain depression.

CLIENT: I can see your point, but even if I agreed with you, there's my family. . . . All my life my parents have been telling me that the whole family is counting on my being a doctor.

A possible origin of C's irrational beliefs is revealed.

THERAPIST: OK, but that is their belief. Does it have to be yours?

T disputes C's illogical assumption.

CLIENT: I just can't let them down.

THERAPIST: What would happen if you did?

CLIENT: They'd be hurt and disappointed. Sometimes I almost think they wouldn't like me any more. That would be awful!

Catastrophizing.

THERAPIST: Well, the worst possible thing that could happen if you don't go to medical school is that your father and mother wouldn't like you, and might even reject you. You aren't even sure this would happen. But, even if they did, does it follow that it would be awful? Could you prove that, logically, I mean?

T points out the lack of evidence.

T models logical analysis of C's thoughts and beliefs.

CLIENT: It's lousy when your own family rejects you.

THERAPIST: I still can't see the logical connection between their rejecting you and things being awful or even lousy. I would agree that it wouldn't exactly be

T continues to challenge C's illogical thoughts.

a pleasant state of affairs. You are equating rejection with catastrophe, and I'd like you to try and convince me one follows from the other.

CLIENT: They wouldn't even want me around . . . like I was a worthless shit. And that would be rotten.

THERAPIST: Well, there you go again, telling yourself that because they would reject you, which means they wouldn't want you around, you are a worthless shit. Again, I don't see the logic.

CLIENT: It would make me feel that way.

THERAPIST: No, I emphatically disagree . . . it's *you* who would make you feel that way. By saying those same things to yourself.

T directly confronts C's idea and introduces the basic premise of REBT.

CLIENT: But I believe it's true.

THERAPIST: I'm still waiting for some logical basis for your belief that rejection means you are worthless, or not going to medical school means you're a shit.

CLIENT: OK, I agree about the medical school bit. I don't *have* to go. But about my parents . . . that's heavy. . . . I was thinking . . . where would I go over the holidays? But I don't spend that much time at home anyway, come to think of it. But, there is money . . . this place is damned expensive and I don't have a scholarship. If they cut off funds, that would be a disaster.

C begins to think rationally.

THERAPIST: There you go again . . . catastrophizing. Prove to me that it would be a disaster.

CLIENT: Well, maybe I was exaggerating a bit. It would be tough, though I suppose I could apply for support, or get a job maybe. In fact, I know I could. But then it would take longer to get through school, and that would be shitty.

THERAPIST: Now you are beginning to make a lot of sense. I agree that it would be shitty . . . but certainly not terrible.

CLIENT: You know, for the first time in weeks I think I feel a little better. Kind of like there is a load off my mind. Is that possible?

> THERAPIST: I don't see why not, but I'm wonder-
> ing what would happen if you'd start
> feeling depressed tonight or tomorrow . . .
> how would you deal with it?

At this point, the therapist suggested that the client rehearse identifying and challenging his irrational ideas.

━━━━━━━━━━━━

Many of the characteristics of REBT can be seen in the therapist-client dialogue in Case 12-2. The therapist is very active in challenging the client's irrational thoughts and models this process for the client. The therapist's style is confrontational, almost argumentative. The client's task is to learn to identify and dispute irrational thoughts and beliefs and then to substitute rational thoughts for them. The client first rehearses these skills in the therapy sessions and then is asked to use them at home, which is what the therapist was leading up to at the end of the dialogue in Case 12-2.

Rational Emotive Education

Rational emotive behavior therapy is used primarily with adults. The basic format of disputing irrational beliefs is not as well suited for children, especially young children, as it is for adults who are more practiced at reasoning verbally.[38] A few cases using standard REBT with children have been reported, but its effectiveness has not been evaluated.[39]

Rational emotive education is an adaptation of REBT for children and adolescents.[40] The curriculum includes identifying emotions and differentiating them from thoughts; learning how thoughts, rather than situations, influence emotions; recognizing rational and irrational thoughts; and dealing with common difficult situations (such as being teased) by using these concepts and skills. Children learn experientially, as through the Expression Guessing Game that involves trying to guess the emotions pantomimed by other children. By playing the game, children discover for themselves that the most reliable way to know what other people are feeling is to ask them.

A small number of studies have indicated that rational emotive education can reduce children's irrational thoughts and anxiety. However, the results of these studies are limited because they are based solely on self-report measures.[41] Generally, self-report measures need to be corroborated by observations made by others. Further, rational emotive education has not always been shown to be superior to no-treatment control conditions.[42] Rational emotive education does not appear to be effective for treating children with serious psychological disorders. Potentially, rational emotive education could prevent psychological disorders, as when it is used to promote healthy parenting.[43] However, longitudinal studies have not been carried out to evaluate this possibility.[44]

◆

Participation Exercise 12-4

I FEEL, THEREFORE I THINK: MAKING THE CONNECTION*

Identifying the cognitions that are associated with our emotions and recognizing how our thoughts may influence the way we feel are essential goals of REBT and rational emotive education. This Participation Exercise will help you become more aware of how your thoughts influence your emotions. Over the next few days, whenever you experience a strong emotion (positive or negative), reflect on what you are thinking at the moment—in other words, what you are saying to yourself. Immediately write the emotion and the associated cognitions on an index card or sheet of paper you carry with you. Divide the card into two columns: the first for the *emotion* you are experiencing and the second for your *cognitions* at the time.

After you have collected a sample of different emotions and associated cognitions, ask yourself the following questions: (1) What did you learn from this exercise? (2) Did you find yourself becoming more aware of your self-talk? (3) What were the basic differences between your cognitions associated with positive emotions and your cognitions associated with negative emotions? (4) Did your emotions seem to come from your thoughts or vice versa? The answers to these questions will give you some insight into the basic assumptions and practices of cognitive restructuring therapies.

◆

Rational Emotive Behavior Therapy in Perspective

Rational emotive behavior therapy is popular among therapists and clients for a number of reasons. Its focus on rationality makes sense! Ellis's theory of the development and maintenance of psychological problems is easy to understand. Further, the "direct, persuasive, and authoritative approach . . . conforms to culturally sanctioned doctor-patient roles."[45] The notoriety of REBT has been enhanced by self-help books based on the REBT approach, many of which have been written by Albert Ellis.[46] Ellis, an outspoken advocate of REBT, draws attention because of his colorful personality, which could be described as inspired and charismatic.[47]

Potentially, REBT could be used to treat any problem maintained by irrational beliefs.[48] Problems that have been treated include stress, generalized anxiety, phobias, unassertive behavior, agoraphobia, obsessions, anger, depression, antisocial behaviors, headaches, stuttering, sexual dysfunctions, obesity, and Type A behaviors.[49] In practice, however, the reliance on direct confrontation of clients' beliefs is likely to be ineffective for a number of disorders, including addictions, paraphilias, panic disorder, anorexia and bulimia, and obsessive-compulsive disorder.[50] In fact, there is evidence that confrontation in therapy generally is associated with clients' noncompliance with treatment procedures.[51] Finally, although variations have been devised for children and adolescents,[52] REBT is more suitable for adults.

* You will need to do this Participation Exercise later.

Despite proponents' enthusiastic claims for the clinical efficacy of REBT, empirical evidence supporting these claims is only modest.[53] Many of the studies evaluating the effectiveness of REBT were poorly designed, so that their findings are inconclusive.[54] One major methodological weakness has been a failure to operationally define REBT.[55] Thus, it is not clear which specific therapy procedures were used in different studies. In general, REBT has been found superior to no-treatment and wait-list control groups,[56] but often REBT is only equivalent to or less effective than other behavior therapies (such as systematic desensitization, relaxation, and exposure therapy). Finally, few long-term follow-up studies exist.

No systematic research has been conducted to identify the essential components of REBT, which leaves important questions unanswered.[57] For example, is strong confrontation of the client's irrational beliefs a necessary component? Would the therapy work as well with a gentler exploration of the client's irrational beliefs rather than direct confrontation?[58] These are critical questions to answer because some clients and therapists may feel uncomfortable with REBT because of its "tough-minded," confrontational approach.[59]

COGNITIVE THERAPY

Aaron Beck[60] conceived of **cognitive therapy** at about the same time Ellis was developing REBT in the early 1960s. Beck and Ellis apparently created their theories and techniques independently.[61] Both therapies are based on the fundamental assumption that psychological disorders are maintained by distorted cognitions, and the therapies share the goal of modifying these cognitions. Both involve cognitive restructuring, but the basic strategies for challenging distorted beliefs differ. Cognitive therapy has the client view beliefs as tentative hypotheses; the client then tests the validity of these hypotheses by gathering evidence that refutes (or supports) them.[62] In contrast, REBT primarily relies on direct instruction, persuasion, and logical disputation to challenge distorted beliefs. The major differences between rational emotive behavior therapy and cognitive therapy are summarized in Table 12-4.

Cognitive therapy evolved from Beck's research on the distorted thinking of depressed clients,[63] and treating depression has been its primary focus. More recently, the scope of cognitive therapy has been widened to include anxiety disorders,[64] including phobias,[65] panic attack,[66] and obsessive-compulsive disorder;[67] marital distress;[68] and personality disorders.[69] Cognitive therapy occasionally has been used to treat suicidal behaviors,[70] anorexia,[71] bulimia,[72] obesity,[73] and schizophrenic delusions.[74]

Cognitive Therapy Theory of Psychological Disorders

Beck's theory of the development and maintenance of psychological disorders shares the same fundamental premises as Ellis's theory. Differences emerge in the specific concepts each theory employs. To begin with, Beck refers to maladaptive (irrational) cognitions as **automatic thoughts**, a

Table 12-4 Major differences between REBT and cognitive therapy

	Rational Emotive Behavior Therapy	*Cognitive Therapy*
APPROACH	Deductive	Inductive
BASIS OF APPROACH	Rationality	Empirical evidence
PROCEDURE	Instruction, persuasion, disputation	Empirical hypothesis testing
MECHANISM	Primarily cognitive restructuring	Combination of cognitive restructuring and overt behavioral interventions
ROLE OF THERAPIST	Model of rational thinking (recognizing and disputing irrational beliefs)	Coinvestigator seeking empirical test of client's beliefs
STYLE OF THERAPIST	Confrontational	Collaborative
ROLE OF HOMEWORK	Practice disputing irrational beliefs and cognitive restructuring	Gather evidence to establish validity of beliefs

term that emphasizes how clients experience their distorted thinking.[75] Specifically, clients report that their distorted thoughts arise as if they were a reflex, without prior reflection or reasoning. Automatic thoughts seem totally plausible and valid at the time, which may help explain their powerful influence on one's emotions and actions.

> Beck's theory recognizes that psychological disorders occur when people perceive the world as threatening. When this happens, there is a functional impairment in normal cognitive processing: Perceptions and interpretations of events become highly selective, egocentric, and rigid. The person has a decreased ability to "turn off" distorted thinking . . . to concentrate, recall, or reason. Corrective functions, which allow reality testing and refinement of global conceptualizations, are weakened.[76]

Thus, the person makes systematic errors in reasoning. For example, children who are anxious tend to misinterpret benign situations as hostile,[77] and adults suffering from panic disorder make catastrophic interpretations of their physical sensations (such as increased heart rate).[78] Beck has identified six common *cognitive distortions* or logical errors frequently made by people experiencing psychological distress (see Table 12-5). Not surprisingly, there is some overlap with the common forms of irrationality Ellis has identified.

Process of Cognitive Therapy

The goals of cognitive therapy are (1) to correct clients' faulty information processing; (2) to modify clients' dysfunctional beliefs that maintain maladaptive behaviors and emotions; and (3) to provide clients with the skills and experiences that create adaptive thinking.[79] The therapist and client collaborate to identify the client's dysfunctional beliefs and challenge their

Table 12-5 Cognitive distortions associated with psychological disorders

Cognitive Distortion	Definition	Example
ARBITRARY INFERENCE	Drawing conclusions without sufficient evidence, or when the evidence is actually contradictory	Believing that you have been laid off from a job because of personal incompetence, although the company has gone out of business
OVERGENERALIZATION	Drawing a general conclusion on the basis of a single incident	Concluding that you will never succeed after failing on the first attempt
SELECTIVE ABSTRACTION	Attending to a detail while ignoring the total context	Feeling rejected because a friend who was rushing to catch a bus did not stop to talk
PERSONALIZATION	Erroneously attributing an external event to yourself	Thinking that people who are laughing are laughing at you
POLARIZED (DICHOTOMOUS) THINKING	Thinking in extremes, in a black-or-white or all-or-none fashion	Believing that you are a pauper after having lost your wallet
MAGNIFICATION AND MINIMIZATION	Viewing something as far more or less important than it is	Thinking that you are a poor writer after getting back a paper with several corrections

validity. Because collaboration between the client and therapist is a key element in cognitive therapy, establishing a good therapeutic relationship is considered a prerequisite for effective treatment.[80] *Empathy*—viewing things from another's perspective—is perhaps the most important element in building a good therapeutic relationship.[81] Thus, the cognitive therapist focuses on the client's ways of viewing the world, which include understanding the client's cognitive distortions.

Cognitive therapists help clients recognize dysfunctional beliefs through a *Socratic dialogue.* This involves the therapist's asking clients a series of easily answerable questions that lead clients to recognize dysfunctional beliefs for themselves—rather than directly pointing out such beliefs, as in REBT. It is particularly important for clients to identify automatic thoughts that influence actions and emotions "reflexively."

The client is encouraged to view automatic thoughts as *hypotheses* that are subject to empirical verification rather than as established facts (that is, "the way things are"). The therapist and client design homework assignments that serve as investigations to test these hypotheses, a process Beck calls **collaborative empiricism.**[82] For instance, a woman believed that a man she found attractive, one of her coworkers in a large office, disliked her because he did not talk to her. The therapist suggested that the woman check out the validity of this hypothesis by observing how frequently the man interacted with other women in the office. She found, much to her surprise, that he rarely spoke to any of the women. Thus, her dysfunctional belief, which was based on arbitrary inference and personalization, was disputed with empirical evidence.

Notice that both cognitive therapy and REBT attempt to change faulty thinking, but they employ different strategies. Cognitive therapy uses *empirical* disputation based on observations of actual events to challenge faulty thinking. In contrast, REBT uses *rational* disputation, focusing directly on the illogical nature of the beliefs.

Once clients in cognitive therapy learn to challenge the validity of their dysfunctional beliefs, they are taught to replace them with adaptive beliefs. The woman in our previous example came to see the man she was attracted to as "uninterested in women in general." This statement not only was more accurate but also was more adaptive in that it allowed her to feel better about herself.

Sometimes empirically testing the validity of a dysfunctional belief reveals that the belief is valid—that it is consistent with what actually is occurring. This would have been the case if the woman had discovered that the man was interacting with other women in the office, excluding only her. In such instances, the client is helped to view the situation in a way that fits the data but does not lead to maladaptive reactions. For example, the woman might have changed her thoughts to: "The man doesn't know what he is missing by not paying attention to me. It is his loss, not mine."

The specific techniques used in cognitive therapy to change clients' dysfunctional thinking fall into two categories: cognitive interventions and overt behavioral interventions.

Cognitive Interventions

Cognitive interventions, which are based on cognitive restructuring, change clients' cognitions directly. For example, to dispel unrealistic fear, the therapist and the client would *analyze faulty logic* the client is using, and the therapist might *provide relevant information* about what makes the fear unrealistic (for instance, people rarely are hurt riding elevators).

The *three-column technique* is a homework procedure used to identify errors in thinking. A sheet of paper is divided into three columns. In the first column, the client writes the anxiety-evoking situation; in the second, automatic thoughts; and in the third, the logical errors in these thoughts (as the example in Figure 12-2 shows). Later, the client is asked to phrase the automatic thoughts as hypotheses to be tested empirically.

Generating alternative interpretations is a critical aspect of cognitive restructuring. For example, a student who is anxious about being one of the last to finish exams could counter the thought "I must be stupid" with more adaptive thoughts, such as "I knew the material well and had a lot to say" and "Writing well-organized answers takes time." The therapist first models generating nonthreatening interpretations of anxiety-evoking events, and then the client rehearses this skill.

Reattribution of responsibility is helpful when clients believe they have more control over potentially negative outcomes than they actually do. A young man who was highly anxious about an upcoming date feared that the woman would not have a good time. Through Socratic dialogue, the therapist

Figure 12-2 Example of a client's use of the three-column technique

Situation	Automatic Thoughts	Logical Errors
Wearing new outfit for first time	People are going to laugh at me.	No evidence
Giving an oral report in class	I froze last time, and I'll freeze again.	Overgeneralization
	I'll die if I don't do well.	Magnification
Waiting for an exam to be turned back	I didn't know the answer to two of the questions so I must have failed.	Overgeneralization
	I was one of the last students to finish. I must be stupid.	Arbitrary inference
	The professor didn't smile at me when I saw him today which has to mean that I did poorly.	Personalization
	If I don't get a good grade on this test, my parents will kill me.	Magnification
Lost job	I'm worthless. I can't do anything right.	Overgeneralization
	I'll never find another job. It's no big deal.	Arbitrary inference Minimalization
Family moved away	They just don't want to be around me anymore.	Personalization
Rejected by date	My life is ruined.	Magnification
Getting a B on a paper	I just have no grasp of the material in this course.	Polarized thinking

helped the man accept that he could plan the evening and enjoy it himself, but he had no control over the woman's feelings.

Decatastrophizing is a specific form of reattribution that is useful when clients anticipate dire consequences, which is common in anxiety disorders. Through Socratic dialogue, the client comes to see the absurdity of highly unlikely consequences and entertains more probable alternative, non-catastrophic outcomes. For example, a headache is much more likely to be due to fatigue, hunger, or stress than to a brain tumor.

Overt Behavioral Interventions

Besides modifying clients' cognitions directly, cognitive therapy changes clients' overt behaviors, which indirectly modifies their cognitions and emotions. Consider the example of a client suffering from depression who believes that she cannot take care of herself. Through a shaping procedure, she starts to dress herself and fix her own meals. Given this experience, the client may be able to reconstrue her thoughts about her abilities and begin to feel less helpless and despondent. The actions clients perform often provide the data to refute their illogical beliefs about themselves and the world (such as "I can't take care of myself").

In general, the more severe the clients' disorders and cognitive distortions, the more reliance is put on overt behavioral interventions, at least at the beginning of therapy. For example, clients with severe depression generally have little interest in engaging in Socratic dialogues and generating alternative interpretations. From their perspective, "Everything is hopeless, so what's the use?" Further, their reasoning abilities may be too impaired to benefit from direct cognitive interventions. Thus, changing their overt behaviors may be the better strategy.[83]

Many different techniques are used in cognitive therapy to change overt behaviors, most of which are not unique to cognitive therapy. For example, in vivo exposure might be used for clients who have specific fears. Social skills training, including assertion training, is appropriate when clients' appraisal of their ineptness is accurate. For instance, a client checked out his belief—"Whenever I make a simple suggestion to my wife, she gets upset"—and he found that it was accurate. When the client and therapist role played how the client made "simple suggestions" to his wife, it became clear that his suggestions were more like commands. Accordingly, the client learned and then practiced more adaptive ways of making suggestions to his wife.

Several overt behavioral interventions are unique to cognitive therapy, including the activity schedule, mastery and pleasure rating, and graded task assignment.

ACTIVITY SCHEDULE

An **activity schedule** is used to plan a client's daily activities and is particularly useful for clients who are anxious or depressed. The client and therapist schedule activities for most hours of each day (see Figure 12-3). An activity schedule gives clients who are anxious a sense of direction and control. It counteracts feelings of disorganization and being overwhelmed and serves to distract clients from anxiety-evoking thoughts. Clients who are depressed often are inactive and have difficulty doing even the simplest tasks. In this case, an activity schedule provides a structure that encourages clients to engage in active behaviors throughout the day.

MASTERY AND PLEASURE RATING

Anxious and depressed clients not only need to be active but also need to feel satisfaction and pleasure from what they are doing. The **mastery and pleasure rating** technique provides clients with feedback about the satisfaction and pleasure they actually are experiencing. *Mastery* refers to a sense of accomplishment, and *pleasure* refers to feelings of enjoyment or satisfaction while performing a task. Clients rate each activity on their

Figure 12-3 Portion of an activity schedule for 45-year-old man suffering from depression

	Monday	Tuesday	Wednesday
8–9	Get out of bed, get dressed	Get out of bed, get dressed	Get out of bed, get dressed
9–10	Clean bathrooms	Do grocery shopping	Vacuum house
10–11	Go to museum	↓	Go to library
11–12	Exercise	Exercise	Exercise or take walk
12–1	Lunch	Lunch with friend	Lunch
1–2	Do therapy homework	↓	Clean bedrooms
2–3	Do laundry	Clean living room	Pay bills
3–4	Housework	Visit with mother	Attend therapy
4–5	Read newspaper	Read newspaper	Read newspaper
5–6	Fix dinner	Go out to dinner	Fix dinner
6–7	Eat dinner with family	Do therapy homework	Eat dinner with family
7–8	Clean kitchen	Take walk	
8–9	Watch TV, read novel	Work on computer	Watch TV, read novel
9–11	↓	Read novel	↓

activity schedule for mastery and for pleasure using a 6-point rating scale (with 0 representing no mastery/pleasure and 5 representing maximum mastery/pleasure).[84] Using a rating scale encourages clients to recognize *partial* successes and *small* pleasures. Mastery and pleasure rating is especially useful for depression because it penetrates "the 'blindness' of depressed clients to situations in which they are successful and their readiness to forget situations that do bring them some satisfaction."[85]

GRADED TASK ASSIGNMENT

A **graded task assignment** encourages a client to perform small sequential steps that lead to a goal. It is a specialized shaping technique that allows the client to progress toward a goal with minimal stress. Case 12-3 illustrates the impact that graded task assignments can have on a client whose activity level is minimal. The therapist was Aaron Beck.

Using Graded Task Assignments to Accelerate Walking in a Client with Severe Depression[86]

Case 12-3

The patient was a 52-year-old man who had spent over a year in a hospital without moving away from his bed. He had many trials of antidepressant medications without any improvement. I saw him for only one visit. At this time, the patient was sitting in a chair next to his bed. After preliminary introductions and general social interchanges, the interview proceeded thus:

THERAPIST: I understand that you haven't moved away from your bedside for a long time. Why is that?

PATIENT: I can't walk.

THERAPIST: Why is that? . . . Are your legs paralyzed?

PATIENT: (irritated) Of course not! I just don't have the energy.

THERAPIST: What would happen if you tried to walk?

PATIENT: I'd fall on my face, I guess.

THERAPIST: What would you say if I told you that you were capable of walking any place in the hospital?

PATIENT: I'd say you were crazy.

THERAPIST: How about testing that out?

PATIENT: What's that?

THERAPIST: Whether I'm crazy.

PATIENT: Please don't bother me.

THERAPIST: You said you don't think you could walk. Many depressed people believe that, but when they try it they find they do better than they expected.

PATIENT: I *know* I can't walk.

THERAPIST: Do you think you could walk a few steps?

PATIENT: No, my legs would cave in.

THERAPIST: I'll bet you can walk from here to the door (about 5 yards).

PATIENT: What happens if I can't do it?

THERAPIST: I'll catch you.

PATIENT: I'm really too weak to do it.

THERAPIST: Suppose I hold your arm. (The patient then took a few steps supported by the therapist. He continued to walk beyond the prescribed five yards—without further assistance. He then walked back to his chair, unassisted.)

THERAPIST: You did better than you expected.

PATIENT: I guess so.

THERAPIST: How about walking down to the end of the corridor (about 20 yards)?

PATIENT: I know I don't have the strength to walk that far.

THERAPIST: How far do you think you can walk?

PATIENT: Maybe to the next room (about 10 yards).

The patient easily walked to the next room and then continued to the end of the corridor. [I] . . . continued to propose specific goals and to elicit the patient's responses to the goals. After successful completion of each task, a greater distance was proposed.

Within 45 minutes, the patient was able to walk freely around the ward. He was thereby able to "reward" himself for his increased activity by being able to obtain a soda from the vending machine. Later, when he extended the range of his activities, he was able to walk to different points in the hospital and gain satisfaction from various recreational activities. Within a few days, he was playing Ping-Pong and going to the hospital snack bar and, in less than a week, he was able to walk around the hospital grounds and enjoy seeing the flowers, shrubs, and trees. Another [natural reinforcer] was the favorable response he received from members of the hospital staff and from the other patients. The patient began to speak about himself in positive terms and to make concrete plans for leaving the hospital permanently—a goal he reached in a month.

The graded task assignments helped the patient become more active and provided him with immediate success experiences. The assignments also served as informal investigations to test his hypothesis that he was too weak to walk. When the man's experiences indicated that his belief about himself was invalid, he was able to view himself differently. In turn, this new perspective allowed him to attempt new behaviors that were consistent with the belief that he was healthy and capable of functioning.

Cognitive Therapy for Schizophrenic Delusions

Delusions—blatantly false beliefs people steadfastly hold despite contrary evidence—are a hallmark of schizophrenia. Recently, cognitive therapists have accepted the challenge of treating these upsetting and dysfunctional forms of thinking.[87]

Cognitive therapy for schizophrenic delusions involves the same basic steps used with depression and anxiety. First, cognitive distortions are identified; then evidence for their validity is sought; and finally adaptive cognitions are substituted for the distorted cognitions. A few special procedures and precautions are required, however, because of the nature and severity of schizophrenic delusions. For example, the client-therapist relationship is especially important because clients must trust the therapist to be able to talk about delusions that are frightening, threatening, and bizarre.[88] Directly challenging schizophrenic delusions is avoided because such confrontation frequently meets with negative reactions.[89] This is especially likely with paranoid delusions, which involve thoughts that people are following, plotting against, and wanting to harm the client.

To help identify specific delusional beliefs, the client is asked to keep a daily log of their occurrences. The log includes an indication of the client's strength of conviction that the delusion is true, which may be rated on a 0-to-100 scale, with 100 representing the strongest belief that the delusion is real.

Cognitive therapy for delusions proceeds in a stepwise fashion. Initially the focus is on beliefs having the lowest conviction ratings. As the client begins to feel more comfortable in therapy, more strongly held delusions are addressed.[90] Clients are encouraged to consider alternative interpretations of events.[91] For instance, a 22-year-old man who was hospitalized for schizophrenia believed that a "haggly witch" followed him around wherever he went.[92] Considering alternative interpretations of his delusion (such as "Maybe I just have a wild imagination") dramatically decreased the frequency and strength of his delusions as well as his need for medication (Thorazine) to control his delusional thoughts.

Clients and therapists collaborate to evaluate empirically the evidence on which delusions are based.[93] For example, a client believed that he had to get angry and shout back at hallucinated voices in order to avoid being physically attacked.[94] The client agreed to refrain from becoming angry and shouting back at the voices and then to observe whether he was attacked. When the client discovered that he was not attacked by the voices, he was greatly relieved and became much less concerned about his safety. Such empirical investigations are useful because they allow clients to draw their own conclusions about the validity of their delusions.[95]

Treatment of delusional beliefs in clients with schizophrenia is an exciting recent application of cognitive therapy. It would be premature, however, to comment on its efficacy because controlled research studies have not yet been completed.

Adaptations of Cognitive Therapy to Diverse Populations

Cognitive therapy primarily has been used with adult outpatients. Increasingly, it is being adapted to other populations, including hospitalized patients[96] and the elderly.[97] Adaptations of cognitive therapy for children have been particularly innovative.[98] For example, the Adolescent Coping with Depression program[99] uses popular cartoon strip characters (such as Garfield) to illustrate how negative thoughts contribute to depression and how positive thoughts can improve mood. This therapy program has been modified for African-American adolescents.[100] Cognitive therapy has been adapted for Turkish children with test anxiety who listened to stories in which characters learned to replace negative thoughts with positive thoughts about test taking.[101]

A large-scale cognitive therapy program was developed for children aged 10 to 13 to prevent depression and related difficulties in school (such as conduct problems, low achievement, and poor peer relations). At-risk children were taught to identify inaccurate and overly pessimistic beliefs and then to replace them with more accurate and optimistic thoughts. The program resulted in significant reductions in depression and improvements in classroom behaviors, which were maintained at a 6-month follow-up.[102]

Cognitive therapy, like all therapies, is most effective when it is tailored for the particular characteristics of the client.[103] For example, a creative adaptation of cognitive therapy for religious clients treated for depression employed religious rationales for the therapy procedures and religious arguments to counter clients' irrational beliefs.[104] The religious-oriented cognitive therapy was more effective than standard cognitive therapy for this population.

Participation Exercise 12-5

TURNING YOUR THINKING UPSIDE DOWN: COGNITIVE RESTRUCTURING*

You can use cognitive restructuring to cope with difficult or stressful situations in your daily life. In this Participation Exercise you will read brief descriptions of everyday situations followed by examples of negative self-statements someone faced with the situations might make. These self-statements are maladaptive because they present the consequences of the situation as so terrible that nothing can be done to cope with them. In fact, the situation may be unfortunate, but it is not necessarily disastrous.

Your task is to think of self-statements that are more positive, optimistic, and adaptive. The self-statements also must be realistic. For example, if your new car is stolen, it would be unrealistic to think, "I didn't need the car" because that is not likely to be true.

For each situation and negative self-statement, write two possible alternative self-statements that are positive, optimistic, adaptive, and realistic. Then compare your self-statements with the examples given in Appendix B.

Situation	Negative Self-Statements
1. Having to hand in a long, difficult assignment the next day	1. "There is just no way I can get this work done for tomorrow."
2. Getting into an automobile accident	2. "Oh no, my father will kill me."
3. Being asked to dance but not being a skillful dancer	3. "I can't dance; I'll make a fool of myself."
4. Losing your job	4. "I'll never get another job."
5. Moving to a new home, away from family and friends	5. "Everything I care about is left behind."
6. Having a roommate with whom you don't get along	6. "We'll never get along. What a horrible year this is going to be!"
7. Breaking up with the person you are in love with	7. "She (or he) was everything to me . . . my whole life. I have nothing else to live for."

* This Participation Exercise can be done before you continue or later.

8. Not getting into graduate school

9. Having to participate in a class discussion

10. Reading a favorite magazine for two hours instead of completing assignments due the next day

8. "I guess I'm just too dumb. I don't know what I'll do."

9. "Everyone else knows more than I do, so I'd better not say anything."

10. "I just blew a couple of hours. If I had only worked for those two hours . . . that really makes me mad. Why am I so dumb? I do this all the time."

Cognitive Therapy in Perspective

Beck's studies of the distorted thinking of depressed clients led him to develop cognitive therapy 35 years ago.[105] Subsequently, it has become clear that distorted thinking also is associated with many other psychological disorders, and the general principles of cognitive therapy appear to be adaptable to a variety of disorders. Specialized cognitive therapy procedures have been designed to treat anxiety,[106] obsessive-compulsive disorder,[107] personality disorders,[108] marital distress,[109] and, recently, schizophrenic delusions.[110] In some cases, such as in the treatment of sexual dysfunctions[111] and obesity,[112] cognitive therapy has been employed along with other behavior therapy treatments to deal with clients' cognitive distortions that are contributing to their problems.

The most substantial body of research on the efficacy of cognitive therapy involves the treatment of depression. Cognitive therapy clearly is an effective treatment for depression.[113] Although most of the controlled studies have been conducted with women, cognitive therapy appears to be equally effective with men suffering from depression.[114] The quality of studies has been especially high (in contrast to outcome research on REBT),[115] and many of the studies have been carried out with true clinical populations. The specific interventions are well-defined, so that clinicians using cognitive therapy and researchers evaluating it are employing standard procedures (which is not the case with REBT[116]).

Overall, it appears that cognitive therapy is an effective treatment for acute episodes of depression[117] and is less effective for chronic depression.[118] Successful cognitive therapy for chronic depression may require more sessions and repetition, narrowing the focus to one or two pivotal problems, and enriching mastery and pleasure exercises.[119]

It is especially noteworthy that cognitive therapy has been shown to be at least as effective in treating depression as medication, even in severe cases.[120] Medication, the most common treatment for depression, has major drawbacks, including possible physical and psychological side effects.

Cognitive therapy also may prevent the recurrence of depression to a greater degree than other approaches.[121] It is possible that cognitive therapy (1) sensitizes clients to the types of cognitions associated with depression and

(2) provides them with coping skills to neutralize potential depression-evoking events (such as substituting adaptive thoughts for automatic thoughts).

Evidence from one large-scale, multisite study carried out by the National Institute of Mental Health has called into question whether cognitive therapy is more effective for depression than other forms of treatment.[122] However, the study has a number of methodological flaws.[123] For example, poor adherence to cognitive therapy procedures by some of the therapists[124] may have contributed to the results. It also may be the case that cognitive therapy is more effective than other therapies in particular circumstances (for example, with patients who have certain characteristics, such as possessing some coping skills).[125] Further research is needed to clarify this issue.[126]

Cognitive therapy integrates a variety of cognitive and overt behavioral interventions[127] and emphasizes the self-control theme of behavior therapy.[128] Two self-control procedures—learning hypothesis-testing skills to examine one's beliefs and between-session practice of skills—are specific components of cognitive therapy that are associated with its effectiveness.[129]

Cognitive therapy is popular with clients and therapists for some of the same reasons that REBT is—namely, it makes sense, and it is based on a theory that is easy to understand. In addition, some clients like cognitive therapy because participating in collaborative empiricism and Socratic dialogue allows them to discover the distortions in their thinking for themselves. Indeed, clients report feeling more control over their thoughts and feelings and greater insight into their problems after completing cognitive therapy.[130]

◆   **In Theory 12-2**

CONSTRUCTIVISM: ALL IN THE EYE OF THE BEHOLDER

The philosophical basis of cognitive restructuring is known as *constructivism,* which holds that people make (construct) their own realities—that is, what is real and meaningful to them.[131] The interpretations we place on events—rather than the events themselves—determine the meaning of events. This idea applies both to external events, such as what other people do in relation to us, and to internal events, such as how we are feeling physically.

To appreciate the usefulness of constructivism, consider how frequently the same event has different meanings for different people. On an unusually hot day in October, some people complain about the heat, while others rejoice about getting a few more days of summer weather. As another example, consider the wide discrepancies among eyewitness accounts of accidents and crimes.[132]

Clients construct the irrational thoughts that maintain their negative emotions and maladaptive behaviors. By the same token, they can reconstruct their thoughts—view situations differently—so that their cognitions lead to positive feelings and adaptive behaviors.

This process is illustrated by the case of M. H., a 44-year-old woman who had decided to leave her job at the end of the year, 4 months away.[133] She had been intensely unhappy at work because her supervisor, Wanda, seemed to be criticizing her constantly. Although M. H. felt good about her decision to leave, she increasingly found going to the office aversive. She dreaded the morning commute, felt "on edge" all day, and was relieved when she left work each day.

M. H.'s therapist suggested that she *reframe* (cognitively reconstrue) her interactions with Wanda in such a way that M. H. would come to view them positively. Specifically, the therapist suggested seeing Wanda's criticisms as validating M. H.'s decision to leave her job. M. H. expanded on this general reframe on her own. Each time Wanda criticized her, M. H. told herself something like, "That was really nice of Wanda to show me, once again, how good my decision was." Initially, such selftalk just made her chuckle or smile. By the second week, M. H. was viewing Wanda as her ally rather than her enemy. On one occasion, she told herself, "How wonderful it is to havea friend like Wanda who, several times a day, reminds me of the wisdom of my decision to leave." Within three weeks, M. H. no longer dreaded going to work, remained relaxed while on the job, and left work feeling good. With the new construction of her work situation, M. H. was able to finish out the year with relatively little stress.

CALVIN AND HOBBES copyright 1986 Watterson. Dist. by UNIVERSAL PRESS SYNDICATE. Reprinted with permission. All rights reserved.

◆ ALL THINGS CONSIDERED: COGNITIVE RESTRUCTURING THERAPY

The order in which we have presented the three cognitive restructuring therapies—thought stopping, REBT, and cognitive therapy—parallels the increasing complexity of the procedures they employ. That order also parallels the increasing reliance on behavioral interventions in these therapies: thought stopping is exclusively a cognitive technique; REBT is more cognitive than behavioral; and cognitive therapy integrates cognitive and behavioral interventions.

Whereas the application of thought stopping is restricted to intrusive thoughts, REBT and cognitive therapy treat a wide range of problems, and they overlap in some of their specific procedures. Although REBT and cognitive therapy share the goal of promoting adaptive thought processes, they take two different approaches to attaining it: rational disputation versus collaborative empiricism. Using rational disputation in REBT, the therapist makes the client aware of dysfunctional thoughts through verbal persuasion; from the client's perspective, it is a "tell me" approach. The focus of collaborative empiricism in cognitive therapy is on the client's self-discovery of dysfunctional thinking through empirical hypothesis testing; it is a "show me" approach. Individual clients differ in their preferences for one of these two distinctive tacks, which makes it important to have two different approaches available. Because cognitive therapy and REBT both require clients to reason using better logic or data, they are likely to exclude clients who have limited cognitive abilities due to intellectual deficits (such as severe mental retardation or serious brain damage) or psychological impairment (for example, autistic disorder).

Cognitive restructuring is a core procedure in thought-stopping, REBT, and cognitive therapy. It also is a part of the cognitive-behavioral coping skills therapies that you will read about next in Chapter 13. Changing our interpretations of life events can have a powerful effect on our overt behaviors, our emotions, and our overall satisfaction and happiness in life.[134]

SUMMARY

1. Cognitive-behavioral therapy changes cognitions that are maintaining conditions of psychological disorders in two ways. Cognitions are modified directly, by cognitive restructuring (substituting adaptive thoughts for maladaptive thoughts), and indirectly, by changing overt behaviors.

2. Cognitive-behavioral therapy consists of two basic models. Cognitive restructuring therapy teaches clients to change distorted and erroneous cognitions that are maintaining their problem behaviors and to substitute more adaptive cognitions. Cognitive-behavioral coping skills therapy teaches clients adaptive responses—both cognitive and overt behavioral—to deal effectively with difficult situations they encounter.

3. Cognitions are operationally defined as self-talk. Four basic methods are used to assess clients' cognitions: interview, self-recording, self-report inventory, and think-aloud procedures.

4. Thought stopping decreases the frequency and duration of disturbing thoughts by interrupting them and substituting competing thoughts.

5. Rational emotive behavior therapy (REBT) employs cognitive restructuring to change irrational thoughts. Ellis's rational emotive theory holds that it is beliefs about events in our lives, rather than the events themselves, that maintain psychological problems.

6. Maladaptive thoughts are illogical because they result from logical errors in thinking, including absolute thinking, overgeneralizing, and catastrophizing. Two themes are common in irrational ideas that lead to psychological problems: personal worthlessness and a sense of duty.

7. The three major operations of REBT are identifying thoughts based on irrational beliefs; challenging the irrational beliefs; and substituting thoughts based on rational beliefs. The therapist challenges the rationality of the client's thoughts; debunks the client's myths about how the world "should be"; and persuades the client to recognize irrational thoughts and to think rationally.

8. REBT is used primarily with adults. Rational emotive education is an adaptation of REBT principles and procedures for children and adolescents.

9. Empirical support for REBT is modest; methodological problems with many studies make definitive conclusions difficult. Nonetheless, REBT is a popular treatment.

10. Cognitive therapy is similar to REBT. Both assume that psychological disorders are maintained by distorted cognitions, and both use cognitive restructuring as a major technique. However, cognitive therapy emphasizes empirical hypothesis testing as a means of changing existing beliefs—rather than disputation and persuasion, as in REBT.

11. The goals of cognitive therapy are to correct faulty information processing; to modify dysfunctional beliefs; and to provide skills and experiences that create adaptive thinking. Cognitive therapy involves a collaborative effort of the client and therapist. Clients are taught to view automatic thoughts (maladaptive cognitions) as hypotheses subject to empirical validation, rather than as established facts. Clients test out the hypotheses in homework assignments in which they make observations to refute (or confirm) the hypotheses.

12. Cognitive therapy procedures that directly change clients' cognitions include analyzing faulty logic, obtaining accurate information, self-recording of automatic thoughts, generating alternative interpretations of events, reattributing responsibility about negative outcomes, and decatastrophizing.

13. Cognitive therapy procedures that indirectly change clients' cognitions and emotions by changing overt behaviors include activity schedule, mastery and pleasure rating, and graded task assignment.

14. Originally developed to treat depression in adults, cognitive therapy has been adapted for other psychological disorders and diverse client populations. These include treatment of schizophrenic delusions as well as anxiety and depression (and related school difficulties) in children and adolescents.

15. Cognitive therapy is an effective treatment for acute episodes of depression, and it may help prevent the recurrence of depression.

16. The philosophical basis of cognitive restructuring is constructivism, which holds that people create their own realities.

REFERENCE NOTES

1. For example, Lazarus & Folkman, 1984.
2. Craighead, 1990b.
3. Cottraux, 1990; Goldfried, Greenberg, & Marmar, 1990.
4. Festinger, 1957; Kelly, 1955.
5. Bandura, 1986a.
6. Beidel & Turner, 1986; Beutler & Guest, 1989.
7. Castaneda, 1972, pp. 218-219.
8. Sokolov, 1972, p. 1.
9. Glass & Arnkoff, 1989.
10. Glass, Merluzzi, Biever, & Larsen, 1982.
11. Ronan, Kendall, & Rowe, 1994.
12. For example, Craighead, Kimball, & Rehak, 1979; Genest & Turk, 1981; White, Davison, Haaga, & White, 1992.
13. Davison, Navarre, & Vogel, 1995.
14. For example, White, Davison, Haaga, & White, 1992; Davison, Navarre, & Vogel, 1995.
15. Wolpe, 1958; compare with Ellis, 1989b.
16. For example, Kenny, Mowbray, & Lalani, 1978.
17. Author's (MDS) clinical files.
18. Upper, 1993.
19. A.B. Kearney, 1993.
20. Dewhurst, 1993.
21. Krop & Burgess, 1993a.
22. Groden, 1993.
23. Jurgela, 1993.
24. Newman & Haaga, 1995.
25. Freeman & Simon, 1989; Gordon, 1983; Guevremont & Spiegler, 1990.
26. Tryon, 1979.
27. For example, Armstrong & Rimm, 1974; Hackmann & McLean, 1975; Kenny, Mowbray, & Lalani, 1978; Rimm, Saunders, & Westel, 1975; Stern, Lipsedge, & Marks, 1973.
28. Ellis, 1995.
29. Ellis & Dryden, 1993.
30. Ellis, 1962, 1994a.
31. Bernard & DiGiuseppe, 1989; Ellis & Bernard, 1985.
32. Ellis & Dryden, 1987.
33. Beck & Weishaar, 1989; Ellis, 1989a.
34. Ellis, 1970.
35. Ellis & Bernard, 1985.
36. Ellis, 1989a; Kopec, Beal, & DiGiuseppe, 1994; Lazarus, 1989b.
37. Rimm & Masters, 1979; dialogue is quoted from pp. 385-387; annotations are original to this text.
38. For example, DiGiuseppe, 1981; Kendall, 1987b.
39. For example, Ellis, 1959; Ellis & Bernard, 1983.
40. Bernard & Joyce, 1984; Knaus, 1974; Knaus, 1985; Knaus & Eyman, 1974; Knaus & McKeever, 1977; Knaus & Haberstroh, 1993; Knaus & Wessler, 1976; Omizo, Cubberly, & Omizo, 1985; Omizo, Lo, & Williams, 1986; Vernon, 1983; Zionts, 1983.
41. Gossette & O'Brien, 1993.
42. Gossette & O'Brien, 1993.
43. Joyce, 1995.
44. Haaga & Davison, 1989a.
45. Mahoney, Lyddon, & Alford, 1989, p. 87.
46. For example, Burns, 1980; Dyer, 1977; Ellis & Harper, 1975.
47. Mahoney, Lyddon, & Alford, 1989.
48. For example, Dryden & Hill, 1993; Ellis, 1994b, 1994c, 1994d, 1994e.
49. Abrams & Ellis, 1994; Haaga & Davison, 1989a; Scholing & Emmelkamp, 1993a, 1993b.
50. Lazarus, 1989b.
51. Meichenbaum, 1991; Patterson & Forgatch, 1985.
52. Bernard, 1990.
53. Franks, 1995; Haaga & Davison, 1989a, 1989b; Hollon & Beck, 1986; Mahoney, Lyddon, & Alford, 1989.
54. Solomon & Haaga, 1995.
55. Haaga & Davison, 1989a, 1989b, 1993; Haaga, Dryden, & Dancey, 1991; Kendall, Haaga, Ellis, Bernard, DiGiuseppe, & Kassinove, 1995.
56. Lyons & Woods, 1991.
57. Haaga & Davison, 1993.
58. Compare with Goldfried, 1988; Goldfried, Decenteceo, & Weinberg, 1974; Haaga & Davison, 1989a.
59. Weinrach, 1995.
60. Beck, 1963, 1976.
61. Bernard & DiGiuseppe, 1989.
62. Hollon & Beck, 1986.
63. Beck, 1967, 1976.
64. For example, Alford, Freeman, Beck, & Wright, 1990; Beck, 1988; Beck & Emery, 1985; Freeman & Simon, 1989.
65. Brown, Heimberg, & Juster, 1995.
66. Laberge, Gauthier, Cote, Plamondon, Cormier, & Van Oppen, 1993.
67. Van Oppen, De Haan, Van Balkom, Spinhoven, Hoogduin, & Van Dyck, 1995.
68. Baucom & Epstein, 1990; Beck, 1988; Dattilio & Padesky, 1990; Epstein & Baucom, 1989.
69. Beck & Freeman, 1989; Young, 1990.
70. Beck, 1967; Freeman & White, 1989.

71. Edgette & Prout, 1989; Simon, 1994; Weishaar, in press.
72. Leitenberg & Rosen, 1988.
73. Kramer & Stalker, 1989.
74. Alford & Beck, 1994; Bentall, Haddock, & Slade, 1994; McNally, 1994.
75. Beck, 1976.
76. Beck & Weishaar, 1989, p. 23.
77. Bell-Dolan, 1995.
78. Otto & Gould, 1995.
79. Beck & Weishaar, 1989.
80. Beck & Emery, 1985; Beck & Freeman, 1989.
81. Burns & Nolen-Hoeksema, 1992.
82. Beck & Weishaar, 1989.
83. Bowers, 1989.
84. Beck, Rush, Shaw, & Emery, 1979.
85. Beck, 1976, p. 272.
86. Beck, 1976, pp. 284-286.
87. Alford & Beck, 1994; Bentall, Haddock, & Slade, 1994; McNally, 1994.
88. Alford & Correia, 1994; Perris, 1989.
89. Alford & Correia, 1994.
90. Alford & Beck, 1994.
91. Alford & Correia, 1994; Himadi, Osteen, & Crawford, 1993.
92. Alford, 1986.
93. Chadwick & Lowe, 1990.
94. Tarrier, 1992.
95. Alford & Beck, 1994.
96. Bowers, 1989; Thase & Wright, 1991.
97. Glanz, 1989.
98. DiGiuseppe, 1989.
99. Clarke, Hawkins, Murphy, Sheeber, Lewinsohn, & Seeley, 1995; Lewinsohn & Rohde, 1993.
100. Lewinsohn, Clarke, & Rohde, 1994.
101. Aydin & Yerin, 1994.
102. Jaycox, Reivich, Gillham, & Seligman, 1994.
103. Lewinsohn, Clarke, & Rohde, 1994.
104. Propst, Ostrom, Watkins, Dean, & Mashburn, 1992.
105. Beck, 1967; Beck, Rush, Shaw, & Emery, 1979.
106. Hollon & Beck, 1994; Otto & Gould, 1995.
107. Van Oppen & Arntz, 1994; Van Oppen, De Hann, Van Balkom, Spinhoven, Hoogduin, & Van Dyck, 1995.
108. Beck & Freeman, 1989.
109. Abrahms, 1983; Baucom & Epstein, 1990; Beck, 1988; Dattilio & Padesky, 1990; Epstein, 1983.
110. Alford & Beck, 1994; Alford & Correia, 1994.
111. McCarthy, 1989.
112. Kramer & Stalker, 1989.
113. For example, Lewinsohn, Clarke, & Rohde, 1994; Pace & Dixon, 1993; Scott, Scott, Tacchi, & Jones, 1994; Shapiro, Rees, Barkham, Hardy, Reynolds, & Startup, 1995; Teasdale, Segal, & Williams, 1995.
114. Thase, Reynolds, Frank, Simons, McGeary, Fasiczka, Garamoni, Jennings, & Kupfer, 1994.
115. For example, Shapiro, Rees, Barkham, Hardy, Reynolds, & Startup, 1995.
116. Haaga & Davison, 1993; Kendall, Haaga, Ellis, Bernard, DiGiuseppe, & Kassinove, 1995.
117. Antonuccio, Danton, & DeNelsky, 1995; Beckham & Watkins, 1989; Blackburn, 1988; Dobson, 1989; Hollon & Beck, 1986; Perris, 1989; Thase, Bowler, & Harden, 1991; Thase, Simons, Cahalane, & McGeary, 1991.
118. Sanderson, Beck, & McGinn, 1994; Thase, Reynolds, Frank, Simons, Garamoni, McGeary, Harden, Fasiczka, & Cahalane, 1994.
119. Thase, 1994.
120. Antonuccio, Danton, & DeNelsky, 1995.
121. Elkin, Shea, Watkins, Imber, Sotsky, Collins, Glass, Pilkonis, Leber, Docherty, Fiester, & Parloff, 1989; Hollon & Beck, 1986; Hollon, Shelton, & Davis, 1993; Shea, 1990; Teasdale, Segal, & Williams, 1995; compare with Otto, Pava, & Sprich-Buckminster, 1995.
122. Elkin, Shea, Watkins, Imber, Sotsky, Collins, Glass, Pilkonis, Leber, Docherty, Fiester, & Parloff, 1989.
123. Otto, Pava, & Sprich-Buckminster, 1995.
124. Hollon, Shelton, & Loosen, 1991.
125. Beckham & Watkins, 1989; Shea, 1990.
126. Thase, 1994.
127. Hollon & Beck, 1994.
128. Newman & Haaga, 1995; O'Leary & Rathus, 1993.
129. Robins & Hayes, 1993.
130. O'Leary & Rathus, 1993.
131. Guidano & Liotti, 1985; Kruglanski & Jaffe, 1988; Mahoney, 1988a, 1988b; Neisser, 1976; Watzlawick, 1984.
132. Loftus, 1979.
133. From the author's (MDS) clinical files.
134. For example, Csikszentmihalyi, 1990; Csikszentmihalyi & Csikszentmihalyi, 1988.

Chapter 13

Cognitive-Behavioral Therapy: Coping Skills

As you know from reading Chapter 12, cognitive restructuring therapy changes distorted and erroneous cognitions, which means that it is appropriate for problems maintained by an *excess of maladaptive thoughts*. In contrast, cognitive-behavioral coping skills therapy—the other model of cognitive-behavioral therapy—is used to treat problems that are maintained by a *deficit of adaptive cognitions*. Here, the focus is not so much on what clients are thinking as on what they are *not* thinking. As with cognitive restructuring therapy, cognitive-behavioral coping skills therapy changes both clients' cognitions and overt behaviors. We will discuss four cognitive-behavioral coping skills therapies: self-instructional training, problem-solving therapy/training, stress inoculation, and cognitive-behavioral couple therapy.

SELF-INSTRUCTIONAL TRAINING

When we are confronted with difficult situations in our daily lives, we often tell ourselves what to do, what to think, and how to feel. When you have a "million" errands to do, you may tell yourself: "Go to the cleaners first because it may close early and then stop by the bank on the way home." During an exam, you may say to yourself: "Stay calm and concentrate. You know this material." While playing tennis, you might think: "Keep your eye on the ball, racket back, step in, follow through." Such directed self-talk is known as *self-instructions*. Self-instructions serve six different functions: (1) preparing to use self-instructions, (2) focusing attention, (3) guiding behavior, (4) providing encouragement, (5) evaluating performance, and (6) reducing anxiety (see Table 13-1). The instructions can be phrased in a variety of ways, as you can see in Table 13-2.

Donald Meichenbaum developed **self-instructional training** to teach people to instruct themselves to cope effectively with difficult situations.[1] It has been used to treat a wide array of problems, ranging from deficits in academic skills of children[2] to the bizarre thoughts and speech of clients with schizophrenia.[3]

Self-instructional training was first used to treat impulsive behaviors in children.[4] Children who act impulsively do not think before acting, which

Donald Meichenbaum

Table 13-1 Functions of self-instructions

Function	Example
PREPARING CLIENT TO USE SELF-INSTRUCTIONS	"Remember to use the self-instructions while you're working on the test."
FOCUSING ATTENTION	"Concentrate. Don't let your mind wander."
GUIDING BEHAVIOR	"All right. Now, check your answer one more time before going on."
PROVIDING ENCOURAGEMENT	"So far, so good. Keep on trying."
EVALUATING PERFORMANCE	"Good work. I got another one right."
REDUCING ANXIETY	"Stay calm. Just relax. I'm doing fine."

Table 13-2 Forms of self-instructions

Form	Example
IMPERATIVE	"Sit and relax for a moment."
FIRST PERSON	"I'd better sit and relax for a moment."
SECOND PERSON	"You need to sit and relax for a moment."
NAME	"Megan, sit and relax for a moment."

has undesirable consequences for them as well as for others. The general goal of self-instructional training for impulsive behaviors is to teach children to think and plan before acting—to "stop, look, and listen" (see Figure 13-1). Five steps are involved.

1. *Cognitive modeling.* An adult model performs a task while verbalizing aloud a deliberate strategy. For example, while engaging in a task involving copying line patterns, the model might say:

> OK, what is it I have to do? You want me to copy the picture with the different lines. I have to go slowly and carefully. OK, draw the line down, down, good; then to the right, that's it; now down some more and to the left. Good, I'm doing fine so far. Remember, go slowly. Now back up again. No, I was supposed to go down. That's

Figure 13-1 Pictures used to encourage and remind children to employ self-instructions to reduce impulsive behaviors
SOURCE: Palkes, Stewart, & Kahana, 1968, p. 819.

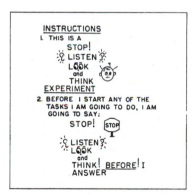

OK. Just erase the line carefully. . . . Good. Even if I make an error I can go on slowly and carefully. I have to go down now. Finished. I did it![5]

2. *Cognitive participant modeling.* The child performs the task as the model verbalizes the instructions aloud.

3. *Overt self-instructions.* The child performs the task while verbalizing the instructions aloud.

4. *Fading of overt self-instructions.* The child performs the task while whispering the instructions.

5. *Covert self-instructions.* Finally, the child performs the task while saying the instructions to herself or himself.

The child first practices these steps with brief, simple tasks (such as tracing lines) and then with lengthier and more complex tasks (such as solving math problems).[6] With young children, the therapy may be presented as a game, with pictorial prompts to remind the child to use self-instructions (see Figure 13-2). Case 13-1 illustrates self-instructional training with a preschool boy.

Figure 13-2 Cue cards for prompting children to use self-instructions to solve problems
SOURCE: Camp, B. W., & Bash, M. A. S. *Think Aloud: Increasing cognitive and social skills—A problem-solving program for children (Primary Level).* Champaign, IL, Research Press, 1981. Reprinted by permission.

What is my problem?

How can I do it?

Am I using my plan?

How did I do?

Case 13-1

IMPROVING A PRESCHOOLER'S ACADEMIC SKILLS THROUGH SELF-INSTRUCTIONAL TRAINING[7]

Five-year-old Paul attended a preschool for children with behavioral and learning problems. Although he was bright and capable of doing his school work, Paul often did not complete his assignments. During work periods, he spent considerable time looking around the classroom and daydreaming. As time was running out, he would rush to complete his work, particularly when recess was the next activity.

The therapist met with Paul 3 times a week for 20 to 30 minutes in a room adjacent to his classroom. The therapist taught Paul to use 4 specific self-instructions: (1) "What do I have to do first?" (problem definition); (2) "Circle all the words that begin with *bl*" (attention focusing and response guidance); (3) "Did I find all the words on the line?" (self-evaluation and error correction); and (4) "Good job. I found all of them" (self-reinforcement). The therapist taught these self-instructions sequentially; only after Paul was using a self-instruction correctly was he taught another.

Two types of recordings of Paul's behaviors were made to assess the effectiveness of the self-instructional training. First, videos of Paul during work periods provided a measure of the time he spent paying attention to his work. Second, a small microphone connected to a tape recorder was attached to Paul's work desk to record self-instructions that Paul said aloud.

The time Paul paid attention to his work increased from 31% before self-instructional training to 72% after training. The improved attention was reflected in an increase in the percentage of problems Paul correctly completed each day, from an average of 32% before training to an average of 79% after training. As Figure 13-3 shows, Paul correctly completed

Figure 13-3 The percentage of problems that Paul correctly completed (points) during the baseline period and after self-instructional training. Note that the percentage of correctly completed problems after training was directly proportional to the percentage of time Paul used overt self-instructions (shaded area).
SOURCE: Adapted from Guevremont, Osnes, & Stokes, 1988.

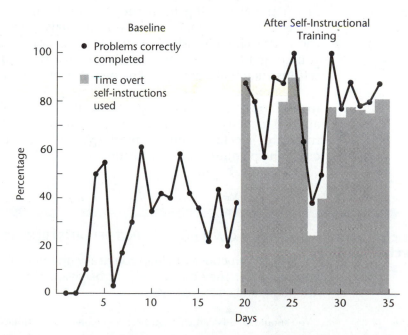

significantly more problems when he used overt self-instructions. On days in which he used few self-instructions, Paul completed fewer problems correctly. Thus, the use of self-instructions was associated with both increased attention to and quality of schoolwork.

Both overt and covert self-instructions have advantages. On the one hand, overt self-instructions can be monitored by others, as you saw in Case 13-1 in which Paul's verbalizations were recorded. Further, overt self-instructions may be more effective because clients may pay better attention to self-instructions when they actually hear them aloud. This is particularly true for young children—as it was for Paul. On the other hand, covert self-instructions do not disturb others, and clients are not embarrassed by others' hearing their self-instructions.

Enhancing the Effects of Self-Instructional Training

A number of factors appear to enhance the effectiveness of self-instructional training for academic problems. Children who are more actively involved in their training (for instance, children who help to generate the self-instructions they use) show greater improvements than children who are passive recipients of training. Not surprisingly, a good relationship with the therapist is associated with better performance.[8] Involving natural change agents (such as parents and teachers) in the training[9] and increasing the number of training sessions[10] also appear to result in greater improvements in children's academic and social behaviors.

Various procedures are used to help clients generalize their self-instructional training from the therapy to the classroom setting. These procedures include making training materials (such as work sheets) similar to those the children will use in the classroom[11] and arranging training situations to simulate normal classroom conditions, such as conducting self-instructional training in the presence of other children.[12] Generalization to different tasks is influenced by the types of self-instructions children are taught. General conceptual instructions that can be applied to many tasks (for instance, "I must go slowly and be careful") result in greater generalization than task-specific instructions (such as "I have to circle the pictures that are the same").[13]

◆

Participation Exercise 13-1

BEING YOUR OWN BOSS: USING SELF-INSTRUCTIONS*

Using self-instructions can help you deal with many difficulties you encounter in your daily life. They can guide your behavior, reduce your anxiety, focus your attention, and encourage you.

* You should do this Participation Exercise before you continue.

For each of the following situations, write a self-instruction that you might find useful. When you have finished, compare your self-instructions with those given in Appendix B.

1. It is Friday evening. You feel overwhelmed with all the studying and assignments you are supposed to complete by Monday.

2. You are tired during a long drive at night. You find that you are having trouble concentrating on driving. Several times you had to quickly steer the car back into your lane as the car wandered into the other lane.

3. You are hurriedly packing for an overnight trip and don't want to forget your essential clothes.

4. You are on a diet, which involves not eating desserts. When you go out with friends after a movie and everyone is ordering pie or ice cream, your resolve is starting to weaken.

5. You are in the last mile of a five-mile run. You are getting very tired and feel like quitting. However, another part of you wants to complete the five miles.

6. You are driving in an unfamiliar area. You stop for directions. The person tells you, "Make a right at the next traffic light. Go about a mile to a stop sign and turn left. Then, in a half mile or so the road ends. Go left there. The restaurant is down about a quarter of a mile on the right."

7. You are about to go into a job interview. You feel confident and relaxed. In fact, you realize you are too relaxed and not at all "psyched" for the interview.

8. You want to ask a classmate for a date. You have gone to the phone, but you are not sure what to say.

Self-Instructional Training in Perspective

Self-instructional training has been used for more than 25 years with a wide array of problems, including impulsive behaviors,[14] schizophrenic behaviors,[15] social withdrawal,[16] anxiety (for example, test,[17] speech,[18] and social anxiety[19]), children's fears,[20] anger,[21] personality disorders,[22] obesity,[23] and eating disorders such as bulimia,[24] as well as deficits in assertive behaviors,[25] problem solving,[26] leisure skills,[27] and creativity.[28] Although it is employed more often with children, self-instructional training sometimes is used with adolescents and adults. For example, adolescents who frequently acted aggressively and displayed angry outbursts were taught coping self-instructions to deal with conflicts.[29] They learned self-instructions to *prepare* to act (for instance, "I'm not going to take it personally"); to *guide* their behaviors during conflicts (such as, "I've got to keep in control"); and to *evaluate* their actions afterwards (for example, "I handled that pretty well").

Self-instructional training has been used to guide job-related tasks of adults with all levels of mental retardation.[30] The training has resulted in significant improvements in work-related on-task behaviors,[31] accuracy of performance,[32] completion of tasks,[33] and punctuality.[34] These findings are impressive because they indicate that cognitive-behavioral therapies can be applied successfully to improve the quality of life (for instance, greater independence) of individuals with significant intellectual impairment.

Although a large number of studies has been conducted to evaluate the efficacy of self-instructional training, the findings have been inconsistent. Whereas self-instructional training has been consistently effective in improving performance on highly specific tasks, applications to more complex problems have been less successful. Overall, self-instructional training is moderately effective when it is (1) applied to narrowly focused problems (2) that are maintained solely by inadequate self-instructions regarding how to proceed with a task. Self-instructional training is less effective as a treatment for broader problems that are likely to be maintained by more than deficits in adaptive cognitions, such as social anxiety. With such problems, self-instructional training can be useful when employed as one of several components of a treatment package.[35]

Research evaluating self-instructional training has four limitations. First, because it is not possible to assess clients' use of covert self-instructions directly, it is difficult to determine the extent to which clients use self-instructions. Second, self-instructional training generally is part of a treatment package,[36] so that the specific effects of the self-instructions remain unknown. Third, much of the research consists of analogue studies in which nonclinical problems were treated (for example, mild anxiety among college students).[37] Thus, not enough is known about the effectiveness of self-instructional training with clinical problems. Fourth, few long-term follow-up assessments have been conducted; thus, the durability of the effects of self-instructional training is not known. These research problems are not an indictment of self-instructional training, but they make it difficult to draw definitive conclusions about the therapy's efficacy. Fortunately, the situation is easily rectifiable with better research.

Problem-Solving Therapy/Training

Problems are a ubiquitous part of life, and problem solving is a broadly useful skill for coping with many of life's difficulties.[38] Moreover, inadequate problem solving is associated with a host of psychological problems in both children and adults, including interpersonal difficulties and depression.[39]

In the present context, *problem solving* refers to a systematic process by which a person generates a variety of potentially effective solutions to a problem, judiciously chooses the best of these solutions, and then implements and evaluates the chosen solution. Problem solving, like reinforcement, was not invented by behavior therapists. Behavior therapists, however, have refined problem-solving procedures and adapted them to treating and preventing psychological problems.

Problem-solving therapy is the application of problem solving to problems for which a client has specifically sought treatment. With adults, it is used to treat stress,[40] depression,[41] agoraphobia,[42] eating disorders,[43] smoking,[44] independent living skills of patients with psychiatric disorders,[45] marital discord,[46] difficulties families face in caring for relatives with schizophrenia,[47] and child abuse.[48] With children and adolescents, applications include anxiety,[49] migraine headaches,[50] aggressive behaviors,[51] anger,[52] assertive social behaviors,[53] classroom behaviors,[54] school adjustment,[55] and parent and adolescent conflicts.[56]

Because problem solving is a broadly applicable coping skill, problem-solving therapy often serves a dual purpose: (1) treating the immediate problems for which clients seek treatment and (2) preparing clients to deal on their own with future problems, which may help prevent psychological disorders from developing.[57] **Problem-solving training** serves only the second function—that is, it teaches problem-solving skills as a general coping strategy for dealing with problems that arise in the course of daily life. The training often is provided for populations who have been identified as being at risk for developing psychological disorders, such as adolescents who have difficulties controlling anger. Prevention-oriented problem-solving training sometimes is incorporated into regular classroom curricula, so that all children learn problem-solving skills.[58] Most of our discussion of the problem-solving method is applicable to both problem-solving therapy and problem-solving training.

Basic Procedures

Thomas D'Zurilla

Problem-solving therapy originally was proposed by Thomas D'Zurilla and Marvin Goldfried.[59] Although a number of different specific models of problem-solving therapy exist, they all divide the problem-solving process into stages or steps.[60] The basic stages are (1) adopting a problem-solving orientation; (2) defining the problem and setting goals; (3) generating alternative solutions; (4) deciding on the best solution; and (5) implementing the solution and evaluating its effects. These stages, shown schematically in Figure 13-4, are cumulative, so that successful completion of each stage depends on skills and information learned in previous stages. Accordingly, if difficulty is encountered in later stages, it may be necessary to return to previous stages (as indicated by the dashed lines in Figure 13-4).

STAGE 1: ADOPTING A PROBLEM-SOLVING ORIENTATION

Marvin Goldfried

Adopting a problem-solving orientation is the first step in implementing problem solving. The client must understand that (1) it is essential to identify problems when they occur so that appropriate action can be taken; (2) problems are a normal part of life, and people can learn to cope with them; and (3) effective problem solving involves carefully assessing alternative courses of action.

Obviously, one must recognize that a problem exists before one can begin to solve it. However, problem recognition is not always as obvious as it might seem. People who lose their jobs easily recognize that they have a problem. However, when individuals develop maladaptive reactions to unchangeable situations—such as being diagnosed with AIDS or the death of a loved one—they are less likely to recognize that a potentially solvable

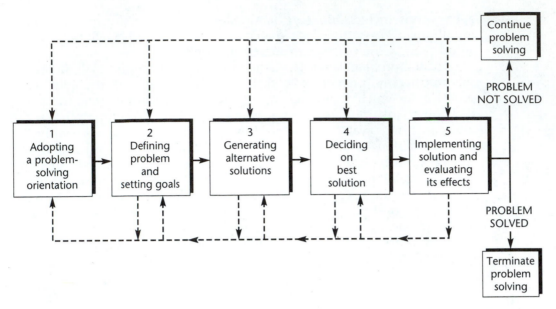

Figure 13-4 Schematic representation of the five stages of problem-solving therapy/training. Dashed lines indicate the possibility that difficulties at one stage may necessitate returning to a prior stage.

problem exists. In this case, it is their *reaction* to the unchangeable situation that is the problem, not the situation itself.

STAGE 2: DEFINING THE PROBLEM AND SETTING GOALS

In the second stage, the therapist helps the client define the problem and formulate goals. A precise definition of the problem is required in order to generate specific solutions. Clearly, it would be difficult to generate useful solutions for the vaguely defined problem: "My roommate and I aren't compatible." In contrast, the following precise definition lends itself to concrete solutions: "My roommate likes to go to sleep early and wake up early, and I prefer just the opposite schedule."

After the problem is precisely defined, goals are formulated. The client must answer the question: "What must happen so that I no longer have the problem?" The goals can focus (1) on the problem situation, (2) on emotional and cognitive reactions to the problem situation, or (3) on both.[61] *Situation-focused* goals are aimed at changing the problem situation itself (such as getting out of debt). *Reaction-focused* goals are aimed at changing one's emotional and cognitive reactions to the problem situation. The nature of the problem—that is, how it is defined—determines the type of goal or goals that are appropriate. For example, when the situation cannot be changed (such as the death of a loved one), only a reaction-focused goal is possible. The client's goals guide the generation of solutions in the third stage. Figure 13-5 shows a work sheet clients can use for the second, third, and fourth stages of problem solving; it has been completed for our hypothetical roommate problem.

STAGE 3: GENERATING ALTERNATIVE SOLUTIONS

In the third stage, the client is taught to generate solutions (courses of action) that might solve the problem. The objective is to come up with as many alternative solutions as possible to maximize the chances of finding a successful one. Possible alternative solutions for our roommate problem are listed in Figure 13-5 (part 2). Clients are encouraged to use *brainstorming*, a procedure in which any possible solution is entertained, no matter how impractical or outlandish it might appear. Although the "wild" ideas may

Figure 13-5 Sample problem-solving work sheet

Problem-Solving Work Sheet

1. *Define Problem and Set Goals*

   a. *Definition of the problem, including important details*:

   Background: My roommate likes to go to bed early and wake up early in the morning. I like to stay up late and sleep in. We are good friends but don't get a lot of time to talk or socialize because of our different schedules. Also, I have to limit myself to quiet activities in the evening because she has gone to bed. I would like to have other friends over in the evening, but this wouldn't be fair to my roommate. In the morning while I'm still sleeping, my roommate's getting up so early frequently wakes me up, and then I have trouble getting back to sleep.

   Specific problem situation: Our different schedules are beginning to interfere with our friendship and cause inconveniences for both of us. I would like to be able to socialize with friends in the evening and sleep in without being awakened by my roommate.

   b. *Specific goals (What must happen so that I no longer have the problem?)*: I have to be able to socialize with friends in the evening because I really enjoy doing this and not be awakened in the morning while my roommate prepares to leave the house.

2. *Generate Alternative Solutions (brainstorm):*   3. *Decide on best solution:*
   (+ + = very good; + = good;
   0 = neutral; – – = bad; – – = very bad)

   a. Just put up with the situation for the rest of the semester.   a. ⎯ – –

   b. Make plans to go over to other friends' places during the evening.   b. +

   c. Move out of the apartment completely.   c. –

   d. Ask some friends what they think I should do.   d. –

   e. Rearrange the house a bit so that we don't interfere with each other in the morning and evening.   e. + +

   f. Start going to bed early and getting up early like my roommate.   f. – –

   g. Take turns so that one day I follow her schedule and the next day she follows mine.   g. +

   h. _____   h. ___

not be viable solutions themselves, they may lead to usable solutions by directing the client's attention in a new direction. For instance, using our roommate problem example, "murdering the roommate" clearly is not a viable solution. However, considering alternative ways to obtain the same effect of this outlandish solution—namely, eliminating the roommate—could prove very useful. Brainstorming, which opens up avenues of solutions that clients might otherwise miss, counters the narrow, rigid thinking that clients in therapy often exhibit.

Brainstorming is a general strategy that is employed in different stages of problem solving.[62] For example, brainstorming can be used to generate alternative goals in the second stage and to identify different consequences of a particular solution in the fourth stage.

STAGE 4: DECIDING ON THE BEST SOLUTION

In the fourth stage, the client chooses the best solution from among the alternatives generated in the third stage. This choice is made by examining the *potential consequences* of each course of action. In other words, what is likely to happen—in the short and long run, for the client and for other people. Using a rating scale to evaluate the alternative solutions is helpful (see Figure 13-5, part 3).

STAGE 5: IMPLEMENTING THE SOLUTION AND EVALUATING ITS EFFECTS

In the final stage, the client implements the solution chosen in the previous stage. Once the solution has had time to take effect, the client evaluates how successful it has been. If the problem has been resolved, therapy is terminated. If the problem has not been resolved, then the client repeats one or more of the previous stages. First, the client would choose another alternative (stage 4). If no acceptable alternatives remain, more solutions would have to be generated (stage 3). Sometimes, the difficulty lies in how the problem was defined or in the goals that were selected, and it is necessary to return to stage 2.

Teaching Problem-Solving Skills to Clients

A variety of behavior therapy procedures are used to teach clients problem solving, including modeling, prompting, self-instructions, shaping, and reinforcement.[63] In the early stages, the therapist may employ *cognitive modeling* to demonstrate the problem-solving process. For example, the therapist might brainstorm aloud about a hypothetical problem in order to illustrate this uninhibited, open-ended procedure, as in the following cognitive-modeling scenario.

> How am I going to get my thesis finished by the June deadline? I could put in more hours, which would mean giving up my daily jogging and watching television . . . even sleeping. Don't evaluate; just come up with ideas. I could hire a typist to make my rough drafts more readable so I could rewrite more quickly. Maybe I could get an

English grad student to help with my gramma and spellin. Of course, I could buy a thesis from one of those companies that sells them . . . or I could bribe the dean.

During the third stage, the therapist *prompts* the client to use brainstorming and *reinforces* the client's ideas, both practical and outrageous. If the client has difficulty with brainstorming, the procedure may need to be *shaped*. The therapist also teaches and encourages the client to *self-reinforce* appropriate problem-solving behaviors. In the final stage, the therapist may have to use other behavior therapy procedures to facilitate the client's actions. For example, if the client feels anxious or inhibited in asking a friend for help, systematic desensitization and assertion training might be employed.

Case 13-2 illustrates the use of problem-solving therapy to reduce an adult client's anxiety related to stressful events that interfered with her studies.

Case 13-2

TREATMENT OF EXAMINATION AND INTERPERSONAL ANXIETY BY PROBLEM-SOLVING THERAPY[64]

G. W., a 32-year-old married female graduate student, initially described her problem as severe test anxiety. Upon questioning, it became clear that her difficulties lay specifically in her inability to cope with domestic and family pressures that interfered with her studies. For example, if her baby-sitter was unable to care for her infant, G. W. could not think of an alternative arrangement that would allow her to attend classes.

Coping desensitization was tried first, but it proved ineffective. Accordingly, G. W. was taught problem-solving skills to help her identify ways to deal with stress-evoking events. Using brainstorming, she generated alternative coping strategies for the problem situations in the anxiety hierarchy that she had constructed during desensitization. She evaluated the alternative solutions by weighing the costs and benefits to herself and others and chose the solution that had the least cost and most benefit. G. W. learned these basic problem-solving steps in a single session. Then, she applied the strategies to cope with events that caused her anxiety and interfered with her studying and evaluated their effectiveness.

Problem-solving therapy was clearly successful. Before treatment, the highest 11 items in G. W.'s anxiety hierarchy evoked 50 to 100 SUDs; after therapy, none of the items produced more than 10 to 15 SUDs. When she entered therapy, G. W. was experiencing an average of 5 panic attacks (overwhelming anxiety) a day; after treatment, she was having less than 1 attack per week. The insomnia, nervousness, and shaking that had occurred before therapy were no longer problematic. Six months after treatment, G. W. reported that she continued to apply the problem-solving strategies to cope successfully with anxiety related to her studies. She also was able to apply problem solving to her deteriorating relationship with her husband.

Table 13-3 Hypothetical problem scenarios used to teach problem-solving skills to boys

You just get in from recess on a very hot day. You are standing in line to get a drink of water. Five other kids are in line in front of you. After a five-minute wait you are finally next in line. Just as you are about to have your turn, another boy in your class cuts in front of you.

You notice that some kids in your neighborhood are playing basketball. You think one of them goes to the same school as you, but you are not sure who the others are. You would like to play with them, but you are not sure they will let you.

After school, you notice some of your classmates smoking cigarettes behind the school building. A couple of the other kids are friends of yours. They call you over and ask you if you want a cigarette. You don't really want to smoke, but you don't want them to dislike you either.

When you arrive at school, another boy in your class begins to laugh at you and tease you about the haircut you just had. You tell him to stop it, but he continues anyway. Soon several other kids begin to tease you also.

Problem-Solving Therapy/Training for Children

George Spivack and Myrna Shure were among the first to apply problem-solving training with children.[65] The same five basic stages used with adults are employed with children. Hypothetical problem scenarios, such as those in Table 13-3, are used to teach problem-solving skills for interpersonal difficulties and aggressive behaviors. Case 13-3 illustrates the use of problem-solving therapy with a preadolescent.

Case 13-3

REDUCING AGGRESSIVE AND DISRUPTIVE BEHAVIORS IN A PREADOLESCENT BOY USING PROBLEM-SOLVING THERAPY[66]

Eleven-year-old Carl was referred for treatment by his teacher because of his aggressive and disruptive classroom behaviors and poor relationships with his classmates. Carl frequently drew attention to himself by engaging in a variety of inappropriate behaviors, such as burping aloud, humming, and leaving his seat. Carl wanted friends, but he was shunned by his classmates, who found his behaviors rude and obnoxious. When faced with a conflict with his teacher or classmates, Carl often acted aggressively—threatening others, yelling obscenities, or storming out of the room. The therapist spoke with Carl's teacher about the specific types of situations that Carl handled ineffectively, and brief scenarios about each problem situation were constructed (similar to those in Table 13-3).

Carl and the therapist met for a total of 18 half-hour sessions over 12 weeks in a private room at Carl's school. The therapist explained the rationale and benefits of "stopping and thinking" before acting and how the therapy could help Carl get along better with his peers and teacher. Carl was taught to think of as many solutions to the problem scenarios as he could. Next, Carl learned to select the best solutions, those that were both realistic and most likely to result in positive, or at least neutral, consequences. If Carl evaluated a solution unrealistically (for example, "If I hit him, he won't bother me anymore"), the therapist reminded him of what the consequences actually were likely to be. Finally, Carl and the therapist discussed how he would implement the chosen solutions and assess their effectiveness.

In later sessions, Carl and the therapist role-played situations that might occur as Carl attempted the solutions. For example, when Carl had decided that he would ask another boy in his class to play with him at recess, the therapist assumed the role of the boy and Carl practiced what he would actually say and do. The therapist provided Carl with feedback about how he was presenting himself and modeled alternative approaches when Carl had difficulty.

Carl learned each of the problem-solving skills, as evidenced by his applying them to the problem scenarios. More importantly, he was able to use the skills to change his behaviors at school. His classroom disruptive behaviors decreased significantly after problem-solving therapy had begun. Before problem-solving therapy, Carl engaged in disruptive behaviors an average of 30% of the time; at the end of therapy, this was reduced to 15%.

Problem-solving therapy/training, with minor procedural differences, is the same for both adults and children, as you can see by comparing Cases 13-2 and 13-3. Problem-solving therapy/training has been used with preschoolers,[67] preadolescents,[68] and adolescents,[69] both individually and in group formats.[70] Problem-solving therapy is especially suitable for adolescents who resist unilateral adult decision and rule making.[71] For example, incorporating family problem-solving therapy into a traditional behavioral child management training program resulted in increased cooperation and compliance on the part of an adolescent boy who was defiant with adults.[72]

Problem-Solving Therapy/Training in Perspective

Problem solving has been applied to diverse problems and populations. A recent example is its use as a major component in cognitive-behavioral interventions for habitual gambling of adolescents[73] and adults.[74] Clients apply problem solving to find ways to gain control of their gambling. (Clients also learn money management skills and coping self-instructions that focus their attention on factual information related to gambling, such as "My winning in the past was due to luck.") Initial studies of this innovative therapy have reported significant reductions in clients' gambling behaviors and increases in clients' feelings of control over their gambling habits.

Problem-solving therapy can help clients solve immediate problems as well as provide them with skills for solving future problems—which exemplifies the self-control theme of behavior therapy. It is especially beneficial for problems that involve conflict or require a decision, such as deciding whether to have a baby, to change jobs, or to drop out of school. Problem-solving therapy also is useful for more serious problems, such as depression, including depressed mood in the elderly.[75] Potentially, problem-solving therapy even might be employed to help clients contemplating suicide consider alternatives to ending their lives.

Some of the factors that appear to be important in effective problem-solving interventions are (1) a positive client-therapist relationship; (2) individualized procedures; (3) the therapist's modeling problem-solving skills; (4) the client's doing homework assignments; and (5) the client's learning specific means of implementing solutions.[76]

The effectiveness of problem-solving therapy/training depends on three sequential outcomes: (1) learning problem-solving skills; (2) applying them to real-life problems; and (3) benefiting from their application (that is, actually solving problems). To evaluate the first outcome, clients' problem-solving skills are assessed before and after therapy/training, often using hypothetical problems. Clients' responses to the problems are recorded and later rated by the therapist. Table 13-4 contains abbreviated scoring guidelines for rating children's problem-solving skills based on their responses to problem scenarios (such as those in Table 13-3, page 352).

The evidence is clear that adults and children can learn problem-solving skills, often very quickly. For example, G. W. in Case 13-2 learned these skills

Table 13-4 Abbreviated guidelines for rating children's problem-solving skills
SOURCE: Adapted from Guevremont & Foster, 1992.

1. *Number of Solutions*
   Solutions are considered separate only if they differ in a significant way. For example, telling the teacher, telling the principal, and telling the playground supervisor all would be considered one solution—that is, telling an authority.

2. *Effectiveness of Solutions*
   The characteristics of an effective solution are that it (1) is nonaggressive, (2) is likely to resolve the problem, and (3) does not result in adverse effects for the child or others. Ratings are as follows:

   1-2 Physical aggression
   3-4 Verbal aggression
     5 Nonaggressive but passive and unlikely to resolve problem
   6-7 Nonaggressive, prosocial, and active attempt to solve problem

3. *Effectiveness of Best Solution*
   Same criteria as used to rate the solutions generated.

4. *Sophistication of Planning*
   Ratings from 1 to 7 are based on the number of the following categories the child's problem-solving skills demonstrate.

   1. Sensitivity to possible consequences
   2. Anticipation of obstacles
   3. Reference to social rules
   4. Goal setting
   5. Amount of detail
   6. Realistic
   7. Sequential

in a single therapy session. That clients can learn problem-solving skills easily has been demonstrated by using hypothetical problem situations with adults with diverse disorders, including schizophrenia, depression, anxiety, and substance abuse.[77] Compared with children who have not been taught problem-solving skills, children receiving problem-solving training are better at defining problems,[78] generating more and better solutions,[79] and evaluating potential consequences of solutions.[80]

Do clients apply and benefit from problem-solving therapy/training? Controlled studies have not consistently found a relationship between children's acquisition of problem-solving skills and their behavioral adjustment.[81] Although children do learn problem-solving skills, changes in their problems at home and in school may not be clinically significant. Studies with adults have resulted in similar findings. One notable exception is an experiment that compared problem-solving therapy with a control condition (social-support therapy) for treating stress in adults.[82] Besides assessing pretherapy and posttherapy problem-solving skills, this study included self-report measures of stress, health, self-esteem, and general life satisfaction. Clients receiving problem-solving therapy showed significant improvements in their problem-solving skills after treatment while, not surprisingly, control clients did not. Moreover, at the end of treatment, clients in problem-solving therapy also showed significantly greater reductions in stress levels and improved self-esteem and life satisfaction than clients in the control group.

What accounts for the disappointing general finding that clients do not apply problem-solving skills they have learned to solving actual problems in their lives? One possibility is that difficulties in daily living are not viewed as problems. This may be true particularly in cases in which reaction-focused goals are appropriate. Because the situation cannot be changed, it appears that the problem has no solution. However, the problem is not the unchangeable situation but rather one's reactions to it. Thus, clients may need more training (in the first stage of problem solving) in viewing life difficulties, including both situations and reactions to situations, as problems.

Another reason that clients fail to apply problem-solving techniques consistently may be that they lack the specific skills required to implement solutions. For instance, clients may not have the requisite *knowledge* and *proficiency* to competently perform the behaviors specified by the solution. This would be the case for a client who decided to confront her boss about unfair treatment but who did not have the appropriate assertive skills to carry out this course of action. Or clients may simply lack the motivation necessary to implement the solution, perhaps because it seems like too much effort.

Traditionally, problem-solving therapy/training has emphasized helping clients generate alternative solutions and selecting the optimal one. However, to get clients to apply in their daily lives the problem-solving skills they have learned, more attention may need to be paid to the first and last stages of problem-solving therapy/training.

Participation   SOLUTIONS, SOLUTIONS, AND MORE SOLUTIONS:
Exercise 13-2   PRACTICING PROBLEM SOLVING*

Solving problems can be fun if you view the process as a challenge. In this Participation Exercise, you will practice two stages of problem solving: generating alternative solutions and choosing the best solution.

Begin by reading the description of Situation 1 and follow the directions for generating solutions and selecting the best solution.

Situation 1. Although the weather report predicts rain, you are skeptical and walk to the library without a raincoat or umbrella. When it is time to come home, it is pouring. You live five blocks from the library and will get soaked walking home. *What could you do?*

Think of as many *different* solutions to the problem as you can. You are interested in *quantity*, not quality. Brainstorm: list any and all solutions, no matter how impractical or "far out" they appear. Of course, don't omit practical or conventional solutions. Even if you find what seems to be the most obvious or best solution, don't stop thinking of additional solutions. Write down your alternative solutions.

Now rate the overall potential consequences of each solution you have generated. Consider (1) how successful you expect the solution to be and (2) whether the solution might have negative consequences for you and others. Use the following scale:

> 5 = very good
> 4 = good
> 3 = neutral
> 2 = bad
> 1 = very bad

Write the ratings next to each solution.

Next, look at all the solutions you've rated 5 (very good), or 4 (good) if none is rated 5. (If you have rated none of your solutions 4 or 5, generate some additional solutions.) From among those solutions, choose the best one—that is, the one you think would result in the most satisfactory consequences.

Now, generate alternative solutions and choose the best one for Situation 2 and then for Situation 3. When you have finished, continue reading the Participation Exercise.

Situation 2. You have a final exam Friday morning. A friend has lost her class notes and asks to borrow yours. You expect it will take a full day to go over the notes, and you plan to do that on Wednesday. You tell your friend that she can have the notes on Thursday morning. However, by Thursday morning you have not yet looked at your notes. You need to spend all day Thursday reviewing the notes, but you have promised your friend that she could have them Thursday morning. *What could you do?*

---

* This Participation Exercise can be done before you continue or later.

Situation 3. You are treating a friend to dinner. When it comes time to pay the bill, you discover that you left your wallet at home. *What could you do?*

Consider what you have learned by doing this Participation Exercise. Did brainstorming help you generate solutions? Were you surprised by the number of different solutions possible for each of the problems? Can you identify any "mental blocks," such as rigid thinking, that impeded your generating alternative solutions? How well do you think the process of selecting the best solution worked? Finally, you may find it enlightening to compare your alternative solutions with someone else who did this Participation Exercise.

STRESS INOCULATION TRAINING

People experience many life events, both large and small, as stressful. We have little control over many potentially stress-evoking events, ranging from earthquakes and deaths of loved ones to academic examinations and flat tires. However, we can control how we *view* and *cope* with such events. *Stress* broadly refers to an array of negative reactions, including anxiety, anger, frustration, conflict, depression, Type A behaviors, and a variety of physical ailments, including headaches, insomnia, fatigue, ulcers, and hypertension.[83]*

Basic Procedures

Stress inoculation training, developed by Donald Meichenbaum, is designed to help clients cope with stress-evoking events. Clients learn coping skills and then practice using them while being exposed to stress-evoking events.[84] The therapy is divided into three phases: (1) conceptualization, (2) coping skills acquisition, and (3) application.

PHASE 1: CONCEPTUALIZATION

The first phase of stress inoculation is educational. The therapist explains that events themselves do not cause negative emotional reactions, such as anxiety or anger; rather, the negative reactions arise from how we perceive these events. Clients are told that they can learn coping skills that will allow them to reconceptualize and deal with potentially stress-evoking events without becoming emotionally upset. Clients are encouraged to view coping as a simple, five-step process:

1. *preparing* for the potentially stress-evoking event,
2. *confronting and coping* with the event,

---

* In everyday usage, the term *stress* is used to refer to both events that result in adverse reactions and to the reactions themselves. This dualism is regretable because it perpetuates the idea that events themselves cause adverse reactions. This idea is counter to not only cognitive-behavioral theorizing but also the prevailing scientific conceptualization of stress (for example, Lazarus & Folkman, 1984).

◆   **In Theory 13-1**

STRESS INOCULATION: PARALLELS WITH BIOLOGICAL IMMUNIZATION

Stress inoculation is a behavioral analogue to *biological immunization,* the process by which a person's defenses against a microorganism are strengthened by exposing the individual to low doses of the microorganism. Biological immunization—such as a measles vaccination—introduces disease-causing organisms into the body in doses too low to produce the physical symptoms of the disease. The body's immune system releases antibodies that fight off or neutralize the disease. These antibodies remain in the system and are available to combat disease-causing microorganisms in the future.

Ernest Poser[85] first proposed the idea of immunizing people to stress-evoking events that result in maladaptive behaviors. *Behavioral immunology* involves exposing people to stress-evoking events in small doses and under safe conditions before they encounter them in real life. Presumably, individuals preexposed to stress-evoking events develop, *on their own,* coping strategies that they can employ with future stress-evoking events.

Stress inoculation does not rely on clients' devising their own coping skills. Instead, clients are directly taught a variety of coping skills that they rehearse while being exposed to controlled doses of stress-evoking events. Coping skills can be thought of as "psychological antibodies" that increase one's resistance to stress. The goal is for clients to be able to activate these stress-fighting coping skills as they encounter real-life stressors.

---

3. *dealing with temporary difficulties* in coping,
4. *assessing* one's performance in coping with the event, and
5. *reinforcing oneself* for successful coping.

PHASE 2: COPING SKILLS ACQUISITION

In the second phase of stress inoculation, the client learns and rehearses coping strategies. Although the specific coping skills depend on the nature of the client's problem, four general coping skills are employed most often: differential muscle relaxation, cognitive restructuring, problem-solving self-instructions, and self-reinforcement/self-efficacy self-instructions.

Most clients who have stress-related problems experience muscle tension, which can be alleviated by *differential muscle relaxation.* Similarly, clients generally have negative thoughts about potentially stress-evoking events and about their ability to cope with them. *Cognitive restructuring* is used to reduce negative thoughts. Table 13-5 gives examples of possible coping self-statements applicable to different problem behaviors.

Clients whose problems are being maintained, in part, by not knowing how to approach and solve problems can benefit from *task-oriented problem-*

Table 13-5 Coping self-statements used in stress inoculation training for fear or anxiety, anger, and pain

Steps in Coping	Fear or Anxiety	Anger	Pain
1. PREPARING	What do I have to do? I can develop a plan to deal with it. Just think about what I can do about it. That is better than getting anxious. Maybe what I think is anxiety is eagerness to confront the situation.	What do I have to do? This is going to upset me, but I know how to deal with it. I can manage the situation. I know how to regulate my anger. Easy does it. Remember to keep your sense of humor.	What is it I have to do? Just think about what I can do about it. Don't worry; worrying won't help anything. I have lots of different strategies I can call on.
2. CONFRONTING AND COPING	One step at a time; I can handle the situation. Don't think about fear; just think about what I have to do. Stay relevant. This anxiety is what the doctor said I would feel. It's a reminder to use my coping exercise. Relax; I'm in control. Take a slow deep breath. Ah, good.	Think of what you want to get out of this. There is no point in getting mad. I'm not going to let him (or her) get to me. Look for the positives. Don't assume the worst or jump to conclusions.	I can meet the challenge. Don't think about the pain, just what I have to do. This tenseness can be an ally, a cue to cope. Just relax, breathe deeply, and use one of the coping strategies.
3. DEALING WITH TEMPORARY DIFFICULTIES	When fear comes, just pause. Keep the focus on the present; what do I have to do? I should expect my fear to rise. Don't try to eliminate fear totally; just keep it manageable.	My muscles are starting to feel tight. Time to relax and slow things down. I have a right to be annoyed, but let's keep the lid on. My anger is a signal of what I need to do. Time to instruct myself. Try to reason it out. Treat each other with respect.	When pain comes, just pause; keep focusing on what I have to do. Just remember, there are different strategies; they'll help me stay in control. When the pain mounts, I can switch to a different strategy; I'm in control. Don't try to eliminate the pain totally; just keep it manageable.
4-5. ASSESSING AND SELF-REINFORCEMENT	*Partially Successful Coping* I didn't handle that as well as I could, but I'll get better. That's better than before. I used coping skills, so I'm making some progress. Don't give up; I'll do better the next time. *Successful Coping* It worked; I did it. I made more out of my fear than it was worth. Wait until I tell my therapist about this.	*Partially Successful Coping* These are difficult situations, and they take time to straighten out. I'll get better at this as I get more practice. Can I laugh about this? It's probably not so serious. *Successful Coping* I handled that one pretty well. It worked. I actually got through that without getting angry. That wasn't as hard as I thought.	*Partially Successful Coping* I didn't cope with pain as well as I could, but I'll get better. That's better than before. I used coping skills, so I'm making some progress. Don't give up; I'll do better the next time. *Successful Coping* Good, I did it. I knew I could do it. Wait until I tell my therapist about which procedures worked best.

SOURCE: Adapted from (fear or anxiety column) Meichenbaum, 1974; (anger) Novaco, 1975; and (pain) Turk, 1975.

Table 13-6 Examples of task-oriented problem-solving self-instructions used in stress inoculation training
SOURCE: Based on Meichenbaum & Deffenbacher, 1988.

Viewing the stressful situation as a problem

  This is not the end of the world, just a problem to be solved.

  It's okay to feel discouraged, but just remember that you can deal with this problem.

Orienting to the stressful situation as a problem

  Just think about what I can do about it.

  Focus on the information I need to gather.

Breaking the stressful situation into smaller units

  What are the steps I need to do?

  How can I break this thing down so I can tackle one piece at a time?

Problem solving

  Set up a plan of action. What is the first thing to do?

  What's my goal? What would I like to happen?

---

solving self-instructions. As the examples in Table 13-6 illustrate, these self-instructions put the problem in perspective and focus the client's attention on concrete problem-solving steps.

Clients will continue to perform coping skills only if they are reinforced. Natural consequences, such as accomplishing goals, cannot be relied on to maintain coping skills, especially when the client is first beginning to cope and may not be successful. Thus, clients are taught individualized *self-reinforcement/self-efficacy self-instructions,* such as the examples in Table 13-7.

In addition to these general coping skills that are applicable to diverse problems, clients also may be taught coping skills that are tailored to specific problems. For fear, the client might learn to gather accurate information about threatening events. For chronic pain, the client might learn to use self-distracting thoughts.

PHASE 3: APPLICATION

In the first two phases of stress inoculation training, clients develop adaptive ways of viewing potentially stress-evoking events and learn coping skills to deal with them. In the third phase, clients apply their new outlooks and coping behaviors. Initially, this is done in the therapy sessions through visualization and role playing of potentially stress-evoking scenes. For example, a client who experiences panic attacks might be asked to visualize

Table 13-7 Self-reinforcement/self-efficacy self-instructions used in stress inoculation training

Keep it up. You're doing great.

Hang in there. You're coping well.

I'm getting better and better at this.

That wasn't as bad as I expected. Next time it will be even easier.

I'm not doing as well as I would like, but I do feel good that I am continuing to try.

having an attack and coping with it (a variation of coping desensitization). Imagining the panic attack can be made more realistic by inducing hyperventilation, a common symptom in panic attacks.[86] *Hyperventilation* is abnormally fast or deep respiration in which excessive amounts of air are taken in, causing tingling in the extremities, buzzing in the ears, and sometimes fainting. It can be induced by sustained blowing into a balloon.

Stress inoculation is one component of John Lochman's Anger Coping Program for children who frequently engage in aggressive behaviors.[87] First, the children are taught coping skills in groups. Then, each client practices implementing anger control strategies while other children taunt and tease the client for 30-second periods. Clients are given feedback on their performance and reinforced for using appropriate coping skills.

In the preceding two examples, the simulated stress-evoking events in which clients practiced coping skills closely resembled those the clients were expected to encounter in their daily lives. However, the simulated stressors need not be the same as the actual events because clients usually are taught *general* coping skills applicable to a wide range of potentially stress-evoking events (which is parallel to coping desensitization; Chapter 9).

THE FAR SIDE copyright 1988 UNIVERSAL PRESS SYNDICATE.

When clients have become proficient in applying coping skills in simulated stress-evoking events during therapy sessions, they are given homework assignments that gradually expose them to increasingly more stress-evoking events, including those for which they initially sought therapy. Clients also are given training in *relapse prevention*, which consists of concrete procedures for handling the inevitable setbacks that occur in coping with real-life events.[88] For example, clients learn to view inevitable failures and setbacks as "learning experiences." The client and the therapist identify high-risk situations—those in which relapses are most likely—and rehearse coping with them. Relapse prevention is a specialized application of stress inoculation that will be described fully in Chapter 15.

Case 13-4 illustrates an innovative application of stress inoculation training to a serious problem that had been unsuccessfully treated during four years of psychoanalytic therapy (three times per week).

ELIMINATING A SELF-MUTILATING BEHAVIOR THROUGH STRESS INOCULATION[89]

Case 13-4

Donna was a 32-year-old mother of two children who was hospitalized because of a severe self-mutilating behavior consisting of "savagely scratching the left side of her face, resulting in an extensive, deep and frequently bleeding scar." Donna had a 15-year history of self-mutilation.

Stress inoculation was the major component of the treatment package that was designed for the client. During the educational phase, Donna kept a daily written log of (1) situations in which she felt the urge to scratch; (2) duration of the urges; (3) thoughts and feelings prior to and during scratching; and (4) thoughts and feelings after scratching. From this information, three situations that triggered her scratching emerged: looking at herself in the mirror; thinking about the scar on her face; and thinking about her estranged husband, who often had humiliated her because of the scratching. The increased tension she felt in these situations was relieved only by vigorous scratching, lasting a few minutes to several hours.

Donna was taught four coping skills: (1) muscle relaxation; (2) self-instructions; (3) covert sensitization; and (4) self-administered physically aversive consequences (slapping the hand that she used to scratch herself). She rehearsed these skills as she looked at herself in a mirror and as she visualized herself with her husband.

After six sessions over a two-week period, Donna's scratching had declined, and she went home for a visit. During the visit, she was unable to cope with a provocative encounter with her husband and reverted to scratching. After another six sessions of therapy, Donna again made a home visit. This time she was able to apply her coping skills to an anxiety-provoking incident involving her husband. This success experience was a turning point for Donna. Thereafter, she reported needing to rely on only two of the coping skills—relaxation and self-instructions—and expressed confidence in her ability to cope.

After 18 sessions, Donna was no longer scratching herself, and she was discharged from the hospital. She continued to keep a daily log. A year after therapy her scratching had not recurred. Donna reported that she no longer had the urge to scratch and that her scar had healed. Further, she had held a full-time job for 6 months and had divorced her husband.

Case 13-4 illustrates that successful treatment of one problem is likely to have positive effects on other problems a client is experiencing; this is an advantage of treating one or two target behaviors at a time. After Donna's scratching had been eliminated, she was able to work full-time, which previously was precluded by her self-mutilating behavior. Additionally, she was able to put her family life in order.

Stress Inoculation Training in Perspective

Stress inoculation has been used to treat and prevent a wide array of problems in adults. The three most common problems have been anxiety,[90] anger,[91] and pain.[92] Examples of the diverse problems to which stress inoculation has been applied include fear of flying,[93] presurgical anxiety,[94] coping with dental examinations,[95] reducing stress in cancer patients,[96] trauma from rape and terrorist attacks,[97] and child abuse.[98] Stress inoculation training can be applied with groups of clients as well as individually.[99] Although stress inoculation most often has been used with adults, there have been applications with children and adolescents, such as for dealing with aggressive behaviors.[100] Unfortunately, controlled research on stress inoculation applications to the problems of children and adolescents is lacking.[101]

Most of the controlled research studies evaluating stress inoculation training have indicated that it is an effective treatment,[102] although a few have not found stress inoculation to be more effective than control conditions.[103] Some studies have yielded impressive results. In one investigation, stress inoculation training was found to be superior to medication in reducing symptoms of anxiety, depression, and subjective feelings of distress in adults.[104] Moreover, in a three-year follow-up, patients given stress inoculation training had significantly fewer hospital readmissions than did patients treated with medication alone. Long-term treatment effects of stress inoculation training also have been found for the treatment of dental phobias.[105] Seventy percent of clients who had received stress inoculation were still going for regular dental check-ups one to four years after treatment.

The essential treatment component in stress inoculation training appears to be learning coping skills. In a complex analysis of the treatment components of stress inoculation for pain, for example, the complete training was compared with each phase alone, with all the possible pairs of phases, and with no treatment.[106] While the complex package was superior to any of the partial treatments, the most substantial contribution to its effectiveness was the acquisition of coping skills. Another study contrasted coping skills alone, exposure to a stress-evoking event alone, and both coping skills and exposure for the treatment of pain.[107] Whereas exposure alone had little effect on pain tolerance, coping skills alone significantly increased pain tolerance (and the combined treatment was even more effective). Because both of these investigations were analogue studies, it remains to be seen whether the findings hold with actual clients.

Stress inoculation training has not been as extensively evaluated as other cognitive-behavioral therapies.[108] One possible reason is that stress inoculation training is a treatment package consisting of components that have been evaluated independently (such as relaxation training, cognitive restructuring, and self-instructions). It is tempting to assume that combining therapies that are known to be effective will result in an even more potent treatment than any single therapy. However, it is possible that a component might be more effective alone than it is in combination with other therapies. Whether the whole is even equal to one of its parts is an empirical question that must be answered by research.

The general strategy of stress inoculation has been examined extensively by David Barlow and his colleagues for treating panic disorder. In this application, the central components of treatment are interoceptive exposure and cognitive restructuring.[109] **Interoceptive exposure** involves inducing the physical sensations of anxiety—for instance, increased heart rate and dizziness can be induced by rapid stair climbing and spinning in a chair. These physical sensations elicit catastrophic thoughts (for example, "I'm having a heart attack") in clients with panic disorder and are presumed to be the major trigger of full-blown panic attacks. After interoceptive exposure is achieved, clients practice cognitive restructuring and other cognitive-behavioral coping strategies (such as relaxation) to decrease their anxiety and prevent a panic attack. This cognitive-behavioral treatment package has been found to be highly effective in treating panic disorder as well as social phobia and generalized anxiety disorder.[110] The treatment package is at least as effective as medication[111] and significantly more efficacious than medication for long-term maintenance.[112]

COGNITIVE-BEHAVIORAL COUPLE THERAPY

Problems in couple relationships—in or out of marriage, between same- or opposite-sex partners—are among the most frequent reasons that adults seek psychological assistance. Because couple relationships are complex and multifaceted, therapy generally involves treatment packages that address different aspects of couples' difficulties. The three basic components of cognitive-behavioral couple therapy are (1) training in communication and problem-solving skills; (2) increasing positive behavior exchanges; and (3) cognitive restructuring. The various approaches to cognitive-behavioral couple therapy differ in the emphasis they place on each of these components.

Skills Training

Communication is the basis for any interpersonal relationship, and poor communication is a common denominator among distressed couples.[113] Communication skills emphasized in cognitive-behavioral couple therapy include listening, restating what the other has said, expressing feelings directly, making requests, giving feedback, and arranging regular times to talk. Distressed couples also tend to have poor problem-solving skills. Both communication and problem-solving skills are taught to couples using standard skills training procedures (see Chapter 11).

Increasing Positive Behavior Exchanges

One goal of cognitive-behavioral couple therapy is to increase couples' *positive behavior exchanges*.[114] Because distressed couples often do not feel especially loving toward one another, the **caring-days technique**, developed by Richard Stuart, has partners act *as if* they cared for each other.[115] They are instructed to perform small, specific, positive behaviors for each other (which is reminiscent of Eliza Doolittle's request in *My Fair Lady*, "If you're in love, show me"). Each partner is asked to answer the question: "What would you like your partner to do that would show you that he or she cares for you?" From a list of caring behaviors, each partner is requested to perform at least five caring behaviors each day, whether or not the other partner also has done so. The couple keep records of their caring behaviors (see Figure 13-6 for an example). Contingency contracts also are employed to promote positive behavior exchanges and implement broader behavior changes in the relationship.[116]

Cognitive Restructuring for Discrepant Cognitions

Discrepancies in partners' cognitions about aspects of their relationship often play a role in creating and maintaining couple problems. The discrepancies may be in (1) *perceptions* about what has occurred; (2) *attributions* about why a partner did something; (3) *expectations* about how things will be; and (4) *assumptions* about how things are or should be (see

Figure 13-6 Record of each partner's caring behaviors

Caring Behaviors Record

Week of June 16

Sandy does for Shelly	Su	Mo	Tu	We	Th	Fr	Sa
Ask how I'm feeling.		✓		✓	✓		
Play Scrabble with me.	✓	✓					
Do the dishes.			✓	✓		✓	✓	✓
Make me a cup of coffee.	✓		✓		✓		
Kiss me when I leave or come home.		✓	✓	✓		✓	
Put the cap on the tooth paste.	✓		✓	✓	✓		✓
Turn lights off.	✓		✓	✓	✓		
Compliment me.	✓		✓	✓	✓	✓	
Say "good night" before going to sleep.	✓	✓				✓	✓
Say "good morning" when I first wake up.						✓	✓

Shelly does for Sandy	Su	Mo	Tu	We	Th	Fr	Sa
Kiss me spontaneously.			✓		✓		✓
Call me at work to say hello.			✓	✓		✓	
Compliment my appearance.		✓	✓		✓		✓
Flush the toilet after using it.		✓	✓		✓	✓	✓
Leave/send me short, loving notes.	✓	✓		✓			
Thank me for something I did.	✓	✓		✓			
Laugh at my jokes.	✓	✓			✓	✓	✓
Keep your dresser neat.	✓		✓	✓			
Ask how my day went.		✓		✓		✓	

Table 13-8).[117] Cognitive restructuring and other cognitive-behavioral therapy procedures are used to deal with these discrepancies. Couples are taught first to evaluate how valid or reasonable their cognitions are and then to modify biased or unrealistic thoughts by substituting more appropriate and adaptive ones.

Acceptance: An Alternative Goal in Couple Therapy

Cognitive-behavioral couple therapy traditionally has focused on changing those behaviors of each partner that are upsetting to the other partner.[118] Recently, Neil Jacobson, a leading researcher in the area of cognitive-behavioral couple therapy, has suggested an alternative goal—namely,

Table 13-8 Common cognitive discrepancies held by distressed couples

Discrepancy	Description	Example
PERCEPTIONS	Partners "see" things differently	PAT: "We haven't talked in months." CHRIS: "We talked just last week."
ATTRIBUTIONS	One partner wrongly infers cause of other's behavior	CHRIS: "I've been waiting for a half hour. You just wanted to keep me waiting." PAT: "I'm late because I had a flat tire on the way here."
EXPECTATIONS	Partners anticipate different outcomes	PAT: "I was looking forward to making love tonight." CHRIS: "I was hoping to watch TV and just drift off to sleep."
ASSUMPTIONS	Partners hold different assumptions	CHRIS: "*You* are supposed to take care of the kids." PAT: "Taking care of *our* children is *our* responsibility."

acceptance of one's partner's upsetting behaviors.[119]* Sometimes, acceptance is the only viable goal because some interpersonal conflicts cannot be resolved. Further, acceptance may be necessary for long-term maintenance of satisfaction in a couple relationship. Acceptance as a goal in couple therapy is not a new idea. However, until recently, concrete methods for promoting acceptance have not been available.[120] Four strategies are employed in behavioral couple therapy to promote acceptance: empathic joining, detachment, tolerance building, and self-care.

Empathic joining refers to the couple's learning to understand and appreciate each other's experience of emotional pain within the relationship, without introducing anger or blame. Empathic joining requires careful listening to one's partner's description of what he or she is experiencing, not judging the experience, and attempting to view the experience from the partner's perspective. The therapist helps the couple understand that the way they view and react to their differences—not the mere fact that they have differences (which is inevitable)—is primarily responsible for their interpersonal distress.[121]

Detachment fosters acceptance through the couple's distancing themselves from their conflicts. The couple are encouraged to talk and think about their difficulties as an "it"—something external to each of them rather than part of them.[122] The "it" becomes a painful, common enemy that they share and cope with together rather than a problem that one partner creates or something that one does to the other. Couples may feel less upset when talking about "it," even though the problem itself has not been resolved.

Tolerance building involves learning ways to become less upset by one's partner's behaviors. Through cognitive restructuring, partners come to view the other's so-called negative behaviors positively. For example "moody"

---

* *Acceptance* should not be confused with the *acceptability* of behavior therapy procedures to clients, one of the criteria of therapy effectiveness (see Chapter 4).

might be reconstrued as "thoughtful"; "picky" as "careful"; and "scatter-brained" as "creative." This process is easier than it might seem because, in fact, most behaviors are not inherently negative or positive. "Positive" and "negative" are evaluations one places on behaviors. Moreover, often the very behaviors that partners view as disturbing when they are experiencing conflict in their relationship are the same behaviors that they found attractive in the past, particularly during courtship.[123]

Finally, acceptance is fostered through *self-care*. The partners are encouraged to develop means of deriving satisfaction and personal fulfillment independent of the relationship. This promotes less dependence on one another for these basic life needs. Couples are asked to facilitate each other's engaging in self-care activities.

At first glance, the idea of promoting acceptance in distressed couples may not seem particularly behavioral. On closer inspection, it turns out to be exemplary of nontraditional therapy procedures that remain well-grounded in behavior therapy.[124] In addition to using specific cognitive-behavioral procedures (such as cognitive restructuring) to foster acceptance, the general approach is action-oriented. Couples are required to engage in specific behaviors to reach the goal of acceptance. This active approach differs from traditional views of acceptance as passive resignation. Further, cognitive-behavioral couple therapy is highly individualized. For example, treatment is guided by an assessment of the maintaining conditions of the particular couple's conflicts rather than by a priori assumptions about what generally leads to conflicts in couples.

Cognitive-Behavioral Couple Therapy in Perspective

A number of well-controlled studies have demonstrated that cognitive-behavioral couple therapy can effectively reduce couple distress.[125] Further, for married couples it has been found to alleviate depression.[126] This is an important finding because almost half the clients who seek treatment for depression have marital difficulties.[127]

Unfortunately, cognitive-behavioral couple therapy is effective for only about two-thirds of couples treated; of these couples, only about two-thirds maintain their improvement over a one- to two-year period.[128] The net result is that less than one-half of couples treated with cognitive-behavioral couple therapy maintain the benefits after therapy. This sobering statistic was the impetus for developing the more durable goal of acceptance for couple therapy.[129] We must wait for future research to tell us if using acceptance as a goal increases the success rate of the therapy.

Couple relationship problems are difficult to treat because of their complex, multifaceted nature and because, over time, patterns of maladaptive interactions have been mutually reinforced. One way around this inevitable hurdle is to prevent such patterns from developing in the first place.[130] Toward this end, Howard Markman has developed a *prevention and relationship enhancement program* that parallels cognitive-behavioral couple therapy.[131] This prevention approach teaches couples, before they develop problems, specific skills that are associated with successful relationships. The skills include communication, problem solving, negotiation of roles and responsibilities, and clarification of values and expectations related to sexuality and intimacy desires. The relationship enhancement skills training approach has led to improved relationship satisfaction and positive perceptions of partners, lower levels of couple violence, and lower rates of separation.[132]

◆ ## All Things Considered: ## Cognitive-Behavioral Coping Skills Therapy

Cognitive-behavioral coping skills therapy is used to treat a wide array of problem behaviors. In contrast to cognitive restructuring therapy (Chapter 12), which is most applicable to adults, cognitive-behavioral coping skills therapy is suitable for children, adolescents, and adults.

In general, the efficacy of cognitive-behavioral coping skills therapy is well-documented by research, especially for emotional problems such as anxiety and depression. However, the complexity of cognitive-behavioral coping skills therapy poses problems for evaluating its effectiveness. The therapy always involves a treatment package, and often the specific contributions of the various components are not assessed. Further, the specific components employed can vary from study to study, even though the same name is used to designate the therapy in each study. These variations may account, in part, for occasional discrepant findings of research evaluating cognitive-behavioral coping skills therapy.

The active nature and self-control themes of behavior therapy are especially evident in cognitive-behavioral coping skills therapy. Because practice and repetition of coping skills are critical to the therapy's success, clients must invest considerable time.[133] Clients are largely responsible for the changes that occur, and the more they are aware that their own efforts have made the difference, the more likely it is that the effects of therapy will generalize and be maintained over time.[134] Further, clients derive a sense of competence from applying coping skills.[135]

Therapies that teach clients coping skills serve two functions. First, they enable clients to deal with the problems for which they have sought therapy. Second, clients may be able to apply the coping skills to future problems in their lives. This is essential in treating *borderline personality disorder,* which is characterized by repeated unstable relationships, extreme mood changes, a negative self-image, and impulsive and often self-destructive behaviors. People with this debilitating disorder appear to have one crisis after another in their lives. Marsha Linehan developed *dialectical behavior therapy* specifically to treat borderline personality disorder.* One of its components is

---

* Dialectical behavior therapy is rooted in a nonbehavioral "worldview" that incorporates Eastern spiritual philosophy and psychoanalytic concepts, in addition to specific behavior therapy components, such as skills training and in vivo exposure.

teaching clients cognitive-behavioral coping skills, including problem solving, relaxation, cognitive restructuring, and assertion training for dealing effectively with stress-evoking events.[136]

◆ ALL THINGS CONSIDERED: COGNITIVE-BEHAVIORAL THERAPY

We will conclude our discussion of cognitive-behavioral therapy, begun in Chapter 12, with some general comments on its current status. In 1968, a group of prominent behavior therapists suggested that "current [behavior therapy] procedures should be modified and new procedures developed to capitalize upon the human organism's unique capacity for cognitive control."[137] Clearly, this recommendation was heeded. Over the next decade, cognitive-behavioral therapy developed, with only minor opposition from those who believed that behavior therapy should deal only with overt behaviors.[138] By 1980, cognitive-behavioral therapy constituted a subfield of behavior therapy,[139] and today it is at the forefront of behavior therapy.[140] The cognitive-behavioral *Zeitgeist* (German for "spirit of the times") within behavior therapy parallels the "cognitive revolution" in psychology.[141] Bandura has argued that *all* behavior therapies are most usefully viewed as cognitive-behavioral.

> The field of psychological change is not well served by false dichotomies that there exist pure cognitive and pure behavioral treatments. One would be hard pressed to find a "behavioral" method that does not rely, at least in part, on cognitive conveyance [mediation], or a "cognitive" method that is devoid of any performance [behavioral] elements.[142]

Cognitive-behavioral therapy epitomizes the self-control theme of behavior therapy.[143] Indeed, a self-control approach is necessary because only clients themselves have direct access to their cognitive processes.

With cognitive restructuring therapy (Chapter 12), clients must possess the requisite cognitive skills, such as the ability to use language to mediate actions and the ability to think abstractly. These abilities are linked to cognitive development,[144] which accounts for the greater effectiveness of cognitive restructuring therapy interventions with adults than with children and adolescents.

In contrast, cognitive-behavioral coping skills therapy (Chapter 13) has been effective with children and adolescents, as well as clients with severe intellectual deficits. However, successful treatment by cognitive-behavioral coping skills therapy requires clients to have relatively high motivation because the treatment procedures are largely self-administered. Youngsters who are referred by adults for treatment of aggressive or impulsive behaviors generally have little motivation to change their behaviors. After all, it is the adults who want these children to behave differently. Thus, children may be capable of learning self-instructions and problem-solving skills, but they cannot be relied on to apply them in their natural environments without additional interventions, such as prompting and reinforcement.[145]

Participation Exercise 13-3

DESIGNING A COGNITIVE-BEHAVIORAL CHANGE PLAN FOR YOUR ANALOGUE TARGET BEHAVIOR*

In Participation Exercise 8-2 you developed (and maybe implemented) a change plan for your analogue target behavior based on consequential behavior therapy procedures. Now that you have learned about another set of interventions—cognitive-behavioral therapy—you can develop a second change plan. Besides giving you a chance to apply what you have learned in Chapters 12 and 13, this Exercise will illustrate how the same target behavior can be treated by diverse treatment strategies.

Examine the target behavior's maintaining conditions that you identified in Participation Exercise 4-3, including both antecedents and consequences. Decide which might be most easily changed with cognitive-behavioral therapy procedures. Then develop a detailed change plan based on cognitive-behavioral interventions (that is, those covered in Chapters 12 and 13). The change plan should be one you could implement on your own rather than what would be done in formal therapy. For example, if you use rational emotive behavior therapy principles and procedures, your plan might include *your* challenging your own illogical thinking rather than a therapist doing the challenging.

When you have completed a written change plan, share it with classmates to get their reactions and suggestions for improving it. Compare your consequential and cognitive-behavioral change plans. What are the general differences and similarities? What are the strengths and limitations of each? What do the answers to these questions tell about the two approaches?

SUMMARY

1. Cognitive-behavioral coping skills therapy treats problems that are maintained by a deficit of adaptive cognitions by changing both cognitions and overt behaviors.
2. In self-instructional training, clients learn to instruct themselves to cope effectively with difficult situations. Self-instructions serve to prepare clients to use self-instructions, focus attention, guide behavior, provide encouragement, evaluate performance, and reduce anxiety.
3. The five steps of self-instructional training are cognitive modeling, cognitive participant modeling, overt self-instructions, fading of overt self-instructions, and covert self-instructions.

* You will need to do this Participation Exercise later.

4. Self-instructional training can be moderately effective when it is applied to narrowly focused problems that are maintained solely by inadequate task-related self-instructions. It is less effective as a treatment for broader problems that are maintained by more than just cognitive deficits.

5. Problem-solving therapy/training teaches clients a systematic strategy for approaching problems. Problem-solving therapy serves the dual purpose of treating clients' immediate problems and preparing clients to deal with future problems on their own. The five stages of problem solving are adopting a problem-solving orientation; defining the problem and selecting goals; generating alternative solutions; choosing the best solution; and implementing the best solution and evaluating its effects. Problem solving is taught to clients by using cognitive modeling, prompting, self-instructions, and reinforcement.

6. Children and adults can learn problem-solving skills, often quickly. However, the degree to which clients apply and benefit from the skills in their everyday lives is questionable.

7. Stress inoculation training helps clients cope with stress by teaching them coping skills and then having clients practice the skills while they are exposed to stress-evoking events. Stress inoculation training consists of three phases: conceptualization, coping skills acquisition, and application. Anxiety, anger, and pain are the most frequently treated problems. The essential component is learning coping skills.

8. Stress inoculation is a behavioral analogue of biological immunization. The coping skills clients learn can be considered "psychological antibodies," which increase resistance to potentially stress-evoking events.

9. The three basic components of behavioral couple therapy are training in communication and problem-solving skills, increasing positive behavior exchanges, and cognitive restructuring. The usual goal of behavioral couple therapy is for each partner to change behaviors that are problematic for the other. An alternative goal is acceptance of the other's behaviors. Another approach, which is proving successful, is to teach clients, before problems develop, specific skills that are associated with successful relationships.

10. Cognitive-behavioral therapy is widely used and accepted, and it epitomizes the self-control theme of behavior therapy.

Reference Notes

1. Meichenbaum & Goodman, 1971.
2. For example, Camp & Bash, 1981; Camp, Blom, Herbert, & Van Doorwick, 1976; Spivack & Shure, 1974.
3. For example, Meichenbaum & Cameron, 1973; Meyers, Mercatoris, & Sirota, 1976.
4. For example, Guevremont, Tishelman, & Hull, 1985.

5. Meichenbaum & Goodman, 1971, p. 117.

6. Meichenbaum, 1977.

7. Guevremont, Osnes, & Stokes, 1988.

8. Kendall & Braswell, 1985.

9. For example, Guevremont, Tishelman, & Hull, 1985.

10. For example, Lochman, 1985; Lochman & Curry, 1986a.

11. For example, Bryant & Budd, 1982; Guevremont, Osnes, & Stokes, 1988.

12. Burgio, Whitman, & Johnson, 1980.

13. For example, Kendall & Wilcox, 1980; Schleser, Meyers, & Cohen, 1981.

14. For example, Kendall & Finch, 1978; Meichenbaum & Goodman, 1971.

15. Bentall, Higson, & Lowe, 1987; Meichenbaum & Cameron, 1973; Meyers, Mercatoris, & Sirota, 1976.

16. Combs & Lahey, 1981.

17. For example, Holroyd, 1976; McCordick, Kaplan, Finn, & Smith, 1979.

18. For example, Cradock, Cotler, & Jason, 1978; Meichenbaum, Gilmore, & Fedoravicius, 1971.

19. For example, Glass, Gottman, & Shmurak, 1976.

20. Kendall, 1994.

21. For example, Camp, Blom, Herbert, & Van Doorwick, 1977; Foreman, 1980.

22. Overhoser & Fine, 1994.

23. For example, Dunkel & Glaros, 1978.

24. For example, Kettlewell, Mizes, & Wasylyshyn, 1992.

25. For example, Carmody, 1978; Craighead, 1979; Jacobs & Cochran, 1982; Kaplan, 1982; Kazdin & Mascitelli, 1982.

26. For example, Labouvie-Vief & Gonda, 1976; Meichenbaum, 1974.

27. Keogh, Faw, Whitman, & Reid, 1984.

28. Meichenbaum, 1975.

29. Ecton & Feindler, 1990.

30. Rusch, Hughes, & Wilson, 1995.

31. For example, Rusch, Morgan, Martin, Riva, & Agran, 1985.

32. For example, Hughes & Rusch, 1989.

33. For example, Rusch, Martin, Lagomarcino, & White, 1987.

34. For example, Sowers, Rusch, Connis, & Cummings, 1980.

35. For example, Kendall & Wilcox, 1980; Lochman & Curry, 1986a; Woodward & Jones, 1980.

36. For example, Guevremont, Osnes, & Stokes, 1988.

37. For example, Denney, Sullivan, & Thiry, 1977; Goren, 1975.

38. For example, D'Zurilla & Chang, 1995.

39. For example, Asarnow & Callan, 1985; Doerfler, Mullins, Griffin, Siegel, & Richards, 1984; D'Zurilla & Nezu, 1982; Lochman & Curry, 1986b; Nezu & D'Zurilla, 1989; Sayers, Bellack, Wade, Bennett, & Fong, 1995; Shure & Spivack, 1972.

40. For example, Meichenbaum & Jaremko, 1982.

41. For example, Arean, Perri, Nezu, Schein, Christopher, & Joseph, 1993; Nezu, Nezu, & Perri, 1989.

42. Kleiner, Marshall, & Spevack, 1987.

43. Black, 1987; Johnson, Corrigan, & Mayo, 1987.

44. Shaffer, Beck, & Boothroyd, 1983.

45. Hansen, St. Lawrence, & Christoff, 1985.

46. Jacobson, 1991; Jacobson & Margolin, 1979; O'Leary & Turkewitz, 1978.

47. Falloon & Coverdale, 1994.

48. Dawson, De Armas, McGrath, & Kelly, 1986; MacMillan, Guevremont, & Hansen, 1989.

49. For example, Kendall & Gerow, 1995.

50. For example, Lascelles, Cunningham, McGrath, & Sullivan, 1989.

51. For example, Kazdin, Esveldt-Dawson, French, & Unis, 1987.

52. Lochman & Curry, 1986a; Lochman, Nelson, & Sims, 1981.

53. Feindler, Ecton, Kingsley, & Dubey, 1986; Feindler, Marriott, & Iwata, 1984.

54. Frisby, 1990.

55. Shure & Spivack, 1980; Spivack & Shure, 1974.

56. Robin & Foster, 1989.

57. For example, Kendall & Gerow, 1995.

58. Weisenberg, Gesten, Carnike, Toro, Rapkin, Davidson, & Cowen, 1981.

59. For example, D'Zurilla, 1986; D'Zurilla & Goldfried, 1971; D'Zurilla & Sheedy, 1991.

60. For example, Spivack & Shure, 1974; D'Zurilla & Goldfried, 1971.

61. Nezu, Nezu, D'Zurilla, & Rothenberg, 1996.

62. Nezu, Nezu, D'Zurilla, & Rothenberg, 1996.

63. Nezu, Nezu, & Houts, 1993; Nezu, Nezu, D'Zurilla, & Rothenberg, 1996; Watson & Kramer, 1995.

64. Mayo & Norton, 1980.

65. Spivack & Shure, 1974.

66. Adapted from Guevremont & Foster, 1992.

67. For example, Sharp, 1981; Spivack & Shure, 1974.

68. For example, Giebink, Stover, & Fahl, 1968; Kazdin, Esveldt-Dawson, French, & Unis, 1987; Weisenberg, Gesten, Carnike, Toro, Rapkin,

Davidson, & Cowen, 1981; Yu, Harris, Solovitz, & Franklin, 1986.

69. Feindler, Marriott, & Iwata, 1984.
70. Feindler, Ecton, Kingsley, & Dubey, 1986.
71. Grothberg, Feindler, White, & Stutman, 1991; Robin & Foster, 1989.
72. Nangle, Carr-Nangle, & Hansen, 1994.
73. Ladouceur, Boisvert, & Dumont, 1994.
74. Bujold, Ladouceur, Sylvain, & Boisvert, 1994.
75. Arean, Perri, Nezu, Schein, Christopher, & Joseph, 1993.
76. Nezu, Nezu, & Houts, 1993; Nezu, Nezu, D'Zurilla, & Rothenberg, 1996.
77. D'Zurilla & Nezu, 1982.
78. Weisenberg, Gesten, Carnike, Toro, Rapkin, Davidson, & Cowen, 1981.
79. For example, Shure & Spivack, 1980; Spivack & Shure, 1974.
80. For example, Sharp, 1981; Yu, Harris, Solovitz, & Franklin, 1986.
81. Yu, Harris, Solovitz, & Franklin, 1986.
82. D'Zurilla & Maschka, 1988.
83. Cofer & Appley, 1964; Lazarus & Folkman, 1984.
84. Meichenbaum, 1977, 1985.
85. Poser, 1970; Poser & King, 1975, 1976; Spiegler, 1980.
86. Barlow & Cerney, 1988.
87. Lochman & Lenhart, 1993.
88. Marlatt & Gordon, 1985.
89. Kaminer & Shahar, 1987; quotation from p. 289.
90. Meichenbaum & Cameron, 1972.
91. Novaco, 1975, 1977a, 1977b.
92. Turk, 1975, 1976.
93. Meichenbaum & Deffenbacher, 1988.
94. For example, Wells, Howard, Nowlin, & Vargas, 1986.
95. For example, Getka & Glass, 1992; Liddell, Di Fazio, Blackwood, & Ackerman, 1994; Moses & Hollandsworth, 1985; Siegel & Peterson, 1980.
96. Elsesser, Van Berkel, Sartory, Biermann-Göcke, & Öhl, 1994.
97. Meichenbaum & Deffenbacher, 1988.
98. Meichenbaum & Deffenbacher, 1988.
99. Meichenbaum & Deffenbacher, 1988.
100. For example, Feindler, Ecton, Kingsley, & Dubey, 1986; Feindler, Marriott, & Iwata, 1984; Lochman & Curry, 1986a; Lochman, Nelson, & Sims, 1981; Wilcox & Dowrick, 1992.
101. Maag & Kotlash, 1994.
102. Meichenbaum, 1985; Meichenbaum & Deffenbacher, 1988.
103. Meichenbaum & Deffenbacher, 1988.
104. Meichenbaum & Deffenbacher, 1988.
105. Liddell, Di Fazio, Blackwood, & Ackerman, 1994.
106. Vallis, 1984.
107. Horan, Hackett, Buchanan, Stone, & Stone, 1977.
108. For example, Maag & Kotlash, 1994.
109. Barlow, 1988; Barlow, 1993; Brown, Antony, & Barlow, 1995; Carter & Barlow, 1993, 1995.
110. Gould & Otto, 1995; Gould, Otto, & Pollack, in press.
111. Otto, Pollack, Sachs, Reiter, Meltzer-Brody, & Rosenbaum, 1993; Pollack, Otto, Kaspi, Hammerness, & Rosenbaum, 1994.
112. Otto & Gould, 1995; Otto, Gould, & Pollack, 1994.
113. For example, Geiss & O'Leary, 1981.
114. For example, Jacobson & Margolin, 1979; Patterson & Reid, 1970.
115. Stuart, 1969, 1980; Wills, Weiss, & Patterson, 1974.
116. Baucom & Epstein, 1990; Jacobson & Margolin, 1979; Stuart, 1969, 1980.
117. Baucom & Epstein, 1990; Beck, 1989.
118. For example, Stuart, 1980.
119. Jacobson, 1991, 1992, 1993.
120. Waller & Spiegler, 1997.
121. Compare with Waller & Spiegler, 1997.
122. Compare with White, 1989, 1995.
123. Waller & Spiegler, 1997.
124. Jacobson, 1992.
125. Baucom & Hoffman, 1986; Hahlweg & Markman, 1988; Jacobson, 1989.
126. For example, Beach & O'Leary, 1992.
127. Beach, Whisman, & O'Leary, 1994.
128. Christensen, Jacobson, & Babcock, in press.
129. Christensen, Jacobson, & Babcock, in press.
130. Jacobson & Addis, 1993; Sullivan & Bradbury, 1996.
131. Markman, Floyd, Stanley, & Lewis, 1986; Markman, Renick, Floyd, Stanley, & Clements, 1993.
132. Hahlweg & Markman, 1988; Markman, Floyd, Stanley, & Storaasli, 1988; Markman, Renick, Floyd, Stanley, & Clements, 1993; Stanley, Markman, St. Peters, & Leber, 1995.
133. Hollon & Beck, 1986.
134. Kopel & Arkowitz, 1975.
135. Compare with Masterpasqua, 1989.
136. Linehan, 1993a, 1993b; Linehan, Armstrong, Suarez, Allmon, & Heard, 1991; Linehan, Heard, & Armstrong, 1993; Linehan & Schmidt, 1995.
137. Davison, D'Zurilla, Goldfried, Paul, & Valins, 1968.

138. For example, Ledwidge, 1978, 1979; Locke, 1979; Mahoney & Kazdin, 1979; Meichenbaum, 1979; Zettle & Hayes, 1982.
139. Spiegler, 1983.
140. Kendall, 1987b.
141. Dember, 1974.
142. Bandura, 1986a, p. 14.
143. For example, Israel, Guile, Baker, & Silverman, 1994; Silverman, Ginsburg, & Kurtines, 1995.
144. Bernard & Joyce, 1984; Morris & Cohen, 1982; Schleser, Meyers, & Cohen, 1981.
145. For example, Kendall, 1993.

PART III

COMPLEX APPLICATIONS

Now that you have digested the appetizers (basic principles) and the main course (behavior therapy), it's time for dessert. The dessert provides a taste of three applications of behavior therapy principles and procedures to complex problems. Chapter 14 describes how behavior therapy procedures are employed to treat and prevent medical disorders. In a related application, Chapter 15 discusses the role that behavior therapy can play in treating psychological disorders whose primary feature is a physical problem. Finally, Chapter 16 explores behavioral community psychology—the creative adaptation of behavior therapy procedures to solve everyday problems faced by individuals and societies.

You will be familiar with most of the behavior therapy procedures described in Chapters 14 through 16, but their applications will be new. Thus, reading these chapters will serve as a review of previous material. It also will show you the versatility and breadth of behavior therapy principles and procedures in dealing with complex and, in some cases, far-reaching human concerns.

Chapter 14

Applications to Behavioral Medicine

T he application of behavioral principles and procedures to physical health and illness has burgeoned over the past two decades. Much of this work is subsumed under the interdisciplinary field known as *behavioral medicine*. This field is devoted to the application of behavioral science, including behavior therapy, to the assessment, treatment, management, rehabilitation, and prevention of physical disease and related behavioral reactions to physical dysfunction.[1]

Behavior therapy serves four functions in dealing with medical disorders: (1) treatment; (2) increasing adherence to medical treatments, such as taking medication; (3) helping patients cope with treatments; and (4) prevention. Table 14-1 describes and gives examples of these four functions. In discussing each of the functions, we will present representative examples of the medical disorders dealt with by behavior therapy. You already are familiar with all the behavior therapies applied to medical disorders (with a few exceptions), but the applications we will describe will be new to you. They provide further illustrations of the versatility of behavior therapy.

TREATMENT OF MEDICAL DISORDERS

Behavior therapy can add to existing medical treatments in three ways. First, behavior therapy can be combined with medical treatments (for example, both relaxation training and medication can be employed to control high blood pressure). Second, behavior therapy may be more desirable than medical treatments that are associated with risk (such as surgery) or with undesirable side effects (such as medication). Third, behavior therapy can play an especially important role in cases for which no viable medical treatments exist (as for certain types of chronic pain). We will illustrate the use of behavior therapy to treat medical disorders by describing its application to two medical problems: essential hypertension and chronic pain.

Table 14-1 Functions of behavior therapy in dealing with medical disorders

Function	Description	Example
TREATMENT	Correct or alleviate a medical condition and the pain and suffering associated with it	Relaxation training to lower blood pressure in patients with essential hypertension
ADHERENCE	Increase patients' following prescribed medical treatments (such as medication, diet, and exercise)	Taking medication at the same time each day so that it will come under stimulus control
COPING	Reduce anxiety, discomfort, and distress associated with medical procedures	Self-instructional training to decrease the anxiety associated with having dental work done
PREVENTION	Reduce the risk of developing disease, including motivating people to engage in healthful behaviors	Assertion training to promote safer sexual practices (such as refusing to engage in unprotected sex)

Essential Hypertension

Cardiovascular disease is the leading cause of death in the United States, claiming about 1 million lives annually.[2] Affecting approximately 15% of the population, high blood pressure is a major contributor to cardiovascular disorders, including heart attacks and strokes, as well as to other physical disorders, such as kidney failure.[3] *Essential hypertension* is chronic high blood pressure with no physical cause that can be treated directly (for convenience, we will shorten the term *essential hypertension* to *hypertension*).

Despite the well-known health hazards of hypertension, providing patients with basic medical information about reducing blood pressure frequently is insufficient to lead to significant reductions.[4] Hypertension most often is treated with medication. Although antihypertensive medication generally is effective in lowering blood pressure, its extended use may actually increase the risk of cardiovascular disease. Further, it is estimated that up to 50% of patients stop taking medication within a year of diagnosis, and a smaller percentage do not take sufficient medication to control their hypertension.[5] Thus, there is a need for nonpharmacological treatments.

Relaxation training and biofeedback sometimes are employed as the sole treatment for mild or moderate hypertension. When relaxation and biofeedback are used in conjunction with medication, it often is possible to lower the drug dosage. Relaxation and biofeedback directly influence blood pressure, in contrast to other nonpharmacological treatments, such as diet and exercise, that indirectly change contributory conditions.

RELAXATION TRAINING

Edmund Jacobson, the father of relaxation training, pioneered the use of relaxation to reduce hypertension.[6] Patients may be taught deep muscle relaxation by a behavior therapist or given instructions (such as on an audiotape) by a physician and practice the skills at home.[7] (Meditation, which is not a behavior therapy, is the other technique for inducing relaxation and also is used to treat hypertension.[8])

There are two approaches to using relaxation to lower blood pressure. One is to set aside one or two 15- to 30-minute periods each day to induce deep muscle relaxation.[9] It is assumed that the relaxed state achieved during these periods will generalize to the remainder of patients' daily activities. The other approach employs differential relaxation as a coping skill, as in coping desensitization (see Chapter 9). The patient is taught to rapidly relax all nonessential muscles (those that are not being used to perform ongoing behaviors) and to tense essential muscles only as much as is needed to perform ongoing behaviors. Then, the patient learns to use environmental or physiological cues to prompt differential relaxation.[10] Clients often use both approaches.[11]

Differential relaxation is a highly useful skill that can help anyone cope with everyday stress-evoking events. Participation Exercise 14-1 will teach you differential relaxation. Although learning differential relaxation will require a number of days of practice, reading the Participation Exercise now will give you a more complete understanding of the technique.

◆

Participation Exercise 14-1

MAKING A DIFFERENCE IN YOUR LIFE WITH DIFFERENTIAL RELAXATION

Differential relaxation allows us to get rid of excess muscle tension as we engage in our normal behaviors. Learning differential relaxation requires that you first learn deep muscle relaxation and then practice relaxing your nonessential muscles during the course of everyday activities.

Part I: Preparation

You will need a comfortable firm surface where you can lie down, such as on a rug, a mat, or a firm bed. The practice location should be free of distractions. Turn off the phone, tell roommates you'll be busy for about an hour, place a "Do Not Disturb" sign on your door, and so on. If you are interrupted, just resume where you left off. Open this book to Table 14-2 and place it close to where you will be lying down, as you will need to refer to it for the specific relaxation instructions for each muscle group.

Part II: Learning Deep Muscle Relaxation

You will learn deep muscle relaxation in two phases. In the first phase, you will tense each muscle group before relaxing it. This procedure will make you aware of the sensations associated with muscle tension. Then, whenever you experience these sensations, you will know that you need to apply differential relaxation. In the second phase of training, you will relax your muscles without first deliberately tensing them, which simulates your using differential relaxation in everyday situations.

PHASE 1: TENSION AND RELAXATION

Lie flat on your back with your legs slightly apart and your arms at your sides. Adjust your body so that you are comfortable. Loosen tight clothing; remove your shoes and any articles of clothing or jewelry that might interfere with the relaxation exercises. To remove visual distractions, close your eyes *lightly*. Keep your eyes lightly shut, except to read the relaxation instructions.

When you are ready to begin, take a few deep breaths. Start with the first of the 16 muscle groups (instruction A1 in Table 14-2, Part A). *Tense those muscles for about 5 seconds* (you may wish to count to yourself, "one-thousand-one, one-thousand-two," and so on). Tense the muscles tightly, but do *not* strain them. You should definitely feel the tension, but it should not hurt. As you tense the muscles, concentrate on the physical sensations you experience.

After 5 seconds of tensing, say "relax" or "calm" to yourself and *gradually relax the muscles you have just tensed. Make your muscles loose; smooth them out.* Continue relaxing your muscles for at least 30 seconds until they feel totally relaxed. As you relax, pay attention to the sensations of relaxation, *noting the difference between the sensations of relaxation and tension.*

Table 14-2 Tensing instructions for learning deep muscle relaxation (Participation Exercise 14-1)

Part A: 16 Muscle Groups	
Muscle Group	*Tensing Instructions*
A1. Dominant hand and forearm (right hand if you're right-handed)	A1. Make a tight fist.
A2. Dominant biceps	A2. Push you elbow down against the floor (or bed), and simultaneously pull the elbow inward toward your body.
A3. Nondominant hand and forearm	A3. Follow instruction A1.
A4. Nondominant biceps	A4. Follow instruction A2.
A5. Upper part of face (forehead and scalp)	A5. Lift your eyebrows as high as you can. (Alternative: Make an exaggerated frown.)[a]
A6. Central part of face (upper cheeks and nose)	A6. Squint your eyes tightly, and simultaneously wrinkle up your nose.
A7. Lower part of face (jaw and lower part of cheeks)	A7. Clench your teeth together, and pull the corners of your mouth back. *Caution:* Do not clench your teeth very hard. Do this just enough to feel tension in your jaw and cheeks.
A8. Neck and throat	A8. Pull your chin down toward your chest, and simultaneously try to keep your chin from touching your chest. (You should feel a small amount of trembling or shaking in your neck.) (Alternative: Press your head against the floor or bed.)[a]
A9. Chest, shoulders, and upper back	A9. Take a deep breath and hold it; at the same time pull your shoulders back as if you were trying to make your shoulder blades touch each other. (Alternative: Pull your shoulders upward as if you were trying to touch your shoulder blades to your ears. It may help to imagine that puppet strings are attached to your shoulders, which are being pulled upward.)[a]
A10. Abdomen	A10. Make your stomach hard, as if you were bracing before being hit in the stomach. (Alternatives: Pull your stomach in as far as it will go. Or push your stomach out as far as it will go.)[a]
A11. Dominant thigh (upper leg)	A11. Keeping your leg straight, lift it a few inches off the floor.

[a]Use the alternative tensing strategy only when the first one presented does not create tension in the appropriate muscle group.

(continued)

Table 14-2 (continued)

Part A: 16 Muscle Groups (continued)	
Muscle Group	Tensing Instructions
A12. Dominant calf (lower leg)	A12. Pull your toes upward toward your head (without moving your legs).
A13. Dominant foot	A13. Point your toes, turn your foot inward, and curl your toes downward (as if you were burying them in the sand). *Caution:* Do not tense these muscles very hard or very long—just enough to feel the tightness under your arch and the ball of your foot for about three to five seconds. (You may also feel some tension in your calf.)
A14. Nondominant thigh	A14. Follow instruction A11.
A15. Nondominant calf	A15. Follow instruction A12.
A16. Nondominant foot	A16. Follow instruction A13.

Part B: 7 Muscle Groups	
Muscle Group	Tensing Instructions
B1. Dominant hand, forearm, and biceps	B1. Hold your arm out in front of you with your elbow bent at about 45 degrees while making a fist. (Alternative: Leave your arm supported on the floor or bed. Bend your arm at the elbow [about 45 degrees], make a fist, and press your elbow down and/or in toward your body.)[a]
B2. Nondominant hand, forearm, and biceps	B2. Follow instruction B1.
B3. Face	B3. At the same time, raise your eyebrows (or frown), squint your eyes, wrinkle your nose, bite down, and pull the corners of your mouth back.[b]
B4. Neck and throat	B4. Follow instruction A8.
B5. Chest, shoulders, upper back, and abdomen	B5. Take a deep breath and hold it, pull your shoulder blades back and together, and make your stomach hard (or pull it in or push it out).
B6. Dominant thigh, calf, and foot	B6. Lift your leg up a few inches off the floor or bed, point your toes, and turn your foot inward.
B7. Nondominant thigh, calf, and foot	B7. Follow instruction B6.

[a]Use the alternative tensing strategy only when the first one presented does not create tension in the appropriate muscle group.
[b]This procedure may be a bit difficult at first, but a few practice sessions will make simultaneous tensing of all the facial muscles relatively easy.

(continued)

Table 14-2   *(continued)*

Part C: 4 Muscle Groups	
Muscle Group	*Tensing Instructions*
C1. Both hands, forearms, and biceps	C1. Follow instruction B1 for both sides.
C2. Face, throat, and neck	C2. Follow instructions B3 and A8 simultaneously.
C3. Chest, shoulders, back, and abdomen	C3. Follow instruction B5.
C4. Both thighs, calves, and feet	C4. Follow instruction B6 for both sides.

Now repeat the tension-relaxation sequence for the same muscle group (instruction A1).

After you have tensed and relaxed the first muscle group (instruction A1) *twice,* proceed to the next muscle group (instruction A2) and go through the tension-relaxation sequence twice. Continue until you have gone through all of the 16 muscle groups (instructions A1 through A16). (This should take about 45 minutes at first and less time as you become familiar with the procedures and proficient at relaxing your muscles.)

After you have tensed and relaxed each of the muscle groups twice, remain in a relaxed state for several minutes. During this period, if you feel tension in any of your muscles, try to relax that tension away by making your muscles loose and smooth.

To end the practice session, slowly count backward from 4 to 1, following the instructions below for each number:

At *4* begin to move your legs and feet.
At *3* move your arms and hands.
At *2* move your head and neck.
At *1* open your eyes.

When you reach *1,* you should feel relaxed and calm, as if you had just awakened from a restful sleep. Sit up slowly. When you are ready, stand up.

Remember two things. First, during your practice, *concentrate on the sensations of tension and relaxation* and do not let your mind wander to other thoughts. Second, *do not fall asleep* while practicing. (However, once you learn deep muscle relaxation, you will be able to use it to help you fall asleep.)

You should devote at least 3 practice sessions to tensing and relaxing each of the 16 muscle groups (instructions A1 through A16) and more if you still are feeling tension in any of your muscles at the end of a session.

Next, follow the instructions just outlined for the seven muscle groups (instructions B1 through B7 in Table 14-2, Part B) for at least two sessions. Finally, spend at least two sessions tensing and relaxing each of the four muscle groups (instructions C1 through C4 in Table 14-2, Part C).

PHASE 2: RELAXATION ONLY

In this phase of training, you will just relax your muscles (without any initial tensing). Begin with the first muscle group (A1), and relax those muscles as deeply as you can. Even when you think your muscles are completely relaxed, it is always possible to relax them a bit more. Proceed through each of the 16 muscle groups (instructions A1 through A16), relaxing each for at least 60 seconds until they are completely relaxed. When you have relaxed all of the 16 muscle groups, follow the same procedure described earlier for concluding the practice session. Remember: now you are *only relaxing* your muscles; do *not* tense them first.

Spend a minimum of 2 sessions relaxing each of the 16 muscle groups, then at least 2 sessions relaxing each of the 7 muscle groups, and finally at least 2 sessions relaxing each of the 4 muscle groups. Many people find that a few muscle groups are especially hard to relax, so you may need to spend more time practicing relaxing "troublesome" muscles.

Part III: Differential Relaxation

When you have completed the two phases of deep muscle relaxation training, you are ready to apply these skills to differential relaxation. In the course of your everyday activities, whenever you experience tension in your nonessential muscles (those not being used to perform your present activity), relax them. In addition, relax any excess tension in your essential muscles. Your muscles should have the minimum tension required to perform your present activity. You can use differential relaxation at almost any time, such as while you are driving your car, eating a meal, standing in line, or sitting in class. Use tension in your muscles as a signal to relax. You may find it helpful to say the self-instruction "relax" or "calm" at the first sign of muscle tension and then proceed to relax the muscles. It is likely that you will discover that you experience more tension in some of your muscles than others, and you may want to devote some additional practice with these specific muscles following the instructions for phase 2.

◆

BIOFEEDBACK

Biofeedback provides a person with information (feedback) about a physiological function, such as blood pressure, to assist the person in modifying that function. The person is "hooked up" to electromechanical equipment, such as a polygraph, that records physiological functions and provides the individual with information about them (see Photo 14-1). For example, a tone or visual display on a computer screen might be used to indicate that blood pressure is below a pre-established level.[12] Patients would be instructed to keep their blood pressure below this predetermined level. Patients report using a variety of strategies, such as visualizing pleasant images, to lower blood pressure. Once patients have learned to lower their blood pressure by using biofeedback, they then need to learn to achieve the same outcome without biofeedback. This involves becoming attuned to the sensations associated with both lower and higher blood pressure during biofeedback training.

Photo 14-1 In biofeedback training, electrodes attached to the client transmit information about a physiological function, such as muscle tension, to electromechanical equipment that provides the client with feedback about a physiological state.

BEHAVIORAL TREATMENT OF HYPERTENSION IN PERSPECTIVE

Relaxation training has been successful in reducing blood pressure.[13] In one series of studies, relaxation training resulted in reductions in blood pressure that persisted throughout the day and also were evident in the evening.[14] The reductions obtained in the clinic generalized to patients' work environments[15] and were maintained in both settings at a 15-month follow-up.[16] The more home practice patients engage in, the more effective the treatment tends to be.[17]

Not all studies have found relaxation training to be effective, however.[18] Although some studies have reported long-term benefits,[19] others have not.[20] Lack of change in some studies may be due to poor compliance with home relaxation practice. Relaxation training appears to be maximally effective when home practice is performed at least twice a day for 15 to 20 minutes and booster sessions of relaxation training with a therapist are provided at follow-up appointments.[21] Although patients may report that they practice relaxation on their own, two studies—one treating hypertension and the other treating anxiety—have documented that patients actually practice less than they report that they do.[22] We will return to the general issue of adherence to medical treatments later in this chapter.

Biofeedback has had modest success in lowering blood pressure,[23] with some studies revealing favorable outcomes[24] and others unfavorable outcomes.[25] The conflicting results are due, in part, to wide variations in the procedures employed in different studies. The failures may be attributable partially to poor generalization to the patients' natural environments, where biofeedback equipment is unavailable.[26]

An advantage of relaxation over biofeedback is that elaborate, expensive equipment is not required. Combining relaxation and biofeedback does not seem to enhance the treatment effectiveness.[27] What may be more critical than the specific treatment (relaxation or biofeedback) are such factors as the way the treatment is individualized for patients; the frequency with which the skills are practiced; how well the skills are learned; and patients' expectations about the efficacy of the treatment.[28]

Although both relaxation and biofeedback are capable of lowering *some* patients' blood pressure, often the magnitude of the change is not sufficient to benefit patients' hypertension. Clearly, individuals differ in their abilities to utilize relaxation[29] and biofeedback.[30] It is important to remember that the results of controlled experiments always represent the *average for a group* of people. Thus, it is possible that one or more patients in an experiment may experience clinically significant changes as a result of relaxation or biofeedback although the average change of the group was not clinically significant.

Medication, the most common treatment for essential hypertension, typically results in a 10% to 30% reduction in blood pressure.[31] In contrast, nonpharmacological treatments, such as relaxation and biofeedback, typically yield less than a 10% reduction.[32] However, relaxation and biofeedback remain useful adjuncts to pharmacological treatment. First, they work well for *some* patients. Second, even limited effectiveness may be beneficial for patients who cannot tolerate hypertensive medication, such as pregnant women and some elderly persons.[33]

Chronic Pain

Pain is the most common problem that patients present to physicians as well as the most frequently cited cause of disability. A distinction usually is made between acute and chronic pain. *Acute pain* is the result of bodily trauma and disappears when the injury heals. Acute pain generally is adaptive in that it signals bodily damage (as when the pain from touching a hot object alerts you to pull your hand away). *Chronic pain* occurs after an injury has healed or when no trauma exists. Pain is considered chronic if its duration is at least 6 months.[34] In the United States, more than 75 million people suffer from chronic pain, and chronic pain results in the loss of 550 million work days and in pain-related disability payments of well over $100 billion annually.[35]

Medication is by far the most frequent treatment for pain, but medication has a number of limitations, especially for chronic pain. First, medication may not fully alleviate patients' pain. Second, many drugs lose their effectiveness over time. Third, long-term use of pain medication may lower people's tolerance for mild forms of pain. Fourth, drugs frequently have undesirable side effects (such as drowsiness). Fifth, more potent pain medications may result in physical addiction. Thus, alternatives to medication are important in the treatment of chronic pain.

Behavioral treatment of chronic pain has two goals: (1) reducing the patient's subjective discomfort (for example, decreasing the intensity or frequency of headaches) or, when this is not possible, (2) increasing the patient's tolerance for pain through coping strategies that minimize life disruptions.

PAIN AS BEHAVIOR

How pain is defined makes a difference. We usually think of pain in terms of the subjective experience of intense discomfort. It may be more useful to view pain as a *behavior* because behaviors can be readily assessed and changed.[36] **Pain behaviors** are overt behaviors that generally indicate a person is experiencing pain—for example, grimacing and saying "Ouch!" In contrast, **well behaviors** are overt behaviors that typically indicate that a person is not experiencing pain, such as smiling. Well behaviors compete with pain behaviors. Common examples of both pain behaviors and well behaviors are listed in Table 14-3.

Pain behaviors, like any other behaviors, are maintained by their antecedents and consequences. A simple example will illustrate this conceptualization.

> Randy is playing a rough game of football with his friends, and his body is becoming badly bruised. However, he does not complain. He continues to play as if nothing hurt. If he did complain, his friends might call him a weakling.
>
> The minute Randy gets home, the story changes. He slumps into a chair, "unable" to move. He tells his mother that he hurts all over, and she offers to help him upstairs and bring him his dinner in bed.

Clearly, the antecedents and consequences in the two situations are different, and it is easy to see how they influence Randy's pain behaviors.

The behavioral conceptualization of pain does not ignore the physical sensation of discomfort caused by the stimulation of pain receptors. The physical sensations of pain are one of the maintaining antecedents of pain

Table 14-3 Examples of pain behaviors and well behaviors

Pain Behaviors	Well Behaviors
Moaning, screaming	Laughing, singing
Grimacing, wincing	Smiling
Talking about the uncomfortable or unbearable sensations	Talking about feeling good
Moving in a guarded, unnatural manner indicating discomfort (for example, limping)	Moving spontaneously, in an unrestricted manner
Reclining or sitting in order to ease pain	Standing or walking
Restricting activities that might result in pain	Engaging in activities that might result in pain
Requesting and taking pain medication	Refusing pain medication
Requesting help moving	Moving by oneself
Using crutches, cane, walker, or wheelchair	Walking without support

behaviors, albeit antecedents that are not amenable to change directly through behavior therapy. In contrast, situational factors (as with Randy) and a person's ability to cope with discomfort can be changed by behavior therapy.

The consequences of exhibiting pain behaviors often are important maintaining conditions.[37] Significant consequences include (1) social reinforcers (such as attention and sympathy); (2) avoidance of responsibilities (for example, missing work); (3) financial compensation (for instance, disability payments); and (4) receipt of pain medication. Just how closely pain behaviors can be associated with social attention is illustrated by the case of a 47-year-old man with chronic lower back pain. Looking at Figure 14-1, you can see that the number of pain behaviors the man exhibited varied with the presence or absence of attention from the hospital staff.

Figure 14-1 Effects of professional staff attention on the pain behaviors of a 47-year-old man with chronic lower back pain
SOURCE: Adapted from Fordyce, 1976, p. 89.

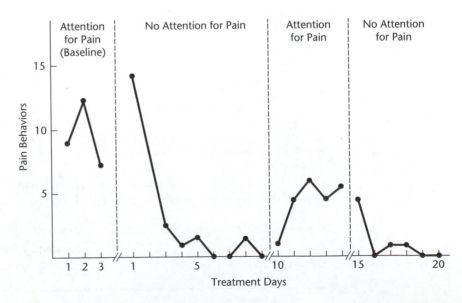

One behavioral treatment of pain involves changing the consequences maintaining the pain behaviors. Let's first look at the prototype for treating pain by changing consequences, which Wilbert Fordyce and his colleagues at the University of Washington Pain Clinic developed 30 years ago.[38]

CHANGING THE CONSEQUENCES OF PAIN BEHAVIORS

The first step in treating pain behaviors is to assess the factors maintaining them. Often, the patient is being reinforced for pain behaviors but not for well behaviors.[39] When this is the case, treatment involves reversing the contingencies: reinforcers are administered for well behaviors and withheld for pain behaviors.

The most frequent reinforcer for pain behaviors is attention from others. Thus, a major focus of the treatment program involves encouraging *everyone* who comes in contact with the patient to ignore or respond matter-of-factly to the patient's pain behaviors in order to extinguish them. At the same time, people are asked to reinforce—as with praise and attention—instances of the patient's well behaviors.

Rest is another reinforcing consequence of pain. Accordingly, rest is made a consequence of activity rather than pain behaviors. First, the amount of activity the patient can tolerate without experiencing pain (pain threshold) is assessed. Then, the initial amount of activity that the patient is required to do is set below the patient's pain threshold. When this criterion is reached, the patient is allowed to rest before going on to the next activity. The hospital staff gives the patient attention and praise for completing the activity criterion. As the patient's tolerance limits increase, criteria for rest are gradually increased.

Medication also results in a variety of reinforcing consequences. Positive reinforcers include the pleasant side effects of pain medication, such as feeling "high," and attention from the person administering the medication. Negative reinforcers include relief from discomfort and being released from unpleasant responsibilities (such as household chores).

Pain medication typically is administered on an as-needed basis. In contrast, during the treatment program, access to medication is made *time-contingent* rather than pain-contingent. Patients are given medication at fixed time intervals, whether or not they request it. Over the course of treatment, the dosage of medication is gradually reduced (and eventually eliminated in many cases).

The treatment program begins in the hospital and continues at home. Systematic procedures are established to ensure that the decrease in pain behaviors generalizes to the patient's home environment and is maintained over time. Toward this end, the patient's spouse and other family members and close friends are asked to participate in the treatment and are trained in the procedures. For example, family and friends learn to withhold reinforcers for the patient's pain behaviors and to administer reinforcers for the patient's well behaviors.

Although family and friends are reinforced for their assistance by observing the patient's progress, this reinforcement may not be sufficient to maintain it over an extended period. Accordingly, procedures are established to assure that the therapeutic endeavors of family and friends are adequately reinforced. For example, patients are instructed to thank family members explicitly for their help.

Part of the program also deals with reestablishing previously reinforcing activities in patients' lives. These activities, which often are natural reinforcers, are made contingent on well behaviors. Suppose a woman's walking, bending, and lifting were increased in the hospital. If the patient had enjoyed shopping, then she would be allowed to go shopping only if she walked to the store. If having friends over had been a favorite activity, the patient would be permitted to entertain only if she did some of the preparatory housework.

TREATMENT PACKAGES FOR CHRONIC PAIN

Because pain is a multifaceted behavior, treatment packages typically are employed. Besides changing the maintaining consequences of pain behaviors, treatment programs often include cognitive-behavioral coping skills therapy, relaxation training, and biofeedback (as well as medication, physical therapy, and exercise).[40]

Relaxation training and biofeedback are widely applied behavior therapies for treating and preventing chronic headaches.[41] For tension headaches, relaxation training and electromyographic (muscle tone) biofeedback appear to be equally effective.[42] For adult migraine headaches, the combination of relaxation training and thermal (skin temperature) biofeedback results in larger reductions in migraine activity than either treatment alone.[43] Thermal biofeedback may be the treatment of choice for children's migraine headaches.[44]

Relaxation training and biofeedback can result in a nearly 50% reduction in patients' tension headaches.[45] Biofeedback-assisted relaxation may be superior to self-relaxation (10 to 15 minutes of relaxing each day while thinking peaceful thoughts) for reducing headaches and medication use,[46] and it appears to result in changes in important physiological functions associated with headache, such as cerebral blood flow velocity.[47] Follow-up studies, for up to three years, show positive results for behavioral treatments of headaches but poor maintenance with medication alone.[48] Further, behavioral treatments for headaches are associated with positive "side effects," such as reduction in anxiety and depression, which do not occur with medication.[49]

Learning differential relaxation allows patients to employ muscle relaxation to cope with pain during the course of their daily activities.[50] Often there are identifiable antecedents to pain that people can use as cues to begin differential relaxation. For example, stress-evoking situations often precipitate headaches as well as other chronic pain problems. To identify those situations in which patients are particularly vulnerable to headaches, patients learn to monitor their headaches, noting the circumstances in which they occur, and this information is recorded in a pain diary (see Figure 14-2).

Figure 14-2 Pain diary format

Time	Pain Situation	Pain Description		Pain Consequences
		Behavior	Thoughts	

In addition to reducing pain, cognitive-behavioral coping skills therapy can help patients live with their chronic pain. Dennis Turk designed a stress inoculation treatment for pain that combines relaxation, breathing exercises, attention diversion, and emotive imagery.[51] These procedures are similar to the Lamaze method of natural childbirth.[52]

BEHAVIORAL TREATMENT OF CHRONIC PAIN IN PERSPECTIVE

Although behavior therapy procedures have been used to treat a variety of pain problems, the majority of research has focused on headaches and lower back pain. Generally, behavioral treatment of chronic pain has been successful.[53] In the majority of cases, however, patients experience a reduction in pain, rather than a complete remission of their pain.[54] The improvement often is substantial enough so that patients can resume normal activities despite still experiencing some physical discomfort. In the case of headaches, treatment gains have been maintained for one to four years without any specific maintenance procedures.[55] An indirect measure of the effectiveness of behavioral treatments for pain is that most pain clinics employ behavior therapy procedures as part of the treatment packages offered to patients.

Turning to specific treatments, changing maintaining consequences of pain behaviors has been shown to be effective in a number of studies.[56] However, its application has been narrow. It has been applied exclusively to pain associated with physical activity (particularly chronic lower back pain), and it has focused on increasing exercise and activity and decreasing medication usage while ignoring emotional and cognitive aspects of pain.[57] Another potential limitation of the consequential approach concerns generalization beyond the treatment setting and long-term maintenance in the client's natural environment.[58] The ultimate success of the treatment may depend on instituting specific procedures to foster generalization and maintenance (such as family members' continuing appropriate contingencies), which has not always been done.

Both relaxation training and biofeedback can be effective in treating headaches.[59] Cognitive-behavioral coping skills approaches also have been successful in treating a variety of types of pain.[60] Treatment outcomes with patients suffering from chronic pain appear to improve when patients are given detailed information about when and how to use coping skills[61] and when coping skills are individualized.[62]

To summarize, four major behavioral interventions have been used to treat chronic pain: changing maintaining consequences, relaxation training, biofeedback, and cognitive-behavioral coping skills therapy. At present, no basis for choosing one treatment over another exists because no treatments have been shown to be consistently superior.[63] This state of affairs is not necessarily bad because individual patients differ widely in their responses to the treatments, implying that there is a need for a variety of effective treatments.[64] Moreover, treatment packages consisting of a combination of the four therapies generally are effective.[65]

ADHERENCE TO MEDICAL REGIMENS

Patients' failure to follow medical advice—for example, to take medication or do rehabilitative exercises—is a major problem for the medical profession.[66] In fact, nonadherence may occur as frequently as 50% of the time.[67] The most effective treatment is worthless for patients who do not avail themselves of it. Early research on increasing adherence to medical regimens attempted to identify the personal characteristics associated with nonadherence, such as educational level and personality traits. However, it appears that there is little or no relationship between patient characteristics and nonadherence.[68] A more useful approach is to view adherence as a *behavior,* rather than a trait,[69] and to develop procedures for accelerating specific adherence behaviors.

Adherence can occur only *if the patient first remembers and then is sufficiently motivated* to follow the prescribed treatment. Prompting is used to help patients remember to perform treatment-related behaviors, and reinforcement is employed to provide motivation.

With many medical regimens, the immediate consequences of "following the doctor's orders" are neutral at best because the benefits are usually delayed. At worst, complying with medical regimens may be distinctly aversive, such as taking bad-tasting medicine and engaging in exhausting physical rehabilitation exercises. In contrast, patients readily adhere to medical regimens that have immediate benefits, such as taking pain medication. We will illustrate behavioral interventions for increasing adherence to three important aspects of medical treatment: taking medication; engaging in health-related behaviors (for example, following a prescribed diet); and keeping appointments.

Taking Medication

Physicians frequently prescribe regular doses of medication for an extended period of time ranging from a week to years, such as for hypertension, seizures, diabetes, and schizophrenia. Stimulus control procedures are used to prompt patients to take medication. Environmental prompts may be as simple as special labels on medicine bottles, such as a picture of a clock with times circled.[70] A more sophisticated prompting device is a portable timer-pill dispenser that sounds a tone when a pill should be taken.[71] The tone continues until a knob is turned that releases a pill into the person's hand. The advent of hand-held computers could facilitate elaborate prompting of medical regimens that could include explicit step-by-step directions for carrying out the procedures.[72]

Naturalistic stimulus control tailors a medication schedule to the patient's daily routine so that regularly occurring activities serve as cues for taking medication. Pill taking might be paired with leaving the house in the morning or meal times.[73]

Merely remembering to take medication may be insufficient to ensure adherence. Accordingly, prompting generally is supplemented with reinforcement. For example, in one study, the combination of telephone reminders and lottery tickets as reinforcers increased taking anticonvulsive medication an average of 43%.[74]

Although prompting and reinforcement can be effective in obtaining adherence to taking medication, adherence may not persist when these procedures are discontinued.[75] Adherence is more likely to be maintained if self-control skills are added to prompting and reinforcement procedures. As an example, one program taught patients with high blood pressure to use

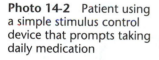

Photo 14-2 Patient using a simple stimulus control device that prompts taking daily medication

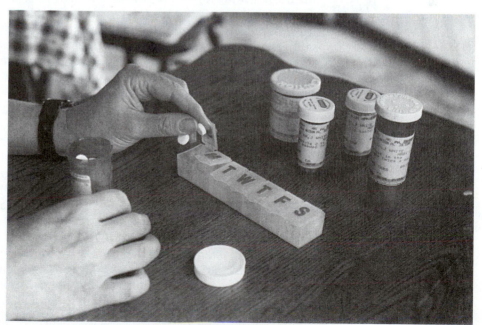

stimulus control procedures (for example, to associate pill taking with daily routines) and self-monitoring (of the medication taken and blood pressure).[76] Additionally, every two weeks the patients' blood pressure was checked. If it was below a set criterion, the patient was given a $4 credit toward the purchase of blood pressure recording equipment. Six months after the intervention, patients' medication adherence (assessed by random urine samples) was 80%, compared with 39% for patients who were not in the program.

Another strategy is to make the consequences of nonadherence unattractive. An example was the use of response cost for failure to take doses of Antabuse (a drug used in the treatment of alcohol dependence).[77] Chronic problem drinkers left "security deposits" with the therapist, from which they forfeited between $5 and $10 for each missed dose during the 3-month treatment contract. The problem drinkers missed only 8% of the scheduled clinic visits and were abstinent during 95% of the treatment days.

Engaging in Health-Related Behaviors

Besides prescribing medication, physicians instruct patients to perform various health-related behaviors, such as maintaining a prescribed diet, engaging in regular exercise, and monitoring bodily-function indicators (such as blood glucose level). However, physicians' instructions alone are not likely to change patients' health-related behaviors. Getting children and adolescents to engage consistently in necessary medical procedures is especially difficult, particularly when multiple behaviors are required.[78] For instance, people with diabetes may have to engage in a variety of health care routines, including maintaining dietary restrictions; self-injecting insulin; testing urine; and taking care of their feet (because of the increased vulnerability to infections due to poor circulation in the extremities). Prompting in the form of visual cues generally has a minimal effect on adherence.[79] Self-monitoring may be an effective intervention for increasing adherence to simple regimens, such as engaging in a single exercise.[80] However, self-monitoring is likely to be ineffective for complex regimens, such as required for diabetes.[81]

Reinforcement results in the most consistent adherence to health-related behaviors.[82] Token economy programs have increased adherence to acceptable levels for children with diabetes[83] and children undergoing hemodialysis.[84] The successful use of a token economy with an 82-year-old man to obtain adherence to diet, exercise, and taking medication after a massive heart attack was described in Case 8-1 (page 184). Contingency contracts have proved useful with children and adolescents as well as with adults. In a program for patients with hemophilia (aged 8 to 15), for example, the use of contingency contracts with token reinforcers resulted in 81% to 90% adherence to exercise and diet over a 6-month period.[85] Other procedures that enhance adherence to prescribed dietary and exercise regimens are self-monitoring, stimulus control, and relapse prevention procedures.[86]

When low adherence is maintained by a skill deficit in the prescribed medical procedure, modeling can increase adherence.[87] For example, parents of children with hemophilia were taught to administer a difficult emergency treatment for bleeding (factor replacement therapy).[88] A nurse practitioner demonstrated the procedure and then gave parents feedback as they rehearsed it. The parents' skill level increased from 15% before the intervention to 92% during the intervention and 97% at follow-up. Modeling also has been helpful in teaching social and coping skills to overcome social barriers to adherence that children and adolescents experience (such as being called "sicky" when abstaining from sports in school).[89] Behavioral child management training for parents is another strategy for enhancing children's adherence to medical regimens, such as prescribed diets for children with cystic fibrosis.[90]

Keeping Medical Appointments

Keeping scheduled medical appointments is a third critical area of adherence. Telephone calls[91] and mailed reminders[92] are simple, relatively low-cost procedures, but they are not always successful.[93] As with the other areas of adherence, reinforcement generally is the most effective strategy. For example, when clients in a treatment program for heroin abuse were given the privilege of taking their methadone (a drug used to treat heroin addiction) at home over the weekend if they made weekly clinic visits, clinic appointments that clients kept increased from 45% to 89%.[94] In a pediatric clinic, the number of appointments that were kept was increased by including parking passes with mailed reminders.[95] The passes allowed parents to park adjacent to the clinic, which saved them time. Similarly, whereas keeping follow-up appointments at a family practice center was unaffected by reminder cards, offering free or reduced-rate appointments significantly increased appointments kept.[96]

COPING WITH MEDICAL PROCEDURES

Medical procedures and hospitalization—even routine visits to the doctor or dentist—produce significant stress and anxiety in many individuals. People fear dying, pain, separation from loved ones, unusual instrumentation and surroundings, and the unknown. Children are particularly vulnerable to these fears. As you saw in Chapter 11, modeling therapy is used to prepare children and adults for medical treatment. Another strategy is to teach patients coping skills to actively reduce their anxiety and discomfort as they prepare for and undergo medical treatment. Using coping skills also can facilitate medical procedures (such as lying still during a lumbar puncture) and aid the recovery process. Specifically, coping skills (1) improve patients' cooperation before, during, and after surgery; (2) reduce the amount of postoperative analgesic medications required; (3) speed recovery and reduce time spent in the hospital; and (4) reduce the amount of time and support patients require from others during recovery.[97]

To cope with painful medical procedures—such as those typically associated with cancer treatment—children have been taught cognitive-behavioral coping skills, such as muscle relaxation, breathing exercises, emotive/distracting imagery, and the use of positive self-statements.[98] A type of desensitization, in which children's preferred activities are paired with stimuli associated with invasive medical procedures, has lowered the distress of children who must repeatedly undergo such procedures.[99] Treatment packages usually are employed and tend to be more effective than single therapies.[100]

Medical procedures need not be painful to cause distress. For example, magnetic resonance imaging (MRI) used for diagnostic purposes may cause claustrophobia (fear of enclosed spaces) because patients are placed in a confined space in which they cannot move. One approach to reducing such anxiety is to administer a pleasant fragrance during the MRI procedure, which may serve to distract or relax the patient.[101] Another approach, employed with young children, is to dispense token reinforcers for lying still during the MRI procedure.[102] After the procedure, the children exchange the tokens for backup reinforcers.

Parents whose children are seriously ill and undergoing medical procedures often experience high levels of stress, which may cause or exacerbate their children's anxiety. In contrast, parents who are calm and effectively deal with their own stress are better able to help their children, such as by serving as coping models for them. Parents' participation in interventions aimed at reducing their children's stress related to medical procedures is beneficial. Pediatric cancer patients undergoing venipuncture, for example, cried significantly less when their parents prompted and reinforced (with praise and token reinforcers) their children's use of a breathing distraction technique.[103] Parents' participation not only is helpful to their children but also can vicariously reduce parents' anxiety.[104]

Parents benefit even more from directly receiving treatment for their anxiety. For instance, parents whose children underwent painful bone marrow aspirations or lumbar punctures for leukemia were given stress inoculation training to deal with their own anxiety.[105] The training consisted of 3 brief (15-minute) training sequences: (1) exposure to a modeling film that provided information and examples of coping behaviors; (2) instruction in using coping-oriented self-statements to counter catastrophic self-statements; and (3) relaxation training (including home practice). Other parents received no direct intervention for their own anxiety but participated in their children's cognitive-behavioral treatment. Parents receiving stress inoculation training reported lower anxiety and used more positive self-statements than parents who only participated in their children's treatment.

Various treatments have been found to be effective in helping children and adults cope with stress associated with dental visits.[106] For example, low-income preschool children who had no previous dental treatment benefited from learning to employ relaxation, breathing exercises, and coping words (such as *calm* and *nice*).[107] The children also were given descriptive information regarding the dental procedures and the sights, sounds, and physical sensations they would experience. These interventions reduced the children's disruptive behaviors, ratings of anxiety and discomfort, and physiological arousal, and they increased children's cooperation.

Systematic desensitization has helped adults who were so anxious about dental treatment that they avoided making appointments even though they needed treatment.[108]

Behavior therapies have been used to reduce the negative physical side effects of medical treatments. For example, nausea and vomiting often occur with chemotherapy for cancer. These extremely noxious side effects generally begin 1 to 2 hours after the injection of the chemical and can persist as long as 24 hours.[109] Some patients also experience anticipatory nausea and vomiting.[110] Relaxation training has been successful in reducing the frequency and severity of nausea and vomiting,[111] and systematic desensitization has been used to treat anticipatory nausea and vomiting.[112]

The physical side effects of cancer treatment and the pain and fatigue caused by the disease itself are horrible enough. In addition, cancer patients often are demoralized by the hospital social environment, which can result in psychological disorders, including anxiety and depression.[113] Cancer patients suffer a substantial loss of important sources of reinforcement.[114] This is especially true for patients in isolation (which may be required because chemotherapy decreases the immune system). These patients' social reinforcers are limited to contact with the medical personnel who care for their needs. Accordingly, one of the few ways patients can control their social contacts is to develop symptoms that require close attention.[115] Case 14-1 describes the treatment of physical symptoms that were maintained by nurses' attention.

Case 14-1

PHYSICAL SYMPTOMS RELATED TO CANCER TREATMENT ALLEVIATED BY EXTINCTION AND DIFFERENTIAL REINFORCEMENT[116]

Two patients with acute leukemia developed symptoms for which no physical cause could be found. Patient 1, a 24-year-old man, had a deep, raspy cough that did not respond to medication. Patient 2, a 63-year-old woman, regurgitated saliva excessively. Both patients were described as outgoing, friendly, and well-adjusted to their illnesses. Their symptoms developed when they were placed in restrictive isolation.

The nursing staff believed that the patients' symptoms worsened in the presence of a staff member. This belief was confirmed by a sophisticated systematic naturalistic observation procedure. Tape recordings were made of the symptoms for 16 hours over the course of 2 days. Three-minute segments were analyzed for (1) the presence of the symptom (for example, loud, repeated exhalation of air or sounds of spitting); (2) a nurse entering (for instance, sounds of the door opening and footsteps); and (3) talking. The assessment revealed that both patients' symptoms were under the stimulus control of the nurses. The symptoms were more likely to occur when a nurse was present (the probabilities were .75 and .82 for Patients 1 and 2, respectively) than when the patients were alone (.25 and .18, respectively).

Treatment involved extinction and differential reinforcement of other behaviors. The nurses did not discuss the patients' symptoms with them at any time. If the symptom continued during standard nursing procedures, the nurse finished the procedures and immediately left the room. However, if the symptom ceased or did not occur, the nurse remained in the room and talked with the patient for a minimum of 10 minutes after the medical procedures had been completed. Within two weeks, both patients' symptoms were eliminated.

PREVENTION OF MEDICAL PROBLEMS

Behavior therapy procedures not only have been employed in the treatment of medical disorders, but they also have been applied to an even more long-range goal: preventing medical problems. Behavioral prevention programs have two major aims. One is to *educate* people about the controllable factors that cause and exacerbate diseases and about specific behaviors that can reduce the risk of developing diseases. The other aim is to *motivate* people to engage in preventive behaviors. We will look at behavioral prevention programs related to cardiovascular disease, women's health care, and AIDS.

Cardiovascular Disease

The Stanford Three Community Study was a multifaceted program for preventing cardiovascular disease that causes serious medical problems, such as heart attacks and strokes.[117] The groups compared in this experiment were entire communities, with populations of about 14,000, located in northern California. (The study became the prototype of whole-community prevention programs.) One community received a mass-media campaign; a second community received a face-to-face intensive instructional program as well as the media campaign; and a third community received no preventive interventions and served as a control group.

The 10-week intensive instruction program was given to a random sample of people who had a high risk of developing cardiovascular disease. The program was administered both individually and in groups and involved the spouses of the high-risk participants. The behavior therapy components included (1) behavioral assessment of each person's health-related behaviors; (2) modeling of healthful behaviors; (3) guided behavior rehearsal of the new healthful behaviors; (4) reinforcement for performing the new behaviors; and (5) procedures to maintain the new behaviors.

Both the media campaign and the intensive instruction successfully (1) increased participants' knowledge of cardiovascular disease and the importance of risk factors; (2) decreased participants' specific high-risk behaviors, such as eating high-cholesterol foods and smoking; and (3) decreased the estimated risk of participants' developing cardiovascular disease. The combination of the media campaign and intensive instruction was more effective than the media campaign alone for high-risk individuals. Since the success of the Stanford Three Community Study, similar programs have been instituted in other parts of the United States and in other countries.[118]

Women's Health Care

Hypertension not only is associated with cardiovascular disease but also increases the risk of other medical problems, including complications in pregnancy. In one study, relaxation was taught to pregnant women in 6 weekly sessions.[119] Compared with women in a control group who received no intervention, women taught relaxation had (1) significantly lower blood pressure throughout pregnancy; (2) fewer hospital admissions for problems related to pregnancy; and (3) substantially shorter stays in the hospital.

Breast cancer, a leading cause of death in women, often is curable if detected early.[120] Regular breast self-examination is the most generally viable means of early detection. Although the self-examination is a simple procedure, a majority of women do not perform it. One program used biweekly postcards and phone calls to prompt women to do their breast self-examinations.[121] Initially, the women participated in a one-hour workshop in which they learned how to examine their breasts. The procedure included placing baby oil on their fingers, palpating their breasts, and placing a sheet of tissue on their chests to absorb the oil. The women were instructed to mail the tissue they used, signed and dated, each time they performed the procedure. This provided a measure of the frequency of self-examinations. Compared with women who received no prompts, women who were prompted either by mail or phone returned more self-examination tissues. However, the frequency of self-examinations decreased over time for both prompted and unprompted women. It is likely that provision of reinforcers for breast self-examination would increase compliance with this important preventive measure.

AIDS

Since it was first identified in 1981, acquired immune deficiency syndrome (AIDS) has become the most serious disease epidemic in the United States,[122] with infection rates rising fastest among heterosexual women.[123] As its name implies, AIDS involves a breakdown in the immune system, rendering the individual vulnerable to a host of diseases. It is caused by the human immunodeficiency virus (HIV), which is transmitted primarily through sexual contact (in semen and vaginal secretions) and direct infusion of contaminated blood (through shared hypodermic needles, blood transfusions, and childbirth).[124] The World Health Organization predicts that 50 to 100 million people will be infected with HIV in the next few years.[125] If current trends continue, it is estimated that more than 1 million people in the United States alone will have developed AIDS by the year 2000.[126]

Because HIV infection is incurable at the present time, it is a prime candidate for prevention. Fortunately, unlike many other life-threatening diseases, the transmission of HIV is linked to specific, identifiable, and

Table 14-4 Behaviors that place people at high risk for AIDS and alternative low-risk behaviors
SOURCE: Adapted from Kelly & St. Lawrence, 1987, p. 9.

High-Risk Behavior	Low-Risk Alternative
Sexual activities that allow bloodstream exposure to semen or blood products (such as unprotected anal intercourse and oral sex to orgasm)	Nonpenetrative sexual acts (such as massage and masturbation) and use of condoms
Sexual contact with multiple partners	Establishment of stable relationships
Frequenting settings where casual or anonymous sexual contacts occur (such as bathhouses and certain pornographic theaters)	Avoidance of high-risk settings and the development of social supports conducive to a nonpromiscuous lifestyle
Excessive use of chemical substances that promote behavioral/sexual disinhibition or impaired judgment	Curtailed use of chemical substances that impair judgment and produce disinhibition

potentially changeable patterns of behavior.[127] Preventive efforts have focused on reducing high-risk activities (see Table 14-4), especially with gay men who, in the United States, presently comprise two-thirds of people with AIDS.[128]

Modest and cost-effective programs have attempted to encourage simple safer-sex practices, such as using condoms. For example, to increase gay bar patrons' taking free condoms, signs were posted as prompts.[129] Printed in large blue and red letters on a 1-by-2-foot poster board, the signs read: "In the State of Alaska 38 people have died from AIDS. Many more have tested positive. Condoms can reduce the spread of AIDS." Commercially printed signs regarding safer-sex practices to prevent HIV infection also were displayed in rest rooms during the intervention periods and reminded patrons that free condoms were available in the bar. The prompting intervention was evaluated by an ABAB reversal study, with baseline and prompting being reversed every 2 weeks. In 3 different bars, condoms were taken an average of 47% more of the time when prompts were displayed. (Of course, this does not mean that the condoms were *used* more as a result of the intervention.)

The primary thrust of behavioral AIDS prevention programs has been to change complex, high-risk sexual behavior patterns by using treatment packages based on the model developed by Jeffrey Kelly and Janet St. Lawrence.[130] Their cognitive-behavioral/skills training model begins with extensive individual assessment, including tests of knowledge of risk behaviors; self-report measures of sexual activity in the recent past; self-monitoring of current risk behaviors; and role-played tests of sexual assertiveness (for instance, refusing a proposition to engage in unsafe sex). The program is conducted in small groups and consists of four basic components.

1. *HIV risk education* involves direct instruction concerning risk factors and ways to reduce them.

2. *Cognitive-behavioral self-management* begins with participants' identifying the maintaining antecedents of their high-risk behaviors (such as

setting, mood, and intoxicant use). Then, strategies for changing the personal and environmental antecedents to lessen risks are taught. Participants generate and practice self-statements emphasizing that safer practices are possible, will reduce anxiety, and are worthwhile (for example, "I can change my sex practices"; "I'll feel better if I change my sex practices"; and "I did well avoiding that high-risk situation").

3. *Assertion training* is aimed at clients' learning to refuse high-risk sexual coercions and to insist on safer sexual activities.

4. *Social skills training* teaches participants how to develop stable relationships involving a mutual commitment to healthy sexual behaviors.

In the final group session, participants identify risk-reduction changes they have made during the program. This session exposes participants to multiple coping models, gives them additional ideas about how they can modify their own behaviors, and strengthens their self-efficacy for reducing high-risk behaviors in their lives.[131]

Cognitive-behavioral/skills training therapies to prevent HIV infection have been tested with adolescents[132] (including New York City runaways[133] and those living in HIV epicenters[134]), gay and bisexual men,[135] inner-city women,[136] college students,[137] and adults with psychiatric disorders.[138] Overall, such interventions appear to reduce high-risk sexual behaviors in a variety of age groups and populations, when compared with information-oriented treatments and no treatment.[139] The most common outcome measures used in these studies are (1) number of sexual partners; (2) number of protected and unprotected occasions of oral, anal, and vaginal intercourse; (3) percentage of time condoms are used; and (4) number of sexual encounters with a high-risk partner.[140] Unfortunately, all of these measures are based on self-reports that ideally should be corroborated by other types of measures (although this is rarely possible with sexual activity).

The long-term maintenance of cognitive-behavioral/skills training to reduce high-risk sexual behaviors has not yet been evaluated thoroughly. Initial studies indicate that the effects diminish over time.[141] For example, a 16-month follow-up assessment of 68 gay and bisexual men who had completed a cognitive-behavioral treatment program showed that 40% of the men had returned to unsafe sexual practices. Relapse was more common in men who were younger and who used alcohol or other drugs in conjunction with their high-risk sexual behaviors.[142]

◆   ## ALL THINGS CONSIDERED: BEHAVIORAL MEDICINE APPLICATIONS

Behavior therapy principles and procedures are proving useful in comprehensive health care. They are especially valuable with regard to helping patients cope with medical treatments and increasing their adherence to medical procedures. Behavior therapy also can play a role in preventing diseases and in providing alternative treatments for some medical disorders.

Medicine has traditionally focused on treatment—that is, on getting the patient well. Concern for the psychological well-being of patients in treatment has been an afterthought at best. For example, the practice of waking sleeping patients in the hospital to give them sleeping medication is more than a well-worn joke. Many people may endure inconveniences and discomfort associated with medical treatments because they adhere to a "no pain, no gain" philosophy. More serious psychological consequences are associated with the intense pain and discomfort brought about by cancer therapy, the dread of undergoing surgery, and the hopelessness and despair caused by chronic illness and its care. Behavior therapy has begun to contribute to alleviating such problems.

Physicians have long recognized that patients' failure to follow prescribed treatment is a major impediment to providing adequate treatment and health care. However, neither physicians' skills nor medical technology is suited to changing the prevailing high rate of nonadherence. In contrast, behavior therapists have a large armamentarium of effective procedures for increasing patients' adherence behaviors.

Prevention of physical illness by promoting healthful behaviors and life-styles also is an area in which behavior therapy procedures are beginning to make a difference. For instance, behavior therapy can influence proper diet, regular exercise, and the elimination of harmful drug habits (such as smoking and heavy drinking), all factors that directly enhance physical health. The major obstacle to implementing behavioral prevention programs is one faced by all prevention endeavors—namely, the prevailing attitude: "If it ain't broke, don't fix it." The benefits of preventive interventions may not become evident until years after the interventions are implemented. Further, because the goal of prevention is always the *absence* of disease, people may not recognize and appreciate the results of preventive measures. Consider the fact that, as you read these words, you are unaware that you are breathing normally or that you are seeing the words clearly. In contrast, you would be aware of labored breathing if you had emphysema or of blurred vision if you had cataracts.

A final contribution made by behavior therapy to medicine is in providing alternative forms of treatment. For some medical conditions, such as certain types of chronic pain, existing medical treatments are inadequate. In other cases, existing medical treatments may be associated with potentially serious negative side effects, as with many drugs. Sometimes the treatments themselves may be potentially life-threatening, such as with certain types of medication. In such instances, behavioral treatments may be preferable, especially if they safely provide comparable results.

Summary

1. The application of behavior therapy to the assessment, treatment, management, rehabilitation, and prevention of physical disease is part of behavioral medicine.

2. Behavior therapy serves four functions in dealing with medical disorders: treatment, increasing adherence to medical treatments, helping patients cope with treatments, and prevention.

3. Relaxation training and biofeedback can directly influence blood pressure, but often the magnitude of the change is not clinically significant. However, the use of relaxation training and biofeedback can lead to a reduction in medication.

4. Pain behaviors—actions that indicate that the person is experiencing sensations of pain—are accessible to assessment and treatment. Well behaviors are overt behaviors that typically indicate a person is not experiencing pain.

5. One approach to treating pain involves changing the consequences that are maintaining pain behaviors. Social attention, rest, and medication are typical reinforcers for pain. Treatment involves extinction of the pain behaviors and reinforcement of well behaviors. Attention and rest are made contingent on well behaviors rather than pain behaviors. Pain medication is made time-contingent rather than pain-contingent.

6. Cognitive-behavioral coping skills treatment packages that include relaxation training and biofeedback also are used to treat pain.

7. Behavioral treatments of pain typically result in reduction, rather than elimination, of pain. The reduction can be substantial enough for patients to resume normal activities.

8. Patients' following medical advice and engaging in health-related behaviors have been increased by means of stimulus control, prompting, reinforcement, teaching patients self-control skills, and making the consequences of nonadherence unpleasant. Reinforcement generally is the most effective technique. When low adherence is maintained by skills deficits, modeling is useful.

9. Cognitive-behavioral coping skills are taught to patients to help them deal with stress associated with medical procedures and hospitalization. These skills are frequently used with children undergoing painful medical procedures. Behavior therapy also is employed to help patients cope with dental visits and to reduce the negative physical side effects of medical treatments.

10. Behavioral interventions have been used to help prevent medical problems by educating people about disease and motivating them to engage in healthful, preventive behaviors.

11. The Stanford Three Community Study was a multifaceted, large-scale prevention program that reduced the risk of cardiovascular disease in three communities.

12. Behavior therapies have been applied to women's health care, including relaxation training to lower hypertension during pregnancy and prompting of breast self-examination.

13. Treatment programs for decreasing high-risk behaviors for HIV infection have used education, cognitive-behavioral coping skills therapy, assertion training, and social skills training.

REFERENCE NOTES

1. Pinkerton, Hughes, & Wenrich, 1982.
2. *Information Please Almanac*, 1989.
3. Appel, Saab, & Holroyd, 1985.
4. Haaga, Davison, Williams, Dolezal, Haleblian, Rosenbaum, Dwyer, Baker, Nezami, & DeQuattro, 1994.
5. Pratt & Jones, 1995.
6. Jacobson, 1929, 1939.
7. Agras, 1981; Brauer, Norlick, Nelson, Farquhar, & Agras, 1979; Lehrer, 1982; McGrady, 1994; McGrady, Olson, & Kroon, 1995.
8. For example, Carrington, 1977.
9. For example, Benson, 1975.
10. For example, Patel, 1977.
11. Appel, Saab, & Holroyd, 1985; McGrady, Olson, & Kroon, 1995.
12. For example, Kristt & Engel, 1975; Tursky, Shapiro, & Schwartz, 1972; Wittrock & Blanchard, 1992.
13. For example, Beiman, Israel, & Johnson, 1978; Haaga, Davison, Williams, Dolezal, Haleblian, Rosenbaum, Dwyer, Baker, Nezami, & DeQuattro, 1994; Rici & Lawrence, 1979; Taylor, Farquhar, Nelson, & Agras, 1977.
14. Agras, Taylor, Kraemer, Allen, & Schneider, 1980.
15. Southam, Agras, Taylor, & Kraemer, 1982.
16. Agras, Southam, & Taylor, 1983; Lynch, Birk, Weaver, Gohara, Leighton, Repka, & Walsh, 1992; Manne, Jacobsen, Gorfinkle, Gerstein, & Redd, 1993.
17. For example, Wittrock, Blanchard, & McCoy, 1988; compare with Hoelscher, Lichstein, Fischer, & Hegarty, 1987.
18. For example, Cottier, Shapiro, & Julius, 1984; Jacob, Shapiro, Reeves, Johnson, McDonald, & Coburn, 1986.
19. Jacobson, 1978.
20. For example, Agras, Taylor, Kraemer, Southam, & Schneider, 1987; Jacob, Wing, & Shapiro, 1987.
21. McGrady, Olson, & Kroon, 1995.
22. Hoelscher, Lichstein, & Rosenthal, 1984; Taylor, Agras, Schneidner, & Allen, 1983.
23. Pickering, 1982.
24. For example, Blanchard, Young, & Haynes, 1975; McGrady, Olson, & Kroon, 1995.
25. For example, Elder & Eustis, 1975.
26. Goldstein, Shapiro, Thananopavarn, & Sambhi, 1982.
27. Pinkerton, Hughes, & Wenrich, 1982; Walsh, Dale, & Anderson, 1977.
28. Bradley & Hughes, 1979; Pinkerton, Hughes, & Wenrich, 1982; Wittrock, Blanchard, & McCoy, 1988.
29. Carlson & Bernstein, 1995; Edinger & Jacobsen, 1982.
30. Miller, 1978.
31. Kaplan, 1983.
32. Appel, Saab, & Holroyd, 1985.
33. McGrady, Olson, & Kroon, 1995.
34. Black, 1975.
35. Bonica, 1986; Osterweis, Mechanic, & Kleinman, 1987.
36. Compare with Kaplan, 1990.
37. Fordyce, 1976.
38. Fordyce, 1976, 1988.
39. Block, Kremer, & Gaylor, 1980; Cairns & Pasino, 1977; Doleys, Crocker, & Patton, 1982; Flor, Kerns, & Turk, 1987.
40. Turk & Meichenbaum, 1989; Turk & Rudy, 1995.
41. Blanchard, 1992; Holroyd & Penzien, 1994.
42. Andrasik & Blanchard, 1987.
43. Holroyd & Penzien, 1994.
44. Blanchard, 1992.
45. Holroyd & Penzien, 1994; Penzien & Holroyd, 1994.
46. McGrady, Wauquier, McNeil, & Gerard, 1994.
47. Wauquier, McGrady, Aloe, Klausner, & Collins, 1995.
48. Lake & Pingel, 1988.
49. Blanchard, 1992; Nicholson & Blanchard, 1993.
50. Linton, 1982; Linton & Melin, 1983.
51. Meichenbaum & Turk, 1976; Turk, 1975, 1976; Turk & Genest, 1979; Turk, Meichenbaum, & Genest, 1983.
52. Lamaze, 1970.
53. For example, Blanchard, 1987; Carey, 1994; Rokke & al'Absi, 1992.
54. For example, Feuerstein & Gainer, 1982.
55. Blanchard, 1987.
56. Anderson, Cole, Gullickson, Hudgens, & Roberts, 1977; Cairns, Thomas, Mooney, & Pau, 1976; Fordyce, 1976; Fordyce, Fowler, & DeLateur, 1968; Fordyce, Fowler, Lehmann, DeLateur, Sand, & Trieschmann, 1973; Fordyce & Steger, 1979; Kerns, Turk, Holzman, & Rudy, 1986; Roberts, 1979; Turner, 1982.
57. Schmidt, Gierlings, & Peters, 1989.

58. Cairns & Pasino, 1977; Dolce, Doleys, Raczynski, Lossie, Poole, & Smith, 1986; Doleys, Crocker, & Patton, 1982.

59. For example, Blanchard, 1987; Blanchard, Applebaum, Radnitz, Morrill, Michultka, Kirsch, Guarnieri, Hillhouse, Evans, Jaccard, & Barron, 1990.

60. Anderson, Lawrence, & Olson, 1981; Blanchard, 1987; Holroyd, Andrasik, & Westbrook, 1977; Reeves, 1976; Steger & Harper, 1977; Turk & Meichenbaum, 1989; Turk, Meichenbaum, & Genest, 1983; Turk & Rudy, 1995.

61. James, Thorn, & Williams, 1993.

62. For example, Osman, Barrios, Osman, Schnekloth, & Troutman, 1994; Rokke & al'Absi, 1992.

63. For example, Blanchard, Theobald, Williamson, Silver, & Brown, 1978; Silver, Blanchard, Williamson, Theobald, & Brown, 1979.

64. For example, Blanchard, Andrasik, Neff, Arena, Ahles, Jurish, Pallmeyer, Saunders, Teders, Barron, & Rodichok, 1982.

65. For example, Anderson, Lawrence, & Olson, 1981; Follick, 1979; Steger & Harper, 1977; Turner & Clancy, 1988; Turner, Heinrich, McCreary, & Dawson, 1979.

66. For example, Gentry, 1971; Haynes, Taylor, & Sackett, 1979; Meichenbaum & Turk, 1987; Zifferblatt, 1975.

67. For example, Gillum & Barsky, 1974; Pratt & Jones, 1995; Sackett & Snow, 1979.

68. Marston, 1970; Sackett & Haynes, 1976.

69. For example, Kasl, 1975; Zifferblatt, 1975.

70. Lima, Nazarian, Charney, & Lahti, 1976.

71. Azrin & Powell, 1969.

72. Newman, Kenardy, Herman, & Taylor, 1996, in press.

73. Compare with Skinner & Vaughan, 1983.

74. Masek, 1982.

75. For example, Masek, 1982.

76. Haynes, Sackett, Gibson, Taylor, Hackett, Roberts, & Johnson, 1976.

77. Bigelow, Strickler, Liebson, & Griffiths, 1976.

78. LaGreca, 1988.

79. For example, Lowe & Lutzker, 1979; compare with Lima, Nazarian, Charney, & Lahti, 1976.

80. For example, LaGreca & Ottinger, 1979; Waggoner & LeLieuvre, 1981.

81. Epstein, Beck, Figueroa, Farkas, Kazdin, Daneman, & Becker, 1981.

82. Epstein, Beck, Figueroa, Farkas, Kazdin, Daneman, & Becker, 1981.

83. Lowe & Lutzker, 1979.

84. Magrab & Papadopoulou, 1977.

85. Greenan, Powell, & Varni, 1984.

86. For example, Brownell & Cohen, 1995; Dubbert, 1992.

87. For example, Gilbert, Johnson, Spillar, McCallum, Silverstein, & Rosenbloom, 1982.

88. Sergis-Deavenport & Varni, 1982, 1983.

89. Follansbee, LaGreca, & Citrin, 1983; Gross, Johnson, Wildman, & Mullett, 1981.

90. Stark, Knapp, Bowen, Powers, Jelalian, Evans, Passero, Mulvihill, & Hovell, 1993.

91. For example, Turner & Vernon, 1976.

92. For example, Nazarian, Mechaber, Charney, & Coulter, 1974.

93. For example, Barkin & Duncan, 1975; Kidd & Euphrat, 1971.

94. Stitzer, Bigelow, Lawrence, Cohen, D'Lugoff, & Hawthorne, 1977.

95. Friman, Finney, Rapoff, & Christophersen, 1985.

96. Rice & Lutzker, 1984.

97. Horne, Vatmanidis, & Careri, 1994.

98. Dahlquist, Gil, Armstrong, Ginsberg, & Jones, 1985; Jay, Elliott, Katz, & Siegel, 1987; Katz, Kellerman, & Ellenberg, 1987; Manne, Redd, Jacobsen, Gorfinkle, Schorr, & Rabkin, 1990; Peterson & Shigetomi, 1981; Rains, 1995.

99. Slifer, Babbitt, & Cataldo, 1995.

100. For example, Peterson & Shigetomi, 1981.

101. Redd, Manne, Peters, Jacobsen, & Schmidt, 1994.

102. Slifer, Cataldo, Cataldo, Llorente, & Gerson, 1993.

103. Manne, Bakeman, Jacobsen, Gorfinkle, & Redd, 1994.

104. For example, Manne, Redd, Jacobsen, Gorfinkle, Schorr, & Rabkin, 1990; Peterson & Shigetomi, 1981.

105. Jay & Elliott, 1990.

106. For example, Nocella & Kaplan, 1982.

107. Siegel & Peterson, 1980.

108. For example, Gatchel, 1980.

109. Redd & Andrykowski, 1982.

110. Morrow & Morrell, 1982.

111. Burish & Lyles, 1979; Burish, Shartner, & Lyles, 1981; Lyles, Burish, Krozely, & Oldham, 1982.

112. Morrow, Asbury, Hammon, Dobkin, Caruso, Pandya, & Rosenthal, 1992; Morrow & Morrell, 1982.

113. Cullen, Fox, & Isom, 1976; Holand, Plumb, Yates, Harris, Tuttolomondo, Holmes, & Holland, 1977.

114. Agras, 1976.

115. Redd, 1980.

116. Redd, 1980.
117. Farquhar, 1978; Maccoby, Farquhar, Wood, & Alexander, 1977; Meyer, Nash, McAlister, Maccoby, & Farquhar, 1980.
118. Farquhar, Maccoby, & Solomon, 1984.
119. Little, Hayworth, Benson, Hall, Beard, Dewhurst, & Priest, 1984.
120. Jansen, 1987.
121. Mayer & Frederiksen, 1986.
122. Kelly & St. Lawrence, 1987.
123. Centers for Disease Control and Prevention, 1994.
124. Hall, 1988.
125. Kelly & St. Lawrence, 1988b.
126. Pheifer & Houseman, 1988.
127. Kelly & St. Lawrence, 1988a.
128. Kelly & St. Lawrence, 1988b.
129. Honnen & Kleinke, 1990.
130. Kelly, St. Lawrence, Hood, & Brasfield, 1989.
131. McKusick, Wiley, Coates, & Morin, 1986.
132. St. Lawrence, Brasfield, Jefferson, Alleyne, O'Bannon, & Shirley, 1995; St. Lawrence, Jefferson, Alleyne, & Brasfield, 1995.
133. Rotheram-Borus, Koopman, Haignere, & Davies, 1991.
134. Walter & Vaughan, 1993.
135. For example, Kelly, St. Lawrence, Hood, & Brasfield, 1989.
136. For example, Hobfoll, Jackson, Lavin, Britton, & Shepherd, 1994: Kelly, Murphy, Washington, Wilson, Koob, Davis, Lepezma, & Davantes, 1994.
137. For example, Sikkema, Winett, & Lombard, 1995.
138. Kalichman, Sikkema, Kelly, & Bulto, 1995.
139. St. Lawrence, Brasfield, Jefferson, Alleyne, O'Bannon, & Shirley, 1995; St. Lawrence, Jefferson, Alleyne, & Brasfield, 1995.
140. For example, Chesney, 1994; Kalichman, Carey, & Johnson, in press; Kelly & Murphy, 1992.
141. Kalichman, Carey, & Johnson, in press.
142. Kelly, St. Lawrence, Hood, & Brasfield, 1989.

Chapter 15

Applications to Psychological Disorders with Primary Physical Characteristics

In addition to its contribution to behavioral medicine (Chapter 14), behavior therapy plays an important role in the treatment of a variety of psychological disorders whose primary feature is a physical problem. We will illustrate this application of behavior therapy with five psychological disorders: enuresis, tics, insomnia, bulimia, and addictive behaviors.

The distinction between these psychological disorders and the medical problems discussed in Chapter 14 is based on the way they are classified in the health professions.[1] For example, while hypertension and pain are considered medical disorders, insomnia and bulimia are viewed as psychological disorders. This distinction is, admittedly, somewhat arbitrary and artificial. Both psychological disorders with primary physical characteristics and medical disorders increasingly are being viewed in terms of an interplay of physical and psychological factors.[2] Psychological factors are both antecedents and consequences of physical problems, which creates a vicious cycle (see Figure 15-1). Once the cycle is started, reciprocal determinism develops so that it is not useful to ask, "Which is causing which?" For example, worrying in bed interferes with falling asleep, and the resulting fatigue over an extended period may affect one's job performance; poor job performance may cause additional worry that makes sleeping even more difficult.

ENURESIS

Enuresis is the inability of people beyond the age of 3 to voluntarily control urination, when no known physical cause is involved. Enuresis most frequently occurs during sleep, so the focus of treatment efforts has been on *nocturnal enuresis,* or bed-wetting. It is a common problem among children, occurring in approximately 15% to 20% of all 5-year-olds, 5% of 10-year-olds, and 2% of 12- to 14-year-olds.[3] Nocturnal enuresis is more prevalent in boys than in girls.[4]

Urination is the natural response to tension in the bladder as it fills up. Normally, bladder tension wakes us when we are sleeping, and we get out of

Figure 15-1 Examples of reciprocal influences between psychological factors and physical problems (arrows show direction of influence)

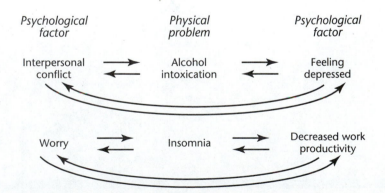

bed and go to the bathroom. The problem in enuresis is that the person is not awakened by bladder tension. Traditional verbal psychotherapy has not been very successful in treating enuresis.[5] In contrast, two behavior therapy procedures—the urine alarm and dry-bed training—have proved to be highly effective.

Urine Alarm

A **urine alarm** is a device that sounds an alarm to wake the child when the child begins to urinate. The original urine alarm, known as the *bell-and-pad*, was developed by Hobart Mowrer and Willie Mowrer in 1938.[6] A specially prepared pad, containing two pieces of bronze screening separated by heavy cotton fabric, is placed under the bed sheet (see Figure 15-2). When urination begins, the urine seeps through the fabric and closes an electrical circuit that sounds an alarm (originally a bell). Through repeated associations between the alarm and bladder tension, bladder tension alone becomes the stimulus that awakens the child before urination starts.

Although the bell-and-pad still is available, a more convenient device generally is used today. It consists of a moisture-sensitive switching system; the sensor end goes inside the client's underpants and is connected to a small alarm that unobtrusively is attached to outer clothing, such as pajamas. This device, which can be purchased over the counter in pharmacies, also is

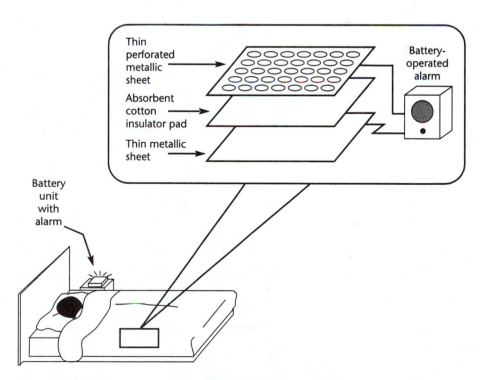

Figure 15-2 Bell-and-pad apparatus used to treat nocturnal enuresis

Thin perforated metallic sheet

Absorbent cotton insulator pad

Thin metallic sheet

Battery-operated alarm

Battery unit with alarm

applicable to diurnal (daytime) enuresis, which affects approximately one percent of children over the age of five.[7]

The urine alarm is an elegantly simple procedure. It has been used for 60 years, and it continues to be highly effective in 70% to 80% of cases.[8] It has been shown to be superior to medication (specifically, imipramine)[9] and traditional psychotherapy.[10] The relapse rate after 6 months has been about 33%, and the predominant reason has been parents' failure to carry out the procedures.[11] The urine alarm has been used alone and as part of treatment packages.[12] Interestingly, the urine alarm tends to be as effective alone as when it is combined with other behavioral treatments.[13]

Dry-Bed Training

Dry-bed training, developed by Nathan Azrin and his associates,[14] is a comprehensive treatment package that employs shaping and overcorrection to teach children the behaviors required to keep the bed dry throughout the night. The steps involved in dry-bed training are outlined in Table 15-1. These procedures illustrate the detail and precision inherent in many behavior therapy procedures.

Table 15-1 Protocol for dry-bed training with parents as trainers
SOURCE: Ethical issues for human services, 1977, pp. v-vi.

I. Training day
  A. Afternoon
    1. Child encouraged to drink favorite beverage to increase urination
    2. Child requested to attempt urination every half hour
      a. If child feels urge to urinate, he is asked to wait for increasingly longer periods of time
      b. If child *has* to urinate, he is asked to lie in bed as if asleep, then jump up and go to the bathroom (role playing what he should do at night); his behavior is then reinforced with a beverage and praise
    3. Child motivated to work at dry beds
      a. Parents and child review inconveniences caused by bed-wetting
      b. Parents contract with child for reinforcers to be given after first dry night and after a specified series of dry nights
      c. Child specifies whom he'd like to tell that he is keeping dry
      d. Child is given a chart to mark his progress
  B. One hour before bedtime with parents watching
    1. Child informed of all phases of procedures
    2. Child role plays cleanliness training (to be used if bed-wetting occurs)
      a. Child required to put on own pajamas
      b. Child required to remove sheets and put them back on
    3. Child role plays positive practice in toileting (to be used if bed-wetting occurs)
      a. Child lies down in bed as if asleep (lights out)
      b. Child counts to 50
      c. Child arises and hurries to bathroom where he tries to urinate
      d. Child returns to bed
      e. Steps a-d repeated 20 times with parents counting

(continued)

Table 15-1   *(continued)*

    C. At bedtime
        1. Child tells parents instructions on accident correction and nighttime awakenings
        2. Child continues to drink fluids
        3. Parents talk to child about reinforcers and express confidence in child
        4. Parents comment on dryness of sheets
        5. Child retires for the night
    D. Hourly awakenings by parents until 1 A.M.
        1. If child is dry
            a. Minimal prompt (light touching) used to awaken (stronger prompt used if child doesn't wake)
            b. Child asked if he needs to urinate
                i. If he can wait another hour
                    (a) Parents praise his urinary control
                    (b) Child returns to bed
                ii. If he must urinate
                    (a) Child goes to bathroom
                    (b) Parents praise him for correct toileting
                    (c) Child returns to bed
            c. Child feels sheets and comments on their dryness
            d. Parents praise child for having dry bed
            e. Child given fluids (discontinued after 11 P.M.)
            f. Child returns to sleep
        2. When an accident has occurred
            a. Parent awakens child and reprimands him for wetting
            b. Parent directs child to bathroom to finish urinating
            c. Child given cleanliness training
                i. Child changes pajamas
                ii. Child removes wet sheets and places them in laundry basket
                iii. Child obtains clean sheets and remakes bed
            d. Positive practice in correct toileting (20 times) performed immediately after cleanliness training
            e. Child reminded that positive practice is necessary before going to bed the next evening
    E. Parents check child half hour earlier than normal waking the next morning
        1. If bed is wet, steps under IIB (below) implemented
 II. Posttraining (after training day)
    A. If bed dry in the morning
        1. Parents point out to child half hour before his usual bedtime that he does not have to practice (because bed was dry that morning) and so he can do what he wants in the half hour before going to bed
        2. Parents point out child's chart that shows his progress toward reinforcers
        3. Parents tell visitors to the home how child is keeping his bed dry
        4. Parents remark on child's success at least three times a day
    B. If bed wet in the morning
        1. Parents wake child half hour earlier, prompt him to check his sheets, and ask him to say what he should do
        2. Child required to change bed and pajamas
        3. Child engages in positive practice in correct toileting (20 times)
        4. Child engages in positive practice (20 times) half hour before bed that night
        5. Child marks chart and is told "We will try again tomorrow"
        6. Parents tell visitors to the home that the child is learning to keep his bed dry

Treatment begins with a night of intensive training. The child is awakened every hour, to urinate if necessary and to be praised for having a dry bed. When an accident occurs, the child goes through a two-phase overcorrection procedure. First comes *cleanliness training,* a form of restitution in which the client changes the wet nightclothes and sheets. Second, there is repeated *positive practice,* which consists of (1) the child lying in bed for a count of 50; (2) then hurrying to the bathroom and attempting to urinate; and (3) finally returning to bed. In addition, during the day the child practices retaining urine in the bladder by using **retention control training**.[15] This procedure involves shaping the retention of increasingly greater amounts of urine (created by frequently drinking favorite beverages) for increasingly longer periods.

Parents can be trained to implement dry-bed training in about an hour and a half,[16] and the child is made largely responsible for carrying out dry-bed training procedures. For example, the therapist first teaches the procedures to the child, who then explains them to the parents and requests their help in carrying them out.[17] The emphasis in dry-bed training is on the child's developing self-control skills and being reinforced for accomplishments. When accidents occur, the child assumes the responsibility of correcting them by cleaning up and then by practicing the behaviors required to prevent accidents in the future.

Dry-bed training eliminates enuresis more quickly and results in longer-lasting effects than the urine alarm.[18] The results of one study with 44 children between the ages of 3 and 15 (average age of 6.8) illustrate the

Photo 15-1 Dry-bed training involves a child's taking responsibility for changing bedding after accidents.

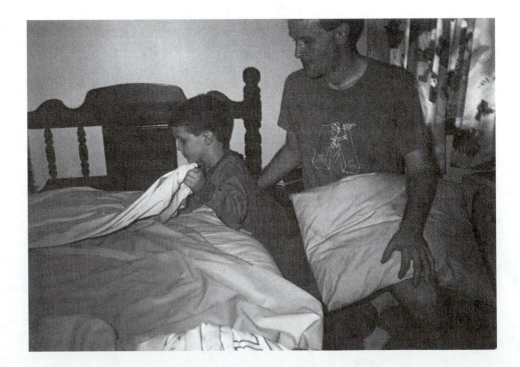

Figure 15-3 Bed-wetting by 44 children with enuresis after office instruction in dry-bed training
SOURCE: Adapted from Azrin, Thienes-Hontos, & Besalel-Azrin, 1979, p. 18.

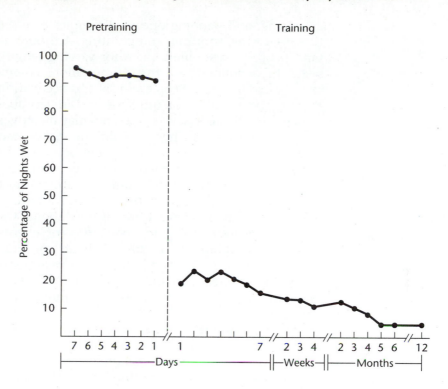

rapidity and long-lasting effectiveness of the treatment.[19] As Figure 15-3 shows, before dry-bed training the children were wetting their beds an average of 92% of the nights. On the first day after the intensive training, bed-wetting was reduced to 18%. At a 5-month follow-up, bed-wetting was occurring on only 4% of the nights, a level that was maintained 1 year later.

Dry-bed training occasionally is used for adults, and one study revealed that 8 of 9 clients who had enuresis most of their lives remained continent at a 6-year follow-up.[20] The principles of dry-bed training have been extended to normal daytime toilet training with impressive results.[21] In the course of normal development, most children learn to use the toilet over a period of several months; parental attempts to hasten the process generally have proved to be of little benefit.[22] Several methods of intensive reinforcement training have been moderately successful in reducing training time to approximately 1 month.[23] In contrast, using the **dry-pants method** (the daytime version of the dry-bed method), children ranging in age from 20 to 36 months have been toilet trained in an average of 4 hours, and the average is 2 hours for children older than 26 months.[24]

TIC DISORDERS

A *tic* is a recurring, sudden, rapid movement or vocalization. Examples of *motor tics* include repetitive neck-jerking, shoulder-twitching, facial grimacing, and slapping oneself. Examples of *vocal tics* include repetitive throat-clearing, snorting, and grunting. Although tics are largely involuntary, people can suppress them for varying lengths of time. Tics usually begin in childhood, are three times more common in males, and are exacerbated by stress. People's social and occupational functioning may be impaired because of social ostracism and anxiety about exhibiting tics in the presence of others. In severe cases, tics may directly interfere with a person's daily functioning, as when eye-blinking makes reading difficult. *Tourette's disorder* is the most serious tic disorder because it involves multiple motor tics and vocal tics that sometimes include uttering obscenities.[25]

Medication is the most common treatment for tics, but it is associated with multiple problems. In the case of Tourette's disorder, for example, reduction in the frequency of tics is only about 50%,[26] and unwanted side effects have been noted in about 80% of clients taking medication.[27] Further, only about 20% to 30% of clients continue taking medication on a long-term basis.[28] Clearly, alternative treatments are needed. The major behavioral treatments for tics are massed negative practice, changing maintaining consequences, relaxation training, self-monitoring, and habit reversal.

Massed negative practice, the most frequently used behavioral treatment for tics, has the client deliberately perform the tic as rapidly as possible. This is done for a set time (for example, 30 minutes), with short rest periods (for instance, 1 minute of rest for each 4 minutes of performing the tic).[29] Negative practice has been moderately successful in reducing the frequency of tics for some people,[30] with an average reduction of about 60%.[31]

Changing the maintaining consequences of tics is the second most frequently employed behavior therapy. Differential reinforcement[32] is effective in reducing tics in children by itself[33] and when combined with other therapies.[34] Consequential deceleration therapies, including contingent electric shock[35] and time out from positive reinforcement,[36] also can reduce tic frequency. However, the treatment effects with deceleration therapies may not generalize from the specific therapy setting and may be only temporary.[37]

Employing deep muscle relaxation is consistently effective in decreasing tics *while* the clients are relaxing.[38] However, the tics tend to return shortly after relaxation sessions.[39]

Self-monitoring can be an effective treatment for tics.[40] Although self-monitoring typically is an assessment procedure (see Chapter 5), it is sometimes specifically used to modify a target behavior. Self-monitoring makes clients more aware of their tics, which is necessary for effective treatment.

In sum, massed negative practice, reinforcement, relaxation training, and self-monitoring all are moderately effective treatments for tics. To increase their effectiveness, various combinations of these treatments generally are used.

Habit Reversal

Habit reversal, by far the most effective treatment package for tics, was developed by Nathan Azrin and his colleagues.[41] Habit reversal incorporates four components: (1) awareness training, (2) competing response training, (3) relaxation training, and (4) reinforcement. Awareness training and competing response training seem to be the critical components.[42]

Awareness training, which includes self-monitoring, involves extensive self-assessment to ensure that the client is aware of (1) the frequency and severity of the tics; (2) their environmental antecedents; and (3) the individual responses that make up the tics. Clients and family members keep a record of when, where, and with whom tics occur. Clients are asked to observe their tics, using a mirror or video, because knowing the specific responses involved is necessary to control tics. Clients also practice detecting the first signs of tics, so that they will be able to stop the tics early in their sequence.

In *competing response training,* clients practice performing a response that (1) competes with the tic; (2) can be sustained for several minutes; (3) is compatible with everyday activities; and (4) is inconspicuous to others.[43] Table 15-2 provides examples of competing responses for various kinds of tics.[44]

Clients are taught muscle relaxation and are instructed to practice it daily. Additionally, they are taught to use relaxation in their daily lives whenever they feel anxious or emit a tic (as in coping desensitization; Chapter 9).

Family members are asked to praise the client when they observe that the client is tic-free or shows a significant reduction in tics. Clients compile a list

Table 15-2 Competing responses for tics used in habit reversal
SOURCE: Based on Azrin & Peterson, 1988b.

Tic	Competing Response
HEAD JERK	Isometric contraction of neck flexor muscles: pull chin down and in, head in, eyes forward
SHOULDER SHRUG	Isometric contraction of shoulder depressor muscles: push elbow toward hip
HEAD SHAKE	Slow isometric contraction of neck muscles with eyes forward until head can be held perfectly still
ARM JERK	Push hand down on thigh or stomach and push elbow in toward hip
LEG JERK	If sitting, place feet on floor and push down; if standing, lock knees
EYE BLINK	Systematic, soft blinking at rate of one blink every 3-5 seconds; frequent downward glance every 5-10 seconds
ORAL VOCAL TICS	Continuous slow, rhythmic breathing through nose with mouth closed
NASAL VOCAL TICS	Continuous slow, rhythmic breathing through mouth

of the negative consequences of emitting tics (such as embarrassment and inconvenience) and the positive consequences of eliminating tics. They write the list on a card that they carry with them and periodically refer to as reminders of the benefits of engaging in habit reversal procedures. Children are given specific reinforcers for completing therapy assignments and reducing tics below a predetermined goal level.

Habit reversal consistently has been shown to be highly effective in treating tics,[45] reducing tics by about 90%, compared with 50% to 60% with drug treatment.[46] It also has been used, often as part of a treatment package, for a variety of other problems, many of which involve "nervous habits."[47] These problems include trichotillomania (hair pulling),[48] thumb sucking,[49] eczema (skin inflammation),[50] bruxism (teeth grinding),[51] temporomandibular disorders (pain in the oral structures),[52] stuttering,[53] and overeating.[54] Habit reversal generally has been found to be superior to other treatments, and it is preferable to aversive treatments that sometimes are used to treat nervous habits. On the downside, habit reversal is an elaborate treatment that requires considerable time from the client, the therapist, and family members.

INSOMNIA

Insomnia involves difficulties in falling asleep or maintaining sleep that cause personal distress and affect one's daytime performance, mood, and general psychological well-being.[55] Insomnia refers to sleep disturbances that are not directly due to a medical condition or the effects of drugs. It is estimated that 15% to 20% of adults suffer from chronic insomnia and 30% to 40% suffer from occasional or transient insomnia.[56] Sedatives or other sleep-inducing drugs constitute the most frequent treatment for adult insomnia. Sedating drugs—usually antihistamines—also are widely prescribed for infant and childhood sleep difficulties.[57] A number of potential problems are associated with using sleep medications, including a deterioration in daytime functioning; "rebound insomnia" (greater difficulty falling asleep after using sleep medication); psychological and physiological dependence on the drug; and financial expense.[58] Given the high prevalence of sleep problems among both children and adults and the significant disadvantages of using drug therapy, psychological treatments play an important role in the treatment of chronic sleep problems. Behavior therapies are among the most effective psychological treatments.[59]

Extinction of Infant and Early Childhood Sleep Problems

Sleep problems in infants and young children (up to age 6) usually involve (1) refusing to go to bed; (2) difficulty in settling down and falling asleep; and (3) nighttime awakening and crying. Such sleep disturbances are chronic problems for 15% to 35% of children under the age of 5.[60] Not surprisingly, parents typically respond to their child's sleep problems with some form of attention, which reinforces the sleep disturbance. When parental attention is the primary maintaining condition of infant and toddler sleep disturbances, extinction is the treatment of choice.[61]

In the standard application of extinction for infant sleep problems, parents refrain from attending to their child after the child is placed in bed. Attention is withheld if the child refuses to go to bed or to sleep and if the child wakes up and cries during the night. This simple procedure is highly effective in decreasing the frequency and duration of awakenings and in improving the child's general sleep quality. The improvements have been shown to last for as long as two years after the treatment ends.[62] A major advantage of extinction is that it is simple for parents to learn. Additionally, extinction, along with stimulus control procedures (which we'll describe in the next section), has been effective in preventing infant sleep problems.[63]

Despite the proven effectiveness of extinction for infant sleep problems, some parents are unwilling to use it because, understandably, they are upset by their child's crying and feel compelled to provide comfort. The temporary, initial increase in the target behavior that is common with extinction (such as crying when the child is put to bed) is another factor that makes extinction unacceptable as a treatment to some parents.[64] Additionally, some critics have argued that extinction is unethical because it damages the parent-child relationship, such as by decreasing the infant's security.[65] In fact, the empirical evidence suggests just the opposite. Infants treated by extinction have shown more security and less emotionality (such as crying) than untreated infants with sleep problems and infants without sleep problems.[66]

Because clients will use a therapy only if it is acceptable, behavior therapists have modified extinction procedures to make them more palatable for parents. The simplest modification allows parents to make a specified number of brief, time-limited checks on their child if the child cries after having been put to bed (for instance, checking for 15 seconds or less, no more often than once every 20 minutes).[67]

Graduated extinction is a more complex modification. It involves either gradually increasing the time the parent ignores the child's bedtime crying[68] or gradually decreasing the time the parent spends attending to the child when the child awakens during the night.[69] The graduated increments are individualized for each family. Parents tend to find modified extinction procedures to be more acceptable,[70] although they are generally less effective than standard extinction procedures.[71]

Behavior Therapy for Adult Insomnia

Adult insomnia is maintained primarily by three antecedent conditions: (1) inappropriate situational cues for sleeping; (2) excessive muscle tension; and (3) excessive sleep-related worry based on erroneous or distorted beliefs. Three behavior therapies are used to change these maintaining conditions: stimulus control, relaxation training, and cognitive restructuring, respectively.

STIMULUS CONTROL

Some people have difficulty falling asleep because, for them, being in bed has strong associations with a host of activities other than sleeping, such as reading, watching TV, snacking, talking on the phone, studying, and worrying about not being able to fall asleep. Stimulus control procedures can be effective when insomnia is maintained by these nonsleep situational cues.

Stimulus control procedures change behaviors by modifying their situational cues. Prompting is a simple example of stimulus control. Generally, stimulus control procedures are part of a treatment package. When behaviors are maintained primarily by situational cues, stimulus control procedures alone can be effective for sleep-onset insomnia.

The stimulus control procedures for insomnia, originally developed by Richard Bootzin,[72] establish a client's bed as a clear-cut cue for sleeping and *only* for sleeping. Clients are instructed to adhere to the following rules that promote good sleep habits.[73]

1. Get into bed *only* when you are sleepy.

2. Use your bed only for sleeping. (The one exception is for sexual behavior, but only if you feel relaxed or sleepy afterwards. If sex leaves you wide awake, engage in it somewhere other than the bed in which you sleep.)

3. If you cannot fall asleep within 15 minutes, get out of bed and go into another room. Return to bed when you are sleepy. If you still cannot fall asleep, repeat this step. (It does not seem to matter what you do when you get out of bed, as long as the activity is not stimulating.)

4. Get up at the same time every morning, regardless of what time you go to bed. (This routine allows you to establish a regular sleep rhythm.)

5. Do not take naps. (Napping can disrupt the regular sleep rhythm and makes it harder to fall asleep at night.)

These stimulus control procedures are highly effective in treating sleep-onset insomnia.[74] They consistently have been shown to be superior to no treatment and to placebo control conditions in decreasing sleep-onset latency (that is, the time it takes to fall asleep).

Stimulus control has been an effective treatment for older adults who often experience sleep-onset problems and frequent nighttime awakenings.[75] In one study with adults aged 47 to 76, stimulus control was combined with *sleep education*, which provides clients with information about practices that facilitate sleep (such as daily exercise) and practices that interfere with sleep (such as consuming alcohol before retiring).[76] This treatment package was compared with sleep education alone, sleep education plus relaxation training, and a no-treatment control group.

Interestingly, all the clients, including those in the control group, showed improvement on self-report measures immediately after treatment, such as the number of nighttime awakenings, feelings of depression, and feelings of being refreshed upon awakening. Because clients in the control group also reported these improvements, it was not possible to conclude that any of the treatments were responsible for the positive changes.

However, at a two-year follow-up, clients who had been taught stimulus control procedures reported shorter sleep-onset latencies and had the highest ratings of sleep quality. It is noteworthy that these clients were still using the stimulus control procedures. Two factors may have accounted for the long-lasting effects: stimulus control procedures are easy to implement, and they become a routine practice. These factors also may explain why, in general, stimulus control consistently is the most effective single treatment for adult insomnia.[77]

Many everyday behaviors besides falling asleep are maintained by situational cues, which means that they can be influenced by stimulus control procedures. Studying is one such behavior that you easily can bring under stimulus control.

Participation Exercise 15-1

DESIGNING STIMULUS CONTROL PROCEDURES TO ENHANCE STUDYING*

Studying is maintained by a host of situational cues, including the time of day, the physical setting, and the presence of other students. You can develop stimulus control rules for increasing the efficiency and effectiveness of your studying.

Using the rules for treating insomnia described earlier as models, make a list of rules to establish situational cues that will remind you to study and will make studying more productive, including increasing concentration and decreasing distractions. Consider the following situational factors and how differences in them affect your studying.

1. *When* you study. This includes the days of the week, the time of day, and the length of study sessions and breaks. What time parameters are optimal for you?

2. *Where* you study. This includes the general location (for instance, at home or at the library) and the specific physical setup (for example, at a desk or on your bed). What factors facilitate your studying (such as ample light and optimal temperature) and inhibit your studying (such as noise and interruptions)?

3. *With whom* you study. Do you study more efficiently with one or more other students or by yourself? If you study by yourself, is your studying facilitated by others' studying around you (such as in a study lounge) or by being alone?

After you have compiled your rules, refer to Appendix B for examples of suggested rules. Finally, you might want to follow your rules and see if they affect your studying.

RELAXATION TRAINING

People who have problems sleeping often report being "all keyed up" and "tense" before going to bed. When insomnia is maintained by muscle

---

* This Participation Exercise can be done before you continue or later.

tension, training in deep muscle relaxation is the treatment of choice. Once clients have learned deep muscle relaxation, they use the relaxation skills when they get into bed to go to sleep. Clients in systematic desensitization sometimes get so relaxed that they fall asleep while visualizing scenes. Although this interferes with systematic desensitization, it is precisely the desired outcome for clients who have difficulty falling asleep.

Deep muscle relaxation consistently has been found to be superior to no treatment for decreasing sleep-onset latency[78] but has not consistently been shown to be superior to placebo conditions.[79] The effectiveness of relaxation training for insomnia can be enhanced by (1) greater individualization of treatment; (2) a larger number of treatment sessions;[80] and (3) increased practice in relaxation exercises between therapy sessions.[81] Standard relaxation training appears to be as effective as electromyographic (muscle tone) biofeedback-assisted relaxation training, particularly for clients with sleep-onset problems. Thus, the additional cost of using biofeedback appears to be unwarranted.[82] Because many clients with chronic insomnia report high levels of daytime anxiety, relaxation training may have the added benefit of serving as a daytime coping skill for dealing with daily stressors.[83]

COGNITIVE RESTRUCTURING

When excessive worry about not sleeping and about the possible negative effects of sleep loss is a major maintaining antecedent of sleep problems, cognitive restructuring may be the treatment of choice. Typically, the worry is the result of faulty or distorted beliefs about sleeping involving one of the following themes: (1) exaggerated ideas about the negative consequences of sleep loss (for instance, "If I don't get a good night's sleep, I'll flunk my exam tomorrow"); (2) unrealistic expectations about what constitutes acceptable sleep requirements (such as "I can't function on less than nine hours of sleep"); and (3) beliefs about not having control over one's sleeping (for example, "I'm 'wired' by the time I get to bed, and with my schedule, I can't do anything about it"). A client's specific sleep-related cognitions can be assessed initially with a direct self-report inventory such as the Personal Beliefs and Attitudes About Sleep inventory that asks clients to rate the degree to which they have common thoughts about sleep problems (see Table 15-3 for sample items).[84]

Table 15-3 Items from the Personal Beliefs and Attitudes About Sleep inventory rated on a scale ranging from *strongly agree* to *strongly disagree* SOURCE: Adapted from Sloan, Hauris, Bootzin, Morin, Stevenson, & Shapiro, 1993.

I am worried that if I go for one or two nights without sleep, I may have a "nervous breakdown."

After a poor night's sleep, I know that it will interfere with my daily activities the next day.

I feel that insomnia is basically the result of aging and there isn't much that can be done about this problem.

My sleep is getting worse all the time and I don't believe anyone can help.

When I sleep poorly on one night, I know that it will disturb my sleep schedule for the whole week.

Cognitive restructuring for insomnia involves three steps: (1) identifying unrealistic, maladaptive sleep-related cognitions; (2) challenging the validity of these cognitions; and (3) replacing unrealistic, maladaptive cognitions with realistic, adaptive ones. For example, "If I don't fall asleep soon, I won't be able to function tomorrow" might be more realistically and adaptively restructured as "I may be tired tomorrow, but I'll still be able to function. And, what I don't get done tomorrow, I can do the next day after a good night's sleep." Note that the adaptive thoughts realistically acknowledge that sleep loss may have some negative consequences, but not the catastrophic consequences predicted by the maladaptive thought. With a more realistic outlook, worry about loss of sleep will diminish, which, in turn, will make it more likely that the person will fall asleep.

Cognitive restructuring for insomnia has been shown to be effective compared with no-treatment control conditions.[85] Although cognitive restructuring can be used as the sole treatment for insomnia, it generally is part of a treatment package.[86]

TREATMENT PACKAGES FOR ADULT INSOMNIA

An example of a treatment package for insomnia is a short-term, structured cognitive-behavioral intervention for adults who had suffered from insomnia for an average of more than 11 years.[87] Therapy was conducted individually and typically required 8 to 10 therapy sessions. Besides cognitive restructuring and stimulus control procedures, the other two major components in the treatment package were sleep education and sleep restriction. *Sleep restriction* involves limiting the time spent in bed to the actual time a client usually sleeps. (If a client typically spends 10 hours in bed but sleeps only 5 hours, the client would be instructed to stay in bed for only 5 hours, no matter how much of that time the client sleeps.) Clients also kept a sleep diary, a self-report measure that included such information as bedtime, arising time, daytime naps, frequency of night awakenings, sleep quality (rated on a 5-point scale), and medication intake. Figure 15-4 shows an excerpt from a sleep diary. Finally, clients who were using sleep medication were offered a withdrawal plan to decrease or eliminate drug usage.

This cognitive-behavioral treatment package resulted in significant reductions in clients' sleep-onset latency, awakenings after sleep onset, and early morning awakenings. Significant reductions in clients' use of sleep medication also occurred. In fact, the number of clients who were habitual users of sleep medication decreased by 54% by the end of therapy. Similar results have been obtained using short-term cognitive-behavioral therapy for older adults (average age 67 years) suffering from insomnia.[88]

Treatment packages for insomnia may be more effective than single therapies, especially when a client's sleeping problems are the result of more than one category of maintaining conditions. For example, stimulus control and relaxation training have been shown to be more effective than stimulus control alone.[89] To decrease dependence on sleep medication, treatment packages that combine medication tapering schedules and cognitive-behavioral procedures have proved successful.[90] Although treatment

Figure 15-4 Excerpt from a sleep diary

Day/date:	**Monday, 2/14**
Naps (Number and duration)	2 11:15 a.m.–12:05 p.m. (50 min.) 3:30–4:00 p.m. (30 min.)
Medication Intake	None
Bedtime	10:30 p.m.
Nighttime Awakenings	12:50 a.m. 3:35 a.m.
Sleep Quality (5-pt. rating)	2
Arising Time	7:10 a.m.

Day/date:	**Tuesday, 2/15**
Naps (Number and duration)	1 11:30 a.m.–12:15 p.m. (45 min.)
Medication Intake	Sominex—2 pills at 10:30 p.m.
Bedtime	11:20 p.m.
Nighttime Awakenings	1:20 a.m. 4:10 a.m.
Sleep Quality (5-pt. rating)	2
Arising Time	7:45 a.m.

packages for insomnia are promising, outcome research has not yet suggested which specific combination of therapies is optimal and which clients are likely to benefit most from treatment packages rather than single therapies.[91]

BULIMIA

To eat or not to eat? That is the question that characterizes eating disorders. The three most prominent eating problems—anorexia, obesity, and bulimia—can be arranged on a weight and eating continuum, as shown in Figure 15-5. *Anorexia* is at the "not eating" end. It is characterized by intense fear of gaining weight; by distorted perceptions about being overweight; and by behaviors designed to keep one's weight significantly below normal— primarily by reducing total food intake drastically and engaging in excessive exercise. Obesity, which involves weighing significantly more than normal, is at the "eating" end. *Bulimia* falls in the middle because people with bulimia *binge* (eat large quantities of food in a brief period) but maintain a normal weight because they *purge* the food they eat (typically by self-induced vomiting and also through the abuse of laxatives and diuretics).[92] Behavior therapy has been applied to all three eating problems. We will

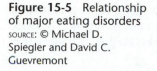

Figure 15-5 Relationship of major eating disorders
SOURCE: © Michael D. Spiegler and David C. Guevremont

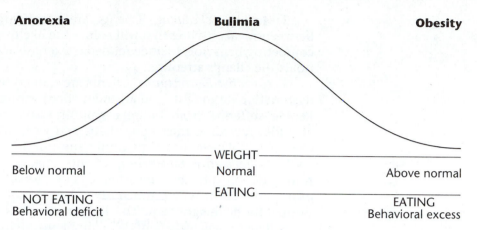

describe the behavioral treatment of bulimia, which employs behavior therapy procedures that have strong empirical support.*

Bulimia is a serious disorder that affects 1% to 3% of women, primarily in industrialized countries, and typically begins in late adolescence or early adulthood. It is rare in males. Recurrent purging after binge eating can result in serious medical problems, especially loss of body fluids and electrolytes as well as teeth destruction caused by stomach acid that is regurgitated.[93]

The behavioral treatment of bulimia generally consists of a comprehensive cognitive-behavioral treatment package that is a rich integration of both behavioral and cognitive procedures.[94] It can be implemented in as few as 20 sessions, individually or in groups. The therapy begins by providing the client with information about bulimia, nutrition, and weight regulation.[95] A combination of the following 8 behavior therapy procedures then is used.

1. *Self-Monitoring.* Self-monitoring of binge eating and purging episodes and the circumstances surrounding them is the clients' first task and continues throughout the treatment. Clients also record their daily food and liquid intake and sometimes the type of food and the time and place of eating. The self-monitoring records help identify maintaining conditions of binge/purge episodes and provide a continuous measure of change.

2. *Stimulus Control.* Clients are taught to design stimulus control procedures, such as eating at specified times, eating in a particular location, and buying only foods that the particular client is less likely to binge on. The aim of these procedures is for clients to develop habits of eating three normal meals a day plus planned snacks.

---

* We have chosen not to include behavioral treatment for anorexia and obesity for the following reasons. Behavioral treatment for anorexia is not well developed and focuses on the use of reinforcement for increasing weight gain in hospitalized clients (Wilson & Fairburn, 1993). Behavioral treatment of obesity typically involves treatment packages with a number of nonbehavioral components, such as diet, exercise, and medication (for example, Kirschenbaum, 1994; Perri, Nezu, & Viegner, 1992). In general, the contribution of the behavioral components has not been established (compare with Wadden, Sternberg, Letizia, Stunkard, & Foster, 1989; Wadden, Stunkard, & Liebschutz, 1988).

3. *Activity Scheduling.* Clients are taught to schedule pleasurable between-meal activities that will reduce the likelihood of binge eating. Such competing behaviors include moderate exercise and engaging in work that holds the client's attention.

4. *Cognitive Restructuring.* Clients are trained to identify and alter their dysfunctional thoughts and attitudes about eating, food, and body image. People suffering from bulimia typically have rigid and perfectionistic attitudes regarding their body shape and weight, eating, and dieting (for example, "I'll never be happy until I am thin").[96]

5. *Collaborative Empiricism.* Clients engage in empirical hypothesis testing designed to challenge their dysfunctional beliefs and thoughts. For example, a client who erroneously believed that she weighed well above normal for her height could check a current table of normal weight ranges.

6. *Problem Solving.* Clients learn problem-solving skills to help them cope with stress-evoking events that have been associated with binge eating. They are encouraged to anticipate these events so the problem solving can be implemented before binge eating is imminent.[97]

7. *Flooding.* Binge eating and the threat of gaining weight typically are highly anxiety-evoking for clients with bulimia. Purging serves to reduce the anxiety, which negatively reinforces purging. Flooding is used to break this vicious cycle.[98] With the therapist present, clients are encouraged to eat the foods on which they typically binge (often high-caloric, sweet, and soft-textured foods that can be rapidly swallowed). Following this exposure, clients are instructed not to vomit (response prevention). The flooding session is terminated only when the strong urge to purge dissipates. During flooding, clients have an opportunity to practice coping skills they have learned, such as cognitive restructuring. Although flooding can be effective, it does not appear to be a necessary treatment component.[99] In some cases, flooding may make the treatment package less effective [100] because of clients' reluctance to participate in the unpleasant flooding procedures.[101]

8. *Relapse Prevention.* Bulimia tends to occur in cycles[102] and is characterized by relapses.[103] Thus, preparing clients for the possibility that the bulimic behaviors will return in the future is important. Accordingly, clients identify high-risk situations for binge eating and rehearse coping strategies that can be used if the situations occur. This may include recruiting and using social support from family and friends. (We will outline the process of relapse prevention more fully later in the chapter.)

The comprehensive cognitive-behavioral treatment package we have just described generally is considered the treatment of choice for bulimia.[104] Well-controlled studies indicate its effectiveness, showing an average reduction in clients' binge eating ranging from 93% to 73% and an average reduction in purging ranging from 94% to 77%.[105] The treatment package consistently is superior to traditional verbal/interpersonal psychotherapies[106] and antidepressant medication (which has been used to treat depression related to bulimia).[107] Long-term maintenance of treatment gains have been found in some,[108] but not all,[109] studies. Cognitive interventions that target clients' maladaptive cognitions that maintain binge eating and purging may be especially important in fostering long-term maintenance of treatment gains.[110] In addition to significantly reducing binge eating and purging, the treatment package consistently improves clients' beliefs and attitudes about their body and weight.[111] Further, most studies show significant improvements in self-esteem, depression, and social functioning.[112]

ADDICTIVE BEHAVIORS AND RELAPSE PREVENTION

Addictive behaviors result in immediate, highly pleasurable consequences and in delayed negative consequences. The immediate pleasurable consequences are so powerful that they override the delayed negative consequences.[113] Consider college students who are drinking heavily at a party and feeling uninhibited, relaxed, and "high." Their drinking behavior is not influenced by the consequences that occur the next day, such as a horrendous hangover and missed classes. The longer-term harmful effects on one's health, interpersonal relations, and job performance associated with alcohol abuse are even further removed from the immediate pleasure experienced while drinking. The same holds true for other forms of substance abuse, as well as other behaviors that are "addictive" in nature, such as gambling and overeating.[114] In a nutshell, then, the major obstacle to treating addictive behaviors is that the maintaining conditions are so reinforcing that clients strongly resist modifying them.

Alcohol abuse, cigarette smoking, and the use of illicit drugs (such as cocaine and heroin) are the most common addictive behaviors treated by behavior therapy. Aversion therapy, cue exposure, and consequential therapies are among the behavior therapies used to treat addictive behaviors.

Aversion therapy pairs the addictive behavior with an aversive stimulus (such as nausea) to "discourage" the client from engaging in the addictive behavior in the future (see Chapter 7). For example, **rapid smoking** is an aversion therapy that requires clients to smoke at the rate of one puff every six seconds; to inhale normally; and to continue smoking rapidly until they cannot tolerate it anymore. In some cases, the aversion created by rapid smoking can have long-term effects in decreasing smoking.[115] However, such results have not been obtained consistently.[116] Further, rapid smoking can cause temporary cardiovascular stress, which makes the procedure unsuitable for anyone who is at risk for cardiovascular disease.[117] Accordingly, rapid smoking is employed infrequently.

In **cue exposure**, the client is exposed to cues associated with the addictive behavior but is prevented from engaging in the addictive behavior, which is similar to flooding. For example, a client with a drinking problem might spend time in a bar. There, the client would experience the visual (such as other people drinking), auditory (such as hearing people order drinks), and olfactory (such as the smell of alcohol) cues associated with drinking. However, the client would refrain from drinking alcohol. Cue exposure by itself can be effective in reducing clients' cravings for the addictive substance.[118] However, it is more effective when clients use specific coping skills, such as differential relaxation, to deal with their cravings.[119] In essence,

Photo 15-2 In cue exposure, a client is exposed to cues associated with an addictive behavior but refrains from engaging in the addictive behavior. Here, the client (at the far right) interacts with others who are drinking in a bar, but he himself does not drink.

clients learn to substitute coping responses for their habitual addictive behaviors when they encounter the salient cues that previously have prompted the addictive behaviors.

Consequential therapies occasionally have been used to reduce addictive behaviors. One approach to substance abuse is to provide clients with attractive reinforcers for abstaining from taking the drug.[120] This strategy proved effective for two clients with schizophrenia who were dependent on cocaine. Paying the clients $25 for each negative urine test significantly reduced their cocaine use.[121] The other approach is response cost, which was illustrated by the case of the African-American client whose abuse of amphetamines was eliminated by the threat of having $50 checks sent to the Ku Klux Klan if he used the drug (Chapter 7, page 145).[122]

The problem with each of these singular behavior therapy approaches is that they are effective only in the short-run. All too often, clients *relapse*— that is, revert to their addictive behaviors—after therapy has ended. This is not surprising because the maintaining conditions of addictive behaviors typically consist of (1) ubiquitous everyday situational cues related to the addictive behavior (such as readily available alcohol at parties and in restaurants) and (2) powerful immediate reinforcers for engaging in the addictive behavior (such as feelings of euphoria from drugs). Clearly, changing these maintaining conditions on a long-term basis is difficult. Relapse prevention provides an alternative strategy.[123]

Relapse Prevention

Alan Marlatt and his colleagues[124] developed an approach to preventing the recurrence of addictive behaviors *after* the behaviors have been successfully eliminated. Central to their relapse prevention model is the distinction between a lapse and a relapse. A *lapse* is a single, isolated violation of abstinence, which does not necessarily lead to a *relapse*, which is a full-blown return to the addictive behavior (that is, to pretreatment levels of substance abuse). Clients are taught to view a lapse as an error and as an opportunity for additional learning.

Relapse prevention provides clients with the cognitive-behavioral coping skills necessary to prevent lapses from escalating into relapses. It consists of four components: (1) identifying high-risk situations; (2) learning coping skills; (3) practicing coping skills; and (4) creating a lifestyle balance. The first three components essentially are a form of stress inoculation.

IDENTIFYING HIGH-RISK SITUATIONS

Relapses are most likely to occur in high-risk situations. Almost three-quarters of all relapses of addictive behaviors are associated with (1) negative emotional states (35%), including frustration, anxiety, depression, anger, and loneliness; (2) social pressure (20%), such as being coaxed to go to a bar; and (3) interpersonal conflicts (16%), such as arguments with a spouse.[125] Clients must become aware of the specific situations that are most likely to trigger their relapse episodes so that they will be prepared to deal with them.

LEARNING COPING SKILLS

The ability to engage in effective coping responses when faced with a high-risk situation decreases the probability of a relapse. Further, successful coping with one high-risk situation tends to increase one's self-efficacy (belief that one can succeed) about being able to cope with other high-risk situations.[126]

Clients are taught cognitive-behavioral coping skills to deal with high-risk situations and keep lapses from turning into relapses. The most common skills clients learn are (1) *assertive behaviors* to help clients deal with social pressures to engage in addictive behaviors; (2) *relaxation and stress management* to reduce tension and discomfort associated with negative emotional states; (3) *social and communication skills* to manage interpersonal conflicts; (4) *problem-solving skills* to deal effectively with problems in their daily lives; and (5) *cognitive restructuring* to change maladaptive addictive-related cognitions (see Table 15-4 that describes the four types of cognitions most often associated with addictive behaviors[127]).

PRACTICING COPING SKILLS

Once clients have learned coping skills, they practice them in simulated high-risk situations. For example, the therapist and client might role play a scenario in which a friend asks the client to go out drinking, and the

Table 15-4 Cognitions associated with addictive behaviors
SOURCE: Based on Liese, 1994.

Cognition	Description	Example
ANTICIPATORY BELIEFS	Expectation of a positive result from engaging in an addictive behavior	"They'll think I'm pretty cool if I get high with them."
RELIEF-ORIENTED BELIEFS	Expectation of reduced discomfort from engaging in an addictive behavior	"I need a cigarette so I can relax."
FACILITATING BELIEFS	Client's giving himself or herself permission to engage in an addictive behavior	"It's only pot. It's not like I'm doing drugs."
AUTOMATIC THOUGHTS	Brief, repetitive, spontaneous mental images related to an addictive behavior that result in urges or cravings	Imagining sipping a cold beer while socializing with friends.

client responds with an appropriately assertive refusal. The two aims of this behavior rehearsal are for the client (1) to learn to recognize high-risk situations and then (2) to "automatically" engage in well-rehearsed coping skills rather than "automatically" reverting to habitual addictive behaviors.

CREATING A LIFESTYLE BALANCE

Feeling burdened by obligations and chores in one's life is a common trigger of addictive behaviors.[128] This occurs when clients perceive that there is an imbalance in their lives between their obligations (what they "should" do, such as go to work) and their desires (what they want to do, such as play golf). The obvious solution is to increase their access to their desires. However, in the case of clients recovering from addictive habits, their desires are likely to involve addictive behaviors. For instance, a client might think: "I deserve a drink for all the work I did today."

Accordingly, clients are encouraged to develop a lifestyle balance between obligations and desires. First, they self-monitor their obligations and desires on a daily basis to identify the degree and nature of the imbalance. Then, where imbalances exist, clients use an activity schedule to increase activities that are both adaptive and enjoyable. The process is viewed as relearning joy or "rejoyment."[129]

EFFECTIVENESS OF RELAPSE PREVENTION FOR ADDICTIVE BEHAVIORS

Cognitive-behavioral relapse prevention has been used as part of the treatment of different types of substance abuse, including alcohol,[130] nicotine,[131] cocaine,[132] marijuana,[133] and opiates.[134] Relapse prevention typically is part of a treatment package. For example, it has been combined with pharmacological treatment,[135] with the Alcoholics Anonymous Twelve-Step Recovery program,[136] and with behavioral couple therapy (when alcohol abuse is present).[137] Two unusual applications of relapse prevention have been to prevent high-risk sexual activity (for HIV infection)[138] and child moles-tation.[139]

The evidence regarding the efficacy of relapse prevention is mixed.[140] Some studies show relapse prevention to be more effective than alternative treatments and no-treatment control conditions. For example, clients receiving transdermal (through the skin) nicotine replacement patches plus relapse prevention training had higher rates of smoking cessation than clients who received only the pharmacological patches.[141] Other studies indicate that relapse prevention is at least equally as effective as alternative therapy approaches.[142] Some studies suggest that the benefits of relapse prevention are most evident with cigarette smoking and with more severe drug abuse.[143] Relapse prevention may decrease the severity of relapses in addition to promoting long-term maintenance.[144]

These positive findings regarding the efficacy of relapse prevention must be viewed cautiously. Some of the studies that support the effectiveness of relapse prevention contain methodological weaknesses, such as not employ-ing control groups[145] and evaluating relapse prevention in the context of a larger treatment package,[146] which cloud the specific contribution of the relapse prevention component. Further, some studies are less supportive of the superiority of relapse prevention compared with other treatments, particularly for cigarette smoking.[147] Taken together, the cumulative evi-dence to date indicates that the efficacy of relapse prevention for addictive behaviors is promising but remains inconclusive.

◆ ALL THINGS CONSIDERED: APPLICATIONS OF BEHAVIOR THERAPY TO PSYCHOLOGICAL DISORDERS WITH PRIMARY PHYSICAL CHARACTERISTICS

Behavior therapy for psychological disorders with primary physical charac-teristics provides psychological treatment alternatives to traditional medical interventions that are more intrusive and have serious negative side effects. The predominant use of sedatives or other sleep-inducing drugs to treat insomnia is a prime example. Prolonged use of sleep medication may actually interfere with sleeping, can lead to diminished daytime functioning, and often results in psychological and physical dependence on the drug.

The effectiveness of behavior therapy in treating psychological disor-ders with primary physical characteristics varies considerably with the par-ticular disorder (as is the case with medical disorders). The five disorders we described—enuresis, tics, insomnia, bulimia, and addictive behaviors—roughly fall on a continuum ranging from narrow impact to broad impact on a person's life. For instance, nocturnal enuresis is limited to one's sleeping time, whereas addictive behaviors generally interfere with almost every sphere of one's life. In general, the narrower the impact of the problem, the easier it is to treat. Behavior therapy interventions for enuresis and tics tend to have a high rate of success, whereas interventions for bulimia and addictive behaviors are less effective.

Although the problems we discussed in this chapter are classified as psychological rather than medical, their physical aspects can have serious medical implications. To begin with, the role of physical factors must be assessed because they may need to be treated directly. For example, bed-wetting can be caused by medication the client is currently taking (such as diuretics) and general medical conditions (such as diabetes); sleep difficulties can be the result of drugs (for instance, amphetamines) and medical conditions (for instance, hyperthyroidism). Additionally, comprehensive treatment often includes both behavior therapy and medical interventions. With bulimia, for instance, electrolyte imbalances and serious loss of tooth enamel are two consequences of purging that require medical attention.

Compared with medical conditions, psychological disorders with primary physical characteristics are more likely to be associated with guilt, embarrassment, and shame and to be clouded in secrecy. This is true for all of the problems you read about in this chapter, with the exception of insomnia. For example, people often try to hide or disguise bed-wetting, binge eating and purging, and tics. The self-conscious distress experienced by clients with these disorders requires an especially good client-therapist relationship. The client must trust the therapist sufficiently to reveal embarrassing behaviors. Also, the therapist must trust the client to be honest and straightforward. In the case of bulimia, for example, the therapist must be able to rely on clients' self-monitoring of binge eating and purging episodes because clients engage in these behaviors privately.

Many of the behavior therapy interventions employed with psychological disorders with primary physical characteristics involve self-control techniques. For example, habit reversal for tic disorders teaches clients to "catch" their maladaptive behaviors early in their sequence and counter them with competing responses. Gaining self-control over so-called involuntary physical disabilities (such as tics) is likely to increase clients' self-efficacy about their ability to modify them. Enhanced self-efficacy may be one of the factors responsible for the success of habit reversal for tics.

The use of treatment packages is another common element in the behavior therapy treatment of psychological disorders with primary physical characteristics. Dry-bed training for enuresis, habit reversal for tics, cognitive-behavioral treatment packages for bulimia, and relapse prevention for addictive behaviors illustrate the multifaceted approach used with these disorders.

It is fitting that we concluded our presentation of behavior therapy interventions for psychological disorders with primary physical characteristics by discussing relapse prevention. Relapse prevention initially was developed for treating substance abuse. However, both the specific procedures and the general principles of relapse prevention are being applied increasingly to other problems, such as high-risk sexual behaviors. Many psychological problems involve long-standing habitual behavior patterns that require continued management and coping. Relapse prevention potentially offers a means of achieving such long-term maintenance.

SUMMARY

1. Behavior therapy treats a variety of psychological disorders whose primary feature is a physical problem. Psychological factors and physical problems influence each other reciprocally.

2. The urine alarm is an efficient and effective treatment of enuresis. An alarm is activated when urine comes in contact with a special pad in the child's underpants or under the bed sheet. Through repeated pairings of the alarm and bladder tension, bladder tension alone comes to awaken the child before urination starts.

3. Dry-bed training is a highly effective treatment package for enuresis that uses shaping and overcorrection to teach children the behaviors required to keep their beds dry throughout the night.

4. Behavioral treatments for tics include massed negative practice (deliberately performing the tic as rapidly as possible), changing maintaining consequences, relaxation training, and self-monitoring. Habit reversal, the most effective treatment, incorporates four components: awareness training, relaxation training, competing response training, and reinforcement. Awareness training and competing response training are the critical components.

5. When infant and toddler sleep problems are maintained by parental attention, extinction, involving withholding attention for nighttime crying, is a simple, effective treatment. Modified forms of extinction are more acceptable to parents but somewhat less effective.

6. For adult insomnia, stimulus control procedures establish a client's being in bed as a clear-cut cue only for sleeping. Relaxation training helps clients reduce muscle tension associated with insomnia prior to going to bed. Cognitive restructuring reduces worry about sleeping by identifying, challenging, and replacing maladaptive beliefs about sleep with adaptive cognitions.

7. Treatment packages involving stimulus control, relaxation training, cognitive restructuring, sleep restriction, and sleep education for insomnia are appropriate when a client's sleeping problems are the result of multiple maintaining conditions.

8. The treatment of choice for bulimia is a comprehensive cognitive-behavioral treatment package that includes self-monitoring, stimulus control, activity scheduling, cognitive restructuring, collaborative empiricism, problem solving, flooding, and relapse prevention. The treatment package reduces binge eating and purging and improves self-image, self-esteem, depression, and social functioning.

9. Behavioral treatments of addictive behaviors include aversion therapy, cue exposure, and consequential therapies. Aversion therapy pairs the addictive behavior with an aversive stimulus to discourage engaging in it. Cue exposure involves exposing the client to cues associated with the addictive behavior and preventing the client from engaging in the addictive behavior. Consequential therapies use reinforcers for abstaining from addictive behaviors and response cost for engaging in addictive behaviors.

10. Relapse prevention is a cognitive-behavioral treatment package that prepares clients who engage in addictive behaviors for future relapses by having them identify high-risk situations; develop coping skills; practice the coping skills before they are needed; and develop a balanced lifestyle. Relapse prevention also may prove to be a general procedure for increasing the long-term maintenance of treatment gains with diverse problem behaviors.

REFERENCE NOTES

1. American Psychiatric Association, 1994; World Health Organization, 1992.
2. Friedman, Sobel, Myers, Caudill, & Benson, 1995; Pallak, Cummings, Dorken, & Henke, 1995; Schell, 1996.
3. Yates, 1970; Lovibond & Coote, 1970; Oppel, Harper, & Rider, 1968.
4. American Psychiatric Association, 1994.
5. For example, Deleon & Mandell, 1966; Werry & Cohrssen, 1965; Yates, 1970.
6. Mowrer & Mowrer, 1938.
7. Friman & Vollmer, 1995.
8. Deleon & Sacks, 1972; Doleys, 1977; Houts, Berman, & Abramson, 1994; Mowrer & Mowrer, 1938; Walker, Milling, & Bonner, 1988.
9. Wagner, Johnson, Walker, Carter, & Witner, 1982.
10. Novick, 1966; Werry & Cohrssen, 1965.
11. Deleon & Sacks, 1972; Doleys, 1977.
12. Azrin, Sneed, & Foxx, 1973; Houts, Peterson, & Whelan, 1986.
13. Houts, Berman, & Abramson, 1994.
14. Azrin, Sneed, & Foxx, 1973.
15. Kimmel & Kimmel, 1970; Paschalis, Kimmel, & Kimmel, 1972.
16. Azrin, Thienes-Hontos, & Besalel-Azrin, 1979.
17. Azrin, Thienes-Hontos, & Besalel-Azrin, 1979.
18. Azrin, Sneed, & Foxx, 1974.
19. Azrin, Thienes-Hontos, & Besalel-Azrin, 1979.
20. Van Son, Van Heesch, Mulder, & Van Londen, 1995; Van Son, Mulder, & Van Londen, 1990.
21. Foxx & Azrin, 1973a, 1973b.
22. For example, Madsen, Hoffman, Thomas, Karopsak, & Madsen, 1969.
23. For example, Madsen, 1965; Madsen, Hoffman, Thomas, Karopsak, & Madsen, 1969; Mahoney, Van Wagenen, & Meyerson, 1971; Pumroy & Pumroy, 1965.
24. Foxx & Azrin, 1973a.
25. American Psychiatric Association, 1994; Bauer & Shea, 1984; Cohen, Leckman, & Shaywitz, 1984.
26. Peterson & Azrin, 1993; Ross & Moldofsky, 1978; Shapiro & Shapiro, 1984; Shapiro, Shapiro, Fulop, Hubbard, Mandeli, Nordlie, & Phillips, 1989.
27. Shapiro & Shapiro, 1984.
28. Cohen, Leckman, & Shaywitz, 1984.
29. Yates, 1958.
30. For example, Browning & Stover, 1971; Clark, 1966; Storms, 1985.
31. Azrin & Peterson, 1988a; Turpin, 1983.
32. For example, Browning & Stover, 1971; Doleys & Kurtz, 1974; Miller, 1970; Schulman, 1974; Tophoff, 1973; Varni, Boyd, & Cataldo, 1978; Wagaman, Miltenberger, & Woods, 1995.
33. Wagaman, Miltenberger, & Williams, 1995.
34. Azrin & Peterson, 1988a.
35. For example, Barr, Lovibond, & Katsaros, 1972; Clark, 1966.
36. For example, Canavan & Powell, 1981; Lahey, McNees, & McNees, 1973; Varni, Boyd, & Cataldo, 1978.
37. For example, Barr, Lovibond, & Katsaros, 1972; Canavan & Powell, 1981; Lahey, McNees, & McNees, 1973.
38. For example, Franco, 1981; Friedman, 1980.
39. Peterson & Azrin, 1990.
40. For example, Billings, 1978; Hutzell, Platzek, & Logue, 1974; Thomas, Abrams, & Johnson, 1971.
41. Azrin & Nunn, 1973.
42. Miltenberger, Fuqua, & McKinley, 1985.
43. Carr, 1995.
44. See Carr, 1995.
45. Azrin & Peterson, 1988a, 1988b, 1990; Finney, Rapoff, Hall, & Christopherson, 1983; Peterson & Azrin, 1993.
46. Peterson & Azrin, 1993.
47. Miltenberger & Fuqua, 1985; Peterson, Campise, & Azrin, 1994; Woods & Miltenberger, 1995.

48. Fleming, 1984; Friman, Finney, & Christophersen, 1984; Friman & O'Connor, 1984; Tarnowski, Rosen, McGrath & Drabman, 1987.

49. Azrin, Nunn, & Frantz-Renshaw, 1980; Christensen & Sanders, 1987.

50. De L. Horne, White, & Varigos, 1989.

51. Bebko & Lennox, 1988.

52. Peterson, Dixon, Talcott, & Kelleher, 1993.

53. For example, Wagaman, Miltenberger, & Arndorfer, 1993; Wagaman, Miltenberger, & Woods, 1995.

54. Nunn, Newton, & Faucher, 1992.

55. For example, Murtagh & Greenwood, 1995; Sloan & Shapiro, 1993.

56. For example, Murtagh & Greenwood, 1995.

57. For example, France & Hudson, 1993.

58. For example, Murtagh & Greenwood, 1995.

59. Lichstein & Riedel, 1994.

60. For example, Blampied & France, 1993; France & Hudson, 1993.

61. For example, France & Hudson, 1990, 1993; Williams, 1959.

62. For example, France & Hudson, 1990.

63. For example, Wolfson, Lacks, & Futterman, 1992.

64. France & Hudson, 1990, 1993.

65. France, 1992.

66. France, 1992.

67. For example, Pritchard & Appleton, 1988.

68. For example, Durand & Mindell, 1990; Rolider & Van Houten, 1984.

69. For example, Lawton, France, & Blampied, 1991.

70. For example, Hall & Nathan, 1992.

71. For example, Lawton, France, & Blampied, 1991.

72. Bootzin, 1972; Bootzin, Epstein, & Wood, 1991.

73. Bootzin & Engle-Friedman, 1987; France & Hudson, 1990.

74. Bootzin & Perlis, 1992; Espie, Lindsay, Brooks, Hood, & Turvey, 1989; Lichstein & Riedel, 1994; Puder, Lacks, Bertelson, & Storandt, 1983.

75. Engle-Friedman, Bootzin, Hazlewood, & Tsao, 1992; Morin & Azrin, 1987, 1988.

76. Engle-Friedman, Bootzin, Hazlewood, & Tsao, 1992.

77. Lichstein & Riedel, 1994.

78. Nicassio, Boylan, & McCabe, 1982.

79. Lacks, Bertelson, Gans, & Kunkel, 1983; Nicassio, Boylan, & McCabe, 1982.

80. Carlson & Hoyle, 1993.

81. Lichstein, 1988; Lichstein & Riedel, 1994.

82. Bootzin & Perlis, 1992; Borkovec, Grayson, & O'Brien, 1979; Hauri, 1981.

83. Bootzin & Perlis, 1992.

84. Sloan, Hauris, Bootzin, Morin, Stevenson, & Shapiro, 1993.

85. Morin, 1993; Morin, Kowatch, Barry, & Walton, 1993.

86. For example, Lichstein & Riedel, 1994; Jacobs, Benson, & Friedman, 1993.

87. Morin, Stone, McDonald, & Jones, 1994.

88. Morin, Kowatch, Barry, & Walton, 1993.

89. Jacobs, Rosenberg, Friedman, Matheson, Peavy, Domar, & Benson, 1993.

90. Morin, Stone, McDonald, & Jones, 1994.

91. Lacks & Morin, 1992; Murtagh & Greenwood, 1995.

92. American Psychiatric Association, 1994.

93. American Psychiatric Association, 1994.

94. Smith, Marcus, & Eldredge, 1994.

95. Olmsted, Davis, Rockert, Irvine, Eagle, & Garner, 1991.

96. For example, Heatherton & Baumeister, 1991.

97. Smith, Marcus, & Eldredge, 1994.

98. Kennedy, Katz, Neitzert, Ralevski, & Mendlowitz, 1995; Leitenberg, 1993.

99. Wilson, Eldredge, Smith, & Niles, 1991.

100. Agras, Schneider, Arnow, Raeburn, & Telch, 1989.

101. Smith, Marcus, & Eldredge, 1994; Sturmey, 1992.

102. Keller, Herzog, Lavori, Bradburn, & Mahoney, 1992.

103. Mitchell, Pyle, Hatsukami, Goff, Glotter, & Harper, 1989.

104. Agras, 1993; Fairburn, Marcus, & Wilson, 1993; Mitchell, Raymond, & Specker, 1993.

105. Wilson & Fairburn, 1993.

106. Kirkley, Schneider, Agras, & Bachman, 1985.

107. Leitenberg, Rosen, Wolf, Vara, Detzer, & Srebnik, 1994; Wilson & Fairburn, 1993.

108. For example, Fairburn, Jones, Peveler, Hope, & O'Connor, 1993.

109. For example, Thackwray, Smith, Bodfish, & Meyers, 1993.

110. Thackwray, Smith, Bodfish, & Meyers, 1993; compare with Wolf & Crowther, 1992.

111. For example, Garner, Rockert, Davis, Garner, Olmsted, & Eagle, 1993.

112. For example, Fairburn, Peveler, Jones, Hope, & Doll, 1993.

113. Spiegler, 1983.

114. For example, Marlatt & Barrett, 1994.

115. Lichtenstein, Harris, Birchler, Wahl, & Schmahl, 1973; Lichtenstein & Rodrigues, 1977.

116. Lando, 1975; Raw & Russell, 1980; Sutherland, Amit, Golden, & Rosenberger, 1975.
117. Dawley & Dillenkoffer, 1975; Hauser, 1974; Horan, Hackett, Nicholas, Linberg, Stone, & Lukaski, 1977; Lichtenstein & Glasgow, 1977; Poole, Sanson-Fisher, German, & Harker, 1980.
118. For example, Lee & Oei, 1993; Monti, Abrams, Kadden, & Cooney, 1989.
119. For example, Monti, Rohsenow, Rubonis, Niaura, Sirota, Colby, Goddard, & Abrams, 1993.
120. For example, Higgins, Budney, Bickel, Foerg, Donham, & Badger, 1994; Shaner, Eckman, & Roberts, 1994.
121. Shaner, Eckman, & Roberts, 1994.
122. Boudin, 1972.
123. Marlatt, 1982; Marlatt & Barrett, 1994; Marlatt & Gordon, 1985.
124. Marlatt & Gordon, 1985.
125. Marlatt & Barrett, 1994.
126. Marlatt & Barrett, 1994.
127. Liese, 1994.
128. Collier & Marlatt, 1995; Marlatt & Tapert, 1993.
129. Collier & Marlatt, 1995.
130. For example, Peterson & Lowe, 1992; Somers & Marlatt, 1992.
131. For example, Dooley & Halford, 1992; Gruder, Mermelstein, Kirkendol, Hedeker, Wong, Schreckengost, Warnecke, Burzette, & Miller, 1993.
132. For example, Carroll, Rounsaville, & Gawin, 1991; Wallace, 1992.
133. For example, Stephens, Roffman, & Simpson, 1994.
134. For example, Chang, Carroll, Behr, & Kosten, 1992.
135. For example, O'Farrell, 1994; O'Farrell, Cutter, Choquette, Floyd, & Bayog, 1992.
136. For example, Minneker-Hugel, Unland, & Buchkremer, 1992.
137. Wells, Peterson, Gainey, Hawkins, & Catalano, 1994.
138. For example, Corrigan, Thompson, & Malow, 1992.
139. Gillies, Hashmall, Hilton, & Webster, 1992.
140. For example, Carroll, 1996; Hollon & Beck, 1994.
141. Minneker-Hugel, Unland, & Buchkremer, 1992.
142. For example, Carroll, Rounsaville, & Gawin, 1991; Wells, Peterson, Gainey, Hawkins, & Catalano, 1994.
143. Carroll, 1996; Carroll, Rounsaville, & Gawin, 1991.
144. Carroll, 1996; Wells, Peterson, Gainey, Hawkins, & Catalano, 1994.
145. For example, Mazur & Michael, 1992.
146. For eample, Chang, Carroll, Behr, & Kosten, 1992.
147. Brown, Lichtenstein, McIntyre, & Harrington-Kostur, 1984; Carmody, 1992; Minneker-Hugel, Unland, & Buchkremer, 1992.

Chapter 16

Beyond Behavior Therapy: Behavioral Community Psychology

The principles and procedures of behavior therapy used to change clients' problem behaviors can be harnessed to change any behaviors. In Chapters 14 and 15, you read about the application of behavior therapy to medical disorders and to psychological disorders with physical characteristics. In this chapter, we will examine some intriguing applications of behavior therapy principles to concerns of daily living that affect individuals and society. These applications fall under the rubric of **behavioral community psychology,** a subfield of behavior therapy that employs behavior therapy technology to deal with problems affecting the population at large.[1] We will describe applications in four areas: promoting safety, reducing and preventing crime, promoting healthful behaviors, and preserving the natural environment.

◆ ▬▬▬▬▬▬▬▬▬▬▬▬▬▬▬▬▬▬▬▬▬▬▬▬▬▬▬▬▬▬▬▬

Participation Exercise 16-1   SOLVING SOCIETAL PROBLEMS WITH BEHAVIORAL INTERVENTIONS*

You already are familiar with the components of behavioral community psychology—that is, the societal problems addressed and the behavior therapy procedures used to deal with them. Combining these components is new to you. You may, however, be able to anticipate some of the ways behavioral procedures have been used to solve societal problems.

For each problem that follows, (1) develop a target behavior; (2) identify its probable maintaining conditions; and (3) choose behavioral procedures that could be used to change the maintaining conditions. Write this information on Work Sheet 16-1.† Figure 16-1 provides an example.

A. Safety
   A1. Wearing seat belts in a car
   A2. Preventing child abduction
   A3. Preventing child molestation
   A4. Teaching children what to do in case of fire
B. Crime Reduction/Prevention
   B1. Reducing shoplifting
   B2. Reducing students' destruction of school property
C. Promoting Healthful Behaviors
   C1. Choosing healthy foods (for example, low-fat and low-calorie foods) in a restaurant
   C2. Taking children for recommended vaccinations
D. Preserving the Natural Environment
   D1. Reducing littering in public places
   D2. Sorting and recycling beverage containers and paper
   D3. Reducing electricity consumed at home
   D4. Reducing automobile use

* You should do this Participation Exercise before you continue.

Figure 16-1 Part of a completed Work Sheet 16-1 (Participation Exercise 16-1)

Problem	Target Behavior	Maintaining Conditions	Intervention
Factory workers exposed to toxic chemicals	Wearing protective clothing	No immediate payoff for compliance because detrimental effects are long-term	Signs to remind (prompt) workers about exposure dangers and small salary bonuses for compliance during periodic, unannounced checks by supervisor

This Participation Exercise can be done in two ways. You can devise interventions for all the problems listed before reading any further, or you can develop interventions for the problems in each of the four areas (safety, crime, healthful behaviors, and environmental concerns) before reading about each area.

As you read this chapter, compare your ideas with the interventions behavioral community psychologists have already implemented. You may, in fact, generate new possibilities that could benefit society.

♦

PROMOTING SAFETY

Changing people's behaviors to make their lives safer has been a prime target of behavioral community psychology. We will illustrate these endeavors by looking at four areas of safety: using seat belts in automobiles; preventing child abduction and sexual abuse; teaching children basic survival skills; and reducing the risks of occupational hazards.

Wearing Seat Belts

Motor vehicle accidents result in more than 45,000 deaths and 500,000 injuries each year.[2] This toll could be reduced by 55% or more with the consistent use of seat belts (also referred to as *safety belts*).[3] Despite widespread educational campaigns and laws aimed at promoting seat belt use,

† You will find this work sheet in Appendix C.

E. Scott Geller

only about 33% to 50% of vehicle occupants buckle up.[4] Behavioral interventions have been moderately successful in promoting seat belt use.

Prompting and incentives are the primary interventions employed to encourage people to wear seat belts (see Figure 16-2).[5] Generally, incentives have proved more potent than prompts alone. Demonstration projects have been conducted in a variety of settings, including fast food restaurants,[6] banks,[7] shopping malls,[8] industries,[9] high schools,[10] and colleges.[11] This work has been spearheaded by E. Scott Geller, a leading researcher and spokesperson in behavioral community psychology.

One of Geller's programs used prompts and an incentive system to motivate seat belt use at a large munitions plant.[12] Seat belt use was assessed on a daily basis at the gate of the industrial complex. Employees were given fliers that (1) prompted seat belt use and (2) provided information about prizes that could be won by workers wearing seat belts. The prizes were gift certificates from local businesses. The fliers given to drivers wearing seat belts contained a contest symbol, which made them eligible to win a prize (see Figure 16-3). The fliers given to drivers not wearing seat belts had no contest symbol but contained the message "Next Time Wear Your Seat Belt and Receive a Chance to Win a Valuable Prize." The intervention was implemented in the afternoon as employees were leaving work.

Before the intervention (during baseline), seat belt use averaged 20% when employees arrived at work in the morning and 17% when they left work in the afternoon. The incentives increased seat belt use to 31% in the

Figure 16-2 Flier to promote seat belt use through prompts and incentives
SOURCE: Courtesy of E. Scott Geller.

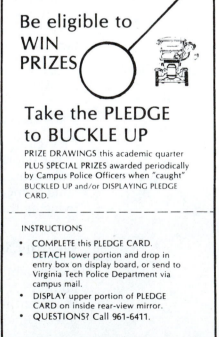

FRONT   BACK

Figure 16-3 Flier that people wearing seat belts received
SOURCE: Courtesy of E. Scott Geller.

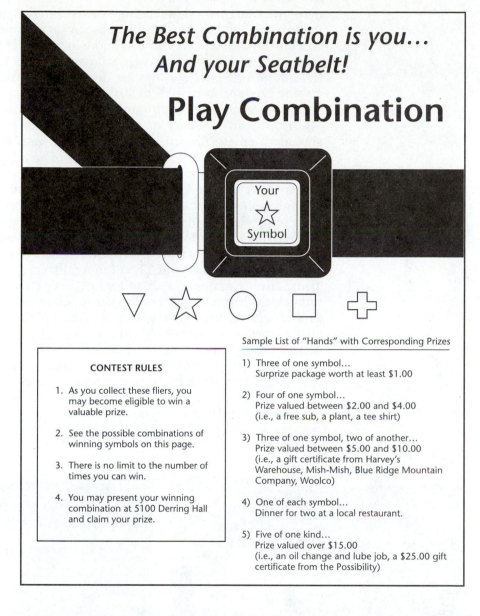

morning and 55% in the afternoon. However, at a 30-day follow-up, the average seat belt use had dropped to approximately baseline levels. More recent seat belt promotion programs have found some residual positive effects of the interventions 6 to 18 months after the seat belt campaigns had ended. Greater involvement of the participants in the intervention is one factor that appears to contribute to an enduring effect.[13]

Prompts alone can increase seat belt use, although generally less effectively than incentives.[14] However, prompts are less expensive, which is an important consideration because seat belt promotion programs are aimed at large groups. Signs are the most economical type of prompt. One program demonstrated that a sign reading "Fasten Safety Belt" posted at the exit of two parking lots increased seat belt use by an average of 23% more than the baseline level in one lot and 10% more in the other lot.[15] Having a woman hold the sign resulted in average increases of 31% and 19%. The success of this prompting program may be due partly to the fact that participants already used seat belts 40% to 50% of the time.

Another program for prompting seat belt use was called "Flash for Life." The front-seat passenger of a stopped vehicle, who was buckled into a shoulder harness, flashed an 11- by 14-inch card that read "Please Buckle Up/I Care" (see Photo 16-1a) to the driver of an adjacent stopped vehicle.[16] If the driver was observed putting on his or her seat belt as a result of the prompt, the "flasher" flipped over the card, which revealed the words "Thank You for Buckling Up" (see Photo 16-1b) to the driver. Besides prompting, the "Flash for Life" program included modeling (the flasher was buckled up) and reinforcement (the "Thank You" sign). Of the nearly 1,100 drivers not using their seat belts who were flashed with the card, 82% turned and looked at the card and 22% of these drivers complied with the request. Thus, the "Flash for Life" procedure was effective in getting 18% of unbuckled drivers to put on their seat belts immediately. The prompter's gender and age (which ranged from 3½ to 23) made no difference in the effectiveness of the intervention. The rate of compliance was higher in a college community (25%) than in a rural town (14%). This was probably due to the fact that the college community had a larger proportion of people with characteristics of individuals who are more likely to use seat belts (for example, highly educated, white-collar, and subcompact car drivers).

Distributing stickers for the dashboard is less effective than posting signs, perhaps because people do not notice the stickers or because they fail to put

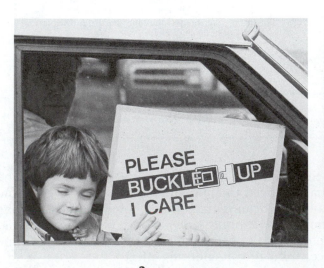

a   b

Photos 16-1a and b   (a) Front-seat passenger (3½-year-old Karly) in a stopped car prompting the driver in an adjacent stopped car to buckle up. (b) When Karly's prompt works, she flips over the flash card to reinforce the driver's buckling up.

them on their dashboards.[17] One way to increase the effectiveness of stickers is to remind people about the consequences of failure to use seat belts (for example, the reduction in workers' compensation benefits for a person who was not wearing a seat belt in an automobile accident).[18] Additionally, prompts may serve to maintain seat belt use even when consequences are no longer in effect. This occurred in two Canadian cities where signs reading "Safety Belt Use Enforced Day & Night" remained posted after police enforcement had ended.[19]

Few behavioral programs have focused on the use of child restraints, despite the fact that automobile crashes are the leading cause of death of children in the United States. Compliance with mandatory laws for child safety seats or belts typically ranges from 10% to 30%.[20] Providing reinforcers to parents[21] or directly to children[22] produces only short-term compliance.

One promising treatment package for young children (average age was 5.1) consisted of education and modeling, assertion training, behavior rehearsal, and reinforcement.[23] A trainer presented facts about seat belt use and described popular role models who use them, such as race car drivers and pilots. The children were taught how to assert themselves about seat belt use (for example, asking for help buckling the belt or requesting that the car not move until the belt is fastened). They also practiced buckling themselves into different types of seat belts. Finally, the children were reinforced with coupons for a lottery (based on very favorable odds) in which they could win small, inexpensive items (such as stickers and coloring books) for wearing their seat belts. Seat belt use was observed unobtrusively by the teachers' aides who walked the children to their parents' cars at the end of the school day.

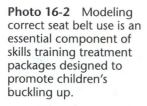

Photo 16-2 Modeling correct seat belt use is an essential component of skills training treatment packages designed to promote children's buckling up.

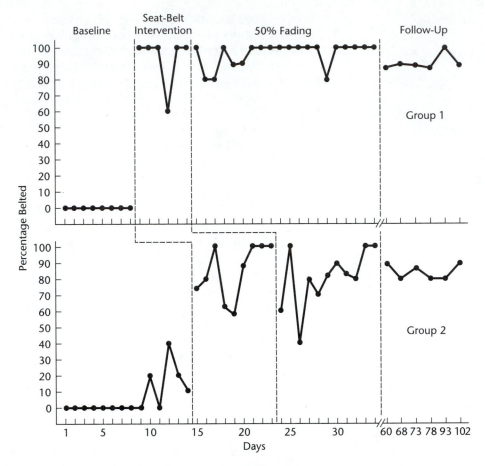

Figure 16-4 Percentage of seat belt use by children in two groups who received skills training to promote seat belt use
SOURCE: Sowers-Hoag, Thyer, & Bailey, 1987.

The program was effective for two groups of eight children. As you can see in Figure 16-4, the children rarely had used seat belts before the training program, and the program dramatically increased their seat belt use. Most impressively, two months after all interventions had been discontinued, the high compliance persisted.

Skills training—including modeling and behavior rehearsal—may be critical treatment components for children. For example, one study compared (1) skills training and reinforcers for buckling up; (2) skills training alone; and (3) noncontingent rewards to increase seat belt use.[24] Both the skills training and the skills training plus reinforcers conditions resulted in significant increases in seat belt use. However, the critical component was the skills training intervention.

Although prompting and reinforcement have had moderate success in fostering seat belt use by adults and children, these procedures may not result in continued use. One strategy for increasing the duration of the effects is to reintroduce the programs periodically, as with booster sessions.[25] Another strategy is for both children and adults to learn and practice relevant skills.

Assertion training, for example, could help some adults to feel less awkward buckling up when other people cavalierly ignore the seat belts.

Programs for promoting seat belt use have been most effective with people who already use seat belts some of the time. Clearly, interventions for people who rarely or never use seat belts need to be developed. It also would be worthwhile to develop behavioral interventions that foster safer driving habits besides wearing seat belts. For example, designated drivers not only reduce the number of alcohol-impaired drivers on the road directly but also serve as positive role models. In one study, using prompts (framed posters and placards) and incentives (free nonalcoholic beer, soda, and coffee) doubled the number of designated drivers at a bar patronized by college students.[26]

Preventing Abduction and Sexual Abuse

Child abduction is a serious problem in the United States and other countries. Only a small percentage of abductors (10% to 17%) use force to lure their victims.[27] Typically, the abductor attempts to develop a relationship with the child or to verbally entice the child, and children usually are unskilled at acting quickly to resist abductors' inducements.[28]

Skills training interventions for teaching children to protect themselves from abduction have been spearheaded by Cheryl Poche.[29] In one of her studies, three preschool children, who appeared susceptible to abduction, were taught abduction prevention skills.[30] Potential susceptibility was assessed by having an adult male role play an abductor who approached the child and asked the child to leave the preschool with him. The "abductor" used three strategies commonly employed to lure children. These strategies are described in Table 16-1, along with the scripts used by the "abductor" in the assessment. A fully appropriate response by a child was operationally defined as follows: succinctly tells the "abductor" that he or she will not go

Table 16-1 Lures used in naturalistic role-played assessment of children's ability to avoid abduction
SOURCE: Based on Poche, Brouwer, & Swearingen, 1981.

Type of Lure	Definition	Role-Played Scenario
SIMPLE	Simple request to go with the abductor	"Abductor" approaches child, says "Hello" or "Hi, there," and engages in small talk (for example, saying"Nice day, isn't it?"). Then "abductor" says, "Would you like to go for a walk?"
AUTHORITY	Request with the implication that an authority figure (such as a parent or teacher) approves	After small talk, "abductor" says, "Would you like to go with me for a walk? Your teacher said that it was all right for you to come with me."
INCENTIVE	Request with the promise of an incentive	After small talk, "abductor" says, "I've got a nice surprise in my car. Would you like to see it?"

Photo 16-3 In child-abduction prevention training, children practice self-protection skills (such as yelling "No" and running away) in response to an adult who role plays an abductor.

with him (for example, "No, I have to ask my teacher") and runs away within three seconds.

The children were taught an appropriate response to each of the three common lures through modeling, behavior rehearsal, feedback, and social reinforcement. The training proceeded as follows:

1. Two adult trainers acted out an abduction situation, with one playing the role of the abductor and the other the child.

2. Then, the child rehearsed responding to the same situation by imitating the responses of the adult model who had played the child's role.

3. Finally, the trainer praised the child's correct responses. If the child responded incorrectly, additional modeling and behavior rehearsal were used.

The results of this training can be seen in Figure 16-5. Before training, the appropriateness of the children's responses, based on a rating from 0 to 6, was near 0. After training it was near 6. To test for generalization of the training, the children were observed in a novel setting in the community after training. All three children were given a rating of 6 for each of the lures. When the two children who remained at the preschool were given a

Figure 16-5
Appropriateness of children's self-protective responses after skills training, evaluated by a multiple baseline study
SOURCE: Adapted from Poche, Brouwer, & Swearingen, 1981.

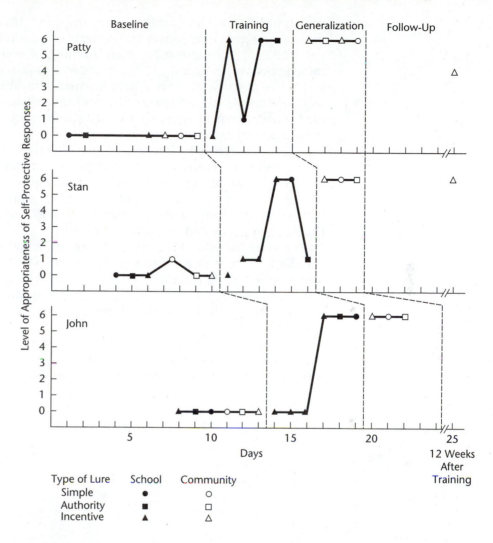

follow-up assessment 12 weeks after training, one was rated 6 and the other 4 (Patty had used an appropriate verbal statement but had remained near the "abductor").

Because all children need to learn self-protective skills, individual training by professionals is not cost-efficient. Books that parents can read to young children to teach them self-protective skills are commercially available. However, the existing books do not appear to equip children with adequate skills to resist abduction effectively,[31] probably because they do not contain the components of successful skills training—namely, modeling, behavior rehearsal, feedback, and reinforcement.[32]

These components were incorporated in a 20-minute interactive video in which child models demonstrate two safety rules: (1) saying "No, I have to go ask my teacher [or parent]" and then (2) quickly running away to the teacher (or parent). After each enticement scene, the narrator asks viewers if the child has done and said the right things.[33] After a pause, the narrator praises appropriate responses and corrects inappropriate ones by saying: "If you said _____ , you're right, good listening! If you said _____ , then I've fooled you. Watch again. . . ."[34] The video also provides an opportunity for viewers to practice what they have learned. The adult in the video directly faces and speaks to the viewers, attempting to entice them. There is a pause for the viewers' responses, after which the narrator provides feedback and praises correct responses.

Children (aged 5 to 7) who saw the video were compared with children who (1) saw the video and engaged in direct behavior rehearsal with the trainer (a police officer who visited schools to teach personal safety); (2) received standard training used in schools (60 minutes of instruction and discussion); or (3) received no formal training. The children's responses to the lures were assessed through role playing.

Viewing the modeling video was significantly more effective than the standard training or no training (see Figure 16-6). However, viewing the video alone was significantly less effective than the combination of viewing the video and behavior rehearsal. This finding indicates that direct practice is important in teaching children to protect themselves from potential abductors.

Beyond preventing abduction, children have been taught how to protect themselves from sexual abuse through behavior therapy procedures. In one program developed by Sandy Wurtele, children as young as four were first

Figure 16-6 Percentage of children in each condition who showed the appropriate verbal and motor responses after training in self-protective skills
SOURCE: Poche, Yoder, & Miltenberger, 1988.

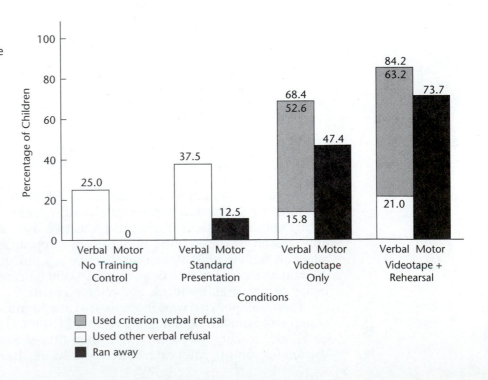

taught when it was appropriate and when it was inappropriate for "bigger people" to touch the children's "private parts," and then the children practiced discriminating between the two sets of conditions.[35] Next, they were taught what to say (for example, "No! Stop that!") and do (for instance, run away or tell someone) if an adult tried to abuse them. Stories presenting a variety of potentially dangerous situations were read to the children, who then rehearsed adaptive responses to the situations. The effectiveness of this program was evaluated by assessing (1) the children's knowledge about sexual abuse through a set of standard questions and (2) the children's skills in dealing with dangerous situations in a role-play procedure called the What If Situations Test. The test consists of six hypothetical situations, three of which are appropriate requests from an adult to touch a child's "private parts" (for example, during a medical examination) and three of which are inappropriate (for instance, by a stranger). The situations are described to the child, and the child is asked (1) whether the request is appropriate; (2) what the child would say and do; (3) whether the child would tell anyone; and (4) if the child would tell someone, to whom and what the child would say. These measures were administered before and after the program as well as in follow-up assessments four to six weeks later. The program effectively increased children's knowledge of sexual abuse and skills for protecting themselves from abuse. Further, the children were not upset by the program,[36] which is an important consideration given the frightening nature of sexual abuse.[37]

Sexual assault on adult women is no less of a problem today than is sexual abuse of children. Self-defense courses for women rely heavily on modeling to teach skills for warding off attackers. Recently, the psychological effects of such courses have been evaluated in controlled research.[38] Besides teaching women the physical skills required to defend themselves, the training can result in a reduction of perceived vulnerability to assault; a reduction of intrusive negative thoughts and anxiety; and an increase in feelings of perceived self-efficacy. Behavioral skills training packages also are used to train professionals who handle sexual harassment complaints in work settings to use appropriate listening and helping behaviors to deal with this sensitive issue.[39]

Teaching Children Basic Survival Skills

A substantial number of children spend extended time without adult supervision. One study found that approximately one-quarter of children in kindergarten through sixth grade were left unsupervised after school.[40] Such children need to be prepared to deal with multiple potential problems, ranging from feeding themselves to dealing with strangers and coping with emergencies, especially accidents. Accidents are a leading cause of death in children and most often occur in the home and in the absence of adult supervision.[41]

Do-it-yourself training manuals for parents and children are cost-effective means of providing such preparation. *Safe at Home* is a manual that uses behavioral interventions to teach children skills in four areas: (1) taking care of themselves (including preparing snacks and engaging in after-school activities); (2) dealing with strangers (for example, answering the door and talking on the telephone to strangers); (3) handling emergencies (for instance, treating cuts and reacting to fire); and (4) looking after younger children.[42] The manual trains parents to implement shaping, prompting, role playing, reinforcement, and extinction procedures to teach the skills to their children.

The effectiveness of this behavioral training manual was compared with that of a widely distributed nonbehavioral manual, *Prepared for Today,*[43] that teaches the same skills through parent-child discussions.[44] Six children, aged 7 to 10, and their parents completed the training in 8 weeks using one of the two manuals. The training was evaluated in a room that was prepared as a life-size "pretend house." The children were asked to show how they would respond to different situations if they were home alone. The children who had been trained with the behavioral manual increased their skills, generalized them to real-life settings, and maintained the skills at a 5-month follow-up. In contrast, children who had been trained with the nonbehavioral manual showed smaller and less consistent increases in their skills, which did generalize to real-life settings and were maintained at the follow-up. However, neither group of children generalized their skills to areas of home safety for which they had not been specifically trained. This finding points to the necessity of providing specific training for all needed skills or, where possible, teaching broadly applicable skills, such as problem solving.

Other safety skills that have been taught to children using behavior therapy principles include crossing streets safely,[45] making emergency phone calls,[46] and dealing with fire.[47] One program successfully taught skills for handling fire emergencies to 5 children, aged 8 and 9.[48] The specific skills for dealing with fire if the child were in bed were (1) sliding to the edge of the bed; (2) rolling out of bed; (3) getting into a crawl position; (4) covering the crack under the door; and (5) rolling on the ground if clothes catch fire. The skills were taught and practiced in the context of 9 home fire emergency situations (for example, "The bedroom door is hot, and you cannot leave through a window without help"). Individual training was conducted in a simulated bedroom. Direct instruction, modeling, behavior rehearsal, shaping, feedback, and reinforcement were used to teach the fire emergency skills. Whereas prior to training the children performed an average of less than 5% of the correct emergency behaviors, during training this figure increased to an average of 74%. At a 2-week posttraining assessment, all 5 children performed perfectly (100%). To assess the social validity of the training, professional firefighters evaluated the children's posttraining performance. The firefighters judged the children's behaviors after training to be significantly less likely than before training to result in their being overcome by smoke, severely burned, or burned to death. Similar approaches have been used to teach fire escape skills to children with severe developmental disabilities, such as autistic disorder.[49]

Photo 16-4 Behavior rehearsal of two fire emergency skills: assuming a crawling position and covering mouth and nose with an article of clothing

Promoting Occupational Safety

Reducing injuries and health hazards in work settings is another area in which behavioral interventions have shown promise.[50] We will look at examples of behavioral interventions used to reduce the hazards of working in a mine and the dangers of exposure to toxic substances.

Mining is a hazardous occupation in which many workers are killed or injured each year. A token economy was instituted to increase safety practices in two open-pit mines.[51] These mines had especially poor safety records; the number of days lost because of injuries was three times the national average at one mine and eight times the national average at the other. Miners who suffered no injuries resulting in lost time or compensation during the month earned a specified number of trading stamps that could be exchanged for a wide selection of merchandise. The higher the injury risk of a miner's job, the more stamps the worker could earn. The miners earned bonus trading stamps for making safety suggestions that were subsequently adopted at the mine. A group contingency also was instituted whereby miners were awarded trading stamps if all the members of their work group remained injury-free during the month.

The token economy resulted in large reductions in (1) the number of days lost from work due to injuries (see Figure 16-7a); (2) the number of lost-time injuries (see Figure 16-7b); and (3) the cost of accidents and injuries (see Figure 16-7c). The number of days lost from work due to injuries changed from 8 times the national average to one-fourth of the national average at one mine and from 3 times to one-twelfth of the national average at the other mine. The token economy remained in effect for more than 11 years with continued impressive results.

Exposure to toxic substances is a major contributor to occupational health problems in the United States.[52] Styrene, for example, is a common industrial chemical with multiple toxic effects, including eye irritation, neurological damage, and cancer. Styrene can enter the body by being inhaled, ingested, or absorbed through the skin. The highest exposure to styrene occurs in industries that produce fiberglass-reinforced plastics.

Figure 16-7a Yearly days lost from work because of work-related injuries in two mines
SOURCE: Fox, Hopkins, & Anger, 1987.

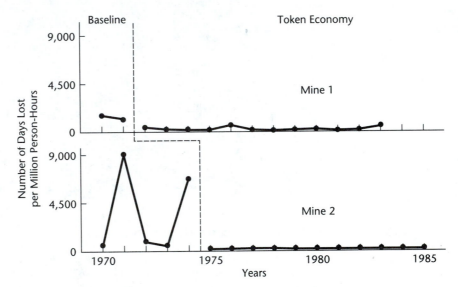

Figure 16-7b Yearly work-related injuries requiring one or more days lost from work in two mines
SOURCE: Fox, Hopkins, & Anger, 1987.

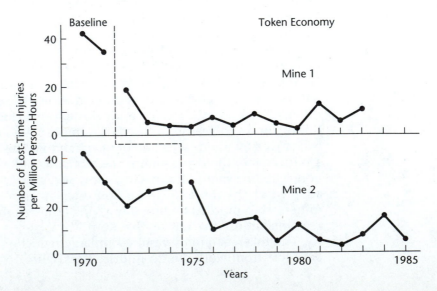

Figure 16-7c Yearly costs resulting from accidents and injuries in two mines
SOURCE: Fox, Hopkins, & Anger, 1987.

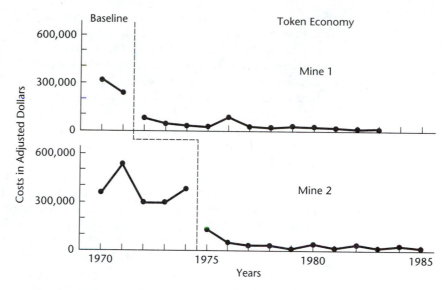

At a plant that manufactured laboratory equipment, a behavioral program was developed to reduce workers' exposure to styrene.[53] Four workers who were engaged in 4 different high-exposure operations were given 10 to 15 minutes of training. Direct instruction, modeling, and prompting were used to teach the workers behaviors that would reduce their exposure to styrene, such as wearing a respirator. After the brief training, the trainer visited each worker twice a day for 1 to 2 minutes to praise the worker's engaging in recommended behaviors and to prompt behaviors not being performed.

These inexpensive on-the-job training and maintenance procedures resulted in an increase in the workers' safety behaviors. Further, air samples taken before and after training indicated that there was a substantial decrease in styrene present in the areas that had had the highest exposure to styrene.

Another cost-effective approach to fostering occupational safety employs *safety coaches*.[54] One worker, serving as the safety coach, systematically observes another worker and provides that worker with constructive feedback about safe and unsafe practices. Potentially, this intervention also can increase the safe work behaviors of the coach because in the act of coaching, the coach learns and is reminded of the safe practices.

Unnecessary exposure to x-rays during routine dental diagnostic screening is a potential health hazard for the population at large. Exposure can be minimized if dental professionals provide patients with lead aprons. Although the use of lead shielding during x-ray examinations is recommended and is required by law in some states,[55] shielding often is not used.[56] One approach to this problem is to educate consumers about the importance of lead shielding.[57] The other approach is to encourage dental professionals to protect their patients with shielding.

In one program, feedback and prompts were employed to encourage dentists and dental assistants to use shielding for their patients.[58] Dental offices that routinely provided shielding for their patients less than 75% of the time were identified by a clever, unobtrusive observation and telephone survey procedure. The license plate numbers of cars in the parking lots of 16 dental offices were recorded, and the names and telephone numbers of their owners were obtained with the cooperation of the state motor vehicle department. The owners were called, and the adult in the household who had the most recent dental appointment was interviewed. That person was asked whether he or she had received an x-ray examination and, if so, whether a lead apron had been provided. The answers to the latter question provided the baseline rate of lead apron use. The same telephone survey method was employed to assess changes in the target behavior.

The 8 dental offices that fell below the 75% criterion of lead apron use received a feedback/prompting package consisting of (1) general information about the dangers of unnecessary x-ray exposure; (2) specific feedback about each individual office's use of lead aprons during the baseline period (from the telephone survey); (3) a respectful request that the dental office provide aprons; and (4) 2 stickers that read "Use Lead Apron" to place directly on the x-ray machine. The remaining 8 offices, which were using shields at least 75% of the time, received specific feedback but no sticker prompts. These offices also received a commendation praising them for their routine use of lead aprons.

These feedback/prompting procedures increased lead apron use in all the dental offices, and these gains were maintained at a 9-month follow-up. During baseline observations, the offices below the 75% criterion provided aprons 30% to 50% of the time; this figure increased to 90% to 100% after the feedback/prompting intervention. The dental offices that originally had had acceptable levels of apron use (at least 75%) also improved, approaching 100% after receiving the feedback/commendation intervention.

REDUCING AND PREVENTING CRIME

Behavioral technology can play a role in preventing minor crimes.[59] For example, shoplifting is one of the most common crimes in the United

Shoplifting is situation specific.
Wizard of Id by permission of Johnny Hart and Creators Syndicate, Inc.

States.[60] Typically, prompts in the form of warning signs are employed to discourage shoplifting. Such general prompts were compared with more specific prompts to reduce shoplifting in the clothing section of a small department store.[61] The general prompts were posted signs stating that shoplifting is stealing, is a crime, and increases prices. The specific prompts consisted of signs reading "Attention Shoppers & Shoplifters—The items you see marked with a red star are items that shoplifters frequently take." Five-inch red stars were mounted on racks holding the targeted clothes. Although both prompts reduced shoplifting, the specific prompts virtually eliminated shoplifting.

Another approach to reducing shoplifting has been to inform employees about the status of thefts in the store.[62] Employees in a grocery store in Uppsala, Sweden, were provided with a list of the most frequently stolen items in three categories of merchandise (candy, hygiene, and jewelry). Employees also were given feedback about actual losses through a graph posted biweekly in the employee lunch room. This simple intervention resulted in clear-cut reductions in the number of stolen items (see Figure 16-8). One or both of two explanations might account for the reductions. Employees may have reduced their own theft of merchandise due to their heightened awareness about shoplifting and the increased threat of detection. Alternatively, employees may have increased their vigilance of customers with respect to the high-risk items, thereby reducing theft by customers.

A different kind of intervention was used to decrease vandalism and disruptive behaviors in elementary and junior high schools.[63] In many schools, teachers' disapproval typically is more prevalent than teachers' approval,[64] and aggressive behaviors are one of the side effects of the use of such negative consequences (see Chapter 7). Assuming that the vandalism and disruptive behaviors in the classroom are maintained by these negative consequences, the goal of the program was to increase the teachers' use of reinforcement.

Teachers were trained in basic behavior therapy procedures for modifying antisocial behaviors through workshops and ongoing consultation. The emphasis was on accelerating prosocial behaviors through positive reinforcement (for example, token systems and group contingency games) rather than directly decelerating antisocial behaviors with negative consequences (such as disapproval, low grades, and disciplinary measures).

Over a 3-year period, teachers in 9 schools received the training and consultation, and they were compared with teachers in 9 other schools who received no training or consultation. The behavioral training and consultation significantly reduced vandalism by an average of 79% (measured by the cost of repairing or replacing damage). At the same time, the frequency of teachers' reinforcement of students increased significantly in the intervention schools, which indicates that the goal of the program was achieved. Moreover, there was a significant decrease in disruptive behaviors in the classroom for students in the intervention schools.

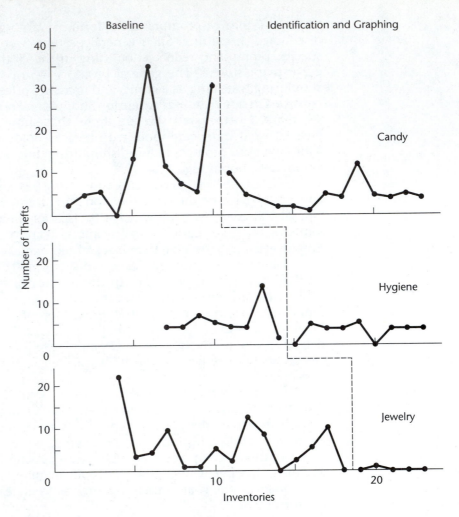

Figure 16-8 Effects on subsequent thefts of informing store employees of items stolen, evaluated by a multiple-baseline design
SOURCE: Carter, Holmstrom, Simpanen, & Melin, 1988, p. 388.

PROMOTING HEALTHFUL BEHAVIORS

In Chapter 14 we described how behavior therapy procedures are used to treat and prevent physical illness. Promoting healthful behaviors is a related application, and we will consider two examples: making healthy food choices and obtaining vaccinations.

Making Healthy Food Choices

Making healthy food choices—a behavior with broad implications for preventing many diseases—can be increased by simple, inexpensive stimulus control procedures. For example, in a cafeteria, labels reading "Lower-Calorie Selection" were placed over the three salads and vegetables that were lowest in calories.[65] The frequency of purchasing lower-calorie salads and vegetables increased from baseline levels immediately after labeling was implemented and then decreased to baseline levels immediately after it was terminated. This pattern indicates that patrons' choices of lower-caloric foods were indeed influenced by the labeling. You can see these changes in Figure 16-9, which shows the results of a combination multiple-baseline, reversal (ABA) study used to evaluate the labeling procedure. Notice that

Figure 16-9   Effects of calorie labeling on the probability of purchasing low-calorie items, evaluated by a combination multiple-baseline, reversal study
SOURCE: Dubbert, Johnson, Schlundt, & Montague, 1984, p. 88.

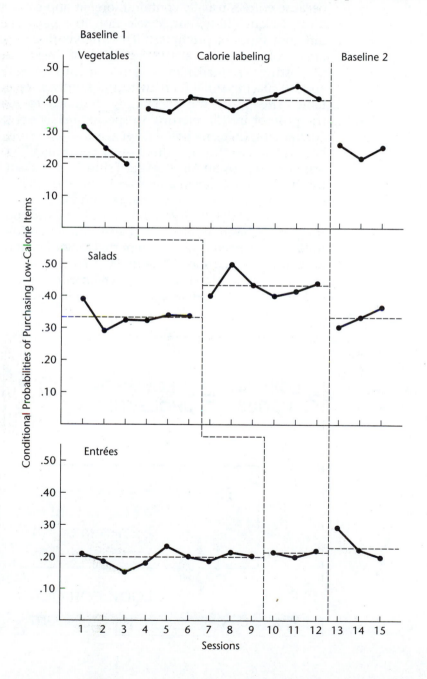

labeling of the lowest-calorie entrées—as opposed to salads and vegetables— did not influence patrons' selections. One explanation, which is consistent with previous findings,[66] is that people's main course selections may be more firmly established and therefore more resistant to change than their preferences for side dishes.

Making healthier entrée selections is an important target behavior because entrées usually contain more fat and calories than other parts of a meal. In one study, entrée selection in a cafeteria was changed using 3 different types of prompts.[67] The intervention consisted of (1) posting a large, colorful poster at the beginning of the food line (see Figure 16-10); (2) posting two smaller low-fat entrée menus where the entrées were located; and (3) placing small fliers (with the same message as the poster) on each table. The poster was specifically designed to maximize the impact of the prompt by (1) referring to specific behaviors that were desirable and convenient; (2) using polite language; and (3) being placed where the target behavior—selecting an entrée—was performed.[68] The prompting package was evaluated by an ABAB reversal study. As you can see in Figure 16-11, the intervention resulted in a substantial increase (85%) in purchases of low-fat entrées; a reduction in low-fat entrée purchases occurred when the prompts were removed (Baseline 2). Finally, low-fat entrée purchases increased when the prompts were implemented again (Intervention 2). Another study that used similar specific prompts reported a significant increase in sales of salads at a national fast food restaurant.[69] The use of prompts (such as verbal reminders and menu fliers) and social reinforcement also has been effective in improving the dietary choices of the elderly.[70]

Figure 16-10
Intervention poster used to prompt selection of low-fat entrées
SOURCE: Mayer, Heins, Vogel, Morrison, Lankester, & Jacobs, 1986, p. 399.

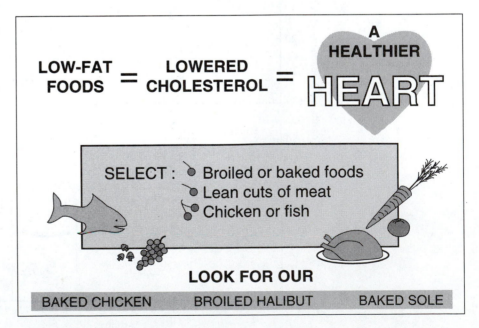

Figure 16-11 Effects of prompts on low-fat entrée selection, evaluated by a reversal study

SOURCE: Mayer, Heins, Vogel, Morrison, Lankester, & Jacobs, 1986, p. 400.

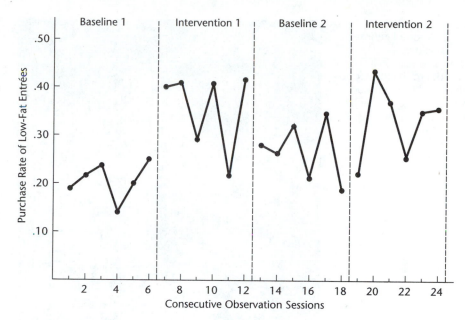

A more complex modeling intervention was used to modify food purchases in a supermarket.[71] The objective was to reduce fat content and increase complex carbohydrate content in shoppers' meals while reducing the cost of their purchases. A 30-minute modeling video, entitled *Optimal Nutrition/Saving Money,* presented a couple's engaging in a variety of behaviors related to purchasing food. In the video, the couple (1) decide to change their dietary habits; (2) gather relevant information; (3) try new practices (such as using a shopping list) and new types of meals (for example, vegetarian); and (4) overcome resistances (for example, false beliefs about nutrition) and obstacles (for instance, the inconvenience of packing nutritious lunches, such as salads).

The effectiveness of this modeling video was compared with (1) direct instruction, (2) participant modeling, (3) discussion about nutrition, and (4) written feedback about the nutritional value of weekly food purchases. The participants in this study were 126 households in a university town (population 40,000). The combination of modeling and feedback was found to be most effective in reducing fat consumption.

In order to reach a wider audience, an automated, interactive nutrition information system was developed.[72] The "Nutrition for a Lifetime System" provides supermarket customers with a series of two- to eight-minute informational videos, which change weekly. Shoppers can test their knowledge of sound food choices and plan food purchases by using a touch screen that accesses a computer program (see Photo 16-5). Initial testing of the system indicated that users decreased their high-fat purchases and increased their high-fiber purchases.

Photo 16-5   The
"Nutrition for a Lifetime
System" allows
shoppers to test their
knowledge of healthy food
choices and to plan food
purchases using interactive
computer programs.

Obtaining Vaccinations

People's reluctance to obtain necessary health care for themselves and their children is a major obstacle for the medical and dental professions. Vaccinations are a prime example. A number of potentially fatal communicable childhood diseases—such as polio, tuberculosis, tetanus, and rubella—are preventable through inoculations. In the United States, where vaccines are readily available, there may be as many as 10,000 reported cases a year of illness due to failure to obtain vaccinations.[73]

Specific prompts and incentives can increase parents' obtaining immunizations for their children. A study evaluating the effects of various prompting and incentive procedures was conducted in a public health clinic with all the local preschool children who needed one or more inoculations (54%; a total of 1133 children).[74] The interventions compared were:

1. *General prompt:* a mailed notice containing general inoculation information and instructions to make an appointment at the clinic

2. *Specific prompt:* a mailed notice containing client-specific information (for example, naming the child and the particular inoculations needed)

3. *Specific prompt with increased access:* the specific prompt along with information on the availability of two special off-hour clinics and additional clinic hours that included child care

4. *Specific prompt with a monetary incentive:* the specific prompt plus a chance to win a $175 lottery if parents brought their children for inoculations

These four interventions were compared with a no-contact control group and a telephone-contact control group (in which families received a telephone request for basic inoculation and demographic information with no reminder to bring their children to the clinic).

The specific prompt with a monetary incentive clearly was the most effective intervention, resulting in the greatest number of inoculations. It was followed by the specific prompt with increased access and then the specific prompt alone. The general prompt resulted in only a slight increase in inoculations compared with the control groups. In a related program, specific prompts (multiple mail and telephone contacts) and incentives (a coupon redeemable for $5 or a selected gift) have been effective in encouraging low-income parents to bring their children for dental care.[75]

Preserving the Natural Environment

Behavioral interventions have been developed to address ecological issues, such as environmental pollution and energy conservation. For the most part, a combination of prompts, incentives, and reinforcers has been tried. Prompts alone generally have had little effect on changing people's environmentally related behaviors. For example, signs, pamphlets, and television commercials have not been successful in reducing littering[76] or promoting energy conservation.[77] Changing maintaining consequences—primarily by providing reinforcers for participating in ecologically sound practices—has proved more potent. We will describe programs that have addressed four ecological issues: littering, recycling, energy conservation, and air pollution.

Reducing Littering

Tangible incentives have been effective in motivating both children and adults to dispose of trash properly. Programs have been carried out in diverse settings, including movie theaters,[78] wilderness recreational areas,[79] zoos,[80] and the yards of low-income urban housing.[81] Money is most frequently offered for cleaning up. Tickets for admission to movies and for soft drinks as well as attractive items for young children (such as Smokey the Bear patches or comic books) also have been effective.

The essential role of incentives in promoting antilitter behaviors was demonstrated in a study that compared six different procedures used in

Photo 16-6 Special trash can used to prompt and encourage proper disposal of trash

neighborhood movie theaters to encourage children to pick up litter and dispose of it properly.[82]

1. *Litterbags:* Children were given litterbags as they entered the theater and were asked to use them while in the theater.

2. *Litterbags and an announcement:* Children were given litterbags, and an announcement was made during intermission asking the children to put their trash in the bags and deposit the bags in cans in the lobby.

3. *Extra trash cans:* Extra trash cans were conspicuously placed around the theater.

4. *Antilitter cartoon:* An antilitter cartoon was shown before the movie.

5. *Litterbags and dimes:* Children were given litterbags and offered dimes for returning the litterbags filled with trash.

6. *Litterbags and tickets:* Children were given litterbags and free tickets to a special children's movie for returning the litterbags filled with trash.

As Figure 16-12 shows, the two incentive procedures—litterbags plus dimes or tickets—resulted in far more trash removal than any of the other procedures.

Figure 16-12 The percentage of litter deposited in movie theater trash cans when different antilitter procedures were in effect. The percentage of litter was determined by comparing the weight of the litter deposited in the trash cans with all the litter in the theater after the show (including litter left on the floor and picked up by staff).

SOURCE: Data from Burgess, Clark, & Hendee, 1971.

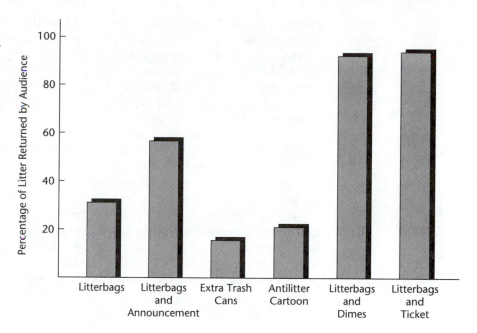

Recycling

Recycling products such as paper, cans, and bottles not only reduces litter but also conserves natural resources.[83] Providing incentives for engaging in recycling behaviors is more effective than simple prompting procedures.[84] This has been demonstrated with children collecting paper in mobile home parks[85] and in schools[86] when they were offered small prizes for recycling and also with university students recycling paper when raffles and contests were used as incentives.[87]

The State of Oregon has employed reinforcement and response cost to promote the recycling of beverage bottles. By law, only returnable bottles are sold in Oregon. A substantial deposit is paid when beverages are purchased, and it is refunded when the bottles are returned. Additionally, heavy fines are imposed for public littering. Research conducted by the Oregon Environmental Council indicates that these procedures have substantially reduced littering.[88] Recycling bottles also has resulted in significant savings in energy because fewer bottles have to be produced and discarded.

Whereas simple prompting procedures (such as reminders through mailings) are not very effective in promoting recycling, more sophisticated prompting procedures can be effective. For example, in a larger-scale study of 6,500 households, weekly recycling pickups that coincided with garbage collection resulted in higher levels of participation than recycling pickups at other times.[89] Coordinating recycling pickups with regular garbage pickups associated a well-practiced behavior—putting out the garbage for collection—with the target behavior—collecting recyclable materials. Distributing distinctive recycling containers for separating recyclable from nonrecyclable items was significantly more effective than using simple prompts alone. Participants commented that the containers helped remind them to collect recyclable materials as well as provided a convenient place to store them. The combination of (1) providing a recycling container; (2) delivering notices to the home the day before each recycling collection; and (3) placing a sticker on the mailbox of participating homes increased participation to 50%, compared with 20% to 25% during the baseline period.

Informational feedback about the success of recycling can serve as a prompt for subsequent recycling. At a university, for example, the number of aluminum cans that were deposited for recycling during the previous week was prominently displayed over recycling receptacles. This intervention resulted in a 65% increase in cans deposited.[90]

Certain characteristics of prompts appear to contribute to their effectiveness in antilitter and recycling interventions: (1) clearly specifying the target behaviors; (2) specifying alternative desirable behaviors when prompts indicate behaviors to be avoided; (3) using polite language; and (4) placing prompts in close proximity to where the target behaviors are to be performed.[91] These characteristics are similar to those identified for effective prompting of selecting healthy foods (page 458).

Conserving Residential Electricity

Ecologically aware people have long known of the limits of our supply of natural energy. However, only in the past quarter of a century—beginning with the onset of the "oil crisis" in the early 1970s—has the importance of conserving energy had widespread impact.

Both periodic feedback and contingent monetary reinforcers have been found effective in reducing residential consumption of electricity.[92] Small experimental programs have demonstrated that families can be induced to conserve electricity.[93] In one experiment, simple feedback was employed to reduce the total residential electricity use of 20 consumers.[94] The families were sent an official-looking form letter each month indicating changes in their energy consumption from previous years (see Figure 16-13). Compared with 20 control consumers who did not receive the feedback, the consumers sent the monthly letters significantly decreased their electricity consumption while the feedback program remained in effect.

Weekly cash payments were given to residents in married student housing in proportion to the amount of electricity they had saved over their individual baseline levels ($3 for a 10% to 19% reduction, $6 for a 20% to 29% reduction, and so on). This procedure resulted in reductions in electricity consumption ranging from 26% to 46%, with an average reduction of 33%, which is substantial.[95]

One-third of all apartment units in the United States have master meters, which means that residents do not pay directly for the electricity they use. Master-metered apartments consume about 35% more electricity than similar individually metered apartments, resulting in an estimated energy waste of 9.1 billion kilowatt hours per year.[96] To deal with this problem, a group contingency was instituted for residents in 166 master-metered

Figure 16-13   Monthly form letter sent to consumer households indicating changes in their energy consumption from previous years
SOURCE: Hayes & Cone, 1981, p. 84.

THIS IS NOT A BILL

Dear Consumer:

   With all the concern over energy conservation, we thought you might like to know whether you are consuming more or less electricity now than in previous years. Based on our records for this address over the last three years, your consumption of electricity this last month was:

_____ % below previous years. Congratulations! You are saving energy.

_____ % above previous years.

(For those of you who would like more detail, this last month you consumed _____ kWh of electricity, compared to the previous average of _____ kWh. At today's prices, this means you saved/spent about an extra $ _____ .)

---

apartments. The residents received biweekly checks equal to $\frac{1}{166}$ of the value of the electricity saved by the building complex. (The savings were calculated by comparing current electricity use with previous use, with current temperatures taken into account.) The residents saved 6.2% (approximately $1500). In a second building complex, residents of 255 apartments were paid 50% of the value of their savings and a onetime bonus of $5 for using 10% less electricity than during their baseline period. These residents saved 6.9% (approximately $1900).

   Modeling has been used on a community-wide basis to promote reduction in electricity consumption.[97] A 20-minute television program, entitled *Summer Breeze,* included the following components: (1) a rationale for conserving energy (for example, that it saves money); (2) a story line in which a couple are upset about their high electric bills, decide to use less energy, and are shown how to save energy and retain comfort (for example, in the summer, closing windows in the morning to trap cool air); and (3) the depiction of potential problems, instructions for overcoming them, and presentation of the positive outcomes of conserving energy. The program was aired on a local cable television station. A single viewing of the program resulted in an overall electricity savings of 10% (23% savings on the electricity used for cooling), with no reported loss of comfort.

A final example of residential electricity conservation concerns the energy consumed through elevator use. In low-rise buildings, elevators are primarily intended for people who cannot use stairs, such as the elderly. However, elevators are used more often than needed by people who could use the stairs, resulting in unnecessary elevator riding and consumption of large amounts of energy. Stimulus control and mildly aversive consequences were instituted to reduce unnecessary elevator use in four-story and five-story buildings in a small college.[98] One stimulus control procedure consisted of posting written feedback about the energy consumed by elevator users above the elevator call buttons. The other presented the same feedback and also included posters requesting that people use the stairs. Neither stimulus control procedure was successful.

In contrast, slowing down the elevator was highly effective in decreasing use. When the time for the door to open and close was increased from a normal 10 seconds to 26 seconds, one-third less energy was consumed. The change not only reduced the number of elevator trips made but also lowered the number of people using the elevators. Interestingly, energy consumption remained low after the slowdown procedure was discontinued. One possible reason is that former elevator users had changed their habits during the intervention period, and their use of the stairs was now maintained by natural reinforcers (such as not having to wait for the elevator and feeling stronger and healthier). Another possibility is that former elevator riders were unaware that the speed had been returned to normal, and they continued to avoid using the "slow" elevator.

Reducing Automobile Travel

Reducing automobile travel has the dual benefit of conserving gasoline and decreasing air pollution. Three basic approaches have been tried to reduce automobile travel: (1) reducing nonessential miles driven; (2) encouraging car pooling; and (3) promoting use of alternative forms of transportation.

One program was designed to get college students to drive fewer nonessential miles in cars.[99] The students were asked to maintain an accurate record of the nonessential miles they drove and were given money or other reinforcers (such as free car servicing or a university parking sticker) for driving fewer miles (which was assessed by periodic odometer checks). This intervention resulted in an average of almost 8 fewer miles driven per day (an average reduction of 21%).

In a business setting, drivers who decreased their mileage were given feedback on how much money they saved on gasoline that week (based on their mileage reductions from their individual baselines) as well as their projected savings in dollars for the year.[100] Drivers who increased their mileage were given feedback on how much this increase would cost them that week as well as projected on an annual basis. Reductions in mileage were reinforced with lottery tickets; the greater the reductions, the more lottery tickets the drivers earned. The drivers given feedback and lottery tickets averaged 7.9 fewer miles per day (a 15% average reduction). In contrast,

Photo 16-7 Access to express lanes is an incentive used to prompt carpooling to conserve gasoline and to reduce air pollution.

drivers in a control condition (no feedback or incentives) averaged 6.9 *more* miles per day (a 17% average increase).

Carpooling is a second approach to conserving gasoline and reducing air pollution. Many communities provide carpoolers with incentives, such as the use of express lanes and free passage on toll roads. One program to promote carpooling offered university students reserved parking spaces and token reinforcers (redeemable for 25 cents in merchandise at participating stores) each time they carpooled to the designated parking lots.[101] The program resulted in small increases in carpooling (10% in one lot and 3% in another, compared with no increases in control lots). However, the changes were maintained with only the incentive of reserved parking (that is, without token reinforcers).

A third approach to reducing automobile use is to encourage people to use alternative forms of transportation.[102] For example, during an 8-day period, people used a specially marked bus in a university community an average of 150% more when they were given tokens (shown in Figure 16-14) exchangeable for a variety of backup reinforcers, including a free bus ride, a cheeseburger, and having one's name in the newspaper for being an "eco-hero."[103] Although the intervention was successful, it did not result in

Figure 16-14 Sample token given for riding a special bus as part of a program to increase use of public transportation SOURCE: Everett, Hayward, & Meyers, 1974, p. 2.

> THANK YOU FOR RIDING ON THE RED STAR BUS
>
> ★ **ONE TOKEN** ★
>
> THESE TOKENS ARE REDEEMABLE FOR ICE CREAM, BEER, PIZZA, COFFEE, CIGARETTES, MOVIES, FLOWERS, RECORDS, ETC. CONSULT THE "BUS TOKEN EXCHANGE SHEET" (AVAILABLE ON THE RED STAR BUS) FOR A COMPLETE LIST OF AVAILABLE GOODIES AND EXCHANGE RATES. TOKENS ARE VALUABLE AND EASILY EXCHANGED AT STORES LISTED ON THE "BUS TOKEN EXCHANGE SHEET."
>
> — THANK YOU FOR BEING ECOLOGICAL —
>
> **GOOD UNTIL END OF TERM**

its intended goal—namely, reducing automobile use. Most of the people who increased their bus use previously had walked to their destinations, whereas only a few regular automobile drivers used the bus. This finding points to the importance of assessing the social validity of changes achieved by behavioral community interventions.[104] In the present case, not only did the intervention fail to impact automobile use but it actually decreased the amount of walking of some people, which certainly is not in the best interests of the individual participants or the community.

◆ ALL THINGS CONSIDERED: BEHAVIORAL COMMUNITY PSYCHOLOGY

Extending the principles and procedures of behavior therapy to everyday concerns of individuals and society is an exciting enterprise. The results of some of the behavioral community psychology projects you have read about are impressive, as, for example, interventions that reduced energy consumption by one-third.[105] The prevention focus of behavioral community psychology is admirable because prevention always is preferable to treatment. It also is noteworthy that behavioral community psychology exemplifies the implementation of behavior therapy procedures in the natural environment.

The accomplishments of behavioral community psychology are limited in one major way. Virtually all the interventions have been applied to relatively small groups of people. In other words, none has been designed for the "masses." This focus on small groups is a liability because the societal problems addressed are far-reaching, affecting large segments of—if not the entire—population. Thus, behavioral community interventions to date cannot be considered practical solutions to the problems they address. They are only demonstration projects that indicate the potential of behavioral community psychology. Furthermore, if they are to have a large-scale impact on global problems, behavioral interventions will require extensive funding, the involvement of governmental agencies, enactment of new legislation, and widespread changes in people's prevailing attitudes and possibly in social customs.

Leading researchers in behavioral community psychology, such as Geller, have acknowledged this problem. However, they believe the problem does not lie with the efficacy of the behavioral technology.[106] Rather, they attribute the limited number of large-scale and long-term applications to inadequate social adoption of the research findings. Clearly, a major challenge for behavioral community psychology is to market the important findings of research and promote the adoption of the valuable technology that is available for solving a number of significant societal problems.

Although interventions have been developed for a wide range of target behaviors of varying complexity, only a limited number of behavior therapy procedures have been used. Prompting and providing incentives or reinforcers are the primary techniques, along with occasional applications of skills training packages.

Reinforcement in the form of monetary and tangible consequences generally is the most potent intervention. This strategy is reminiscent of Skinner's vision of a Utopian society based on principles of positive reinforcement, which he described in his novel, *Walden Two*.[107] Feedback about the effects of performing the target behavior also can be effective. Although incentives and reinforcement generally are more effective than prompting alone, prompting can be a successful change strategy. Specific prompts (for example, identifying items frequently shoplifted) tend to be more effective than general prompts (for example, signs about shoplifting).[108] Effective prompting procedures are considerably more cost-effective than providing monetary or tangible incentives and reinforcers. Cost is a critical issue in behavioral community psychology because ultimately the interventions must influence large groups of people.[109]

Skills training packages, although employed less frequently than reinforcement and prompting, may prove to be the optimal intervention for many of the behaviors targeted by behavioral community psychology programs. Long-term maintenance of the behavior changes is enhanced by learning useful skills that are naturally reinforced. In contrast, prompting and reinforcement usually are terminated at some point, at which time people's behaviors typically return to their preintervention levels.

Two potential problems may arise with skills training packages. First, just because people learn skills (such as how to prevent sexual abuse or handle emergencies) does not mean that they will use the skills in real-life situations. Determining the ultimate success of skills training programs is problematic because the appropriate follow-up data are difficult to obtain. For example, in the case of teaching children to avoid abduction, it would be necessary to trace children in the program who were later confronted by abductors to determine how they responded. A second potential problem with skills training packages is that they can be costly for large numbers of people.

The degree of change obtained by behavioral community psychology interventions varies with target behaviors. Some of the target behaviors for which only small changes have been obtained are highly resistant to change.

For example, automobile seat belt use appears to be a difficult habit to foster. Consider that buckling up is easy to do, has been proven to prevent serious injuries and death, and may be mandated by law. Nonetheless, less than half the population wears seat belts.[110] Even small changes, however, can be meaningful in community-based interventions, in that the interventions often are ultimately aimed at millions of people. For instance, suppose just 10% of a small city of 50,000 people began to wear their seat belts. This would mean that 5,000 people would be significantly safer on the streets and highways.

Summary

1. Behavioral community psychology involves the application of behavior therapy principles and procedures to problems affecting the population at large.
2. Seat belt use has been increased by prompting and providing incentives and reinforcers. Incentives and reinforcers are more costly but are generally more effective than prompts alone.
3. Children have been taught self-protection skills to prevent abduction, to protect themselves from sexual abuse, and to take care of themselves when they are at home alone. Procedures used include modeling, behavior rehearsal, feedback, and reinforcement.
4. Safety practices of miners have been increased and maintained with a long-term token economy. Exposure to toxic substances has been reduced by teaching workers to take precautions. Prompts and feedback have been successful in promoting the use of lead shields by dental professionals to reduce patients' unnecessary exposure to x-rays.
5. Shoplifting has been reduced through prompts and feedback to both customers and employees. Vandalism in public schools has been reduced by training teachers to modify students' antisocial behaviors by reinforcing prosocial behaviors.
6. Prompting and reinforcement have been employed to encourage adults to make healthy food choices and to obtain vaccinations for their children.
7. Littering has been reduced by providing incentives and reinforcers for proper disposal of trash.
8. Recycling has been increased by reinforcement and specific prompts.
9. Both periodic feedback and contingent monetary reinforcers are effective in reducing residential electrical consumption. Modeling through the media also is useful. Elevator use has been reduced by applying aversive consequences for riding the elevator.
10. Automobile travel has been decreased by using reinforcement and feedback either to decrease nonessential miles driven or to increase carpooling.
11. With most behavioral community interventions, monetary and tangible consequences generally are the most effective interventions, but feedback and prompting also can be effective. Skills training is more likely to

promote continued practice of adaptive behaviors. Because large numbers of people are affected by behavioral community interventions, small changes can make an impact.

REFERENCE NOTES

1. For example, Fantuzzo & Thompson, 1991; Glenwick & Jason, 1980; Jason & Glenwick, 1984.
2. Bigelow, 1982.
3. Federal Register, 1984.
4. Geller, 1991.
5. For example, Berry & Geller, 1991; Hagenzieker, 1991; Ludwig & Geller, 1991.
6. Cope, Moy, & Grossnickle, 1988.
7. Geller, Johnson, & Pelton, 1982; Johnson & Geller, 1984.
8. Elman & Killebrew, 1987.
9. Geller, 1983; Geller & Hahn, 1984.
10. Campbell, Hunter, Stewart, & Stutts, 1982.
11. Geller, Paterson, & Talbott, 1982; Rudd & Geller, 1985.
12. Geller, 1983.
13. Geller, Rudd, Kalsher, Streff, & Lehman, 1987.
14. For example, Cope, Moy, & Grossnickle, 1988.
15. Williams, Thyer, Bailey, & Harrison, 1989.
16. Geller, Bruff, & Nimmer, 1985.
17. Cope, Moy, & Grossnickle, 1988.
18. Rogers, Rogers, Bailey, Runkle, & Moore, 1988.
19. Malenfant & Van Houten, 1988; Roberts & Turner, 1986.
20. Roberts & Turner, 1986.
21. Roberts & Turner, 1986.
22. Roberts & Fanurik, 1986.
23. Sowers-Hoag, Thyer, & Bailey, 1987.
24. Geller, 1989b.
25. Geller, 1989b.
26. Brigham, Meier, & Goodner, 1995.
27. Groth, 1980.
28. For example, Poche, Brouwer, & Swearingen, 1981.
29. Miltenberger & Thiesse-Duffy, 1988; Poche, Brouwer, & Swearingen, 1981; Poche, Yoder, & Miltenberger, 1988.
30. Poche, Brouwer, & Swearingen, 1981.
31. Miltenberger & Thiesse-Duffy, 1988; Poche, Yoder, & Miltenberger, 1988.
32. Carroll, Miltenberger, & O'Neil, 1992.
33. Poche, Yoder, & Miltenberger, 1988.
34. Poche, Yoder, & Miltenberger, 1988, p. 255.
35. Wurtele, Currier, Gillispie, & Franklin, 1991.
36. Wurtele, 1990; Wurtele, Currier, Gillispie, & Franklin, 1991; Wurtele, Marrs, & Miller-Perrin, 1987.
37. For example, Brazelton, 1987.
38. Ozer & Bandura, 1990.
39. Blaxall, Parsonson, & Robertson, 1993.
40. Chira, 1994; Peterson, 1989; Peterson, Bartelstone, Kern, & Gillies, 1995.
41. For example, Peterson, Bartelstone, Kern, & Gillies, 1995; Tokuhata, Colflesh, Digon, & Mann, 1972.
42. Peterson, 1984.
43. Boy Scouts of America, 1982.
44. Peterson, 1984.
45. Yeaton & Bailey, 1983.
46. Jones & Kazdin, 1980; Rosenbaum, Creedon, & Drabman, 1981.
47. Jones & Kazdin, 1980.
48. Jones, Kazdin, & Haney, 1981.
49. Bigelow, Huynen, & Lutzker, 1993.
50. For example, Fellner & Sulzer-Azaroff, 1984; Komaki, Barwick, & Scott, 1978; Roberts & Geller, 1995; Sulzer-Azaroff, 1982; Sulzer-Azaroff, Harris, & McCann, 1994; Zohar & Fussfeld, 1981.
51. Fox, Hopkins, & Anger, 1987.
52. For example, National Institute for Occupational Safety and Health, 1983.
53. Hopkins, Conrad, Dangel, Fitch, Smith, & Anger, 1986.
54. Geller, in press.
55. American Dental Association, 1972, 1974.
56. Laws, 1974.
57. For example, Food and Drug Administration, 1980.
58. Greene & Neistat, 1983.
59. For example, Carter, Hansson, Holmberg, & Melin, 1979; Carter, Kindstedt, & Melin, 1995; McNees, Gilliam, Schnelle, & Risley, 1979; McNees, Kennon, Schnelle, Kirchner, & Thomas, 1980; Switzer, Deal, & Bailey, 1977.
60. Weinstein, 1974.
61. McNees, Egli, Marshall, Schnelle, Schnelle, & Risley, 1976.
62. Carter, Holmstrom, Simpanen, & Melin, 1988.

63. Mayer, Butterworth, Nafpakitis, & Sulzer-Azaroff, 1983.
64. For example, Thomas, Presland, Grant, & Glynn, 1978.
65. Dubbert, Johnson, Schlundt, & Montague, 1984.
66. Zifferblatt, Wilbur, & Pinsky, 1980a, 1980b.
67. Mayer, Heins, Vogel, Morrison, Lankester, & Jacobs, 1986.
68. Geller, Winett, & Everett, 1982.
69. Wagner & Winett, 1988.
70. Stock & Milan, 1993.
71. Winett, Kramer, Walker, Malone, & Lane, 1988.
72. Winett, Moore, Wagner, Hite, Leahy, Neubauer, Walberg, Walker, Lombard, Geller, & Mundy, 1991.
73. Notifiable Diseases, 1983.
74. Yokley & Glenwick, 1984.
75. Reiss & Bailey, 1982; Reiss, Piotrowski, & Bailey, 1976.
76. Kazdin, 1977b; Kohlenberg & Phillips, 1973.
77. For example, Hayes & Cone, 1977, 1981; Kohlenberg, Phillips, & Proctor, 1976; Winett & Nietzel, 1975.
78. For example, Burgess, Clark, & Hendee, 1971.
79. For example, Clark, Burgess, & Hendee, 1972; Powers, Osborne, & Anderson, 1973.
80. For example, Kohlenberg & Phillips, 1973.
81. Chapman & Risley, 1974.
82. Burgess, Clark, & Hendee, 1971.
83. For example, Geller, Chaffee, & Ingram, 1975; Geller, Wylie, & Farris, 1971; Reid, Luyben, Rawers, & Bailey, 1976; Witmer & Geller, 1976.
84. Geller, Chaffee, & Ingram, 1975; Hamad, Cooper, & Semb, 1977; Luyben & Bailey, 1979; Witmer & Geller, 1976.
85. Luyben & Bailey, 1979.
86. Hamad, Cooper, & Semb, 1977.
87. Geller, Chaffee, & Ingram, 1975; Witmer & Geller, 1976.
88. *Oregon's Bottle Bill: The 1977 Report*, 1977.
89. Jacobs, Bailey, & Crews, 1984.
90. Larson, Houlihan, & Goernert, 1995.
91. Austin, Hatfield, Grindle, & Bailey, 1993; Geller, 1980a, 1980b.
92. For example, Becker, 1978; Palmer, Lloyd, & Lloyd, 1978; Seligman & Darley, 1977; Winett, Kagel, Battalio, & Winkler, 1978; Winett, Kaiser, & Haberkorn, 1977; Winett, Neale, & Grier, 1979; Winett & Nietzel, 1975.
93. For example, Hayes & Cone, 1977.
94. Hayes & Cone, 1981.
95. Hayes & Cone, 1977.
96. Slavin, Wodarski, & Blackburn, 1981.
97. Winett, Leckliter, Chinn, Stahl, & Love, 1985.
98. Van Houten, Nau, & Merrigan, 1981.
99. Foxx & Hake, 1977; Hake & Foxx, 1978.
100. Foxx & Schaeffer, 1981.
101. Jacobs, Fairbanks, Poche, & Bailey, 1982.
102. For example, Deslauriers & Everett, 1977; Everett, Hayward, & Meyers, 1974.
103. Everett, Hayward, & Meyers, 1974.
104. Geller, 1987.
105. Hayes & Cone, 1977; Van Houten, Nau, & Merrigan, 1981.
106. Geller, 1989a.
107. Skinner, 1948.
108. McNees, Egli, Marshall, Schnelle, Schnelle, & Risley, 1976.
109. For example, Geller, Berry, Ludwig, Evans, Gilmore, & Clarke, 1990.
110. Geller, 1991.

PART IV

Issues

Having finished dessert, it is time to sit back and reflect on your elaborate dinner. To help you do this, we have prepared an assortment of stimulating issues (in place of coffee). First, Chapter 17 presents ethical issues in the practice of behavior therapy. Then, in Chapter 18, we offer the chef's selection of the strengths and challenges to behavior therapy, seasoned with some spicy controversies surrounding the future of behavior therapy.

Chapter 17

Ethical Issues in Behavior Therapy

Many of the ethical questions that arise in the practice of behavior therapy have been alluded to in previous chapters. Two salient ethical issues are depriving clients of their rights and harming clients. With respect to these concerns, we will consider clients' vulnerability to ethical violations and the ways in which clients are protected in behavior therapy from ethical violations. To begin your exploration of ethical issues, take three minutes to complete Participation Exercise 17-1 before reading further. It will sensitize you to the issues that will be discussed in the chapter.

◆

Participation Exercise 17-1

ASSESSING YOUR OPINIONS ABOUT ETHICAL ISSUES IN BEHAVIOR THERAPY

The purpose of this Participation Exercise is to assess your opinions about the ethical issues that will be raised in this chapter and to have you start thinking about them. List the numbers 1 through 10 on a sheet of paper. Then, using the following scale, write the letter(s) that best represent(s) your opinion about each statement. As you do so, think of the arguments you would make if you were asked to defend your opinions.

AA = strongly agree
A = moderately agree
a = slightly agree
d = slightly disagree
D = moderately disagree
DD = strongly disagree

1. Behavior therapy poses ethical problems that do not exist with other forms of psychotherapy.
2. After successful behavior therapy, clients have fewer options for behaving than they did before therapy.
3. The behavior therapist establishes the goals of treatment for the client.
4. Aversive behavior therapy procedures result in long-term ill effects for clients.
5. The potency of aversive procedures has led to their widespread use in behavior therapy.
6. Behavior therapy increases clients' personal freedom.
7. Clients in behavior therapy have little control over their treatment.
8. The particular behavior therapy procedures employed are selected by the therapist.
9. Treatments that involve discomfort and pain are ethical.
10. Clients who are considered incompetent to make decisions about their own welfare should, nonetheless, have input regarding their treatment.

Save your ratings because you will use them in Participation Exercise 17-2.

◆

ETHICAL ISSUES IN PERSPECTIVE

It is important to keep in mind that the ethical issues pertaining to the practice of behavior therapy are relevant to all psychotherapies. Further, these issues arise whenever one person's behavior is to be changed directly or indirectly by another person, as in education, advertising, and religion.

Early Ethical Concerns About Behavior Therapy

In Chapter 2, you read about how behavior therapy was met with severe criticism and skepticism in its formative years. Some of these criticisms involved ethical concerns that were in large measure artifacts of the time. For example, one ethical criticism involved the possible danger that people would be controlled by behavior therapy techniques. In part, this may be due to misunderstandings of the meaning of some of the technical terminology behavior therapists used, such as references to "controlling variables," "experimental control," and the "manipulation of contingencies." Additionally, by coincidence, behavior therapy emerged in a period of heightened concern about external control (for example, by the government); about the invasion of personal privacy (as through electronic eavesdropping and computer storage of personal information); and about the abuse of civil liberties (for instance, of institutionalized patients and prisoners). "Reacting to the seemingly unchecked growth of these influences, many citizens . . . [came] to adopt positions that are highly critical of any and all behavior influence efforts."[1]

A number of early ethical criticisms of behavior therapy arose out of confusion about what behavior therapy is and what it is not. These criticisms occurred most frequently when the term *behavior modification* was used (rather than behavior therapy). *Behavior modification* was mistakenly confused with *any* procedure that modifies behavior, including psychosurgery (such as lobotomies and implanting electrodes in the brain), electroconvulsive shock therapy (ECT), drugs, brainwashing, sensory deprivation, and even torture.[2] A survey of articles indexed under *behavior modification* in the *New York Times* over a five-year period revealed that the term was incorrectly used approximately half of the time.[3] In some cases, the treatment procedures had absolutely no relationship to behavior therapy. For example, the use of a drug that causes a brief period of paralysis of the muscles (including those of the respiratory system) as punishment for prisoners was *erroneously* described as behavior modification.[4]

The extent to which the name of a therapy procedure can influence people's perceptions of it is illustrated by a study titled "A Rose by Any Other Name . . . : Labeling Bias and Attitudes Toward Behavior Modification."[5] In this study, undergraduate and graduate students evaluated a video of a teacher using reinforcement procedures in a special education class. All of the students saw the same video, but half were told that it illustrated "behavior modification" and half were told that it illustrated "humanistic education." Interestingly, students who believed that they had seen "humanistic education" illustrated (1) gave the teacher significantly more favorable ratings and (2) considered the teaching method significantly more likely to promote academic learning and emotional growth.

Current State of Affairs

Early misconceptions and unwarranted fears about behavior therapy certainly contributed to erroneous reports of unethical practices. At the same time, ethical violations have occasionally arisen in behavior therapy, and there are a small number of well-documented incidents. Most of them have been perpetrated against people who have little or no power—especially institutionalized individuals, such as prison inmates.[6] To help prevent such incidents, behavior therapists have developed guidelines for the ethical practice of behavior therapy.[7] For example, a checklist of ethical issues that should be considered whenever therapeutic procedures are applied has been developed.[8] These issues—each formulated as a question—are presented in Table 17-1 (along with some preliminary comments by the committee that wrote the checklist).

CONTROL AND FREEDOM IN BEHAVIOR THERAPY

Many ethical criticisms of behavior therapy are related to claims that its practices manipulate or control clients and therefore rob them of their personal freedom.

Providing Clients with Alternatives

One important aspect of freedom involves having *alternatives* from which to choose. People are free when they have options in their lives. Behavior therapy increases clients' personal freedom by providing them with alternative ways of behaving. This effect is most obvious for techniques that accelerate desirable behaviors. For instance, when modeling and reinforcement are used to provide clients with new skills, the clients' freedom is increased. This is equally true for the child with mental retardation who learns to ask for assistance and for the business executive who learns appropriate assertive behaviors to use in complex social interactions. In fact, competency-based treatments that involve skills training can enhance self-efficacy, independent functioning, and the overall quality of life even for clients with serious, chronic psychiatric disorders.[9]

Behavior therapies that decelerate undesirable behaviors also provide clients with alternatives. A woman whose excessive drinking has been alleviated by aversion therapy is freer because now she has many more options in her life. She is able to engage in activities that had been impaired by intoxication, including holding a job and enjoying sex. With either acceleration or deceleration behavior therapy procedures, *after successful treatment the client has more options for behaving than before treatment.*

Table 17-1 Checklist of ethical issues for human services

SOURCE: Ethical issues for human services, 1977, pp. v-vi.

Rather than recommending a list of prescriptions and proscriptions, the committee agreed to focus on critical ethical issues of central importance to human services.

On each of the issues described below, ideal interventions would have maximum involvement by the person whose behavior is to be changed, and the fullest possible consideration of societal pressures on that person, the therapist, and the therapist's employer. The committee recognizes that the practicalities of actual settings sometimes require exceptions, and that there certainly are occasions when exceptions can be consistent with ethical practice. Even though some exceptions may eventually be necessary, the committee feels that each of these issues should be explicitly considered.

The questions related to each issue have deliberately been cast in a general manner that applies to all types of interventions, and not solely or specifically to the practice of behavior therapy. The committee felt strongly that issues directed specifically to behavior therapists might imply erroneously that behavior therapy was in some way more in need of ethical concern than non-behaviorally-oriented therapies.

In the list of issues, the term *client* is used to describe the person whose behavior is to be changed; *therapist* is used to describe the professional in charge of the intervention; *treatment* and *problem*, although used in the singular, refer to any and all treatments and problems being formulated with this checklist. The issues are formulated so as to be relevant across as many settings and populations as possible. Thus, they need to be qualified when someone other than the person whose behavior is to be changed is paying the therapist, or when that person's competence or the voluntary nature of that person's consent is questioned. For example, if the therapist has found that the client does not understand the goals or methods being considered, the therapist should substitute the client's guardian or other responsible person for *client*, when reviewing the issues below.

A. Have the goals of treatment been adequately considered?
   1. To ensure that the goals are explicit, are they written?
   2. Has the client's understanding of the goals been assured by having the client restate them orally or in writing?
   3. Have the therapist and client agreed on the goals of therapy?
   4. Will serving the client's interests be contrary to the interests of other persons?
   5. Will serving the client's immediate interests be contrary to the client's long-term interest?

B. Has the choice of treatment methods been adequately considered?
   1. Does the published literature show the procedure to be the best one available for that problem?
   2. If no literature exists regarding the treatment method, is the method consistent with generally accepted practice?
   3. Has the client been told of alternative procedures that might be preferred by the client on the basis of significant differences in discomfort, treatment time, cost, or degree of demonstrated effectiveness?
   4. If a treatment procedure is publicly, legally, or professionally controversial, has formal professional consultation been obtained, has the reaction of the affected segment of the public been adequately considered, and have the alternative treatment methods been more closely reexamined and reconsidered?

C. Is the client's participation voluntary?
   1. Have possible sources of coercion on the client's participation been considered?
   2. If treatment is legally mandated, has the available range of treatments and therapists been offered?
   3. Can the client withdraw from treatment without a penalty or financial loss that exceeds actual clinical costs?

(continued)

Table 17-1 Checklist of ethical issues for human services *(continued)*

D. When another person or an agency is empowered to arrange for therapy, have the interests of the subordinated client been sufficiently considered?
   1. Has the subordinated client been informed of the treatment objectives and participated in the choice of treatment procedures?
   2. Where the subordinated client's competence to decide is limited, have the client as well as the guardian participated in the treatment discussions to the extent that the client's abilities permit?
   3. If the interests of the subordinated person and the superordinate persons or agency conflict, have attempts been made to reduce the conflict by dealing with both interests?
E. Has the adequacy of treatment been evaluated?
   1. Have quantitative measures of the problem and its progress been obtained?
   2. Have the measures of the problem and its progress been made available to the client during treatment?
F. Has the confidentiality of the treatment relationship been protected?
   1. Has the client been told who has access to the records?
   2. Are records available only to authorized persons?
G. Does the therapist refer the clients to other therapists when necessary?
   1. If treatment is unsuccessful, is the client referred to other therapists?
   2. Has the client been told that if dissatisfied with the treatment, referral will be made?
H. Is the therapist qualified to provide treatment?
   1. Has the therapist had training or experience in treating problems like the client's?
   2. If deficits exist in the therapist's qualifications, has the client been informed?
   3. If the therapist is not adequately qualified, is the client referred to other therapists, or has supervision by a qualified therapist been provided? Is the client informed of the supervisory relation?
   4. If the treatment is administered by mediators, have the mediators been adequately supervised by a qualified therapist?

Client's Role in Choosing Therapy Goals and Procedures

In behavior therapy, clients actively participate in making decisions about their treatment. The client plays the primary role in setting goals for therapy. The therapist may facilitate the client's goal setting by helping the client clarify what he or she wants to achieve and by guiding the client toward realistic goals. In the final analysis, however, it is the client who decides what the goals of therapy are to be. Once goals have been established, the therapist helps the client state these goals so that they are specific, unambiguous, and measurable. In cases where the client is incapable of formulating goals, the primary role in goal setting is assumed by the person who is legally responsible for the client.

Although behavior therapists are the experts in the methods used to attain treatment goals, the client is the one who will undergo the treatment. Accordingly, clients in behavior therapy play a role in selecting the particular therapy procedures to be used. In most cases, several different behavior therapies are likely to be effective for the client's problem. Before any treatment begins, the therapist describes each of the viable alternative therapy procedures to the client. The descriptions include (1) the underlying rationale; (2) what the therapy entails; (3) what the client will be expected to do; (4) an estimate of how long it will take the therapy to work; and (5) the general success rate of the therapy for the type of problem the client is experiencing. Finally, the therapist lists the advantages and disadvantages of each therapy. For example, both systematic desensitization and flooding may alleviate a client's fear of flying. Desensitization is likely to take longer and be less "painful," whereas the reverse is true for flooding. Financial cost is another consideration. In the treatment of specific phobias, for instance, exposure therapies tend to be more costly ($4,000 on average) than cognitive-behavioral therapies ($1,000 on average) although they may be equally effective.[10]

Armed with information about the available alternative behavior therapy procedures, the client can ask informed questions and make an informed choice, including refusing any of the treatments suggested. This process not only gives clients freedom of choice regarding therapy but also increases the chances of the treatment's success because of their active involvement in selecting their treatment.[11]

In practice, clients tend to rely heavily on the therapist's suggestions and advice. This is true because clients consider the therapist to be the authority in these matters and because clients beginning therapy are not always capable of thinking clearly. Still, in behavior therapy, the availability of alternative therapies provides the optimal conditions under which clients are free to choose how they will deal with their problems. This, incidently, is not the case with many other psychotherapies.

Terminating Treatment: Who Decides?

In behavior therapy, continual assessment of target behaviors is used to indicate whether therapy is effective—unlike other therapies, which rely on the therapist's subjective judgment about the client's progress. Because the treatment goals in behavior therapy are stated in clear-cut, measurable terms, clients are aware of how therapy is proceeding. The client as well as the behavior therapist know when the goals have been met and therapy is no longer necessary. Having ready access to data about their progress makes clients in behavior therapy informed, fully enfranchised partners in their treatment. This is another way in which behavior therapy enhances the client's personal freedom.

ETHICAL ISSUES IN THE USE OF AVERSIVE PROCEDURES

Aversive procedures—physically aversive consequences and aversion therapy—are the behavior therapies that have come under closest scrutiny regarding ethical concerns. Because these treatments involve physical discomfort or pain, they have the *potential* for impinging on clients' fundamental human rights. Some people believe that aversive treatments should not be used at all and especially not with clients who are vulnerable to abuse and unable to make informed decisions about their own treatment.[12]

In considering the ethicality of aversive procedures, two points should be kept in mind. First, the aversive stimulus is relatively brief and has no long-term ill effects. For example, when electric shock is used, it is administered for only a second or two. The sharp, stinging sensation that the client experiences lasts no more than a few minutes, and no permanent tissue damage results. Second, there is nothing inherently unethical about treatment involving discomfort or pain. After all, we do not think it is unethical to have our teeth drilled at the dentist or to receive an injection to prevent or cure a disease—not to mention the extreme discomfort people who undergo certain cancer treatments must endure. We do not consider these treatments unethical because their unpleasantness is outweighed by their benefits.

The potential for harm by aversive procedures has been exaggerated due to widely held misconceptions about the extent and nature of aversive procedures used in behavior therapy. After briefly examining these misconceptions, we will discuss the ethical issues relevant to the actual use of aversive procedures in behavior therapy.

Misconceptions About Aversive Procedures in Behavior Therapy

A widespread misconception about aversive procedures is that they are used extensively in behavior therapy. Indeed, some people even think of aversive procedures as synonymous with behavior therapy. In fact, aversive procedures constitute a small proportion of behavior therapy techniques (as you have seen from reading this book), and they are employed infrequently.[13] One reason for their limited use is that aversive procedures generally are relatively weak treatments, especially for producing lasting change.

The myth that aversive behavior therapy procedures are powerful and evil forces has been spurred by exaggerated and inaccurate popular depictions of techniques that only remotely resemble behavior therapy procedures. The most notable example is *A Clockwork Orange,* a popular book and movie. In the story, a young man named Alex has committed a series of sadistic and brutal attacks on innocent people. He is taken to a prison hospital for treatment. Strapped to a chair with his eyelids pinned open, Alex is forced to watch films depicting violence while experiencing drug-induced nausea and panic. Alex's pleas to terminate the treatment are ignored by the hospital staff. Supposedly, after a few such treatments, even the thought of violence makes him extremely anxious, and Alex is considered to be cured of his antisocial behaviors. First of all, the so-called treatment is *not* an example of behavior therapy because aversion therapy never involves restraining clients and subjecting them to treatment against their will. Further, the story is grossly inaccurate about the potential of aversive conditioning.[14] In fact, it is extremely difficult, and often impossible, to change a person's behavior when the individual does not want to change.[15] Thus, the procedures depicted in *A Clockwork Orange* are science fiction, not science.

Principle of Utility

Aversive techniques usually are employed as a last resort, when other therapy procedures have failed to decelerate serious debilitating behaviors. In each case, a cost-benefit analysis must be made. Does the potential outcome of therapy—the reduction of a serious, maladaptive behavior—outweigh the potential negative effects of the aversive procedure, such as temporary discomfort? This question follows from the ethical *principle of utility*, which holds that an action is morally right if, when compared with alternative actions, it produces more benefit than harm.[16] Case 17-1 addresses the question "Do the ends justify the means?"—which summarizes the fundamental ethical dilemma involved in using aversive procedures to reduce self-destructive behaviors.[17]

Case 17-1

TREATING SELF-DESTRUCTIVE BEHAVIORS WITH PHYSICALLY AVERSIVE CONSEQUENCES[18]

A colleague . . . showed us a deeply moving film. The heroine was an institutionalized primary-grade girl. She . . . [frequently engaged in head banging], so a padded football helmet was put on her head. Because she could take it off, her hands were tied down in her crib. She kept tossing her neck and tore out her hair at every opportunity. She accordingly had a perpetually bruised face on a hairless head, with a neck almost as thick as that of a horse. She was nonverbal.

My colleague and his staff carefully planned a program for her, using all kinds of reinforcers. She was remanded to their program, but persisted in her typical behavior. In desperation, the ultimate weapon was unwrapped. When she tossed her head, my colleague yelled "Don't!" simultaneously delivering a sharp slap to her cheek. She subsided for a brief period, tossed again, and the punishment was delivered. My colleague reports that less than a dozen slaps were ever delivered and the word "Don't!" yelled even from across the room was effective. Its use was shortly down to once a week and was discontinued in a few weeks. In the meantime, the football helmet was removed and the girl began to eat at the table. She slept in a regular bed. Her hair grew out, and she turned out to be a very pretty little blonde girl with delicate features and a delicate neck. In less than a year, she started to move toward joining a group of older girls whose behavior, it was hoped, she would [imitate]. She smiled often.

[When the girl's] . . . parents discovered that she had been slapped . . . , they immediately withdrew her from the custody of my colleague's staff. The last part of the film shows her back at the institution. She is strapped down in her crib. Her hands are tied to a side. She is wearing a football helmet. Her hair is torn out, her face is a mass of bruises and her neck is almost as thick as that of a horse.

What ethical issues do you see raised by this case? Before reading on, take a moment to list them.

To begin with, the therapist violated ethical guidelines by not completely informing the girl's parents about the treatment procedures. When this case occurred 25 years ago, behavior therapists were not as sensitized as they are today to the importance of fully disclosing treatment procedures and obtaining consent for their use.

The case also raises another critical ethical issue. Given the self-destructive nature of the girl's behaviors, do you think the treatment was ethically justified? Looking at the case from a different perspective, was it ethical to stop the treatment? Was the principle of utility violated?

Finally, consider a recent case of a 31-year-old man with a severe developmental disability who engaged in voluntary vomiting that was life threatening.[19] Because alternative nonaversive treatments could not be found, two behavior therapists recommended that short-term contingent electric shock be used. After a court ruled against this recommendation, the man was subjected to an intrusive medical procedure (permanent nasogastric intubation) and a severely restricted environment for the next year. How would you evaluate the ethicality of the conservative decision made in this case? Was the principle of utility violated?

The principle of utility also may be applicable when clients voluntarily seek treatment for psychological problems that seriously interfere with their living normal lives. In the treatment of sexual deviations (such as exhibitionism or pedophilia) and substance abuse, aversion therapy can be an important component of a comprehensive treatment package that includes procedures to accelerate alternative, socially desirable behaviors. The brief discomfort experienced in aversion therapy is minimal compared with the extensive interference with work and family life, the social ostracism, and the self-depreciation that result from long-standing socially unacceptable and personally maladaptive behaviors.[20]

Misuse, Abuse, and Safeguards

Aversive procedures are sometimes misused and abused. Misuse is usually perpetrated by nonprofessional change agents who have had minimal training and experience with the procedures. For example, aversive consequences often need to be applied only briefly in order to be effective.[21] Inexperienced change agents, including some behavior therapists, may continue the aversive consequences long after they have had their desired effect. This practice is not only unlikely to produce a further decrease in the target behavior, but it is likely to produce negative side effects, such as aggressive behaviors. Moreover, such treatment justifiably would be considered harsh.

Abuses of aversive techniques are more likely to arise when the deceleration target behavior is disturbing to others, as when a patient on a psychiatric ward disrupts the ongoing activities with inappropriate outbursts. Overburdened ward staff may apply aversive procedures because they are, in the short run, more efficient. Often it is easier to devise an aversive consequence to stop disturbing behaviors immediately than to identify and then accelerate alternative, competing prosocial behaviors gradually. However, the client's best interests must take precedence over other people's interests.

A variety of guidelines has been proposed to promote the ethical use of aversive procedures, including the following.

1. Aversive procedures should be considered only after it is clear that alternatives are not possible or would be ineffective or inefficient.[22]
2. Whenever possible, deceleration therapies that are not *physically* aversive (such as response cost and time out from positive reinforcement) should be tried before physically aversive procedures are employed.
3. If a physically aversive procedure is used, a physician should be consulted to be sure that it will be medically safe for the client.
4. The client or the client's legal guardian must be aware of the nature of the treatment and agree to it.
5. The procedures should be implemented only by a competent professional.
6. Aversive techniques should be used along with procedures that simultaneously accelerate alternative behaviors to take the place of the behaviors being eliminated.
7. Clear-cut measures of the target behavior should be collected before and after therapy to document its effectiveness (or ineffectiveness).

Such guidelines for the *ethical* use of aversive procedures supplement the guidelines for the *effective* use of aversive consequences presented in Chapter 7. Another means of safeguarding clients from potentially harmful therapies is to have special committees monitor their use.[23] These committees should consist of both professionals and concerned laypeople who are competent to evaluate treatment ethicality.[24] Finally, institutionalized clients would benefit from an independent ombudsman who was available to hear clients' complaints and ensure that they received proper consideration.[25]

Ethical problems are far less likely to arise when clients freely volunteer to receive aversive procedures. For example, few people would consider it unethical for consenting adults to subject themselves to a series of mild shocks in order to eliminate their desire to drink alcohol. In contrast, ethical issues regarding aversive procedures are prominent in the treatment of clients who are *required* to be in therapy, such as adults committed to institutions.

◆   ## ALL THINGS CONSIDERED: ETHICAL ISSUES IN BEHAVIOR THERAPY

Our discussion of ethical issues in the practice of behavior therapy has focused on the concerns most frequently voiced by critics. In closing, we would like to highlight some characteristics of behavior therapy that specifically serve to protect clients' rights.

To begin with, there are two practices common in behavior therapy that help protect clients' rights. First, clients are presented with detailed information about the specific therapy procedures that are appropriate for their particular problems. Second, clients participate in the choice of the therapy procedures that will be employed.[26]

The scientific approach that is a hallmark of behavior therapy contributes to ethical practices in a number of ways. The detailed specification of goals and target behaviors make the process of evaluating the success of therapy clear-cut and public. This practice also minimizes the chances that therapy will continue longer than necessary. Psychotherapy sometimes is prolonged because clients are overly dependent on their therapists. While this dependence may be inappropriate, it is not unethical. In contrast, it is unethical for therapists to prolong therapy because of *their* dependence on clients. Therapists are made vulnerable to this pitfall because they receive some of their most potent reinforcers from their clients, including the satisfaction of helping others and, of course, money. Again, the practice of continually evaluating clients' progress in behavior therapy provides a partial safeguard against therapists' inappropriately prolonging treatment.

Additionally, behavior therapists use empirically tested therapy procedures, assuring that clients are receiving effective treatment. Besides being effective, behavior therapies are relatively brief as compared with many other psychotherapies. Alleviating psychological distress as quickly as possible is certainly an ethical practice.

The collaboration between therapist and client—which is an essential element of behavior therapy—also serves to protect clients' rights. Clients are active participants in the therapy process, including being responsible for carrying out aspects of the therapy on their own. Such involvement decreases the chances that clients will become victims of ethical violations.

We began our discussion about ethical issues by noting the heightened scrutiny that behavior therapy received in its formative years. In concluding, it is worth noting that this heightened scrutiny may have been a blessing in disguise. By alerting behavior therapists to potential ethical violations, the early scrutiny may have contributed to the sensitivity to clients' welfare inherent in the practice of behavior therapy.

Before reading this chapter, you were asked to assess your opinions about ethical issues related to behavior therapy (in Participation Exercise 17-1). Participation Exercise 17-2 will give you a chance to reassess your opinions in light of what you have learned and thought about while reading this chapter.

◆ ▬▬▬▬▬▬▬▬▬▬▬▬▬▬▬▬▬▬▬▬▬▬▬▬▬▬▬▬▬▬▬▬▬▬▬▬

Participation   **REASSESSING YOUR OPINIONS ABOUT ETHICAL ISSUES**
Exercise 17-2   **IN BEHAVIOR THERAPY***

Has reading this chapter modified any of your opinions about the ethical issues related to behavior therapy? For now, do *not* refer to your prereading opinions

* This Participation Exercise can be done before you continue or later.

from Participation Exercise 17-1. List the numbers 1 to 10 on a sheet of paper. Using the following scale, write the letter(s) that best represent(s) your *present* opinion about each statement. Start at the *bottom* of your numbered sheet with number 10 and work up.

AA = strongly agree
A = moderately agree
a = slightly agree
d = slightly disagree
D = moderately disagree
DD = strongly disagree

10. Clients who are considered incompetent to make decisions about their own welfare should, nonetheless, have input regarding their treatment.
9. Treatments that involve discomfort and pain are ethical.
8. The particular behavior therapy procedures employed are selected by the therapist.
7. Clients in behavior therapy have little control over their treatment.
6. Behavior therapy increases clients' personal freedom.
5. The potency of aversive procedures has led to their widespread use in behavior therapy.
4. Aversive behavior therapy procedures result in long-term ill effects for clients.
3. The behavior therapist establishes the goals of treatment for the client.
2. After successful behavior therapy, clients have fewer options for behaving than they did before therapy.
1. Behavior therapy poses ethical problems that do not exist with other forms of psychotherapy.

Now, compare the ratings you just made with those you made before reading this chapter (in Participation Exercises 17-1). Consider the ethical issues about which you have changed your opinion. What is the direction of the changes? What new information or ideas have changed your opinions?

◆

Summary

1. Two salient ethical issues faced by behavior therapy are depriving clients of their rights and harming clients.
2. A number of early ethical criticisms of behavior therapy arose because of a heightened concern about the possible dangers of external control and because of confusion about what constitutes behavior therapy.
3. Many ethical criticisms of behavior therapy are based on claims that it controls clients and thus reduces their personal freedom. However, after successful behavior therapy, clients have more options for behaving than before therapy, which increases their personal freedom. Clients' freedom is protected in behavior therapy because clients actively participate in

choosing goals and therapy procedures as well as in deciding when the goals have been achieved and therapy can be terminated.

4. Aversive procedures have come under the closest scrutiny regarding ethical violations. In fact, aversive procedures constitute a small proportion of behavior therapy techniques and are used infrequently. When aversive procedures are used, a cost-benefit analysis of potential benefits and negative effects is performed for each case.

5. Misuses and abuses of aversive procedures most often are perpetrated by change agents who have limited experience with the procedures and who employ them because they are easier to implement than alternative therapy approaches.

6. The characteristics of behavior therapy that serve to protect clients' rights include clients' being given detailed information about therapy procedures and having a choice of procedures; the detailed specification of goals and target behaviors; a reliance on empirically tested therapy procedures; the relative brevity of behavior therapy; and the collaborative relationship between the client and therapist.

REFERENCE NOTES

1. Davison & Stuart, 1975, p. 756.
2. Franks & Wilson, 1978.
3. Turkat & Feuerstein, 1978.
4. Reimringer, Morgan, & Bramwell, 1970.
5. Woolfolk, Woolfolk, & Wilson, 1977.
6. For example, Cotter, 1967.
7. For example, Davison, 1976; Davison & Stuart, 1975; Stolz, 1977.
8. Ethical issues for human services, 1977.
9. Hunter, 1995.
10. Turner, Beidel, Spaulding, & Brown, 1995.
11. Bandura, 1969.
12. Tustin, Pennington, & Byrne, 1994.
13. Guevremont & Spiegler, 1990.
14. Franks & Wilson, 1975.
15. Bandura, 1969.
16. Beauchamp & Walters, 1978.
17. For example, Lovaas & Simmons, 1969.
18. Goldiamond, 1974, pp. 62-63.
19. Mudford, 1995.
20. Bandura, 1969.
21. For example, Lovaas & Simmons, 1969.
22. Carr & Durand, 1985; Emerson, 1993.
23. For example, Risley & Twardosz, 1974.
24. Kassirer, 1974.
25. Bootzin, 1975, p. 152.
26. Compare with Richard, 1995.

Chapter 18

Contemporary Behavior Therapy in Perspective: Strengths, Challenges, and Controversies

Having come this far in the book, you know what behavior therapy is and have seen the wide range of assessment and therapy procedures it employs as well as the broad spectrum of problems it treats. What, then, is left for this last chapter? Deciding on the content of the final chapter has not been easy. There still are things we want to share with you about behavior therapy, and this is our last chance to do so. We have decided on three topics. First, we think it is important to review the major strengths of contemporary behavior therapy. However, not to rest on the laurels of the field, we then will suggest some critical challenges that we believe behavior therapists must meet in the future. Finally, we will comment on two current controversies that involve a change in the identity of the field of behavior therapy. In brief, then, the chapter covers where behavior therapy is, where it should be going, and where it may end up.

MAJOR STRENGTHS OF BEHAVIOR THERAPY

What do you consider the major strengths of behavior therapy? Before reading further, take a moment to jot them down.

We have chosen to highlight five strengths of behavior therapy: (1) effectiveness, (2) efficiency, (3) breadth and complexity of applications, (4) precision in specifying goals and procedures, and (5) accountability.

Effectiveness

The bottom line for any psychotherapy is its success, which is measured in terms of *change*. The question is: How much has the client changed with respect to the goals of therapy? Because the goals in behavior therapy are specific, clear-cut, and measurable, the success of treatment is easy to determine for an *individual* client.*

In contrast, making statements about the *general* effectiveness of behavior therapy is a complex task. Determining the effectiveness of a particular behavior therapy requires asking a series of qualifying questions, including: "For what target behavior?" "For which client population?" and "In what context?" Further, the effectiveness of therapy must be evaluated vis-à-vis alternatives, such as other forms of treatment as well as placebo effects and no treatment. People with psychological disorders sometimes improve without the benefit of psychotherapy, a phenomenon known as *spontaneous remission*. Spontaneous remission does not happen simply because time passes. Rather, positive changes in the person's life (such as a change of job or improved marital relations) comprise the major factor that accounts for spontaneous remission. In assessing the effectiveness of therapy, it is

---

* Strictly speaking, the fact that a client's goals have been met does not mean that the change was due to the therapy. It always is possible that some other factors occurring at the same time as the therapy (such as changes in home or work life) were responsible. Controlled research, such as a single subject reversal or multiple baseline study, is necessary to draw conclusions about the effectiveness of therapy procedures.

important to determine whether the rate of improvement for a particular treatment is significantly greater than the rate of spontaneous remission.

Finally, even when carefully qualified questions are asked, a host of practical, methodological, and ethical problems may make it difficult to carry out meaningful research.[1] Consider the different criteria used to assess the effectiveness of therapy: generalizability, meaningfulness, durability of change, and acceptability. To their credit, behavior therapists are increasingly examining the effectiveness of their treatments in terms of each of these variables.[2] Interestingly, this research ethic has had an impact beyond behavior therapy in that it has served to encourage proponents of other forms of psychotherapy to conduct outcome research.[3]

Behavior therapy arguably has the broadest and strongest empirical base of any form of psychotherapy.[4] Further, a number of behavior therapy procedures are currently the best available treatments for some specific problem areas (for example, exposure as a treatment for anxiety disorders).[5]

It is noteworthy that behavior therapy fares well in comparison to drug therapy, which is the most frequently employed treatment for psychological disorders. Despite the effectiveness of many drug treatments, behavior therapy is a desirable form of treatment because (1) pharmacological therapies are not useful for situational or life adjustment problems (which constitute about half of all referrals for therapy); (2) behavior therapy works just as well as drug treatments for many disorders and may reduce relapse; (3) most clients prefer to avoid drug therapies; (4) a significant minority of clients do not respond favorably to drug treatments; and (5) many clients cannot tolerate medications because of undesirable side effects.[6]

Efficiency

The efficiency of a therapy is another important factor in assessing its value. Efficient therapies are those that (1) achieve the goals of therapy quickly and (2) are cost-effective for both therapists and clients, in terms of time and money.

Behavior therapy often brings about change relatively quickly, especially compared with traditional verbal psychotherapies. This is due to two factors. First, many behavior therapy techniques are fast-acting because they directly change the present maintaining conditions of the target behavior. Occasionally, the target behavior is altered almost immediately (as when powerful reinforcers are eliminated completely for a maladaptive behavior and provided exclusively for alternative, adaptive behaviors).

A second factor responsible for change in a relatively short time is that behavior therapy is not limited to therapy *sessions*. In fact, clients in behavior therapy often engage in the majority of their therapeutic work outside the therapy sessions. For example, for every hour in a therapy session, a client might do 4 hours of homework. If therapy involves 20 weekly, one-hour sessions, then the total amount of therapy is 80 hours, not 20.[7] Interestingly, over the course of a year and a half of once-a-week therapy sessions, a client in verbal psychotherapy might spend an equivalent number of hours.

However, the client in behavior therapy would have been helped more than a year earlier.

Besides shortening the duration of therapy, homework assignments are cost-effective because the therapist is not needed. Similarly, therapists' time is saved when nonprofessional change agents—such as parents, teachers, and partners—are trained to implement therapy procedures in clients' natural environments.

In the era of health care reform and managed care, brief treatment is critical.[8] Fortunately, behavior therapists are equipped to provide effective short-term therapies, even for serious problems.[9] Nonetheless, the health care industry's search for briefer therapy for clients undoubtedly will force behavior therapists to look even more carefully at essential and facilitative components of various therapies and to reduce treatments to their core elements.[10]

Breadth and Complexity of Applications

Behavior therapy is broadly applied, serving clients of all ages and with various cultural backgrounds who exhibit the gamut of psychological disorders.[11] Behavior therapy has met the needs of certain groups of clients for whom traditional verbal psychotherapy has been ineffective, including infants, young children, the elderly,[12] people with low intelligence, and people who cannot speak.[13] Clients who cannot afford expensive, long-term therapy have benefited from relatively efficient and therefore less costly behavior therapy. Behavior therapy has made inroads in the treatment of disorders that are relatively unresponsive to other forms of psychological treatment, such as schizophrenia, attention deficit hyperactivity disorders, and a number of physical problems, such as pain, enuresis, and tic disorders. Finally, behavior therapy is implemented in settings in which traditional psychotherapy is not typically employed, including the home, schools, industry, and the community.

An early criticism of behavior therapy was that it dealt only with simple problems. From your reading about behavior therapy, it should be clear that many *complex* problems are treated by contemporary behavior therapy. Behavioral treatment of psychological trauma, depression, chronic pain, and couple relationship problems are but a few examples.

The wide breadth of application of behavior therapy notwithstanding, behavior therapy is not the optimal or even an effective form of treatment in some cases.[14] For instance, some clients are not receptive to the general behavioral approach, including how behavior therapy is conducted. Consider two of the defining themes of behavior therapy, its active nature and emphasis on the present. Some people would prefer to talk about a problem and learn about its origin rather than to develop coping skills and practice them in their daily lives in order to change the current maintaining conditions of their problem.[15] As another example, behavior therapists *teach* and *give advice*. The directive style inherent in behavior therapy does not fare well with clients who prefer to act independently and resist being told what to do (even when the advice is presented as an alternative or suggestion).[16] Clearly, behavior therapy does not work for everyone. It is not a panacea, despite its arguably being the most widely applicable form of therapy.

Precision in Specifying Goals and Procedures

In behavior therapy, goals are defined in unambiguous, measurable terms, which provide both client and therapist with explicit criteria for evaluating the therapy's success. Thus, it is clear how well the therapy is working and when it can be terminated. In contrast, many types of psychotherapy employ goals that are implicit and vaguely defined (for example, "gaining insight"). In such cases, the criterion of progress and success often amounts to the therapist's subjective opinion.

The procedures employed in behavior therapy also are clearly specified, as in detailed treatment manuals.[17] This practice has four benefits. First, therapists are able to use the precise therapy procedures that have been found to be effective. (Of course, the basic procedures are tailored for each individual case.) Second, therapists are able to explain to clients exactly what will happen in therapy, allowing clients to give informed consent about treatment. Third, detailed descriptions of therapy procedures are invaluable in training behavior therapists. Finally, independent researchers can test the efficacy of behavioral interventions because the procedures are clearly specified. In contrast, when procedures are loosely defined, different studies may be testing treatments that are at least partly different.

The emphasis in behavior therapy on precision in specifying therapy goals and procedures is consistent with contemporary managed health care requirements.[18] Clearly defined and measurable goals make it possible to determine whether therapy needs to be continued.[19] Detailing therapy procedures provides a check on the appropriateness and quality of the treatment being offered.

Accountability

The existence of a strong empirical base for the effectiveness of behavior therapy procedures is due to the commitment behavior therapists have to evaluating the treatment procedures scientifically. Not only have behavior therapists accepted the difficult challenge of conducting psychotherapy outcome studies, but they also have been loud and stringent critics of their own research.[20]

Behavior therapy has been scrutinized by considerably more well-designed empirical research than any other form of psychotherapy. Unfortunately, the relative paucity of studies evaluating the effectiveness of many other psychotherapies makes it difficult to compare their effectiveness with behavior therapy. The strong empirical foundation of behavior therapies is one reason that they often are listed as treatments of choice by managed health care organizations that determine if a treatment is appropriate for a particular client before they will pay for it.[21]

CHALLENGES

The strengths of behavior therapy notwithstanding, behavior therapy currently faces a number of challenges that need to be met. Again, you might find it instructive to make a list of significant challenges that you believe exist. We will highlight five challenges: (1) enhancing durability of change; (2) preventing psychological disorders and problems; (3) matching clients to therapy; (4) treating culturally diverse clients; and (5) employing technology in behavior therapy.

Durability of Change

Ideally, changes that occur in a client's target behaviors as a result of behavior therapy will endure over time. However, this goal, which behavior therapy shares with all psychotherapies, is not easy to attain.[22] A major reason is that treatment focuses on initiating changes in clients' behaviors, and the process of *initiating* change and the process of *maintaining* change often are different. Thus, it is important that therapy include specific strategies designed to promote long-term maintenance of change.

PROMOTING DURABILITY: DURING THERAPY

Two broad strategies are employed *during* behavior therapy to foster durability of treatment gains: (1) providing clients with self-control coping skills and (2) structuring clients' natural environments. Teaching clients self-control coping skills is the easier and more frequently used strategy. The aim is for clients to use the coping skills to handle any recurrences of the problem in the future. Problem solving, self-instructions, cognitive restructuring, and muscle relaxation are examples of such self-control coping skills. Central to the success of this approach is clients' understanding that behavior therapy is an educational enterprise designed to help them cope more adaptively with their problems rather than to "cure" them of their ills.[23]

The second strategy for promoting durability of treatment gains during behavior therapy is to ensure that the client's natural environment will provide the necessary antecedents and consequences to maintain the new adaptive behaviors developed in therapy. This strategy is more complicated and requires more time than teaching clients coping skills. Contact with and sometimes training of people in the client's natural environments often are necessary. For instance, parents may be taught to apply the same reinforcement contingencies that are being used in therapy to promote adaptive behaviors with their children at home.

Even with such deliberate strategies to promote long-term maintenance, durability of treatment gains is not guaranteed. It is impossible to anticipate all of the future life events that may interfere with clients' dealing effectively with the problems that were treated in therapy. Further, the less related a client's future problems are to the problems specifically focused on in treatment, the less likely it is that the treatment gains will endure. Finally, if problems do not recur for some time after therapy has been terminated, it is likely that the client will have lost some proficiency in the coping skills learned in therapy.

Despite these obstacles, behavior therapies probably promote long-term maintenance as well as or better than most other therapies. (It is not possible to say this definitively because long-term maintenance data are unavailable for many other therapies.) With some disorders, both immediate effectiveness and long-term effectiveness of behavioral interventions are very impressive. For example, outcome studies of cognitive-behavioral treatment of panic disorder indicate that panic attacks are eliminated in over 80% of clients immediately after treatment (which is as good or better than existing drug therapies). Further, clients maintain these gains for at least 2 years.[24]

Nonetheless, in many cases long-term maintenance of treatment gains in behavior therapy is far from optimal in an absolute sense.[25] In other words, even if behavior therapy does as well as or better than other treatments, the extent of long-term maintenance may be less than desirable. For example, only about half the couples treated by cognitive-behavioral couple therapy retain the benefits after two years.[26]

PROMOTING DURABILITY: AFTER THERAPY

To help increase the chances of long-term maintenance of treatment gains, behavior therapists increasingly are relying on posttherapy interventions. Relapse prevention is the most comprehensive posttherapy approach for promoting long-term maintenance. It was originally developed for preventing substance-abuse relapses (see Chapter 15). Clients learn to identify high-risk situations for relapse; develop specific coping skills to use in these situations; practice the skills; and develop a balanced lifestyle that decreases the need for the previous maladaptive behaviors.

A second approach to enhancing the durability of change is to offer clients booster sessions after therapy has ended. In essence, clients are given one or more brief refresher sessions. Booster sessions commonly are employed after aversion therapy because the treatment effects tend to deteriorate over time but can be renewed with periodic booster sessions.[27]

A third, recently proposed approach for fostering lasting change is to provide *maintenance treatment* for extended periods of time after therapy has terminated—even for the remainder of a client's life. This is a radical idea for behavior therapists for two reasons. First, behavior therapy has a tradition of providing effective treatment in a relatively short time. Second, the approach superficially resembles traditional long-term psychotherapy which behavior therapists often criticize. However, maintenance treatment is different than traditional long-term psychotherapy, in which the therapy *itself*—that is, the process of initiating change—requires years to complete.

Specifically, maintenance treatment is less intense and less frequent than the initial treatment, and it is available to clients either on a regular basis (for example, once every six months) or on an as-needed basis, often over many years. Maintenance treatment has been suggested for such divergent populations and problems as couples experiencing distress[28] and adolescents' engaging in delinquent behaviors.[29] The need for maintenance treatment in many cases is based on the sobering fact that

> no matter how potent the technology, after treatment ends other salient life events gradually become more important in influencing the course of . . . functioning. . . . The solution cannot simply be more and better therapy technology during the active therapy phase. Rather, maintenance may be facilitated to a greater extent by creating a context for the therapist to remain a continuing presence in the lives of [clients]. . . .[30]

Maintenance treatment is an exciting idea, albeit one that has yet to be tried and tested.

Although behavior therapy is among the most effective forms of intervention for many disorders, treatment effects often deteriorate over time.[31] Indeed, promoting the long-term maintenance of therapeutic change has been and remains the most difficult challenge for behavior therapy (as well as other psychotherapies).[32]

Prevention

The overall objective of behavior therapy is to alleviate the human suffering that results from psychological disorders that interfere with people's personal lives and create societal problems. Clearly, behavior therapy has made major advances toward this goal. Behavioral principles and procedures could make an even greater contribution if they were employed more extensively to *prevent* the occurrence of psychological disorders in the first place. Some behavior therapy procedures are immediately applicable to prevention, such as stress inoculation and problem-solving therapy. Others must be adapted because there are fundamental differences between treatment and prevention[33] (just as there are differences between treatment and long-term maintenance[34]).

Prevention might be especially germane to problems for which behavior therapy has been least effective. Addictive behaviors, for example, are notoriously resistant to change, largely because of the powerful immediate consequences associated with them. While behavior therapy has been among the most effective psychotherapies in treating addictive behaviors,[35] the success rate is far below that achieved with many other problems. In some cases, continued efforts to improve interventions have made little difference.[36] One reason may be that addictive habits and lifestyles are extremely difficult to change. The solution may lie in *preventing* addictive behaviors. Although prevention programs for addictive behaviors that target school-age children and adolescents do exist, often they merely provide information or advice. The popular "Just Say No" campaign, for example, is not likely to be very effective because it does not equip youngsters with the assertive skills required to successfully follow the advice. In contrast, there are cognitive-behavioral programs for preventing of depression that teach children and adolescents coping skills to deal with stress-evoking events that are likely to trigger depression. These programs usually are offered to groups identified as being at greater risk for developing depression, such as children from households containing significant parental conflict[37] and adolescents whose parents have depressive disorders.[38]

Prevention is unquestionably needed with problems for which no effective treatment exists. Currently, the prime example is AIDS. Although AIDS cannot be cured, it can be prevented. Behavioral interventions have shown some promise in helping to prevent people from being infected with HIV (see Chapter 14).[39]

The idea of a behavioral prevention technology is not new.[40] You have read about behavioral programs developed to prevent couple relationship problems (Chapter 13), medical disorders (Chapter 14), and accidents and crime (Chapter 16), for example. However, the number of preventive efforts is very small relative to treatment efforts. Also, behavioral preventive interventions have been narrow in scope, focusing on children and adolescents[41] and principally on medical disorders and associated psychological disorders (such as fear of surgery). The potential for preventing problems using behavioral interventions is great, and it is an important challenge for the future.

Matching Clients to Therapy

The idea of matching clients to specific psychotherapies is intuitively appealing. The client-therapy match can be based on the nature of the psychological disorder or problem as well as on characteristics of the client, including personal beliefs, lifestyle, and ethnicity. Attempts to meet these goals have met with very limited success.[42]

Behavior therapists recently have joined the quest for good client-therapy matches.[43] With very few disorders and problems is it possible to identify a single, optimal therapy—that is, a treatment of choice. Even when a treatment of choice exists, it certainly is not the treatment of choice for all clients. For example, the treatment of choice for panic disorders,[44] developed by David Barlow and his colleagues,[45] is a cognitive-behavioral treatment package that includes exposure to simulated panic attacks. Clearly, this would not be an appropriate therapy for clients who might be susceptible to heart attacks. Thus, matching in terms of disorder/problem has its limitations.

Clients can be matched to therapies in terms of their personal characteristics in a variety of ways. On an intuitive level, therapists can use their clinical judgment, or clients can choose the type of therapy they believe fits them best. Preferably, the matching process would be guided by a body of empirical findings that indicates that particular behavior therapies are most effective for clients with certain characteristics.[46] These are intriguing possibilities that have yet to be tried and evaluated systematically. Thus, they remain another challenge for the future.

Culturally Competent Behavior Therapy

Added to the challenge of matching clients to therapy is the need for behavior therapists to become more responsive to *specific* issues of ethnic and cultural diversity. Behavior therapy is sensitive to differences among clients in a broad sense. Treatments are designed based on the unique maintaining conditions of the client's target behavior, and standard therapy procedures are tailored for each client.[47] Nonetheless, behavior therapists have paid very little attention to issues of race, gender, ethnicity, and sexual orientation.[48] These issues can affect the usefulness and outcome of therapy.[49] As just one example, some African-American clients' distrust of European-American therapists may reflect a healthy response to the realities of racism. However, a culturally insensitive therapist may misinterpret this "cultural paranoia" as clinical paranoia.

Assessment methods should be chosen with the client's cultural background in mind. For instance, many Native Americans value paying attention to the *actions* of others rather than to their verbal accounts, and they believe that asking questions is rude.[50] Accordingly, a Native American client might have more confidence in systematic naturalistic observations than interviews as a means of assessment. Another critical assessment issue is that people from different cultures differ in the way they communicate subjective discomfort. For instance, Chinese and Southeast Asian refugees in the United States frequently express depression through somatic complaints, such as headaches and chest pains.[51]

Providing behavior therapy that is sensitive to differences among clients of varying cultural backgrounds is challenging.[52] To begin with, clients' cultural identities impact their preferences for type of therapy and therapist style. For instance, many Asian clients prefer a directive approach in therapy (in which they are told what to do by an authority figure),[53] and therapy with many Hispanic clients is more effective when the therapist allows for a period of familiarizing "small talk" prior to goal-directed activities.[54]

The particular therapy procedures chosen must take into account unique aspects of the client's cultural identity.[55] For example, because Native Americans value action over words, they are more likely to find the collaborative empiricism of cognitive therapy (that is, actually gathering evidence for one's beliefs) more acceptable than the rational disputation of rational emotive behavior therapy. Further, the way in which standard therapy procedures are individualized for the client must be culturally sensitive. Thus, attempting to increase eye contact as part of social skills training with Navajos might be inappropriate because, in their culture, extended eye contact is viewed as aggressive.[56]

This last example raises the complex issue of working with people who live both in their own minority culture and in a very different mainstream culture. Among the knotty questions behavior therapists must answer are: What standards of social validity are used to judge the effectiveness of therapy with clients from cultural minorities?[57] And, how do these standards change during the course of a client's acculturation process? Many people superficially appear to be bicultural, but, in fact, they may be more firmly rooted in one of the cultures. Thus, therapists must ascertain where clients place themselves culturally and then approach them from the appropriate cultural perspective.

Effective therapy with clients from diverse backgrounds requires that the therapist become knowledgeable about as well as open and sensitive to issues such as (1) what is considered normal and abnormal behavior in the client's culture (for instance, seeing and speaking with entities from the spirit world may be regarded as normal); (2) clients' culturally based conceptions of their problems; (3) relevant information about the client's culture, such as the roles that individuals play in a family (for example, Japanese women traditionally behave unassertively); and (4) who are appropriate and inappropriate behavior change agents (for instance, in some Southeast Asian cultures, a woman is not permitted to be alone with a man other than her husband).[58]

Behavior therapists have only recently begun to attend to the impact of cultural diversity as well as other forms of diversity, such as age,[59] gender,[60] and sexual orientation.[61] Most of the work so far has consisted of proposing general guidelines for working with clients from diverse backgrounds. As with client-therapy matching, it will be important in the future to develop empirically based recommendations about how behavior therapy can optimally serve diverse clients.

Technological Advances and Behavior Therapy

Behavior therapy has utilized simple technology more than most other forms of psychotherapy. Some examples you have read about include mechanical devices for recording behaviors (Chapter 5); the battery-operated device for individually administering response cost to students in a classroom (Chapter 7); the Self-Injurious Behavior Inhibiting System for automatically delivering shock when the client begins the self-injurious behavior (Chapter 7); and the use of video modeling (Chapter 11). Occasionally, more sophisticated and costly technology has been utilized, such as biofeedback (Chapter 14) and, recently, virtual reality for exposure therapy (Chapter 9).

For the most part, however, behavior therapy has not made extensive use of technology. In one way, this is a virtue. Technology often makes procedures complicated and costly, whereas simplicity has distinct advantages in therapy. All other things being equal, the simpler therapy procedures are, the more likely they are to work, especially when clients administer treatment procedures themselves.

Nonetheless, there are ways in which behavior therapy could utilize existing and future technology, especially technology that is readily accessible and relatively inexpensive.[62] For example, clients could use home computers with modems to transmit information to the therapist. At the beginning of therapy, for example, clients could transmit completed assessment forms, such as self-report inventories. During therapy, clients could keep the therapist informed of the outcome of ongoing homework assignments, such as self-monitoring and practicing coping skills. This would allow therapists to provide feedback and modify assignments before the next therapy session, which, in some cases, might reduce the number of therapy sessions required.

Hand-held (palmtop) computers have recently been employed in the treatment of panic disorder.[63] The computer, which clients carry with them at all times, serves three purposes: (1) prompting clients to self-monitor the frequency and severity of their panic attacks; (2) prompting them to perform homework assignments; and (3) guiding clients through in vivo exposure, cognitive restructuring, and breathing exercises. Similar functions also might be served by portable cellular phones. These examples point to the challenge for behavior therapists: to use available technology to enhance the efficiency and effectiveness of therapy procedures.

CURRENT CONTROVERSIES

Despite the diversity of procedures used in behavior therapy, there is a cohesiveness to the field. All behavior therapies have certain themes and characteristics in common (which we first described in Chapter 1), which make them members of a single family of psychotherapy. Recently, two controversial developments have arisen that threaten the integrity and identity of behavior therapy. First, behavior therapy is becoming less pure (less behavioral) as it incorporates therapy procedures from other types of psychotherapy. Second, behavior therapy research is shifting from the study of therapy—that is, how we treat disorders—to the study of the nature of disorders.

In discussing each of these developments, we will not only describe the basic issues but also present our personal opinions about them. We have chosen to depart from the generally neutral stance we have assumed throughout the book regarding controversial issues for two reasons. First, we want to stimulate debate on the issues, which is sparked by advocating a strong position. Second, we do have definite opinions about the two issues that may affect the future of behavior therapy, and we would like to share them with you.

Effects of Psychotherapy Integration

In the early days of behavior therapy, single treatments were more prevalent than treatment packages. Today, clients often benefit from a combination of two or more behavior therapy procedures, either simultaneously or sequentially, in comprehensive treatment packages. Behavior therapists now are more aware of the limitations of specific interventions, and they recognize that, in many cases, optimal treatment may require more than one *behavioral* approach.

In the search for optimal treatments for their clients, behavior therapists are increasingly going beyond behavioral treatment packages and incorporating interventions from *nonbehavioral* forms of treatment into behavior therapy treatment plans. This approach is consistent with a general trend toward *psychotherapy integration,* which involves incorporating treatment strategies from two or more different types of therapy.[64] An early example of integration in behavior therapy was implosive therapy, which melded psychoanalytic theory with behavioral procedures. The use of medication along with behavior therapy (for example, in the treatment of anxiety,[65] hypertension,[66] and attention deficit disorders[67]) is the most common form of integration in behavior therapy.

Combining medication with behavior therapy is an example of *technical eclecticism,* which involves using a variety of different treatment procedures that are selected based on the empirical evidence of their effectiveness for a particular disorder.[68] Another example of technical eclecticism is Arnold Lazarus's *multimodal therapy*, which combines effective nonbehavioral interventions with effective behavioral interventions.[69] It is important to note that the multimodal therapist remains firmly rooted in the behavioral approach to therapy while using some nonbehavioral treatment procedures.[70]

The merits of integration and eclecticism are the subject of debate among behavior therapists.[71] Central to the debate is the issue of the integrity of behavior therapy. *At some point, integrating nonbehavioral treatment procedures into behavior therapy renders the treatment something other than behavior therapy.* The precise point at which this change occurs is difficult to define (just as it is not easy to specify how much milk must be added to coffee for it no longer to be coffee).

Behavior therapists are becoming more interested in nonbehavioral approaches. For instance, over the past few years, an increasing number of presentations on nonbehavioral approaches to therapy have been made at the annual meeting of the Association for Advancement of Behavior Therapy.[72] This trend means that the practice of behavior therapy as it has been known for the past 40 years—and as we have presented it in this book—is becoming diluted and less pure.

We believe that the challenge of psychotherapy integration for behavior therapy is to incorporate nonbehavioral treatments without violating the fundamental behavioral approach, which would preserve the integrity of behavior therapy. Whether this can be done remains to be seen.

Is Behavior Therapy in an Identity Crisis?

A related issue that affects the integrity of behavior therapy is the changing focus of research done by behavior therapists. Much current research deals with the nature and characteristics of psychological disorders. For example, between 1984 and 1989 about half the studies published in *Behavior Therapy,* arguably the most prestigious journal in the field, fell into this category.[73]

Because *therapy* (including assessment) is the focus of behavior therapy, the shift of research from therapy to the nature of psychological disorders is altering the identity of the field. Proponents of this shift now consider the term *behavior therapy* to signify much more than an approach to treatment. The term has been broadened to include the study of abnormal psychology or psychopathology.[74]

Research on the nature of psychological disorders clearly is a worthwhile endeavor and certainly has implications for the practice of behavior therapy. However, we believe that to establish such an all-encompassing purview for behavior therapy is an overly ambitious goal. In attempting to "do it all,"[75] behavior therapy's mission becomes too broad.

Broadening the purview of behavior therapy relegates behavior *therapy* (treatment) to a less prominent role in the field that bears its name. It means that less attention is being paid to developing, refining, and understanding treatment and assessment. We think this trend is regrettable because the field of behavior therapy has certainly not completed its fundamental mission—namely, to provide clients with effective, long-lasting treatment.

◆ ALL THINGS CONSIDERED: BEHAVIOR THERAPY

In its relatively brief history, behavior therapy has come a long way. It started as a new family of kids in the psychotherapy neighborhood that previously had been populated by one dominant family, psychoanalysis. Accordingly, behavior therapy initially had a hard time being accepted. When verbal taunts (such as that it treated only the simplest problems or that it resulted in symptom substitution) did not scare behavior therapy away, the old-timers placed seemingly impossible barriers in its path. Behavior therapists were allowed to treat only the most difficult cases, those for whom established therapies had been ineffective. Believing they were omnipotent, as youngsters often do, the new kids enthusiastically accepted the challenge. The result was some remarkable successes with so-called hopeless clients. The established family had no choice but to allow the new family, which by that time had grown considerably, to take up legitimate residence in the neighborhood.

At this point, the kids began to fight among themselves (which was predictable now that their common external adversaries had quieted down). Some of the kids began to *think*—a process that most of the other kids did not trust because they did not directly observe it. The result of this infighting was an informal division into a behavioral side of the family and a cognitive-behavioral side. The cognitive-behavioral side now outnumbers the behavioral side.[76] The two sides still squabble occasionally, but, for the most part, they acknowledge being part of the same family—behavior therapy. The behavior therapy family has grown considerably over the past 40 years in both number and stature. Today, it is the predominant cohesive family in the psychotherapy neighborhood. Whether this cohesiveness will continue remains to be seen, especially in light of recent loosening of family ties, manifest in intermarriages (integration with other therapies) and a changing family structure (loss of identity).

The stature of behavior therapy in the current practice of psychotherapy is based largely on its effectiveness which is substantiated by strong empirical support. Nonetheless, behavior therapy is not a panacea. The effectiveness of behavior therapy in general varies with different disorders and client populations. Further, not all clients favor the behavioral approach, with its emphasis on direct, concrete solutions to psychological problems.

Looking ahead, the advent of managed health care has raised many issues regarding the future of the treatment of psychological disorders. While it is too early to know all the implications of a predominant managed health care system, three imperatives are clear. First, accountability is essential. Therapists will be required to specify (1) the problems being treated; (2) clear-cut goals and criteria for determining if the goals have been met; and (3) the specific treatment procedures being employed.[77] Accountability should be an easy requirement for behavior therapists to meet because precision and measurement are essential elements of their approach. Second, the treatments used must be proven to be effective for the psychological disorder being treated.[78] Fortunately, behavior therapists use therapy procedures that have strong empirical support.[79] Third, managed health care emphasizes short-term and cost-effective treatment. Generally, behavior therapy is relatively brief, involving fewer therapy sessions and less overall professional time than many other types of therapy.[80] Further, the emphasis on teaching clients self-control coping skills is cost-effective. What all this means is that behavior therapy should fare well in the era of managed health care.[81]

The commitment to empirical accountability in behavior therapy has resulted in almost continual change in the field. Behavior therapists have remained open to new ideas, examining empirical evidence to determine their merit. A prime example is the wide acceptance of cognitive factors into a therapeutic approach that initially had focused exclusively on overt behaviors. The fact that behavior therapists are self-critical is another example of their open-mindedness. Recently, the limitations of behavior therapy have been increasingly recognized and accepted.[82] Additionally, behavior therapists generally are committed to finding alternative approaches and procedures that take acknowledged limitations into account. An example is the recognition that the durability of treatment effects is not assured by procedures instituted during therapy. Thus, posttherapy procedures, including protracted maintenance treatment, may be necessary with some problems and client populations.

The field of behavior therapy is characterized by continual assessment and responsiveness to change. For us, this quality makes being behavior therapists exciting and challenging. We hope that you, as students of behavior therapy, share our enthusiasm.

◆ ▬▬▬▬▬▬▬▬▬▬▬▬▬▬▬▬▬▬▬▬▬▬▬▬▬▬▬▬▬▬▬▬▬▬

Participation Exercise 18-1

ASSESSING YOUR AFTERTHOUGHTS ABOUT CONTEMPORARY BEHAVIOR THERAPY*

You began your introduction to behavior therapy by judging whether 14 statements about behavior therapy were valid (in Participation Exercise 1-1). You learned that all the statements are predominantly false; they all are commonly held misconceptions about behavior therapy. At this point, you should know why each of the statements is false. As a final review of your understanding of

* This Participation Exercise can be done before you continue or later.

contemporary behavior therapy, read each of the 14 statements again and write specific reasons why each is false. When you have finished, compare your reasons with those in Appendix B.

1. Behavior therapy is the application of well-established laws of learning.
2. Behavior therapy directly changes symptoms.
3. A trusting relationship between client and therapist is not important in behavior therapy.
4. Behavior therapy does not deal with problems of feelings, such as depression and low self-esteem.
5. Generally, little verbal interchange takes place between the therapist and client in behavior therapy.
6. The client's cooperation is not necessary for behavior therapy to be successful.
7. Most clients in behavior therapy can be successfully treated in fewer than five sessions.
8. Behavior therapy is not applicable to changing mental processes such as thoughts.
9. Positive reinforcement works better with children than with adults.
10. Many behavior therapy procedures use painful or aversive treatments.
11. Behavior therapy primarily deals with relatively simple problems, such as phobias (for example, fear of snakes) or undesirable habits (for instance, smoking).
12. Behavior therapy uses biological treatments such as drugs and psychosurgery (for example, lobotomies).
13. The behavior therapist establishes the goals for the client.
14. The behavior therapist is directly responsible for the success of therapy.

Summary

1. Five major strengths of behavior therapy are its effectiveness, efficiency, breadth and complexity of applications, precision in specifying goals and procedures, and accountability.
2. One major challenge for behavior therapy is to design procedures that increase the durability of change when treatment ends. The two major strategies employed during behavior therapy are teaching clients self-control coping skills and assuring that clients' natural environments provide the necessary antecedents and consequences to maintain treatment gains. These strategies are limited because they cannot anticipate all life events that will affect clients after therapy.
3. Three posttherapy strategies are used to promote durability of treatment gains. First, relapse prevention is a procedure that prepares clients for future relapses by identifying high-risk situations, developing coping skills, practicing the coping skills before they are needed, and developing a balanced lifestyle. Second, clients can receive booster sessions. Third, a recent proposal is to provide clients with maintenance treatment, that is

less frequent and intense than the initial treatment, for an indefinite period following therapy itself.

4. A second major challenge for behavior therapy is to develop prevention programs using behavioral principles and techniques. Prevention is especially germane to problems for which behavior therapies have been least effective or for which there is no available treatment.

5. Matching clients with the optimal therapy for their individual disorders or problems and with the therapist's style to fit their personal preferences is a third challenge.

6. Providing assessment and therapy procedures that are sensitive to culturally and otherwise diverse clients is a fourth challenge.

7. Behavior therapy has not made extensive use of existing technology, and using available technology to enhance the efficiency and effectiveness of behavior therapy procedures is a fifth challenge.

8. Two controversial recent developments are threatening the integrity and identity of behavior therapy. First, behavior therapy is becoming less behavioral as it incorporates therapy procedures from other types of psychotherapy, a practice known as psychotherapy integration. Second, behavior therapy research is shifting from the study of therapy to the study of the nature of the disorders, which may be stretching the purview of the field too far.

9. Because behavior therapy emphasizes accountability, has demonstrated effectiveness, and is relatively brief, the field should fare well in the era of managed health care.

REFERENCE NOTES

1. Bergin & Strupp, 1972; Gottman & Markman, 1978; Strupp, 1978.
2. For example, Risley, 1995.
3. Goldfried & Castonguay, 1993.
4. Barlow, 1994; Goldfried & Castonguay, 1993.
5. For example, Barlow, 1994.
6. Barlow, 1994; Bergan, 1995; Strosahl, 1995.
7. Compare with White, 1995.
8. For example, Barnett, 1996; Bracero, 1996; Cantor, 1995.
9. For example, Giles, 1991; Giles, Prial, & Neims, 1993.
10. Bergan, 1995; Strosahl, 1995.
11. For example, Agras & Berkowitz, 1994; Chen, 1995; Cottraux, 1993; Simos & Dimitriou, 1994.
12. For example, Hersen & Van Hasselt, 1992; Lemsky, 1996; Malec, 1995; Nicholson & Blanchard, 1993; Wisocki, 1994.
13. For example, Cottraux, 1993.
14. Smith, Klevstrand, & Lovaas, 1995.
15. For example, Goldfried & Castonguay, 1993.
16. Gaston, Goldfried, Greenberg, Horvath, Raue, & Watson, 1995.
17. For example, Dobson & Shaw, 1989; Meichenbaum, 1994; compare with Addis & Carpenter, 1997.
18. Hayes, 1995.
19. For example, Cavaliere, 1995.
20. Christensen, Jacobson, & Babcock, in press; Franks, 1995; Franks, Wilson, Kendall, & Foreyt, 1990; Jacobson, 1989, 1991; Kazdin & Wilson, 1978; Paul, 1969b.
21. Addis & Carpenter, 1997; Giles, 1991; Giles, Prial, & Neims, 1993; Strosahl, 1995, 1996.
22. For example, Barlow, 1994; Milne & Kennedy, 1993.
23. For example, Nelson & Politano, 1993.
24. Barlow, 1994.
25. For example, Chorpita, 1995; Shea, Elkin, Imber, Sotsky, Watkins, Collins, Pilkonis, Beckham, Glass, Dolan, & Parloff, 1992.
26. Christensen, Jacobson, & Babcock, in press.

27. Rachman & Teasdale, 1969; Voegtlin, Lemere, Broz, & O'Hollaren, 1941.
28. Jacobson, 1989.
29. Wolf, Braukmann, & Ramp, 1987.
30. Jacobson, 1989, p. 329.
31. Kendall, 1989.
32. Barlow, 1994; Chorpita, 1995; Shea, Elkin, Imber, Sotsky, Watkins, Collins, Pilkonis, Beckham, Glass, Dolan, & Parloff, 1992.
33. Spiegler, 1983.
34. Jacobson, 1989.
35. For example, Foreyt, 1987, 1990.
36. For example, Bennett, 1987.
37. Jaycox, Reivich, Gillham, & Seligman, 1994.
38. Clarke, Hawkins, Murphy, Sheeber, Lewinsohn, & Seeley, 1995.
39. Honnen & Kleinke, 1990; Kelly & St. Lawrence, 1988b; Kelly, St. Lawrence, Hood, & Brasfield, 1989; Roffman, Gilchrist, Stephens, & Kirkham, 1988.
40. Poser, 1970; Spiegler, 1980.
41. For example, Church, Forehand, Brown, & Holmes, 1990; Clarke, Hawkins, Murphy, Sheeber, Lewinsohn, & Seeley, 1995; Hammond & Prothow-Stith, 1991; Jaycox, Reivich, Gillham, & Seligman, 1994.
42. Lambert & Bergin, 1994.
43. Eifert, Forsyth, & Schauss, 1994.
44. Lambert & Bergin, 1994.
45. Barlow & Cerney, 1988.
46. Longabaugh, Wirtz, Beattie, Noel, & Stout, 1995.
47. Tanaka-Matsumi & Higginbotham, 1994.
48. Iwamasa & Smith, 1996; Purcell, Campos, & Perilla, 1996.
49. Hatch, Friedman, & Paradis, 1996; Landrine & Klonoff, 1995; Paradis, Friedman, Hatch, & Ackerman, 1996.
50. Reyna, 1996; Waller, in press.
51. Tanaka-Matsumi & Higginbotham, 1994.
52. Iwamasa, 1996; Martin, 1995.
53. Chen, 1995.
54. Waller, in press.
55. Fudge, 1996; Simos & Dimitriou, 1994; Tanaka-Matsumi & Higginbotham, 1994.
56. Tanaka-Matsumi & Higginbotham, in press.
57. Tanaka-Matsumi & Higginbotham, 1994.
58. Tanaka-Matsumi & Higginbotham, in press; Tanaka-Matsumi & Seiden, 1994.
59. For example, Lemsky, 1996; McGrady, Olson, & Kroon, 1995; Malec, 1995; Nicholson & Blanchard, 1993; Zeiss & Steffen, 1996.
60. For example, McNair, 1996; Thase, Reynolds, Frank, Simons, McGeary, Fasiczka, Garamoni, Jennings, & Kupfer, 1994.
61. Chesney & Folkman, 1994; Hunter & Schaecher, 1994; Kelly & St. Lawrence, 1990; Mylott, 1994; Purcell, Campos, & Perilla, 1996; Schneiderman, Antoni, Ironson, LaPerriere, & Fletcher, 1992; Ussher, 1990.
62. For example, Gale, 1996.
63. Newman, Kenardy, Herman, & Taylor, 1996, in press.
64. For example, Arkowitz, 1992a, 1992b, 1995; Davison, 1995; Goldfried, 1995; Goldfried, Castonguay, & Safran, 1992; Goldfried, Wiser, & Raue, 1992; Norcross & Goldfried, 1992.
65. Wilson, 1984.
66. For example, Blanchard, McCoy, Musso, Gerardi, Pallmeyer, Gerardi, Koch, Siracusa, & Andrasik, 1986.
67. For example, Satterfield, Satterfield, & Cantwell, 1981.
68. Lazarus, 1995; Lazarus & Beutler, 1993.
69. Lazarus, 1989a.
70. Lazarus, 1985, 1989a, 1989c.
71. For example, Lazarus, 1989a, 1989c; Wolpe, 1976.
72. For example, Greenberg, 1990; Marmar, 1990.
73. Craighead, 1990a; Peterson, 1992.
74. Craighead, 1990b.
75. Craighead, 1990b.
76. Craighead, 1990b.
77. For example, Cavaliere, 1995.
78. For example, Strosahl, 1995, 1996.
79. Spiegler & Guevremont, 1994.
80. For example, Bergan, 1995; Strosahl, 1995.
81. For example, Giles, 1991; Giles, Prial, & Neims, 1993; compare with Cone, Alexander, Lichtszajn, & Mason, 1996.
82. Goldfried & Castonguay, 1993.

Appendix A

Guidelines for Choosing a Behavior Therapist*

After the decision to seek therapy has been made, an individual may feel unsure about how to choose a therapist. Persons seeking therapy often find that they have no standards to use in evaluating potential therapists. There are many competent therapists of varying theoretical persuasions. The purpose of this guide is to provide you with information that might be useful in selecting a behavior therapist. No guideline can provide strict rules for selecting the best therapist for a particular individual. We can, however, suggest questions you might ask and areas of information you might want to cover with a potential behavior therapist before you make a final decision.

WHAT IS BEHAVIOR THERAPY?

There is no single definition of behavior therapy. Although some common points of view are shared by most behavior therapists, there is a wide diversity among those persons who call themselves behavior therapists. The definition that follows is meant to give you a general idea of what behavior therapy is. It is not, however, an absolute definition. The particular behavior therapist you select may agree with some parts of it and disagree with other parts. The following definition is adapted from "Behavior Modification: Perspective on a Current Issue," published by the National Institute of Mental Health:

> Behavior therapy is a particular kind of therapy that involves the application of findings from behavioral science research to help

* The "Guidelines" were written by Marsha Linehan, Ph.D. (University of Washington, Seattle), during her tenure as Membership Chairperson of the Association for Advancement of Behavior Therapy, with a committee consisting of Richard Bootzin, Ph.D., Joseph Cautela, Ph.D., Perry London, Ph.D., Morris Perloff, Ph.D., Richard Stuart, D.S.W., and Todd Risley, Ph.D.

individuals change in ways they would like to change. There is an emphasis in behavior therapy on checking up on how effective the therapy is by monitoring and evaluating the individual's progress. Most behaviorally-oriented therapists believe that the current environment is most important in affecting the person's present behavior. Early life experiences, long time intrapsychic conflicts, or the individual's personality structure are considered to be of less importance than what is happening in the person's life at the present time. The procedures used in behavior therapy are generally intended to improve the individual's self-control by expanding the person's skills, abilities, and independence.

QUALIFICATIONS AND TRAINING NECESSARY FOR PARTICULAR MENTAL HEALTH PROFESSIONALS

Behavior therapy can be done by a number of different mental health professionals. Competent behavior therapists are trained in many different disciplines, and the distinction between different types of mental health professions can sometimes be confusing. Therefore, we have listed below a brief description of the training received by different types of professionals who may offer behavior therapy.

Psychiatric Social Workers

A psychiatric social worker must have a college degree, plus at least two years of graduate training in a program accredited by the Council on Social Work Education. A psychiatric social worker who is certified by the Academy of Certified Social Workers (ACSW) must have a master's or doctoral degree in Social Work (M.S.W. or D.S.W.) from a program approved by the Council on Social Work Education, two years of post-degree experience in the practice of social work, and membership in the National Association of Social Workers. In addition, the certified psychiatric social worker must pass a written exam and submit several professional references. Licensing procedures vary from state to state.

Psychologists

Psychologists usually have doctoral degrees (Ph.D., Ed.D., or Psy.D.) from graduate programs approved by the American Psychological Association. The *National Register of Health Service Providers in Psychology* lists psychologists who have a doctoral degree from a regionally accredited university, have at least two years of supervised experience in health services, one of which is postdoctoral, and are licensed or certified by the state for the independent practice of psychology. After five years of post-doctoral experience, a psychologist may apply for credentials from the American Board of Professional Psychology. This involves a review by the Board of the applicant's experience and an examination that the applicant must pass. Licensing or certification procedures vary from state to state.

Psychiatrists

A psychiatrist must have a medical degree. Although technically an individual can practice psychiatry having had four years of medical school and a one-year medical internship, most psychiatrists continue their training in a three-year residency program in psychiatry. Psychiatrists who have Board certification have had two years of post-residency experience in practicing psychiatry and must have passed an examination given by the American Board of Psychiatry and Neurology.

PRACTICAL INFORMATION ABOUT THERAPISTS

You have the right to obtain the following information about any potential therapist. This information may be obtained from the referral person, over the phone with the therapist, or at your first visit with the therapist. Although you may not feel that all this information is relevant, you will need a substantial amount of it in order to evaluate whether a particular therapist would be good for you.

Your first session with a therapist should always be a consultation. This session does not commit you to working with the therapist. The goals in the first session should be to find out whether therapy would be useful for you and whether this particular therapist is likely to be helpful to you. During this session you may want to discuss with your therapist any values which are particularly important to you. If your therapist's views are very different from yours, you may want to find a therapist more compatible with you. An important aspect of therapy for you will be the relationship between you and the therapist. This first session is a time for you to determine whether you will feel comfortable and confident working with this particular therapist.

The following are things you need to know about a prospective therapist.

Training and Qualifications

An earlier section of this guide gives a description of the qualifications and amount of training necessary for an individual to obtain a particular mental health–related degree. You should find out whether the individual therapist is licensed or certified by your state. If the person is not licensed or certified by your state, you may want to ask whether the person is being supervised by another mental health professional.

Because behavior therapists vary in types of training, there are no set rules on which professional qualifications would be best for any given person. It is common, though, for clients to want to know about the training, experience, and other professional qualifications of a potential therapist. Good therapists will not mind being asked questions about their qualifications and will freely give you any professional information which you request. If a therapist does not answer your questions, you should consult another therapist.

Fees

Many people feel uncomfortable asking about fees. However, it is important information which a good therapist will be quite willing to give a potential client. The following are financial questions you may want to cover with a therapist. This information may be obtained over the phone or during your first visit. You will want to know:

1. How much does the therapist charge per session?
2. Does the therapist charge according to income (sliding scale)?
3. Does the therapist charge for the initial session? (Since many therapists *do* charge for the initial session, you should get this information before your first visit.)
4. Is there a policy concerning vacations and missed or cancelled sessions? Is there a charge?
5. Will your health insurance cover you if you see this therapist?
6. Will the therapist want you to pay after each session, or will you be billed periodically?

Other Questions

The following are other questions you may want to ask a potential therapist:

1. How many times a week will the therapist want to see you?
2. How long will each session last?
3. How long does the therapist expect treatment to last? (Some therapists only do time-limited therapy, whereas others set no such limits.)
4. What are some of the treatment approaches likely to be used?
5. Does the therapist accept phone calls at the office or at home?
6. When your therapist is out of town or otherwise unavailable, is there someone else you can call if an emergency arises?
7. Are there any limitations on confidentiality?

QUESTIONS TO ASK WHEN DECIDING ON A THERAPIST

A behavior therapist will devote the first few sessions to assessing the extent and causes of the concerns which you have. Generally, your therapist will be asking quite specific questions about the concerns or problems causing you distress and about when and where these occur. As the assessment progresses, you can expect that you and your therapist will arrive at mutually agreeable goals for how you want to change. If you cannot agree on the goals of therapy, you should consider finding another therapist.

Once the initial goals are decided upon, you can expect the therapist to discuss with you one or more approaches for helping you reach your goals. As you continue therapy, you can expect your therapist to continually evaluate with you your progress toward these goals. If you are not progressing, or if progress is too slow, your therapist will most likely suggest modifying or changing the treatment approach. At each of these points you may want to ask yourself the following questions:

1. Do you understand what the therapist has asked you to do?
2. Do the therapist's instructions seem relevant to your objectives?
3. Do you believe that following these instructions is likely to help you make significant progress?
4. Has the therapist given you a choice of alternative therapy approaches?
5. Has the therapist explained possible side effects of the therapy?
6. Do you know what the therapist's own values are, to the extent that they are relevant to your problem?

WHAT TO DO IF YOU ARE DISSATISFIED WITH YOUR THERAPIST

Talk with Your Therapist

People often feel angry or frustrated at times about their therapy. If you do, you should discuss these concerns, dissatisfactions, and questions with the therapist. A good therapist will be open to hearing them and discussing your dissatisfactions with you.

Get a Second Opinion

If you feel that the issues and problems you have raised with your therapist are not being resolved, you may want to consider asking for a consultation with another professional. Usually the therapist you are seeing can suggest someone you can consult. If your therapist objects to your consulting another professional, you should change to another therapist who will not object.

Consider Changing Therapists

Many people feel that it is never acceptable to change therapists once therapy has begun. This is simply not true. Good therapists realize that they might not be appropriate for every person.

The most important thing you need to ask yourself when deciding to continue with a particular therapist is "Am I changing in the direction I want to change?" If you do not feel that you are improving, and if, after discussing this with your therapist, it does not appear likely to you that you will improve with this therapist, you should consult another therapist.

How to Get the Names of Behavior Therapists

If you don't already have the name of a therapist, you might try some of the following suggestions:

1. Ask for recommendations from your family physician, friends, and relatives.

2. Look through the Association for Advancement of Behavior Therapy Membership Directory. AABT is not a certifying organization, and not all members listed offer behavior therapy. However, you might call persons listed in the directory to ask for a referral. Members are listed by city and state, as well as alphabetically.

3. Call your state psychological association or district psychiatric association, and ask for a referral. You can locate your state psychological association by writing or calling the American Psychological Association, 750 First Street, N.E., Washington, DC 20002, phone (202) 336-5000. Only certified or licensed persons will be referred by these organizations. District psychiatric associations can be found by calling or writing the American Psychiatric Association, 1400 "K" Street, N.W., Washington, DC 20005, phone (202) 682-6000.

4. Call the university psychology, social work, or medical school psychiatry departments in your area and ask for a referral. Ask to speak with someone in clinical or counseling psychology, the chairperson of the social work department, or the chairperson of the department of psychiatry.

5. Call your local community mental health clinic. The clinic may have a behavior therapist on the staff or be able to give you a referral.

6. Look in the directories of the American Psychological Association and the American Psychiatric Association. Copies of these directories should be in your public library. Members in these organizations will often be able to give you a referral.

7. Look in the *National Register of Health Service Providers in Psychology* published by the Council of National Health Service Providers in Psychology, 1120 "G" Street, N.W., Suite 330, Washington, DC 20005, phone (202) 783-7663. Persons listed might be able to give you a referral.

8. Look in the National Association of Social Workers' *Register of Clinical Social Workers* published by the National Association of Social Workers, 750 First Street, N.E., Suite 700, Washington, DC 20002, phone (202) 408-8600. Persons listed might be able to give you a referral.

Appendix B

Answers for Participation Exercises

Participation Exercise 3-1: DISTINGUISHING BETWEEN TRAITS AND BEHAVIORS

1. T	5. T	9. T	13. B	17. T
2. B	6. T	10. B	14. T	18. T
3. B	7. B	11. T	15. T	19. T
4. B	8. T	12. B	16. B	20. B

Participation Exercise 3-2: TRANSLATING TRAITS INTO BEHAVIORS

1. *Sociable*
   Attending social events
   Meeting new people
   Inviting people to your house
   Talking with strangers
   Going places where people
      often gather
   Being with other people rather
      than being alone

2. *Hostile*
   Criticizing someone slanderously
   Striking a person
   Spreading rumors about someone
   Fighting
   Defacing someone's property

3. *Helpful*
   Giving a hitchhiker a lift
   Tutoring a student
   Lending money to a friend
   Doing volunteer work
   Changing a flat tire for a
      stranger
   Giving someone good advice

4. *Thrifty*
   Budgeting your money
   Using a car pool
   Making your own clothes
   Sharing an apartment
   Shopping at sales

(continued)

5. *Dependable*
Being on time
Keeping a promise
Adhering to a schedule
Paying back borrowed money

6. *Smart*
Getting good grades in school
Scoring high on an I.Q. test
Reading difficult books
Writing a book
Speaking several languages
fluently
Solving complex problems

7. *Patient*
Sticking to a long, frustrating task
until it is completed
Answering a rude customer
politely
Cheerfully waiting for a late
person
Tutoring a "slow" student
Calmly teaching a beginning
driver
Sitting attentively through a
boring lecture

8. *Healthy*
Exercising regularly
Eating nutritious foods
Sleeping an appropriate number
of hours each night
Passing a physical examination
Attending a health spa
Bringing blood pressure to
normal

Participation Exercise 3-3:   Distinguishing Between Overt and Covert Behaviors

1. O	5. O	9. C	13. O	17. C
2. C	6. C	10. O	14. C	18. O
3. O	7. C	11. C	15. O	19. C
4. C	8. O	12. C	16. O	20. O

Participation Exercise 3-4: FINDING OVERT BEHAVIORAL ANCHORS FOR COVERT BEHAVIORS

1. *Silent reading*
   Looking at a page of a book (for a reasonable time)
   Eyes moving across lines of page
   Lip movements while looking at page
   Turning pages (at reasonable time intervals)

2. *Worrying*
   Pacing
   Saying you are worried
   Biting your fingernails
   Chain smoking

3. *Feeling happy*
   Smiling
   Laughing
   Saying you are happy
   Telling jokes
   Playing
   "Jumping for joy"

4. *Being interested (in a particular topic)*
   Looking at the person talking to you
   Taking courses on a subject
   Asking questions about a subject
   Working in a field of interest
   Talking about the interest

5. *Listening (to a speaker)*
   Looking directly at the speaker
   Taking notes on what the speaker is saying
   Verbally disagreeing with the speaker
   Asking questions about the talk
   Telling others about what the speaker had to say

6. *Liking (a particular person)*
   Often speaking with the person
   Smiling in the company of the person
   Giving presents to the person
   Saying you like the person
   Inviting the person to do things with you
   Writing to the person often

Participation Exercise 3-5: IDENTIFYING ANTECEDENTS AND CONSEQUENCES

Antecedents	*Consequences*
1. *Calling the police*	
Hot evening	Reported the crime
Sitting in her apartment	Was thanked by police
Looking out window	Police rushed to the scene
Saw attack	Felt she did the right thing

(continued)

Antecedents	Consequences

2. *Going to a play*
   Play was in town
   Juanita read about play
   Play received good reviews
   Got a pass for the play
   Juanita expected to earn
     extra credits

Earned extra credits
Was disappointed
Felt she wasted her time
Her grade was boosted

3. *Getting up late*
   Got to bed very late
   Was intoxicated
   Forgot to set the alarm

Missed the bus to work
Missed two important clients

4. *Cooking a fancy meal*
   Parents coming for visit
   Brendan wanted to make a
     good impression
   Perfect situation for trying
     new recipe
   He enjoyed preparing fancy
     meals

His kitchen was messed up
The meal was a success
Parents enjoyed his meal
Brendan enjoyed the meal
Brendan felt satisfied

5. *Shopping for new clothes*
   Jane needed new clothes
   Saved enough money to go
     shopping
   Took family car
   Obtained directions to shopping
     mall

She had a new wardrobe
She felt good
People complimented her

6. *Pulling a fire alarm*
   Saw alarm box
   Wanted to impress his friends
   Thought of the excitement if he
     pulled the alarm
   Read the instructions
   Saw no one was around

Fire trucks came
Crowd gathered
Fire chief was angry
Chief announced it was a false
  alarm
Investigation ensued

Participation Exercise 4-1: FINDING COMPETING ACCELERATION TARGET BEHAVIORS TO SUBSTITUTE FOR UNDESIRABLE BEHAVIORS

Deceleration	*Acceleration*
1. *Eating junk food between meals*	Eating only fruits between meals Only drinking between meals Eating only at mealtime Buying only healthy foods
2. *Cramming for exams*	Studying 2 hours per day a week before exam Putting all books away at 11 P.M. the night before exam Scheduling nonstudy activities the night before exam
3. *Blowing an entire paycheck*	Immediately depositing part of check into bank account Sticking to a budget Having paycheck automatically deposited Having someone else hold your money for you Immediately paying off all bills
4. *Using foul language*	Using only decent language Using a nonsense word when angry Counting to 10 when frustrated Stamping feet instead of swearing
5. *Leaving lights on that are not in use*	Shutting lights off immediately after use Turning lights on only when needed Working with daylight only Shutting lights off when leaving room
6. *Wasting time*	Having more planned than you can complete Following a schedule Having activity prepared for free times Carrying a portable hobby (such as reading, knitting)

(continued)

	Deceleration	*Acceleration*
7.	*Being late for classes*	Arriving 5 minutes early to class
8.	*Procrastinating in paying bills*	Paying all bills within 3 days of receipt
		Having someone pay all bills for you
9.	*Littering*	Using garbage cans
		Carrying litter bag with you
		Using nondisposable items (such as glasses instead of paper cups)

Participation Exercise 4-2:   RESURRECTING THE DEAD: IDENTIFYING AND CORRECTING DEAD PERSON BEHAVIORS

Dead Person Instruction	*Live Person Instruction*
"Don't be impolite."	"Be polite."
	"Chew with your mouth closed."
	"Please excuse yourself."
	"Say 'please'!"
DO NOT LITTER	PLACE TRASH IN CANS
	TAKE GARBAGE WITH YOU
	CLEAN UP BEFORE LEAVING
	KEEP AREA CLEAN
"No running in the hallway"	"Walk down the hallway."
	"Walk slowly."
DO NOT ENTER	USE OTHER DOOR
	TRY ANOTHER ENTRANCE
	USE ELEVATOR ONLY

(continued)

Dead Person Instruction	*Live Person Instruction*
"Don't cry; big boys don't cry."	"Be proud that you're doing so much better." "Put a smile on your face for effort." "Keep on trying; you'll get it." "Go sit down on the chair for a few minutes if you're going to keep crying!"
"Don't eat with your fingers."	"Use your fork to eat that." "Try using a spoon." "Keep your fork and knife in your hands while you eat."
DO NOT FEED THE ANIMALS	IF YOU ARE THINKING OF GIVING OUR ANIMALS FOOD, PLEASE WALK AWAY IMMEDIATELY KEEP ALL FOOD OUT OF REACH OF ANIMALS GIVE FOOD TO OTHER PEOPLE ONLY PLACE FOOD ON TABLE WHILE VIEWING THE ANIMALS
"I don't want to hear another word out of you."	"Walk silently back to your room." "Place both hands over your mouth and go back to your bed."
NO LEFT TURN	MAKE A RIGHT TURN YOU MUST GO STRAIGHT TURN RIGHT OR GO STRAIGHT
"Don't look at other students' tests."	"Keep your eyes on your own tests." "Look straight ahead only."
DO NOT WRITE BELOW THE RED LINE	WRITE ABOVE THE RED LINE PUT YOUR PENCIL DOWN WHEN YOU COME TO THE RED LINE
"No diving off the side."	"You may jump off the side only." "Stay in the water at all times."
"Don't hit your sister when she takes your toy."	"Tell someone when your sister takes your toy." "Ask your sister to give your toy back to you." "Find another toy to play with when your sister takes your toy."

Participation Exercise 5-1: WHAT, WHEN, WHERE, HOW, AND HOW OFTEN? BEHAVIORAL INTERVIEWING

1. What does your daughter say or do that leads you to say her self-concept is so poor?

   What happens after she says or does these things?

   When does she seem to lack self-confidence?

   How often do these situations occur?

   Are there situations in which she appears to have more self-confidence?

   How often does she fail at things that she tries?

   What exactly do you mean when you say "she fails"?

2. What are you thinking about when you feel like you're going to explode?

   How often do you feel this way?

   When did this pressure seem to begin?

   When do you usually feel the most pressure?

   Where do you feel that you are going to explode? In your head? In your stomach?

   What happens immediately after you get these feelings?

3. What does your son do when he is behaving like a monster?

   Where does this typically occur?

   How often does your son act this way?

   What happens immediately before he begins acting like a monster?

   What happens after he acts this way?

   When did these behaviors first begin?

4. What do you actually do when you are "at each others' throats?"

   How long will these conflicts typically last?

   Where do they take place?

   What are you generally thinking about when these conflicts begin?

   What are you typically doing when the conflicts begin?

   How do the conflicts generally end?

5. What do you say to yourself when you feel that you have avoided a responsibility?

   How does avoiding responsibilities make you feel?

   How often do you have these thoughts and feelings?

   What specifically do you think is "stupid" about your attitude?

   When do you usually feel this way?

◆

Participation Exercise 7-3:   NOVEL OVERCORRECTION

1. Littering

Restitution:

Clean the mess up.
Pay for workers to clean up the littering.

Positive Practice:

Spend several hours for an entire week picking up garbage.
Empty all trash cans in the park for a week.
Hand out fliers urging people to dispose of garbage properly.
Post signs about keeping the park free of litter.

2. Misspelling

Restitution:

Rewrite the paper without spelling errors.
Apologize to person reading the paper for being careless.

Positive Practice:

Correctly write misspelled words 50 times.
Memorize the spelling of commonly misspelled words.
Spend several hours correcting spelling errors in other students' papers.

3. Leaving clothes out

Restitution:

Put clothes where they belong.
Apologize to roommates (and other people who live in the house).

Positive Practice:

Empty drawers and closets and return the clothes to their proper storage locations several times.
Put roommates' clothes away for them for one week.
Go through the entire house and return all misplaced items to their proper storage locations.

4. Being late

Restitution:

Apologize to anyone inconvenienced.

Positive Practice:

Arrive at the next 10 appointments 15 minutes early.

(continued)

5. **Trashing lawn**

   Restitution:

   Clean and repair damage caused to neighbor's lawn.
   Apologize to neighbor.
   Apologize to other neighbors likely to have seen your "handiwork."
   Pay for all clean-up and repair of property.

   Positive Practice:

   Mow and care for neighbor's lawn for a month.
   Mow several other neighbors' lawns once for free.
   Volunteer to do work on the grounds at local park.
   Spend an entire day working for a landscaper for no pay.

6. **Leaving lights on**

   Restitution:

   Turn all unnecessary lights off.
   Apologize to others in the house for failing to turn lights off.

   Positive Practice:

   Inspect house three times a day for a week for any lights that are unnecessarily on.
   Make a list of all electrical appliances in house and inspect house three times a day for a week for any appliances that are unnecessarily on.

7. **Putting dishes in the sink**

   Restitution:

   Wash the dishes you just put in the sink.
   Apologize to the other people living in the house.

   Positive Practice:

   Wash and dry all dishes for one week.
   Take all dishes out of cupboards and wash them.
   Volunteer to wash dishes at a local soup kitchen.

Participation Exercise 12-5: COGNITIVE RESTRUCTURING

1. "If I work real hard, I may be able to get it all done for tomorrow."
   "This is going to be tough but it is still possible to do it."
   "It will be a real challenge finishing this assignment for tomorrow."
   "If I don't get it finished, I'll just have to ask the teacher for an extension."

(continued)

2. "What's done is done; I'll just have to make the best of it."
   "I'll just have to figure out a way that I can pay for this."
   "This is going to cost me, but thank God no one was injured."
   "Maybe my father will understand if I explain it to him calmly."

3. "I'm sure there are others who aren't great dancers either."
   "Hey, it's all for fun. So what if I don't dance well."
   "There's still time to learn. I'll ask my cousin to give me a few quick lessons."
   "I'll just do what everyone else does. Maybe no one will even notice."

4. "I'll just have to look harder for another job."
   "There will be rough times ahead, but I've dealt with rough times before."
   "Hey, maybe my next job will be a better deal altogether."
   "There are agencies that can probably help me get some kind of a job."

5. "I'll miss everyone, but it doesn't mean we can't stay in touch."
   "Just think of all the new people I'm going to meet."
   "I guess it will be kind of exciting moving to a new home."
   "Now I'll have two places to call home."

6. "Maybe I'll find he (she) is not so bad a person after all."
   "Just because we are roommates doesn't mean we have to be friends."
   "If it doesn't work out maybe I can find a way to switch roommates."
   "Maybe if I act friendly toward him (her), he (she) will act better toward me."
   "Just because I don't get along with my roommate doesn't mean my whole year is going to be bad."

7. "I really thought our relationship would work, but it's not the end of the world."
   "Maybe we can try again in the future."
   "I'll just have to try to keep myself busy and not let it bother me."
   "It sure is hard to accept, but I'll just have to live with it."
   "If I met him (her), there is no reason why I won't meet someone else someday."

8. "I'll just have to reapply next year."
   "There are things I can do with my life other than going to grad school."
   "I guess a lot of good students get turned down. It's just so damn competitive."
   "I can still get a half-decent job I can enjoy."
   "This could be a good thing for me. It will give me time to think about my future."
   "Perhaps there are a few other programs that I could apply to."

9. "I have as much to say as anyone else in the class."
   "My ideas may be different, but they're still valid."
   "It's OK to be a bit nervous; I'll relax as I start talking."
   "I might as well say something; how bad could it sound?"
   "I may as well speak up; I'm sure half the class feels the same way I do."

(continued)

10. "Now I'm really behind. I'll just have to put in a few extra hours later to make it up."

"Hey, I enjoyed reading the magazines. I think it was almost worth falling behind."

"There will be time in the morning to finish my work. I'll just have to get up a little earlier."

"Just because I blew those 2 hours doesn't mean I have to give up and blow the next 2 hours."

"I should know better, but I guess I don't. So I'll just get into the work now."

Participation Exercise 13-1:

BEING YOUR OWN BOSS: USING SELF-INSTRUCTIONS

1. "Just relax and take one thing at a time."
"Get yourself organized before starting anything."
"Monday is still a ways away."
"Keep your mind on one thing at a time."

2. "Keep your eyes on the road."
"I've got to keep focusing on the lights."
"Not much longer to go."

3. "Slow it down. Don't forget to check the list."
"Pants, shirts, ties, and shoes." (repeated)
"What do I need for tomorrow? Think."

4. "Keep focusing on the salad menu, that's it."
"Come on, you've come too far to turn back."
"You can do it."

5. "One step at a time."
"Almost there; got to keep pushing."
"Don't give up; stay with it."
"Keep your mind on your breathing."

6. "Right, left, left, right." (repeated)
"Look for the traffic light and stop signs."
"Okay, almost there. You're going to make it."

7. "This is my big chance."
"Got to give it all I have."
"Getting this job will be great."

8. "Calm down. Just act naturally."
"Don't forget to talk slowly."
"Remember, this is all for fun."

Participation Exercise 15-1:

DESIGNING STIMULUS CONTROL PROCEDURES TO ENHANCE STUDYING

1. Study at set times each day.

2. Tell others what your study times are and ask them not to disturb you during those times.

3. Study in the same place (such as at the desk in your room).

4. Use your study location *only* to study (for instance, write letters and pay bills somewhere else).

5. Keep all necessary study materials (such as pads, pens, and highlighter) in the same location, and do not remove them from that location.

6. Make the study location free of distractions.

7. Before studying, make a list of what you will attempt to accomplish during the study period and prioritize the tasks.

8. When you are studying, do nothing else (for example, do not listen to background music, answer the telephone, or eat).

9. Study with other people only if (a) you are actually collaborating on study tasks (for example, preparing a group project or quizzing one another) or (b) the other people will not distract you.

10. If you begin to daydream while you are studying, leave the designated study area.

Participation Exercise 18-1:

AFTERTHOUGHTS ABOUT CONTEMPORARY BEHAVIOR THERAPY

Note: The following explanations are overviews only; see the appropriate parts of the text for full explanations.

1. To begin with, there are no "well-established laws of learning." Instead, a number of *theories* of learning exist. Some, but not all, behavior therapy procedures do use various *principles* of learning, such as reinforcement, modeling, and extinction. Although learning theories frequently are used to explain how behavioral interventions work, behavior therapy is not accurately defined in terms of the explanatory theories.

2. Behavior therapy directly changes the *maintaining conditions* of problem behaviors (symptoms), thereby indirectly changing the problem behaviors.

3. A trusting relationship is crucial in behavior therapy for a variety of reasons. For example, a trusting relationship is necessary for the client to be candid with the therapist and follow the therapist's directives and for the therapist to have confidence that the client is providing accurate information. In behavior therapy, a trusting relationship facilitates the treatment procedures. In contrast, in other forms of therapy, such as insight-oriented therapies (for example, psychoanalysis), the trusting relationship itself is the primary treatment procedure.

(continued)

4. Feelings are covert behaviors that constitute one of the most frequently treated types of problems. Feelings may be treated directly (as in exposure therapy for anxiety) and indirectly (as in shaping increasingly more active behaviors for depression).

5. Verbal interchange is usually the major means by which the client and the behavior therapist communicate. However, behavior therapy is an action-oriented therapy that involves much more than just talking about the client's problems.

6. Psychotherapy, of any variety, is highly unlikely to be effective without the cooperation of the client. Furthermore, behavior therapy generally involves the active participation of clients in their therapy so that their cooperation is critical.

7. Behavior therapy usually brings about changes in problem behaviors in considerably fewer therapy sessions than many other forms of psychotherapy (especially verbal, insight-oriented therapies) but generally not in as few as five sessions.

8. Cognitive-behavioral therapy procedures directly deal with clients' mental processes or cognitions that are either maintaining overt problem behaviors or are themselves covert problem behaviors.

9. Reinforcement procedures are as effective with adults as with children, although many of the specific, generalized reinforcers are different for children and adults.

10. Few behavior therapy procedures involve painful or aversive treatments. Further, aversive procedures are used in a small minority of cases, usually after nonaversive procedures have been tried and have failed. Moreover, because aversive procedures are deceleration therapies, they must be supplemented with acceleration therapies, which comprise the vast majority of behavior therapy procedures.

11. Behavior therapy treats a wide array of complex human problems. However, the focus of behavior therapy is on target behaviors, which are relatively simple aspects of (complex) problem behaviors.

12. Biological treatments, such as drug therapy and psychosurgery, are *not* part of behavior therapy.

13. In behavior therapy, clients decide on their goals for therapy. However, because clients often do not have well-defined goals, behavior therapists may have to help clients generate realistic and clearly delineated goals for therapy.

14. Clients in behavior therapy are actively involved in their treatment, especially in terms of carrying out vital homework assignments. Clearly, then, clients share responsibility with their behavior therapists for the success of treatment.

Work Sheets for Participation Exercises

WORK SHEET 3-1

Antecedents	Behavior	Consequences
	Calling the police	
	Going to a play	
	Getting up late	
	Cooking a fancy meal	
	Shopping for new clothes	
	Pulling a fire alarm	

WORK SHEET 4-1

Part I

I. *Situation/Context*	II. *Instruction*	III. *Live Person Behavior*
Parent to child	"Don't be impolite."	
Sign in park	DO NOT LITTER	
Teacher to student	"No running in the hallway."	
Sign on one of two side-by-side doors	DO NOT ENTER	
Parent to young boy having trouble tying his shoe	"Don't cry; big boys don't cry."	
Parent to child at dinner table	"Don't eat with your fingers."	
Sign at petting zoo	DO NOT FEED THE ANIMALS	
Parent to child being put to bed	"I don't want to hear another word out of you."	
Traffic sign at fork in road	NO LEFT TURN	
Teacher to student	"Don't look at other students' tests."	
Instructions on a written form	DO NOT WRITE BELOW THE RED LINE	
Lifeguard to swimmer	"No diving off the side."	
Parent to child	"Don't hit your sister when she takes your toy."	

WORK SHEET 4-1, continued

Part II

I. Situation/Context	II. Instruction	III. Live Person Behavior

WORK SHEET 5-1

_____ Paces	_____ Strokes beard
_____ Fumbles with notes	_____ Tells jokes
_____ Arrives late	_____ Stutters
_____ Speaks in monotone	_____ Loses train of thought
_____ Talks with hands	_____ Argues with students
_____ Smiles	_____ Reads notes
_____ Taps pen on desk	_____ Fiddles with clothing
_____ Pauses for long time	_____ Repeats self
_____ Plays with hair	_____ Drinks coffee in class
_____ Talks rapidly	_____ Ridicules students
_____ Hums	_____ Listens attentively to students
_____ Dismisses class early	_____ Gives hard exams
_____ Checks watch	_____ Tells personal stories
_____ Sits on desk	_____ Falls asleep
_____ Coughs	_____ Cracks knuckles
_____ Makes eye contact	_____ Uses blackboard
_____ Speaks softly	_____ Talks to students before class
_____ Keeps class late	_____ Talks to students after class
_____ Picks nose	_____ Cancels class
_____ Rubs eyes	_____ Takes attendance

WORK SHEET 5-1: DUPLICATE FORM

_____ Paces	_____ Strokes beard
_____ Fumbles with notes	_____ Tells jokes
_____ Arrives late	_____ Stutters
_____ Speaks in monotone	_____ Loses train of thought
_____ Talks with hands	_____ Argues with students
_____ Smiles	_____ Reads notes
_____ Taps pen on desk	_____ Fiddles with clothing
_____ Pauses for long time	_____ Repeats self
_____ Plays with hair	_____ Drinks coffee in class
_____ Talks rapidly	_____ Ridicules students
_____ Hums	_____ Listens attentively to students
_____ Dismisses class early	_____ Gives hard exams
_____ Checks watch	_____ Tells personal stories
_____ Sits on desk	_____ Falls asleep
_____ Coughs	_____ Cracks knuckles
_____ Makes eye contact	_____ Uses blackboard
_____ Speaks softly	_____ Talks to students before class
_____ Keeps class late	_____ Talks to students after class
_____ Picks nose	_____ Cancels class
_____ Rubs eyes	_____ Takes attendance

WORK SHEET 5-2

Activity	Subjective Feeling	Activity Level	Combined Rating	Heart Rate
Resting	1	1	1	(Resting Rate)
A1.				
A2.				
A3.				
B1.				
B2.				
B3.				

WORK SHEET 6-1

	Frequency	Pleasantness	Frequency × Pleasantness
Attending a concert			
Attending a club meeting			
Being with my parents			
Being alone			
Complimenting or praising someone			
Cooking			
Dancing			
Dating			
Daydreaming			
Doing volunteer work			
Doing art work			
Driving			
Eating out			
Eating snacks			
Exercising			
Getting up early in the morning			
Getting dressed up			
Getting/giving a massage or back rub			
Going to a mall			
Going to the movies			
Going to a party			
Helping someone			
Listening to or watching the news			
Listening to music			
Listening to radio talk shows			

WORK SHEET 6-1, continued

	Frequency	Pleasantness	Frequency × Pleasantness
Playing videogames			
Playing sports			
Playing a musical instrument			
Playing with a pet			
Playing board games			
Reading the newspaper			
Reading fiction			
Riding a bike			
Staying up late			
Saying prayers			
Shopping			
Skating			
Sleeping late			
Straightening up (house or car)			
Taking a walk			
Taking a nap			
Taking a shower			
Talking on the telephone			
Teaching someone			
Telling stories and jokes			
Watching a TV program			
Watching a video			
Watching sports events			
Watching people			
Writing letters			

WORK SHEET 8-1

BASELINE

Chore	Frequency	Sum
1.		
2.		
3.		
4.		

WORK SHEET 8-2

WAY TO EARN POINTS

		A Chores	B Points Earned
Most Unpleasant	1.		40
	2.		30
	3.		20
Least Unpleasant	4.		10

BACKUP REINFORCERS

		C Activities	D Point Cost
Most Enjoyable	1.		25
	2.		20
	3.		10
Least Enjoyable	4.		5

WORK SHEET 8-3

TOKEN ECONOMY

Chore	Frequency	Sum
1.		
2.		
3.		
4.		

WORK SHEET 8-4

REVERSAL

Chore	Frequency	Sum
1.		
2.		
3.		
4.		

WORK SHEET 8-5

Points Earned	Points Spent	Point Balance

WORK SHEET 8-5, continued

Points Earned	Points Spent	Point Balance

WORK SHEET 9-1

Situation:			
Date	SUDs	Feelings and thoughts	What is happening

WORK SHEET 12-1

Musturbatory Thoughts	Rational Rebuttal	Rational Thoughts

WORK SHEET 16-1

Problem	Target Behavior	Maintaining Conditions	Intervention
A1. Wearing seat belts in car			
A2. Preventing child abduction			
A3. Preventing child molestation			
A4. Teaching children what to do in case of fire			

WORK SHEET 16-1, continued

Problem	Target Behavior	Maintaining Conditions	Intervention
B1. Reducing shoplifting			
B2. Reducing students' destruction of school property			
C1. Choosing healthy foods in a restaurant			
C2. Taking children for recommended vaccinations			

(continued)

WORK SHEET 16-1, continued

Problem	Target Behavior	Maintaining Conditions	Intervention
D1. Reducing littering in public places			
D2. Sorting and recycling beverage containers and paper			
D3. Reducing electricity consumed at home			
D4. Reducing the use of automobiles			

ABA study Single subject reversal study consisting of three phases: baseline (A), treatment (B), and reversal (to baseline) (A).

ABAB study Single subject reversal study consisting of four phases: baseline (A), treatment (B), reversal (to baseline) (A), and reinstatement of treatment (B).

ABC model Temporal sequence of antecedents, behavior, and consequences.

acceleration target behavior Adaptive behavior increased in therapy.

acceptability Outcome measure that assesses how palatable therapy procedures are to clients.

activity schedule List of the day's activities used in cognitive therapy to provide structure in clients' lives and motivate them to remain active.

adaptation period Initial period in systematic naturalistic observation in which observations are made but the data are not used. Its purpose is to allow the client to become accustomed to the observer's presence in order to reduce reactivity.

analogue experiment Experiment in which the conditions of the study are similar, but not identical, to the conditions that exist in actual clinical practice.

antecedents Events that occur or that are present before a behavior is performed.

anxiety hierarchy List of events that elicit anxiety, ranked in order of increasing anxiety.

anxiety-induction therapy Exposure therapy in which the client's level of anxiety is heightened initially in order to reduce it eventually.

assertion training Specific skills training procedures used to teach assertive behaviors.

assertive behaviors Actions that secure and maintain what one is entitled to without infringing on the rights of others.

automatic thoughts Cognitive therapy term for maladaptive thoughts that appear to arise reflexively, without prior deliberation or reasoning.

aversion-relief therapy Aversion therapy in which the relief following the termination of the aversive stimulus is associated with a competing adaptive behavior.

aversion therapy Treatment that directly decelerates a maladaptive behavior by associating it with a distinctly unpleasant stimulus.

backup reinforcer Actual reinforcer that can be purchased with tokens in a token economy.

baseline Repeated measurement of the natural occurrence of a target behavior prior to the introduction of a treatment. It provides a standard to evaluate changes in a target behavior after a treatment has been introduced.

behavior Anything a person does.

behavioral child management training Treatment package taught to parents consisting of acceleration and deceleration behavior therapy procedures to effectively manage their children's behavioral problems.

behavioral community psychology Subfield of behavior therapy that uses behavior therapy technology to deal with problems affecting the population at large.

behavioral deficit Adaptive behavior that clients are not performing often enough, long enough, or strongly enough.

behavioral excess Maladaptive behavior that clients are performing too often, for too long, or too strongly.

behavior rehearsal Therapy procedure in which a client practices performing a target behavior.

biofeedback Feedback giving clients specific information about their physiological processes.

booster treatment Additional treatment after therapy has been terminated, designed to promote the long-term maintenance of therapeutic gains.

brief/graduated exposure therapy Treatment in which the client is exposed to an anxiety-evoking event for a short period and in a gradual manner that minimizes anxiety.

caring-days technique Behavioral couple therapy procedure in which each partner deliberately performs behaviors that the other partner believes show caring.

checklist List of potential problem behaviors; someone who knows the client well checks those behaviors that are problematic for the client.

clinical significance Change following therapy that is meaningful for the client.

cognitive-behavioral coping skills therapy Treatment that teaches clients specific skills (both cognitive and overt actions) to deal effectively with difficult situations.

cognitive-behavioral therapy Treatment that changes cognitions that are the maintaining conditions of psychological disorders.

cognitive restructuring Technique of recognizing maladaptive thoughts and substituting adaptive ones for them.

cognitive restructuring therapy Treatment that teaches clients to substitute adaptive cognitions for the distorted and erroneous cognitions that are maintaining their problem behaviors.

cognitive therapy Cognitive restructuring therapy that emphasizes empirically testing hypotheses about the validity of maladaptive beliefs and substituting adaptive beliefs for them.

collaborative empiricism Cognitive therapy process in which the therapist and client work together to phrase the client's irrational beliefs as hypotheses and design homework "experiments" so the client can test these hypotheses.

competing responses Two behaviors that cannot easily be performed simultaneously.

consequences Events that occur as a result of a behavior being performed.

consequential deceleration therapy Treatment that directly decelerates a maladaptive behavior by changing its consequences.

contingency contract Written agreement between a client and one or more other people which specifies the relationship between performing target behaviors and their consequences.

continuous reinforcement schedule Schedule of reinforcement in which the target behavior is reinforced every time it is performed.

control group Group of clients in a therapy outcome experiment who do not receive the therapy so that they can be compared with a group of clients who receive the therapy.

coping desensitization Variation of systematic desensitization in which clients use specific anxiety-related bodily sensations as cues to actively cope with anxiety.

coping model Model who initially experiences difficulty performing a target behavior and gradually becomes competent.

covert behavior Behavior that other people cannot directly observe, such as thinking and feeling.

covert behavior rehearsal Procedure in which clients visualize themselves performing a target behavior.

covert modeling Procedure in which clients visualize a model's behaviors.

covert sensitization Aversion therapy in which an aversive stimulus and a maladaptive target behavior are associated completely in the client's imagination.

cue exposure Therapy procedure that exposes clients to cues associated with their addictive behaviors but prevents them from engaging in the addictive behaviors.

dead person rule Rule that reminds therapists to make target behaviors active—namely, never ask a client to "do" something a dead person can "do."

deceleration target behavior Maladaptive behavior decreased in therapy.

deep muscle relaxation Process of reducing muscle tension, used as a competing response to anxiety.

differential reinforcement Reinforcing an acceleration target behavior that is an alternative to the deceleration target behavior.

differential reinforcement of competing behaviors Procedure for indirectly decelerating a maladaptive behavior by reinforcing behaviors that compete with the deceleration target behavior.

differential reinforcement of incompatible behaviors Procedure for indirectly decelerating a maladaptive behavior by reinforcing behaviors incompatible with the deceleration target behavior.

differential reinforcement of low response rates Procedure for indirectly decelerating a maladaptive behavior by reinforcing less frequent performance of the target behavior.

differential reinforcement of other behaviors Procedure for indirectly decelerating a maladaptive behavior by reinforcing any behaviors other than the deceleration target behavior.

differential relaxation Relaxing all muscles not essential to the behaviors being performed.

direct self-report inventory Questionnaire containing brief statements or questions requiring simple, discrete answers that are used to provide information about a client's problem behaviors.

dry-bed training Treatment package for enuresis using shaping and overcorrection to teach clients the behaviors required to keep their beds dry throughout the night.

dry-pants method Daytime version of dry-bed training.

emotive imagery Procedure in which pleasant thoughts are used as competing responses for anxiety.

environment All external influences on behaviors.

exposure therapy Treatment for anxiety, fear, and other negative emotional responses that exposes clients, under carefully controlled conditions, to the situations or events that create the negative emotions.

extinction Process of withdrawing or withholding reinforcers to decrease maladaptive behaviors.

eye movement desensitization and reprocessing (EMDR) Exposure-based treatment that involves imaginal flooding, cognitive restructuring, and the induction of rapid, rhythmic eye movements in clients aimed at alleviating upsetting memories about traumatic experiences.

fading Process of gradually withdrawing prompts as the client performs the acceleration target behavior more frequently.

fear survey schedule Direct self-report inventory containing a list of situations and objects that may elicit fear or anxiety, which clients rate on a numerical scale of severity.

flooding Prolonged/intense in vivo or imaginal exposure to highly anxiety-evoking stimuli without the opportunity to avoid or escape from them.

follow-up assessment (or **follow-up**) Measurement of the client's functioning some time after therapy has been terminated to determine the durability of treatment effects.

generalized imitation The basic ability to learn by observing others and imitating them.

generalized reinforcer Consequence of a behavior that functions as a reinforcer for many people.

graded task assignment Cognitive therapy shaping technique in which clients are encouraged to perform small sequential steps leading to a goal.

group contingency Procedure in which the behaviors of a group of clients as a whole determine the consequences for each member of the group.

group hierarchy Common anxiety hierarchy used for all the clients in group systematic desensitization.

habit reversal Treatment package for tics incorporating awareness training, relaxation training, competing response training, and reinforcement.

homework assignments Specific therapeutic activities clients carry out on their own in their everyday environments.

implosive therapy Imaginal, prolonged/intense exposure therapy in which the client visualizes exaggerated scenes that include hypothesized stimuli related to the client's anxiety.

individual contingency Procedure in which the behaviors of an individual client determine the consequences for that client.

intermittent reinforcement schedule Schedule of reinforcement in which only some of the occurrences of a target behavior are reinforced.

interobserver reliability Extent to which two or more observers agree on their observations of a client's behaviors.

interoceptive exposure Therapy procedure that induces physical sensations of anxiety so that clients can practice using cognitive-behavioral coping skills to decrease anxiety.

interrater reliability Extent to which two or more raters agree on their ratings of a client's behaviors.

in vivo Term used to designate therapy procedures implemented in the client's natural environment (Latin for "in life").

in vivo exposure therapy Brief/graduated exposure to an actual anxiety-evoking event.

in vivo flooding Prolonged/intense exposure to an actual anxiety-evoking event.

live model Model who is actually present ("in the flesh").

long-term maintenance (of treatment gains) Durability over time of changes in the target behavior after therapy.

maintaining antecedents Prerequisites and situational cues that are present before a behavior is performed which set the stage for the behavior to occur.

maintaining consequences Events that occur as a result of a behavior being performed that increase the likelihood that the behavior will be repeated.

maintaining conditions Antecedents and consequences of a behavior that cause the behavior to be performed.

massed negative practice Treatment for tics in which the client deliberately performs the tic as rapidly as possible.

mastery and pleasure rating Cognitive therapy technique in which clients rate the degree of success and enjoyment they experience in doing daily activities.

mastery model Model who, from the outset, performs a target behavior competently.

model Person who demonstrates behaviors for another person (the observer).

modeling Therapy procedures in which a client observes a person demonstrating some behavior from which the client can benefit.

modes of behavior The four dimensions of behavior assessed and treated in behavior therapy—namely, overt actions, cognitions, emotions, and physiological responses.

multimethod assessment Use of two or more methods to gather information about a target behavior and its maintaining conditions.

multimodal assessment Assessment of two or more of the four modes of behavior.

multiple baseline study Single subject study in which baseline measures are obtained on two or more target behaviors; then the same therapy procedure is applied sequentially to each of the target behaviors. (In variations, the therapy is applied sequentially to the same target behavior either for two or more clients or in two or more settings.)

natural model Person in a client's natural environment who exhibits behaviors that the client can benefit from observing.

natural reinforcer A reinforcer that is readily available to clients in their natural environments.

negative reinforcement Process that occurs when the removal or avoidance of an event as a consequence of a behavior increases the likelihood that the behavior will be repeated.

negative reinforcer An event that is removed or avoided as a consequence of a behavior being performed which increases the likelihood that the behavior will be repeated.

observer In modeling therapy, person who observes a model demonstrating a behavior.

overcorrection Consequential deceleration therapy in which a client corrects the effects of a maladaptive behavior (restitution) and then intensively practices an appropriate adaptive behavior (positive practice).

overt behavior Behavior that can be directly observed by other people.

pain behaviors Overt behaviors generally indicating that a person is experiencing pain.

participant modeling Treatment in which the therapist models the target behavior for the client and then physically prompts the client to perform the target behavior.

perceived self-efficacy A person's belief that he or she can master a situation or be successful at performing a task.

physically aversive consequences Physically painful or unpleasant consequences used to decelerate a maladaptive target behavior.

positive reinforcement Process by which an event that is presented as a consequence of a behavior increases the likelihood that the behavior will be repeated.

positive reinforcer An event presented as a consequence of a behavior, which increases the likelihood that the behavior will be repeated.

Premack principle Principle stating that if a higher-probability behavior is made contingent on a lower-probability behavior, the frequency of the lower-probability behavior will increase; thus, the higher-probability behavior serves as a reinforcer for the lower-probability behavior.

problem-solving therapy The application of problem solving to a problem for which a client has specifically sought treatment.

problem-solving training Procedures that teach people to use problem solving as a general coping skill for dealing with problems that arise in daily life.

prolonged/intense exposure therapy Treatment in which the client is exposed to highly anxiety-evoking event for a lengthy period of time (in order to ultimately reduce the anxiety).

prompt Cue that reminds or instructs a client to perform a behavior.

prompting Reminding or instructing a client to perform a behavior.

punishment Process by which the consequence of a target behavior results in the behavior being performed less frequently in the future.

rapid smoking Aversion therapy procedure that makes smoking distasteful by requiring clients to smoke rapidly until they cannot tolerate it anymore.

rating scale List of potential problem behaviors; someone who knows the client well rates the frequency or severity of each behavior for the client.

rational emotive behavior therapy (REBT) Cognitive restructuring therapy in which clients directly confront their irrational thoughts and replace them with rational thoughts.

rational emotive education Training in which children and adolescents learn how the basic principles and procedures of rational emotive behavior therapy can be applied in their daily lives.

reactivity Phenomenon in which people's behaviors change because they know they are being observed.

reinforcement Process by which the consequences of a behavior increase the likelihood that the behavior will be repeated.

reinforcer A consequence of a behavior that increases the likelihood that the behavior will be repeated.

reinforcer sampling Procedure for making a generalized reinforcer a reinforcer for an individual client; the client first receives the generalized reinforcer noncontingently, then contingently when the client comes to value it.

reinforcing agent A person who dispenses reinforcers.

relapse prevention Procedure for promoting long-term maintenance that involves identifying situations in which clients are likely to relapse, developing skills to cope with such situations, and creating a lifestyle balance that decreases the chances of relapse.

response cost Consequential deceleration therapy in which a client's access to a valued item or privilege is removed as a consequence of performing a maladaptive behavior.

response prevention Exposure therapy procedure in which the client remains exposed to the threatening situation without engaging in anxiety-reducing responses.

retention control training Procedure used to treat enuresis that involves shaping the retention of increasingly greater amounts of urine for increasingly longer periods.

reversal phase Phase in a reversal study in which the therapy is withdrawn temporarily while the target behavior continues to be measured.

reversal studies Single subject studies in which the therapy is applied to the target behavior and then is withdrawn temporarily to determine whether the therapy is causing the change in the target behavior.

role playing Assessment or therapy technique in which clients act as if they were in actual problem situations to provide the therapist with samples of how they typically behave in the situations (assessment) or to practice skills to cope with the situations (therapy).

self-control approach Training clients to initiate, conduct, and evaluate behavior therapy procedures to change their own problem behaviors.

self-instructional training Cognitive-behavioral coping skills therapy that teaches clients to instruct themselves verbally (often silently) to cope effectively with difficult situations.

self-managed exposure Exposure therapy procedure in which clients expose themselves to anxiety-evoking events on their own.

self-modeling Therapy procedure in which clients serve as their own models, usually by observing themselves on videotape.

self-recording (self-monitoring) Clients' observing and keeping records of their own behaviors.

self-reinforcement Process by which clients administer reinforcers to themselves for performing target behaviors.

self-talk What people "say" to themselves when they are thinking.

shaping Reinforcing components of a target behavior that are successively closer approximations of the complete target behavior.

simulated observation Observing a client's behaviors under conditions set up to resemble those in the client's natural environment.

single subject studies Research methods that systematically compare target behaviors of individuals when they are treated and when they are not treated to evaluate the effectiveness of the therapy.

situational cues Maintaining antecedents that set the stage for a behavior to occur.

situation-specific Term used to indicate that behaviors are influenced by the environmental context in which they are performed.

skills training Treatment package—including modeling, behavior rehearsal, and reinforcement—used to teach clients skills.

social reinforcers Reinforcers consisting of attention and affirmation from other people.

social skills Interpersonal competencies needed to interact successfully with others.

social validity Outcome measure that evaluates whether a client's behaviors following therapy are similar to the behaviors of individuals judged to be functioning adaptively.

stimulus control The influence of situational cues on a behavior.

stimulus control procedures Procedures that change behaviors by modifying their situational cues, such as prompting.

stress inoculation training Cognitive-behavioral coping skills therapy in which clients learn coping skills for dealing with stressful situations and then practice the skills while being exposed to stressors.

Subjective Units of Discomfort scale Scale clients use to rate the level of anxiety they experience in anxiety-evoking situations; usually the scale ranges from 0, representing total calm, to 100, representing the highest level of anxiety the client can imagine.

SUDs Subjective Units of Discomfort.

symbolic model Model who is observed indirectly, such as on television, in books, and in one's imagination.

systematic desensitization Exposure therapy in which the client imagines successively more anxiety-evoking situations while engaging in a behavior that competes with anxiety.

systematic naturalistic observation Observation and recording of a client's specific, predetermined overt behaviors as they occur in the client's natural environment.

tangible reinforcers Valued material objects that serve as reinforcers.

target behavior Aspect of a client's problem that is relatively narrow and discrete and that can be clearly defined and easily measured; the focus of treatment in behavior therapy.

theft reversal Specific form of overcorrection in which a thief is required to return stolen items to the victim or purchase similar items for the victim as a consequence of stealing.

therapist-assisted exposure In vivo exposure therapy procedure in which the therapist guides the client through the exposure.

thought stopping Therapy procedure in which clients interrupt disturbing thoughts by saying "Stop!" (usually silently) and then substitute a pleasant thought for the disturbing thought.

time out from positive reinforcement (or **time out**) Consequential deceleration therapy in which a client's access to generalized reinforcers is temporarily withdrawn after the client engages in a maladaptive behavior, often by placing the client in a time-out room or area.

time-out room Isolated room in which a client spends a time-out period with no access to generalized reinforcers.

token economy A system for motivating clients in which they earn token reinforcers for adaptive behaviors and lose tokens for maladaptive behaviors; the tokens are exchanged for backup reinforcers.

token reinforcers Symbolic reinforcers, such as poker chips or points, that can be exchanged for desired tangible reinforcers and reinforcing activities.

tokens Symbolic reinforcers, such as poker chips or points, that clients earn for performing adaptive behaviors and lose for performing maladaptive behaviors.

treatment package Treatment consisting of two or more therapy procedures.

urine alarm   Device to treat enuresis that sounds an alarm to wake the child when the child begins to urinate; eventually the child associates bladder tension with awakening.

vicarious consequences   Consequences of a model's behaviors that indicate the consequences that observers are likely to receive for imitating the model.

vicarious extinction   Process by which a client's fear is reduced by observing a model perform the feared behavior without incurring negative consequences.

vicarious negative consequences   Consequences of a model's acts that decrease the likelihood that an observer will imitate the model.

vicarious reinforcement   Process by which the consequences of a model's acts increase the likelihood that an observer will imitate the model.

well behaviors   Overt behaviors generally indicating that a person is not experiencing pain.

ABRAHMS, J. L. (1983). Cognitive-behavioral strategies to induce and enhance a collaborative set in distressed couples. In A. Freeman (Ed.), *Cognitive therapy with couples and groups* (pp. 125-155). New York: Plenum.

ABRAMOWITZ, J. S. (1996). Variants of exposure and response prevention in the treatment of obsessive-compulsive disorder: A meta-analysis. *Behavior Therapy, 27,* 583-600.

ABRAMS, M., & ELLIS, A. (1994). Rational emotive behaviour therapy in the treatment of stress. *British Journal of Guidance and Counselling, 22,* 39-50.

ACHENBACH, T. M. (1978). The Child Behavior Profile, I: Boys aged 6-11. *Journal of Consulting and Clinical Psychology, 46,* 478-488.

ACIERNO, R., HERSEN, M., VAN HASSELT, V. B., TREMONT, G., & MEUSER, K. T. (1994). Review of the validation and dissemination of eye-movement desensitization and reprocessing: A scientific and ethical dilemma. *Clinical Psychology Review, 14,* 287-299.

ACIERNO, R., TREMONT, G., LAST, C., & MONTGOMERY, D. (1994). Tripartite assessment of the efficacy of eye-movement desensitization in a multi-phobic patient. *Journal of Anxiety Disorders, 8,* 259-276.

ADAMS, C. D., & KELLEY, M. L. (1992). Managing sibling aggression: Overcorrection as an alternative to time-out. *Behavior Therapy, 23,* 707-717.

ADDIS, M. E., & CARPENTER, K. M. (1997). Treatment manuals and the future of behavior therapy. *the Behavior Therapist, 20,* 53-55.

AGIGIAN, H. (1996, September 18). Personal communication.

AGRAS, W. S. (1976). Behavior modification in the general hospital psychiatric unit. In H. Leitenberg (Ed.), *Handbook of behavior modification and behavior therapy* (pp. 547-565). Englewood Cliffs, NJ: Prentice-Hall.

AGRAS, W. S. (1981). Behavioral approaches to the treatment of essential hypertension. *International Journal of Obesity, 5* (Suppl. 1), 173-181.

AGRAS, W. S. (1993). Short-term psychological treatments for binge eating. In C. G. Fairburn & G. T. Wilson (Eds.), *Binge eating: Nature, assessment and treatment* (pp. 270-286). New York: Guilford.

AGRAS, W. S., & BERKOWITZ, R. I. (1994). Behavior therapy. In R. E. Hales, S. C. Yudofsky, & J. A. Talbott (Eds.), *The American Psychiatric Press textbook of psychiatry* (2nd ed., pp. 1061-1081). Washington, DC: American Psychiatric Press.

AGRAS, W. S., KAZDIN, A. E., & WILSON, G. T. (1979). *Behavior therapy: Toward an applied clinical science.* San Francisco: W. H. Freeman.

AGRAS, W. S., SCHNEIDER, J. A., ARNOW, B., RAEBURN, S. D., & TELCH, C. F. (1989). Cognitive-behavioral treatment with and without exposure plus response-prevention of bulimia nervosa: A reply to Leitenberg and Rosen. *Journal of Consulting and Clinical Psychology, 57,* 778-779.

AGRAS, W. S., SOUTHAM, M. A., & TAYLOR, C. B. (1983). Long-term persistence of relaxation-induced blood pressure lowering during the working day. *Journal of Consulting and Clinical Psychology, 51,* 792-794.

AGRAS, W. S., TAYLOR, C. B., KRAEMER, H. C., ALLEN, R. A., & SCHNEIDER, J. A. (1980). Relaxation training: Twenty-four-hour blood pressure reductions. *Archives of General Psychiatry, 37,* 859-863.

AGRAS, W. S., TAYLOR, C. B., KRAEMER, H. C., SOUTHAM, M. A., & SCHNEIDER, J. A. (1987). Relaxation treatment for essential hypertension at the worksite: II. The poorly controlled hypertensive. *Psychosomatic Medicine, 49,* 264-273.

AIKEN, L. R. (1996). *Personality assessment: Methods and practices* (2nd ed.). Seattle: Hogrefe & Huber.

AJIBOLA, O., & CLEMENT, P. W. (1995). Differential effects of methylphenidate and self-reinforcement on attention-deficit hyperactive disorder. *Behavior Modification, 19,* 211-233.

ALBERTI, R., & EMMONS, M. (1995). *Your perfect right* (7th ed.). San Luis Obispo, CA: Impact Publishers.

ALFORD, B. A. (1986). Behavioral treatment of schizophrenic delusions: A single-case experimental analysis. *Behavior Therapy, 17,* 637-644.

ALFORD, B. A., & BECK, A. T. (1994). Cognitive therapy of delusional beliefs. *Behaviour Research and Therapy, 32,* 369-380.

ALFORD, B. A., & CORREIA, C. J. (1994). Cognitive therapy of schizophrenia: Theory and empirical status. *Behavior Therapy, 25,* 17-33.

ALFORD, B. A., FREEMAN, A., BECK, A. T., & WRIGHT, F. (1990). Brief focused cognitive therapy of panic disorder. *Psychotherapy, 27,* 230-234.

ALLEN, K. D., DANFORTH, J. S., & DRABMAN, R. S. (1989). Videotaped modeling and film distraction for fear reduction in adults undergoing hyperbaric oxygen therapy. *Journal of Consulting and Clinical Psychology, 57,* 554-558.

ALLEN, K. E., TURNER, K. K., & EVERETT, P. M. (1970). A behavior modification classroom for Head Start children with problem behaviors. *Exceptional Children, 37,* 119-127.

ALLEN, S. N., & BLOOM, S. L. (1994). Group and family treatment of post-traumatic stress disorder. *The Psychiatric Clinics of North America, 8,* 425-438.

Altmaier, E. M., & Bernstein, D. N. (1981). Counselor trainees' problem-solving skills. *Counselor Education and Supervision, 20,* 285-291.

Altmaier, E. M., Leary, M. R., Halpern, S., & Sellers, J. E. (1985). Effects of stress inoculation and participant modeling on confidence and anxiety: Testing predictions of self-efficacy theory. *Journal of Social and Clinical Psychology, 3,* 500-505.

American Dental Association. (1972). Recommendations in radiographic practices. *Journal of American Dental Association, 84,* 1108.

American Dental Association. (1974). *Guide to dental materials and devices.* Chicago: Author.

American Psychiatric Association. (1987). *Diagnostic and statistical manual of mental disorders* (3rd ed., rev.). Washington, DC: Author.

American Psychiatric Association. (1994). *Diagnostic and statistical manual of mental disorders* (4th ed.). Washington, DC: Author.

Anant, S. S. (1968). The use of verbal aversion (negative conditioning) with an alcoholic: A case report. *Behaviour Research and Therapy, 6,* 695-696.

Anderson, N. B., Lawrence, P. S., & Olson, T. W. (1981). Within-subject analysis of autogenic training and cognitive coping training in the treatment of tension headache pain. *Journal of Behavior Therapy and Experimental Psychiatry, 12,* 219-223.

Anderson, T. P., Cole, T. M., Gullickson, G., Hudgens, A., & Roberts, A. H. (1977). Behavior modification of chronic pain: A treatment program by a multidisciplinary team. *Clinical Orthopedics, 129,* 96-100.

Andersson, G., Melin, L., Scott, B., & Lindberg, P. (1995). An evaluation of a behavioural treatment approach to hearing impairment. *Behaviour Research and Therapy, 33,* 283-292.

Andrasik, F., & Blanchard, E. B. (1987). Task force report on the biofeedback treatment of tension headache. In J. P. Hatch, J. D. Rugh, & J. G. Fisher (Eds.), *Biofeedback studies in clinical efficacy* (pp. 281-321). New York: Plenum.

Anesko, K. M., & O'Leary, S. G. (1982). The effectiveness of brief parent training for the management of children's homework problems. *Child and Family Behavior Therapy, 4,* 113-126.

Anton, W. D. (1976). An evaluation of outcome variables in the systematic desensitization of test anxiety. *Behaviour Research and Therapy, 14,* 217-224.

Antonuccio, D. O., Danton, W. G., & DeNelsky, G. Y. (1995). Psychotherapy versus medication for depression: Challenging the conventional wisdom with data. *Professional Psychology: Research and Practice, 26,* 574-585.

Appel, M. A., Saab, P. G., & Holroyd, K. A. (1985). Cardiovascular disorders. In M. Hersen & A. S. Bellack (Eds.), *Handbook of clinical behavior therapy with adults* (pp. 381-416). New York: Plenum.

Arean, P. A., Perri, M. G., Nezu, A. M., Schein, R. L., Christopher, F., & Joseph, T. X. (1993). Comparative effectiveness of social problem-solving therapy and reminiscence therapy as treatments for depression in older adults. *Journal of Consulting and Clinical Psychology, 61,* 1003-1010.

Arkowitz, H. (1992a). Integrative theories of therapy. In D. K. Freedheim (Ed.), *History of psychotherapy: A century of change* (pp. 261-303). Washington, DC: American Psychological Association.

Arkowitz, H. (1992b, Summer). Psychotherapy integration: Bringing psychotherapy back to psychology. *The General Psychologist,* 11-20.

Arkowitz, H. (1995). Common factors or processes of change in psychotherapy? *Clinical Psychology: Science and Practice, 2,* 94-100.

Armstrong, D., & Rimm, D. C. (1974). *Thought stopping-covert assertion vs. systematic desensitization in the treatment of snake phobias.* Unpublished master's thesis, Southern Illinois University, Carbondale.

Arnarson, E. O. (1994). The saga of behavioural cognitive intervention. *Behavioural and Cognitive Psychotherapy, 22,* 105-109.

Arnkoff, D. B., & Glass, C. R. (1992). Cognitive therapy and psychotherapy: A century of change. In D. K. Freedheim (Ed.), *History of psychotherapy: A century of change* (pp. 657-694). Washington, DC: American Psychological Association.

Asarnow, J. R., & Callan, J. W. (1985). Boys with peer adjustment problems: Social cognitive processes. *Journal of Consulting and Clinical Psychology, 53,* 80-87.

Ashem, B., & Donner, L. (1968). Covert sensitization with alcoholics: A controlled replication. *Behaviour Research and Therapy, 6,* 7-12.

Asylum on the front porch: Community life for the mentally retarded. (1974). *Innovations, 1,* 11-14.

Atthowe, J. M., Jr., & Krasner, L. (1968). Preliminary report on the application of contingent reinforcement procedures (token economy) on a "chronic" psychiatric ward. *Journal of Abnormal Psychology, 73,* 37-43.

Austin, J., Hatfield, D. B., Grindle, A. C., & Bailey, J. S. (1993). Increasing recycling in office environments: The effects of specific, informative cues. *Journal of Applied Behavior Analysis, 26,* 247-253.

Axelrod, S., Brantner, J. P., & Meddock, T. D. (1978). Overcorrection: A review and critical analysis. *Journal of Special Education, 12,* 367-391.

Aydin, G., & Yerin, O. (1994). The effect of a story-based cognitive behavior modification procedure on reducing children's test anxiety before and after cancellation of an important examination. *International Journal for the Advancement of Counselling, 17,* 149-161.

Ayllon, T. (1963). Intensive treatment of psychotic behavior by stimulus satiation and food reinforcement. *Behaviour Research and Therapy, 1,* 53-61.

Ayllon, T. (1965). Some behavioral problems associated with eating in chronic schizophrenic patients. In L. P. Ullmann & L. Krasner (Eds.), *Case studies in behavior modification* (pp. 73-84). New York: Holt, Rinehart & Winston.

Ayllon, T., & Azrin, N. H. (1965). The measurement and reinforcement of behavior of psychotics. *Journal of the Experimental Analysis of Behavior, 8,* 357-383.

Ayllon, T., & Azrin, N. H. (1968). *The token economy: A motivational system for therapy and rehabilitation.* New York: Appleton-Century-Crofts.

Ayllon, T., Layman, D., & Kandel, H. J. (1975). A behavioral-educational alternative to drug control of hyperactive children. *Journal of Applied Behavior Analysis, 8,* 137-146.

Ayllon, T., & Michael, J. (1959). The psychiatric nurse as a behavioral engineer. *Journal of the Experimental Analysis of Behavior, 2,* 323-334.

Ayllon, T., & Roberts, M. D. (1974). Eliminating discipline problems by strengthening academic performance. *Journal of Applied Behavior Analysis, 7,* 71-76.

Azrin, N. H., Gottlieb, L., Hughart, L., Wesolowski, M. D., & Rahn, T. (1975). Eliminating self-injurious behavior by educative procedures. *Behaviour Research and Therapy, 13,* 101-111.

Azrin, N. H., & Holz, W. C. (1966). Punishment. In W. K. Honig (Ed.), *Operant behavior: Areas of research and application* (pp. 380-447). New York: Appleton-Century-Crofts.

Azrin, N. H., McMahon, P. T., Donahue, B., Besalel, V. A., Lapinski, K. J., Kogan, E. S., Acierno, R. E., & Galloway, E. (1994). Behavior therapy for drug abuse: A controlled treatment outcome study. *Behaviour Research and Therapy, 32,* 857-866.

Azrin, N. H., & Nunn, R. G. (1973). Habit reversal: A method of eliminating nervous habits and tics. *Behaviour Research and Therapy, 11,* 619-628.

Azrin, N. H., Nunn, R. G., & Frantz-Renshaw, S. (1980). Habit reversal treatment of thumbsucking. *Behaviour Research and Therapy, 18,* 395-399.

Azrin, N. H., & Peterson, A. L. (1988a). Behavior therapy for Tourette's Syndrome and tic disorders. In D. J. Cohen, R. D. Bruun, & J. F. Leckman (Eds.), *Tourette's Syndrome and tic disorders: Clinical understanding and treatment* (pp. 238-255). New York: Wiley.

Azrin, N. H., & Peterson, A. L. (1988b). Habit reversal for the treatment of Tourette Syndrome. *Behaviour Research and Therapy, 26,* 347-351.

Azrin, N. H., & Peterson, A. L. (1990). Treatment of Tourette Syndrome by habit reversal: A waiting-list control group comparison. *Behavior Therapy, 21,* 305-318.

Azrin, N. H., & Powell, J. (1968). Behavioral engineering: The reduction of smoking behavior by a conditioning apparatus and procedure. *Journal of Applied Behavior Analysis, 1,* 193-200.

Azrin, N. H., & Powell, J. (1969). Behavioral engineering: The use of response priming to improve prescribed self-medication. *Journal of Applied Behavior Analysis, 2,* 39-42.

Azrin, N. H., & Powers, M. A. (1975). Eliminating classroom disturbances of emotionally disturbed children by positive practice procedures. *Behavior Therapy, 6,* 525-534.

Azrin, N. H., Sneed, T. J., & Foxx, R. M. (1973). Dry bed: A rapid method of eliminating bedwetting (enuresis) of the retarded. *Behaviour Research and Therapy, 11,* 427-434.

Azrin, N. H., Sneed, T. J., & Foxx, R. M. (1974). Dry-bed training: Rapid elimination of childhood enuresis. *Behaviour Research and Therapy, 12,* 147-156.

Azrin, N. H., & Thienes, P. M. (1978). Rapid elimination of enuresis by intensive learning without a conditioning apparatus. *Behavior Therapy, 9,* 342-354.

Azrin, N. H., Thienes-Hontos, P., & Besalel-Azrin, V. (1979). Elimination of enuresis without a conditioning apparatus: An extension by office instruction of the child and parents. *Behavior Therapy, 10,* 14-19.

Azrin, N. H., & Wesolowski, M. D. (1974). Theft reversal: An overcorrection procedure for eliminating stealing by retarded persons. *Journal of Applied Behavior Analysis, 7,* 577-581.

Azrin, N. H., & Wesolowski, M. D. (1975). Eliminating habitual vomiting in a retarded adult by positive practice and

self-correction. *Journal of Behavior Therapy and Experimental Psychiatry, 6,* 145-148.

Babcock, R. A., Sulzer-Azaroff, B., Sanderson, M., & Scibak, J. (1992). Increasing nurses' use of feedback to promote infection-control practices in a head-injury treatment center. *Journal of Applied Behavior Analysis, 25,* 621-627.

Baer, D. M., & Guess, D. (1971). Receptive training of adjectival inflections in mental retardates. *Journal of Applied Behavior Analysis, 4,* 129-139.

Baer, D. M., & Guess, D. (1973). Teaching productive noun suffixes to severely retarded children. *American Journal of Mental Deficiency, 77,* 498-505.

Baer, L., Hurley, J. D., Minichiello, W. E., Ott, B. D., Penzel, F., & Ricciardi, J. (1992). EMDR workshop: Disturbing issues? *the Behavior Therapist, 15,* 110-111.

Baer, R. A., Osnes, P. G., & Stokes, T. F. (1983). Training generalized correspondence between verbal behavior at school and nonverbal behavior at home. *Education and Treatment of Children, 6,* 379-388.

Baer, R. A., Williams, J. A., Osnes, P. G., & Stokes, T. F. (1983). Generalized verbal control and correspondence training. *Behavior Modification, 9,* 477-489.

Baggs, K., & Spence, S. H. (1990). Effectiveness of booster sessions in the maintenance and enhancement of treatment gains following assertion training. *Journal of Consulting and Clinical Psychology, 58,* 845-854.

Bailey, J. S., Timbers, G. D., Phillips, E. L., & Wolf, M. M. (1971). Modification of articulation errors of pre-delinquents by their peers. *Journal of Applied Behavior Analysis, 4,* 265-281.

Bailey, J. S., Wolf, M. M., & Phillips, E. L. (1970). Home-based reinforcement and the modification of pre-delinquents' classroom behavior. *Journal of Applied Behavior Analysis, 3,* 223-233.

Bakken, J., Miltenberger, R. G., & Schauss, S. (1993). Teaching parents with mental retardation: Knowledge versus skills. *American Journal of Mental Retardation, 97,* 405-417.

Ballard, K. D., & Crooks, T. J. (1984). Videotape modeling for preschool children with low levels of social interaction and low peer involvement in play. *Journal of Abnormal Child Psychology, 12,* 95-110.

Bandura, A. (1969). *Principles of behavior modification.* New York: Holt, Rinehart & Winston.

Bandura, A. (Ed.). (1971). *Psychological modeling: Conflicting theories.* Chicago: Aldine-Atherton.

Bandura, A. (1976). Effecting change through participant modeling. In J. D. Krumboltz & C. E. Thoresen (Eds.), *Counseling methods* (pp. 248-265). New York: Holt, Rinehart & Winston.

Bandura, A. (1977a). Self-efficacy: Toward a unifying theory of behavioral change. *Psychological Review, 84,* 191-215.

Bandura, A. (1977b). *Social learning theory.* Englewood Cliffs, NJ: Prentice-Hall.

Bandura, A. (1978). Reflections on self-efficacy. In S. Rachman (Ed.), *Advances in behaviour research and therapy* (Vol. 1, pp. 237-269). Oxford: Pergamon.

Bandura, A. (1984). Recycling misconceptions of perceived self-efficacy. *Cognitive Therapy and Research, 8,* 231-255.

Bandura, A. (1986a). From thought to action: Mechanisms of personal agency. *New Zealand Journal of Psychology, 15,* 1-17.

Bandura, A. (1986b). *Social foundations of thought and action: A social cognitive theory.* Englewood Cliffs, NJ: Prentice-Hall.

BANDURA, A. (1988). Self-efficacy conception of anxiety. *Anxiety Research, 1,* 77-98.

BANDURA, A. (1989). Human agency in social cognitive theory. *American Psychologist, 44,* 1175-1184.

BANDURA, A. (1997). *Self-efficacy: The exercise of control.* San Francisco: W. H. Freeman.

BANDURA, A., JEFFERY, R. W., & GAJDOS, E. (1975). Generalizing change through participant modeling with self-directed mastery. *Behaviour Research and Therapy, 13,* 141-152.

BANDURA, A., JEFFERY, R. W., & WRIGHT, C. L. (1974). Efficacy of participant modeling as a function of response instruction aids. *Journal of Abnormal Psychology, 83,* 56-64.

BANDURA, A., & WALTERS, R. H. (1963). *Social learning and personality development.* New York: Holt, Rinehart & Winston.

BANKART, B., & ELLIOTT, R. (1974). Extinction of avoidance in rats: Response availability and stimulus presentation effects. *Behaviour Research and Therapy, 12,* 53-56.

BARCLAY, D. R., & HOUTS, A. C. (1995). Parenting skills: A review and developmental analysis of training content. In W. O'Donohue & L. Krasner (Eds.), *Handbook of psychological skills training: Clinical techniques and applications* (pp. 195-228). Boston: Allyn and Bacon.

BARKIN, R. M., & DUNCAN, R. (1975). Broken appointments: Questions, not answers. *Pediatrics, 55,* 747-748.

BARKLEY, R. A. (1987). *Defiant children: A clinician's manual for parent training.* New York: Guilford.

BARKLEY, R. A. (1989). *Defiant children.* New York: Guilford.

BARKLEY, R. A., GUEVREMONT, D. C., ANASTOPOULOS, A. D., & FLETCHER, K. (1992). A comparision of three family therapy programs for treating family conflicts in adolescents with attention deficit hyperactivity disorder. *Journal of Consulting and Clinical Psychology, 60,* 450-462.

BARLOW, D. H. (1988). *Anxiety and its disorders: The nature and treatment of anxiety and panic.* New York: Guilford.

BARLOW, D. H. (1993). Covert sensitization for paraphilia. In J. R. Cautela & A. J. Kearney (Eds.), *Covert conditioning casebook* (pp. 185-198). Pacific Grove, CA: Brooks/Cole.

BARLOW, D. H. (1994). Psychological interventions in the era of managed competition. *Clinical Psychology: Science and Practice, 1,* 109-122.

BARLOW, D. H., & CERNEY, J. A. (1988). *Psychological treatment of panic.* New York: Guilford.

BARLOW, D. H., & HERSEN, M. (1984). *Single case experimental designs: Strategies for studying behavior change* (2nd ed.). New York: Pergamon Press.

BARLOW, D. H., LEITENBERG, H., & AGRAS, W. S. (1969). Experimental control of sexual deviation through manipulation of the noxious scene in covert sensitization. *Journal of Abnormal Psychology, 74,* 597-601.

BARLOW, D. H., O'BRIEN, G. T., & LAST, C. A. (1984). Couples treatment of agoraphobia. *Behavior Therapy, 15,* 41-58.

BARNETT, J. E. (1996). Managed care: Time to fight or flee? *Psychotherapy Bulletin, 31,* 54-58.

BARR, R. F., LOVIBOND, S. H., & KATSAROS, E. (1972). Gilles de la Tourette's syndrome in a brain-damaged child. *Medical Journal of Australia, 2,* 372-374.

BARRIOS, B. A. (1988). On the changing nature of behavioral assessment. In A. S. Bellack & M. Hersen (Eds.), *Behavioral assessment: A practical handbook* (3rd ed., pp. 3-41). Elmsford, NY: Pergamon.

BARRY, J. V. (1958). *Alexander Maconochie of Norfolk Island: A study of a pioneer in penal reform.* London: Oxford University Press.

BARRY, N. J., & OVERMANN, P. B. (1977). Comparison of the effectiveness of adult and peer models with EMR children. *American Journal of Mental Deficiency, 82,* 33-36.

BARTON, E. J., & ASCIONE, F. R. (1984). Direct observation. In T. H. Ollendick & M. Hersen (Eds.), *Child behavioral assessment* (pp. 166-194). Elmsford, NY: Pergamon.

BARTON, E. S., GUESS, D., GARCIA, E., & BAER, D. M. (1970). Improvement of retardates' mealtime behaviors by time-out procedures using multiple base-line techniques. *Journal of Applied Behavior Analysis, 3,* 77-84.

BAUCOM, D. H., & EPSTEIN, N. (1990). *Cognitive-behavioral marital therapy.* New York: Brunner/Mazel.

BAUCOM, D. H., & HOFFMAN, J. A. (1986). The effectiveness of marital therapy: Current status and applications to the clinical setting. In N. S. Jacobson & A. S. Gurman (Eds.), *Clinical handbook of marital therapy* (pp. 597-620). New York: Guilford.

BAUER, A. M., & SHEA, T. M. (1984). Tourette Syndrome: A review and educational implications. *Journal of Autism and Developmental Disorders, 14,* 69-80.

BAUM, C. J., & FOREHAND, R. (1981). Long-term follow-up of parent training by use of multiple outcome measures. *Behavior Therapy, 12,* 643-652.

BAXTER, L. R., SCHWARTZ, J. M., BERGMAN, K. S., SZUBA, M. P., GUZE, B. H., MAZZIOTTA, J. C., AKAZRAJU, A., SELIN, C. E., FERNG, H. K., MUNFORD, P., & PHELPS, M. E. (1992). Caudate glucose metabolic rate changes with both drug and behavior therapy for obsessive-compulsive disorder. *Archives of General Psychiatry, 49,* 681-689.

BEACH, S. R. H., & O'LEARY, K. D. (1992). Treating depression in the context of marital discord: Outcome predictors of response of marital therapy versus cognitive therapy. *Behavior Therapy, 23,* 507-528.

BEACH, S. R. H., WHISMAN, M. A., & O'LEARY, K. D. (1994). Marital therapy for depression: Theoretical foundation, current status, and future directions. *Behavior Therapy, 25,* 345-371.

BEAUCHAMP, T. L., & WALTERS, L. (EDS.). (1978). *Contemporary issues in bioethics.* Encino, CA: Dickenson.

BEBKO, J. M., & LENNOX, C. (1988). Teaching the control of diurnal bruxism to two children with autism using a simple cueing procedure. *Behavior Therapy, 19,* 249-255.

BECK, A. T. (1963). Thinking and depression. *Archives of General Psychiatry, 9,* 324-333.

BECK, A. T. (1967). *Depression: Clinical, experimental, and theoretical aspects.* New York: Hoeber.

BECK, A. T. (1972). *Depression: Causes and treatment.* Philadelphia: University of Pennsylvania Press.

BECK, A. T. (1976). *Cognitive therapy and the emotional disorders.* New York: International Universities Press.

BECK, A. T. (1988). Cognitive approaches to panic disorder: Theory and therapy. In S. Rachman & J. D. Maser (Eds.), *Panic: Psychological perspectives* (pp. 91-109). Hillsdale, NJ: Lawrence Erlbaum.

BECK, A. T. (1989). *Love is never enough.* New York: Harper & Row (Perennial Library).

BECK, A. T., & EMERY, G. (1985). *Anxiety disorders and phobias: A cognitive perspective.* New York: Basic Books.

BECK, A. T., & FREEMAN, A. (1989). *Cognitive therapy of personality disorders.* New York: Guilford.

BECK, A. T., RUSH, A. J., SHAW, B. F., & EMERY, G. (1979). *Cognitive therapy of depression.* New York: Guilford.

BECK, A. T., & WEISHAAR, M. (1989). Cognitive therapy. In A. Freeman, K. M. Simon, L. E. Beutler, & H. Arkowitz (Eds.), *Comprehensive handbook of cognitive therapy* (pp. 21-36). New York: Plenum.

BECKER, L. S. (1978). Joint effect of feedback and goal setting on performance: A field study of residential energy conservation. *Journal of Applied Psychology, 63,* 428-433.

BECKER, R. E., & HEIMBERG, R. G. (1988). Assessment of social skills. In A. S. Bellack & M. Hersen (Eds.), *Behavioral assessment: A practical handbook* (3rd ed., pp. 365-395). Elmsford, NY: Pergamon.

BECKER, W. (1971). *Parents are teachers: A child management program.* Champaign, IL.: Research Press.

BECKHAM, E. E., & WATKINS, J. T. (1989). Process and outcome in cognitive therapy. In A. Freeman, K. M. Simon, L. E. Beutler, & H. Arkowitz (Eds.), *Comprehensive handbook of cognitive therapy* (pp. 583-596). New York: Plenum.

BEIDEL, D. C., & TURNER, S. M. (1986). A critique of the theoretical bases of cognitive-behavioral theories and therapy. *Clinical Psychology Review, 6,* 177-197.

BEIDEL, D. C., TURNER, S. M., & MORRIS, T. L. (1995). A new inventory to assess childhood social anxiety and phobia: The social phobia and anxiety inventory for children. *Psychological Assessment, 7,* 73-79.

BEIMAN, I., ISRAEL, E., & JOHNSON, S. A. (1978). During training and posttraining effects of live and taped extended progressive relaxation, self-relaxation, and electromyogram biofeedback. *Journal of Consulting and Clinical Psychology, 46,* 314-321.

BELCHIC, J. K., & HARRIS, S. L. (1994). The use of multiple peer exemplars to enhance the generalization of play skills to the siblings of children with autism. *Child and Family Behavior Therapy, 16,* 1-24.

BELLACK, A. S., & HERSEN, M. (EDS.). (1988). *Behavioral assessment: A practical handbook* (3rd ed.). Elmsford, NY: Pergamon.

BELLACK, A. S., HERSEN, M., & TURNER, S. M. (1979). Relationship of role playing and knowledge of appropriate behavior to assertion in the natural environment. *Journal of Consulting and Clinical Psychology, 47,* 670-678.

BELLACK, A. S., MORRISON, R. L., WIXTED, J. T., & MUESER, K. T. (1990). An analysis of social competence in schizophrenia. *British Journal of Psychiatry, 156,* 809-818.

BELLACK, A. S., & MUESER, K. T. (1994). Schizophrenia. In L. W. Craighead, W. E. Craighead, A. E. Kazdin, & M. J. Mahoney (Eds.), *Cognitive and behavioral interventions: An empirical approach to mental health problems.* Needham Heights, MA: Allyn and Bacon.

BELL-DOLAN, D. J. (1995). Social cue interpretation of anxious children. *Journal of Clinical Child Psychology, 24,* 1-10.

BENNETT, W. (1987). Dietary treatments of obesity. In R. J. Wurtman & J. J. Wurtman (Eds.), *Human obesity* (pp. 250-263). New York: New York Academy of Sciences.

BENSON, H. (1975). *The relaxation response.* New York: Morrow.

BENTALL, R., HIGSON, P., & LOWE, C. (1987). Teaching self-instructions to chronic schizophrenic patients: Efficacy and generalization. *Behavioural Psychotherapy, 15,* 58-76.

BENTALL, R. P., HADDOCK, G., & SLADE, P. D. (1994). Cognitive behavior therapy for persistent auditory hallucinations: From theory to therapy. *Behavior Therapy, 25,* 51-66.

BENTON, M. K., & SCHROEDER, H. E. (1990). Social skills training with schizophrenics: A meta-analytic evaluation. *Journal of Consulting and Clinical Psychology, 58,* 741-747.

BERGAN, J. (1995). Behavioral training and the new mental health: Are we learning what we need to know? *the Behavior Therapist, 18,* 161-164, 166.

BERGIN, A. E., & STRUPP, H. H. (EDS.). (1972). *Changing frontiers in the science of psychotherapy.* Chicago: Aldine-Atherton.

BERNARD, M. E. (1990). Rational-emotive therapy with children and adolescents: Treatment strategies. *School Psychology Review, 19,* 294-303.

BERNARD, M. E., & DIGIUSEPPE, R. (1989). Rational-emotive therapy today. In M. E. Bernard & R. DiGiuseppe (Eds.), *Inside rational-emotive therapy: A critical appraisal of the theory and therapy of Albert Ellis* (pp. 1-7). San Diego: Academic Press.

BERNARD, M. E., & JOYCE, M. R. (1984). *Rational-emotive therapy with children and adolescents: Theory, treatment strategies, preventative methods.* New York: Wiley.

BERNSTEIN, D. A., & BORKOVEC, T. D. (1973). *Progressive relaxation training: A manual for the helping professions.* Champaign, IL: Research Press.

BERRY, T. D., & GELLER, E. S. (1991). A single-subject approach to evaluating vehicle safety belt reminders: Back to basics. *Journal of Applied Behavior Analysis, 24,* 45-51.

BEUTLER, L. E., & GUEST, P. D. (1989). The role of cognitive change in psychotherapy. In A. Freeman, K. M. Simon, L. E. Beutler, & H. Arkowitz (Eds.), *Comprehensive handbook of cognitive therapy* (pp. 123-142). New York: Plenum.

BIGELOW, B. E. (1982, August). *The federal answer to the safety belt issue.* Symposium presented at the meeting of the American Psychological Association, Washington, DC.

BIGELOW, G., LIEBSON, I., & GRIFFITHS, R. (1974). Alcoholic drinking: Suppression by a brief time-out procedure. *Behaviour Research and Therapy, 12,* 107-115.

BIGELOW, G., STRICKLER, D., LIEBSON, L., & GRIFFITHS, R. (1976). Maintaining disulfiram ingestion among outpatient alcoholics: A security-deposit contingency contracting procedure. *Behaviour Research and Therapy, 14,* 378-381.

BIGELOW, K. M., HUYNEN, K. B., & LUTZKER, J. R. (1993). Using a changing criterion design to teach fire escape to a child with developmental disabilities. *Journal of Developmental and Physical Disabilities, 5,* 121-128.

BILLINGS, A. (1978). Self-monitoring in the treatment of tics: A single subject analysis. *Journal of Behavior Therapy and Experimental Psychiatry, 9,* 339-342.

BLACK, D. (1987). A minimal intervention program and a problem-solving program for weight control. *Cognitive Therapy and Research, 11,* 107-120.

BLACK, R. G. (1975). The chronic pain syndrome. *Surgical Clinics of North America, 55,* 4.

BLACKBURN, I. M. (1988). An appraisal of cognitive trials of cognitive therapy for depression. In C. Perris, I. M. Blackburn, & H. Perris (Eds.), *Cognitive psychotherapy* (pp. 329-364). Heidelberg: Springer.

BLAMPIED, N. M., & FRANCE, K. G. (1993). A behavioral model of infant sleep disturbance. *Journal of Applied Behavior Analysis, 26,* 477-492.

BLAMPIED, N. M., & KAHAN, E. (1992). Acceptability of alternative punishments: A community survey. *Behavior Modification, 16,* 400-413.

BLANCHARD, E. B. (1970). The relative contributions of modeling, informational influences, and physical contact in the extinction of phobic behavior. *Journal of Abnormal Psychology, 76,* 55-61.

BLANCHARD, E. B. (1987). Long-term effects of behavioral treatment of chronic headache. *Behavior Therapy, 18,* 375-385.

BLANCHARD, E. B. (1992). Psychological treatment of benign headache disorders. *Journal of Consulting and Clinical Psychology, 60,* 537-551.

BLANCHARD, E. B., ANDRASIK, F., NEFF, D. F., ARENA, J. G., AHLES, T. A., JURISH, S. E., PALLMEYER, T. P., SAUNDERS, N. L., TEDERS, S. J., BARRON, K. D., & RODICHOK, L. D. (1982). Biofeedback and relaxation training with three kinds of headaches: Treatment effects and their prediction. *Journal of Consulting and Clinical Psychology, 50,* 562-575.

BLANCHARD, E. B., APPLEBAUM, K. A., RADNITZ, C. L., MORRILL, B., MICHULTKA, D., KIRSCH, C., GUARNIERI, P., HILLHOUSE, J., EVANS, D. D., JACCARD, J., & BARRON, K. D. (1990). A controlled evaluation of thermal biofeedback and thermal biofeedback combined with cognitive therapy in the treatment of vascular headache. *Journal of Consulting and Clinical Psychology, 58,* 216-224.

BLANCHARD, E. B., MCCOY, G. C., MUSSO, A., GERARDI, M. A., PALLMEYER, T. P., GERARDI, R. J., KOCH, P. A., SIRACUSA, K., & ANDRASIK, F. (1986). A controlled comparison of thermal biofeedback and relaxation training in the treatment of essential hypertension: I. Short-term and long-term outcome. *Behavior Therapy, 17,* 563-579.

BLANCHARD, E. B., THEOBALD, D. E., WILLIAMSON, D. A., SILVER, B. V., & BROWN, D. A. (1978). Temperature biofeedback in the treatment of migraine headaches. *Archives of General Psychiatry, 35,* 581-588.

BLANCHARD, E. B., YOUNG, L. D., & HAYNES, M. R. (1975). A simple feedback system for the treatment of elevated blood pressure. *Behavior Therapy, 6,* 241-245.

BLAXALL, M. D. C., PARSONSON, B. S., & ROBERTSON, N. R. (1993). The development and evaluation of sexual harassment contact person training package. *Behavior Modification, 17,* 148-163.

BLOCK, A. R., KREMER, E. F., & GAYLOR, M. (1980). Behavioral treatment of chronic pain: The spouse as a discriminative cue for pain behaviors. *Pain, 9,* 243-252.

BLOXHAM, G., LONG, C. G., ALDERMAN, N., & HOLLIN, C. R. (1993). The behavioral treatment of self-starvation and severe self-injury in a patient with borderline personality disorder. *Journal of Behavior Therapy and Experimental Psychiatry, 24,* 261-267.

BLY, R. (1990). *Iron John: A book about men.* Reading, MA: Addison-Wesley.

BONICA, J. J. (1986). Status of pain research and therapy. *Seminars in Anesthesia, 5,* 82-99.

BOOTZIN, R. R. (1972). Stimulus control treatment for insomnia. *Proceedings of the 80th annual convention of the American Psychological Association, 7,* 395-396.

BOOTZIN, R. R. (1975). *Behavior modification and therapy: An introduction.* Cambridge, MA: Winthrop.

BOOTZIN, R. R., & ENGLE-FRIEDMAN, M. (1987). Sleep disturbances. In B. Edelstein & L. Carstensen (Eds.), *Handbook of clinical gerontology* (pp. 238-251). Elmsford, NY: Pergamon.

BOOTZIN, R. R., EPSTEIN, D., & WOOD, J. M. (1991). Stimulus control instructions. In P. Hauri (Ed.), *Case studies in insomnia* (pp. 19-28). New York: Plenum.

BOOTZIN, R. R., & PERLIS, M. L. (1992). Nonpharmacologic treatments of insomnia. *Journal of Clinical Psychiatry, 53,* 37-41.

BORKOVEC, T. D. (1970). *The comparative effectiveness of systematic desensitization and implosive therapy and the effect of expectancy manipulation on the elimination of fear.* Unpublished doctoral dissertation, University of Illinois, Champaign.

BORKOVEC, T. D. (1972). Effects of expectancy on the outcome of systematic desensitization and implosive treatments for analogue anxiety. *Behavior Therapy, 3,* 29-40.

BORKOVEC, T. D., & COSTELLO, E. (1993). Efficacy of applied relaxation and cognitive-behavioral therapy in the treatment of generalized anxiety disorder. *Journal of Consulting and Clinical Psychology, 61,* 611-619.

BORKOVEC, T. D., GRAYSON, J. B., & O'BRIEN, G. T. (1979). Relaxation treatment of pseudoinsomnia and idiopathic insomnia: An electroencephalographic evaluation. *Journal of Applied Behavior Analysis, 12,* 37-54.

BORKOVEC, T. D., & MATHEWS, A. M. (1988). Treatment of nonphobic anxiety disorders: A comparison of nondirective, cognitive, and coping desensitization therapy. *Journal of Consulting and Clinical Psychology, 56,* 877-884.

BORKOVEC, T. D., & WHISMAN, M. A. (1996). Psychosocial treatment for generalized anxiety disorder. In M. R. Mavissakalian & R. F. Prien (Eds.), *Long term treatments of anxiety disorders* (pp. 171-199). Washington, DC: American Psychiatric Press.

BORNSTEIN, P. H., HAMILTON, S. B., & BORNSTEIN, M. T. (1986). Self-monitoring procedures. In A. Ciminero, K. Calhoun, & H. Adams (Eds.), *Handbook of behavioral assessment* (2nd ed., pp. 176-225). New York: Wiley.

BOUDEWYNS, P. A., STWERTKA, S. A., HYER, L. A., ALBRECHT, J. W., & SPERR, E. V. (1993). Eye movement desensitization and reprocessing: A pilot study. *Behavior Therapy, 16,* 30-33.

BOUDIN, H. M. (1972). Contingency contracting as a therapeutic tool in deceleration of amphetamine use. *Behavior Therapy, 3,* 602-608.

BOULOUGOURIS, J. C., MARKS, I. M., & MARSET, P. (1971). Superiority of flooding (implosion) to desensitization for reducing pathological fear. *Behaviour Research and Therapy, 9,* 7-16.

BOWERS, W. A. (1989). Cognitive therapy with inpatients. In A. Freeman, K. M. Simon, L. E. Beutler, & H. Arkowitz (Eds.), *Comprehensive handbook of cognitive therapy* (pp. 583-596). New York: Plenum.

BOY SCOUTS OF AMERICA. (1982). *Prepared for today.* Dallas: Author.

BRACERO, W. (1996). The story hour: Narrative and multicultural perspectives on managed care and time-limited psychotherapy. *Psychotherapy Bulletin, 31,* 59-65.

BRADLEY, R. W., & HUGHES, H. (1979). *Blood pressure biofeedback and relaxation training: The effects of home practice on reduction of blood pressure in persons with essential hypertension.* Unpublished manuscript.

BRAUER, A. P., NORLICK, L., NELSON, E., FARQUHAR, J. W., & AGRAS, W. S. (1979). Relaxation therapy for essential hypertension: A Veterans Administration outpatient study. *Journal of Behavioral Medicine, 2,* 21-29.

BRAUKMANN, C. J., & WOLF, M. M. (1987). Behaviorally based group homes for juvenile offenders. In E. K. Morris & C. J. Braukmann (Eds.), *Behavioral approaches to crime and delinquency: A handbook of applications, research, and concepts* (pp. 135-159). New York: Plenum.

BRAUKMANN, C. J., WOLF, M. M., & KIRIGIN RAMP, K. A. (1985). *Follow-up of group home youths into young adulthood*

(Progress Rep., Grant MH20030). Lawrence: University of Kansas, Achievement Place Research Project.

BRAZELTON, T. B. (1987, June). Are we frightening our children? *Family Circle*, pp. 98, 100, 124.

BREINER, J. L., & FOREHAND, R. (1981). An assessment of the effects of parent training on clinic-referred children's school behavior. *Behavioral Assessment, 3,* 31-42.

BRICKES, W. A., & BRICKES, D. D. (1970). Development of receptive vocabulary in severely retarded children. *American Journal of Mental Deficiency, 74,* 599-607.

BRIGHAM, F. J., BAKKEN, J. P., SCRUGGS, T. E., & MASTROPIERE, M. A. (1992). Cooperative behavior management: Strategies for promoting a positive classroom environment. *Education and Training in Mental Retardation, 27,* 3-12.

BRIGHAM, T. A., MEIER, S. M., & GOODNER, V. (1995). Increasing designated driving with a program of prompts and incentives. *Journal of Applied Behavior Analysis, 28,* 83-84.

BRISTOL, M. M., & SLOANE, H. N. (1974). Effects of contingency contracting on study rate and test performance. *Journal of Applied Behavior Analysis, 7,* 271-285.

BROWN, D. K., KRATOCHWILL, T. R., & BERGAN, J. R. (1982). Teaching interviewing skills for problem identification: An analogue study. *Behavioral Assessment, 4,* 63-73.

BROWN, E. J., HEIMBERG, R. G., & JUSTER, H. R. (1995). Social phobia subtype and avoidant personality disorder: Effect on severity of social phobia, impairment, and outcome of cognitive-behavioral treatment. *Behavior Therapy, 26,* 467-486.

BROWN, R. A., LICHTENSTEIN, E., MCINTYRE, K. O., & HARRINGTON-KOSTUR, J. (1984). Effects of nicotine fading and relapse prevention on smoking cessation. *Journal of Consulting and Clinical Psychology, 52,* 307-309.

BROWN, T. A., ANTONY, M. M., & BARLOW, D. H. (1995). Diagnostic comorbidity in panic disorder: Effect on treatment outcome and course of comorbid diagnoses following treatment. *Journal of Consulting and Clinical Psychology, 63,* 408-418.

BROWNELL, K. D., & COHEN, L. R. (1995). Adherence to dietary regimens 1: An overview of research. *Behavioral Medicine, 20,* 149-154.

BROWNING, R. M., & STOVER, D. O. (1971). *Behavior modification in child treatment: An experimental and clinical approach.* Chicago: Aldine-Atherton.

BRYANT, L. E., & BUDD, K. S. (1982). Self-instructional training to increase independent work performance in preschoolers. *Journal of Applied Behavior Analysis, 15,* 259-271.

BUCELL, M. (1979). *An empirically derived self-report inventory for the assessment of assertive behavior.* Unpublished doctoral dissertation, Kent State University, Kent, OH.

BUCHER, B., & LOVAAS, O. I. (1968). Use of aversive stimulation in behavior modification. In M. R. Jones (Ed.), *Miami Symposium on the Prediction of Behavior 1967: Aversive stimulation* (pp. 77-145). Coral Gables, FL: University of Miami Press.

BUDD, K. S., WORKMAN, D. E., LEMSKY, C. M., & QUICK, D. M. (1994). The children's headache assessment scale (CHAS): Factor structure and psychometric properties. *Journal of Behavioral Medicine, 17,* 159-179.

BUJOLD, A., LADOUCEUR, R., SYLVAIN, C., & BOISVERT, J. (1994). Treatment of pathological gamblers: An experimental study. *Journal of Behavior Therapy and Experimental Psychiatry, 25,* 275-282.

BURGESS, R. L., CLARK, R. N., & HENDEE, J. C. (1971). An experimental antilitter procedure. *Journal of Applied Behavior Analysis, 4,* 71-75.

BURGIO, L. D., WHITMAN, T. L., & JOHNSON, M. R. (1980). A self-instructional package for increasing attending behavior in educable mentally retarded children. *Journal of Applied Behavior Analysis, 13,* 443-459.

BURISH, T. G., & LYLES, J. N. (1979). Effectiveness of relaxation training in reducing the aversiveness of chemotherapy in the treatment of cancer. *Journal of Behavior Therapy and Experimental Psychiatry, 10,* 357-361.

BURISH, T. G., SHARTNER, C. D., & LYLES, J. N. (1981). Effectiveness of multiple-site EMG biofeedback and relaxation training in reducing the aversiveness of cancer chemotherapy. *Biofeedback and Self-Regulation, 6,* 523-535.

BURMAN, B., MARGOLIN, G., & JOHN, R. S. (1993). America's angriest home videos: Behavioral contingencies observed in home reenactments of marital conflict. *Journal of Consulting and Clinical Psychology, 61,* 28-39.

BURNS, D. (1980). *Feeling good.* New York: Morrow.

BURNS, D. D., & NOLEN-HOEKSEMA, S. (1992). Therapeutic empathy and recovery from depression in cognitive-behavioral therapy: A structural equation model. *Journal of Consulting and Clinical Psychology, 60,* 441-449.

BUSHELL, D., JR. (1978). An engineering approach to the elementary classroom: The Behavior Analysis Follow Through Project. In C. A. Catania & T. A. Brigham (Eds.), *Handbook of applied behavior analysis: Social and instructional processes* (pp. 525-563). New York: Irvington.

BUSS, A. H., PLOMIN, R., & WILLERMAN, L. (1973). The inheritance of temperaments. *Journal of Personality, 41,* 513-524.

BUTLER, G. (1985). Exposure as a treatment for social phobia: Some instructive difficulties. *Behaviour Research and Therapy, 23,* 651-657.

CAHOON, D. D. (1968). Symptom substitution and the behavior therapies: A reappraisal. *Psychological Bulletin, 69,* 149-156.

CAIRNS, D., & PASINO, J. A. (1977). Comparison of verbal reinforcement and feedback in operant treatment of disability due to low back pain. *Behavior Therapy, 8,* 621-630.

CAIRNS, D., THOMAS, L., MOONEY, V., & PAU, J. B. (1976). A comprehensive treatment approach to chronic low back pain. *Pain, 2,* 301-308.

CALAMARI, J. E., FABER, S. D., HITSMAN, B. L., & POPPE, C. J. (1994). Treatment of obsessive compulsive disorder in the elderly: A review and case example. *Journal of Behavior Therapy and Experimental Psychiatry, 25,* 95-104.

CALLAHAN, E. J., & LEITENBERG, H. (1973). Aversion therapy for sexual deviation: Contingent electric shock and covert sensitization. *Journal of Abnormal Psychology, 81,* 60-73.

CAMP, B. W., & BASH, M. A. S. (1981). *Think aloud: Increasing social and cognitive skills—A problem-solving program for children (primary level).* Champaign, IL: Research Press.

CAMP, B. W., BLOM, G. E., HERBERT, F., & VAN DOORWICK, W. J. (1977). "Think aloud": A program for developing self-control in young aggressive boys. *Journal of Abnormal Child Psychology, 5,* 157-169.

CAMPBELL, B. J., HUNTER, W. W., STEWART, J. R., & STUTTS, J. C. (1982). *Increasing safety belt use through an incentive program.* Final report for Innovative Grant Project 4-A22 from the U. S. Department of Transportation, University of North Carolina Highway Safety Research Center, Chapel Hill, NC.

CAMPBELL, J. (1988). *The power of myth*. New York: Doubleday.

CAMPBELL, R. V., & LUTZKER, J. R. (1993). Using functional equivalence training to reduce severe challenging behavior: A case study. *Journal of Developmental and Physical Disabilities, 5,* 203-215.

CANAVAN, A. G. M., & POWELL, G. E. (1981). The efficacy of several treatments of Gilles de la Tourette's syndrome as assessed in a single case. *Behaviour Research and Therapy, 19,* 549-556.

CANTOR, D. W. (1995). Maintaining our professional integrity in the era of managed care. *Psychotherapy Bulletin, 30,* 27-28.

CAREY, R. G., & BUCHER, B. B. (1981). Identifying the educative and suppressive effects of positive practice and restitutional overcorrection. *Journal of Applied Behavior Analysis, 14,* 71-80.

CAREY, R. G., & BUCHER, B. B. (1986). Positive practice overcorrection: Effects of reinforcing correct performance. *Behavior Modification, 10,* 73-92.

CAREY, T. S. (1994). Chronic back pain: Behavioral interventions and outcomes in a changing healthcare environment. *Behavioral Medicine, 20,* 113-117.

CARLSON, C. R., & BERNSTEIN, D. A. (1995). Relaxation skills training: Abbreviated progressive relaxation. In W. O'Donohue & L. Krasner (Eds.), *Handbook of psychological skills training: Clinical techniques and applications* (pp. 20-35). Boston: Allyn and Bacon.

CARLSON, C. R., & HOYLE, R. H. (1993). Efficacy of abbreviated progressive muscle relaxation training: A quantitative review of behavioral medicine research. *Journal of Consulting and Clinical Psychology, 61,* 1059-1067.

CARMODY, T. P. (1978). Rational-emotive, self-instructional, and behavioral assertion training: Facilitating maintenance. *Cognitive Therapy and Research, 2,* 241-254.

CARMODY, T. P. (1992). Preventing relapse in the treatment of nicotine addiction: Current issues and future directions. *Journal of Psychoactive Drugs, 24,* 131-158.

CARR, E. G., & CARLSON, J. I. (1993). Reduction of severe behavior problems in the community using a multicomponent treatment approach. *Journal of Applied Behavior Analysis, 26,* 157-172.

CARR, E. G., & DURAND, V. M. (1985). Reducing behavior problems through functional communication training. *Journal of Applied Behavior Analysis, 18,* 111-126.

CARR, J. E. (1995). Competing responses for the treatment of Tourette syndrome and tic disorders. *Behaviour Research and Therapy, 33,* 455-456.

CARRINGTON, P. (1977). *Freedom in meditation*. New York: Anchor Press/Doubleday.

CARROLL, K. M. (1996). Relapse prevention as a psychosocial treatment: A review of controlled clinical trials. *Experimental and Clinical Psychopharmacology, 4,* 46-54.

CARROLL, K. M., ROUNSAVILLE, B. J., & GAWIN, F. H. (1991). A comparative trial of psychotherapies for ambulatory cocaine abusers: Relapse prevention and interpersonal psychotherapy. *American Journal of Drug and Alcohol Abuse, 17,* 229-247.

CARROLL, L. A., MILTENBERGER, R. G., & O'NEIL, H. K. (1992). A review and critique of research evaluating child sexual abuse prevention programs. *Education and Treatment of Children, 15,* 335-354.

CARSTENSEN, L. L., & FISHER, J. E. (1991). Problems of the institutionalized elderly. In P. A. Wisocki (Ed.), *Handbook of clinical behavior therapy for the elderly client* (pp. 337-362). New York: Plenum.

CARTER, M. M., & BARLOW, D. H. (1993). Interoceptive exposure in the treatment of panic disorder. In L. VandeCreek, S. Knapp, & T. L. Jackson (Eds.), *Innovations in clinical practice: A source book* (Vol. 12, pp. 329-336). Sarasota, FL: Professional Resource Press/Professional Resource Exchange.

CARTER, M. M., & BARLOW, D. H. (1995). Learned alarms: The origins of panic. In W. T. O'Donohue & L. Krasner (Eds.), *Theories of behavior therapy: Exploring behavior change* (pp. 209-228). Washington, DC: American Psychological Association.

CARTER, N., HANSSON, L., HOLMBERG, B., & MELIN, L. (1979). Shoplifting reduction through the use of specific signs. *Journal of Organizational Behavior Management, 2,* 73-84.

CARTER, N., HOLMSTROM, H., SIMPANEN, M., & MELIN, L. (1988). Theft reduction in a grocery store through product identification and graphing of losses for employees. *Journal of Applied Behavior Analysis, 21,* 385-389.

CARTER, N., KINSTEDT, A., & MELIN, L. (1995). Increased sales and thefts of candy as a function of sales promotion activities: Preliminary findings. *Journal of Applied Behavior Analysis, 28,* 81-82.

CARTWRIGHT, D. E. (1955). Effectiveness of psychotherapy: A critique of the spontaneous remission argument. *Journal of Counseling Psychology, 2,* 290-296.

CASTANEDA, C. A. (1972). *A separate reality: Further conversations with Don Juan*. New York: Pocket Books.

CAUCE, A. M. (1995, May). *Consequences of introducing culture/diversity into the research context*. Paper presented at the Conference on Marital and Family Therapy Outcome and Process Research: State of the Science, Philadelphia.

CAUTELA, J. R. (1966). Treatment of compulsive behavior by covert sensitization. *Psychological Record, 16,* 33-41.

CAUTELA, J. R. (1967). Covert sensitization. *Psychological Reports, 20,* 459-468.

CAUTELA, J. R. (1970). The use of covert sensitization in the treatment of alcoholism. *Psychotherapy: Theory, Research and Practice, 7,* 86-90.

CAUTELA, J. R. (1971). Covert sensitization for the treatment of sexual deviations. *Psychological Record, 21,* 37-48.

CAUTELA, J. R. (1972). Rationale and procedures for covert conditioning. In R. D. Rubin, H. Fensterheim, J. D. Henderson, & L. P. Ullmann (Eds.), *Advances in behavior therapy* (pp. 85-96). New York: Academic Press.

CAUTELA, J. R. (1982). Covert conditioning with children. *Journal of Behavior Therapy and Experimental Psychiatry, 13,* 209-214.

CAUTELA, J. R. (1993). Insight in behavior therapy. *Journal of Behavior Therapy and Experimental Psychiatry, 24,* 155-159.

CAUTELA, J. R., & BARON, M. G. (1969). *The behavior therapy treatment of self-destructive behavior*. Unpublished manuscript, Boston College.

CAUTELA, J. R., & KASTENBAUM, R. (1967). A reinforcement survey schedule for use in therapy, training, and research. *Psychological Reports, 20,* 1115-1130.

CAUTELA, J. R., & KEARNEY, A. J. (1993). *Covert conditioning casebook*. Pacific Grove, CA: Brooks/Cole.

CAUTELA, J. R., & WISOCKI, P. A. (1969). The use of male and female therapists in the treatment of homosexual behavior. In R. D. Rubin & C. M. Franks (Eds.), *Advances in behavior therapy* (pp. 165-174). New York: Academic Press.

CAVALIERE, F. (1995, October). Payers demand increased provider documentation. *APA Monitor, 26,* p. 41.

CAYNER, J. J., & KILAND, J. R. (1974). Use of brief time out with three schizophrenic patients. *Journal of Behavior Therapy and Experimental Psychiatry, 5,* 141-145.

CENTERS FOR DISEASE CONTROL AND PREVENTION. (1994). *HIV/AIDS surveillance report.* Atlanta: Author.

CERVONE, D., & PEAKE, P. K. (1986). Anchoring, efficacy, and action: The influence of judgmental heuristics on self-efficacy judgments and behavior. *Journal of Personality and Social Psychology, 50,* 492-501.

CERVONE, D., & SCOTT, W. D. (1995). Self-efficacy theory of behavioral change: Foundations, conceptual issues, and therapeutic implications. In W. O'Donohue & L. Krasner (Eds.), *Theories of behavior therapy* (pp. 349-383). Washington, DC: American Psychological Association.

CHADWICK, B. A., & DAY, R. C. (1971). Systematic reinforcement: Academic performance of underachieving students. *Journal of Applied Behavior Analysis, 4,* 311-319.

CHADWICK, P. D. J., & LOWE, C. F. (1990). Measurement and modification of delusional beliefs. *Journal of Consulting and Clinical Psychology, 58,* 225-232.

CHAMBLESS, D. L. (1985). Agoraphobia. In M. Hersen & A. S. Bellack (Eds.), *Handbook of clinical behavior therapy with adults* (pp. 49-87). New York: Plenum.

CHAMBLESS, D. L., FOA, E. B., GROVES, G. A., & GOLDSTEIN, A. J. (1982). Exposure and communications training in the treatment of agoraphobia. *Behaviour Research and Therapy, 20,* 219-231.

CHANDLER, G. M., BURCK, H. D., & SAMPSON, J. P. (1986). A generic computer program for systematic desensitization: Description, construction and case study. *Journal of Behavior Therapy and Experimental Psychiatry, 17,* 171-174.

CHANG, G., CARROLL, K. M., BEHR, H. M., & KOSTEN, T. R. (1992). Improving treatment outcome in pregnant opiate-dependent women. *Journal of Substance Abuse Treatment, 9,* 327-330.

CHAPMAN, C., & RISLEY, T. R. (1974). Antilitter procedures in an urban high-density area. *Journal of Applied Behavior Analysis, 7,* 377-383.

CHAPMAN, S., FISHER, W., PIAZZA, C. C., & KURTZ, P. F. (1993). Functional assessment and treatment of life-threatening drug ingestion in a dually diagnosed youth. *Journal of Applied Behavior Analysis, 26,* 255-256.

CHARLOP, M. H., & MILSTEIN, J. P. (1989). Teaching autistic children conversational speech using video modeling. *Journal of Applied Behavior Analysis, 22,* 275-285.

CHARLOP, M. H., SCHREIBMAN, L., & TRYON, A. S. (1983). Learning through observation: The effects of peer modeling on acquisition and generalization in autistic children. *Journal of Abnormal Child Psychology, 11,* 355-366.

CHEN, C. P. (1995). Counseling applications of RET in a Chinese cultural context. *Journal of Rational-Emotive and Cognitive Behavior Therapy, 13,* 117-129.

CHESNEY, M. A. (1994). Prevention of HIV and STD infections. *Preventive Medicine, 23,* 655-660.

CHESNEY, M. A., & FOLKMAN, S. (1994). Psychological impact of HIV disease and implications for intervention. *Psychiatric Clinics of North America, 17,* 163-182.

CHIRA, S. (1994, October 6). Left alone at home: O.K., or a danger? *The New York Times,* pp. C1, C8.

CHORPITA, B. F. (1995). Eventual responders: What do we do when treatments do not work? *the Behavior Therapist, 18,* 140-141.

CHRISTENSEN, A., JACOBSON, N. S., & BABCOCK, J. C. (in press). Integrative behavioral couple therapy. In N. S. Jacobson & A. S. Gurman (Eds.), *Clinical handbook of marital therapy* (2nd ed.). New York: Guilford.

CHRISTENSEN, A. P., & SANDERS, M. R. (1987). Habit reversal and differential reinforcement of other behaviour in the treatment of thumb-sucking: An analysis of generalization and side-effects. *Journal of Child Psychology and Psychiatry and Allied Disciplines, 28,* 281-295.

CHRISTOPHERSEN, E. R. (1977). *Little people: Guidelines for common sense child rearing.* Lawrence, KS: H & H Enterprises.

CHURCH, P., FOREHAND, R., BROWN, C., & HOLMES, T. (1990). Prevention of drug abuse: Examination of the effectiveness of a program with elementary school children. *Behavior Therapy, 21,* 339-347.

CLARK, D. F. (1966). Behaviour therapy of Gilles de la Tourette's syndrome. *British Journal of Psychiatry, 112,* 771-778.

CLARK, G. R., BUSSONE, A., & KIVITZ, M. S. (1974). Elwyn Institute's community living program. *The Challenge, 17,* 14-15.

CLARK, G. R., KIVITZ, M. S., & ROSEN, M. (1972). From research to community living. *Human Needs, 1,* 25-28.

CLARK, R. N., BURGESS, R. L., & HENDEE, J. C. (1972). The development of antilitter behavior in a forest campground. *Journal of Applied Behavior Analysis, 5,* 1-5.

CLARKE, G. N., HAWKINS, W., MURPHY, M., SHEEBER, L. B., LEWINSOHN, P. M., & SEELEY, J. R. (1995). Targeted prevention of unipolar depressive disorder in an at-risk sample of high school adolescents: A randomized trial of a group cognitive intervention. *Journal of the American Academy of Child and Adolescent Psychiatry, 34,* 312-321.

CLEES, T. J. (1994-95). Self-recording of students' daily schedules of teachers' expectancies: Perspectives on reactivity, stimulus control, and generalization. *Exceptionality, 5,* 113-129.

CLOITRE, M. (1995). An interview with Edna Foa. *the Behavior Therapist, 18,* 177-181.

CLUM, G. A., CLUM, G. A., & SURLS, R. (1993). A meta-analysis of treatment for panic disorder. *Journal of Consulting and Clinical Psychology, 61,* 317-326.

COCCO, N., & SHARPE, L. (1993). An auditory variant of eye movement desensitization in a case of childhood post-traumatic stress disorder. *Journal of Behavior Therapy and Experimental Psychiatry, 24,* 373-377.

COFER, C. N., & APPLEY, M. H. (1964). *Motivation: Theory and research.* New York: Wiley.

COHEN, D. J., LECKMAN, J. F., & SHAYWITZ, B. (1984). *A physician's guide to diagnosis and treatment of Tourette syndrome: A neurologial multiple tic disorder.* New York: Tourette Syndrome Association.

COLLIER, W. C., & MARLATT, G. A. (1995). Relapse prevention. In A. J. Goreczny (Ed.), *Handbook of health and rehabilitation psychology* (pp. 307-321). New York: Plenum.

COMBS, M. L., & LAHEY, B. B. (1981). A cognitive social skills training program: Evaluation with young children. *Behavior Modification, 5,* 39-60.

CONE, J. D. (1993). The current state of behavioral assessment. *European Journal of Psychological Assessment, 9,* 175-181.

CONE, J. D. (in press). Psychometric considerations: Concepts, contents, and methods. In M. Hersen & A. S. Bellack (Eds.), *Behavioral assessment: A practical handbook* (4th ed.). Des Moines, IA: Allyn and Bacon.

Cone, J. D., Alexander, K., Lichtszajn, J. L., & Mason, R. L. (1996). Reengineering clinical training curricula to meet challenges beyond the year 2000. *the Behavior Therapist, 19,* 65-70.

Connell, M. C., Carta, J. J., & Baer, D. M. (1993). Programming generalization of in-class transition skills: Teaching preschoolers with developmental delays to self-assess and recruit contingent teacher praise. *Journal of Applied Behavior Analysis, 26,* 345-352.

Conrin, J., Pennypacker, H. S., Johnston, J., & Rast, J. (1982). Differential reinforcement of other behavior to treat chronic rumination of mental retardates. *Journal of Behavior Therapy and Experimental Psychiatry, 13,* 325-329.

Constantino, G., Malgady, R. G., & Rogler, L. G. (1986). Cuento therapy: A culturally sensitive modality for Puerto Rican children. *Journal of Consulting and Clinical Psychology, 54,* 639-645.

Cooper, J. O., Heron, T. E., & Heward, W. L. (1987). *Applied behavior analysis.* Columbus, OH: Merrill.

Cope, J. G., Moy, S. S., & Grossnickle, W. F. (1988). The behavioral impact of an advertising campaign to promote safety belt use. *Journal of Applied Behavior Analysis, 21,* 277-280.

Corrigan, P., Schade, M., & Liberman, J. P. (1992). Social skills training. In R. P. Liberman (Ed.), *Handbook of psychiatric rehabilitation* (pp. 95-126). New York: Macmillan.

Corrigan, S. A., Thompson, K. E., & Malow, R. M. (1992). A psychoeducational approach to prevent HIV transmission among injection drug users. *Psychology of Addictive Behaviors, 6,* 114-119.

Costenbader, V., & Reading-Brown, M. (1995). Isolation timeout used with students with emotional disturbance. *Exceptional Children, 61,* 353-363.

Cotharin, R. L., & Mikulas, W. L. (1975). Systematic desensitization of racial emotional responses. *Journal of Behavior Therapy and Experimental Psychiatry, 6,* 347-348.

Cotter, L. H. (1967). Operant conditioning in a Vietnamese mental hospital. *American Journal of Psychiatry, 124,* 23-28.

Cottier, C., Shapiro, K., & Julius, S. (1984). Treatment of mild hypertension with progressive muscle relaxation: Predictive value of indexes of sympathetic tone. *Archives of Internal Medicine, 144,* 1954-1958.

Cottraux, J. (1990). "Cogito ergo sum": Cognitive-behavior therapy in France. *the Behavior Therapist, 13,* 189-190.

Cottraux, J. (1993). Behavioral psychotherapy applications in the medically ill. *Psychotherapy and Psychosomatics, 60,* 116-128.

Cottraux, J., Mollard, E., Bouvard, M., & Marks, I. (1993). Exposure therapy, Fluvoxamine, or combination treatment in obsessive-compulsive disorder: One-year follow up. *Psychiatry Research, 49,* 63-75.

Cousins, N. (1979). *Anatomy of an illness.* New York: Norton.

Cousins, N. (1989). *Head first: The biology of hope.* New York: Dutton.

Cowley, G. (1994, June 20). Waving away the pain. *Newsweek, 123,* 70-71.

Cox, B. J., Fergus, K. D., & Swinson, R. P. (1994). Patient satisfaction with behavioral treatments for panic disorder with agoraphobia. *Journal of Anxiety Disorders, 8,* 193-206.

Cradock, C., Cotler, S., & Jason, L. A. (1978). Primary prevention: Immunization of children for speech anxiety. *Cognitive Therapy and Research, 2,* 389-396.

Craig, K. D. (1986). Social modeling influences: Pain in context. In R. A. Sternbach (Ed.), *The psychology of pain* (2nd ed., pp. 67-95). New York: Raven Press.

Craighead, L. W. (1979). Self-instructional training for assertive-refusal behavior. *Behavior Therapy, 10,* 529-543.

Craighead, W. E. (1990a). The changing nature of behavior therapy. *Behavior Therapy, 21,* 1-2.

Craighead, W. E. (1990b). There's a place for us: All of us. *Behavior Therapy, 21,* 3-23.

Craighead, W. E., Kazdin, A. E., & Mahoney, M. J. (1976). *Behavior modification: Principles, issues, and applications.* Boston: Houghton Mifflin.

Craighead, W. E., Kimball, W. H., & Rehak, P. J. (1979). Mood changes, physiological responses, and self-statements during social rejection imagery. *Journal of Consulting and Clinical Psychology, 47,* 385-396.

Creer, T. L., & Miklich, D. R. (1970). The application of a self-modeling procedure to modify inappropriate behavior: A preliminary report. *Behaviour Research and Therapy, 8,* 91-92.

Critchfield, T. S., & Vargas, E. A. (1991). Self-recording, instructions, and public self-graphing. *Behavior Modification, 15,* 95-112.

Csikszentmihalyi, M. (1990). *Flow: The psychology of optimal experience.* New York: Harper & Row.

Csikszentmihalyi, M., & Csikszentmihalyi, I. S. (Eds.). (1988). *Optimal experience: Psychological studies of flow in consciousness.* New York: Cambridge University Press.

Cullen, J. W., Fox, B. H., & Isom, R. N. (1976). *Cancer: The behavioral dimension.* New York: Raven Press.

Cunliffe, T. (1992). Arresting youth crime: A review of social skills training with young offenders. *Adolescence, 27,* 891-899.

Cunningham, C. E., & Linscheid, T. R. (1976). Elimination of chronic infant ruminating by electric shock. *Behavior Therapy, 7,* 231-234.

Dahlquist, L. M., Gil, K. M., Armstrong, F. D., Ginsberg, A., & Jones, B. (1985). Behavioral management of children's distress during chemotherapy. *Journal of Behavior Therapy and Experimental Psychiatry, 16,* 325-329.

Daley, M. F. (1969). The "Reinforcement Menu": Finding effective reinforcers. In J. D. Krumboltz & C. E. Thoresen (Eds.), *Behavioral counseling: Cases and techniques* (pp. 42-45). New York: Holt, Rinehart & Winston.

Dalton, A. J., Rubino, C. A., & Hislop, M. W. (1973). Some effects of token rewards on school achievement of children with Down's syndrome. *Journal of Applied Behavior Analysis, 6,* 251-259.

Danaher, B. G. (1974). Theoretical foundations and clinical applications of the Premack principle: Review and critique. *Behavior Therapy, 5,* 307-324.

Daniels, L. K. (1974). Rapid extinction of nail biting by covert sensitization: A case study. *Journal of Behavior Therapy and Experimental Psychiatry, 5,* 91-92.

Dapcich-Miura, E., & Hovell, M. F. (1979). Contingency management of adherence to a complex medical regimen in an elderly heart patient. *Behavior Therapy, 10,* 193-201.

Date, A. (1996). On maintaining an empirical orientation in an "alternative ways of knowing" world. *the Behavior Therapist, 19,* 86.

Dattilio, F. M., & Padesky, C. A. (1990). *Cognitive therapy with couples*. Sarasota, FL: Professional Resource Exchange.

Davis, P. K., & Chittum, R. (1994). A group-oriented contingency to increase leisure activities of adults with traumatic brain injury. *Journal of Applied Behavior Analysis, 27,* 553-554.

Davis, R. A. (1979). The impact of self-modeling on problem behaviors in school-age children. *School Psychology Digest, 8,* 128-132.

Davison, G. C. (1976). Homosexuality: The ethical challenge. *Journal of Consulting and Clinical Psychology, 44,* 157-162.

Davison, G. C. (1995). A failure of early behavior therapy (circa 1960): Or why I learned to stop worrying and to embrace psychotherapy integration. *Journal of Psychotherapy Integration, 5,* 107-112.

Davison, G. C., D'Zurilla, T. J., Goldfried, M. R., Paul, G. L., & Valins, S. (1968, August). In M. R. Goldfried (Chair), *Cognitive processes in behavior modification.* Symposium presented at the meeting of the American Psychological Association, San Francisco.

Davison, G. C., & Lazarus, A. A. (1995). The dialectics of science and practice. In S. C. Hayes, V. M. Follette, R. M. Dawes, & K. E. Grady (Eds.), *Scientific standards of psychological practice: Issues and recommendations* (pp. 95-120). Reno, NV: Context Press.

Davison, G. C., Navarre, S. G., & Vogel, R. S. (1995). The articulated thoughts in simulated situations paradigm: A think-aloud approach to cognitive assessment. *Current Directions in Psychological Science, 4,* 29-33.

Davison, G. C., & Stuart, R. B. (1975). Behavior therapy and civil liberties. *American Psychologist, 30,* 755-763.

Dawe, G. F., & Hart, D. S. (1986, June). *Covert modeling and rehearsal in the treatment of social anxiety.* Paper presented at the meeting of the Canadian Psychological Association, Toronto.

Dawley, H. H., & Dillenkoffer, R. L. (1975). Minimizing the risks in rapid smoking treatment. *Journal of Behavior Therapy and Experimental Psychiatry, 6,* 174.

Dawson, B., de Armas, A., McGrath, M. L., & Kelly, J. A. (1986). Cognitive problem-solving training to improve child-care judgement of child neglectful parents. *Journal of Family Violence, 1,* 209-221.

Day, L., & Reznikoff, M. (1980). Preparation of children and parents for treatment at a children's psychiatric clinic through videotaped modeling. *Journal of Consulting and Clinical Psychology, 48,* 303-304.

Deitz, S. M. (1977). An analysis of programming DRL schedules in educational settings. *Behaviour Research and Therapy, 15,* 103-111.

Deitz, S. M., & Repp, A. C. (1973). Decreasing classroom misbehavior through the use of DRL schedules of reinforcement. *Journal of Applied Behavior Analysis, 6,* 457-463.

Deitz, S. M., Repp, A. C., & Deitz, D. E. D. (1976). Reducing inappropriate classroom behavior of retarded students through three procedures of differential reinforcement. *Journal of Mental Deficiency Research, 20,* 155-170.

Deleon, G., & Mandell, W. (1966). A comparison of conditioning and psychotherapy in the treatment of functional enuresis. *Journal of Clinical Psychology, 22,* 326-330.

Deleon, G., & Sacks, S. (1972). Conditioning functional enuresis: A four-year follow-up. *Journal of Consulting and Clinical Psychology, 39,* 299-300.

de L. Horne, D. J., White, A. E., & Varigos, G. A. (1989). A preliminary study of psychological therapy in the management of atopic eczema. *British Journal of Medical Psychology, 62,* 241-248.

Dember, W. N. (1974). Motivation and the cognitive revolution. *American Psychologist, 29,* 161-168.

de Moor, W. (1970). Systematic desensitization versus prolonged high intensity stimulation (flooding). *Journal of Behavior Therapy and Experimental Psychiatry, 1,* 45-52.

Denney, D. R., Sullivan, B. J., & Thiry, M. R. (1977). Participant modeling and self-verbalization training in the reduction of spider fears. *Journal of Behavior Therapy and Experimental Psychiatry, 8,* 247-253.

Derby, K. M., Wacker, D. P., Sasso, G., Steege, M., Northup, J., Cigland, K., & Asinus, J. (1992). Brief functional assessment techniques to evaluate aberrant behavior in an outpatient setting: A summary of 79 cases. *Journal of Applied Behavior Analysis, 25,* 713-721.

DeRisi, W. J., & Butz, G. (1975). *Writing behavioral contracts: A case simulation practice manual.* Champaign, IL: Research Press.

Deslauriers, B. C., & Everett, P. B. (1977). The effects of intermittent and continuous token reinforcement on bus ridership. *Journal of Applied Psychology, 62,* 369-375.

Dewhurst, D. T. (1993). Using the self-control triad to treat tension headache in a child. In J. R. Cautela & A. J. Kearney (Eds.), *Covert conditioning casebook* (pp. 75-81). Pacific Grove, CA: Brooks/Cole.

Diament, C., & Wilson, G. T. (1975). An experimental investigation of the effects of covert sensitization in an analogue eating situation. *Behavior Therapy, 6,* 499-509.

DiGiuseppe, R. (1989). Cognitive therapy with children. In A. Freeman, K. M. Simon, L. E. Beutler, & H. Arkowitz (Eds.), *Comprehensive handbook of cognitive therapy* (pp. 515-533). New York: Plenum.

DiGiuseppe, R. A. (1981). Cognitive therapy with children. In G. Emery, S. D. Hollon, & R. C. Bedrosian (Eds.), *New directions in cognitive therapy: A casebook* (pp. 50-67). New York: Guilford.

Dobson, K. S. (1989). A meta-analysis of the efficacy of cognitive therapy for depression. *Journal of Consulting and Clinical Psychology, 57,* 414-419.

Dobson, K. S., & Shaw, B. F. (1989). The use of treatment manuals in cognitive therapy: Experiences and issues. *Journal of Consulting and Clinical Psychology, 56,* 673-681.

Doerfler, L. A., Mullins, L. L., Griffin, N. J., Siegel, L. J., & Richards, C. S. (1984). Problem-solving deficits in depressed children, adolescents, and adults. *Cognitive Therapy and Research, 8,* 489-500.

Dolce, J. J., Doleys, D. M., Raczynski, J. M., Lossie, J., Poole, L., & Smith, M. (1986). The role of self-efficacy expectancies in the prediction of pain tolerance. *Pain, 27,* 261-272.

Doleys, D. M. (1977). Behavioral treatment of nocturnal enuresis in children: A review of the recent literature. *Psychological Bulletin, 84,* 30-54.

Doleys, D. M., Crocker, M., & Patton, D. (1982). Response of patients with chronic pain to exercise quotas. *Physical Therapy, 62,* 1111-1114.

Doleys, D. M., & Kurtz, P. S. (1974). A behavioral treatment program for Gilles de la Tourette syndrome. *Psychological Reports, 35,* 43-48.

DONNER, L., & GUERNEY, B. G. (1969). Automated group desensitization for test anxiety. *Behaviour Research and Therapy, 7,* 1-13.

DONOHUE, B. C., VAN HASSELT, V. B., & HERSEN, M. (1994). Behavioral assessment and treatment of social phobia: An evaluative review. *Behavior Modification, 18,* 262-288.

DOOLEY, R. T., & HALFORD, W. K. (1992). A comparison of relapse prevention with nicotine gum or nicotine fading in modification of smoking. *Australian Psychologist, 27,* 186-191.

DOSTER, J. A. (1972). Effects of instructions, modeling, and role rehearsal on interview verbal behavior. *Journal of Consulting and Clinical Psychology, 39,* 202-209.

DOUGHER, M. J. (1993). Covert sensitization in the treatment of deviant sexual arousal. In J. R. Cautela & A. J. Kearney (Eds.), *Covert conditioning casebook* (pp. 199-207). Pacific Grove, CA: Brooks/Cole.

DOWNS, A. F. D., ROSENTHAL, T. L., & LICHSTEIN, K. L. (1988). Modeling therapies reduce avoidance of bath-time by the institutionalized elderly. *Behavior Therapy, 19,* 359-368.

DOWRICK, P. W. (1978). Suggestions for the use of edited video replay in training behavioral skills. *Journal of Practical Approaches to Developmental Handicap, 2,* 21-24.

DOWRICK, P. W. (1979). Single dose medication to create a self model film. *Child Behavior Therapy, 1,* 193-198.

DOWRICK, P. W. (1983). Video training of alternatives to cross-gender identity behaviors in a 4-year-old boy. *Child and Family Behavior Therapy, 5,* 59-65.

DOWRICK, P. W. (1986). *Social survival for children: A trainer's resource book.* New York: Brunner/Mazel.

DOWRICK, P. W. (1991). *Practical guide to using video in the behavioral sciences.* New York: Wiley.

DOWRICK, P. W. (1994). Video psychology. In R. J. Corsini (Ed.), *Encyclopedia of psychology* (2nd ed., pp. 566-567). New York: Wiley.

DOWRICK, P. W. (1996, January 2). Personal communication.

DOWRICK, P. W., BEN, K., & WEIDLE, J. (1995, January). *Video futures: New strategies for difficult transitions.* Invited presentation at 11th Annual Pacific Rim Conference, Hawaii University Affiliated Program for Developmental Disabilities, Honolulu.

DOWRICK, P. W., & HOOD, M. (1978). Transfer of talking behaviours across settings using faked films. In T. Glynn & S. McNaughton (Eds.), *Behaviour analysis in New Zealand* (pp. 78-87). Auckland, New Zealand: University of Auckland.

DOWRICK, P. W., & RAEBURN, J. M. (1977). Video editing and medication to produce a therapeutic self model. *Journal of Consulting and Clinical Psychology, 45,* 1156-1158.

DOWRICK, P. W., & RAEBURN, J. M. (1995). Self-modeling: Rapid skill training for children with physical disabilities. *Journal of Developmental and Physical Disabilities, 7,* 25-37.

DRYDEN, W., & HILL, L. K. (EDS.). (1993). *Innovations in rational-emotive therapy.* Newbury Park, CA: Sage.

DUBBERT, P. M. (1992). Exercise in behavioral medicine. *Journal of Consulting and Clinical Psychology, 60,* 613-618.

DUBBERT, P. M., JOHNSON, W. J., SCHLUNDT, D. G., & MONTAGUE, N. W. (1984). The influence of caloric information on cafeteria food choices. *Journal of Applied Behavior Analysis, 16,* 85-92.

DUCHARME, J. M., PONTES, E., GUGER, S., CROZIER, K., LUCAS, H., & POPYNICK, M. (1994). Errorless compliance to parental requests II: Increasing clinical practicality through abbreviation of treatment parameters. *Behavior Therapy, 25,* 469-487.

DUCHARME, J. M., & POPYNICK, M. (1993). Errorless compliance to parental requests: Treatment effects and generalization. *Behavior Therapy, 24,* 209-226.

DUCHARME, J. M., & VAN HOUTEN, R. (1994). Operant extinction in the treatment of severe maladaptive behavior: Adapting research to practice. *Behavior Modification, 18,* 139-170.

DULEY, S. M., CANCELLI, A. A., KRATOCHWILL, T. R., BERGAN, J. R., & MEREDITH, K. E. (1983). Training and generalization of motivational analysis interview assessment skills. *Behavioral Assessment, 5,* 281-293.

DUNKEL, L. D., & GLAROS, A. G. (1978). Comparison of self-instructional and stimulus control treatments for obesity. *Cognitive Therapy and Research, 2,* 75-78.

DUPAUL, G. J., GUEVREMONT, D. C., & BARKLEY, R. A. (1992). Behavioral treatment of attention-deficit hyperactivity disorder in the classroom: The use of the attention training system. *Behavior Modification, 16,* 204-225.

DURAND, V. M., & MINDELL, J. A. (1990). Behavioral treatment of multiple childhood sleep disorders. *Behavior Modification, 14,* 37-49.

DYER, W. (1977). *Your erroneous zones.* New York: Funk & Wagnalls.

D'ZURILLA, T. J. (1986). *Problem-solving therapy: A social competence approach to clinical intervention.* New York: Springer.

D'ZURILLA, T. J., & CHANG, E. C. (1995). The relations between social problem solving and coping. *Cognitive Therapy and Research 19,* 547-562.

D'ZURILLA, T. J., & GOLDFRIED, M. R. (1971). Problem solving and behavior modification. *Journal of Abnormal Psychology, 78,* 107-126.

D'ZURILLA, T. J., & MASCHKA, G. (1988, November). *Outcome of a problem-solving approach to stress management: I. Comparison with social support.* Paper presented at the meeting of the Association for Advancement of Behavior Therapy, New York.

D'ZURILLA, T., & NEZU, A. (1982). Social problem solving in adults. In P. Kendall (Ed.), *Advances in cognitive-behavioral research and therapy* (Vol. 1, pp. 285-315). New York: Academic Press.

D'ZURILLA, T. J., & SHEEDY, C. F. (1991). Relation between social problem-solving ability and subsequent level of psychological stress in college students. *Journal of Personality and Social Psychology, 61,* 841-846.

ECTON, R. B., & FEINDLER, E. L. (1990). Anger control training for temper control disorders. In E. L. Feindler & G. R. Kalfus (Eds.), *Adolescent behavior therapy handbook* (pp. 351-371). New York: Springer.

EDELMAN, R. E., & CHAMBLESS, D. L. (1993). Compliance during sessions and homework in exposure-based treatment of agoraphobia. *Behaviour Research and Therapy, 31,* 767-773.

EDELMAN, R. E., & CHAMBLESS, D. L. (1995). Adherence during sessions and homework in cognitive-behavioral group treatment of social phobia. *Behaviour Research and Therapy, 33,* 573-577.

EDGETTE, J. S., & PROUT, M. F. (1989). Cognitive and behavioral approaches to the treatment of anorexia nervosa. In

A. Freeman, K. M. Simon, L. E. Beutler, & H. Arkowitz (Eds.), *Comprehensive handbook of cognitive therapy* (pp. 367-384). New York: Plenum.

EDINGER, J. D., & JACOBSEN, R. (1982). Incidence and significance of relaxation treatment side effects. *the Behavior Therapist, 5,* 137-138.

EGEL, A. L., RICHMAN, G. S., & KOEGEL, R. L. (1981). Normal peer models and autistic children's learning. *Journal of Applied Behavior Analysis, 14,* 3-12.

EIFERT, G. H., FORSYTH, J. P., & SHAUSS, S. L. (1994, November). Behavior therapy in the next 25 years: Redefining the context for a science of effective behavior change. In G. H. Eifert (Chair), *Putting the science of behavior back into the practice of behavior therapy.* Symposium presented at the meeting of the Association for Advancement of Behavior Therapy, San Diego.

EIFERT, G. H., & WILSON, P. H. (1991). The triple response approach to assessment: A conceptual and methodological reappraisal. *Behaviour Research and Therapy, 29,* 283-292.

EISLER, R. M., HERSEN, M., & MILLER, P. M. (1973). Effects of modeling on components of assertive behavior. *Journal of Behavior Therapy and Experimental Psychiatry, 4,* 1-6.

EISLER, R. M., HERSEN, M., MILLER, P. M., & BLANCHARD, E. B. (1975). Situational determinants of assertive behaviors. *Journal of Consulting and Clinical Psychology, 43,* 330-340.

EITZEN, D. S. (1975). The effects of behavior modification on the attitudes of delinquents. *Behaviour Research and Therapy, 13,* 295-299.

ELDER, S. T., & EUSTIS, N. K. (1975). Instrumental blood pressure conditioning in outpatient hypertensives. *Behaviour Research and Therapy, 13,* 185-188.

ELKIN, I., SHEA, M. T., WATKINS, J. T., IMBER, S. D., SOTSKY, S. M., COLLINS, J. F., GLASS, D. R., PILKONIS, P. A., LEBER, W. R., DOCHERTY, J. P., FIESTER, S. J., & PARLOFF, M. B. (1989). National Institute of Mental Health Treatment of Depression Collaborative Research Program: General effectiveness of treatments. *Archives of General Psychiatry, 46,* 971-982.

ELLIS, A. (1959). *Psychotherapy session with an eight year old female bedwetter.* Cassette recording. New York: Institute for Rational-Emotive Therapy.

ELLIS, A. (1962). *Reason and emotion in psychotherapy.* New York: Lyle Stuart.

ELLIS, A. (1970). *The essence of rational psychotherapy: A comprehensive approach in treatment.* New York: Institute for Rational Living.

ELLIS, A. (1989a). Comments on my critics. In M. E. Bernard & R. DiGiuseppe (Eds.), *Inside rational-emotive therapy: A critical appraisal of the theory and therapy of Albert Ellis* (pp. 199-233). San Diego: Academic Press.

ELLIS, A. (1989b). The history of cognition in psychotherapy. In A. Freeman, K. M. Simon, L. E. Beutler, & H. Arkowitz (Eds.), *Comprehensive handbook of cognitive therapy* (pp. 5-20). New York: Plenum.

ELLIS, A. (1994a). A corrective note on O'Donohue and Szymanski's study of logical analysis and REBT's use of empirical hypothesis testing as well as logical analysis. *Journal of Rational-Emotive and Cognitive-Behavior Therapy, 12,* 73-76.

ELLIS, A. (1994b). Ellis, Albert. *Current Biography, 65,* 6-10.

ELLIS, A. (1994c). General semantics and rational emotive behavior therapy. In P. D. Johnston, D. D. Bourland, & J. Klein (Eds.), *More E-prime: To be or not II* (pp. 213-

240). Concord, CA: International Society for General Semantics.

ELLIS, A. (1994d). Post-traumatic stress disorder (PTSD): A rational emotive behavioral theory. *Journal of Rational-Emotive and Cognitive-Behavior Therapy, 12,* 3-25.

ELLIS, A. (1994e). Radical behavioral treatment of private events: A response to Michael Dougher. *the Behavior Therapist, 17,* 219-221.

ELLIS, A. (1995). Changing rational-emotive therapy (RET) to rational-emotive behavior therapy (REBT). *Journal of Rational-Emotive and Cognitive-Behavior Therapy, 13,* 85-89.

ELLIS, A., & BERNARD, M. E. (EDS.). (1983). *Rational-emotive approaches to the problems of childhood.* New York: Plenum.

ELLIS, A., & BERNARD, M. E. (1985). What is rational-emotive therapy (RET)? In A. Ellis & R. M. Grieger (Eds.), *Handbook of rational-emotive therapy* (pp. 1-30). New York: Springer.

ELLIS, A., & DRYDEN, W. (1987). *The practice of rational-emotive therapy.* New York: Springer.

ELLIS, A., & DRYDEN, W. (1993). A therapy by any other name? An interview. *The Rational Emotive Therapist, 1,* 34-37.

ELLIS, A., & HARPER, R. A. (1975). *A new guide to rational living.* North Hollywood, CA: Wilshire.

ELMAN, D., & KILLEBREW, T. J. (1987). Incentives and seat belts: Changing a resistant behavior through extrinsic motivation. *Journal of Applied Social Psychology, 8,* 72-83.

ELSESSER, K., VAN BERKEL, M., SARTORY, G., BIERMANN-GÖCKE, W., & ÖHL, S. (1994). The effects of anxiety management training on psychological variables and immune parameters in cancer patients: A pilot study. *Behavioural and Cognitive Psychotherapy, 22,* 13-23.

EMERSON, E. (1993). Challenging behaviours and severe learning disabilities: Recent developments in behavioural analysis and intervention. *Behavioural and Cognitive Psychotherapy, 21,* 171-198.

EMMELKAMP, P. M. G. (1982). *Phobic and obsessive-compulsive disorders: Theory, research, and practice.* New York: Plenum.

EMMELKAMP, P. M. G. (1994). Behavior therapy with adults. In A. E. Bergin & S. L. Garfield (Eds.), *Handbook of psychotherapy and behavior change* (4th ed., pp. 379-427). New York: Wiley.

EMMELKAMP, P. M. G., DE HAAN, E., & HOOGDUIN, C. A. L. (1990). Marital adjustment and obsessive-compulsive disorder. *British Journal of Psychiatry, 156,* 55-60.

EMMELKAMP, P. M. G., & WESSELS, H. (1975). Flooding in imagination versus flooding *in vivo*: A comparison with agoraphobics. *Behaviour Research and Therapy, 13,* 7-15.

ENGLE-FRIEDMAN, M., BOOTZIN, R. R., HAZLEWOOD, L., & TSAO, C. (1992). An evaluation of behavioral treatments for insomnia in the older adult. *Journal of Clinical Psychology, 48,* 77-90.

EPSTEIN, L. H., BECK, S., FIGUEROA, J., FARKAS, G., KAZDIN, A. E., DANEMAN, D., & BECKER, D. (1981). The effects of targeting improvements in urine glucose on metabolic control in children with insulin dependent diabetes. *Journal of Applied Behavior Analysis, 14,* 365-375.

EPSTEIN, L. H., & MASEK, B. J. (1978). Behavioral control of medicine compliance. *Journal of Applied Behavior Analysis, 11,* 1-9.

EPSTEIN, N. (1983). Cognitive therapy with couples. In A. Freeman (Ed.), *Cognitive therapy with couples and groups* (pp. 107-123). New York: Plenum.

EPSTEIN, N., & BAUCOM, D. H. (1989). Cognitive-behavioral marital therapy. In A. Freeman, K. M. Simon, L. E. Beutler, & H. Arkowitz (Eds.), *Comprehensive handbook of cognitive therapy* (pp. 491-513). New York: Plenum.

ESPIE, C. A., LINDSAY, W. R., BROOKS, D. N., HOOD, E. H., & TURVEY, T. (1989). A controlled comparative investigation of psychological treatments for chronic sleep-onset insomnia. *Behaviour Research and Therapy, 27,* 79-88.

Ethical issues for human services. (1977). *Behavior Therapy, 8,* v-vi.

EVANS, J. H., FERRE, L., FORD, L. A., & GREEN, J. L. (1995). Decreasing attention deficit hyperactivity disorder symptoms utilizing an automated classroom reinforcement device. *Psychology in the Schools, 32,* 210-219.

EVANS, P. D., & KELLAM, A. M. P. (1973). Semi-automated desensitization: A controlled clinical trial. *Behaviour Research and Therapy, 11,* 641-646.

EVERETT, P. B., HAYWARD, C. S., & MEYERS, A. W. (1974). The effects of a token economy procedure on bus ridership. *Journal of Applied Behavior Analysis, 7,* 1-9.

EYSENCK, H. J. (1952). The effects of psychotherapy: An evaluation. *Journal of Consulting Psychology, 16,* 319-324.

FAIRBURN, C. G., JONES, R., PEVELER, R. C., HOPE, R. A., & O'CONNOR, M. E. (1993). Psychotherapy and bulimia nervosa: The long-term effects of interpersonal psychotherapy, behavior therapy, and cognitive behavior therapy for bulimia nervosa. *Archives of General Psychiatry, 50,* 419-428.

FAIRBURN, C. G., MARCUS, M. D., & WILSON, G. T. (1993). Cognitive-behavioral therapy for binge eating and bulimia nervosa: A comprehensive treatment manual. In C. G. Fairburn & G. T. Wilson (Eds.), *Binge eating: Nature, assessment and treatment* (pp. 361-404). New York: Guilford.

FAIRBURN, C. G., PEVELER, R. C., JONES, R., HOPE, R. A., & DOLL, H. (1993). Predictors of 12-month outcome in bulimia nervosa and the influence of attitudes to shape and weight. *Journal of Consulting and Clinical Psychology, 61,* 696-698.

FALLOON, I. R. H., & COVERDALE, J. H. (1994). Cognitive-behavioural family interventions for major mental disorders. Special issue: Behaviour therapy and schizophrenia: I. *Behaviour Change, 11,* 213-222.

FALS-STEWART, W., MARKS, A. P., & SCHAFER, J. (1993). A comparison of behavioral group therapy and individual behavior therapy in treating obsessive-compulsive disorder. *Journal of Mental and Nervous Disease, 181,* 189-193.

FANTUZZO, J. W., & THOMPSON, D. W. (1991). Behavioral community psychology: A timely and potent synergy. *the Behavior Therapist, 14,* 28.

FARQUHAR, J. W. (1978). The community-based model of lifestyle intervention trials. *American Journal of Epidemiology, 108,* 103-111.

FARQUHAR, J. W., MACCOBY, N., & SOLOMON, D. S. (1984). Community applications of behavioral medicine. In W. D. Gentry (Ed.), *Handbook of behavioral medicine* (pp. 437-478). New York: Guilford.

FEDERAL REGISTER. (1984, July). *Federal motor vehicle safety standards: Occupant crash protection, Final Rule 48 (No. 138).* Washington, DC: U.S. Department of Transportation.

FEINDLER, E. L., ECTON, R. B., KINGSLEY, D., & DUBEY, D. R. (1986). Group anger-control training for institutionalized psychiatric male adolescents. *Behavior Therapy, 17,* 109-123.

FEINDLER, E. L., MARRIOTT, S. A., & IWATA, M. (1984). Group anger-control training for junior high school delinquents. *Cognitive Therapy and Research, 8,* 299-311.

FELDMAN, M. P., & MACCULLOCH, M. J. (1971). *Homosexual behavior: Therapy and assessment.* Elmsford, NY: Pergamon.

FELL, C. (TRANS. AND ED.). (1975). *Egils sage.* London: J. M. Dent & Sons.

FELLNER, D. J., & SULZER-AZAROFF, B. (1984). Increasing industrial safety practices and conditions through posted feedback. *Journal of Safety Research, 15,* 7-21.

FERRITOR, D. E., BUCKHOLDT, D., HAMBLIN, R. L., & SMITH, L. (1972). The noneffects of contingent reinforcement for attending behavior on work accomplished. *Journal of Applied Behavior Analysis, 5,* 7-17.

FESTINGER, L. (1957). *A theory of cognitive dissonance.* Stanford, CA: Stanford University Press.

FEUERSTEIN, M., & GAINER, J. (1982). Chronic headache: Etiology and management. In D. M. Doleys, R. L. Meredith, & A. R. Ciminero (Eds.), *Behavioral medicine: Assessment and treatment strategies* (pp. 199-249). New York: Plenum.

FINNEY, J. W., MILLER, K. M., & ADLER, S. P. (1993). Changing protective and risky behaviors to prevent child-to-parent transmission of cytomegalovirus. *Journal of Applied Behavior Analysis, 26,* 471-472.

FINNEY, J. W., RAPOFF, M. A., HALL, C. L., & CHRISTOPHERSON, E. R. (1983). Replication and social validation of habit reversal treatment for tics. *Behavior Therapy, 14,* 116-126.

FISHER, E., & THOMPSON, J. K. (1994). A comparative evaluation of cognitive-behavioral therapy (CBT) versus exercise therapy (ET) for the treatment of body image disturbance: Preliminary findings. *Behavior Modification, 18,* 171-185.

FIXSEN, D. L., PHILLIPS, E. L., PHILLIPS, E. A., & WOLF, M. M. (1976). The teaching-family model of group home treatment. In W. E. Craighead, A. E. Kazdin, & M. J. Mahoney, *Behavior modification: Principles, issues, and applications* (pp. 310-320). Boston: Houghton Mifflin.

FLEECE, L. (1995). [Review of the book *The therapeutic relationship in behavioural psychotherapy*]. *the Behavior Therapist, 18,* 142.

FLEMING, I. (1984). Habit reversal treatment for trichotillomania: A case study. *Behavioural Psychotherapy, 12,* 73-80.

FLOR, H., KERNS, R. D., & TURK, D. C. (1987). The role of spouse reinforcement, perceived pain, and activity levels of chronic pain patients. *Journal of Psychosomatic Research, 31,* 251-259.

FOA, E. B., & ROTHBAUM, B. O. (1989). Behavioural psychotherapy for post-traumatic stress disorder. *International Review of Psychiatry, 1,* 219-226.

FOA, E. B., ROTHBAUM, B. O., & KOZAK, M. J. (1989). Behavioral treatments for anxiety and depression. In P. C. Kendall & D. Watson (Eds.), *Anxiety and depression: Distinctive and overlapping features* (pp. 413-454). New York: Academic Press.

FOA, E. B., ROTHBAUM, B. O., RIGGS, D. S., & MURDOCK, T. B. (1991). Treatment of posttraumatic stress disorder in rape victims: A comparison between cognitive-behavioral procedures and counseling. *Journal of Consulting and Clinical Psychology, 59,* 715-723.

FOA, E. B., STEKETEE, G. S., TURNER, R. M., & FISCHER, S. C. (1980). Effectiveness of imaginal exposure to feared disasters in obsessive-compulsive checkers. *Behaviour Research and Therapy, 18,* 449-455.

FOLLANSBEE, D. J., LAGRECA, A. M., & CITRIN, W. S. (1983). Coping skills training for adolescents with diabetes. *Diabetes, 32* (Suppl. 1), 147. (Abstract)

FOLLICK, M. J. (1979, September). *An outpatient based behaviorally oriented approach to the management of chronic pain.* Paper presented at the meeting of the American Psychological Association, New York.

FOOD AND DRUG ADMINISTRATION. (1980). *Get the picture on protection.* Rockville, MD: Author.

FORBES, D., CREAMER, M., & RYCROFT, P. (1994). Eye movement desensitization and reprocessing in posttraumatic stress disorder: A pilot study using assessment measures. *Journal of Behavior Therapy and Experimental Psychiatry, 25,* 113-120.

FORDYCE, W. (1976). *Behavioral methods for chronic pain and illness.* St. Louis: Mosby.

FORDYCE, W. E. (1988). Pain and suffering: A reappraisal. *American Psychologist, 43,* 276-283.

FORDYCE, W. E., FOWLER, R. S., & DELATEUR, B. (1968). An application of behavior modification techniques to a problem of chronic pain. *Behaviour Research and Therapy, 6,* 105-107.

FORDYCE, W. E., FOWLER, R. S., LEHMANN, J. F., DELATEUR, B. J., SAND, P. L., & TRIESCHMANN, R. B. (1973). Operant conditioning in the treatment of chronic pain. *Archives of Physical Medicine and Rehabilitation, 54,* 399-408.

FORDYCE, W. E., & STEGER, J. C. (1979). Chronic pain. In O. F. Pomerleau & J. P. Brady (Eds.), *Behavioral medicine: Theory and practice* (pp. 125-153). Baltimore: Williams & Wilkins.

FOREHAND, R., & KING, H. E. (1977). Noncompliant children: Effects of parent training on behavior and attitude. *Behavior Modification, 1,* 93-108.

FOREHAND, R., & LONG, N. (1988). Outpatient treatment of the acting-out child: Procedures, long-term follow-up data, and clinical problems. *Archives in Behaviour Research and Therapy, 10,* 129-177.

FOREHAND, R. L., & MCMAHON, R. J. (1981). *Helping the noncompliant child: A clinician's guide to parent training.* New York: Guilford.

FOREMAN, S. A. (1980). A comparison of cognitive training and response cost procedures in modifying aggressive behavior of elementary school children. *Behavior Therapy, 11,* 594-600.

FOREYT, J. P. (1987). The addictive disorders. In G. T. Wilson, C. M. Franks, P. C. Kendall, & J. P. Foreyt (Eds.), *Review of behavior therapy: Theory and practice* (Vol. 11, pp. 187-233). New York: Guilford.

FOREYT, J. P. (1990). The addictive disorders. In C. M. Franks, G. T. Wilson, P. C. Kendall, & J. P. Foreyt (Eds.), *Review of behavior therapy: Theory and practice* (Vol. 12, pp. 178-224). New York: Guilford.

FOREYT, J. P., & HAGEN, R. L. (1973). Covert sensitization: Conditioning or suggestions? *Journal of Abnormal Psychology, 82,* 17-23.

FOSTER, S. L., BELL-DOLAN, D. J., & BURGE, D. A. (1988). Behavioral observation. In A. S. Bellack & M. Hersen (Eds.), *Behavioral assessment: A practical handbook* (3rd ed., pp. 119-160). Elmsford, NY: Pergamon.

FOSTER, S. L., & CONE, J. D. (1980). Current issues in direct observation. *Behavioral Assessment, 2,* 313-338.

FOSTER, S. L., & CONE, J. D. (1986). Design and use of direct observation. In A. R. Ciminero, K. S. Calhoun, & H. A. Adams (Eds.), *Handbook of behavioral assessment* (2nd ed., pp. 253-324). New York: Wiley.

FOX, D. K., HOPKINS, B. L., & ANGER, W. K. (1987). The long-term effects of a token economy on safety performance in open-pit mining. *Journal of Applied Behavior Analysis, 20,* 215-224.

FOX, R. A., & DESHAW, J. M. (1993a). Milestone reinforcer survey. *Education and Training in Mental Retardation, 28,* 257-261.

FOX, R. A., & DESHAW, J. M. (1993b). *Milestone reinforcer survey manual.* Rockford, IL: Milestone, Inc.

FOXX, R. M., & AZRIN, N. H. (1972). Restitution: A method of eliminating aggressive-disruptive behavior of retarded and brain damaged patients. *Behaviour Research and Therapy, 10,* 15-27.

FOXX, R. M., & AZRIN, N. H. (1973a). Dry pants: A rapid method of toilet training children. *Behaviour Research and Therapy, 11,* 435-442.

FOXX, R. M., & AZRIN, N. H. (1973b). *Toilet training the retarded: A rapid program for day and night time independent toileting.* Champaign, IL: Research Press.

FOXX, R. M., & FAW, G. D. (1990). Long-term follow-up of echolalia and question answering. *Journal of Applied Behavior Analysis, 23,* 387-396.

FOXX, R. M., FAW, G. D., & WEBER, G. (1991). Producing generalization of inpatient adolescents' social skills with significant adults in a natural environment. *Behavior Therapy, 22,* 85-99.

FOXX, R. M., & HAKE, D. F. (1977). Gasoline conservation: A procedure for measuring and reducing the driving of college students. *Journal of Applied Behavior Analysis, 10,* 61-74.

FOXX, R. M., MARTELLA, R. C., & MARCHAND-MARTELLA, N. E. (1989). The acquisition, maintenance, and generalization of problem-solving skills by closed head-injured adults. *Behavior Therapy, 20,* 61-76.

FOXX, R. M., & SCHAEFFER, M. H. (1981). A company-based lottery to reduce the personal driving of employees. *Journal of Applied Behavior Analysis, 14,* 273-285.

FRAME, C. L., & MATSON, J. L. (1987). *Handbook of assessment in childhood psychopathology: Applied issues in differential diagnosis and treatment evaluation.* New York: Plenum.

FRANCE, K. G. (1992). Behavioral characteristics and security in sleep disturbed infants treated with extinction. *Journal of Pediatric Psychology, 17,* 467-475.

FRANCE, K. G., & HUDSON, S. M. (1990). Behavior management of infant sleep disturbance. *Journal of Applied Behavior Analysis, 23,* 91-98.

FRANCE, K. G., & HUDSON, S. M. (1993). Management of infant sleep disturbance: A review. *Clinical Psychology Review, 13,* 635-647.

FRANCO, D. D. (1981). Habit reversal and isometric tensing with motor tics. *Dissertation Abstracts International, 42,* 3418B.

FRANCO, D. P., CHRISTOFF, K. A., CRIMMINS, D. B., & KELLY, J. A. (1983). Social skills training for an extremely shy young adolescent: An empirical case study. *Behavior Therapy, 14,* 568-575.

FRANCO, H., GALANTER, M., CASTEÑEDA, R., & PATERSON, J. (1995). Combining behavioral and self-help approaches in the inpatient management of dually diagnosed patients. *Journal of Substance Abuse, 12,* 227-232.

FRANKS, C. M. (1963). Behavior therapy, the principles of conditioning and the treatment of the alcoholic. *Quarterly Journal of Studies on Alcohol, 24,* 511-529.

FRANKS, C. M. (1969). Introduction: Behavior therapy and its Pavlovian origins: Review and perspectives. In C. M. Franks (Ed.), *Behavior therapy: Appraisal and status* (pp. 1-26). New York: McGraw-Hill.

FRANKS, C. M. (1995). RET, REBT and Albert Ellis. *Journal of Rational-Emotive and Cognitive-Behavior Therapy, 13,* 91-95.

FRANKS, C. M., & WILSON, G. T. (EDS.). (1973). *Annual review of behavior therapy: Theory and practice* (Vol. 1). New York: Brunner/Mazel.

FRANKS, C. M., & WILSON, G. T. (EDS.). (1975). *Annual review of behavior therapy: Theory and practice* (Vol. 3). New York: Brunner/Mazel.

FRANKS, C. M., & WILSON, G. T. (EDS.). (1976). *Annual review of behavior therapy: Theory and practice* (Vol. 4). New York: Brunner/Mazel.

FRANKS, C. M., & WILSON, G. T. (EDS.). (1978). *Annual review of behavior therapy: Theory and practice* (Vol. 6). New York: Brunner/Mazel.

FRANKS, C. M., WILSON, G. T., KENDALL, P. C., & FOREYT, J. P. (1990). *Review of behavior therapy: Theory and practice* (Vol. 12). New York: Guilford.

FREEMAN, A., & SIMON, K. M. (1989). Cognitive therapy of anxiety. In A. Freeman, K. M. Simon, L. E. Beutler, & H. Arkowitz (Eds.), *Comprehensive handbook of cognitive therapy* (pp. 347-365). New York: Plenum.

FREEMAN, A., & WHITE, D. M. (1989). The treatment of suicidal behavior. In A. Freeman, K. M. Simon, L. E. Beutler, & H. Arkowitz (Eds.), *Comprehensive handbook of cognitive therapy* (pp. 321-346). New York: Plenum.

FREUD, S. (1955). Analysis of a phobia in a five-year-old boy. In J. Strachey (Ed. and Trans.), *The standard edition of the complete psychological works of Sigmund Freud* (Vol. 10). London: Hogarth. (Originally published 1909.)

FRIEDMAN, R., SOBEL, D., MYERS, P., CAUDILL, M., & BENSON, H. (1995). Behavioral medicine, clinical health psychology, and cost offset. *Health Psychology, 14,* 509-518.

FRIEDMAN, S. (1980). Self-control in the treatment of Gilles de la Tourette's syndrome: Case study with 18-month follow-up. *Journal of Consulting and Clinical Psychology, 48,* 400-402.

FRIMAN, P. C., FINNEY, J. W., & CHRISTOPHERSEN, E. R. (1984). Behavioral treatment of trichotillomania: An evaluative review. *Behavior Therapy, 15,* 249-265.

FRIMAN, P. C., FINNEY, J. W., RAPOFF, M. A., & CHRISTOPHERSEN, E. R. (1985). Improving pediatric appointment keeping with reminders and reduced response requirements. *Journal of Applied Behavior Analysis, 18,* 315-321.

FRIMAN, P. C., & O'CONNOR, W. A. (1984). The integration of hypnotic and habit reversal techniques in the treatment of trichotillomania. *the Behavior Therapist, 7,* 166-167.

FRIMAN, P. C., & VOLLMER, D. (1995). The successful use of the nocturnal urine alarm for diurnal enuresis. *Journal of Applied Behavior Analysis, 28,* 89-90.

FRISBY, C. (1990). A teacher inservice model for problem solving in classroom discipline: Suggestions for the school psychologist. *School Psychology Quarterly, 5,* 211-232.

FRISCH, M. B., & FROBERG, W. (1987). Social validation of assertion strategies for handling aggressive criticism: Evidence for consistency across situations. *Behavior Therapy, 18,* 181-191.

FRUEH, B. C. (1995). Self-administered exposure therapy by a Vietnam veteran with PTSD. *American Journal of Psychiatry, 152,* 1831-1832.

FRUEH, B. C., TURNER, S. M., & BEIDEL, D. C. (1995). Exposure therapy for combat-related PTSD: A critical review. *Clinical Psychology Review, 15,* 799-817.

FUDGE, R. C. (1996). The use of behavior therapy in the development of ethnic consciousness: A treatment model. *Cognitive and Behavioral Practice, 3,* 317-335.

GALE, B. M. (1996). Is this the year you become friends with technology? *the Behavior Therapist, 19,* 82-83.

GAMBRILL, E. (1985). Social skill training with the elderly. In L. L'Abate & M. A. Milan (Eds.), *Handbook of social skills training and research* (pp. 326-327). New York: Wiley.

GAMBRILL, E. (1995a). Assertion skills training. In W. O'Donohue & L. Krasner (Eds.), *Handbook of psychological skills training: Clinical techniques and applications* (pp. 81-118). Boston: Allyn and Bacon.

GAMBRILL, E. (1995b). Helping shy, socially anxious, and lonely adults: A skill-based contextual approach. In W. O'Donohue & L. Krasner (Eds.), *Handbook of psychological skills training: Clinical techniques and applications* (pp. 247-286). Boston: Allyn and Bacon.

GAMBRILL, E. D., & RICHEY, C. A. (1975). An assertion inventory for use in assessment and research. *Behavior Therapy, 6,* 550-561.

GARLAND, J. (1985). Adaptation skills in the elderly, their supporters and careers. Special issue: Sharing psychological skills: Training non-psychologists in the use of psychological techniques. *British Journal of Medical Psychology, 58,* 267-274.

GARNER, D. M., ROCKERT, W., DAVIS, R., GARNER, M. V., OLMSTEAD, M. P., & EAGLE, M. (1993). Comparison of cognitive-behavioral and supportive-expressive therapy for bulimia nervosa. *American Journal of Psychiatry, 150,* 37-46.

GASTON, L., GOLDFRIED, M. R., GREENBERG, L. S., HORVATH, A. O., RAUE, P. J., & WATSON, J. (1995). The therapeutic alliance in psychodynamic, cognitive-behavioral, and experimental therapies. *Journal of Psychotherapy Integration, 5,* 1-26.

GATCHEL, R. J. (1980). Effectiveness of two procedures for reducing dental fear: Group-administered desensitization and group education and discussion. *Journal of the American Dental Association, 101,* 634-637.

GAUTHIER, J., & PELLERIN, D. (1982). Management of compulsive shoplifting through covert sensitization. *Journal of Behavior Therapy and Experimental Psychiatry, 13,* 73-75.

GEER, J. H. (1965). The development of a scale to measure fear. *Behaviour Research and Therapy, 3,* 45-53.

GEISS, S. K., & O'LEARY, K. D. (1981). Therapist ratings of frequency and severity of marital problems: Implications for research. *Journal of Marital and Family Therapy, 7,* 515-520.

GELLER, E. S. (1980a). Applications of behavioral analysis for litter control. In D. Glenwick & L. Jason (Eds.), *Behavioral community psychology: Progress and prospects* (pp. 254-283). New York: Praeger.

GELLER, E. S. (1980b). Saving environmental resources through waste reduction and recycling: How the behavioral community psychologist can help. In G. L. Martin & J. G. Osborne (Eds.), *Helping in the community: Behavioral applications* (pp. 55-102). New York: Plenum.

GELLER, E. S. (1983). Rewarding safety belt usage at an industrial setting: Test of treatment generality and response maintenance. *Journal of Applied Behavior Analysis, 16*, 189-202.

GELLER, E. S. (1987). Environmental psychology and applied behavior analysis: From strange bedfellows to a productive marriage. In D. Stokols & I. Altman (Eds.), *Handbook of environmental psychology* (Vol. 1, pp. 361-388). New York: Wiley.

GELLER, E. S. (1989a). Applied behavior analysis and social marketing: An integration for environmental preservation. *Journal of Social Issues, 45*, 17-36.

GELLER, E. S. (1989b). Intervening to increase children's use of safety belts. *Alcohol, Drugs and Driving, 5*, 37-59.

GELLER, E. S. (1991). Preventing trauma from vehicle crashes with behavioral community psychology. *the Behavior Therapist, 14*, 33-35.

GELLER, E. S. (in press). Safety coaching: Key to achieving a total safety culture. *Professional Safety.*

GELLER, E. S., BERRY, T. D., LUDWIG, T. D., EVANS, R. E., GILMORE, M. R., & CLARKE, S. W. (1990). A conceptual framework for developing and evaluating behavior change interventions for injury control. *Health Education Research: Theory & Practice, 5*, 125-137.

GELLER, E. S., BRUFF, C. D., & NIMMER, J. G. (1985). "Flash for Life": Community-based prompting for safety belt promotion. *Journal of Applied Behavior Analysis, 18*, 309-314.

GELLER, E. S., CHAFFEE, J. L., & INGRAM, R. E. (1975). Promoting paper recycling on a university campus. *Journal of Environmental Systems, 5*, 39-57.

GELLER, E. S., & HAHN, H. A. (1984). Promoting safety belt use at industrial sites: An effective program for blue collar employees. *Professional Psychology: Research and Practice, 15*, 553-564.

GELLER, E. S., JOHNSON, R. P., & PELTON, S. L. (1982). Community-based interventions for encouraging safety belt use. *American Journal of Community Psychology, 10*, 183-195.

GELLER, E. S., PATERSON, L., & TALBOTT, E. (1982). A behavioral analysis of incentive prompts for motivating seat belt use. *Journal of Applied Behavior Analysis, 15*, 403-415.

GELLER, E. S., RUDD, J. R., KALSHER, M. J., STREFF, F. M., & LEHMAN, G. R. (1987). Employer-based programs to motivate safety belt use: A review of short-term and long-term effects. *Journal of Safety Research, 18*, 1-17.

GELLER, E. S., WINETT, R. A., & EVERETT, P. B. (1982). *Preserving the environment: New strategies for behavior change.* New York: Pergamon.

GELLER, E. S., WYLIE, R. G., & FARRIS, J. C. (1971). An attempt at applying prompting and reinforcement toward pollution control. *Proceedings of the 79th Annual Convention of the American Psychological Association, 6*, 701-702. (Summary)

GENEST, M., & TURK, D. C. (1981). Think-aloud approaches to cognitive assessment. In T. V. Merluzzi, C. R. Glass, & M. Genest (Eds.), *Cognitive assessment* (pp. 233-269). New York: Guilford.

GENTRY, W. D. (1971). Noncompliance to medical regimen. In R. B. Williams & W. D. Gentry (Eds.), *Behavioral approaches to medical treatment.* Cambridge, MA: Ballinger.

GETKA, E. J., & GLASS, C. R. (1992). Behavioral and cognitive-behavioral approaches to the reduction of dental anxiety. *Behavior Therapy, 23*, 433-448.

GIEBINK, J. W., STOVER, D., & FAHL, M. (1968). Teaching adaptive responses to frustration to emotionally disturbed boys. *Journal of Consulting and Clinical Psychology, 32*, 366-368.

GILBERT, B. O., JOHNSON, S. B., SPILLAR, R., MCCALLUM, M., SILVERSTEIN, J. H., & ROSENBLOOM, A. (1982). The effects of a peer-modeling film on children learning to self-inject insulin. *Behavior Therapy, 13*, 186-193.

GILES, T. R. (1991). Managed mental health care and effective psychotherapy: A step in the right direction? *Journal of Behaviour Therapy and Experimental Psychiatry, 22*, 83-86.

GILES, T. R., PRIAL, E. M., & NEIMS, D. M. (1993). Evaluating psychotherapies: A comparison of effectiveness. *International Journal of Mental Health, 22*, 43-65.

GILLIES, L. A., HASHMALL, J. M., HILTON, N. Z., & WEBSTER, C. D. (1992). Relapse prevention in pedophiles: Clinical issues and program development. Special issue: Violence and its aftermath. *Canadian Psychology, 33*, 199-210.

GILLUM, R. F., & BARSKY, A. J. (1974). Diagnosis and management of patient noncompliance. *Journal of the American Medical Association, 228*, 1563-1567.

GIRARDEAU, F. L., & SPRADLIN, J. E. (1964). Token rewards in a cottage program. *Mental Retardation, 2*, 345-351.

GLANZ, M. D. (1989). Cognitive therapy with the elderly. In A. Freeman, K. M. Simon, L. E. Beutler, & H. Arkowitz (Eds.), *Comprehensive handbook of cognitive therapy* (pp. 467-489). New York: Plenum.

GLASGOW, R. E. (1975). *In vivo* prolonged exposure in treatment of urinary retention. *Behavior Therapy, 6*, 701-702.

GLASS, C. R., & ARNKOFF, D. B. (1989). Behavioral assessment of social anxiety and social phobia. *Clinical Psychology Review, 9*, 75-90.

GLASS, C. R., & ARNKOFF, D. B. (1992). Behavior therapy. In D. K. Freedheim (Ed.), *History of psychotherapy: A century of change* (pp. 587-628). Washington, DC: American Psychological Association.

GLASS, C. R., & ARNKOFF, D. B. (1994). Validity issues in self-statement measures of social phobia and social anxiety. *Behaviour Research and Therapy, 32*, 255-267.

GLASS, C. R., GOTTMAN, J. M., & SHMURAK, S. H. (1976). Response acquisition and cognitive self-statement modification approaches to dating skills training. *Journal of Counseling Psychology, 23*, 520-526.

GLASS, C. R., MERLUZZI, T. V., BIEVER, J. L., & LARSEN, K. H. (1982). Cognitive assessment of social anxiety: Development and validation of a self-statement questionnaire. *Cognitve Therapy and Research, 6*, 37-55.

GLENWICK, D., & JASON, L. (EDS.). (1980). *Behavioral community psychology: Progress and prospects.* New York: Praeger.

GLYNN, E. L. (1970). Classroom applications of self-determined reinforcement. *Journal of Applied Behavior Analysis, 3*, 123-132.

GLYNN, S. M. (1990). Token economy approaches for psychiatric patients. *Behavior Modification, 14*, 383-407.

GOETZ, E. M., HOLMBERG, M. C., & LeBLANC, J. M. (1975). Differential reinforcement of other behavior and noncontingent reinforcement as control procedures during the modification of a preschooler's compliance. *Journal of Applied Behavior Analysis, 8*, 77-82.

GOLD, S. R., LETOURNEAU, E. J., & O'DONOHUE, W. (1995). Sexual interaction skills. In W. O'Donohue & L. Krasner (Eds.), *Handbook of psychological skills training: Clinical techniques and applications* (pp. 229-246). Boston: Allyn and Bacon.

GOLDFRIED, M. R. (1971). Systematic desensitization as training in self-control. *Journal of Consulting and Clinical Psychology, 37*, 228-234.

GOLDFRIED, M. R. (1988). Application of rational restructuring to anxiety disorders. *The Counseling Psychologist, 16,* 50-68.

GOLDFRIED, M. R. (1995). *From cognitive-behavior therapy to psychotherapy integration: An evolving view.* New York: Springer.

GOLDFRIED, M. R., & CASTONGUAY, L. G. (1993). Behavior therapy: Redefining strengths and limitations. *Behavior Therapy, 24,* 505-526.

GOLDFRIED, M. R., CASTONGUAY, L. G., & SAFRAN, J. D. (1992). Core issues and future directions in psychotherapy integration. In J. C. Norcross & M. R. Goldfried (Eds.), *Handbook of psychotherapy integration* (pp. 593-616). New York: Basic Books.

GOLDFRIED, M. R., & DAVISON, G. C. (1994). *Clinical behavior therapy* (Exp. ed.). New York: Wiley.

GOLDFRIED, M. R., DECENTECEO, E. T., & WEINBERG, L. (1974). Systematic rational restructuring as a self-control technique. *Behavior Therapy, 5,* 247-254.

GOLDFRIED, M. R., GREENBERG, L. S., & MARMAR, C. (1990). Individual psychotherapy: Process and outcome. *Annual Review of Psychology, 41,* 659-688.

GOLDFRIED, M. R., & ROBINS, C. (1983). Self-schema, cognitive bias and the processing of therapeutic experience. In P. C. Kendall (Ed.), *Advances in cognitive-behavioral research and therapy* (Vol. 2, pp. 35-81). New York: Academic Press.

GOLDFRIED, M. R., & SPRAFKIN, J. N. (1974). *Behavioral personality assessment.* Morristown, NJ: General Learning Press.

GOLDFRIED, M. R., WISER, S. L., & RAUE, P. J. (1992). On the movement toward psychotherapy integration. *Journal of Psychotherapy Practice and Research, 1,* 213-224.

GOLDIAMOND, I. (1974). Toward a constitutional approach to social problems: Ethical and constitutional issues raised by applied behavior analysis. *Behaviorism, 2,* 1-79.

GOLDSTEIN, H., & MOUSETIS, L. (1989). Generalized language learning by children with severe mental retardation: Effects of peers' expressive modeling. *Journal of Applied Behavior Analysis, 22,* 245-259.

GOLDSTEIN, I. B., SHAPIRO, D., THANANOPAVARN, C., & SAMBHI, M. P. (1982). Comparison of drug and behavioral treatments of essential hypertension. *Health Psychology, 1,* 7-26.

GORDON, C. M., & CAREY, M. P. (1995). Penile tumescence monitoring during morning naps to assess male erectile functioning: An initial study of healthy men of varied ages. *Archives of Sexual Behavior, 24,* 291-307.

GORDON, P. K. (1983). Switching attention from obsessional thoughts: An illustrative case study. *Journal of Psychiatric Treatment and Evaluation, 5,* 171-174.

GOREN, E. (1975). *A comparison of systematic desensitization and self-instruction in the treatment of phobias.* Unpublished master's thesis, Rutgers University.

GOSSETTE, R. L., & O'BRIEN, R. M. (1993). Efficacy of rational emotive therapy (RET) with children: A critical reappraisal. *Journal of Behavior Therapy and Experimental Psychiatry, 24,* 15-25.

GOTTMAN, J., & RUSHE, R. (1995). Communication skills and social skills approaches to treating ailing marriages: A recommendation for a new marital therapy called "Minimal Marital Therapy." In W. O'Donohue & L. Krasner (Eds.), *Handbook of psychological skills training: Clinical techniques and applications* (pp. 287-305). Boston: Allyn and Bacon.

GOTTMAN, J. M., & MARKMAN, H. J. (1978). Experimental designs in psychotherapy research. In S. L. Garfield & A. E. Gergin (Eds.), *Handbook of psychotherapy and behavior change: An empirical analysis* (2nd ed., pp. 23-62). New York: Wiley.

GOULD, M. S., & SHAFFER, D. (1986). The impact of suicide in television movies: Evidence of imitation. *New England Journal of Medicine, 31,* 690-694.

GOULD, R. A., & OTTO, M. W. (1995). Cognitive-behavioral treatment of social phobia and generalized anxiety disorder. In M. H. Pollack, M. W. Otto, & J. F. Rosenbaum (Eds.), *Challenges in psychiatric treatment: Pharmacological and psychosocial strategies* (pp. 171-200). New York: Guilford.

GOULD, R. A., OTTO, M. W., & POLLACK, M. H. (in press). A meta-analysis of treatment outcome for panic disorder. *Clinical Psychology Review.*

GRAUBARD, P. S., ROSENBERG, H., & MILLER, M. B. (1974). Student applications of behavior modification to teachers and environments or ecological approaches to social deviancy. In R. Ulrich, T. Stachnik, & J. Mabry (Eds.), *Control of human behavior* (Vol. 3, pp. 421-436). Glenview, IL: Scott, Foresman.

GRAVES, R., OPENSHAW, D., & ADAMS, G. R. (1992). Adolescent sex offenders and social skills training. *International Journal of Offender Therapy and Comparative Criminology, 36,* 139-153.

GRAZIANO, A. M., deGIOVANNI, I. S., & GARCIA, K. A. (1979). Behavioral treatment of children's fears: A review. *Psychological Bulletin, 86,* 804-830.

GREEN, L. (1978). Temporal and stimulus factors in self-monitoring of obese persons. *Behavior Therapy, 8,* 328-341.

GREENAN, E., POWELL, C., & VARNI, J. W. (1984). *Adherence to therapeutic exercise by children with hemophilia.* Unpublished manuscript. Cited in LaGreca, A. M. (1988). Adherence to prescribed medical regimens. In D. K. Routh (Ed.), *Handbook of pediatric psychology* (pp. 299-320). New York: Guilford.

GREENBERG, B. (1992, January). Personal communication.

GREENBERG, L. S. (1990, November). *The emotional bond: The therapeutic alliance in experiential therapy.* Paper presented at the meeting of the Association for Advancement of Behavior Therapy, San Francisco.

GREENE, B. F., & NEISTAT, M. D. (1983). Behavioral analysis in consumer affairs: Encouraging dental professionals to provide consumers with shielding from unnecessary X-ray exposure. *Journal of Applied Behavior Analysis, 16,* 13-27.

GREYSON, J. B., FOA, E. A., & STEKETEE, G. (1985). Obsessive-compulsive disorder. In M. Hersen & A. S. Bellack (Eds.), *Handbook of clinical behavior therapy with adults* (pp. 133-165). New York: Plenum.

GRIFFITHS, R., BIGELOW, G., & LIEBSON, I. (1974). Suppression of ethanol self-administration in alcoholics by contingent time-out from social interactions. *Behaviour Research and Therapy, 12,* 327-334.

GRODEN, J. (1993). The use of covert procedures to reduce severe aggression in a person with retardation and behavioral disorders. In J. R. Cautela & A. J. Kearney (Eds.), *Covert conditioning casebook* (pp. 144-152). Pacific Grove, CA: Brooks/Cole.

GROSS, A. M., JOHNSON, W. G., WILDMAN, H. E., & MULLETT, M. (1981). Coping skills training with insulin dependent preadolescent diabetics. *Child Behavior Therapy, 3,* 141-153.

GROSS, A. M., & WIXTED, J. T. (1988). Assessment of child behavior problems. In A. S. Bellack & M. Hersen (Eds.),

Behavioral assessment: A practical handbook (3rd ed., pp. 578-608). Elmsford, NY: Pergamon.

GROTH, A. N. (1980). *Men who rape: The psychology of the offender.* New York: Plenum.

GROTHBERG, E. H., FEINDLER, E. L., WHITE, C. B., & STUTMAN, S. S. (1991). Using anger management for prevention of child abuse. In P. Keller & S. Heyman (Eds.), *Innovations in clinical practice: A source book* (Vol. 10, pp. 5-21). Sarasota, FL: Professional Resource Press/Professional Resource Exchange.

GRUDER, C. L., MERMELSTEIN, R. J., KIRKENDOL, S., HEDEKER, D., WONG, S. C., SCHRECKENGOST, J., WARNECKE, R. B., BURZETTE, R., & MILLER, T. Q. (1993). Effects of social support and relapse prevention training as adjuncts to a televised smoking-cessation intervention. *Journal of Consulting and Clinical Psychology, 61,* 113-120.

GUESS, D. (1969). A functional analysis of receptive and productive speech: Acquisition of the plural morpheme. *Journal of Applied Behavior Analysis, 2,* 55-64.

GUESS, D., & BAER, D. M. (1973). An analysis of individual differences in generalization between receptive and productive language in retarded children. *Journal of Applied Behavior Analysis, 6,* 311-329.

GUEVREMONT, D. C. (1987). *A contingency contract to reduce fighting among siblings.* Unpublished manuscript, West Virginia University.

GUEVREMONT, D. C. (1990). Social skills and peer relationship training. In R. A. Barkley, *Attention deficit hyperactivity disorder* (pp. 540-572). New York: Guilford.

GUEVREMONT, D. C., & DUMAS, M. C. (1996). *Impact of multiple setting events on social interactions of children with ADHD.* Unpublished manuscript, Blackstone Valley Psychological Institute, North Smithfield, RI.

GUEVREMONT, D. C., DUPAUL, G. J., & BARKLEY, R. A. (1990). Diagnosis and assessment of Attention Deficit Hyperactivity Disorder in children. *Journal of School Psychology, 28,* 51-78.

GUEVREMONT, D. C., & FOSTER, S. L. (1992). Impact of social problem solving on the behavior of aggressive boys: Generalization, maintenance, and social validation. *Journal of Abnormal Child Psychology, 26,* 112-121.

GUEVREMONT, D. C., OSNES, P. G., & STOKES, T. F. (1986a). Preparation for effective self-management: The development of generalized verbal control. *Journal of Applied Behavior Analysis, 19,* 99-104.

GUEVREMONT, D. C., OSNES, P. G., & STOKES, T. F. (1986b). Programming maintenance following correspondence training with children. *Journal of Applied Behavior Analysis, 19,* 215-219.

GUEVREMONT, D. C., OSNES, P. G., & STOKES, T. F. (1988). The functional role of verbalizations in the generalization of self-instructional training with children. *Journal of Applied Behavior Analysis, 21,* 45-55.

GUEVREMONT, D. C., & SPIEGLER, M. D. (1990, November). *What do behavior therapists really do?: A survey of the clinical practice of AABT members.* Paper presented at the meeting of the Association for Advancement of Behavior Therapy, San Francisco.

GUEVREMONT, D. C., TISHELMAN, A. C., & HULL, D. B. (1985). Teaching generalized self-control to attention-deficit boys with mothers as adjunct therapists. *Child and Family Behavior Therapy, 7,* 23-36.

GUIDANO, V. F., & LIOTTI, G. (1985). A constructivistic foundation for cognitive therapy. In M. J. Mahoney & A. Freeman (Eds.), *Cognition and psychotherapy* (pp. 101-142). New York: Plenum.

HAAGA, D. A., & DAVISON, G. C. (1993). An appraisal of rational-emotive therapy. *Journal of Consulting and Clinical Psychology, 61,* 215-220.

HAAGA, D. A., DRYDEN, W., & DANCEY, C. P. (1991). Measurement of rational-emotive therapy in outcome studies. *Journal of Rational-Emotive and Cognitive-Behavior Therapy, 9,* 73-93.

HAAGA, D. A. F. (1990). Issues in relating self-efficacy to smoking relapse: Importance of an "Achilles' heel" situation and of prior quitting experience. *Journal of Substance Abuse, 2,* 191-200.

HAAGA, D. A. F., & DAVISON, G. C. (1989a). Outcome studies of rational-emotive therapy. In M. E. Bernard & R. DiGiuseppe (Eds.), *Inside rational-emotive therapy: A critical appraisal of the theory and therapy of Albert Ellis* (pp. 155-197). San Diego: Academic Press.

HAAGA, D. A. F., & DAVISON, G. C. (1989b). Slow progress in rational-emotive therapy outcome research: Etiology and treatment. *Cognitive Therapy and Research, 13,* 493-508.

HAAGA, D. A. F., DAVISON, G. C., WILLIAMS, M. E., DOLEZAL, S. L., HALEBLIAN, J., ROSENBAUM, J., DWYER, J. H., BAKER, S., NEZAMI, E., & DEQUATTRO, V. (1994). Mode-specific impact of relaxation training for hypertensive men with Type A behavior pattern. *Behavior Therapy, 25,* 209-223.

HACKMANN, A., & McLEAN, C. (1975). A comparison of flooding and thought stopping in the treatment of obsessional neurosis. *Behaviour Research and Therapy, 13,* 263-269.

HAGENZIEKER, M. P. (1991). Enforcement of incentives? Promoting safety belt use among military personnel in the Netherlands. *Journal of Applied Behavior Analysis, 24,* 24-30.

HAGOPIAN, L. P., & SLIFER, K. J. (1993). Treatment of separation anxiety disorder with graduated exposure and reinforcement targeting school attendance: A controlled case study. *Journal of Anxiety Disorders, 7,* 271-280.

HAHLWEG, K., & MARKMAN, H. J. (1988). Effectiveness of behavioral marital therapy: Empirical status of behavioral techniques in preventing and alleviating marital distress. *Journal of Consulting and Clinical Psychology, 56,* 440-447.

HAKE, D. F., & FOXX, R. M. (1978). Promoting gasoline conservation: The effects of reinforcement, a leader, and self-recording. *Behavior Modification, 2,* 339-369.

HALL, A. C., & NATHAN, P. R. (1992, July). *The management of night wakening and settling problems in young children: Efficacy of a behavioral group parent training programme.* Paper presented at the Fourth World Congress of Behavior Therapy, Queensland, Australia.

HALL, N. R. S. (1988). The virology of AIDS. *American Psychologist, 43,* 907-913.

HALL, R. V., & HALL, M. C. (1982). *How to negotiate a behavioral contract.* Austin, TX: Pro-Ed.

HAMAD, C. D., COOPER, D., & SEMB, G. (1977). Resource recovery: The use of a contingency to increase paper recycling in an elementary school. *Journal of Applied Psychology, 62,* 768-772.

HAMMOND, W. R., & PROTHOW-STITH, D. (1991, November). *Skills training for violence prevention with African American youth.* Clinical forum discussion presented at the meeting of the

Association for Advancement of Behavior Therapy, New York.

Hannie, T. J., Jr., & Adams, H. E. (1974). Modification of agitated depression by flooding: A preliminary study. *Journal of Behavior Therapy and Experimental Psychiatry, 5,* 161-166.

Hansen, D. J., MacMillan, V. M., & Shawchuck, C. R. (1990). Social isolation. In E. L. Feindler & G. R. Kalfus (Eds.), *Adolescent behavior therapy handbook* (pp. 165-190). New York: Springer.

Hansen, D. J., St. Lawrence, J. S., & Christoff, K. A. (1985). Effects of interpersonal problem-solving training with chronic aftercare patients on problem-solving component skills and effectiveness of solutions. *Journal of Consulting and Clinical Psychology, 53,* 167-174.

Harbert, T. L., Barlow, D. H., Hersen, M., & Austin, J. B. (1974). Measurement and modification of incestuous behavior: A case study. *Psychological Reports, 34,* 79-86.

Haring, T. G., Breen, C. G., Weiner, J., Kennedy, C. H., & Bednerah, F. (1995). Using videotape modeling to facilitate generalized purchasing skills. *Journal of Behavioral Education, 5,* 29-53.

Harris, S. L., & Romanczyk, R. G. (1976). Treating self-injurious behavior of a retarded child by overcorrection. *Behavior Therapy, 7,* 235-239.

Harris, V. W., & Sherman, J. A. (1974). Homework assignments, consequences, and classroom performance in social studies and mathematics. *Journal of Applied Behavior Analysis, 7,* 505-519.

Hartmann, D. P. (1982). Assessing the dependability of observational data. In D. P. Hartmann (Ed.), *New directions for methodology of social and behavioral science: Using observers to study behavior* (pp. 51-65). San Francisco: Jossey-Bass.

Hartmann, D. P., & Wood, D. D. (1982). Observational methods. In A. S. Bellack, M. Hersen, & A. E. Kazdin (Eds.), *International handbook of behavior modification and therapy* (pp. 109-138). New York: Plenum.

Hatch, M. L., Friedman, S., & Paradis, C. M. (1996). Behavioral treatment of obsessive-compulsive disorder in African Americans. *Cognitive and Behavioral Practice, 3,* 303-315.

Haughton, E., & Ayllon, T. (1965). Production and elimination of symptomatic behavior. In L. P. Ullmann & L. Krasner (Eds.), *Case studies in behavior modification* (pp. 94-98). New York: Holt, Rinehart & Winston.

Hauri, P. (1981). Treating psychophysiological insomnia with biofeedback: A replication study. *Biofeedback and Self-Regulation, 7,* 752-758.

Hauser, R. (1974). Rapid smoking as a technique of behavior modification: Caution in selection of subjects. *Journal of Consulting and Clinical Psychology, 42,* 625.

Hay, W. M., Hay, L. R., & Nelson, R. O. (1977). The adaptation of covert modeling procedures in the treatment of chronic alcoholism and obsessive-compulsive behavior: Two case reports. *Behavior Therapy, 8,* 70-76.

Hayes, S. C. (1995). Working with managed care: Lessons from the acceptance and committment therapy training project. *the Behavior Therapist, 18,* 184-186.

Hayes, S. C., & Cone, J. D. (1977). Reducing residential electrical energy use: Payments, information, and feedback. *Journal of Applied Behavior Analysis, 10,* 425-436.

Hayes, S. C., & Cone, J. D. (1981). Reduction of residential consumption of electricity through simple monthly feedback. *Journal of Applied Behavior Analysis, 14,* 81-88.

Haynes, R. B., Sackett, D. L., Gibson, E. S., Taylor, D. W., Hackett, B. C., Roberts, R. S., & Johnson, A. L. (1976). Improvement of medication compliance in uncontrolled hypertension. *Lancet, 1,* 1265-1268.

Haynes, R. B., Taylor, D. W., & Sackett, D. L. (Eds.). (1979). *Compliance with health care.* Baltimore: Johns Hopkins University Press.

Haynes, S. N. (1978). *Principles of behavioral assessment.* New York: Gardner.

Haynes, S. N., Spain, E. H., & Oliveira, J. (1993). Identifying causal relationships in clinical assessment. *Psychological Assessment, 5,* 281-291.

Heatherton, T. F., & Baumeister, R. F. (1991). Binge eating as escape from self-awareness. *Psychological Bulletin, 110,* 86-108.

Heaton, R. C., & Safer, D. J. (1982). Secondary school outcome following a junior high school behavioral program. *Behavior Therapy, 13,* 226-231.

Hedberg, A. G., & Campbell, L. (1974). A comparison of four behavioral treatments of alcoholism. *Journal of Behavior Therapy and Experimental Psychiatry, 5,* 251-256.

Heiman, G. A. (1995). *Research methods in psychology.* Boston: Houghton Mifflin.

Heimberg, R. G., Salzman, D. G., Holt, C. S., & Blendell, K. A. (1993). Cognitive-behavioral group treatment for social phobia: Effectiveness at five-year followup. *Cognitive Therapy and Research, 17,* 325-339.

Herbert, J. D., & Mueser, K. T. (1992). Eye movement desensitization: A critique of the evidence. *Journal of Behavior Therapy and Experimental Psychiatry, 23,* 169-174.

Hermann, J. A., de Montes, A. I., Dominguez, B., Montes, F., & Hopkins, B. L. (1973). Effects of bonuses for punctuality on the tardiness of industrial workers. *Journal of Applied Behavior Analysis, 6,* 563-570.

Hersen, M., Eisler, R. M., Miller, P. M., Johnson, M. B., & Pinkston, S. G. (1973). Effects of practice, instructions, and modeling on components of assertive behavior. *Behaviour Research and Therapy, 11,* 443-451.

Hersen, M., Kazdin, A. E., Bellack, A. S., & Turner, S. M. (1979). Effects of live modeling, covert modeling and rehearsal on assertiveness in psychiatric patients. *Behaviour Research and Therapy, 17,* 369-377.

Hersen, M., & van Hasselt, V. (1992). Behavioral assessment and treatment of anxiety in the elderly. *Clinical Psychology Review, 12,* 619-640.

Heward, W. L., Dardig, J. C., & Rossett, A. (1979). *Working with parents of handicapped children.* Columbus, OH: Charles E. Merrill.

Hicks, D. J. (1965). Imitation and retention of film-mediated aggressive peer and adult models. *Journal of Personality and Social Psychology, 2,* 97-100.

Higgins, S. T., Budney, A. J., Bickel, W. K., Foerg, F. E., Donham, R., & Badger, G. J. (1994). Incentives improve outcome in outpatient behavioral treatment of cocaine dependence. *Archives of General Psychiatry, 51,* 568-576.

Higgins, S. T., Budney, A. J., Bickel, W. K., Hughes, J. R., Foerg, F., & Badger, G. (1993). Achieving cocaine abstinence with a behavioral approach. *American Journal of Psychiatry, 150,* 763-769.

Hill, P. (1989). Behavioural psychotherapy with children. *International Review of Psychiatry, 1,* 257-266.

HILLIARD, R. B. (1993). Single-case methodology in psychotherapy process and outcome research. *Journal of Consulting and Clinical Psychology, 61,* 373-380.

HIMADI, B., OSTEEN, F., & CRAWFORD, E. (1993). Delusional verbalizations and beliefs. *Behavioral Residential Treatment, 8,* 229-242.

HOBFOLL, S. E., JACKSON, A. P., LAVIN, J., BRITTON, P. J., & SHEPHERD, J. B. (1994). Reducing inner-city women's AIDS risk activities: A study of single, pregnant women. *Health Psychology, 13,* 397-403.

HODGES, L. F., ROTHBAUM, B. O., KOOPER, R., OPDYKE, D., MEYER, T., DE GRAFF, J. J., & WILLIFORD, J. S. (1994). *Presence as the defining factor in a VR application: Virtual reality graded exposure in the treatment of acrophobia.* (Tech. Rep. #GIT-GVU-94-6). Atlanta: Georgia Institute of Technology.

HODGSON, R. J., & RACHMAN, S. (1970). An experimental investigation of the implosive technique. *Behaviour Research and Therapy, 8,* 21-27.

HOELSCHER, T. J., LICHSTEIN, K. L., FISCHER, S., & HEGARTY, T. B. (1987). Relaxation treatment of hypertension: Do home relaxation tapes enhance treatment outcome? *Behavior Therapy, 18,* 33-37.

HOELSCHER, T. J., LICHSTEIN, K. L., & ROSENTHAL, T. L. (1984). Objective vs. subjective assessment of relaxation compliance among anxious individuals. *Behaviour Research and Therapy, 22,* 187-193.

HOGAN, R. A. (1968). The implosive technique. *Behaviour Research and Therapy, 6,* 423-432.

HOGAN, R. A. (1969). Implosively oriented behavior modification: Therapy considerations. *Behaviour Research and Therapy, 7,* 177-184.

HOGAN, R. A., & KIRCHNER, J. H. (1967). A preliminary report of the extinction of learned fears via a short term implosive therapy. *Journal of Abnormal Psychology, 72,* 106-111.

HOLAND, J., PLUMB, M., YATES, J., HARRIS, S., TUTTOLOMONDO, A., HOLMES, J., & HOLLAND, J. F. (1977). Psychological response of patients with acute leukemia to germ-free environments. *Cancer, 36,* 871-879.

HOLDEN, A. E., & BARLOW, D. H. (1986). Heart rate and heart rate variability recorded in vivo in agoraphobics and nonphobics. *Behavior Therapy, 17,* 26-42.

HOLLON, S. D., & BECK, A. T. (1986). Research on cognitive therapies. In S. L. Garfield & A. E. Bergin (Eds.), *Handbook of psychotherapy and behavior change* (3rd ed., pp. 443-482). New York: Wiley.

HOLLON, S. D., & BECK, A. T. (1994). Cognitive and cognitive behavioral therapies. In A. E. Bergin & S. L. Garfield (Eds.), *Handbook of psychotherapy and behavior change* (4th ed., pp. 428-466). New York: Wiley.

HOLLON, S. D., SHELTON, R. C., & DAVIS, D. D. (1993). Cognitive therapy for depression: Conceptual issues and clinical efficacy. *Journal of Consulting and Clinical Psychology, 61,* 270-275.

HOLLON, S. D., SHELTON, R. C., & LOOSEN, P. T. (1991). Cognitive therapy and pharmacotherapy for depression. *Journal of Consulting and Clinical Psychology, 59,* 88-99.

HOLROYD, K. A. (1976). Cognition and desensitization in the group treatment of test anxiety. *Journal of Consulting and Clinical Psychology, 44,* 991-1001.

HOLROYD, K. A., ANDRASIK, F., & WESTBROOK, T. (1977). Cognitive control of tension headache. *Cognitive Therapy and Research, 1,* 121-133.

HOLROYD, K. A., & PENZIEN, D. B. (1994). Psychosocial interventions in the management of recurrent headache disorders 1: Overview and effectiveness. *Behavioral Medicine, 20,* 53-63.

HOMME, L. E. (1971). *How to use contingency contracting in the classroom.* Champaign, IL: Research Press.

HOMME, L. E., C'DE BACA, P., DEVINE, J. V., STEINHORST, R., & RICKERT, E. J. (1963). Use of the Premack principle in controlling the behavior of nursery school children. *Journal of the Experimental Analysis of Behavior, 6,* 544.

HONNEN, T. J., & KLEINKE, C. L. (1990). Prompting bar patrons with signs to take free condoms. *Journal of Applied Behavior Analysis, 23,* 215-217.

HOPKINS, B. L., CONRAD, R. J., DANGEL, R. F., FITCH, H. G., SMITH, M. J., & ANGER, W. K. (1986). Behavioral technology for reducing occupational exposure to styrene. *Journal of Applied Behavior Analysis, 19,* 3-11.

HORAN, J. J., HACKETT, G., BUCHANAN, J. D., STONE, C. I., & STONE, D. D. (1977). Coping with pain: A component analysis of stress inoculation. *Cognitive Therapy and Research, 1,* 211-221.

HORAN, J. J., HACKETT, G., NICHOLAS, W. C., LINBERG, S. E., STONE, C. I., & LUKASKI, H. C. (1977). Rapid smoking: A cautionary note. *Journal of Consulting and Clinical Psychology, 45,* 341-343.

HORAN, J. J., & JOHNSON, R. G. (1971). Coverant conditioning through a self-management application of the Premack principle: Its effect on weight reduction. *Journal of Behavior Therapy and Experimental Psychiatry, 2,* 243-249.

HORNE, A. M., & MATSON, J. L. (1977). A comparison of modeling, desensitization, flooding, study skills, and control groups for reducing test anxiety. *Behavior Therapy, 8,* 1-8.

HORNE, D. J., VATMANIDIS, P., & CARERI, A. (1994). Preparing patients for invasive medical and surgical procedures 1: Adding behavioral and cognitive interventions. *Behavioral Medicine, 20,* 5-13.

HORNER, R. D., & KEILITZ, I. (1975). Training mentally retarded adolescents to brush their teeth. *Journal of Applied Behavior Analysis, 8,* 301-309.

HOSFORD, R. (1974). *Using the self as a model to promote behavioral change.* Paper presented at the meeting of the University of Wisconsin Fourth Annual Symposium in Counseling, Madison.

HOSFORD, R., & BROWN, S. (1975). Innovations in behavioral approaches to counseling. *Focus on Guidance, 8,* 1-11.

HOUTS, A. C., BERMAN, J. S., & ABRAMSON, H. (1994). Effectiveness of psychological and pharmacological treatments for nocturnal enuresis. *Journal of Consulting and Clinical Psychology, 62,* 737-745.

HOUTS, A. C., PETERSON, J. K., & WHELAN, J. P. (1986). Prevention of relapse in Full-Spectrum Home Training for primary enuresis: A components analysis. *Behavior Therapy, 17,* 462-469.

HRYDOWY, E. R., STOKES, T. F., & MARTIN, G. (1984). Training elementary students to prompt teacher praise. *Education and Treatment of Children, 7,* 99-108.

HUGHES, C., & RUSCH, F. R. (1989). Teaching supported employees with severe mental retardation to solve problems. *Journal of Applied Behavior Analysis, 22,* 365-372.

HUMPHREYS, L., FOREHAND, R., McMAHON, R., & ROBERTS, M. (1978). Parent behavioral training to modify child noncompliance: Effects on untreated siblings. *Journal of Behavior Therapy and Experimental Psychiatry, 9,* 235-238.

HUNT, J. G., FITZHUGH, L. C., & FITZHUGH, K. B. (1968). Teaching "exit-ward" patients appropriate personal appearance by using reinforcement techniques. *American Journal of Mental Deficiency, 73,* 41-45.

HUNT, J. G., & ZIMMERMAN, J. (1969). Stimulating productivity in a simulated sheltered workshop setting. *American Journal of Mental Deficiency, 74,* 43-49.

HUNTER, J., & SCHAECHER, R. (1994). AIDS prevention for lesbian, gay, and bisexual adolescents. Special Issue: HIV/AIDS. *Families in Society, 75,* 346-354.

HUNTER, R. H. (1995). Benefits of competency-based treatment programs. *American Psychologist, 50,* 509-513.

HUTZELL, R., PLATZEK, D., & LOGUE, P. (1974). Control of Gilles de la Tourette's syndrome by self-monitoring. *Journal of Behavior Therapy and Experimental Psychiatry, 5,* 71-76.

Information please almanac: Atlas and yearbook, 1990 (43rd ed.). (1989). Boston: Houghton Mifflin.

INGHAM, R. J., & ANDREWS, G. (1973). An analysis of a token economy in stuttering therapy. *Journal of Applied Behavior Analysis, 6,* 219-229.

ISAACS, W., THOMAS, I., & GOLDIAMOND, I. (1960). Application of operant conditioning to reinstate verbal behavior in psychotics. *Journal of Speech and Hearing Disorders, 25,* 8-12.

ISRAEL, A. C., GUILE, C. A., BAKER, J. E., & SILVERMAN, W. K. (1994). An evaluation of enhanced self-regulation training in the treatment of childhood obesity. *Journal of Pediatric Psychology, 19,* 737-749.

ITARD, J. M. G. (1962). *The wild boy of Aveyron.* New York: Appleton-Century-Crofts.

IWAMASA, G. Y. (1996). Introduction to the special series: Ethnic and cultural diversity in cognitive and behavioral practice. *Cognitive and Behavioral Practice, 3,* 209-213.

IWAMASA, G. Y., & SMITH, S. K. (1996). Ethnic diversity in behavioral psychology. *Behavior Modification, 20,* 45-59.

IWATA, B. A. (1987). Negative reinforcement in applied behavior analysis: An emerging technology. *Journal of Applied Behavior Analysis, 20,* 361-378.

IWATA, B. A. (1994). Functional analysis methodology: Some closing comments. *Journal of Applied Behavior Analysis, 27,* 413-418.

IWATA, B. A., VOLLMER, T. R., & ZARCONE, J. R. (1990). The experimental (functional) analysis of behavior disorders: Methodology, applications, and limitations. In A. C. Repp & N. N. Singh (Eds.), *Perspectives on the use of nonaversive and aversive interventions for persons with developmental disabilities* (pp. 301-330). Sycamore, IL: Sycamore Publishing.

JACKSON, H. J., & FRANCEY, S. M. (1985). The use of hypnotically induced covert modelling in the desensitization of an escalator phobia. *Australian Journal of Clinical and Experimental Hypnosis, 13,* 55-58.

JACOB, R. G., SHAPIRO, A. P., REEVES, R. A., JOHNSON, A. M., McDONALD, R. H., & COBURN, C. (1986). Relaxation therapy for hypertension: Comparison of effects with concomitant placebo, diuretic and beta-blocker. *Archives of Internal Medicine, 146,* 2335-2340.

JACOB, R. G., WING, R., & SHAPIRO, A. P. (1987). The behavioral treatment of hypertension: Long-term effects. *Behavior Therapy, 18,* 325-352.

JACOBS, G. D., BENSON, H., & FRIEDMAN, R. (1993). Home-based central nervous system assessment of a multifactor behavioral intervention for chronic sleep-onset insomnia. *Behavior Therapy, 24,* 159-174.

JACOBS, G. D., ROSENBERG, P. A., FRIEDMAN, R., MATHESON, J., PEAVY, G. M., DOMAR, A. D., & BENSON, H. (1993). Multifactor behavioral treatment of chronic sleep-onset insomnia using stimulus control and the relaxation response: A preliminary study. *Behavior Modification, 17,* 498-509.

JACOBS, H. E., BAILEY, J. S., & CREWS, J. I. (1984). Development and analysis of a community-based resources recovery program. *Journal of Applied Behavior Analysis, 17,* 127-145.

JACOBS, H. E., FAIRBANKS, D., POCHE, C. E., & BAILEY, J. S. (1982). Multiple incentives in encouraging car pool formation on a university campus. *Journal of Applied Behavior Analysis, 15,* 141-149.

JACOBS, M. K., & COCHRAN, S. D. (1982). The effects of cognitive restructuring on assertive behavior. *Cognitive Therapy and Research, 6,* 63-76.

JACOBSON, E. (1929). *Progressive relaxation.* Chicago: University of Chicago Press.

JACOBSON, E. (1934). *You must relax.* Chicago: University of Chicago Press.

JACOBSON, E. (1939). Variations of blood pressure with skeletal muscle tension and relaxation. *Annals of Internal Medicine, 12,* 1194-1212.

JACOBSON, E. (1978). Relaxation technology applied to hypertensives. *Archives für Arzneitherapie, 2,* 152. Cited in J. Wolpe (1990), *The practice of behavior therapy* (4th ed.). Elmsford, NY: Pergamon.

JACOBSON, J. W., MULICK, J. A., & SCHWARTZ, A. A. (1995). A history of facilitated communciation: Science, pseudoscience, and antiscience. *American Psychologist, 50,* 750-765.

JACOBSON, N. S. (1985). The role of observational measures in behavior therapy outcome research. *Behavioral Assessment, 7,* 297-308.

JACOBSON, N. S. (1988). Defining clinically significant change: An introduction. *Behavior Therapy, 10,* 131-132.

JACOBSON, N. S. (1989). The maintenance of treatment gains following social learning-based marital therapy. *Behavior Therapy, 20,* 325-336.

JACOBSON, N. S. (1991, September). *Marital therapy: Theory and treatment considerations.* Workshop sponsored by the Rhode Island Psychological Association, Warwick.

JACOBSON, N. S. (1992). Behavioral couple therapy: A new beginning. *Behavior Therapy, 23,* 493-506.

JACOBSON, N. S. (1993). Introduction to special section on couples and couple therapy. *Journal of Consulting and Clinical Psychology, 61,* 5.

JACOBSON, N. S., & ADDIS, M. E. (1993). Research on couples and couple therapy: What do we know, where are we going? *Journal of Consulting and Clinical Psychology, 61,* 85-93.

JACOBSON, N. S., FOLLETTE, W. C., & REVENSTORF, D. (1984). Psychotherapy outcome research: Methods for reporting variability and evaluating clinical significance. *Behavior Therapy, 15,* 336-352.

JACOBSON, N. S., & MARGOLIN, G. (1979). *Marital therapy: Strategies based on social learning and behavior exchange principles.* New York: Brunner/Mazel.

JAMES, J. E. (1985). Desensitization treatment of agoraphobia. *British Journal of Clinical Psychology, 24,* 133-134.

JAMES, J. E. (1986). Review of the relative efficacy of imaginal and *in vivo* flooding in the treatment of clinical fear. *Behavioural Psychotherapy, 14,* 183-191.

JAMES, L. D., THORN, B. E., & WILLIAMS, D. A. (1993). Goal specification in cognitive-behavioral therapy for chronic headache pain. *Behavior Therapy, 24,* 305-320.

JAMES, S. D., & EGEL, A. L. (1986). A direct prompting strategy for increasing reciprocal interactions between handicapped and nonhandicapped siblings. *Journal of Applied Behavior Analysis, 19,* 173-186.

JANDA, L. H., & RIMM, D. C. (1972). Covert sensitization in the treatment of obesity. *Journal of Abnormal Psychology, 80,* 37-42.

JANNOUN, L., MUNBY, M., CATALAN, J., & GELDER, M. (1980). A home-based treatment program for agoraphobia: Replication and controlled evaluation. *Behavior Therapy, 11,* 294-305.

JANSEN, M. (1987). Women's health issues: An emerging priority for health psychology. In G. C. Stone, S. M. Weiss, J. D. Matarazzo, N. E. Miller, J. Rodin, C. D. Belar, M. J. Follick, & J. E. Singer (Eds.), *Health psychology: A discipline and a profession* (pp. 249-264). Chicago: University of Chicago Press.

JANSSON, L., & ÖST, L. G. (1982). Behavioral treatments for agoraphobia: An evaluation review. *Clinical Psychology Review, 2,* 42-58.

JASON, L., & GLENWICK, D. (1984). Behavioral community psychology: A review of recent research. In M. Hersen, R. M. Eisler, & P. M. Miller (Eds.), *Progress in behavior modification* (Vol. 18, pp. 85-121). New York: Academic Press.

JASON, L. A. (1985). Using a token-actuated timer to reduce television viewing. *Journal of Applied Behavior Analysis, 18,* 269-272.

JAY, S. M., & ELLIOTT, C. H. (1990). A stress inoculation program for parents whose children are undergoing painful medical procedures. *Journal of Consulting and Clinical Psychology, 58,* 799-804.

JAY, S. M., ELLIOTT, C. H., KATZ, E., & SIEGEL, E. (1987). Cognitive-behavioral and pharmacologic interventions for children's distress during painful medical procedures. *Journal of Consulting and Clinical Psychology, 55,* 860-865.

JAY, S. M., ELLIOTT, C. H., OZOLINS, M., OLSON, R. A., & PRUITT, S. D. (1985). Behavioral management of children's distress during painful medical procedures. *Behaviour Research and Therapy, 23,* 513-520.

JAYCOX, L. H., REIVICH, K. J., GILLHAM, J., & SELIGMAN, M. E. P. (1994). Prevention of depressive symptoms in school children. *Behaviour Research and Therapy, 32,* 801-816.

JENSEN, B. J., & HAYES, S. N. (1986). Self-report questionnaires and inventories. In A. R. Ciminero, K. S. Calhoun, & H. A. Adams (Eds.), *Handbook of behavioral assessment* (2nd ed., pp. 150-179). New York: Wiley.

JOHNSON, R. P., & GELLER, E. S. (1984). Contingent versus noncontingent rewards for promoting seat belt usage. *American Journal of Community Psychology, 12,* 113-122.

JOHNSON, S. M., & BOLSTAD, O. D. (1973). Methodological issues in naturalistic observation: Some problems and solutions for field research. In L. A. Hamerlynck, L. C. Handy, & E. J. Mash (Eds.), *Behavior change: Methodology, concepts, and practice.* Champaign, IL: Research Press.

JOHNSON, W. G., CORRIGAN, S. A., & MAYO, L. L. (1987). Innovative treatment approaches to bulimia nervosa. Special issue: Recent advances in behavioral medicine. *Behavior Modification, 11,* 373-388.

JONES, M. C. (1924). A laboratory study of fear: The case of Peter. *Pedagogical Seminar, 31,* 308-315.

JONES, R. J., & TIMBERS, G. D. (1983). *Professional parenting for juvenile offenders* (Final Report, Grant MH15776). Morgantown, NC: BIABH Study Center.

JONES, R. T., & KAZDIN, A. E. (1980). Teaching children how and when to make emergency telephone calls. *Behavior Therapy, 11,* 509-521.

JONES, R. T., KAZDIN, A. E., & HANEY, J. I. (1981). Social validation and training of emergency fire skills for potential injury prevention and life saving. *Journal of Applied Behavior Analysis, 14,* 249-260.

JORGENSEN, R. S., & CAREY, M. P. (1994). Supplementing relaxation training with "Aromatherapy": An in-depth comparison of two clients. *Anxiety Disorders Practice Journal, 1,* 59-76.

JOYCE, M. R. (1995). Emotional relief for parents: Is rational-emotive parent education effective? *Journal of Rational-Emotive and Cognitive-Behavior Therapy, 13,* 55-75.

JURGELA, A. R. (1993). The use of covert conditioning to treat self-injurious behavior. In J. R. Cautela & A. J. Kearney (Eds.), *Covert conditioning casebook* (pp. 172-184). Pacific Grove, CA: Brooks/Cole.

KAESTLE, C. F. (Ed.). (1973). *Joseph Lancaster and the monitorial school movement: A documentary history.* New York: Teachers College Press.

KAHLE, A. L., & KELLEY, M. L. (1994). Children's homework problems: A comparison of goal setting and parent training. *Behavior Therapy, 25,* 275-290.

KAHN, J. S., KEHLE, T. J., JENSON, W. R., & CLARK, E. (1990). Comparison of cognitive-behavioral, relaxation, and self-modeling interventions for depression among middle-school students. *School Psychology Review, 19,* 196-211.

KALAWSKY, R. S. (1993). *The science of virtual reality and virtual environments.* Reading, MA: Addison-Wesley.

KALICHMAN, S. C., CAREY, M. P., & JOHNSON, B. T. (in press). Prevention of sexually transmitted HIV infection: A meta-analytic review of the behavioral outcome literature. *Annals of Behavioral Medicine.*

KALICHMAN, S. C., SIKKEMA, K., KELLY, J. A., & BULTO, M. (1995). Use of a brief behavioral skills intervention to prevent HIV infection among chronic mentally ill adults. *Psychiatric Services, 46,* 275-280.

KALLMAN, W. M., HERSEN, M., & O'TOOLE, D. H. (1975). The use of social reinforcement in a case of conversion reaction. *Behavior Therapy, 6,* 411-413.

KALMUSS, D. (1984). The intergenerational transmission of marital aggression. *Journal of Marriage and the Family, 46,* 11-19.

KAMINER, Y., & SHAHAR, A. (1987). The stress inoculation training management of self-mutilating behavior: A case study. *Journal of Behavior Therapy and Experimental Psychiatry, 18,* 289-292.

KAPLAN, D. A. (1982). Behavioral, cognitive, and behavioral-cognitive approaches to group assertion training therapy. *Cognitive Therapy and Research, 6,* 301-314.

KAPLAN, H. S. (1974). *The new sex therapy: Active treatment of sexual dysfunctions.* New York: Brunner/Mazel.

KAPLAN, H. S. (1975). *The illustrated manual of sex therapy*. New York: Quadrangle.

KAPLAN, N. M. (1983). Mild hypertension: When and how to treat. *Archives of Internal Medicine, 143,* 255-259.

KAPLAN, R. M. (1990). Behavior as the central outcome in health care. *American Psychologist, 45,* 1211-1220.

KASL, S. V. (1975). Issues in patient adherence to health care regimens. *Journal of Human Stress, 1,* 5-17.

KASSIRER, L. B. (1974). Behavior modification for patients and prisoners: Constitutional ramifications of enforced therapy. *Journal of Psychiatry and Law, 2,* 245-302.

KATZ, E., KELLERMAN, J., & ELLENBERG, L. (1987). Hypnosis in the reduction of acute pain and distress in children with cancer. *Journal of Pediatric Psychology, 12,* 379-394.

KAZDIN, A. E. (1972). Response cost: The removal of conditioned reinforcers for therapeutic change. *Behavior Therapy, 3,* 533-546.

KAZDIN, A. E. (1973). Covert modeling and the reduction of avoidance behavior. *Journal of Abnormal Psychology, 81,* 87-95.

KAZDIN, A. E. (1974a). Comparative effects of some variations of covert modeling. *Journal of Behavior Therapy and Experimental Psychiatry, 5,* 225-231.

KAZDIN, A. E. (1974b). Covert modeling, model similarity, and reduction of avoidance behavior. *Behavior Therapy, 5,* 325-340.

KAZDIN, A. E. (1974c). The effect of model identity and fear-relevant similarity on covert modeling. *Behavior Therapy, 5,* 624-635.

KAZDIN, A. E. (1974d). Effects of covert modeling and modeling reinforcement on assertive behavior. *Journal of Abnormal Psychology, 83,* 240-252.

KAZDIN, A. E. (1974e). Reactive self-monitoring: The effects of response desirability, goal setting, and feedback. *Journal of Counsulting and Clinical Psychology, 5,* 704-716.

KAZDIN, A. E. (1976). Effects of covert modeling, multiple models, and model reinforcement on assertive behavior. *Behavior Therapy, 7,* 211-222.

KAZDIN, A. E. (1977a). Assessing the clinical or applied importance of behavior change through social validation. *Behavior Modification, 1,* 427-452.

KAZDIN, A. E. (1977b). Extensions of reinforcement techniques to socially and environmentally relevant behaviors. In M. Hersen, R. M. Eisler, & P. M. Miller (Eds.), *Progress in behavior modification* (Vol. 4, pp. 39-67). New York: Academic Press.

KAZDIN, A. E. (1977c). *The token economy: A review and evaluation*. New York: Plenum.

KAZDIN, A. E. (1978). *History of behavior modification: Experimental foundations of contemporary research*. Baltimore: University Park Press.

KAZDIN, A. E. (1979). Vicarious reinforcement and punishment in operant programs for children. *Child Behavior Therapy, 1,* 13-36.

KAZDIN, A. E. (1980). Acceptability of alternative treatments for deviant child behavior. *Journal of Applied Behavior Analysis, 13,* 259-273.

KAZDIN, A. E. (1987). *Conduct disorders in childhood and adolescence*. Newbury Park, CA: Sage.

KAZDIN, A. E. (1989). *Behavior modification in applied settings* (4th ed.). Pacific Grove, CA: Brooks/Cole.

KAZDIN, A. E. (1992). *Research design in clinical psychology* (2nd ed.). Boston: Allyn and Bacon.

KAZDIN, A. E. (1993). Evaluation in clinical practice: Clinically sensitive and systematic methods of treatment delivery. *Behavior Therapy, 24,* 11-45.

KAZDIN, A. E. (1994). *Behavior modification in applied settings* (5th ed.). Pacific Grove, CA: Brooks/Cole.

KAZDIN, A. E., ESVELDT-DAWSON, K., FRENCH, N. H., & UNIS, A. S. (1987). Problem-solving skills training and relationship therapy in the treatment of antisocial child behavior. *Journal of Consulting and Clinical Psychology, 55,* 76-85.

KAZDIN, A. E., & GEESEY, S. (1977). Simultaneous-treatment design comparisons of the effects of reinforcers for one's peers versus for oneself. *Behavior Therapy, 8,* 682-693.

KAZDIN, A. E., & MASCITELLI, S. (1982). Behavioral rehearsal, self-instructions, and homework practice in developing assertiveness. *Behavior Therapy, 13,* 346-360.

KAZDIN, A. E., & WILCOXON, L. A. (1976). Systematic desensitization and nonspecific treatment effects: A methodological evaluation. *Psychologial Bulletin, 83,* 729-758.

KAZDIN, A. E., & WILSON, G. T. (1978). *Evaluation of behavior therapy: Issues, evidence, and research strategies*. Cambridge, MA: Ballinger.

KEANE, T. M., FAIRBANK, J. A., CADDELL, J. M., & ZIMERING, R. T. (1989). Implosive (flooding) therapy reduces symptoms of PTSD in Vietnam combat veterans. *Behavior Therapy, 20,* 245-260.

KEANE, T. M., FAIRBANK, J. A., CADDELL, J. M., ZIMERING, R. T., & BENDER, M. E. (1985). A behavioral approach to assessing and treating post-traumatic stress disorder in Vietnam veterans. In C. R. Figley (Ed.), *Trauma and its wake* (pp. 257-294). New York: Brunner/Mazel.

KEARNEY, A. B. (1993). The use of covert conditioning in the treatment of obsessive compulsive disorder. In J. R. Cautela & A. J. Kearney (Eds.), *Covert conditioning casebook* (pp. 22-37). Pacific Grove, CA: Brooks/Cole.

KEARNEY, A. J. (1993). The use of covert conditioning in a hypnotic context to treat anticipatory anxiety and post-operative pain. In J. R. Cautela & A. J. Kearney (Eds.), *Covert conditioning casebook* (pp. 99-107). Pacific Grove, CA: Brooks/Cole.

KEHLE, T. J., CLARK, E., JENSON, W. R., & WAMPOLD, B. E. (1986). Effectiveness of self-observation with behavior disordered elementary school children. *School Psychology Review, 15,* 289-295.

KEHLE, T. J., OWEN, S. V., & CRESSY, E. T. (1990). The use of self-modeling as an intervention in school psychology: A case study of an elective mute. *School Psychology Review, 19,* 115-121.

KELLAM, A. M. P. (1969). Shop lifting treated by aversion to a film. *Behaviour Research and Therapy, 7,* 125-127.

KELLER, F. S. (1968). "Good-bye, teacher. . .". *Journal of Applied Behavior Analysis, 1,* 79-89.

KELLER, M. B., HERZOG, D. B., LAVORI, P. W., BRADBURN, I. S., & MAHONEY, E. M. (1992). The naturalistic history of bulimia nervosa: Extraordinary high rates of chronicity, relapse, recurrence, and psychosocial morbidity. *International Journal of Eating Disorders, 12,* 1-9.

KELLEY, M. L. (1990). *School-home notes: Promoting children's classroom success*. New York: Guilford.

KELLY, G. A. (1955). *The psychology of personal constructs*. New York: Norton.

KELLY, J. A., & MURPHY, D. A. (1992). Psychological interventions with AIDS and HIV: Prevention and treatment. *Journal of Consulting and Clinical Psychology, 60,* 576-585.

KELLY, J. A., MURPHY, D., WASHINGTON, C., WILSON, T., KOOB, J., DAVIS, D., LEPEZMA, G., & DAVANTES, B. (1994). Effects of HIV/AIDS prevention groups for high-risk women in urban primary health care clinics. *American Journal of Public Health, 84,* 1918-1922.

KELLY, J. A., & ST. LAWRENCE, J. (1987). The prevention of AIDS: Roles for behavioral intervention. *Scandinavian Journal of Behaviour Therapy, 16,* 5-19.

KELLY, J. A., & ST. LAWRENCE, J. S. (1988a). *The AIDS health crisis: Psychological and social intervention.* New York: Plenum.

KELLY, J. A., & ST. LAWRENCE, J. S. (1988b). AIDS prevention and treatment: Psychology's role in the health crisis. *Clinical Psychology Review, 8,* 255-284.

KELLY, J. A., & ST. LAWRENCE, J. S. (1990). The impact of community-based groups to help persons reduce HIV infection risk behaviours. *AIDS-Care, 2,* 25-36.

KELLY, J. A., ST. LAWRENCE, J. S., HOOD, H. V., & BRASFIELD, T. L. (1989). Behavioral intervention to reduce AIDS risk activities. *Journal of Consulting and Clinical Psychology, 57,* 60-67.

KENDALL, P. C. (1987a). Behavioral assessment and methodology. In G. T. Wilson, C. M. Franks, P. C. Kendall, & J. P. Foreyt (Eds.), *Review of behavior therapy: Theory and practice* (Vol. 11, pp. 40-83). New York: Guilford.

KENDALL, P. C. (1987b). Cognitive processes and procedures in behavior therapy. In G. T. Wilson, C. M. Franks, P. C. Kendall, & J. P. Foreyt (Eds.), *Review of behavior therapy: Theory and practice* (Vol. 11, pp. 114-153). New York: Guilford.

KENDALL, P. C. (1989). The generalization and maintenance of behavior change: Comments, considerations, and the "no-cure" criticism. *Behavior Therapy, 20,* 357-364.

KENDALL, P. C. (1993). Cognitive-behavioral therapies with youth: Guiding theory, current status, and emerging developments. *Journal of Consulting and Clinical Psychology, 61,* 235-247.

KENDALL, P. C. (1994). Treating anxiety disorders in children: Results of a randomized clinical trial. *Journal of Consulting and Clinical Psychology, 62,* 100-110.

KENDALL, P. C., & BRASWELL, L. (1985). *Cognitive-behavioral therapy for impulsive children.* New York: Guilford.

KENDALL, P. C., & FINCH, A. J. (1978). A cognitive-behavioral treatment for impulsivity: A group comparison study. *Journal of Consulting and Clinical Psychology, 46,* 110-118.

KENDALL, P. C., & GEROW, M. A. (1995). *Long-term follow-up of a cognitive-behavioral therapy for anxiety-disordered youth.* Unpublished manuscript.

KENDALL, P. C., HAAGA, D. A. F., ELLIS, A., BERNARD, M., DiGIUSEPPE, R., & KASSINOVE, H. (1995). Rational-emotive therapy in the 1990s and beyond: Current status, recent revisions, and research questions. *Clinical Psychology Review, 15,* 169-185.

KENDALL, P. C., NAY, W. R., & JEFFERS, J. (1975). Timeout duration and contrast effects: A systematic evaluation of a successive treatments design. *Behavior Therapy, 6,* 609-615.

KENDALL, P. C., & NORTON-FORD, J. D. (1982). Therapy outcome research methods. In P. C. Kendall & J. N. Butcher (Eds.), *Handbook of research methods in clinical psychology* (pp. 429-460). New York: Wiley.

KENDALL, P. C., & WILCOX, L. E. (1980). Cognitive-behavioral treatment for impulsivity: Concrete versus conceptual training in non-self-controlled problem children. *Journal of Consulting and Clinical Psychology, 48,* 80-91.

KENNEDY, C. H., & ITKONEN, T. (1993). Effects of setting events on the problem behavior of students with severe disabilities. *Journal of Applied Behavior Analysis, 26,* 321-327.

KENNEDY, S. H., KATZ, R., NEITZERT, C. S., RALEVSKI, E., & MENDLOWITZ, S. (1995). Exposure with response prevention treatment of anorexia nervosa-bulimic subtype and bulimia nervosa. *Behaviour Research and Therapy, 33,* 685-689.

KENNY, F. T., MOWBRAY, R. M., & LALANI, S. (1978). Faradic disruption of obsessive ideation in the treatment of obsessive neurosis. *Behavior Therapy, 9,* 209-221.

KENT, R. N., & FOSTER, S. (1977). Direct observational procedures: Methodological issues in naturalistic settings. In A. R. Ciminero, K. S. Calhoun, & H. E. Adams (Eds.), *Handbook of behavioral assessment* (pp. 279-328). New York: Wiley.

KEOGH, D. A., FAW, G. D., WHITMAN, T. L., & REID, D. H. (1984). Enhancing leisure skills in severely retarded adolescents through a self-instructional treatment package. *Analysis and Intervention in Developmental Disabilities, 4,* 333-351.

KERN, J. M. (1982). Predicting the impact of assertive, empathic-assertive, and nonassertive behavior: The assertiveness of the assertee. *Behavior Therapy, 13,* 486-498.

KERN, J. M., CAVELL, T. A., & BECK, B. (1985). Predicting differential reactions to males' versus females' assertions, empathic-assertions, and nonassertions. *Behavior Therapy, 16,* 63-75.

KERNS, R. D., TURK, D. C., HOLZMAN, A. D., & RUDY, T. E. (1986). Comparison of cognitive-behavioral and behavioral approaches to outpatient treatment of chronic pain. *Clinical Journal of Pain, 1,* 195-203.

KETTLEWELL, P. W., MIZES, J. S., & WASYLYSHYN, N. A. (1992). A cognitive-behavioral group treatment of bulimia. *Behavior Therapy, 23,* 657-670.

KIDD, A. H., & EUPHRAT, J. L. (1971). Why prospective outpatients fail to make or keep appointments. *Journal of Clinical Psychology, 27,* 94-95.

KILPATRICK, D. G., & BEST, C. L. (1984). Some cautionary remarks on treating sexual assault victims with implosion. *Behavior Therapy, 15,* 421-423.

KIMMEL, H. D., & KIMMEL, E. (1970). An instrumental conditioning method for treatment of enuresis. *Journal of Behavior Therapy and Experimental Psychiatry, 1,* 121-124.

KIRBY, K. C., FOWLER, S. A., & BEAR, D. M. (1991). Reactivity in self-recording: Obtrusiveness of recording procedure and peer comments. *Journal of Applied Behavior Analysis, 24,* 487-498.

KIRIGIN, K. A., BRAUKMANN, C. J., ATWATER, J., & WOLF, M. M. (1982). An evaluation of Achievement Place (Teaching-Family) group homes for juvenile offenders. *Journal of Applied Behavior Analysis, 15,* 1-16.

KIRKLAND, K., & HOLLANDSWORTH, J. G. (1980). Effective test taking: Skills-acquisition versus anxiety-reduction technique. *Journal of Consulting and Clinical Psychology, 48,* 431-439.

KIRKLEY, B. G., SCHNEIDER, J. A., AGRAS, W. S., & BACHMAN, J. A. (1985). Comparison of two group treatments for bulimia. *Journal of Consulting and Clinical Psychology, 53,* 43-48.

KIRSCHENBAUM, D. S. (1994). *Weight loss through persistence: Making science work for you.* Oakland, CA: New Harbinger Publications.

KLEINER, L., MARSHALL, W. L., & SPEVACK, M. (1987). Training in problem solving and exposure treatment for agoraphobic with panic attacks. *Journal of Anxiety Disorders, 1*, 219-238.

KLEINKNECHT, R. A. (1993). Rapid treatment of blood and injection phobias with eye movement desensitization. *Journal of Behavior Therapy and Experimental Psychiatry, 24*, 211-217.

KLEINKNECHT, R. A., & BERNSTEIN, D. A. (1979). Short term treatment of dental avoidance. *Journal of Behavior Therapy and Experimental Psychiatry, 10*, 311-315.

KLEINKNECHT, R. A., & MORGAN, M. P. (1992). Treatment of posttraumatic stress disorder with eye movement desensitization and reprocessing. *Journal of Behavior Therapy and Experimental Psychiatry, 23*, 43-49.

KLESGES, R. C., MALOTT, J. M., & UGLAND, M. (1984). The effects of graded exposure and parental modeling on the dental phobias of a four-year-old girl and her mother. *Journal of Behavior Therapy and Experimental Psychiatry, 15*, 161-164.

KLINGMAN, A., MELAMED, B. G., CUTHBERT, M. I., & HERMECZ, D. A. (1984). Effects of participant modeling on information acquisition and skill utilization. *Journal of Consulting and Clinical Psychology, 52*, 414-422.

KLORMAN, R., HILPERT, P. L., MICHAEL, R., LAGANA, C., & SVEEN, O. B. (1980). Effects of coping and mastery modeling on experienced and inexperienced pedodontic patients' disruptiveness. *Behavior Therapy, 11*, 156-168.

KNAPCZYK, D. R., & LIVINGSTON, G. (1973). Self-recording and student teacher supervision: Variables within a token economy structure. *Journal of Applied Behavior Analysis, 6*, 481-486.

KNAUS, W. (1974). *Rational-emotive education: A manual for elementary school teachers.* New York: Institute for Rational Living.

KNAUS, W., & EYMAN, W. (1974). Progress in rational-emotive education. *Rational Living, 9*, 27-29.

KNAUS, W., & MCKEEVER, C. (1977). Rational-emotive education with learning disabled children. *Journal of Learning Disabilities, 10*, 10-14.

KNAUS, W., & WESSLER, R. (1976). Rational-emotive problem simulation. *Rational Living, 11*, 8-11.

KNAUS, W. J. (1985). Student burnout: A rational-emotive education treatment approach. In A. Ellis & M. Bernard (Eds.), *Clinical applications of rational-emotive therapy* (pp. 257-276). New York: Plenum.

KNAUS, W. J., & HABERSTROH, N. (1993). A rational-emotive education program to help disruptive mentally retarded clients develop self-control. In W. Dryden & L. K. Hill (Eds.), *Innovations in rational-emotive therapy* (pp. 201-217). Newbury Park, CA: Sage.

KNIGHT, M. F., & MCKENZIE, H. S. (1974). Elimination of bedtime thumbsucking in home settings through contingent reading. *Journal of Applied Behavior Analysis, 7*, 33-38.

KOHLENBERG, R., & PHILLIPS, T. (1973). Reinforcement and rate of litter depositing. *Journal of Applied Behavior Analysis, 6*, 391-396.

KOHLENBERG, R., PHILLIPS, T., & PROCTOR, W. (1976). A behavioral analysis of peaking in residential electrical energy consumers. *Journal of Applied Behavior Analysis, 9*, 13-18.

KOHLENBERG, R. J., & TSAI, M. (1991). *Functional analytic psychotherapy: Creating intense and curative therapeutic relationships.* New York: Plenum.

KOHLENBERG, R. J., & TSAI, M. (1994). Functional analytic psychotherapy: A radical behavioral approach to treatment and integration. *Journal of Psychotherapy Integration, 4*, 175-201.

KOHLENBERG, R. J., & TSAI, M. (1995). Functional analytic psychotherapy: A behavioral approach to intensive treatment. In W. T. O'Donohue & L. Krasner (Eds.), *Theories of behavior therapy: Exploring behavior change* (pp. 637-658). Washington, DC: American Psychological Association.

KOMAKI, J., BARWICK, K. D., & SCOTT, L. R. (1978). A behavioral approach to occupational safety: Pinpointing and reinforcing safe performance in a food manufacturing plant. *Journal of Applied Psychology, 63*, 424-445.

KOPEC, A. M., BEAL, D., & DIGIUSEPPE, R. (1994). Training in RET: Disputational strategies. *Journal of Rational-Emotive and Cognitive-Behavior Therapy, 12*, 47-60.

KOPEL, S., & ARKOWITZ, H. (1975). The role of attribution and self-perception in behavior change: Implications for behavior therapy. *General Psychology Monographs, 92*, 175-212.

KORNFELD, A. D. (1989). Mary Cover Jones and the Peter case: Social learning versus conditioning. *Journal of Anxiety Disorders, 3*, 187-195.

KORNHABER, R. C., & SCHROEDER, H. E. (1975). Importance of model similarity on extinction of avoidance behavior in children. *Journal of Consulting and Clinical Psychology, 43*, 601-607.

KOZAK, M. J., FOA, E. B., & STEKETEE, G. (1988). Process and outcome of exposure treatment with obsessive-compulsives: Psychophysiological indicators of emotional processing. *Behavior Therapy, 19*, 157-169.

KRAKAUER, J. (1995, October). Loving them to death. *Outside, 20,* pp. 72-80, 82, 142-143.

KRAMER, F. M., & STALKER, L. A. (1989). Treatment of obesity. In A. Freeman, K. M. Simon, L. E. Beutler, & H. Arkowitz (Eds.), *Comprehensive handbook of cognitive therapy* (pp. 385-401). New York: Plenum.

KRAPFL, J. E. (1967). *Differential ordering of stimulus presentation and semi-automated versus live treatment in the systematic desensitization of snake phobia.* Unpublished doctoral dissertation, University of Missouri.

KRASNER, L. (1976). Behavior modification: Ethical issues and future trends. In H. Leitenberg (Ed.), *Handbook of behavior modification and behavior therapy* (pp. 627-649). Englewood Cliffs, NJ: Prentice-Hall.

KRISTT, D. A., & ENGEL, B. T. (1975). Learned control of blood pressure in patients with high blood pressure. *Circulation, 51*, 370-378.

KROP, H., & BURGESS, D. (1993a). Use of covert conditioning to treat excessive masturbation. In J. R. Cautela & A. J. Kearney (Eds.), *Covert conditioning casebook* (pp. 208-216). Pacific Grove, CA: Brooks/Cole.

KROP, H., & BURGESS, D. (1993b). The use of covert modeling in the treatment of a sexual abuse victim. In J. R. Cautela & A. J. Kearney (Eds.), *Covert conditioning casebook* (pp. 153-158). Pacific Grove, CA: Brooks/Cole.

KRUGLANSKI, A. W., & JAFFE, Y. (1988). Curing by knowing: The epistemic approach to cognitive therapy. In L. Y. Abramson (Ed.), *Social cognition and clinical psychology: A synthesis* (pp. 254-291). New York: Guilford.

KUTCHINS, H., & KIRK, S. A. (1995). Should DSM be the basis for teaching social work practice in mental health? No! *Journal of Social Work Education, 31,* 159-168.

LABERGE, B., GAUTHIER, J. G., CÔTÉ, G., PLAMONDON, J., & CORMIER, H. J. (1993). Cognitive-behavioral therapy of panic disorder with secondary major depression: A preliminary investigation. *Journal of Consulting and Clinical Psychology, 61,* 1028-1037.

LABOUVIE-VIEF, G., & GONDA, J. (1976). Cognitive strategy training and intellectual performance in the elderly. *Journal of Gerontology, 31,* 327-332.

LACKS, P., BERTELSON, A. D., GANS, L., & KUNKEL, J. (1983). The effectiveness of three behavioral treatments for different degrees of sleep-onset insomnia. *Behavior Therapy, 14,* 593-605.

LACKS, P., & MORIN, C. M. (1992). Recent advances in the assessment and treatment of insomnia. *Journal of Consulting and Clinical Psychology, 60,* 586-594.

LADOUCEUR, R. (1983). Participant modeling with or without cognitive treatment for phobias. *Journal of Consulting and Clinical Psychology, 51,* 942-944.

LADOUCEUR, R., BOISVERT, J., & DUMONT, J. (1994). Cognitive-behavioral treatment for adolescent pathological gamblers. *Behavior Modification, 18,* 230-242.

LaGRECA, A. M. (1988). Adherence to prescribed medical regimens. In D. K. Routh (Ed.), *Handbook of pediatric psychology* (pp. 299-320). New York: Guilford.

LaGRECA, A. M., & OTTINGER, D. R. (1979). Self-monitoring and relaxation training in the treatment of medically ordered exercise in a 12-year-old female. *Journal of Pediatric Psychology, 4,* 49-54.

LAHEY, B. B., & DRABMAN, R. S. (1974). Facilitation of the acquisition and retention of sight word vocabulary through token reinforcement. *Journal of Applied Behavior Analysis, 7,* 307-312.

LAHEY, B. B., McNEES, M. P., & McNEES, M. C. (1973). Control of an obscene "verbal tic" through time out in an elementary classroom. *Journal of Applied Behavior Analysis, 6,* 101-104.

LAKE, A. E., & PINGEL, J. D. (1988). Brief versus extended relaxation: Relationship to improvement at follow-up in mixed headache patients. *Medical Psychotherapy, 1,* 119-129.

LAMAZE, F. (1970). *Painless childbirth.* Chicago: Henry Regery.

LAMBERT, M. J., & BERGIN, A. E. (1994). The effectiveness of psychotherapy. In A. E. Bergin & S. L. Garfield (Eds.), *Handbook of psychotherapy and behavior change* (4th ed., pp. 143-189). New York: Wiley.

LAMONTAGNE, Y., & MARKS, I. M. (1973). Psychogenic urinary retention: Treatment of prolonged exposure. *Behavior Therapy, 4,* 581-585.

LANCASTER, J. (1805). *Improvements in education, as it respects the industrious classes of the community* (3rd ed.). London: Darton and Harvey.

LANDERS, S. (1990, March). Phobias: A stepchild garners new respect. *APA Monitor, 21,* p. 18.

LANDO, H. A. (1975). A comparison of excessive and rapid smoking in the modification of chronic smoking behavior. *Journal of Consulting and Clinical Psychology, 43,* 350-355.

LANDRINE, H., & KLONOFF, E. (1995). Cultural diversity and the silence of behavior therapy. *the Behavior Therapist, 18,* 187-189.

LANG, P. J. (1969). The mechanics of desensitization and the laboratory study of fear. In C. M. Franks (Ed.), *Behavior therapy: Appraisal and status* (pp. 160-191). New York: McGraw-Hill.

LANG, P. J., MELAMED, B. G., & HART, J. A. (1970). A psychophysiological analysis of fear modification using an automated desensitization procedure. *Journal of Abnormal Psychology, 76,* 220-234.

LARSON, K., & AYLLON, T. (1990). The effects of contingent music and differential reinforcement on infantile colic. *Behaviour Research and Therapy, 28,* 119-125.

LARSON, M. E., HOULIHAN, D., & GOERNERT, P. N. (1995). Effects of informational feedback on aluminum can recycling. *Behavioral Interventions, 10,* 111-117.

LASCELLES, M., CUNNINGHAM, S., McGRATH, P., & SULLIVAN, M. (1989). Teaching coping skills to adolescents with migraine. *Journal of Pain and Symptom Management, 4,* 135-145.

LaVIGNA, G. W., & DONNELLAN, A. M. (1986). *Alternatives to punishment: Solving behavior problems with non-aversive strategies.* New York: Irvington.

LAVIN, N. I., THORPE, J. G., BARKER, J. C., BLAKEMORE, C. B., & CONWAY, C. G. (1961). Behaviour therapy in a case of transvestism. *Journal of Nervous and Mental Disease, 133,* 346-353.

LAWS, P. (1974). *A consumer's guide to avoiding unnecessary radiation exposure.* Washington, DC: Public Citizen, Inc.

LAWSON, D. M., & MAY, R. B. (1970). Three procedures for the extinction of smoking behavior. *Psychological Record, 20,* 151-157.

LAWTON, C., FRANCE, K. G., & BLAMPIED, N. M. (1991). Treatment of infant sleep disturbance by graduated extinction. *Child and Family Behavior Therapy, 13,* 39-56.

LAZARUS, A. A. (1959). The elimination of children's phobias by deconditioning. *Medical Proceedings, 5,* 261-265.

LAZARUS, A. A. (1961). Group therapy of phobic disorders by systematic desensitization. *Journal of Abnormal and Social Psychology, 63,* 505-510.

LAZARUS, A. A. (1966). Broad-spectrum behaviour therapy and the treatment of agoraphobia. *Behaviour Research and Therapy, 4,* 95-97.

LAZARUS, A. A. (1967). In support of technical eclecticism. *Psychological Reports, 21,* 415-416.

LAZARUS, A. A. (1971). *Behavior therapy and beyond.* New York: McGraw-Hill.

LAZARUS, A. A. (1973). On assertive behavior: A brief note. *Behavior Therapy, 4,* 697-699.

LAZARUS, A. A. (1976). *Multimodal behavior therapy.* New York: Springer.

LAZARUS, A. A. (Ed.). (1985). *Casebook of multimodal therapy.* New York: Guilford.

LAZARUS, A. A. (1989a). *The practice of multimodal therapy.* Baltimore: Johns Hopkins University Press.

LAZARUS, A. A. (1989b). The practice of rational-emotive therapy. In M. E. Bernard & R. DiGiuseppe (Eds.), *Inside rational-emotive therapy: A critical appraisal of the theory and therapy of Albert Ellis* (pp. 95-112). San Diego: Academic Press.

LAZARUS, A. A. (1989c). Why I am an eclectic (not an integrationist). *The British Journal of Guidance and Counselling, 17,* 248-258.

LAZARUS, A. A. (1995). Different types of eclecticism and

integration: Let's be aware of the dangers. *Journal of Psychotherapy Integration, 5,* 27-39.

LAZARUS, A. A., & ABRAMOVITZ, A. (1962). The use of "emotive imagery" in the treatment of children's phobias. *Journal of Mental Science, 108,* 191-195.

LAZARUS, A. A., & BEUTLER, L. E. (1993). On technical eclecticism. *Journal of Counseling and Development, 71,* 381-385.

LAZARUS, A. A., DAVISON, G. C., & POLEFKA, D. A. (1965). Classical and operant factors in the treatment of a school phobia. *Journal of Abnormal Psychology, 70,* 225-229.

LAZARUS, R. S., & FOLKMAN, S. (1984). *Stress, appraisal, and coping.* New York: Springer.

LEDWIDGE, B. (1978). Cognitive behavior modification: A step in the wrong direction? *Psychological Bulletin, 85,* 353-375.

LEDWIDGE, B. (1979). Cognitive behavior modification: A rejoinder. *Cognitive Therapy and Research, 3,* 133-140.

LEE, E. S. (1951). Negro intelligence and selective migration: A Philadelphia test of the Klineberg hypothesis. *American Review, 16,* 227-232.

LEE, N. K., & OEI, T. P. S. (1993). Exposure and response prevention in anxiety disorders: Implications for treatment and relapse prevention in problem drinkers. *Clinical Psychology Review, 13,* 619-632.

LEHRER, P. M. (1982). How to relax and how not to relax: A reevaluation of the work of Edmund Jacobson—I. *Behaviour Research and Therapy, 20,* 417-428.

LEITENBERG, H. (1976). Behavioral approaches to treatment of neuroses. In H. Leitenberg (Ed.), *Handbook of behavior modification and behavior therapy* (pp. 124-167). Englewood Cliffs, NJ: Prentice-Hall.

LEITENBERG, H. (1993). Treatment of bulimia nervosa. In T. R. Giles (Ed.), *Handbook of effective psychotherapy* (pp. 279-302). New York: Plenum.

LEITENBERG, H., BURCHARD, D., BURCHARD, N., FULLER, E. J., & LYSAGHT, T. V. (1977). Using positive reinforcement to suppress behavior: Some experimental comparisons with sibling conflict. *Behavior Therapy, 8,* 168-182.

LEITENBERG, H., GROSS, J., PETERSON, J., & ROSEN, J. C. (1984). Analysis of an anxiety model in the process of change during exposure plus response prevention treatment of bulimia nervosa. *Behavior Therapy, 15,* 3-20.

LEITENBERG, H., & ROSEN, J. C. (1988). Cognitive-behavioral treatment of bulimia nervosa. In M. Hersen, R. M. Eisler, & P. M. Miller (Eds.), *Progress in behavior modification* (Vol. 23, pp. 11-32). Newbury Park, CA: Sage.

LEITENBERG, H., ROSEN, J. C., WOLF, J., VARA, L. S., DETZER, M. J., & SREBNIK, D. (1994). Comparison of cognitive-behavior therapy and desipramine in the treatment of bulimia nervosa. *Behaviour Research and Therapy, 32,* 37-45.

LEMSKY, C. M. (1996). Adapting behavioral interventions for brain injured older adults. *the Behavior Therapist, 19,* 9-12.

LENNOX, D. B., MILTENBERGER, R. G., & DONNELLY, D. R. (1987). Response interruption and DRL for the reduction of rapid eating. *Journal of Applied Behavior Analysis, 20,* 279-284.

LERMAN, D. C., & IWATA, B. A. (1995). Prevalence of the extinction burst and its attenuation during treatment. *Journal of Applied Behavior Analysis, 28,* 93-94.

LERMAN, D. C., & IWATA, B. A. (1996). Developing a technology for the use of operant extinction in clinical settings: An examination of basic and applied research. *Journal of Applied Behavior Analysis, 29,* 345-382.

LESTER, D. (1987). Indirect evidence for effects of suggestion in suicide: A critical mass hypothesis. *Psychological Reports, 61,* 576.

LEVIN, R. B., & GROSS, A. M. (1984). Reactions to assertive versus nonassertive behavior. *Behavior Modification, 8,* 581-592.

LEVIS, D. J. (1979). The infrahuman avoidance model of symptom maintenance and implosive therapy. In J. D. Keehn (Ed.), *Psychopathology in animals* (pp. 257-277). New York: Academic Press.

LEVIS, D. J. (1980). Implementing the technique of implosive therapy. In A. Goldstein & E. B. Foa (Eds.), *Handbook of behavioral interventions: A clinical guide* (pp. 92-151). New York: Wiley.

LEVIS, D. J. (1985). Implosive theory: A comprehensive extension of conditioning theory of fear/anxiety to psychopathology. In S. Reiss & R. R. Bootzin (Eds.), *Theoretical issues in behavior therapy* (pp. 49-82). New York: Academic Press.

LEVIS, D. J. (1988). Observations and experience from clinical practice: A critical ingredient for advancing behavioral theory and therapy. *the Behavior Therapist, 11,* 95-99.

LEVIS, D. J. (1991). A clinician's plea for a return to the development of nonhuman models of psychopathology: New clinical observations in need of laboratory study. In M. R. Denny (Ed.), *Fear, avoidance, and phobias: A fundamental analysis* (pp. 395-427). Hillsdale, NJ: Lawrence Erlbaum.

LEVIS, D. J. (1993). The power of extrapolating basic laboratory principles: The behavioural-cognitive approach of implosive therapy. *Behaviour Change, 10,* 154-161.

LEVIS, D. J., & CARRERA, R. N. (1967). Effects of 10 hours of implosive therapy in the treatment of outpatients: A preliminary report. *Journal of Abnormal Psychology, 72,* 504-508.

LEVIS, D. J., & HARE, N. (1977). A review of the theoretical rationale and empirical support for the extinction approach of implosive (flooding) therapy. In M. Hersen, R. M. Eisler, & P. M. Miller (Eds.), *Progress in behavior modification* (Vol. 2, pp. 300-376). New York: Academic Press.

LEVIS, D. J., & MALLOY, P. F. (1982). Research in infrahuman and human conditioning. In G. T. Wilson & C. M. Franks (Eds.), *Contemporary behavior therapy* (pp. 65-118). New York: Guilford.

LEVITT, E. E. (1957). The results of psychotherapy with children: An evaluation. *Journal of Consulting Psychology, 21,* 189-196.

LEVITT, E. E. (1963). Psychotherapy with children: A further evaluation. *Behaviour Research and Therapy, 1,* 45-51.

LEWINSOHN, P. M., CLARKE, G. N., & ROHDE, P. (1994). Psychological approaches to the treatment of depression in adolescents. In W. M. Reynolds & H. F. Johnston (Eds.), *Handbook of depression in children and adolescents* (pp. 309-344). New York: Plenum.

LEWINSOHN, P. M., & ROHDE, P. (1993). The cognitive-behavioral treatment of depression in adolescents: Research and suggestions. *The Clinical Psychologist, 46,* 177-183.

LIBB, J. W., & CLEMENTS, C. B. (1969). Token reinforcement in an exercise program for hospitalized geriatric patients. *Perceptual and Motor Skills, 28,* 957-958.

LIBERMAN, R. P., KOPELOWICZ, A., & YOUNG, A. S. (1994). Biobehavioral treatment and rehabilitation of schizophrenia. *Behavior Therapy, 25,* 89-107.

LIBERMAN, R. P., VACCARO, J. V., & CORRIGAN, P. W. (in press). Psychiatric rehabilitation. In H. I. Kaplan & B. J. Sadock (Eds.), *Comprehensive textbook of psychiatry*. Baltimore: Williams and Wilkins.

LIBERMAN, R. P, WALLACE, C. J., BLACKWELL, G., ECKMAN, T. A., VACCARO, J. V., & KUEHNEL, T. G. (1993). Innovations in skills training for the seriously mentally ill: The UCLA social and independent living skills modules. *Innovations and Research, 2*, 43-60.

LIBERMAN, R. P., WALLACE, C. J., BLACKWELL, G. A., & VACCARO, J. V. (1993, November). *Integrating skills training with assertive case management in the rehabilitation of persons with schizophrenia*. Paper presented at a meeting of Psychiatric Research in the Department of Veterans Affairs, Washington, DC.

LICHSTEIN, K. L. (1988). *Clinical relaxation strategies*. New York: Wiley.

LICHSTEIN, K. L., & RIEDEL, B. W. (1994). Behavioral assessment and treatment of insomnia: A review with an emphasis on clinical application. *Behavior Therapy, 25*, 659-688.

LICHTENSTEIN, E., & DANAHER, B. G. (1976). Modification of smoking behavior: A critical analysis of theory, research, and practice. In M. Hersen, R. M. Eisler, & P. M. Miller (Eds.), *Progress in behavior modification* (Vol. 3, pp. 79-132). New York: Academic Press.

LICHTENSTEIN, E., & GLASGOW, R. E. (1977). Rapid smoking: Side effects and safeguards. *Journal of Consulting and Clinical Psychology, 45*, 815-821.

LICHTENSTEIN, E., HARRIS, D. E., BIRCHLER, G. R., WAHL, J. M., & SCHMAHL, D. P. (1973). Comparison of rapid smoking, warm, smoky air and attention-placebo in the modification of smoking behavior. *Journal of Consulting and Clinical Psychology, 40*, 92-98.

LICHTENSTEIN, E., & RODRIGUES, M. R. P. (1977). Long-term effects of rapid smoking treatment for dependent cigarette smokers. *Addictive Behaviors, 2*, 109-112.

LICK, J. R. (1975). Expectancy, false galvanic skin response feedback and systematic desensitization in the modification of a phobic behavior. *Journal of Consulting and Clinical Psychology, 43*, 557-567.

LIDDELL, A., DI FAZIO, L., BLACKWOOD, J., & ACKERMAN, C. (1994). Long-term follow-up of treated dental phobics. *Behaviour Research and Therapy, 32*, 605-610.

LIEBERT, R. M., & SPIEGLER, M. D. (1994). *Personality: Strategies and issues* (7th ed.). Pacific Grove, CA: Brooks/Cole.

LIESE, B. S. (1994). Brief therapy, crisis intervention and the cognitive therapy of substance abuse. *Crisis Intervention, 1*, 11-29.

LIMA, J., NAZARIAN, L., CHARNEY, E., & LAHTI, C. (1976). Compliance with short-term antimicrobial therapy: Some techniques that help. *Pediatrics, 57*, 383-386.

LINDSLEY, O. R. (1956). Operant conditioning methods applied to research in chronic schizophrenia. *Psychiatric Research Reports, 5*, 118-139.

LINDSLEY, O. R. (1960). Characteristics of the behavior of chronic psychotics as revealed by free-operant conditioning methods. *Diseases of the Nervous System* (Monograph Supplement), *21*, 66-78.

LINDSLEY, O. R. (1963). Free-operant conditioning and psychotherapy. *Current Psychiatric Therapies, 3*, 47-56.

LINDSLEY, O. R. (1966). An experiment with parents handling behavior at home. *Johnstone Bulletin* (Johnstone Training Center, Bordentown, NJ), *9*, 27-36.

LINDSLEY, O. R. (1968). A reliable wrist counter for recording behavior rates. *Journal of Applied Behavior Analysis, 1*, 77-78.

LINEHAN, M. M. (1993a). *Cognitive-behavioral treatment of borderline personality disorder*. New York: Guilford.

LINEHAN, M. M. (1993b). *Skill training manual for treating borderline personality disorder*. New York: Guilford.

LINEHAN, M. M., ARMSTRONG, H. E., SUAREZ, A., ALLMON, D., & HEARD, H. L. (1991). Cognitive-behavioral treatment of chronically parasuicidal borderline patients. *Archives of General Psychiatry, 48*, 1060-1064.

LINEHAN, M. M., HEARD, L., & ARMSTRONG, H. E. (1993). Naturalistic follow-up of a behavioral treatment for chronically parasuicidal borderline patients. *Archives of General Psychiatry, 50*, 971-974.

LINEHAN, M. M., & SCHMIDT, H., III. (1995). The dialectics of effective treatment of borderline personality disorders. In W. T. O'Donohue & L. Krasner (Eds.), *Theories of behavior therapy: Exploring behavior change* (pp. 553-584). Washington, DC: American Psychological Association.

LINSCHEID, T. R., HARTEL, F., & COOLEY, N. (1993). Are aversive procedures durable? A five year follow-up of three individuals treated with contingent electric shock. *Child and Adolescent Mental Health Care, 3*, 67-76.

LINSCHEID, T. R., IWATA, B. A., RICKETTS, R. W., WILLIAMS, D. E., & GRIFFIN, J. C. (1990). Clinical evaluation of the self-injurious behavior inhibiting system (SIBIS). *Journal of Applied Behavior Analysis, 23*, 53-78.

LINSCHEID, T. R., PEJEAU, C., COHEN, S., & FOOTO-LENZ, M. (1994). Positive side effects in the treatment of SIB using the self-injurious behavior inhibiting system (SIBIS): Implications for operant and biochemical explanations of SIB. *Research in Developmental Disabilities, 15*, 81-90.

LINTON, S. J. (1982). Applied relaxation as a method of coping with chronic pain: A therapist's guide. *Scandinavian Journal of Behaviour Therapy, 11*, 161-174.

LINTON, S. J., & MELIN, L. (1983). Applied relaxation in the management of chronic pain. *Behavioural Psychotherapy, 11*, 337-350.

LIPKE, H., & BOTKIN, A. (1992). Brief case studies of eye movement desensitization and reprocessing with chronic post-traumatic stress disorder. *Psychotherapy, 29*, 591-595.

LITTLE, B. C., HAYWORTH, J., BENSON, P., HALL, F., BEARD, R. W., DEWHURST, V., & PRIEST, R. G. (1984). Treatment of hypertension in pregnancy by relaxation and biofeedback. *Lancet, 1*, 865-867.

LOCHMAN, J. E. (1985). Effects of different treatment lengths in cognitive behavioral interventions with aggressive boys. *Child Psychiatry and Human Development, 16*, 45-56.

LOCHMAN, J. E., & CURRY, J. F. (1986a). Effects of social problem-solving training and self-instruction training with aggressive boys. *Journal of Clinical Child Psychology, 15*, 159-164.

LOCHMAN, J. E., & CURRY, J. F. (1986b). Situational social problem-solving skills and self-esteem of aggressive and nonaggressive boys. *Journal of Abnormal Child Psychology, 14*, 605-617.

LOCHMAN, J. E., & LENHART, L. A. (1993). Anger coping intervention for aggressive children: Conceptual models and outcome effects. *Clinical Psychology Review, 13*, 785-805.

LOCHMAN, J. E., NELSON, W. M., III, & SIMS, J. P. (1981). A cognitive-behavioral program for use with aggressive children. *Journal of Clinical Child Psychology, 13,* 527-538.

LOCKE, E. A. (1979). Behavior modification is not cognitive and other myths: A reply to Ledwidge. *Cognitive Therapy and Research, 3,* 119-126.

LOFTUS, E. (1979). *Eyewitness testimony.* Cambridge, MA: Harvard University Press.

LOHR, J. M., KLEINKNECHT, R. A., CONLEY, A. T., DAL CERRO, S., SCHMIDT, J., & SONNTAG, M. E. (1992). A methodological critique of the current status of eye movement desensitization (EMD). *Journal of Behavior Therapy and Experimental Psychiatry, 23,* 159-167.

LOHR, J. M., TOLIN, D. F., & MONTGOMERY, R. W. (1996, January). Differing opinions on EMDR [Letter to the editor]. *APA Monitor,* pp. 3-4.

LONG, P., FOREHAND, R., WIERSON, M., & MORGAN, A. (1993). Does parent training with young noncompliant children have long-term effects? *Behaviour Research and Therapy, 32,* 101-107.

LONGABAUGH, R. L., WIRTZ, P. W., BEATTIE, M. C., NOEL, N., & STOUT, R. (1995). Matching treatment focus to patient social investment and support: 18-month follow-up results. *Journal of Consulting and Clinical Psychology, 63,* 296-307.

LOVAAS, O. I. (1977). *The autistic child: Language development through behavior modification.* New York: Irvington.

LOVAAS, O. I. (1987). Behavioral treatment and normal educational and intellectual functioning in young autistic children. *Journal of Consulting and Clinical Psychology, 55,* 3-9.

LOVAAS, O. I., & SIMMONS, J. Q. (1969). Manipulation of self-destruction in three retarded children. *Journal of Applied Behavior Analysis, 2,* 143-157.

LOVIBOND, S. H., & COOTE, M. A. (1970). Enuresis. In C. G. Costello (Ed.), *Symptoms of psychopathology: A handbook* (pp. 373-396). New York: Wiley.

LOWE, K., & LUTZKER, J. R. (1979). Increasing compliance to a medical regimen with a juvenile diabetic. *Behavior Therapy, 10,* 57-64.

LUBETKIN, B. S., & FISHMAN, S. T. (1974). Electrical aversion therapy with a chronic heroin user. *Journal of Behavior Therapy and Experimental Psychiatry, 5,* 193-195.

LUBORSKY, L. (1954). A note on Eysenck's article "The effects of psychotherapy: An evaluation." *British Journal of Psychology, 45,* 129-131.

LUCIC, K. S., STEFFEN, J. J., HARRIGAN, J. A., & STUEBING, R. C. (1991). Progressive relaxation training: Muscle contraction before relaxation? *Behavior Therapy, 22,* 249-256.

LUDWIG, T. D., & GELLER, E. S. (1991). Improving the driving practices of pizza deliverers: Response generalization and moderating effects of driving history. *Journal of Applied Behavior Analysis, 24,* 31-44.

LUISELLI, J. K. (1993). Training self-feeding skills in children who are deaf and blind. *Behavior Modification, 17,* 457-473.

LUISELLI, J. K., & GREENRIDGE, A. (1982). Behavioral treatment of high-rate aggression in a rubella child. *Journal of Behavior Therapy and Experimental Psychiatry, 13,* 152-157.

LUYBEN, P. D., & BAILEY, J. S. (1979). The effects of rewards and proximity of containers on newspaper recycling. *Environment and Behavior, 9,* 539-557.

LYLES, J. M., BURISH, T. G., KROZELY, M. G., & OLDHAM, R. K. (1982). Efficacy of relaxation training and guided imagery in reducing the aversiveness of cancer chemotherapy. *Journal of Consulting and Clinical Psychology, 50,* 509-524.

LYNCH, D. J., BIRK, T. J., WEAVER, M. T., GOHARA, A. F., LEIGHTON, R. F., REPKA, F. J., & WALSH, M. E. (1992). Adherence to exercise interventions in the treatment of hypercholesterolemia. *Journal of Behavioral Medicine, 15,* 365-377.

LYONS, L. C., & WOODS, P. J. (1991). The efficacy of rational-emotive therapy: A quantitative view of the outcome research. *Clinical Psychology Review, 11,* 357-369.

MAAG, J. W., & KOTLASH, J. (1994). Review of stress inoculation training with children and adolescents: Issues and recommendations. *Behavior Modification, 18,* 443-469.

McADAM, D. B., & CUVO, A. J. (1994). Textual prompts as an antecedent cue self-management strategy for persons with mild disabilities. *Behavior Modification, 18,* 47-65.

McCAFFREY, R. J., & FAIRBANK, J. A. (1985). Behavioral assessment and treatment of accident-related posttraumatic stress disorder: Two case studies. *Behavior Therapy, 16,* 404-416.

McCAIN, A. P., & KELLEY, M. L. (1993). Managing the classroom behavior of an ADHD preschooler: The efficacy of a school-home note intervention. *Child and Family Behavior Therapy, 15,* 33-44.

McCAIN, A. P., & KELLEY, M. L. (1994). Improving classroom performance in underachieving adolescents: The additive effects of response cost to a school-home note system. *Child and Family Behavior Therapy, 16,* 27-41.

McCANN, D. L. (1992). Post-traumatic stress disorder due to devastating burns overcome by a single session of eye movement desensitization. *Journal of Behavior Therapy and Experimental Psychiatry, 23,* 319-323.

McCARTHY, B. (1989). A cognitive-behavioral approach to sex therapy. In A. Freeman, K. M. Simon, L. E. Beutler, & H. Arkowitz (Eds.), *Comprehensive handbook of cognitive therapy* (pp. 435-447). New York: Plenum.

McCARTHY, G. W., & CRAIG, K. D. (1995). Flying therapy for flying phobia. *Aviation, Space, and Environmental Medicine, 66,* 1179-1184.

McCATHIE, H., & SPENCE, S. H. (1991). What is the Revised Fear Survey Schedule for Children measuring? *Behaviour Research and Therapy, 29,* 495-502.

MACCOBY, N., FARQUHAR, J. W., WOOD, P. D., & ALEXANDER, J. (1977). Reducing the risk of cardiovascular disease: Effects of a community-based campaign on knowledge and behavior. *Journal of Community Health, 3,* 100-114.

McCONAGHY, N. (1988). Assessment of sexual dysfunction and deviation. In A. S. Bellack & M. Hersen (Eds.), *Behavioral assessment: A practical handbook* (3rd ed., pp. 490-541). Elmsford, NY: Pergamon.

McCONNELL, J. V. (1990). Negative reinforcement and positive punishment. *Teaching of Psychology, 17,* 247-249.

McCORDICK, S. M., KAPLAN, R. M., FINN, M. E., & SMITH, S. H. (1979). Cognitive behavior modification and modeling for test anxiety. *Journal of Consulting and Clinical Psychology, 47,* 419-420

MacCUBREY, J. (1971). Verbal operant conditioning with young institutionalized Down's syndrome children. *American Journal of Mental Deficiency, 75,* 676-701.

MACE, F. C. (1994). The significance and future of functional analysis methodologies. *Journal of Applied Behavior Analysis, 27,* 385-392.

McFall, R. M., & Lillesand, D. B. (1971). Behavior rehearsal with modeling and coaching in assertion training. *Journal of Abnormal Psychology, 77,* 313-323.

McFall, R. M., & Marston, A. R. (1970). An experimental investigation of behavior rehearsal in assertive training. *Journal of Abnormal Behavior, 76,* 295-303.

McGlynn, F. D., & Cornell, C. E. (1985). Simple phobia. In M. Hersen & A. S. Bellack (Eds.), *Handbook of clinical behavior therapy with adults* (pp. 23-48). New York: Plenum.

McGlynn, F. D., Moore, P. M., Rose, M. P., & Lazarte, A. (1995). Effects of relaxation training on fear and arousal during in vivo exposure to a caged snake among DSM-III-R simple (snake) phobics. *Journal of Behavior Therapy and Experimental Psychiatry, 26,* 1-8.

McGrady, A. (1994). Effects of group relaxation training and thermal biofeedback on blood pressure and related physiological and psychological variables in essential hypertension. *Biofeedback and Self-Regulation, 19,* 51-66.

McGrady, A., Olson, R. P., & Kroon, J. S. (1995). Biobehavioral treatment of essential hypertension. In M. S. Schwartz (Ed.), *Biofeedback: A practitioner's guide* (pp. 445-467). New York: Guilford.

McGrady, A., Wauquier, A., McNeil, A., & Gerard, G. (1994). Effects of biofeedback-assisted relaxation on migraine headache and changes in cerebral blood flow velocity in the middle cerebral artery. *Headache, 34,* 424-428.

MacKenzie-Keating, S. E., & McDonald, L. (1990). Overcorrection: Reviewed, revisited, and revised. *The Behavior Analyst, 13,* 39-48.

McKusick, L., Wiley, J., Coates, T. J., & Morin, S. F. (1986, November). *Predictors of AIDS behavioral risk reduction: The AIDS behavioral research project.* Paper presented at the New Zealand AIDS Foundation Prevention Education Planning Workshop, Auckland.

McLaughlin, T. F. (1982). An analysis of token reinforcement: A control group comparison with special education youth employing measures of clinical significance. *Child and Family Behavior Therapy, 3,* 43-50.

MacMillan, V., Guevremont, D. C., & Hansen, D. J. (1989). Problem-solving training with a multi-distressed abusive mother. *Journal of Family Violence, 3,* 69-81.

McNair, L. D. (1996). African American women and behavior therapy: Integrating theory, culture, and clinical practice. *Cognitive and Behavioral Practice, 3,* 337-349.

McNally, R. J. (1994). Introduction to the special series: Innovations in cognitive-behavioral approaches to schizophrenia. *Behavior Therapy, 25,* 1-4.

McNamee, G., O'Sullivan, G., Lelliott, P., & Marks, I. M. (1989). Telephone-guided treatment for housebound agoraphobics with panic disorder: Exposure vs. relaxation. *Behavior Therapy, 20,* 491-497.

McNees, M. P., Egli, D. S., Marshall, D. S., Schnelle, R. S., Schnelle, J. F., & Risley, T. R. (1976). Shoplifting prevention: Providing information through signs. *Journal of Applied Behavior Analysis, 9,* 399-405.

McNees, M. P., Gilliam, S. W., Schnelle, J. F., & Risley, T. R. (1979). Controlling employee theft through time and product identification. *Journal of Organizational Behavior Management, 2,* 113-119.

McNees, M. P., Kennon, M., Schnelle, J. F., Kirchner, R. E., & Thomas, M. M. (1980). An experimental analysis of a program to reduce retail theft. *American Journal of Community Psychology, 8,* 379-385.

McNeil, C. B., Clemens-Mowrer, L., Gurwitch, R. H., & Funderburk, B. W. (1994). Assessment of a new procedure to prevent timeout escape in preschoolers. *Child and Family Behavior Therapy, 16,* 27-35.

Maconochie, A. (1848). *The mark system.* London: John Ollivier.

MacPhillamy, D., & Lewinsohn, P. M. (1971). *The Pleasant Events Schedule.* Eugene: University of Oregon. (Mimeo)

Madsen, C. H. (1965). Positive reinforcement in the toilet training of a normal child. In L. P. Ullmann & L. Krasner (Eds.), *Case studies in behavior modification* (pp. 305-307). New York: Holt, Rinehart & Winston.

Madsen, C. H., Hoffman, M., Thomas, D. R., Koropsak, E., & Madsen, C. K. (1969). Comparison of toilet training techniques. In D. M. Gelfand (Ed.), *Social learning in childhood* (pp. 104-112). Pacific Grove, CA: Brooks/Cole.

Madsen, C. K., Greer, R. D., & Madsen, C. H. (1975). *Research in music behavior: Modifying music behavior in the classroom.* New York: Teachers College Press.

Maeda, M. (1985). The effects of combinations of vicarious reinforcement on the formation of assertive behaviors in covert modeling. *Japanese Journal of Behavior Therapy, 10,* 34-44. (English abstract)

Magrab, P. R., & Papadopoulou, Z. L. (1977). The effects of a token economy on dietary compliance for children on hemodialysis. *Journal of Applied Behavior Analysis, 10,* 573-578.

Mahoney, K., van Wagenen, R. K., & Meyerson, L. (1971). Toilet training of normal and retarded children. *Journal of Applied Behavior Analysis, 4,* 173-181.

Mahoney, M. J. (1988a). Constructive metatheory: I. Basic features and historical foundations. *International Journal of Personal Construct Psychology, 1,* 1-35.

Mahoney, M. J. (1988b). Constructive metatheory: II. Implications for psychotherapy. *International Journal of Personal Construct Psychology, 1,* 299-315.

Mahoney, M. J., & Kazdin, A. E. (1979). Cognitive behavior modification: Misconceptions and premature evacuation. *Psychological Bulletin, 86,* 1044-1049.

Mahoney, M. J., Lyddon, W. J., & Alford, D. J. (1989). An evaluation of the rational-emotive theory of psychotherapy. In M. E. Bernard & R. DiGiuseppe (Eds.), *Inside rational-emotive therapy: A critical appraisal of the theory and therapy of Albert Ellis* (pp. 69-94). San Diego: Academic Press.

Mahrer, A. R., Nordin, S., & Miller, L. S. (1995). If a client has this kind of problem, prescribe that kind of post-session behavior. *Psychotherapy, 32,* 194-203.

Malec, J. F. (1995). Behavior therapy and cognitive decline in the elderly. *the Behavior Therapist, 18,* 161-169.

Malenfant, J. E. L., & van Houten, R. (1988). The effects of nighttime seat belt enforcement on seat belt use by tavern patrons: A preliminary analysis. *Journal of Applied Behavior Analysis, 21,* 271-276.

Maletzky, B. M. (1974). "Assisted" covert sensitization in the treatment of exhibitionism. *Journal of Consulting and Clinical Psychology, 42,* 34-40.

Maletzky, B. M. (1993). Assisted covert sensitization: Application to a bisexual pedophile. In J. R. Cautela & A. J. Kearney (Eds.), *Covert conditioning casebook* (pp. 217-234). Pacific Grove, CA: Brooks/Cole.

Malleson, N. (1959). Panic and phobia. *Lancet, 1,* 225-227.

Maloney, D. M., Fixsen, D. L., & Phillips, E. L. (1981). The Teaching-Family model: Research and dissemination in a service program. *Children and Youth Services Review, 3,* 343-355.

MALONEY, K. B., & HOPKINS, B. L. (1973). The modification of sentence structure and its relationship to subjective judgments of creativity in writing. *Journal of Applied Behavior Analysis, 6,* 425-433.

MANN, R. A. (1972). The behavior-therapeutic use of contingency contracting to control an adult behavior problem: Weight control. *Journal of Applied Behavior Analysis, 5,* 99-109.

MANN, R. A. (1976). The use of contingency contracting to facilitate durability of behavior change: Weight loss maintenance. *Addictive Behaviors, 1,* 245-249.

MANNE, S. L., BAKEMAN, R., JACOBSEN, P. B., GORFINKLE, K., & REDD, W. H. (1994). An analysis of a behavioral intervention for children undergoing venipuncture. *Health Psychology, 13,* 556-566.

MANNE, S. L., JACOBSEN, P. B., GORFINKLE, K., GERSTEIN, F., & REDD, W. H. (1993). Treatment adherence difficulties among children with cancer: The role of parenting style. *Journal of Pediatric Psychology, 18,* 47-62.

MANNE, S. L., REDD, W. H., JACOBSEN, P. B., GORFINKLE, K., SCHORR, O., & RABKIN, B. (1990). Behavioral interventions to reduce child and parent distress during venipuncture. *Journal of Consulting and Clinical Psychology, 58,* 565-572.

MARAFIOTE, R. A. (1993). On EMDR and controlled outcome studies. *the Behavior Therapist, 17,* 22-24.

MARCUS, B. A., & VOLLMER, T. R. (1995). Effects of differential negative reinforcement on disruption and compliance. *Journal of Applied Behavior Analysis, 28,* 229-230.

MARGOLIN, G., MICHELLI, J., & JACOBSON, N. (1988). Assessment of marital dysfunction. In A. S. Bellack & M. Hersen (Eds.), *Behavioral assessment: A practical handbook* (3rd ed., pp. 441-489). Elmsford, NY: Pergamon.

MARKMAN, H. J., FLOYD, F. J., STANLEY, S. M., & LEWIS, H. (1986). Prevention. In N. S. Jacobson & A. S. Gurman (Eds.), *Clinical handbook of marital therapy* (pp. 173-195). New York: Guilford.

MARKMAN, H. J., FLOYD, F. J., STANLEY, S. M., & STORAASLI, R. D. (1988). Prevention of marital distress: A longitudinal investigation. *Journal of Consulting and Clinical Psychology, 56,* 210-217.

MARKMAN, H. J., LEBER, B., CORDOVA, A. D., & ST. PETERS, M. (1995). Behavioral observation and family psychology: Strange bedfellows or happy marriage? *Journal of Family Psychology, 9,* 371-379.

MARKMAN, H. J., RENICK, M. J., FLOYD, F. J., STANLEY, S. M., & CLEMENTS, M. (1993). Preventing marital distress through communication and conflict management training: A 4- and 5-year follow-up. *Journal of Consulting and Clinical Psychology, 61,* 70-77.

MARKS, I. (1978). Behavioral psychotherapy of adult neurosis. In S. L. Garfield & A. E. Bergin (Eds.), *Handbook of psychotherapy and behavior change: An empirical analysis* (2nd ed., pp. 493-547). New York: Wiley.

MARKS, I. M. (1987). *Fears, phobias, and rituals: Panic, anxiety and their disorders.* New York: Oxford University Press.

MARLATT, G. A. (1982). Relapse prevention: A self-control program for the treatment of addictive behaviors. In R. B. Stuart (Ed.), *Adherence, compliance, and generalization in behavioral medicine* (pp. 329-378). New York: Brunner/Mazel.

MARLATT, G. A., & BARRETT, K. (1994). Relapse prevention. In M. Galanter & H. D. Kleber (Eds.), *The textbook of substance abuse treatment* (pp. 285-299). Washington, DC: American Psychiatric Press.

MARLATT, G. A., & GORDON, J. R. (EDS.). (1985). *Relapse prevention: Maintenance strategies in the treatment of addictive behaviors.* New York: Guilford.

MARLATT, G. A., & TAPERT, S. F. (1993). Harm reduction: Reducing the risks of addictive behaviors. In J. S. Baer, G. A. Marlatt, & R. J. McMahon (Eds.), *Addictive behaviors across the lifespan* (pp. 243-273). Newbury Park, CA: Sage.

MARMAR, C. R. (1990, November). *Implications of empirical findings for the psychodynamic theory of the therapeutic alliance.* Paper presented at the meeting of the Association for Advancement of Behavior Therapy, San Francisco.

MARQUIS, J. N. (1972). An expedient model for behavior therapy. In A. A. Lazarus (Ed.), *Clinical behavior therapy* (pp. 41-72). New York: Brunner/Mazel.

MARQUIS, J. N. (1991). A report on seventy-eight cases treated by eye movement desensitization. *Journal of Behavior Therapy and Experimental Psychiatry, 22,* 187-192.

MARQUIS, J. N., MORGAN, W. G., & PIAGET, G. W. (1971). *A guidebook for systematic desensitization* (2nd ed.). Palo Alto, CA: Veterans' Workshop, Veterans Administration Hospital.

MARSHALL, W. L., GAUTHIER, J., CHRISTIE, M. M., CURRIE, D. W., & GORDON, A. (1977). Flooding therapy: Effectiveness, stimulus characteristics, and the value of brief *in vivo* exposure. *Behaviour Research and Therapy, 15,* 79-87.

MARSHALL, W. L., GAUTHIER, J., & GORDON, A. (1979). The current status of flooding therapy. In M. Hersen, R. M. Eisler, & P. M. Miller (Eds.), *Progress in behavior modification* (Vol. 7, pp. 205-275). New York: Academic Press.

MARSTON, M. V. (1970). Compliance with medical regimens: A review of the literature. *Nursing Research, 19,* 312-323.

MARTIN, G., & PEAR, J. (1996). *Behavior modification: What it is and how to do it* (5th ed.). Upper Saddle River, NJ: Prentice Hall.

MARTIN, S. (1995, October). Ethnic issues deeply entwined in family therapy. *APA Monitor, 26,* p. 38.

MASEK, B. J. (1982). Compliance and medicine. In D. M. Doleys, R. L. Meredith, & A. R. Ciminero (Eds.), *Behavioral medicine: Assessment and treatment strategies* (pp. 527-545). New York: Plenum.

MASTERPASQUA, F. (1989). A competence paradigm for psychological practice. *American Psychologist, 44,* 1366-1371.

MASTERS, J. C., BURISH, T. G., HOLLON, S. D., & RIMM, D. C. (1987). *Behavior therapy: Techniques and empirical findings* (3rd ed.). San Diego: Harcourt Brace Jovanovich.

MASTERS, W. H., & JOHNSON, V. E. (1970). *Human sexual inadequacy.* Boston: Little, Brown.

MATHEWS, A. M., GELDER, M. G., & JOHNSTON, D. W. (1981). *Agoraphobia: Nature and treatment.* New York: Guilford.

MATHEWS, A. M., JOHNSTON, D. W., LANCASHIRE, M., MUNBY, M., SHAW, P. M., & GELDER, M. G. (1976). Imaginal flooding and exposure to real phobic situations: Treatment outcome with agoraphobic patients. *British Journal of Psychology, 129,* 362-371.

MATHEWS, A. M., TEASDALE, J., MUNBY, M., JOHNSTON, D. W., & SHAW, P. A. (1977). A home-based treatment for agoraphobia. *Behavior Therapy, 8,* 915-924.

MATSON, J. L., SEVIN, J. A., & BOX, M. L. (1995). Social skills in children. In W. O'Donohue & L. Krasner (Eds.). *Handbook of psychological skills training: Clinical techniques and applications* (pp. 36-53). Boston: Allyn and Bacon.

Mattick, R. P., & Peters, L. (1988). Treatment of severe social phobia: Effects of guided exposure with and without cognitive restructuring. *Journal of Consulting and Clinical Psychology, 56,* 251-260.

Mavissakalian, M., & Barlow, D. H. (Eds.). (1981). *Phobia: Psychological and pharmacological treatment.* New York: Guilford.

Mayer, G. R., Butterworth, T., Nafpakitis, M., & Sulzer-Azaroff, B. (1983). Preventing school vandalism and improving discipline: A three-year study. *Journal of Applied Behavior Analysis, 16,* 353-369.

Mayer, J. A., & Frederiksen, L. W. (1986). Encouraging long-term compliance with breast self-examination: The evaluation of prompting strategies. *Journal of Behavioral Medicine, 9,* 179-189.

Mayer, J. A., Heins, J. M., Vogel, J. M., Morrison, D. C., Lankester, L. D., & Jacobs, A. L. (1986). Promoting low-fat entree choices in a public cafeteria. *Journal of Applied Behavior Analysis, 19,* 397-402.

Mayhew, G. L., & Harris, F. C. (1978). Some negative side effects of a punishment procedure for stereotyped behavior. *Journal of Behavior Therapy and Experimental Psychiatry, 9,* 245-251.

Mayo, L. L., & Norton, G. R. (1980). The use of problem solving to reduce examination and interpersonal anxiety. *Journal of Behavior Therapy and Experimental Psychiatry, 11,* 287-289.

Mazaleski, J. L., Iwata, B. A., Vollmer, T. R., Zarcone, J. R., & Smith, R. G. (1993). Analysis of the reinforcement and extinction components in contingencies with self-injury. *Journal of Applied Behavior Analysis, 26,* 143-156.

Mazur, T., & Michael, P. M. (1992). Outpatient treatment for adolescents with sexually inappropriate behavior. *Journal of Offender Rehabilitation, 18,* 191-203.

Meadowcroft, P., Hawkins, R. P., Trout, B. A., Grealish, E. M., & Stark, L. J. (1982, September). *Making foster-family-based treatment accountable: The issue of quality control.* Paper presented at the meeting of the American Psychological Association, Washington, DC.

Mealiea, W. L., & Nawas, M. M. (1971). The comparative effectiveness of systematic desensitization and implosive therapy in the treatment of snake phobia. *Journal of Behavior Therapy and Experimental Psychiatry, 2,* 85-94.

Meharg, S. S., & Woltersdorf, M. A. (1990). Therapeutic uses of videotape self-modeling: A review. *Advances in Behaviour Research and Therapy, 12,* 85-99.

Mehta, M. (1990). A comparative study of family-based and patient-based behavioral management in obsessive-compulsive disorder. *British Journal of Psychiatry, 157,* 133-135.

Meichenbaum, D. (1971). Examination of model characteristics in reducing avoidance behavior. *Journal of Personality and Social Psychology, 17,* 298-307.

Meichenbaum, D. (1974). Self-instructional training: A cognitive prosthesis for the aged. *Human Development, 17,* 273-280.

Meichenbaum, D. (1975). Enhancing creativity by modifying what subjects say to themselves. *American Educational Research Journal, 12,* 129-145.

Meichenbaum, D. (1977). *Cognitive-behavior modification: An integrative approach.* New York: Plenum.

Meichenbaum, D. (1979). Cognitive behavior modification: The need for a fairer assessment. *Cognitive Therapy and Research, 3,* 127-132.

Meichenbaum, D. (1991, February-March). *Cognitive behavioral therapy.* Workshop sponsored by the Institute for the Advancement of Human Behavior (Portola Valley, CA), Chicago.

Meichenbaum, D. (1994). *A clinical handbook/practical therapist manual for assessing and treating adults with post-traumatic stress disorder (PTSD).* Waterloo, Ontario: Institute Press.

Meichenbaum, D., & Cameron, R. (1972). *Stress inoculation: A skills training approach to anxiety management.* Unpublished manuscript, University of Waterloo, Ontario.

Meichenbaum, D., & Cameron, R. (1973). Training schizophrenics to talk to themselves: A means of developing attentional controls. *Behavior Therapy, 4,* 515-534.

Meichenbaum, D., Gilmore, B., & Fedoravicius, A. (1971). Group insight vs. group desensitization in treating speech anxiety. *Journal of Consulting and Clinical Psychology, 36,* 410-421.

Meichenbaum, D., & Goodman, J. (1971). Training impulsive children to talk to themselves: A means of developing self-control. *Journal of Abnormal Psychology, 77,* 115-126.

Meichenbaum, D., & Jaremko, M. E. (Eds.). (1982). *Stress prevention and management: A cognitive-behavioral approach.* New York: Plenum.

Meichenbaum, D., & Turk, D. (1976). The cognitive-behavioral management of anxiety, anger and pain. In J. Davison (Ed.), *The behavioral management of anxiety, depression and pain* (pp. 1-34). New York: Brunner/Mazel.

Meichenbaum, D., & Turk, D. (1987). *Facilitating treatment adherence: A practitioner's guidebook.* New York: Plenum.

Meichenbaum, D. H. (1985). *Stress inoculation training.* Elmsford, NY: Pergamon.

Meichenbaum, D. H., & Deffenbacher, J. L. (1988). Stress inoculation training. *The Counseling Psychologist, 16,* 69-90.

Melamed, B. G. (1979). Behavioral approaches to fear in dental settings. In M. Hersen, R. M. Eisler, & P. M. Miller (Eds.), *Progress in behavior modification* (Vol. 7, pp. 172-205). New York: Academic Press.

Melamed, B. G., Hawes, R. R., Helby, E., & Glick, J. (1975). Use of filmed modeling to reduce uncooperative behavior of children during dental treatment. *Journal of Dental Research, 54,* 797-801.

Melamed, B. G., & Siegel, L. J. (1975). Reduction of anxiety in children facing hospitalization and surgery by use of filmed modeling. *Journal of Consulting and Clinical Psychology, 43,* 511-521.

Melamed, B. G., Weinstein, D., Hawes, R., & Katkin-Borland, M. (1975). Reduction of fear-related dental management problems with use of filmed modeling. *Journal of the American Dental Association, 90,* 822-826.

Menzies, R. G., & Clarke, J. C. (1993). A comparison of in vivo and vicarious exposure in the treatment of childhood water phobia. *Behaviour Research and Therapy, 31,* 9-15.

Messer, S. C., & Gross, A. M. (1995). Childhood depression and family interaction: A naturalistic observation study. *Journal of Clinical Child Psychology, 24,* 77-88.

Metz, J. R. (1965). Conditioning generalized imitation in autistic children. *Journal of Experimental Child Psychology, 2,* 389-399.

Meyer, A. J., Nash, J. D., McAlister, A. L., Maccoby, N., & Farquhar, J. W. (1980). Skills training in a cardiovascular health education campaign. *Journal of Consulting and Clinical Psychology, 48,* 129-142.

MEYER, R. G. (1975). A behavioral treatment of sleepwalking associated with test anxiety. *Journal of Behavior Therapy and Experimental Psychiatry, 6,* 167-168.

MEYER, V., ROBERTSON, J., & TATLOW, A. (1975). Home treatment of an obsessive-compulsive disorder by response prevention. *Journal of Behavior Therapy and Experimental Psychiatry, 6,* 37-38.

MEYERS, A., MERCATORIS, M., & SIROTA, A. (1976). Use of covert self-instruction for the elimination of psychotic speech. *Journal of Consulting and Clinical Psychology, 44,* 480-483.

MICHAEL, J. (1975). Positive and negative reinforcement, a distinction that is no longer necessary; or, a better way to talk about bad things. *Behaviorism, 3,* 33-44.

MIDDLETON, M. B., & CARTLEDGE, G. (1995). The effects of social skills instruction and parental involvement on the aggressive behaviors of African American males. *Behavioral Medicine, 19,* 192-210.

MIKULAS, W. L., & COFFMAN, M. F. (1989). Home-based treatment of children's fear of the dark. In C. E. Schaefer & J. M. Briesmeister (Eds.), *Handbook of parent training: Parents as co-therapists for children's behavior problems* (pp. 179-202). New York: Wiley.

MIKULAS, W. L., COFFMAN, M. F., DAYTON, D., FRAYNE, C., & MAIER, P. L. (1985). Behavioral bibliotherapy and games for treating fear of the dark. *Child and Family Behavior Therapy, 7,* 1-7.

MILAN, M. A. (1987). Token economy programs in closed institutions. In E. K. Morris & C. J. Braukmann (Eds.), *Behavioral approaches to crime and delinquency: A handbook of applications, research, and concepts* (pp. 195-222). New York: Plenum.

MILGROM, P., MANCL, L., KING, B., & WEINSTEIN, P. (1995). Origins of childhood dental fear. *Behaviour Research and Therapy, 33,* 313-319.

MILLER, A. L. (1970). Treatment of a child with Gilles de la Tourette's syndrome using behavior modification techniques. *Journal of Behavior Therapy and Experimental Psychiatry, 1,* 319-321.

MILLER, H. R., & NAWAS, M. M. (1970). Control of aversive stimulus termination in systematic desensitization. *Behaviour Research and Therapy, 8,* 57-61.

MILLER, N. E. (1978). Biofeedback and visceral learning. *Annual Review of Psychology, 29,* 373-404.

MILLER, P. M. (1972). The use of behavioral contracting in the treatment of alcoholism: A case report. *Behavior Therapy, 3,* 593-596.

MILNE, D., & KENNEDY, S. (1993). The utility of consumer satisfaction data: A case study in organizational behaviour management. *Behavioural and Cognitive Psychotherapy, 21,* 281-291.

MILTENBERGER, R. G., & FUQUA, R. W. (1985). A comparison of contingent vs. non-contingent competing response practice in the treatment of nervous habits. *Journal of Behavior Therapy and Experimental Psychiatry, 16,* 195-200.

MILTENBERGER, R. G., FUQUA, R. W., & McKINLEY, T. (1985). Habit reversal with muscle tics: Replication and component analysis. *Behavior Therapy, 16,* 39-50.

MILTENBERGER, R. G., & THIESSE-DUFFY, E. (1988). Evaluation of home-based programs for teaching personal safety skills to children. *Journal of Applied Behavior Analysis, 21,* 81-87.

MINEKA, S. (1985). Animal models of anxiety-based disorders: Their usefulness and limitations. In A. Tuma & J. Maser (Eds.), *Anxiety and the anxiety disorders* (pp. 199-244). Hillsdale, NJ: Erlbaum.

MINEKA, S., & ZINBARG, R. (1991). Animal models of psychopathology. In C. E. Walker (Ed.), *Clinical psychology: Historical and research foundations* (pp. 51-86). New York: Plenum.

MINKIN, N., BRAUKMANN, C. J., MINKIN, B. L., TIMBERS, G. D., TIMBERS, B. J., FIXSEN, D. L., PHILLIPS, E. L., & WOLF, M. M. (1976). The social validation and training of conversational skills. *Journal of Applied Behavior Analysis, 9,* 127-139.

MINNEKER-HUGEL, E., UNLAND, H., & BUCHKREMER, G. (1992). Behavioral relapse prevention strategies in smoking cessation. *The International Journal of the Addictions, 27,* 627-634.

MINOR, S. W., LEONE, C., & BALDWIN, R. T. (1984). A comparison of in vivo and imaginal participant modeling. *Journal of Clinical Psychology, 40,* 717-720.

MINOR, S. W., MINOR, J. W., & WILLIAMS, P. P. (1983). A participant modeling procedure to train parents of developmentally disabled infants. *Journal of Psychology, 115,* 107-111.

MISCHEL, W. (1968). *Personality and assessment.* New York: Wiley.

MISCHEL, W. (1973). On the empirical dilemmas of psychodynamic approaches: Issues and alternatives. *Journal of Abnormal Psychology, 82,* 335-344.

MITCHELL, J. E., PYLE, R. L., HATSUKAMI, D., GOFF, G., GLOTTER, D., & HARPER, J. (1989). A 2-5 year follow-up study of patients treated for bulimia nervosa. *International Journal of Eating Disorders, 8,* 157-165.

MITCHELL, J. E., RAYMOND, N., & SPECKER, S. (1993). A review of the controlled trials of pharmacotherapy and psychotherapy in the treatment of bulimia nervosa. *International Journal of Eating Disorders, 14,* 229-247.

MONTGOMERY, R. W. (1993). *An empirical investigation of eye movement desensitization.* Unpublished dissertation, Georgia State University.

MONTI, P. M., ABRAMS, D. B., KADDEN, R. M., & COONEY, N. L. (1989). *Treating alcohol dependence.* New York: Guilford.

MONTI, P. M., ROHSENOW, D. J., RUBONIS, A. V., NIAURA, R. S., SIROTA, A. D., COLBY, S. M., GODDARD, P., & ABRAMS, D. B. (1993). Cue exposure with coping skills treatment for male alcoholics: A preliminary investigation. *Journal of Consulting and Clinical Psychology, 61,* 1011-1019.

MOORE, N. (1965). Behavior therapy in bronchial asthma: A controlled study. *Journal of Psychosomatic Research, 9,* 257-276.

MOORE, V., & CALLIAS, M. (1987). A systematic approach to teaching reading and spelling to a nine-year-old boy with severely impaired literacy skills. *Educational Psychology, 7,* 103-115.

MORGAN, W. G. (1974). The shaping game: A teaching technique. *Behavior Therapy, 5,* 271-272.

MORGANSTERN, K. P. (1973). Implosive therapy and flooding procedures: A critical review. *Psychological Bulletin, 79,* 318-334.

MORGANSTERN, K. P. (1976). Behavioral interviewing: The initial stages of assessment. In M. Hersen & A. S. Bellack (Eds.), *Behavioral assessment: A practical approach* (pp. 51-76). Oxford: Pergamon.

MORIN, C. M. (1993). *Insomnia: Psychological assessment and management.* New York: Guilford.

MORIN, C. M., & AZRIN, N. H. (1987). Stimulus control and imagery training in treating sleep-maintenance insomnia. *Journal of Consulting and Clinical Psychology, 55*, 260-262.

MORIN, C. M., & AZRIN, N. H. (1988). Behavioral and cognitive treatments of geriatric insomnia. *Journal of Consulting and Clinical Psychology, 56*, 748-753.

MORIN, C. M., KOWATCH, R. A., BARRY, T., & WALTON, E. (1993). Cognitive-behavior therapy for late-life insomnia. *Journal of Consulting and Clinical Psychology, 61*, 137-146.

MORIN, C. M., STONE, J., McDONALD, K., & JONES, S. (1994). Psychological management of insomnia: A clinical replication series with 100 patients. *Behavior Therapy, 25*, 291-309.

MORRIS, C. W., & COHEN, R. (1982). Cognitive considerations in cognitive behavior modification. *School Psychological Review, 11*, 14-20.

MORRIS, R. J., & KRATOCHWILL, T. R. (1983). *Treating children's fears and phobias.* Elmsford, NY: Pergamon.

MORRISON, R. L. (1988). Structured interviews and rating scales. In A. S. Bellack & M. Hersen (Eds.), *Behavioral assessment: A practical handbook* (3rd ed., pp. 252-277). Elmsford, NY: Pergamon.

MORROW, G. R. (1986). Effect of the cognitive hierarchy in the systematic desensitization treatment of anticipatory nausea in cancer patients: A component comparison with relaxation only, counseling, and no treatment. *Cognitive Therapy and Research, 10*, 421-446.

MORROW, G. R., ASBURY, R., HAMMON, S., DOBKIN, P., CARUSO, L., PANDYA, K., & ROSENTHAL, S. (1992). Comparing the effectiveness of behavioral treatment for chemotherapy-induced nausea and vomiting when administered by oncologists, oncology nurses, and clinical psychologists. *Health Psychology, 11*, 250-256.

MORROW, G. R., & MORRELL, C. (1982). Behavioral treatment for the anticipatory nausea and vomiting induced by cancer chemotherapy. *New England Journal of Medicine, 307*, 1476-1480.

MOSES, A. N., & HOLLANDSWORTH, J. G. (1985). Relative effectiveness of education alone versus stress inoculation training in treatment of dental phobia. *Behavior Therapy, 16*, 531-537.

MOWRER, O. H. (1960). *Learning theory and the symbolic processes.* New York: Wiley.

MOWRER, O. H., & MOWRER, W. M. (1938). Enuresis: A method for its study and treatment. *American Journal of Orthopsychiatry, 8*, 436-447.

MUDFORD, O. C. (1995). An intrusive and restrictive alternative to contingent shock. *Behavioral Interventions, 10*, 87-99.

MUNBY, M., & JOHNSTON, D. W. (1980). Agoraphobia: The long-term follow-up of behavioural treatment. *British Journal of Psychiatry, 137*, 418-427.

MURTAGH, D. R. R., & GREENWOOD, K. M. (1995). Identifying effective psychological treatments for insomnia: A meta-analysis. *Journal of Consulting and Clinical Psychology, 63*, 79-89.

MYLOTT, K. (1994). Twelve irrational ideas that drive gay men and women crazy. *Journal of Rational-Emotive and Cognitive-Behavior Therapy, 12*, 61-71.

NANGLE, D. W., CARR-NANGLE, R. E., & HANSEN, D. J. (1994). Enhancing generalization of a contingency-management intervention through the use of family problem-solving training: Evaluation with a severely conduct-disordered adolescent. *Child and Family Behavior Therapy, 15*, 65-76.

NATHAN, P. E. (1976). Alcoholism. In H. Leitenberg (Ed.), *Handbook of behavior modification and behavior therapy* (pp. 3-44). Englewood Cliffs, NJ: Prentice-Hall.

NATIONAL INSTITUTE FOR OCCUPATIONAL SAFETY AND HEALTH. (1983). *Criteria for a recommended standard: Occupational exposure to styrene* (DHHS Publication No. NIOSH 83-119). Washington, DC: U.S. Government Printing Office.

NAWAS, M. M., WELSCH, W. V., & FISHMAN, S. T. (1970). The comparative effectiveness of pairing aversive imagery with relaxation, neutral tasks and muscular tension in reducing snake phobia. *Behaviour Research and Therapy, 6*, 63-68.

NAZARIAN, L. F., MECHABER, J., CHARNEY, E., & COULTER, M. P. (1974). Effects of a mailed appointment reminder on appointment keeping. *Pediatrics, 5*, 49-52.

NEEF, N. A., BILL-HARVEY, D., SHADE, D., IEZZI, M., & deLORENZO, T. (1995). Exercise participation with videotaped modeling: Effects on balance and gait in elderly residents of care facilities. *Behavior Therapy, 26*, 135-151.

NEISSER, U. (1976). *Cognition and reality.* San Francisco: W. H. Freeman.

NEISWORTH, J. T., & MOORE, F. (1972). Operant treatment of asthmatic responding with the parent as therapist. *Behavior Therapy, 3*, 95-99.

NELSON, W. M., & POLITANO, P. M. (1993). The goal is to say "goodbye" and have the treatment effects generalize and maintain: A cognitive-behavioral view of termination. *Journal of Cognitive Psychotherapy, 7*, 251-263.

NEMETZ, G. H., CRAIG, K. D., & REITH, G. (1978). Treatment of female sexual dysfunction through symbolic modeling. *Journal of Consulting and Clinical Psychology, 46*, 62-73.

NESBITT, E. B. (1973). An escalator phobia overcome in one session of flooding *in vivo. Journal of Behavior Therapy and Experimental Psychiatry, 4*, 405-406.

NEVO, O., & SHAPIRA, J. (1988). The use of humor by pediatric dentists. *Journal of Children in Contemporary Society, 20*, 171-178.

NEWMAN, C. F., & HAAGA, D. A. F. (1995). Cognitive skills training. In W. O'Donohue & L. Krasner (Eds.), *Handbook of psychological skills training: Clinical techniques and applications* (pp. 119-143). Boston: Allyn and Bacon.

NEWMAN, M. G., HOFMANN, S. G., TRABERT, W., ROTH, W. T., & TAYLOR, C. B. (1994). Does behavioral treatment of social phobia lead to cognitive changes? *Behavior Therapy, 25*, 503-517.

NEWMAN, M. G., KENARDY, J., HERMAN, S., & TAYLOR, C. B. (1996). The use of hand-held computers as an adjunct to cognitive-behavior therapy. *Computers in Human Behavior, 12*, 135-143.

NEWMAN, M. G., KENARDY, J., HERMAN, S., & TAYLOR, C. B. (in press). Comparison of palmtop computer assisted brief cognitive behavioral treatment to cognitive behavioral treatment for panic disorder. *Journal of Consulting and Clinical Psychology.*

NEWTON, T., HARTLEY, P., & STURMEY, P. (1993). Treatment evaluation for eating disorders by clients with eating disorders. *Behavioural and Cognitive Psychotherapy, 21*, 371-374.

New tool: "Reinforcement" for good work. (1971, December 18). *Business Week*, 76-77.

Neziroglu, F. A., & Yaryura-Tobias, J. A. (1993). Exposure, response prevention, and cognitive therapy in the treatment of body dysmorphic disorder. *Behavior Therapy, 24,* 431-438.

Nezu, A. (1996). The main thing. *the Behavior Therapist, 19,* 36-39.

Nezu, A. M., & D'Zurilla, T. J. (1989). Social problem solving and negative affective conditions. In P. C. Kendall & D. Watson (Eds.), *Anxiety and depression: Distinctive and overlapping features* (pp. 285-315). San Diego: Academic Press.

Nezu, A. M., Nezu, C. M., D'Zurilla, T. J., & Rothenberg, J. L. (1996). Problem-solving therapy. In Kantor, J. S. (Ed.), *Clinical depression during addiction recovery: Processes, diagnosis, and treatment* (pp. 187-219). New York: Marcel Dekker.

Nezu, A. M., Nezu, C. M., & Perri, M. G. (1989). *Problem-solving therapy for depression: Theory, research, and clinical guidelines.* New York: Wiley.

Nezu, C. M., Nezu, A. M., & Houts, P. S. (1993). Multiple applications of problem-solving principles in clinical practice. In K. T. Kuehlwein & H. Rosen (Eds.), *Cognitive therapies in action: Evolving innovative practice* (pp. 353-378). San Francisco: Jossey-Bass.

Nicassio, P. M., Boylan, M. B., & McCabe, T. G. (1982). Progressive relaxation, EMG biofeedback and biofeedback placebo in the treatment of sleep-onset insomnia. *British Journal of Medical Psychology, 55,* 159-166.

Nicholson, N. L., & Blanchard, E. B. (1993). A controlled evaluation of behavioral treatment of chronic headache in the elderly. *Behavior Therapy, 24,* 395-408.

Nietzel, M. T., Bernstein, D. A., & Russell, R. L. (1988). Assessment of anxiety and fear. In A. S. Bellack & M. Hersen (Eds.), *Behavioral assessment: A practical handbook* (3rd ed., pp. 280-312). Elmsford, NY: Pergamon.

Nocella, J., & Kaplan, R. (1982). Training children to cope with dental treatment. *Journal of Pediatric Psychology, 7,* 175-178.

Nomellini, S., & Katz, R. C. (1983). Effects of anger control training on abusive parents. *Cognitive Therapy and Research, 7,* 57-68.

Norcross, J. C., & Goldfried, M. R. (Eds.). (1992). *Handbook of psychotherapy integration.* New York: Basic Books.

Notifiable diseases. (1983). *Center for Disease Control Morbidity and Mortality Weekly Report, 31,* 702-705.

Novaco, R. (1977a). A stress-inoculation approach to anger management in the training of law enforcement officers. *American Journal of Community Psychology, 5,* 327-346.

Novaco, R. (1977b). Stress inoculation: A cognitive therapy for anger and its application to a case of depression. *Journal of Consulting and Clinical Psychology, 45,* 600-608.

Novaco, R. W. (1975). *Anger control: The development and evaluation of an experimental treatment.* Lexington, MA: Lexington Books.

Novick, J. (1966). Symptomatic treatment of acquired and persistent enuresis. *Journal of Abnormal Psychology, 71,* 363-368.

Nunes, D. L., Murphy, R. J., & Ruprecht, M. L. (1977). Reducing self-injurious behavior of severely retarded individuals through withdrawal-of-reinforcement procedures. *Behavior Modification, 1,* 499-516.

Nunn, R. G., Newton, K. S., & Faucher, P. (1992). 2.5 year follow-up of weight and body mass index values in the Weight Control for Life Program: A descriptive analysis. *Addictive Behaviors, 17,* 579-585.

O'Banion, D. R., & Whaley, D. L. (1981). *Behavior contracting: Arranging contingencies of reinforcement.* New York: Springer.

O'Connor, R. D. (1969). Modification of social withdrawal through symbolic modeling. *Journal of Applied Behavior Analysis, 2,* 15-22.

O'Donohue, W., & Krasner, L. (Eds.). (1995a). *Handbook of psychological skills training: Clinical techniques and applications.* Boston: Allyn and Bacon.

O'Donohue, W., & Krasner, L. (1995b). Psychological skills training. In W. O'Donohue & L. Krasner (Eds.), *Handbook of psychological skills training: Clinical techniques and applications* (pp. 1-19). Boston: Allyn and Bacon.

O'Donohue, W., & Noll, J. (1995). Problem-solving skills. In W. O'Donohue & L. Krasner (Eds.), *Handbook of psychological skills training: Clinical techniques and applications* (pp. 144-160). Boston: Allyn and Bacon.

O'Donohue, W. T., Fisher, J. E., & Krasner, L. (1986). Behavior therapy and the elderly: A conceptual and ethical analysis. *International Journal of Aging and Human Development, 23,* 1-15.

O'Farrell, T. J. (1994). Marital therapy and spouse-involved treatment with alcoholic patients. *Behavior Therapy, 25,* 391-406.

O'Farrell, T. J., Cutter, H. S. G., Choquette, K. A., Floyd, F. J., & Bayog, R. D. (1992). Behavioral marital therapy for male alcoholics: Marital and drinking adjustment during the two years after treatment. *Behavior Therapy, 23,* 529-549.

Oldenburg, D. (1994, April 12). In the eye of the beholder. *The Washington Post,* p. E5.

O'Leary, K. D. (1972). The assessment of psychopathology in children. In H. C. Quay & J. S. Werry (Eds.), *Psychopathological disorders of childhood* (pp. 234-272). New York: Wiley.

O'Leary, K. D., & Rathus, J. H. (1993). Clients' perceptions of therapeutic helpfulness in cognitive and marital therapy for depression. *Cognitive Therapy and Research, 17,* 225-233.

O'Leary, K. D., & Turkewitz, H. (1978). Marital therapy from a behavioral perspective. In T. J. Paolino & B. S. McCrady (Eds.), *Marriage and marital therapy: Psychoanalytic, behavioral and systems theory perspectives* (pp. 240-297). New York: Brunner/Mazel.

O'Leary, K. D., & Wilson, G. T. (1975). *Behavior therapy: Application and outcome.* Englewood Cliffs, NJ: Prentice-Hall.

Ollendick, T. H. (1979). Fear reduction techniques with children. In M. Hersen, R. M. Eisler, & P. M. Miller (Eds.), *Progress in behavior modification* (Vol. 8, pp. 127-168). New York: Academic Press.

Ollendick, T. H. (1983). Reliability and validity of the Revised Fear Survey Schedule for Children (FSSC-R). *Behaviour Research and Therapy, 21,* 685-692.

Ollendick, T. H., & Cerny, J. A. (1981). *Clinical behavior therapy with children.* New York: Plenum.

Ollendick, T. H., & Matson, J. L. (1978). Overcorrection: An overview. *Behavior Therapy, 9,* 830-842.

Olmsted, M. P., Davis, R., Rockert, W., Irvine, M. J., Eagle, M., & Garner, D. M. (1991). Efficacy of a brief group psychoeducational intervention for bulimia nervosa. *Behaviour Research and Therapy, 29,* 71-83.

OLSON, R. L., & ROBERTS, M. W. (1987). Alternative treatments for sibling aggression. *Behavior Therapy, 18,* 243-250.

OMIZO, M. M., CUBBERLY, W. E., & OMIZO, S. A. (1985). The effects of rational-emotive education groups on self-concept and locus of control among learning disabled children. *Exceptional Child, 32,* 13-19.

OMIZO, M. M., LO, F. G., & WILLIAMS, E. (1986). Rational-emotive education, self-concept, and locus of control among learning disabled students. *Journal of Humanistic Education and Development, 25,* 58-69.

O'NEILL, R. E., HORNER, R. H., ALBIN, R. W., STOREY, K., & SPRAGUE, J. R. (1990). *Functional analysis of problem behavior: A practical assessment guide.* Pacific Grove, CA: Brooks/Cole.

OPPEL, W. C., HARPER, P. A., & RIDER, R. V. (1968). Social, psychological and neurological factors associated with nocturnal enuresis. *Pediatrics, 42,* 627-641.

Oregon's bottle bill: The 1977 report. (1977). State of Oregon Department of Environmental Quality.

OSBORN, E. L. (1986). Effects of participant modeling and desensitization on childhood warm water phobia. *Journal of Behavior Therapy and Experimental Psychiatry, 17,* 117-119.

OSMAN, A., BARRIOS, F. X., OSMAN, J. R., SCHNEKLOTH, R., & TROUTMAN, J. A. (1994). The pain anxiety symptoms scale: Psychometric properties in a community sample. *Journal of Behavioral Medicine, 17,* 511-522.

ÖST, L., WESTLING, B. E., & HELLSTRÖM, K. (1993). Applied relaxation, exposure in vivo and cognitive methods in the treatment of panic disorder with agoraphobia. *Behaviour Research and Therapy, 31,* 383-394.

ÖST, L. G. (1989). One-session treatment for specific phobias. *Behaviour Research and Therapy, 27,* 1-7.

OSTERWEIS, M., MECHANIC, D., & KLEINMAN, A. (1987). *Pain and disability: Clinical, behavioral, and public policy perspectives.* New York: National Academy Press.

OSTROFF, R. B., & BOYD, J. H. (1987). Television and suicide: Comment. *New England Journal of Medicine, 316,* 876-877.

OTTO, M. W., & GOULD, R. A. (1995). Maximizing treatment-outcome for panic disorder: Cognitive-behavioral strategies. In M. H. Pollack, M. W. Otto, & J. F. Rosenbaum (Eds.), *Challenges in psychiatric treatment: Pharmacological and psychosocial strategies* (pp. 113-140). New York: Guilford.

OTTO, M. W., GOULD, R. A., & POLLACK, M. H. (1994). Cognitive-behavioral treatment of panic disorder: Considerations for the treatment of patients over the long term. *Psychiatric Annals, 24,* 307-315.

OTTO, M. W., PAVA, J. A., & SPRICH-BUCKMINSTER, S. (1995). Treatment of major depression: Applications and efficacy of cognitive-behavior therapy. In M. H. Pollack, M. W. Otto, & J. F. Rosenbaum (Eds.), *Challenges in psychiatric treatment: Pharmacological and psychosocial strategies* (pp. 31-52). New York: Guilford.

OTTO, M. W., PENAVA, S. J., POLLACK, R. A., & SMOLLER, J. W. (1995). Cognitive-behavioral and pharmacologic perspectives on the treatment of post-traumatic stress disorder. In M. H. Pollack, M. W. Otto, & J. F. Rosenbaum (Eds.), *Challenges in psychiatric treatment: Pharmacological and psychosocial strategies* (pp. 219-260). New York: Guilford.

OTTO, M. W., & POLLACK, M. H. (1994). Treatment strategies for panic disorder: A debate. *Harvard Review of Psychiatry, 2,* 166-170.

OTTO, M. W., POLLACK, M. H., MELTZER-BRODY, S., & ROSENBAUM, J. F. (1992). Cognitive-behavioral therapy for benzodiazepine discontinuation in panic disorder patients. *Psychopharmacology Bulletin, 28,* 123-130.

OTTO, M. W., POLLACK, M. H., SACHS, G. S., REITER, S. R., MELTZER-BRODY, S., & ROSENBAUM, J. F. (1993). Discontinuation of benzodiazepine treatment: Efficacy of cognitive-behavioral therapy for patients with panic disorder. *American Journal of Psychiatry, 150,* 1485-1490.

OVERHOSER, J. C., & FINE, M. A. (1994). Cognitive-behavioral treatment of excessive interpersonal dependency: A four-stage psychotherapy model. *Journal of Cognitive Psychotherapy: An International Quarterly, 8,* 55-70.

OWUSU-BEMPAH, J. P., & HOWITT, D. (1985). The effects of self-modeling on cigarette smoking behavior. *Current Psychological Research and Reviews, 4,* 133-142.

OZER, E. M., & BANDURA, A. (1990). Mechanisms governing empowerment effects: A self-efficacy analysis. *Journal of Personality and Social Psychology, 58,* 472-486.

PACE, G. M., IVANCIC, M. T., EDWARDS, J. L., IWATA, B. A., & PAGE, T. J. (1985). Assessment of stimulus preference and reinforcer value with profoundly retarded individuals. *Journal of Applied Behavior Analysis, 18,* 249-255.

PACE, T. M., & DIXON, D. N. (1993). Changes in depressive self-schemata and depressive symptoms following cognitive therapy. *Journal of Counseling Psychology, 40,* 288-294.

PAGE, A. C., & CRINO, R. D. (1993). Eye-movement desensitisation: A simple treatment for post-traumatic stress disorder? *Australian and New Zealand Journal of Psychiatry, 27,* 288-293.

PALLAK, M., CUMMINGS, N., DORKEN, H., & HENKE, C. (1995). Effect of mental health treatment on medical costs. *Mind/Body Medicine, 1,* 7-12.

PALMER, M. H., LLOYD, M. E., & LLOYD, K. E. (1978). An experimental analysis of electricity conservation procedures. *Journal of Applied Behavior Analysis, 10,* 665-672.

PAQUIN, M. J. (1977). The treatment of a nail-biting compulsion by covert sensitization in a poorly motivated client. *Journal of Behavior Therapy and Experimental Psychiatry, 8,* 181-183.

PARADIS, C. M., FRIEDMAN, S., HATCH, M. L., & ACKERMAN, R. (1996). Cognitive behavioral treatment of anxiety disorders in Orthodox Jews. *Cognitive and Behavioral Practice, 3,* 271-288.

PARK, W. D., & WILLIAMS, G. T. (1986). Encouraging elementary school children to refer themselves for counseling. *Elementary School Guidance and Counseling, 21,* 8-14.

PASCHALIS, A. P., KIMMEL, H. D., & KIMMEL, E. (1972). Further study of diurnal instrumental conditioning in the treatment of enuresis nocturna. *Journal of Behavior Therapy and Experimental Psychiatry, 3,* 253-256.

PATEL, C. (1977). Biofeedback-aided relaxation and meditation in the management of hypertension. *Biofeedback and Self-Regulation, 2,* 1-41.

PATTERSON, G. R. (1974). Interventions for boys with conduct problems: Multiple settings, treatments, and criteria. *Journal of Consulting and Clinical Psychology, 42,* 471-481.

PATTERSON, G. R. (1975). *Families: Applications of social learning to family life.* Champaign, IL: Research Press.

PATTERSON, G. R. (1982). *Coercive family processes.* Eugene, OR: Castalia Press.

PATTERSON, G. R., CHAMBERLAIN, P., & REID, J. B. (1982). A comparative evaluation of a parent-training program. *Behavior Therapy, 13,* 638-650.

PATTERSON, G. R., & FORGATCH, M. S. (1985). Therapist behavior as a determinant for client noncompliance: A paradox for the behavior modifier. *Journal of Consulting and Clinical Psychology, 53,* 846-851.

PATTERSON, G. R., & GULLION, M. E. (1976). *Living with children: New methods for parents and teachers.* Champaign, IL: Research Press.

PATTERSON, G. R., RAY, R. S., SHAW, D. A., & COBB, T. A. (1969). *A manual for coding of family interactions.* New York: Microfiche Publications.

PATTERSON, G. R., & REID, J. B. (1970). Reciprocity and coercion: Two facets of social systems. In C. Neuringer & J. L. Michael (Eds.), *Behavior modification in clinical psychology* (pp. 133-177). New York: Appleton-Century-Crofts.

PATTERSON, G. R., & REID, J. B. (1973). Interventions for families of aggressive boys: A replication study. *Behaviour Research and Therapy, 11,* 383-394.

PATTERSON, G. R., REID, J. B., & DISHION, T. J. (1992). *Antisocial boys.* Eugene, OR: Castalia Press.

PAUL, G. L. (1966). *Insight vs. desensitization in psychotherapy.* Stanford, CA: Stanford University Press.

PAUL, G. L. (1967). Insight vs. desensitization in psychotherapy two years after termination. *Journal of Consulting Psychology, 31,* 333-348.

PAUL, G. L. (1969a). Behavior modification research: Design and tactics. In C. M. Franks (Ed.), *Behavior therapy: Appraisal and status* (pp. 29-62). New York: McGraw-Hill.

PAUL, G. L. (1969b). Outcome of systematic desensitization: II. Controlled investigations of individual treatment, technique variations, and current status. In C. M. Franks (Ed.), *Behavior therapy: Appraisal and status* (pp. 105-159). New York: McGraw-Hill.

PAUL, G. L., & LENTZ, R. J. (1977). *Psychosocial treatment of chronic mental patients: Milieu vs. social learning programs.* Cambridge, MA: Harvard University Press.

PAUL, G. L., & SHANNON, D. T. (1966). Treatment of anxiety through systematic desensitization in therapy groups. *Journal of Abnormal Psychology, 71,* 124-135.

PAVLOV, I. P. (1927). *Conditioned reflexes.* New York: Liveright.

PEDALINO, E., & GAMBOA, V. U. (1974). Behavior modification and absenteeism: Intervention in one industrial setting. *Journal of Applied Psychology, 59,* 694-698.

PEED, S., ROBERTS, M., & FOREHAND, R. (1977). Evaluation of the effectiveness of a standardized parent training program in altering the interaction of mothers and their noncompliant children. *Behavior Modification, 1,* 323-350.

PENISTON, E. (1975). Reducing problem behaviors in the severely and profoundly retarded. *Journal of Behavior Therapy and Experimental Psychiatry, 6,* 295-299.

PENZIEN, D. B., & HOLROYD, K. A. (1994). Psychosocial interventions in the management of recurrent headache disorders 2: Description of treatment techniques. *Behavioral Medicine, 20,* 64-73.

PERRI, M. G., NEZU, A. M., & VIEGNER, B. J. (1992). *Improving the long-term management of obesity: Theory, research, and clinical guidelines.* New York: Wiley.

PERRIS, C. (1989). *Cognitive therapy with schizophrenic patients.* New York: Guilford.

PERSONS, J. (1994). Is behavior therapy boring? *the Behavior Therapist, 17,* 190.

PETERSON, A. L., & AZRIN, N. H. (1990, November). *A comparison of behavioral procedures for the treatment of Tourette syndrome.* Paper presented at the meeting of the Association for Advancement of Behavior Therapy, San Francisco.

PETERSON, A. L., & AZRIN, N. H. (1993). Behavioral and pharmacological treatments for Tourette syndrome: A review. *Applied and Preventive Psychology, 2,* 231-242.

PETERSON, A. L., CAMPISE, R. L., & AZRIN, N. H. (1994). Behavioral and pharmacological treatments for tic and habit disorders: A review. *Developmental and Behavioral Pediatrics, 15,* 430-441.

PETERSON, A. L., DIXON, D. C., TALCOTT, W., & KELLEHER, W. J. (1993). Habit reversal treatment of temporomandibular disorders: A pilot investigation. *Journal of Behavior Therapy and Experimental Psychiatry, 24,* 49-55.

PETERSON, D. R. (1968). *The clinical study of social behavior.* New York: Appleton-Century-Crofts.

PETERSON, L. (1984). Teaching home safety and survival skills to latch key children: A comparison of two manuals and methods. *Journal of Applied Behavior Analysis, 17,* 279-293.

PETERSON, L. (1989). Latchkey children's preparation for self-care: Overestimated, underrehearsed, and unsafe. *Journal of Clinical Child Psychology, 18,* 36-43.

PETERSON, L. (1992). Behavior Therapy—Not just "behavior therapy." *the Behavior Therapist, 15,* 87.

PETERSON, L., BARTELSTONE, J., KERN, T., & GILLIES, R. (1995). Parents' socialization of children's injury prevention: Description and some initial parameters. *Child Development, 66,* 224-235.

PETERSON, L., & BELL-DOLAN, D. (1995). Treatment outcome research in child psychology: Realistic coping with the "Ten Commandments of Methodology." *Journal of Clinical Child Psychology, 24,* 149-162.

PETERSON, L., & RIDLEY-JOHNSON, R. (1980). Pediatric hospital response to survey on prehospital preparation for children. *Journal of Pediatric Psychology, 5,* 1-7.

PETERSON, L., SCHULTHEIS, K., RIDLEY-JOHNSON, R., MILLER, D. J., & TRACY, K. (1984). Comparison of three modeling procedures on the presurgical and postsurgical reactions of children. *Behavior Therapy, 15,* 197-203.

PETERSON, L., & SHIGETOMI, C. (1981). The use of coping techniques to minimize anxiety in hospitalized children. *Behavior Therapy, 12,* 1-14.

PETERSON, P. L., & LOWE, J. B. (1992). Preventing fetal alcohol exposure: A cognitive behavioral approach. *The International Journal of the Addictions, 27,* 613-626.

PETRONKO, M. R., HARRIS, S. L., & KORMANN, R. J. (1994). Community-based behavioral training approaches for people with mental retardation and mental illness. *Journal of Consulting and Clinical Psychology, 62,* 49-54.

PHEIFER, W., & HOUSEMAN, C. (1988). Bereavement and AIDS: A framework for intervention. *Journal of Psychosocial Nursing, 26,* 21-26.

PHILLIPS, D., FISCHER, S. C., & SINGH, R. (1977). A children's reinforcement survey schedule. *Journal of Behavior Therapy and Experimental Psychiatry, 8,* 131-134.

PHILLIPS, E. L. (1968). Achievement Place: Token reinforcement procedures in a home-style rehabilitation setting for "pre-delinquent" boys. *Journal of Applied Behavior Analysis, 1,* 213-223.

PHILLIPS, E. L., PHILLIPS, E. A., FIXSEN, D. L., & WOLF, M. M. (1971). Achievement Place: Modification of the behaviors of pre-delinquent boys within a token economy. *Journal of Applied Behavior Analysis, 4,* 45-59.

PHILLIPS, E. L., PHILLIPS, E. A., WOLF, M. M., & FIXSEN, D. L. (1973). Achievement Place: Development of the elected manager system. *Journal of Applied Behavior Analysis, 6,* 541-561.

PICKERING, T. G. (1982). Nonpharmacologic methods of treatment of hypertension: Promising but unproved. *Cardiovascular Reviews and Reports, 3,* 82-88.

PIERCE, K. L., & SCHREIBMAN, L. (1994). Teaching daily living skills to children with autism in unsupervised settings through pictorial self-management. *Journal of Applied Behavior Analysis, 27,* 471-481.

PIERCE, T. W. (1995). Skills training in stress management. In W. O'Donohue & L. Krasner (Eds.), *Handbook of psychological skills training: Clinical techniques and applications* (pp. 306-319). Boston: Allyn and Bacon.

PIGOTT, H. E., & GONZALES, F. P. (1987). The efficacy of videotape self-modeling to treat an electively mute child. *Journal of Clinical Child Psychology, 16,* 106-110.

PIGOTT, H. E., & HEGGIE, D. L. (1986). Interpreting the conflicting results of individual versus group contingencies on classrooms: The targeted behavior as a mediating variable. *Child and Family Behavior Therapy, 7,* 1-15.

PINKERTON, S. S., HUGHES, H., & WENRICH, W. W. (1982). *Behavioral medicine: Clinical applications.* New York: Wiley.

PINKSTON, E. M., LINSK, N. L., & YOUNG, R. N. (1988). Home-based behavioral family therapy of the impaired elderly. *Behavior Therapy, 19,* 331-344.

PITMAN, R. K., ALTMAN, B., GREENWALD, E., LONGPRE, R. E., MACKLIN, M. L., POIRE, R. E., & STEKETEE, G. S. (1991). Psychiatric complications during flooding therapy for posttraumatic stress disorder. *Journal of Clinical Psychiatry, 52,* 17-20.

PITMAN, R. K., ORR, S. P., ALTMAN, B., LONGPRE, R. E., POIRE, R. E., & LASKO, N. B. (1993, May). *A controlled study of EMDR treatment for post-traumatic stress disorder.* Paper presented at the 146th annual meeting of the American Psychiatric Association, Washington, DC.

PITTS, C. E. (1976). Behavior modification—1787. *Journal of Applied Behavior Analysis, 9,* 146.

POCHE, C., BROUWER, R., & SWEARINGEN, M. (1981). Teaching self-protection to young children. *Journal of Applied Behavior Analysis, 14,* 169-176.

POCHE, C., YODER, P., & MILTENBERGER, R. (1988). Teaching self-protection to children using television techniques. *Journal of Applied Behavior Analysis, 21,* 253-261.

POLING, A., & RYAN, C. (1982). Differential-reinforcement-of-other-behavior schedules. *Behavior Modification, 6,* 3-21.

POLLACK, M. H., OTTO, M. W., KASPI, S. P., HAMMERNESS, P. G., & ROSENBAUM, J. F. (1994). Cognitive behavior therapy for treatment-refractory panic disorder. *Journal of Clinical Psychiatry, 55,* 200-205.

POLLACK, M. J., FLEMING, R. K., & SULZER-AZAROFF, B. (1994). Enhancing professional performance through organizational change. *Behavioral Interventions, 9,* 27-42.

POOLE, A. D., SANSON-FISHER, R. W., GERMAN, G. A., & HARKER, J. (1980). The rapid-smoking technique: Some physiological effects. *Behaviour Research and Therapy, 18,* 581-586.

POSER, E., & KING, M. (1975). Strategies for the prevention of maladaptive fear responses. *Canadian Journal of Behavioural Science, 7,* 279-294.

POSER, E. G. (1970). Toward a theory of behavioral prophylaxis. *Journal of Behavior Therapy and Experimental Psychiatry, 1,* 39-43.

POSER, E. G., & KING, M. C. (1976). Primary prevention of fear: An experimental approach. In I. G. Sarason & C. D. Spielberger (Eds.), *Stress and anxiety, III* (pp. 325-344). New York: Hemisphere.

POWELL, E. (1996). *Sex on your terms.* Needham Heights, MA: Allyn and Bacon.

POWERS, L. E., SINGER, G. H. S., STEVENS, T., & SOWERS, J. (1992). Behavioral parent training in home and community generalization settings. *Education and Training in Mental Retardation, 27,* 13-27.

POWERS, R. B., OSBORNE, J. G., & ANDERSON, E. G. (1973). Positive reinforcement of litter removal in the natural environment. *Journal of Applied Behavior Analysis, 6,* 579-586.

POWERS, S. W., & ROBERTS, M. W. (1995). Simulation training with parents of oppositional children: Preliminary findings. *Journal of Clinical Child Psychology, 24,* 89-97.

PRATT, J., & JONES, T. (1995). Noncompliance with therapy: An ongoing problem in treating hypertension. *Primary Cardiology, 21,* 34-38.

PREMACK, D. (1965). Reinforcement theory. In D. Levine (Ed.), *Nebraska symposium on motivation* (pp. 123-180). Lincoln: University of Nebraska Press.

PRINCE, D., & DOWRICK, P. W. (1984, November). *Self-modeling in the treatment of depression: Implications for video in behavior therapy.* Paper presented at the meeting of the Association for Advancement of Behavior Therapy, Philadelphia.

PRINCE, H. T., II. (1975). *The effects of covert behavioral rehearsal, modeling, and vicarious consequences in assertive training.* Unpublished doctoral dissertation, University of Texas at Austin.

PRITCHARD, A., & APPLETON, P. (1988). Management of sleep problems in preschool children. *Early Child Development and Care, 34,* 227-240.

PROCHASKA, J., SMITH, N., MARZILLI, R., COLBY, J., & DONOVAN, W. (1974). Remote-control aversive stimulation in the treatment of head-banging in a retarded child. *Journal of Behavior Therapy and Experimental Psychiatry, 5,* 285-289.

PROPST, L. R., OSTROM, R., WATKINS, P., DEAN, T., & MASHBURN, D. (1992). Comparative efficacy of religious and nonreligious cognitive-behavioral therapy for the treatment of clinical depression in religious individuals. *Journal of Consulting and Clinical Psychology, 60,* 94-103.

PUDER, R., LACKS, P., BERTELSON, A. D., & STORANDT, M. (1983). Short-term stimulus control treatment of insomnia in older adults. *Behavior Therapy, 14,* 424-429.

PUK, G. (1991). Treating traumatic memories: A case report on the eye movement desensitization procedure. *Journal of Behavior Therapy and Experimental Psychiatry, 22,* 149-151.

PUMROY, D. K., & PUMROY, S. S. (1965). Systematic observation and reinforcement technique in toilet training. *Psychological Reports, 16,* 467-471.

PURCELL, D. W., CAMPOS, P. E., & PERILLA, J. L. (1996). Therapy with lesbians and gay men: A cognitive behavioral perspective. *Cognitive and Behavioral Practice, 3,* 391-415.

RABAVILAS, A. D., BOULOUGOURIS, J. C., & STEFANIS, C. (1976). Duration of flooding sessions in the treatment of obsessive-compulsive patients. *Behaviour Research and Therapy, 14,* 349-355.

RACHMAN, S. (1959). The treatment of anxiety and phobic reactions by systematic desensitization psychotherapy. *Journal of Abnormal and Social Psychology, 58,* 259-263.

RACHMAN, S. (1967). Systematic desensitization. *Psychological Bulletin, 67,* 93-103.

RACHMAN, S. (1972). Clinical application of observational learning, imitation and modeling. *Behavior Therapy, 3,* 379-397.

RACHMAN, S. (1990). *Fear and courage* (2nd ed.). New York: W. H. Freeman.

RACHMAN, S., & EYSENCK, H. J. (1966). Reply to a "critique and reformulation" of behavior therapy. *Psychological Bulletin, 65,* 165-169.

RACHMAN, S., & HODGSON, R. (1980). *Obsessions and compulsions.* Englewood Cliffs, NJ: Prentice-Hall.

RACHMAN, S., & TEASDALE, J. (1969). *Aversion therapy and behaviour disorders: An analysis.* Coral Gables, FL: University of Miami Press.

RACHMAN, S. J., & WILSON, G. T. (1980). *The effects of psychological therapy* (2nd enlarged ed.). Oxford: Pergamon.

RAINS, J. C. (1995). Treatment of obstructive sleep apnea in pediatric patients: Behavioral intervention for compliance with nasal continuous positive airway pressure. *Clinical Pediatrics, 34,* 535-541.

RAMIREZ, S. Z., & KRATOCHWILL, T. R. (1990). Development of the Fear Survey Schedule for Children With and Without Mental Retardation. *Behavioral Assessment, 12,* 457-470.

RAO, N., MOELY, B. E., & LOCKMAN, J. J. (1987). Increasing social participation in preschool social isolates. *Journal of Clinical Child Psychology, 16,* 178-183.

RASING, E. J., CONINX, F., DUKER, P. C., & VAN DEN HURK, A. J. (1994). Acquisition and generalization of social behavior in language-disabled deaf adolescents. *Behavior Modification, 18,* 411-442.

RATHUS, S. A. (1973). A 30-item schedule for assessing assertive behavior. *Behavior Therapy, 4,* 398-406.

RAUE, P. J., CASTONGUAY, L. G., & GOLDFRIED, M. R. (1993). The working alliance: A comparison of two therapies. *Psychotherapy Research, 3,* 197-207.

RAUE, P. J., & GOLDFRIED, M. R. (1994). The therapeutic alliance in cognitive-behavior therapy. In A. O. Horvath & L. S. Greenberg (Eds.), *The working alliance: Theory, research, and practice* (pp. 131-152). New York: Wiley.

RAW, M., & RUSSELL, M. A. H. (1980). Rapid smoking, cue exposure and support in the modification of smoking. *Behaviour Research and Therapy, 18,* 363-372.

RAW, S. D. (1993). Does psychotherapy research teach us anything about psychotherapy? *the Behavior Therapist, 16,* 75-76.

RAYMOND, D. D., DOWRICK, P. W., & KLEINKE, C. L. (1993). Affective responses to seeing oneself for the first time on unedited videotape. *Counseling Psychology Quarterly, 6,* 193-200.

REDD, W. (1980). Stimulus control and extinction of psychosomatic symptoms in cancer patients in protective isolation. *Journal of Consulting and Clinical Psychology, 48,* 448-455.

REDD, W. H., & ANDRYKOWSKI, M. A. (1982). Behavioral intervention in cancer treatment: Controlling aversion reactions to chemotherapy. *Journal of Consulting and Clinical Psychology, 50,* 1018-1029.

REDD, W. H., MANNE, S. L., PETERS, B., JACOBSEN, P. B., & SCHMIDT, H. (1994). Fragrance administration to reduce anxiety during MR imaging. *Journal of Magnetic Resonance, 4,* 623-626.

REEVES, J. L. (1976). EMG-biofeedback reduction of tension headache: A cognitive skills-training approach. *Biofeedback and Self-Regulation, 1,* 217-225.

REHM, L. P. (1988). Assessment of depression. In A. S. Bellack & M. Hersen (Eds.), *Behavioral assessment: A practical handbook* (3rd ed., pp. 313-364). Elmsford, NY: Pergamon.

REID, D. H., LUYBEN, P. L., RAWERS, F. A., & BAILEY, J. S. (1976). The effects of prompting and proximity of containers on newspaper recycling behavior. *Environment and Behavior, 8,* 471-482.

REID, J. B., EDDY, M., BANK, L., & FETROW, R. (1994, November). *Some preliminary findings from a universal prevention program for conduct disorder.* Paper presented at the Fourth Annual National Prevention Conference, Washington, DC.

REID, J. B., HINJOSA-RIVERA, G., & LOEBER, R. A. (1980). *A social learning approach to the outpatient treatment of children who steal.* Unpublished manuscript, Oregon Social Learning Center, Eugene.

REID, R. (1996). Research in self-monitoring with students with learning disabilities: The present, the prospects, the pitfalls. *Journal of Learning Disabilities, 29,* 317-331.

REIMRINGER, M. J., MORGAN, S. W., & BRAMWELL, P. F. (1970). Succinylcholine as a modifier of acting-out behavior. *Clinical Medicine, 77,* 28-29.

REISINGER, J. J., & ORA, J. P. (1977). Parent-child and home interaction during toddler management training. *Behavior Therapy, 8,* 771-786.

REISS, M., PIOTROWSKI, W., & BAILEY, J. (1976). Behavioral community psychology: Encouraging low-income parents to seek dental care for their children. *Journal of Applied Behavior Analysis, 9,* 387-398.

REISS, M. L., & BAILEY, J. S. (1982). Visiting the dentist: A behavioral community analysis of participation in a dental screening and referral program. *Journal of Applied Behavior Analysis, 15,* 353-362.

RENFREY, G., & SPATES, C. R. (1994). Eye movement desensitization: A partial dismantling study. *Journal of Behavior Therapy and Experimental Psychiatry, 23,* 231-239.

RENFREY, G. S. (1992). Cognitive-behavior therapy and the Native American client. *Behavior Therapy, 23,* 321-340.

REYNA, T. (1996). Personal communication.

RICE, J. M., & LUTZKER, J. R. (1984). Reducing noncompliance to follow-up appointment keeping at a family practice center. *Journal of Applied Behavior Analysis, 17,* 303-311.

RICHARD, J. (1995). Behavioral treatment of an atypical case of obsessive compulsive disorder. *the Behavior Therapist, 18,* 134-135.

RICHARDS, D. A., LOVELL, K., & MARKS, I. M. (1994). Post-traumatic stress disorder: Evaluation of a behavioral treatment program. *Journal of Traumatic Stress, 7,* 669-680.

RICHARDSON, F. C., & SUINN, R. M. (1973). A comparison of traditional systematic desensitization, accelerated massed desensitization, and anxiety management training in the treatment of mathematics anxiety. *Behavior Therapy, 4,* 212-218.

RICI, D. M., & LAWRENCE, P. S. (1979, December). *The effectiveness of group-administered relaxation training as an adjunctive therapy for essential hypertension.* Paper presented at the meeting of the Association for Advancement of Behavior Therapy, San Francisco.

RIETVELD, C. M. (1983). The training of choice behaviours in Down's Syndrome and nonretarded preschool children. *Australia and New Zealand Journal of Developmental Disabilities, 9,* 75-83.

RIMM, D. C., DEGROOT, J. C., BOORD, P., HEIMAN, J., & DILLOW, P. V. (1971). Systematic desensitization of an anger response. *Behaviour Research and Therapy, 9,* 273-280.

RIMM, D. C., & MASTERS, J. C. (1979). *Behavior therapy: Techniques and empirical findings* (2nd ed.). New York: Academic Press.

RIMM, D. C., SAUNDERS, W. D., & WESTEL, W. (1975). Thought stopping and covert assertion in the treatment of snake phobias. *Journal of Consulting and Clinical Psychology, 43,* 92-93.

RISLEY, T. R. (1968). The effects and side effects of punishing the autistic behaviors of a deviant child. *Journal of Applied Behavior Analysis, 1,* 21-34.

RISLEY, T. R. (1995). Get a life! Positive behavioral intervention for challenging behavior through Life Arrangement and Life Coaching. In L. K. Koegel, R. L. Koegel, & G. Dunlap (Eds.), *Community, school, family, and social inclusion through positive behavioral support.* Baltimore: Brookes Publishing.

RISLEY, T. R., & TWARDOSZ, S. (1974, January). *Suggesting guidelines for the humane management of the behavior problems of the retarded.* Unpublished manuscript, Johnny Cake Child Study Center.

RITTER, B. (1968a). Effect of contact desensitization on avoidance behavior, fear ratings, and self-evaluative statements. *Proceedings of the American Psychological Association* (pp. 527-528). Washington, DC: American Psychological Association.

RITTER, B. (1968b). The group desensitization of children's snake phobias using vicarious and contact desensitization procedures. *Behaviour Research and Therapy, 6,* 1-6.

RITTER, B. (1969a). Eliminating excessive fears of the environment through contact desensitization. In J. D. Krumboltz & C. E. Thoresen (Eds.), *Behavioral counseling: Cases and techniques* (pp. 168-178). New York: Holt, Rinehart & Winston.

RITTER, B. (1969b). Treatment of acrophobia with contact desensitization. *Behaviour Research and Therapy, 7,* 41-45.

RITTER, B. (1969c). The use of contact desensitization, demonstration-plus-relaxation and demonstration alone in the treatment of acrophobia. *Behaviour Research and Therapy, 7,* 157-164.

RIVERA, D., & SMITH, D. D. (1988). Using a demonstration strategy to teach midschool students with learning disabilities how to compute long division. *Journal of Learning Disabilities, 21,* 77-81.

ROBERTS, A. (1979). The behavioral treatment of pain. In M. Ferguson & C. B. Taylor (Eds.), *A comprehensive handbook of behavioral medicine* (pp. 171-189). New York: Spectrum.

ROBERTS, A. E. (1969). Development of self-control using Premack's differential rate hypothesis: A case study. *Behaviour Research and Therapy, 7,* 341-344.

ROBERTS, D. S., & GELLER, E. S. (1995). An "actively caring" model for occupational safety: A field test. *Applied and Preventive Psychology, 4,* 53-59.

ROBERTS, M. C., & FANURIK, D. (1986). Rewarding elementary school children for their use of safety belts. *Health Psychology, 5,* 185-196.

ROBERTS, M. C., & TURNER, D. S. (1986). Rewarding parents for their children's use of safety seats. *Journal of Pediatric Psychology, 11,* 25-36.

ROBIN, A. L., & FOSTER, S. L. (1989). *Negotiating parent adolescent conflict: A behavioral-family-systems approach.* New York: Guilford.

ROBINS, C. J., & HAYES, A. M. (1993). An appraisal of cognitive therapy. *Journal of Consulting and Clinical Psychology, 61,* 205-214.

ROFFMAN, R. A., GILCHRIST, L. D., STEPHENS, R. S., & KIRKHAM, M. A. (1988, November). Relapse prevention with gay or bisexual males at risk for AIDS due to ongoing unsafe sexual behavior. In J. A. Kelly (Chair), *Behavioral intervention to prevent AIDS: Current status and future directions.* Symposium presented at the meeting of the Association for Advancement of Behavior Therapy, New York.

ROGERS, R. W., ROGERS, J. S., BAILEY, J. S., RUNKLE, W., & MOORE, B. (1988). Promoting safety belt use among state employees: The effects of prompting and a stimulus-control intervention. *Journal of Applied Behavior Analysis, 21,* 263-269.

ROKKE, P. D., & AL'ABSI, M. (1992). Matching pain coping strategies to the individual: A prospective validation of the cognitive coping strategy inventory. *Journal of Behavioral Medicine, 15,* 611-625.

ROLIDER, A., & VAN HOUTEN, R. (1984). Training parents to use extinction to eliminate nighttime crying by gradually increasing the criteria for ignoring crying. *Education and Treatment of Children, 7,* 119-124.

ROLLINGS, J. P., BAUMEISTER, A. A., & BAUMEISTER, A. A. (1977). The use of overcorrection procedures to eliminate the stereotyped behaviors of retarded individuals: An analysis of collateral behaviors and generalization of suppressive effects. *Behavior Modification, 1,* 29-46.

ROMANO, J. M., & BELLACK, A. S. (1980). Social validation of a component model of assertive behavior. *Journal of Consulting and Clinical Psychology, 48,* 478-490.

RONAN, K., KENDALL, P. C., & ROWE, M. (1994). Negative affectivity in children: Development and validation of a self-statement questionnaire. *Cognitive Therapy and Research 18,* 509-528.

RORTVEDT, A. K., & MILTENBERGER, R. G. (1994). Analysis of a high-probability instructional sequence and time-out in the treatment of child noncompliance. *Journal of Applied Behavior Analysis, 27,* 327-330.

ROSEKRANS, M. A. (1967). Imitation of children as a function of perceived similarity to a social model and vicarious reinforcement. *Journal of Personality and Social Psychology, 7,* 307-315.

ROSEN, G. M. (1995). On the origin of eye movement desensitization. *Journal of Behavior Therapy and Experimental Psychiatry, 26,* 121-122.

ROSEN, G. M. (1996). Level II training for EMDR: One commentator's view. *the Behavior Therapist, 19,* 76-77.

Rosen, G. M., Glasgow, R. E., & Barrera, M. (1976). A controlled study to assess the clinical efficacy of totally self-administered systematic desensitization. *Journal of Consulting and Clinical Psychology, 44,* 208-217.

Rosen, H. S., & Rosen, L. A. (1983). Eliminating stealing: Use of stimulus control with an elementary student. *Behavior Modification, 7,* 56-63.

Rosenbaum, M. S., Creedon, D. L., & Drabman, R. S. (1981). Training preschool children to identify emergency situations and make emergency calls. *Behavior Therapy, 12,* 425-435.

Rosenhan, D. L. (1973). On being sane in insane places. *Science, 179,* 250-258.

Rosenthal, R. (1969). Interpersonal expectations: Effects of the experimenter's hypothesis. In R. Rosenthal & R. L. Rosnow (Eds.), *Artifact in behavioral research* (pp. 181-277). New York: Academic Press.

Rosenthal, T. L., Linehan, K. S., Kelley, J. E., Rosenthal, R. H., Theobald, D. E., & Davis, A. F. (1978). Group aversion by imaginal, vicarious and shared recipient-observer shocks. *Behaviour Research and Therapy, 16,* 421-427.

Rosenthal, T. L., & Reese, S. L. (1976). The effects of covert and overt modeling on assertive behavior. *Behaviour Research and Therapy, 14,* 463-470.

Rosenthal, T. L., Rosenthal, R. H., & Chang, A. F. (1977). Vicarious, direct and imaginal aversion in habit control: Outcomes, heart rates, and subjective perceptions. *Cognitive Therapy and Research, 1,* 143-159.

Rosenthal, T. L., & Steffek, B. D. (1991). Modeling applications. In F. H. Kanfer & A. P. Goldstein (Eds.), *Helping people change* (4th ed., pp. 70-122). New York: Pergamon.

Ross, D. M., Ross, S. A., & Evans, T. A. (1971). The modification of extreme social withdrawal by modeling with guided participation. *Journal of Behavior Therapy and Experimental Psychiatry, 2,* 273-279.

Ross, L. (1977). The intuitive psychologist and his shortcomings. In L. Berkowitz (Ed.), *Advances in experimental social psychology* (Vol. 10, pp. 173-220). New York: Academic Press.

Ross, M. S., & Moldofsky, H. (1978). A comparison of pimozide and haloperidol in the treatment of Gilles de la Tourette's Syndrome. *American Journal of Psychiatry, 135,* 585-587.

Rothbaum, B. O. (1992). The behavioral treatment of trichotillomania. *Behavioural Psychotherapy, 20,* 85-90.

Rothbaum, B. O., Hodges, L. F., Kooper, R., Opdyke, D., Williford, J. S., & North, M. (1995a). Effectiveness of computer-generated (virtual reality) graded exposure in the treatment of acrophobia. *The American Journal of Psychiatry, 152,* 626-628.

Rothbaum, B. O., Hodges, L. F., Kooper, R., Opdyke, D., Williford, J. S., & North, M. (1995b). Virtual reality graded exposure in the treatment of acrophobia: A case report. *Behavior Therapy, 26,* 547-554.

Rotheram-Borus, M. J., Koopman, C., Haignere, C., & Davies, M. (1991). Reducing HIV sexual risk behaviors among runaway adolescents. *Journal of the American Medical Association, 266,* 1237-1241.

Rowan-Szal, G. A., Joe, G. W., Chatham, L. R., & Simpson, D. D. (1994). A simple reinforcement system for methadone clients in a community-based treatment program. *Journal of Substance Abuse Treatment, 11,* 217-223.

Rudd, J. R., & Geller, E. S. (1985). A university-based incentive program to increase safety belt use: Toward cost-effective institutionalization. *Journal of Applied Behavior Analysis, 18,* 215-226.

Rusch, F. R., Hughes, C., & Wilson, P. G. (1995). Utilizing cognitive strategies in the acquisition of employment skills. In W. O'Donohue & L. Krasner (Eds.), *Handbook of psychological skills training: Clinical techniques and applications* (pp. 363-382). Boston: Allyn and Bacon.

Rusch, F. R., Martin, J. E., Lagomarcino, T. R., & White, D. M. (1987). Teaching task sequencing via verbal mediation. *Education and Training in Mental Retardation, 22,* 229-235.

Rusch, F. R., Morgan, T. K., Martin, J. E., Riva, M., & Agran, M. (1985). Competitive employment: Teaching mentally retarded employees self-instructional strategies. *Applied Research in Mental Retardation, 6,* 389-407.

Rushall, B. S., & Siedentop, D. (1972). *The development and control of behavior in sport and physical education.* Philadelphia: Lea & Febiger.

Rychtarik, R. G., Silverman, W. K., Landingham, W. P. V., & Prue, D. M. (1984). Treatment of an incest victim with implosive therapy: A case study. *Behavior Therapy, 15,* 410-420.

Sachs, D. A. (1975). Behavioral techniques in a residential nursing home facility. *Journal of Behavior Therapy and Experimental Psychiatry, 26,* 123-127.

Sackett, D. L., & Haynes, R. B. (Eds.). (1976). *Compliance with therapeutic regimens.* Baltimore: Johns Hopkins University Press.

Sackett, D. L., & Snow, J. C. (1979). The magnitude of compliance and noncompliance. In R. B. Haynes, D. W. Taylor, & D. L. Sackett (Eds.), *Compliance with health care* (pp. 11-22). Baltimore: Johns Hopkins University Press.

Sahakian, B., & Charlesworth, G. (1994). Masked bereavement presenting as agoraphobia. *Behavioural and Cognitive Psychotherapy, 22,* 177-180.

Saigh, P. A. (1986). *In vitro* flooding in the treatment of a 6-yr-old boy's posttraumatic stress disorder. *Behaviour Research and Therapy, 24,* 685-688.

Saigh, P. A. (1987). *In vitro* flooding of an adolescent's posttraumatic stress disorder. *Journal of Clinical Child Psychology, 16,* 147-150.

St. Lawrence, J. S. (1987). Assessment of assertion. In M. Hersen, R. M. Eisler, & P. M. Miller (Eds.), *Progress in behavior modification* (Vol. 12, pp. 152-190). Newbury Park, CA: Sage.

St. Lawrence, J. S., Brasfield, T. L., Jefferson, K. W., Alleyne, E., O'Bannon, R. E., & Shirley, A. (1995). Cognitive behavioral intervention to reduce African American adolescents' risk for HIV infection. *Journal of Consulting and Clinical Psychology, 58,* 432-436.

St. Lawrence, J. S., Hansen, D. J., Cutts, T. F., Tisdelle, D. A., & Irish, J. D. (1985). Situational context: Effects on perceptions of assertive and unassertive behavior. *Behavior Therapy, 16,* 51-62.

St. Lawrence, J. S., Jefferson, K. W., Alleyne, E., & Brasfield, T. L. (1995). Comparison of education versus behavioral skills training interventions in lowering sexual HIV-risk behavior of substance-dependent adolescents. *Journal of Consulting and Clinical Psychology, 63,* 154-157.

SANDERSON, A., & CARPENTER, R. (1992). Eye movement desensitization versus image confrontation: A single-session crossover study of 58 phobic subjects. *Journal of Behavior Therapy and Experimental Psychiatry, 23,* 269-275.

SANDERSON, W. C., BECK, A. T., & McGINN, L. K. (1994). Cognitive therapy for generalized anxiety disorder: Significance of comorbid personality disorders. *Journal of Cognitive Psychotherapy, 8,* 13-18.

SAPER, Z., BLANK, M. K., & CHAPMAN, L. (1995). Implosive therapy as an adjunct treatment in a psychotic disorder: A case report. *Journal of Behavior Therapy and Experimental Psychiatry, 26,* 157-160.

SARASON, I. G. (1975). Test anxiety and the self-disclosing coping model. *Journal of Consulting and Clinical Psychology, 43,* 148-153.

SATTERFIELD, J. H., SATTERFIELD, B. T., & CANTWELL, D. P. (1981). Three-year multi-modality treatment of 100 hyperactive boys. *Journal of Pediatrics, 98,* 650-655.

SAUNDERS, D. G. (1976). A case of motion sickness treated by systematic desensitization and *in vivo* relaxation. *Journal of Behavior Therapy and Experimental Psychiatry, 7,* 381-382.

SAYERS, M. D., BELLACK, A. S., WADE, J. H., BENNETT, M. E., & FONG, P. (1995). An empirical method for assessing social problem solving in schizophrenia. *Behavior Modification, 19,* 267-289.

SCHAPP, C., BENNUN, I., SCHINDLER, L., & HOOGDUIN, K. (1993). *The therapeutic relationship in behavioural psychotherapy.* New York: Wiley.

SCHELL, B. J. (1996). Chronic disease and psychotherapy: Part I. *Psychotherapy Bulletin, 31,* 21-25.

SCHERER, M. W., & NAKAMURA, C. Y. (1968). A fear survey schedule for children (FSS-C): A factor analytic comparison with manifest anxiety. *Behaviour Research and Therapy, 6,* 173-182.

SCHIFF, R., SMITH, N., & PROCHASKA, J. (1972). Extinction of avoidance in rats as a function of duration and number of blocked trails. *Journal of Comparative and Physiological Psychology, 81,* 356-359.

SCHLESER, R., MEYERS, A., & COHEN, R. (1981). Generalization of self-instructions: Effects of general versus specific content, active rehearsal, and cognitive level. *Child Development, 52,* 335-340.

SCHMIDT, A. J. M., GIERLINGS, R. E. H., & PETERS, M. L. (1989). Environment and interoceptive influences on chronic low back pain behavior. *Pain, 38,* 137-143.

SCHMIDT, U. (1989). Behavioural psychotherapy for eating disorders. *International Review of Psychiatry, 1,* 245-256.

SCHMITZ, J. M., RHOADES, H., & GRABOWSKI, J. (1994). A menu of potential reinforcers in a methodone maintenance program. *Journal of Substance Abuse Treatment, 11,* 425-431.

SCHNEIDERMAN, N., ANTONI, M. H., IRONSON, G., LaPERRIERE, A., & FLETCHER, M. A. (1992). Applied psychological science and HIV-1 spectrum disease. *Applied and Preventive Psychology, 1,* 67-82.

SCHNELLE, J. F., KIRCHNER, R. E., MACRAE, J. W., McNEES, M. P., ECK, R. H., SNODGRASS, S., CASEY, J. D., & USELTON, P. H. (1978). Police evaluation research: An experimental and cost-benefit analysis of a helicopter patrol in a high crime area. *Journal of Applied Behavior Analysis, 11,* 11-21.

SCHNELLE, J. F., KIRCHNER, R. E., McNEES, M., & LAWLER, J. M. (1975). Social evaluation research: The evaluation of two police patrolling strategies. *Journal of Applied Behavior Analysis, 8,* 353-365.

SCHOLING, A., & EMMELKAMP, P. M. G. (1993a). Cognitive and behavioural treatments of fear of blushing, sweating or trembling. *Behaviour Research and Therapy, 31,* 155-170.

SCHOLING, A., & EMMELKAMP, P. M. G. (1993b). Exposure with and without cognitive therapy for generalized social phobia: Effects of individual and group treatment. *Behaviour Research and Therapy, 31,* 667-681.

SCHROEDER, H. E., & BLACK, M. J. (1985). Unassertiveness. In M. Hersen & A. S. Bellack (Eds.), *Handbook of clinical behavior therapy with adults* (pp. 509-530). New York: Plenum.

SCHULMAN, M. (1974). Control of tics by maternal reinforcement. *Journal of Behavior Therapy and Experimental Psychiatry, 5,* 95-96.

SCHUMAKER, J., & SHERMAN, J. A. (1970). Training generative verb usage by imitation and reinforcement procedures. *Journal of Applied Behavior Analysis, 3,* 273-287.

SCHWARTZ, J. M., STOESSEL, P. W., BAXTER, L. R., MARTIN, K. M., & PHELPS, M. E. (1996). Systematic changes in cerebral glucose metabolic rate after successful behavior modification treatment of obsessive-compulsive disorder. *Archives of General Psychiatry, 53,* 109-113.

SCHWARZER, R. (Ed.). (1992). *Self-efficacy: Thought control of action.* New York: Hemisphere.

SCHWITZGEBEL, L., & SCHWITZGEBEL, K. (1973). *Psychotechnology: Electronic control of mind and behavior.* New York: Holt, Rinehart & Winston.

SCOTT, C. S., SCOTT, J. L., TACCHI, M. J., & JONES, R. H. (1994). Abbreviated cognitive therapy for depression: A pilot study in primary care. *Behavioural and Cognitive Psychotherapy, 22,* 57-64.

SELIGMAN, C., & DARLEY, J. M. (1977). Feedback as a means of decreasing residential energy consumption. *Journal of Applied Psychology, 62,* 363-368.

SELIGSON, M. R., & PETERSON, K. E. (EDS.). (1992). *AIDS prevention and treatment: Hope, humor, & healing.* New York: Hemisphere.

SERGIS-DEAVENPORT, E., & VARNI, J. W. (1982). Behavioral techniques in teaching hemophilia factor replacement procedures to families. *Pediatric Nursing, 8,* 416-419.

SERGIS-DEAVENPORT, E., & VARNI, J. W. (1983). Behavioral assessment and management of adherence to factor replacement therapy in hemophilia. *Journal of Pediatric Psychology, 8,* 367-377.

SHAFFER, H., BECK, J., & BOOTHROYD, P. (1983). The primary prevention of smoking onset: An inoculation approach. *Journal of Psychoactive Drugs, 15,* 177-184.

SHAFTO, F., & SULZBACHER, S. (1977). Comparing treatment tactics with a hyperactive preschool child: Stimulant medication and programmed teacher intervention. *Journal of Applied Behavior Analysis, 10,* 13-20.

SHANER, A., ECKMAN, T. A., & ROBERTS, L. (1994, November). *Monetary reinforcement for cocaine abstinence in cocaine dependent schizophrenia.* Poster presented at the meeting of the Association for Advancement of Behavior Therapy, San Diego.

SHAPIRO, A. K., & SHAPIRO, E. (1984). Controlled study of pimozide vs. placebo in Tourette's syndrome. *Journal of the American Academy of Child Psychiatry, 23,* 161-173.

SHAPIRO, D. A., REES, A., BARKHAM, M., HARDY, G., REYNOLDS, S., & STARTUP, M. (1995). Effects of treatment duration and severity of depression on the maintenance of gains after cognitive-behavioral and psychodynamic-interpersonal psychotherapy. *Journal of Consulting and Clinical Psychology, 63,* 378-387.

Shapiro, E., Shapiro, A. K., Fulop, G., Hubbard, M., Mandeli, J., Nordlie, J., & Phillips, R. A. (1989). Controlled study of haloperidol, pimozide, and placebo for the treatment of Gilles de la Tourette's syndrome. *Archives of General Psychiatry, 46,* 722-730.

Shapiro, E. S., Albright, T. S., & Ager, C. L. (1986). Group versus individual contingencies in modifying two disruptive adolescents' behavior. *Professional School Psychology, 1,* 105-116.

Shapiro, F. (1989a). Efficacy of the eye movement desensitization procedure in the treatment of traumatic memories. *Journal of Traumatic Stress Studies, 2,* 199-223.

Shapiro, F. (1989b). Eye movement desensitization: A new treatment for post-traumatic stress disorder. *Journal of Behavior Therapy and Experimental Psychiatry, 20,* 211-217.

Shapiro, F. (1995). *Eye movement desensitization and reprocessing: Basic principles, protocols, and procedures.* New York: Guilford.

Shapiro, M. B. (1951). An experimental approach to diagnostic psychological testing. *Journal of Mental Science, 98,* 748-764.

Shapiro, M. B. (1952). Experimental studies of a perceptual anomaly. II. Confirmatory and explanatory experiments. *Journal of Mental Science, 98,* 605-617.

Shapiro, M. B. (1957). Experimental method in the psychological description of the individual psychiatric patient. *International Journal of Social Psychiatry, 3,* 89-102.

Shapiro, M. B. (1961a). A method of measuring psychological changes specific to the individual psychiatric patient. *British Journal of Medical Psychology, 34,* 151-155.

Shapiro, M. B. (1961b). The single case in fundamental clinical research. *British Journal of Medical Psychology, 34,* 255-262.

Shapiro, M. B. (1966). The single case of clinical-psychological research. *Journal of General Psychology, 74,* 3-23.

Sharp, K. (1981). Impact of interpersonal problem-solving training on preschoolers' social competency. *Journal of Applied Developmental Psychology, 2,* 129-143.

Sharpe, L., Tarrier, N., & Rotundo, N. (1994). Treatment of delayed post-traumatic stress disorder following sexual abuse: A case example. *Behavioural and Cognitive Psychotherapy, 22,* 233-242.

Shea, M. T. (Panelist). (1990, November). In K. S. Dobson (Moderator), *Cognitive therapy and interpersonal therapy: What do the collaborative study results tell us and where do we go from here?* Panel discussion presented at the meeting of the Association for Advancement of Behavior Therapy, San Francisco.

Shea, M. T., Elkin, I., Imber, S. D., Sotsky, S. M., Watkins, J. T., Collins, J. F., Pilkonis, P. A., Beckham, E., Glass, D. R., Dolan, R. T., & Parloff, M. B. (1992). Course of depressive symptoms over follow-up: Findings from the National Institute of Mental Health Treatment of Depression Collaborative Research Program. *Archives of General Psychiatry, 49,* 782-787.

Shipley, R. H., & Boudewyns, P. A. (1980). Flooding and implosive therapy: Are they harmful? *Behavior Therapy, 11,* 503-508.

Shipley, R. H., Butt, J. H., & Horwitz, E. A. (1979). Preparation to re-experience a stressful medical examination: Effect of repetitious videotape exposure and coping style. *Journal of Consulting and Clinical Psychology, 47,* 485-492.

Shipley, R. H., Butt, J. H., Horwitz, B., & Farbry, J. E. (1978). Preparation for a stressful medical procedure: Effect of stimulus pre-exposure and coping style. *Journal of Consulting and Clinical Psychology, 46,* 499-507.

Shipley, R. H., Mock, L. A., & Levis, D. J. (1971). Effects of several response prevention procedures on activity, avoidance responding, and conditioned fear in rats. *Journal of Comparative and Physiological Psychology, 77,* 256-270.

Shorkey, C., & Himle, D. P. (1974). Systematic desensitization treatment of a recurring nightmare and related insomnia. *Journal of Behavior Therapy and Experimental Psychiatry, 5,* 97-98.

Shure, M. B., & Spivack, G. (1972). Means ends thinking, adjustment and social class among elementary school-aged children. *Journal of Consulting and Clinical Psychology, 38,* 348-353.

Shure, M. B., & Spivack, G. (1980). Interpersonal problem-solving as a mediator of behavioral adjustment in preschool and kindergarten children. *Journal of Applied Developmental Psychology, 1,* 29-44.

Siegel, L. J., & Peterson, L. (1980). Stress reduction in young dental patients through coping skills and sensory information. *Journal of Consulting and Clinical Psychology, 48,* 785-787.

Sikkema, K., Winett, R. A., & Lombard, D. N. (1995). Development and evaluation of an HIV risk reduction program for female college students. *AIDS Education and Prevention, 7,* 145-159.

Silver, B. V., Blanchard, E. B., Williamson, D. A., Theobald, D. E., & Brown, D. A. (1979). Temperature biofeedback and relaxation training in the treatment of migraine headache: One year follow-up. *Biofeedback and Self-Regulation, 4,* 359-366.

Silverman, W. H. (1986). Client-therapist cooperation in the treatment of compulsive hand washing. *Journal of Behavior Therapy and Experimental Psychiatry, 17,* 39-42.

Silverman, W. K., Ginsburg, G. S., & Kurtines, W. M. (1995). Clinical issues in treating children with anxiety and phobic disorders. *Cognitive and Behavioral Practice, 2,* 93-117.

Silverman, W. K., & Rabian, B. (1994). Specific phobias. In T. H. Ollendick, N. J. King, & W. Yule (Eds.), *International handbook of phobic and anxiety disorders in children and adolescents* (pp. 87-109). New York: Plenum.

Simmons, T. (1993). *A season in the air.* New York: Fawcett Columbine.

Simon, K. M. (1994). A rapid stabilization cognitive group therapy program for psychiatric inpatients. *Clinical Psychology and Psychotherapy, 1,* 286-297.

Simos, G., & Dimitriou, E. (1994). Cognitive-behavioural treatment of culturally bound obsessional ruminations: A case report. *Behavioural and Cognitive Psychotherapy, 2,* 325-330.

Singh, N. N., Dawson, M. J., & Manning, P. (1981). Effects of spaced responding DRL on the stereotyped behavior of profoundly retarded persons. *Journal of Applied Behavior Analysis, 14,* 521-526.

Sipich, J. F., Russell, R. K., & Tobias, L. L. (1974). A comparison of covert sensitization and "non-specific" treatment in the modification of smoking behavior. *Journal of Behavior Therapy and Experimental Psychiatry, 5,* 201-203.

SISSON, L. A., VAN HASSELT, V. B., & HERSEN, M. (1993). Behavioral interventions to reduce maladaptive responding in youth with dual sensory impairment: An analysis of direct and concurrent effects. *Behavior Modification, 17,* 164-188.

SKEELS, H. M. (1966). Adult status of children with contrasting early life experiences. *Monographs of the Society for Research in Child Development, 31* (Whole No. 3).

SKINNER, B. F. (1948). *Walden two.* New York: Macmillan.

SKINNER, B. F. (1953). *Science and human behavior.* New York: Macmillan.

SKINNER, B. F. (1954). A new method for the experimental analysis of the behavior of psychotic patients. *Journal of Nervous and Mental Disease, 120,* 403-406.

SKINNER, B. F., SOLOMON, H. C., & LINDSLEY, O. R. (1953, November 30). *Studies in behavior therapy: Status Report I.* Waltham, MA: Metropolitan State Hospital.

SKINNER, B. F., SOLOMON, H. C., LINDSLEY, O. R., & RICHARDS, M. E. (1954, May 31). *Studies in behavior therapy: Status Report II.* Waltham, MA: Metropolitan State Hospital.

SKINNER, B. F., & VAUGHAN, M. E. (1983). *Enjoy old age.* New York: Norton.

SLAVIN, R. E., WODARSKI, J. S., & BLACKBURN, B. L. (1981). A group contingency for electricity conservation in master-metered apartments. *Journal of Applied Behavior Analysis, 14,* 357-363.

SLIFER, K. J., BABBITT, R. L., & CATALDO, M. D. (1995). Simulation and counterconditioning as adjuncts to pharmacotherapy for invasive pediatric procedures. *Journal of Developmental and Behavioral Pediatrics, 16,* 133-141.

SLIFER, K. J., CATALDO, M. F., CATALDO, M. D., LLORENTE, A. M., & GERSON, A. C. (1993). Behavior analysis of motion control for pediatric neuroimaging. *Journal of Applied Behavior Analysis, 26,* 469-470.

SLOAN, E. P., HAURIS, P., BOOTZIN, R., MORIN, C., STEVENSON, M., & SHAPIRO, C. M. (1993). The nuts and bolts of behavioral therapy for insomnia. *Journal of Psychosomatic Research, 37* (Suppl. 1), 19-37.

SLOAN, E. P., & SHAPIRO, C. M. (1993). [Editorial] *Journal of Psychosomatic Research, 37,* 1-2.

SLOANE, R. B., STAPLES, F. R., CRISTOL, A. H., YORKSTON, N. H., & WHIPPLE, K. (1975). *Psychotherapy versus behavior therapy.* Cambridge, MA: Harvard University Press.

SMITH, D. D., & LOVITT, T. C. (1975). The use of modeling techniques to influence acquisition of computational arithmetic skills in learning disabled children. In E. Ramp & G. Semb (Eds.), *Behavior analysis: Areas of research and application* (pp. 283-308). Englewood Cliffs, NJ: Prentice-Hall.

SMITH, D. E., MARCUS, M. D., & ELDREDGE, K. L. (1994). Binge eating syndromes: A review of assessment and treatment with an emphasis on clinical application. *Behavior Therapy, 25,* 635-658.

SMITH, F. A., & LINSCHEID, T. R. (1994). Effect of parental acceptance or rejection of a proposed aversive intervention on treatment acceptability. *American Journal on Mental Retardation, 99,* 262-269.

SMITH, M. L., & GLASS, G. V. (1977). Meta-analysis of psychotherapy outcome studies. *American Psychologist, 32,* 752-760.

SMITH, R. E. (1973). The use of humor in the counterconditioning of anger responses: A case study. *Behavior Therapy, 4,* 576-580.

SMITH, R. E., & GREGORY, P. B. (1976). Covert sensitization by induced anxiety in the treatment of an alcoholic. *Journal of Behavior Therapy and Experimental Psychiatry, 7,* 31-33.

SMITH, R. G., IWATA, B. A., VOLLMER, T. R., & ZARCONE, J. R. (1993). Experimental analysis and treatment of multiply controlled self-injury. *Journal of Applied Behavior Analysis, 26,* 183-196.

SMITH, T., KLEVSTRAND, M., & LOVAAS, O. I. (1995). Behavioral treatment of Rett's disorder: Ineffectiveness in three cases. *American Journal of Mental Retardation, 100,* 317-322.

SOBELL, L. C. (1994). AABT coming of middle age. *the Behavior Therapist, 17,* 179-180.

SOKOLOV, A. N. (1972). *Inner speech and thought.* New York: Plenum.

SOLOMON, A., & HAAGA, D. A. F. (1995). Rational-emotive behavior therapy research: What we know and what we need to know. *Journal of Rational-Emotive and Cognitive Behavior Therapy, 13,* 179-191.

SOLOMON, R. L. (1964). Punishment. *American Psychologist, 19,* 239-253.

SOLOMON, R. W., & WAHLER, R. G. (1973). Peer reinforcement control of classroom problem behavior. *Journal of Applied Behavior Analysis, 6,* 49-56.

SOMERS, J. M., & MARLATT, G. A. (1992). Alcohol problems. In P. H. Wilson (Ed.), *Principles and practice of relapse prevention* (pp. 23-42). New York: Guilford.

SOUTHAM, M. A., AGRAS, W. S., TAYLOR, C. B., & KRAEMER, H. C. (1982). Relaxation training: Blood pressure lowering during the working day. *Archives of General Psychiatry, 39,* 715-717.

SOWERS, J., RUSCH, F. R., CONNIS, R. T., & CUMMINGS, L. E. (1980). Teaching mentally retarded adults to time manage in a vocational setting. *Journal of Applied Behavior Analysis, 13,* 119-128.

SOWERS-HOAG, K. M., THYER, B. A., & BAILEY, J. S. (1987). Promoting automobile safety belt use by young children. *Journal of Applied Behavior Analysis, 20,* 133-138.

SPECTOR, I. P., CAREY, M. P., JORGENSEN, R. S., MEISLER, A. W., & CARNRIKE, C. L. M., II. (1993). Cue-controlled relaxation and "Aromatherapy" in the treatment of speech anxiety. *Behavioural and Cognitive Psychotherapy, 21,* 239-253.

SPIEGLER, M. D. (1970, January). A modeling approach. In J. Schwartz (Chair), *Alternatives within behavior modification.* Symposium presented at the meeting of the California State Psychological Association, Monterey.

SPIEGLER, M. D. (1980, November). Behavioral primary prevention: Introduction and overview. In M. D. Spiegler (Chair), *Behavioral primary prevention: A challenge for the 1980s.* Symposium presented at the meeting of the Association for Advancement of Behavior Therapy, New York.

SPIEGLER, M. D. (1983). *Contemporary behavioral therapy.* Palo Alto, CA: Mayfield.

SPIEGLER, M. D. (1989, March). *Teaching behavior modification experientially through individual behavior change projects: A five-year study.* Paper presented at Teaching of Psychology: Ideas and Innovations, Philadelphia.

SPIEGLER, M. D., & AGIGIAN, H. (1977). *The Community Training Center: An educational-behavioral-social systems model for rehabilitating psychiatric patients.* New York: Brunner/Mazel.

SPIEGLER, M. D., COOLEY, E. J., MARSHALL, G. J., PRINCE, H. T., II, PUCKETT, S. P., & SKENAZY, J. A. (1976). A self-control versus a counterconditioning paradigm for systematic desensitization: An experimental comparison. *Journal of Counseling Psychology, 23,* 83-86.

SPIEGLER, M. D., & GUEVREMONT, D. C. (1994, November). *The relationship between behavior therapy practice and research.* Paper presented at the meeting of the Association for Advancement of Behavior Therapy, San Diego.

SPIEGLER, M. D., & LIEBERT, R. M. (1970). Some correlates of self-reported fear. *Psychological Reports, 26,* 691-695.

SPIEGLER, M. D., LIEBERT, R. M., MCMAINS, M. J., & FERNANDEZ, L. E. (1969). Experimental development of a modeling treatment to extinguish persistent avoidance behavior (pp. 45-51). In R. D. Rubin & C. M. Franks (Eds.), *Advances in behavior therapy, 1968.* New York: Academic Press.

SPIVACK, G., & SHURE, M. B. (1974). *Social adjustment of young children.* San Francisco: Jossey-Bass.

SPRADLIN, J. E., & GIRARDEAU, F. L. (1966). The behavior of moderately and severely retarded persons. In N. R. Ellis (Ed.), *International review of research in mental retardation* (Vol. 1, pp. 257-298). New York: Academic Press.

SPRING, F. L., SIPICH, J. F., TRIMBLE, R. W., & GOECKNER, D. J. (1978). Effects of contingency and noncontingency contracts in the context of a self-control-oriented smoking modification program. *Behavior Therapy, 9,* 967-968.

STAMBAUGH, E. E., II. (1977). Audio-taped flooding in outpatient treatment of somatic complaints. *Journal of Behavior Therapy and Experimental Psychiatry, 8,* 173-176.

STAMPFL, T. G. (1961, May). *Implosive therapy: A learning theory derived psychodynamic therapeutic technique.* Colloquium presented at the University of Illinois, Champaign.

STAMPFL, T. G. (1966). Implosive therapy, Part I: The theory. In S. G. Armitage (Ed.), *Behavioral modification techniques in the treatment of emotional disorder* (pp. 12-21). Battle Creek, MI: V. A. Hospital Publications.

STAMPFL, T. G. (1970). Implosive therapy: An emphasis on covert stimulation. In D. J. Levis (Ed.), *Learning approaches to therapeutic behavior change.* Chicago: Aldine.

STAMPFL, T. G., & LEVIS, D. J. (1967). Essentials of implosive therapy: A learning-theory-based psychodynamic behavioral therapy. *Journal of Abnormal Psychology, 72,* 496-503.

STAMPFL, T. G., & LEVIS, D. J. (1973). *Implosive therapy: Theory and technique.* Morristown, NJ: General Learning Press.

STANLEY, M. A., & TURNER, S. M. (1995). Current status of pharmacological and behavioral treatment of obsessive-compulsive disorder. *Behavior Therapy, 26,* 163-186.

STANLEY, S. M., MARKMAN, H. J., ST. PETERS, M., & LEBER, D. (1995). Strengthening marriages and preventing divorce: New directions in prevention research. *Family Relations, 44,* 392-401.

STAR, T. Z. (1986). Group social skills training: A comparison of two coaching programs. *Techniques, 2,* 24-38.

STARK, L. J., COLLINS, F. L., OSNES, P. G., & STOKES, T. F. (1986). Using reinforcement and cueing to increase healthy snack food choices in preschoolers. *Journal of Applied Behavior Analysis, 19,* 367-379.

STARK, L. J., KNAPP, L. G., BOWEN, A. M., POWERS, S. W., JELALIAN, E., EVANS, S., PASSERO, M. A., MULVIHILL, M. M., & HOVELL, M. (1993). Increasing calorie consumption in children with cystic fibrosis: Replication with 2-year follow-up. *Journal of Applied Behavior Analysis, 26,* 435-450.

STARK, L. J., POWERS, S. W., JELALIAN, E., RAPE, R. N., & MILLER, D. L. (1994). Modifying problematic mealtime interactions of children with cystic fibrosis and their parents via behavioral parent training. *Journal of Pediatric Psychology, 19,* 751-768.

STARTUP, M., & EDMONDS, J. (1994). Compliance with homework assignments in cognitive-behavioral psychotherapy for depression: Relation to outcome and methods of enhancement. *Cognitive Therapy and Research, 18,* 567-579.

STEED, S. E., BIGELOW, K. M., HUYNEN, K. B., & LUTZKER, J. R. (1995). The effects of planned activities training, low-demand schedule, and reinforcement sampling on adults with developmental disabilities who exhibit challenging behaviors. *Journal of Developmental and Physical Disabilities, 7,* 303-316.

STEGER, J., & HARPER, R. (1977, April). *EMG biofeedback versus in vivo self-monitored relaxation training in the treatment of tension headaches.* Paper presented at the meeting of the Western Psychological Association, Seattle.

STEINMARK, S. W., & BORKOVEC, T. D. (1974). Active and placebo treatment effects on moderate insomnia under counterdemand and positive demand instructions. *Journal of Abnormal Psychology, 83,* 157-163.

STEKETEE, G. (1994). Behavioral assessment and treatment planning with obsessive compulsive disorder: A review emphasizing clinical application. *Behavior Therapy, 25,* 613-633.

STEKETEE, G., & LAM, J. (1993). Obsessive-compulsive disorder. In T. R. Giles (Ed.), *Handbook of effective psychotherapy* (pp. 253-278). New York: Plenum.

STEPHENS, R. S., ROFFMAN, R. A., & SIMPSON, E. E. (1994). Treating adult marijuana dependence: A test of the relapse prevention model. *Journal of Consulting and Clinical Psychology, 62,* 92-99.

STERN, R. S., LIPSEDGE, M. S., & MARKS, I. M. (1973). Obsessive ruminations: A controlled trial of thought-stopping technique. *Behaviour Research and Therapy, 11,* 659-662.

STEWART, M. A. (1961). Psychotherapy by reciprocal inhibition. *American Journal of Psychiatry, 118,* 175-177.

STITZER, M., BIGELOW, G., LAWRENCE, C., COHEN, J., D'LUGOFF, B., & HAWTHORNE, J. (1977). Medication take-home as a reinforcer in a methadone maintenance program. *Addictive Behaviors, 2,* 9-14.

STOCK, L. Z., & MILAN, M. A. (1993). Improving dietary practices of elderly individuals: The power of prompting, feedback, and social reinforcement. *Journal of Applied Behavior Analysis, 26,* 379-387.

STOLZ, S. B. (1977). Why no guidelines for behavior modification? *Journal of Applied Behavior Analysis, 10,* 349-367.

STOLZ, S. B., & ASSOCIATES. (1978). *Ethical issues in behavior modification: Report of the American Psychological Association Commission.* San Francisco: Jossey-Bass.

STONE, G. W. (1994, May 9). Magic fingers. *New York, 27,* pp. 32-37.

STOREY, K., DANKO, C. D., ASHWORTH, R., & STRAIN, P. S. (1994). Generalization of social skills intervention for preschoolers with social delays. *Education and Treatment of Children, 17,* 29-51.

STOREY, K., LAWRY, J. R., ASHWORTH, R., DANKO, C. D., & STRAIN, P. S. (1994). Functional analysis and intervention for disruptive behaviors of a kindergarten student. *Journal of Educational Research, 87,* 361-370.

STORMS, L. (1985). Massed negative practice as a behavioral treatment of Gilles de la Tourette's syndrome. *American Journal of Psychotherapy, 39,* 277-281.

STRAHLEY, R. F. (1965). *Systematic desensitization and counterphobic treatment of an irrational fear of snakes.* Unpublished doctoral dissertation, University of Tennessee.

STRAIN, P. S. (Ed.). (1981). *The utilization of classroom peers as behavior change agents.* New York: Plenum.

STRAIN, P. S., SHORES, R. E., & KERR, M. M. (1976). An experimental analysis of "spillover" effects on the social interaction of behaviorally handicapped preschool children. *Journal of Applied Behavior Analysis, 9,* 31-40.

STRAUSS, C. A. (1986). An operant approach to increasing performance of household chores: A case study using behavioral consultation. *Psychological Reports, 58,* 738.

STRAVYNSKI, A., BELISLE, M., MARCOUILLER, M., LAVELLEE, Y. J., & ELIE, R. (1994). The treatment of avoidant personality disorder by social skills training in the clinic or in real-life settings. *Canadian Journal of Psychiatry, 39,* 377-383.

STRAVYNSKI, A., & GREENBERG, D. (1989). Behavioural psychotherapy for social phobia and dysfunction. *International Review of Psychiatry, 1,* 207-217.

STROSAHL, K. (1995). Behavior therapy 2000: A perilous journey. *the Behavior Therapist, 18,* 130-133.

STROSAHL, K. (1996). Behavior therapy 2000: Three "gold mine-land mine" themes in Generation 2 of health care reform. *the Behavior Therapist, 19,* 52-54.

STRUPP, H. H. (1966). *Who needs intrapsychic factors in clinical psychology?* Paper presented at the Albert Einstein College of Medicine, New York.

STRUPP, H. H. (1978). Psychotherapy research and practice: An overview. In S. L. Garfield & A. E. Gergin (Eds.), *Handbook of psychotherapy and behavior change: An empirical analysis* (2nd ed., pp. 3-22). New York: Wiley.

STRUPP, H. H. (1995). The psychotherapist's skills revisited. *Clinical Psychology: Science and Practice, 2,* 70-74.

STUART, R. B. (1967). Behavioral control of overeating. *Behaviour Research and Therapy, 5,* 357-365.

STUART, R. B. (1969). Operant-interpersonal treatment for marital discord. *Journal of Consulting and Clinical Psychology, 33,* 675-682.

STUART, R. B. (1971). Behavioral contracting with the families of delinquents. *Journal of Behavior Therapy and Experimental Psychiatry, 2,* 1-11.

STUART, R. B. (1980). *Helping couples change: A social learning approach to marital therapy.* New York: Guilford.

STUART, R. B., & LOTT, L. A., JR. (1972). Behavioral contracting with delinquents: A cautionary note. *Journal of Behavior Therapy and Experimental Psychiatry, 3,* 161-169.

STURGIS, E. T., & GRAMLING, S. (1988). Psychophysiological assessment. In A. S. Bellack & M. Hersen (Eds.), *Behavioral assessment: A practical handbook* (3rd ed., pp. 213-251). Elmsford, NY: Pergamon.

STURMEY, P. (1992). Treatment acceptability for anorexia nervosa: Effect of treatment type, problem severity, and treatment outcome. *Behavioural Psychotherapy, 20,* 91-93.

SUAREZ, Y., McCUTCHEON, B. A., & ADAMS, H. E. (1976). Flooding and systematic desensitization: Efficacy in subclinical phobias as a function of arousal. *Journal of Consulting and Clinical Psychology, 44,* 872.

SUAREZ, Y., PETERS, R. D., CROWE, M. J., EASTERLING, K., & ADAMS, C. (1988, August). *Self vs. therapist control of escape for treatment of phobias.* Paper presented at the meeting of the American Psychological Association, Atlanta.

SULLIVAN, K. T., & BRADBURY, T. N. (1996). Preventing marital dysfunction: The primacy of secondary strategies. *the Behavior Therapist, 19,* 33-36.

SULLIVAN, M. A., & O'LEARY, S. G. (1990). Maintenance following reward and cost token programs. *Behavior Therapy, 21,* 139-149.

SULZER-AZAROFF, B. (1982). Behavioral approaches to occupational health and safety. In L. W. Frederiksen (Ed.), *Handbook of organizational behavior management* (pp. 505-538). New York: Wiley.

SULZER-AZAROFF, B., HARRIS, T. C., & McCANN, K. B. (1994). Beyond training: Organizational performance management techniques. *Occupational Medicine, 9,* 321-339.

SUTHERLAND, A., AMIT, Z., GOLDEN, N., & ROSENBERGER, Z. (1975). Comparison of three behavioral techniques in the modification of smoking behavior. *Journal of Consulting and Clinical Psychology, 43,* 443-447.

SWAGGART, B., GAGNON, E., BOCK, S. J., EARLES, T. L., QUINN, C. P., MYLES, B. S., & SIMPSON, R. L. (1995). Using social stories to teach social and behavioral skills to children with autism. *Focus on Autistic Behavior, 10,* 1-16.

SWAN, G. E., & MacDONALD, M. L. (1978). Behavior therapy in practice: A national survey of behavior therapists. *Behavior Therapy, 9,* 799-807.

SWINSON, R. P., FERGUS, K. D., COX, B. J., & WICKWIRE, K. (1995). Efficacy of telephone-administered behavioral therapy for panic disorder with agoraphobia. *Behaviour Research and Therapy, 33,* 465-469.

SWINSON, R. P., & KUCH, K. (1989). Behavioural psychotherapy for agoraphobia. *International Review of Psychiatry, 1,* 195-205.

SWITZER, E. B., DEAL, T. E., & BAILEY, J. S. (1977). The reduction of stealing in second graders using a group contingency. *Journal of Applied Behavior Analysis, 10,* 267-272.

SZYMANSKI, J., & O'DONOHUE, W. (1995). Self-appraisal skills. In W. O'Donohue & L. Krasner (Eds.). *Handbook of psychological skills training: Clinical techniques and applications* (pp. 161-179). Boston: Allyn and Bacon.

TANAKA-MATSUMI, J., & HIGGINBOTHAM, H. N. (1994). Clinical application of behavior therapy across ethnic and cultural boundaries. *the Behavior Therapist, 17,* 123-126.

TANAKA-MATSUMI, J., & HIGGINBOTHAM, H. N. (in press). Behavioral approaches to counseling across cultures. In P. B. Pedersen, J. G. Draguns, W. J. Lonner, & J. E. Trimble (Eds.), *Counseling across cultures* (4th ed.). Thousand Oaks, CA: Sage.

TANAKA-MATSUMI, J., & SEIDEN, D. Y. (1994, November). *Functional analytic approaches to cross-cultural therapy.* Paper presented at the meeting of the Association for Advancement of Behavior Therapy, San Diego.

TARAS, M. E., MATSON, J. L., & LEARY, C. (1988). Training social interpersonal skills in two autistic children. *Journal of Behavior Therapy and Experimental Psychiatry, 19,* 275-280.

TARNOWSKI, K. J., ROSEN, L. A., McGRATH, M. L., & DRABMAN, R. S. (1987). A modified habit reversal procedure in a recalcitrant case of trichotillomania. *Journal of Behavior Therapy and Experimental Psychiatry, 18,* 157-163.

TARNOWSKI, K. J., SIMONIAN, S. J., BEKENY, P., & PARK, A. (1992). Acceptability of interventions for childhood depression. *Behavior Modification, 16,* 103-117.

TARRIER, N. (1992). Management and modification of residual positive psychotic symptoms. In M. Birchwood & N. Tarrier (Eds.), *Innovations in the psychological management of schizophrenia* (pp. 147-169). Chichester, U.K.: Wiley.

TATE, B. G., & BAROFF, G. S. (1966). Aversive control of self-injurious behavior in a psychotic boy. *Behaviour Research and Therapy, 4,* 281-287.

TAYLOR, C. B., AGRAS, W. S., SCHNEIDNER, J. A., & ALLEN, R. A. (1983). Adherence to instructions to practice relaxation exercises. *Journal of Consulting and Clinical Psychology, 51,* 952-953.

TAYLOR, C. B., FARQUHAR, J. W., NELSON, E., & AGRAS, W. S. (1977). Relaxation therapy and high blood pressure. *Archives of General Psychiatry, 34,* 339-342.

TAYLOR, D. W. A. (1971). A comparison of group desensitization with two control procedures in the treatment of test anxiety. *Behaviour Research and Therapy, 9,* 281-284.

TEASDALE, J. D., SEGAL, Z., & WILLIAMS, J. M. G. (1995). How does cognitive therapy prevent depressive relapse and why should attention control (mindfulness) training help? *Behaviour Research and Therapy, 33,* 25-39.

THACKWRAY, D. E., SMITH, M. C., BODFISH, J. W., & MEYERS, A. W. (1993). A comparison of behavioral and cognitive-behavioral interventions for bulimia nervosa. *Journal of Consulting and Clinical Psychology, 61,* 639-645.

THASE, M. E. (1994). After the fall: Perspectives on cognitive behavioral treatment of depression in the "post-collaborative" era. *the Behavior Therapist, 17,* 48-52.

THASE, M. E., BOWLER, K., & HARDEN, T. (1991). Cognitive behavior therapy of endogenous depression: Part 2: Preliminary findings in 16 unmedicated inpatients. *Behavior Therapy, 22,* 469-477.

THASE, M. E., REYNOLDS, C. F., FRANK, E., SIMONS, A. D., GARAMONI, G. D., McGEARY, J., HARDEN, T., FASICZKA, A. L., & CAHALANE, J. F. (1994). Response to cognitive-behavioral therapy in chronic depression. *The Journal of Psychotherapy Practice and Research, 3,* 204-214.

THASE, M. E., REYNOLDS, C. F., FRANK, E., SIMONS, A. D., McGEARY, J., FASICZKA, A. L., GARAMONI, G. G., JENNINGS, J. R., & KUPFER, D. J. (1994). Do depressed men and women respond similarly to cognitive behavior therapy? *The American Journal of Psychiatry, 151,* 500-505.

THASE, M. E., SIMONS, A. D., CAHALANE, J. F., & McGEARY, J. (1991). Cognitive behavior therapy of endogenous depression: Part 1: An outpatient clinical replication series. *Behavior Therapy, 22,* 457-467.

THASE, M. E., & WRIGHT, J. H. (1991). Cognitive behavior therapy manual for depressed inpatients: A treatment protocol outline. *Behavior Therapy, 22,* 579-595.

THELEN, M. H., FRY, R. A., FEHRENBACH, P. A., & FRAUTSCHI, N. M. (1979). Therapeutic videotape and film modeling: A review. *Psychological Bulletin, 86,* 701-720.

THOMAS, D. R., BECKER, W. C., & ARMSTRONG, M. (1968). Production and elimination of disruptive classroom behavior by systematically varying teacher's behavior. *Journal of Applied Behavior Analysis, 1,* 35-45.

THOMAS, E. J., ABRAMS, K. S., & JOHNSON, J. (1971). Self-monitoring and reciprocal inhibition in the modification of multiple tics of Gilles de la Tourette's syndrome. *Journal of Behavior Therapy and Experimental Psychiatry, 2,* 159-171.

THOMAS, J. D., PRESLAND, I. E., GRANT, M. D., & GLYNN, T. (1978). Natural rates of teacher approval in grade 7 classrooms. *Journal of Applied Behavior Analysis, 11,* 91-94.

THOMPSON, J. K. (1992). Body image: Extent of disturbance, associated features, theoretical models, assessment methodologies, intervention strategies, and a proposal for a new DSM-IV diagnostic category—body image disorder. In M. Hersen, R. M. Eisler, & P. M. Miller (Eds.), *Progress in behavior modification* (Vol. 28, pp. 3-54). Sycamore, IL: Sycamore.

THORESEN, C. E., & MAHONEY, M. J. (1974). *Behavioral self-control.* New York: Holt, Rinehart & Winston.

THORNDIKE, E. L. (1911). *Animal intelligence: Experimental studies.* New York: Macmillan.

THORNDIKE, E. L. (1931). *Human learning.* New York: Century.

THORNDIKE, E. L. (1933). *An experimental study of rewards.* New York: Teachers College Press.

THORPE, J. G., SCHMIDT, E., BROWN, P. T., & CASTELL, D. (1964). Aversion-relief therapy: A new method for general application. *Behaviour Research and Therapy, 2,* 71-82.

THYER, B. A. (1985). Audio-taped exposure therapy in a case of obsessional neurosis. *Journal of Behavior Therapy and Experimental Psychiatry, 16,* 271-273.

TIMBERLAKE, E. M. (1981). Child abuse and externalized aggression: Preventing a delinquent lifestyle. In R. J. Hunner & Y. E. Walker (Eds.), *Exploring the relationship between child abuse and delinquency* (pp. 43-51). Montclair, NJ: Allanheld, Osmun.

TIMBERLAKE, W., & FARMER-DOUGAN, V. A. (1991). Reinforcement in applied settings: Figuring out ahead of time what will work. *Psychological Bulletin, 110,* 379-391.

TIMBERS, G. D., TIMBERS, B. J., FIXSEN, D. L., PHILLIPS, E. L., & WOLF, M. M. (1973, August). *Achievement Place for pre-delinquent girls: Modification of inappropriate emotional behaviors with token reinforcement and instructional procedures.* Paper presented at the meeting of the American Psychological Association, Montreal.

TOKUHATA, G. K., COLFLESH, V., DIGON, E., & MANN, L. (1972). *Childhood injuries caused by consumer products.* Harrisburg: Pennsylvania Department of Health, Division of Research and Biostatistics.

TOOLEY, J. T., & PRATT, S. (1967). An experimental procedure for the extinction of smoking behavior. *Psychological Record, 17,* 209-218.

TOPHOFF, M. (1973). Massed practice, relaxation, and assertion training in the treatment of Gilles de la Tourette's syndrome. *Journal of Behavior Therapy and Experimental Psychiatry, 4,* 71-73.

TORGERSEN, A. M. (1985). Temperamental differences in infants and 6-year-old children: A follow-up study of twins. In J. Strelau, F. Farley, & A. Gale (Eds.), *The biological bases of personality and behavior* (Vol. 1, pp. 227-239). New York: Hemisphere.

TROWER, P. (1995). Adult social skills: State of the art and future directions. In W. O'Donohue & L. Krasner (Eds.). *Handbook of psychological skills training: Clinical techniques and applications* (pp. 54-80). Boston: Allyn and Bacon.

TRUAX, C. B., SHAPIRO, J. G., & WARGO, D. G. (1968). The effects of alternate sessions and vicarious therapy pretraining on group psychotherapy. *International Journal of Group Psychotherapy, 18,* 186-198.

TRULL, T. J., NIETZEL, M. T., & MAIN, A. (1988). The use of meta-analysis to assess the clinical significance of behavior therapy for agoraphobia. *Behavior Therapy, 19,* 527-538.

TRYON, G. S. (1979). A review and critique of thought stopping research. *Journal of Behavior Therapy and Experimental Psychiatry, 10,* 189-192.

TRYON, W. W. (1995). Neural networks for behavior therapists: What they are and why they are important. *Behavior Therapy, 26,* 295-318.

TRYON, W. W., & PINTO, L. P. (1994). Comparing activity measurements and ratings. *Behavior Modification, 18,* 251-261.

TURK, D. (1975). *Cognitive control of pain: A skill training approach.* Unpublished manuscript, University of Waterloo, Ontario.

TURK, D. (1976). *An expanded skills training approach for the treatment of experimentally induced pain.* Unpublished doctoral dissertation, University of Waterloo, Ontario.

TURK, D. C., & GENEST, M. (1979). Regulation of pain: The application of cognitive and behavioral techniques for prevention and remediation. In P. Kendall & S. Hollon (Eds.), *Cognitive behavioral interventions: Theory, research, and prevention* (pp. 287-319). New York: Academic Press.

TURK, D. C., & MEICHENBAUM, D. (1989). A cognitive-behavioural approach to pain management. In P. D. Wall & R. Melzack (Eds.), *Textbook of pain* (2nd ed.). London: Churchill Livingstone.

TURK, D. C., MEICHENBAUM, D., & GENEST, M. (1983). *Pain and behavioral medicine.* New York: Guilford.

TURK, D. C., & RUDY, T. E. (1995). Strategies and tactics in the treatment of persistent pain patients. In W. O'Donohue & L. Krasner (Eds.). *Handbook of psychological skills training: Clinical techniques and applications* (pp. 339-362). Boston: Allyn and Bacon.

TURKAT, I. D., & FEUERSTEIN, M. (1978). Behavior modification and the public misconception. *American Psychologist, 33,* 194.

TURNER, A. J., & VERNON, J. C. (1976). Prompts to increase attendance in a community mental health center. *Journal of Applied Behavior Analysis, 9,* 141-145.

TURNER, J., HEINRICH, R., MCCREARY, C., & DAWSON, E. (1979, April). *Evaluation of two behavioral interventions for chronic low back pain.* Paper presented at the meeting of the Society of Behavioral Medicine, San Fransisco.

TURNER, J. A. (1982). Comparison of group progressive-relaxation training and cognitive-behavioral group therapy. *Journal of Consulting and Clinical Psychology, 50,* 757-765.

TURNER, J. A., & CLANCY, S. (1988). Comparison of operant behavioral and cognitive-behavioral group treatment for chronic low back pain. *Journal of Consulting and Clinical Psychology, 56,* 261-266.

TURNER, S. M., BEIDEL, D. C., & JACOB, R. G. (1994). Social phobia: A comparison of behavior therapy and atenolol. *Journal of Consulting and Clinical Psychology, 62,* 350-358.

TURNER, S. M., BEIDEL, D. C., SPAULDING, S. A., & BROWN, J. M. (1995). The practice of behavior therapy: A national survey of cost and methods. *the Behavior Therapist, 18,* 1-4.

TURPIN, G. (1983). The behavioral management of tic disorders: A critical review. *Advances in Behaviour Research and Therapy, 5,* 203-245.

TURSKY, B., SHAPIRO, D., & SCHWARTZ, G. E. (1972). Automated constant cuff pressure system to measure average systolic blood pressure in men. *IEEE Transactions on Biomedical Engineering, 19,* 271-276.

TUSTIN, R. D., PENNINGTON, B., & BYRNE, M. (1994). Intrusiveness of interventions: Ratings by psychologists. *Behaviour Change, 11,* 68-100.

TWYMAN, J. S., JOHNSON, H., BUIE, J. D., & NELSON, C. M. (1994). The use of a warning procedure to signal a more intrusive timeout contingency. *Behavioral Disorders, 19,* 243-253.

ULLMANN, L. P., & KRASNER, L. (EDS.). (1965). *Case studies in behavior modification.* New York: Holt, Rinehart & Winston.

ULMAN, J. D., & KLEM, J. L. (1975). [Communication] *Journal of Applied Behavior Analysis, 8,* 210.

UPPER, D. (1993). The use of covert reinforcement and thought stopping in treating a young woman's sexual anxiety. In J. R. Cautela & A. J. Kearney (Eds.), *Covert conditioning casebook* (pp. 235-244). Pacific Grove, CA: Brooks/Cole.

USSHER, J. M. (1990). Cognitive behavioural couples therapy with gay men referred for counselling in an AIDS setting: A pilot study. *AIDS-Care, 2,* 43-51.

UTZ, S. W. (1994). The effect of instructions on cognitive strategies and performance in biofeedback. *Journal of Behavioral Medicine, 17,* 291-308.

VAAL, J. J. (1973). Applying contingency contracting to a school phobic: A case study. *Journal of Behavior Therapy and Experimental Psychiatry, 4,* 371-373.

VALENTI-HEIN, D. C., YARNOLD, P. R., & MUESER, K. T. (1994). Evaluation of the Dating Skills Program for improving heterosocial interactions in people with mental retardation. *Behavior Modification, 18,* 32-46.

VALINS, S., & RAY, A. (1967). Effects of cognitive desensitization on avoidance behavior. *Journal of Personality and Social Psychology, 7,* 345-350.

VALLIS, T. M. (1984). A complete component analysis of stress inoculation for pain tolerance. *Cognitive Therapy and Research, 8,* 313-329.

VAN BALKOM, A. J. L. M., VAN OPPEN, P., VERMEULEN, A. W. A., VAN DYCK, R., NAUTA, M. C. E., & VORST, H. C. M. (1994). A meta-analysis on the treatment of obsessive compulsive disorder: A comparison of antidepressants, behavior, and cognitive therapy. *Clinical Psychology Review, 14,* 359-381.

VAN HOUTEN, R., NAU, P. A., & MERRIGAN, M. (1981). Reducing elevator energy use: A comparison of posted feedback and reduced elevator convenience. *Journal of Applied Behavior Analysis, 14,* 377-387.

VAN OPPEN, P., & ARNTZ, A. (1994). Cognitive therapy for obsessive-compulsive disorder. *Behaviour Research and Therapy, 32,* 79-87.

VAN OPPEN, P., DE HANN, E., VAN BALKOM, A. J. L. M., SPINHOVEN, P., HOOGDUIN, K., & VAN DYCK, R. (1995). Cognitive therapy and exposure *in vivo* in the treatment of obessive-compulsive disorder. *Behaviour Research and Therapy, 33,* 379-390.

VAN SON, M., VAN HEESCH, N., MULDER, G., & VAN LONDEN, A. (1995). The effectiveness of dry bed training for nocturnal enuresis in adults: A 3, 5, and 6 years follow-up. *Behaviour Research and Therapy, 33,* 557-559.

VAN SON, M. J., MULDER, G., & VAN LONDEN, A. (1990). The effectiveness of dry bed training for nocturnal enuresis in adults. *Behaviour Research and Therapy, 28,* 347-349.

VARGAS, J. S., & SHANLEY, D. (1995). Academic skills. In W. O'Donohue & L. Krasner (Eds.), *Handbook of psychological skills training: Clinical techniques and applications* (pp. 180-194). Boston: Allyn and Bacon.

VARNI, J. W., BOYD, E. F., & CATALDO, M. F. (1978). Self-monitoring, external reinforcement, and timeout procedures in the control of high rate tic behaviors in a hyperactive child. *Journal of Behavior Therapy and Experimental Psychiatry, 9,* 353-358.

VARNI, J. W., KATZ, E. R., COLEGROVE, R., JR., & DOLGIN, M. (1993). The impact of social skills training on the adjustment of children with newly diagnosed cancer. *Journal of Pediatric Psychology, 18,* 751-767.

VAUGHAN, K., ARMSTRONG, M. F., GOLD, R., O'CONNOR, N., JENNEKE, W., & TARRIER, N. (1994). A trial of eye movement desensitization compared to image habituation training and applied muscle relaxation in post-traumatic stress disorder. *Journal of Behavior Therapy and Experimental Psychiatry, 25,* 283-291.

VENTIS, W. L. (1973). Case history: The use of laughter as an alternative response in systematic desensitization. *Behavior Therapy, 4,* 120-122.

VERNON, A. (1983). Rational-emotive education. In A. Ellis & M. Bernard (Eds.), *Rational-emotive approaches to the problems of childhood* (pp. 467-484). New York: Plenum.

VERNON, D. T. A. (1974). Modeling and birth order in responses to painful stimuli. *Journal of Personality and Social Psychology, 29,* 794-799.

VOEGTLIN, W. L., LEMERE, F., BROZ, W. R., & O'HOLLAREN, P. (1941). Conditioned reflex therapy of chronic alcoholism. *Quarterly Journal of Studies on Alcohol, 2,* 505-511.

VOELTZ, L. M., & EVANS, I. M. (1982). The assessment of behavioral interrelationships in child behavior therapy. *Behavioral Assessment, 4,* 131-165.

VOLLMER, T. R., IWATA, B. A., ZARCONE, J. R., SMITH, R. G., & MAZALESKI, J. L. (1993). The role of attention in the treatment of attention-maintained self-injurious behavior: Noncontingent reinforcement and differential reinforcement of other behavior. *Journal of Applied Behavior Analysis, 26,* 9-21.

WADDEN, T. A., STERNBERG, J. A., LETIZIA, K. A., STUNKARD, A. J., & FOSTER, G. D. (1989). Treatment of obesity by a very low calorie diet, behavior therapy, and their combination: A five-year perspective. *International Journal of Obesity, 13,* 39-46.

WADDEN, T. A., STUNKARD, A. J., & LIEBSCHUTZ, J. (1988). Three-year follow-up of the treatment of obesity by a very low calorie diet, behavior therapy, and their combination. *Journal of Consulting and Clinical Psychology, 56,* 925-928.

WADE, T. C., BAKER, T. B., & HARTMANN, D. P. (1979). Behavior therapists' self-reported views and practices. *the Behavior Therapist, 2,* 3-6.

WAGAMAN, J. R., MILTENBERGER, R. G., & ARNDORFER, R. E. (1993). Analysis of a simplified treatment for stuttering in children. *Journal of Applied Behavior Analysis, 26,* 53-61.

WAGAMAN, J. R., MILTENBERGER, R. G., & WILLIAMS, D. E. (1995). Treatment of a vocal tic by differential reinforcement. *Journal of Behavior Therapy and Experimental Psychiatry, 26,* 35-39.

WAGAMAN, J. R., MILTENBERGER, R. G., & WOODS, D. (1995). Long-term follow-up of a behavioral treatment for stuttering in children. *Journal of Applied Behavior Analysis, 28,* 233-234.

WAGGONER, C. D., & LeLIEUVRE, R. B. (1981). A method to increase compliance to exercise regimens in rheumatoid arthritis patients. *Journal of Behavioral Medicine, 4,* 191-201.

WAGNER, J. L., & WINETT, R. A. (1988). Prompting one low-fat, high-fiber selection in a fast-food restaurant. *Journal of Applied Behavior Analysis, 21,* 179-185.

WAGNER, M. K., & BRAGG, R. A. (1970). Comparing behavior modification approaches to habit decrement—Smoking. *Journal of Consulting and Clinical Psychology, 34,* 258-263.

WAGNER, W., JOHNSON, S. B., WALKER, D., CARTER, R., & WITNER, J. (1982). A controlled comparison of two treatments of nocturnal enuresis. *Journal of Pediatrics, 101,* 302-307.

WAHLER, R. G. (1969). Oppositional children: A quest for parental reinforcement control. *Journal of Applied Behavior Analysis, 2,* 159-170.

WAHLER, R. G., & GRAVES, M. G. (1983). Setting events in social networks: Ally or enemy in child behavior therapy? *Behavior Therapy, 14,* 19-36.

WALKER, C. E., HEDBERG, A., CLEMENT, P. W., & WRIGHT, L. (1981). *Clinical procedures for behavior therapy.* Englewood Cliffs, NJ: Prentice-Hall.

WALKER, C. E., MILLING, L. S., & BONNER, B. L. (1988). Incontinence disorders: Enuresis and encopresis. In D. K. Routh (Ed.), *Handbook of pediatric psychology* (pp. 363-397). New York: Guilford.

WALKER, W. R., FREEMAN, R. F., & CHRISTENSEN, D. K. (1994). Restricting environmental stimulation (REST) to enhance cognitive behavioral treatment for obsessive compulsive disorder with schizotypal personality disorder. *Behavior Therapy, 25,* 709-719.

WALLACE, B. C. (1992). Treating crack cocaine dependence: The critical role of relapse prevention. *Journal of Psychoactive Drugs, 24,* 131-158.

WALLER, M. A. (1977). The incongruity of congruence. *Journal of Couples Therapy, 7,* 83-98.

WALLER, M. A., & SPIEGLER, M. D. (1997). A cross-cultural perspective on couple differences. *Journal of Couples Therapy, 7,* 83-98.

WALSH, P., DALE, A., & ANDERSON, D. E. (1977). Comparison of biofeedback pulse wave velocity and progressive relaxation in essential hypertensives. *Perceptual and Motor Skills, 44,* 839-843.

WALTER, H., & VAUGHAN, R. (1993). AIDS risk reduction among a multiethnic sample of urban high school students. *Journal of the American Medical Association, 270,* 725-730.

WALTON, D., & MATHER, M. D. (1963). The relevance of generalization techniques to the treatment of stammering and phobic symptoms. *Behaviour Research and Therapy, 1,* 121-125.

WASIK, B. H. (1970). The application of Premack's generalization on reinforcement to the management of classroom behavior. *Journal of Experimental Child Psychology, 10,* 33-43.

WASSERMAN, I. M. (1984). Imitation and suicide: A reexamination of the Werther effect. *American Sociological Review, 49,* 427-436.

WATSON, D. L., & THARP, R. G. (1972). *Self-directed behavior: Self-modification for personal adjustment.* Pacific Grove, CA: Brooks/Cole.

WATSON, D. L., & THARP, R. G. (1989). *Self-directed behavior: Self-modification for personal adjustment* (5th ed.). Pacific Grove, CA: Brooks/Cole.

WATSON, J. B. (1914). *Behavior: An introduction to comparative psychology.* New York: Holt.

WATSON, J. P., MULLETT, G. E., & PILLAY, H. (1973). The effects of prolonged exposure to phobic situations upon agoraphobic patients treated in groups. *Behaviour Research and Therapy, 11,* 531-545.

WATSON, T. S., ALLEN, S. J., & ALLEN, K. D. (1993). Ventricular fold dysphonia: Application of biofeedback technology to a rare voice disorder. *Behavior Therapy, 24,* 439-446.

WATSON, T. S., & KRAMER, J. J. (1995). Teaching problem solving skills to teachers-in-training: An analogue experimental analysis of three methods. *Journal of Behavioral Education, 5,* 295-317.

WATZLAWICK, P. (Ed.). (1984). *The invented reality.* New York: Norton.

WAUQUIER, A., McGRADY, A., ALOE, L., KLAUSNER, T., & COLLINS, B. (1995). Changes in cerebral blood flow velocity, associated with biofeedback-assisted relaxation treatment of migraine headaches, are specific for the middle cerebral artery. *Headache, 35,* 358-362.

WEBSTER-STRATTON, C. (1981a). Modification of mothers' behaviors and attitudes through videotape modeling group discussion. *Behavior Therapy, 12,* 634-642.

WEBSTER-STRATTON, C. (1981b). Videotape modeling: A method of parent education. *Journal of Clinical Child Psychology, 10,* 93-97.

WEBSTER-STRATTON, C. (1982a). Long-term effects of a videotape modeling parent education program: Comparison of immediate and 1-year follow-up results. *Behavior Therapy, 13,* 702-714.

WEBSTER-STRATTON, C. (1982b). Teaching mothers through videotape modeling to change their children's behaviors. *Journal of Pediatric Psychology, 7,* 279-294.

WEBSTER-STRATTON, C. (1984). Randomized trial of two parent-training programs for families with conduct disordered children. *Journal of Consulting and Clinical Psychology, 52,* 666-678.

WEBSTER-STATTON, C., KOLPACOFF, M., & HOLLINGSWORTH, T. (1988). Self-administered videotape therapy for families with conduct problem children: Comparison with two cost-effective treatments and a control group. *Journal of Consulting and Clinical Psychology, 57,* 558-566.

WEIDNER, F. (1970). *In vivo* desensitization of a paranoid schizophrenic. *Journal of Behavior Therapy and Experimental Psychiatry, 1,* 79-81.

WEINRACH, S. G. (1995). Rational emotive behavior therapy: A tough-minded therapy for a tender-minded profession. *Journal of Counseling and Development, 73,* 296-300.

WEINSTEIN, G. W. (1974, April). The truth about teenage shoplifting. *Parents' Magazine,* pp. 42-43, 60-61.

WEINSTEIN, M. (1988). Preparation of children for psychotherapy through videotaped modeling. *Journal of Clinical Child Psychology, 17,* 131-136.

WEISENBERG, R. P., GESTEN, E. L., CARNIKE, C. L., TORO, P. A., RAPKIN, B. D., DAVIDSON, E., & COWEN, E. L. (1981). Social problem-solving skills training: A competence-building intervention with second-to-fourth-grade children. *American Journal of Community Psychology, 9,* 411-423.

WEISHAAR, M. E. (in press). Developments in cognitive therapy theory and practice. In W. Dryden (Ed.), *Developments in psychotherapy.* London: Sage.

WELCH, M. W., & GIST, J. W. (1974). *The open token economy system: A handbook for a behavioral approach to rehabilitation.* Springfield, IL: Charles C Thomas.

WELLS, E. A., PETERSON, P. L., GAINEY, R. R., HAWKINS, J. D., & CATALANO, R. F. (1994). Outpatient treatment for cocaine abuse: A controlled comparison of relapse prevention and twelve-step approaches. *American Journal of Drug and Alcohol Abuse, 20,* 1-17.

WELLS, J. K., HOWARD, G. S., NOWLIN, W. F., & VARGAS, M. J. (1986). Presurgical anxiety and postsurgical pain and adjustment: Effects of a stress inoculation procedure. *Journal of Consulting and Clinical Psychology, 54,* 831-835.

WELLS, K. C. (1994). Parent and family management training. In L. W. Craighead, W. E. Craighead, A. E. Kazdin, & M. J. Mahoney (Eds.), *Cognitive and behavioral interventions: An empirical approach to mental health problems* (pp. 251-266). Boston: Allyn and Bacon.

WELLS, K. C., & EGAN, J. (1988). Social learning and systems family therapy for childhood oppositional disorder: Comparative treatment outcome. *Comprehensive Psychiatry, 29,* 138-146.

WELLS, K. C., GRIEST, D. C., & FOREHAND, R. (1980). The use of a self-control package to enhance temporal generality of a parent training program. *Behaviour Research and Therapy, 18,* 347-353.

WERRY, J. S., & COHRSSEN, J. (1965). Enuresis: An etiologic and therapeutic study. *Journal of Pediatrics, 67,* 423-431.

WHISMAN, M. A. (1993). Mediators and moderators of change in cognitive therapy of depression. *Psychological Bulletin, 114,* 248-265.

WHITE, G. D., NIELSON, G., & JOHNSON, S. M. (1972). Time-out duration and the suppression of deviant behavior in children. *Journal of Applied Behavior Analysis, 5,* 111-120.

WHITE, J. A., DAVISON, G. C., HAAGA, D. A. F., & WHITE, K. L. (1992). Cognitive bias in the articulated thoughts of depressed and nondepressed psychiatric patients. *Journal of Nervous and Mental Disease, 180,* 77-81.

WHITE, M. (1989). *Selected papers.* Adelaide, South Australia: Dulwich Centre Publications.

WHITE, M. (1995, March). *Re-authoring lives.* Workshop presented in Mansfield, MA.

WHITE-BLACKBURN, G., SEMB, S., & SEMB, G. (1977). The effects of a good-behavior contract on the classroom behaviors of sixth-grade students. *Journal of Applied Behavior Analysis, 10,* 312.

WICKRAMASEKERA, I. (1976). Aversive behavior rehearsal for sexual exhibitionism. *Behavior Therapy, 7,* 167-176.

WILCOX, D., & DOWRICK, P. W. (1992). Anger management with adolescents. *Residential Treatment for Children and Youth, 9,* 29-38.

WILKIE, E. A., KIVITZ, M. S., CLARK, G. R., BYER, M. J., & COHEN, J. S. (1968). Developing a comprehensive rehabilitation program within an institutional setting. *Mental Retardation, 6,* 35-38.

WILLERMAN, L. (1979). *The psychology of individual and group differences.* San Francisco: W. H. Freeman.

WILLIAMS, C. D. (1959). The elimination of tantrum behavior by extinction procedures: Case report. *Journal of Abnormal and Social Psychology, 59,* 269.

WILLIAMS, D. E., KIRKPATRICK-SANCHEZ, S., & CROCKER, W. T. (1994). A long-term follow-up of treatment for severe self-injury. *Research in Developmental Disabilities, 15,* 487-501.

WILLIAMS, D. E., & WILLIAMS, J. W. (1995). Contingencies for dangerous behavior. *American Journal of Psychiatry, 152,* 1696.

WILLIAMS, M., THYER, B. A., BAILEY, J. S., & HARRISON, D. F. (1989).

Promoting safety belt use with traffic signs and prompters. *Journal of Applied Behavior Analysis, 22,* 71-76.

WILLIAMS, S. L., DOOSEMAN, G., & KLEIFIELD, E. (1984). Comparative effectiveness of guided mastery and exposure treatments for intractable phobias. *Journal of Consulting and Clinical Psychology, 52,* 505-518.

WILLIAMS, S. L., TURNER, S. M., & PEER, D. F. (1985). Guided mastery and performance desensitization treatments for severe acrophobia. *Journal of Consulting and Clinical Psychology, 53,* 237-247.

WILLIAMS, S. L., & ZANE, G. (1989). Guided mastery and stimulus exposure treatments for severe performance anxiety in agoraphobics. *Behaviour Research and Therapy, 27,* 237-245.

WILLIAMSON, D. A., DAVIS, C. J., & PRATHER, R. C. (1988). Assessment of health-related disorders. In A. S. Bellack & M. Hersen (Eds.), *Behavioral assessment: A practical handbook* (3rd ed., pp. 396-440). Elmsford, NY: Pergamon.

WILLIAMSON, D. A., WILLIAMSON, S. H., WATKINS, P. C., & HUGHES, H. H. (1992). Increasing cooperation among children using dependent group-oriented reinforcement contingencies. *Behavior Modification, 16,* 414-425.

WILLIS, R. W., & EDWARDS, J. A. (1969). A study of the comparative effectiveness of systematic desensitization and implosive therapy. *Behaviour Research and Therapy, 7,* 387-395.

WILLS, T. A., WEISS, R. L., & PATTERSON, G. R. (1974). A behavioral analysis of the determinants of marital satisfaction. *Journal of Consulting and Clinical Psychology, 42,* 802-811.

WILSON, D. D., ROBERTSON, S. J., HERLONG, L. H., & HAYNES, S. N. (1979). Vicarious effects of time out in the modification of aggression in the classroom. *Behavior Modification, 3,* 97-111.

WILSON, G. T. (1978). On the much discussed nature of the term "behavior therapy." *Behavior Therapy, 9,* 89-98.

WILSON, G. T. (1982). Adult disorders. In G. T. Wilson & C. M. Franks (Eds.), *Contemporary behavior therapy: Conceptual and empirical foundations* (pp. 505-562). New York: Guilford.

WILSON, G. T. (1984). Fear reduction methods and the treatment of anxiety disorders. In C. M. Franks, G. T. Wilson, P. C. Kendall, & K. D. Brownell (Eds.), *Review of behavior therapy: Theory and practice* (Vol. 10, pp. 87-122). New York: Guilford.

WILSON, G. T. (1990). Fear reduction methods and the treatment of anxiety disorders. In C. M. Franks, G. T. Wilson, P. C. Kendall, & J. P. Foreyt (Eds.), *Review of behavior therapy: Theory and practice* (Vol. 12, pp. 72-102). New York: Guilford.

WILSON, G. T., ELDREDGE, K. L., SMITH, D. E., & NILES, B. (1991). Cognitive-behavioral treatment with and without response prevention for bulimia. *Behaviour Research and Therapy, 29,* 575-583.

WILSON, G. T., & FAIRBURN, C. G. (1993). Cognitive treatment for eating disorders. *Journal of Consulting and Clinical Psychology, 61,* 261-269.

WILSON, G. T., O'LEARY, K. D., & NATHAN, P. E. (1992). *Abnormal psychology.* Englewood Cliffs, NJ: Prentice-Hall.

WILSON, G. T., ROSSITER, E., KLEIFIELD, E. I., & LINDHOLM, L. (1986). Cognitive-behavioral treatment of bulimia nervosa: A controlled evaluation. *Behaviour Research and Therapy, 24,* 277-288.

WILSON, G. T., & TRACEY, D. A. (1976). An experimental analysis of aversive imagery versus electrical aversive conditioning in the treatment of chronic alcoholics. *Behaviour Research and Therapy, 14,* 41-51.

WILSON, J. Q., & HERRNSTEIN, R. J. (1985). *Crime and human nature.* New York: Simon & Schuster.

WILSON, K., & GALLOIS, C. (1993). *Assertion and its social context.* New York: Pergamon.

WILSON, M. D., & MCREYNOLDS, L. V. (1973). A procedure for increasing oral reading rate in hard of hearing children. *Journal of Applied Behavior Analysis, 6,* 231-239.

WINCZE, J. P., & CAIRD, W. K. (1976). The effects of systematic desensitization and video desensitization in the treatment of sexual dysfunction in women. *Behavior Therapy, 7,* 335-342.

WINETT, R. A., KAGEL, J., BATTALIO, R., & WINKLER, R. (1978). The effects of rebates, feedback, and information on electricity conservation. *Journal of Applied Psychology, 63,* 73-80.

WINETT, R. A., KAISER, S., & HABERKORN, G. (1977). The effects of monetary rebates and daily feedback on electricity conservation. *Journal of Environmental Systems, 6,* 327-339.

WINETT, R. A., KRAMER, K. D., WALKER, W. B., MALONE, S. W., & LANE, M. K. (1988). Modifying food purchases in supermarkets with modeling, feedback, and goal-setting procedures. *Journal of Applied Behavior Analysis, 21,* 73-80.

WINETT, R. A., LECKLITER, I. N., CHINN, D. E., STAHL, B., & LOVE, S. Q. (1985). Effects of television modeling on residential energy conservation. *Journal of Applied Behavior Analysis, 18,* 33-44.

WINETT, R. A., MOORE, J. F., WAGNER, J. L., HITE, L. A., LEAHY, M., NEUBAUER, T. E., WALBERG, J. L., WALKER, W. B., LOMBARD, D., GELLER, E. S., & MUNDY, L. L. (1991). Altering shoppers' supermarket purchases to fit nutritional guidelines: An interactive information system. *Journal of Applied Behavior Analysis, 24,* 95-105.

WINETT, R. A., NEALE, M. S., & GRIER, H. C. (1979). Effects of self-monitoring and feedback on residential electricity consumption. *Journal of Applied Behavior Analysis, 12,* 173-185.

WINETT, R. A., & NIETZEL, M. T. (1975). Behavioral ecology: Contingency management of consumer energy use. *American Journal of Community Psychology, 3,* 123-133.

WINETT, R. A., & WINKLER, R. C. (1972). Current behavior modification in the classroom: Be still, be quiet, be docile. *Journal of Applied Behavior Analysis, 5,* 499-504.

WISOCKI, P. A. (1994). The experience of worry among the elderly. In G. C. L. Davey & F. Tallis (Eds.), *Worrying: Perspectives on theory, assessment and treatment* (pp. 247-261). Chichester, U. K.: Wiley.

WITMER, J. F., & GELLER, E. S. (1976). Facilitating paper recycling: Effects of prompts, raffles, and contests. *Journal of Applied Behavior Analysis, 9,* 315-322.

WITTROCK, D. A., & BLANCHARD, E. B. (1992). Thermal biofeedback treatment of mild hypertension: A comparison of effects on conventional and ambulatory blood pressure measures. *Behavior Modification, 16,* 283-304.

WITTROCK, D. A., BLANCHARD, E. B., & MCCOY, G. C. (1988). Three studies on the relation of process to outcome in the treatment of essential hypertension with relaxation and thermal biofeedback. *Behaviour Research and Therapy, 26,* 53-66.

WOLF, E. M., & CROWTHER, J. H. (1992). An evaluation of behavior and cognitive-behavioral group interventions for the treatment of bulimia nervosa in women. *International Journal of Eating Disorder, 22,* 503-517.

WOLF, M. M. (1978). Social validity: The case for subjective measurement or how applied behavior analysis is finding its heart. *Journal of Applied Behavior Analysis, 11,* 203-214.

WOLF, M. M., BRAUKMANN, C. J., & RAMP, K. A. (1987). Serious delinquent behavior as part of a significantly handicapping condition: Cures and supportive environments. *Journal of Applied Behavior Analysis, 20,* 347-359.

WOLFE, D. A., & SANDLER, J. (1981). Training abusive parents in effective child management. *Behavior Modification, 5,* 320-335.

WOLFE, D. A., & WEKERLE, C. (1993). Treatment strategies for child physical abuse and neglect: A critical progress report. *Clinical Psychology Review, 13,* 473-500.

WOLFSON, A., LACKS, P., & FUTTERMAN, A. (1992). Effects of parent training on infant sleeping patterns, parents' stress, and perceived parental competence. *Journal of Consulting and Clinical Psychology, 60,* 41-48.

WOLPE, J. (1958). *Psychotherapy by reciprocal inhibition.* Stanford, CA: Stanford University Press.

WOLPE, J. (1976). Behavior therapy and its malcontents: II. Multimodal eclecticism, cognitive exclusivism and "exposure" empiricism. *Journal of Behavior Therapy and Experimental Psychiatry, 7,* 109-116.

WOLPE, J. (1990). *The practice of behavior therapy* (4th ed.). Elmsford, NY: Pergamon.

WOLPE, J., & ABRAMS, J. (1991). Post-traumatic stress disorder overcome by eye movement desensitization: A case report. *Journal of Behavior Therapy and Experimental Psychiatry, 22,* 39-43.

WOLPE, J., & LANG, P. J. (1964). A fear survey schedule for use in behavior therapy. *Behaviour Research and Therapy, 2,* 27-30.

WOLPE, J., & LAZARUS, A. A. (1966). *Behavior therapy techniques: A guide to the treatment of neurosis.* New York: Pergamon.

WONG, S. E., MARTINEZ-DIAZ, J. A., MASSEL, H. K., EDELSTEIN, B. A., WIEGAND, W., BOWEN, L., & LIBERMAN, R. P. (1993). Conversation skills training with schizophrenic inpatients: A study of generalization across settings and conversants. *Behavior Therapy, 24,* 285-304.

WOODS, D. W., & MILTENBERGER, R. G. (1995). Habit reversal: A review of applications and variations. *Journal of Behavior Therapy and Experimental Psychiatry, 26,* 123-131.

WOODWARD, R., & JONES, R. B. (1980). Cognitive restructuring treatment: A controlled trial with anxious patients. *Behaviour Research and Therapy, 18,* 401-407.

WOOLFOLK, A. E., WOOLFOLK, R. L., & WILSON, G. T. (1977). A rose by another name. . . : Labeling bias and attitudes toward behavior modification. *Journal of Consulting and Clinical Psychology, 45,* 184-191.

WOOLFOLK, R. L., & DEVER, S. (1979). Perceptions of assertion: An empirical analysis. *Behavior Therapy, 10,* 404-411.

WORLD HEALTH ORGANIZATION. (1992). *International classification of diseases and related health problems* (10th rev.). Geneva: Author.

WURTELE, S. K. (1990). Teaching personal safety skills to four-year-old children: A behavioral approach. *Behavior Therapy, 21,* 25-32.

WURTELE, S. K., CURRIER, L. L., GILLISPIE, E. I., & FRANKLIN, C. F. (1991). The efficacy of a parent-implemented program for teaching preschoolers personal safety skills. *Behavior Therapy, 22,* 69-83.

WURTELE, S. K., MARRS, S. R., & MILLER-PERRIN, C. J. (1987). Practice makes perfect? The role of participant modeling in sexual abuse prevention programs. *Journal of Consulting and Clinical Psychology, 55,* 599-602.

WYSOCKI, T., HALL, G., IWATA, B., & RIORDAN, M. (1979). Behavioral management of exercise: Contracting for aerobic points. *Journal of Applied Behavior Analysis, 12,* 55-64.

YATES, A. J. (1958). The application of learning theory to the treatment of tics. *Journal of Abnormal and Social Psychology, 56,* 175-182.

YATES, A. J. (1970). *Behavior therapy.* New York: Wiley.

YEATON, W. H., & BAILEY, J. S. (1983). Utilization analysis of a pedestrian training program. *Journal of Applied Behavior Analysis, 16,* 203-216.

YOKLEY, J. M., & GLENWICK, D. S. (1984). Increasing the immunization of preschool children: An evaluation of applied community interventions. *Journal of Applied Behavior Analysis, 17,* 313-325.

YOUNG, J. E. (1990). *Cognitive therapy for personality disorders: A schema-focused approach.* Sarasota, FL: Professional Resource Exchange.

YU, P., HARRIS, G. E., SOLOVITZ, B. L., & FRANKLIN, L. (1986). A social problem-solving intervention for children at high risk for later psychopathology. *Journal of Clinical Child Psychology, 13,* 30-40.

YULE, W., SACKS, B., & HERSOV, L. (1974). Successful flooding treatment of a noise phobia in an eleven-year-old. *Journal of Behavior Therapy and Experimental Psychiatry, 5,* 209-211.

ZEISS, A. M., & STEFFEN, A. (1996). Treatment issues with elderly clients. *Cognitive and Behavioral Practice, 3,* 371-389.

ZEITLIN, S. B., NETTEN, K. A., & HODDER, S. L. (1995). Thought suppression: An experimental investigation of spider phobics. *Behaviour Research and Therapy, 33,* 407-413.

ZETTLE, R. D., & HAYES, S. C. (1982). Rule-governed behavior: A potential theoretical framework for cognitive-behavioral therapy. In P. C. Kendall (Ed.), *Advances in cognitive-behavioral research and therapy* (Vol. 1, pp. 73-118). New York: Academic Press.

ZIFFERBLATT, S. M. (1975). Increasing patient compliance through the applied analysis of behavior. *Preventive Medicine, 4,* 173-182.

ZIFFERBLATT, S. M., WILBUR, C. S., & PINSKY, J. I. (1980a). Changing cafeteria eating habits. *Journal of the American Dietetic Association, 76,* 15-20.

ZIFFERBLATT, S. M., WILBUR, C. S., & PINSKY, J. I. (1980b). Influence of ecological events on cafeteria food selections. *Journal of the American Dietetic Association, 76,* 9-14.

ZIMMERMAN, J., STUCKEY, T. E., GARLICK, B. J., & MILLER, M. (1969). Effects of token reinforcement on productivity in multiple handicapped clients in a sheltered workshop. *Rehabilitation Literature, 30,* 34-41.

ZIONTS, P. (1983). A strategy for understanding and correcting irrational beliefs in pupils: The rational-emotive approach. *Pointer, 27,* 13-17.

ZOHAR, D., & FUSSFELD, N. (1981). Modifying earplug wearing behavior by behavior modification techniques: An empirical evaluation. *Journal of Organizational Behavior Management, 3,* 41-52.

Subject Index

NOTE: Pages on which definitions appear are either in **boldface type** or under "defined." Disorders and problems are listed under "Problems (treated by behavior therapy)." Illustrations and footnotes (designated by "n" following page number) are included.

for the Experimental Analysis of Behavior, Inc. Reprinted by permission. **448, Figure 16-6,** Adapted from Poche [Knowles], C., Yoder, P., & Miltenberger, R. (1988). Teaching Self-Protection to Children Using Television. *Journal of Applied Behavior Analysis, 21,* 253-261. Copyright © 1988 by Society for the Experimental Analysis of Behavior, Inc. Reprinted by permission. **452-453, Figure 16-7a-c,** From Fox, D. K., Hopkins, B. L., & Anger, W. K. (1987). The Long-Term Effects of a Token Economy on Safety Performance in Open-Pit Mining. *Journal of Applied Behavior Analysis, 20,* 215-224. Copyright © 1987 by Society for the Experimental Analysis of Behavior, Inc. Reprinted by permission. **455, Figure 16-8,** From Carter, N., Holnstrom, H., Simpanen, M., & Melin, L. (1988). Theft Reduction in a Grocery Store Through Product Identification and Graphing of Losses for Employees. *Journal of Applied Behavior Analysis, 21,* 385-389. Copyright © 1988 by Society for the Experimental Analysis of Behavior, Inc. Reprinted by permission. **457, Figure 16-9,** From Dubbert, P. M., Johnson, W. J., Schlundt, D. G., & Montegue, N. W. (1984). The Influence of Caloric Information on Cafeteria Food Choices. *Journal of Applied Behavior Analysis, 16,* 85-92. Copyright © 1984 by Society for the Experimental Analysis of Behavior, Inc. Reprinted by permission. **458, Figure 16-10,** From Mayer, J. A., Heins, J. M., Vogel, J. M., Morrison, D. C., Lankester, L. D., & Jacobs, A. L. (1986). Promoting Low-Fat Entree Choices in a Public Cafeteria. *Journal of Applied Behavior Analysis, 19,* 399. Copyright 1986 by Society for the Experimental Analysis of Behavior, Inc. Reprinted by permission. **459, Figure 16-11,** From Mayer, J. A., Heins, J. M., Vogel, J. M., Morrison, D. C., Lankester, L. D., & Jacobs, A. L. (1986). Promoting Low-Fat Entree Choices in a Public Cafeteria. *Journal of Applied Behavior Analysis, 19,* 399. Copyright 1986 by Society for the Experimental Analysis of Behavior, Inc. Reprinted by permission. **465, Figure 16-13,** From Hayes, C. S., & Cone, J. D. (1981). Reduction of Residential Consumption of Electricity Through Simple Monthly Feedback. *Journal of Applied Behavior Analysis, 14,* 84. Copyright © 1981 by Society for the Experimental Analysis of Behavior, Inc. Reprinted by permission. **470-480, Table 17-1,** From Ethical Issues for Human Services by Association for the Advancement of Behavior Therapy, Inc. *Behavior Therapy, 8(5),* v-vi. Reprinted by permission. **483, Case 17-1,** Excerpt from Goldiamond, I. (1974). Toward a Constitutional Approach to Social Problems: Ethical and Constitutional Issues Raised by Applied Behavior Analysis. *Behaviorism, 2,* 1-79. Copyright © 1974 by Cambridge Center for Behavioral Studies. Excerpted by permission. **507, Appendix A,** From Linehan, M. *Guidelines.* Written during her tenure as Membership Chairperson of the Association for the Advancement of Behavior Therapy. Reprinted by permission of the publisher and author.

Photo credits: 15, Archives of the History of American Psychology, University of Akron, Akron, Ohio, 44304. **16 (top),** The Bettman Archive; **(margin),** Courtesy of Vassar College Libraries/Archives of the History of American Psychology, University of Akron, Akron, Ohio, 44304. **17 (top),** Photograph courtesy of the University of Illinois Archives, Record Series 15/19/25, Box 1. **18 (margin, top),** Photograph by Mark Gerson, FBIPP, London, Courtesy of Dr. H. J. Eysenck; **(margin, middle),** Courtesy of Harvard University Archives; **(margin, bottom),** Courtesy of University of Kansas, University Archives. **19 (margin, middle),** Courtesy of Teodoro Ayllon; **(margin, bottom),** Courtesy of Nathan Azrin. **20 (margin, top),** Courtesy of Joseph Wolpe; **(margin, bottom),** Courtesy of Stanley Rachman. **21 (margin),** Photo by Chuck Painter, News and Publication Service, Stanford University. **22,** Courtesy of Cyril Franks. **52 (left),** Elizabeth Crews/Stock, Boston; **(right),** Barbara Alper/Stock, Boston. **89, 96,** Copyright © 1997 by Michael D. Spiegler and David C. Guevremont. **97,** Cary Wolinsky/Stock, Boston. **101, 123, 128, 142, 144,** Copyright © 1997 by Michael D. Spiegler and David C. Guevremont. **153,** The Johns Hopkins University Applied Physics Laboratory. **184, 201,** Copyright © 1997 by Michael D. Spiegler and David C. Guevremont. **229,** Courtesy of Georgia Tech TelePhoto. **246 (margin, top),** Courtesy of the University of Wisconsin-Milwaukee; **(margin, bottom),** Courtesy of Donald Levis. **269,** Courtesy of the Eden Institute. **274,** Courtesy of Peter W. Dowrick. **290,** Copyright © 1997 by Michael D. Spiegler and David C. Guevremont. **293,** Courtesy of Barbara C. Melamed. **311 (margin),** Albert Ellis, Ph.D., Director, Institute for Rational Emotive Therapy. **321 (margin),** Courtesy of the University of Pennsylvania Medical Center. **340 (margin),** Courtesy of University of Waterloo, Ontario, Canada. **347 (margin, top),** Courtesy of Thomas D'Zurilla; **(margin, bottom),** Courtesy of Marvin R. Goldfried. **387, 395, 414, 428,** Copyright © 1997 by Michael D. Spiegler and David C. Guevremont. **440, 442,** Courtesy of E. Scott Geller. **443, 446, 451,** Copyright © 1997 by Michael D. Spiegler and David C. Guevremont. **460,** Developed and field tested at Virginia Tech, with support from the National Cancer Institute (R. Winett, J. Moore, and J. Rankin). **462,** Courtesy of E. Scott Geller.